Quick-Access Guide to World Radio

RADIO
DATABASE
INTERNATIONAL

Editor-in-Chief:	Lawrence Magne
Editor:	Tony Jones
Contributing Editors:	Goeff Cosier, Noel Green, Baba Ngala, Greg Shafritz
Consulting Editors:	Larry Miller, Don Jensen

Special Contributors: Rogildo Fontenelle Aragão, J.M. Brinker, John G. Cook, Antonio Ribeiro da Motta, DXFL/Isao Ugusa, Arnold Hartley, John C. Herkimer, Robert Hill, Edward J. Insinger, Graham L. Mytton, Toshimichi Ohtake, RNM/Tetsuya Hirahara, Lars Rydén, Simo Soininen, Don Swampoe, URSC/Shigenori Aoki, Jan van der Horst, David L. Walcutt, George Wood

---

Systems Manager:	John A. Campbell
Systems Development/ Implementation:	Richard Mayell
Programmer-Analysts:	Roger Cumming, Mark Goodman, David Lau-kee, John Leather, Sara Young
Systems Contributors:	David D. Meisel, Jon Pastor
Laboratory:	Sherwood Engineering Inc.
Marketing & Distribution Manager:	Mary W. Kroszner
Production Manager:	Larry Miller
Advertising Representative:	Mary W. Kroszner
Publicity Writing:	RJ Hill
Cover Layout:	Glenn Brown
Cover Photo:	Walter Wick
Cover Model Construction:	Joan Steiner

Copyright © 1986 International Broadcasting Services, Ltd.
P.O. Box 300, Penn's Park, PA 18943 USA

Inside This Edition...

I magine a day when you'll be able to turn on your radio and out of the speaker will come reports direct from the news fronts of the world. "No mercy to the traitors!" screams the Leader. "Infidels will die!" cry the throngs. Switch channels and you're suddenly at a track and field event in Moscow, then a concert from the Aldeburgh Festival, then a news studio in Tokyo. Another channel up, you find a breaking report on the latest air disaster near Madrid.

While imagination always has played a major part in radio listening, there's no need to imagine world radio. Now it's as close as the controls on your set and nearly as easy to hear as your local AM station.

Every day, hundreds of stations weave a tapestry of news, information and entertainment programs from the four corners of the globe, occupying more channels than all of cable and satellite TV combined. And, oh, the music! Music of every variety, music from every people, music from every land, music for every heart.

RADIO DATABASE INTERNATIONAL gives you everything you need to know about the riches of world radio in a straightforward, easy-to-access guide prepared by the foremost authorities in the field. Included are...

- Complete coverage of world radio from the tiniest station in Nepal to the largest broadcasters of Europe.
- No-nonsense grapics that let you see clearly which stations you can hear at what time.
- Major stations listed alphabetically by country with at-a-glance schedules.
- World's first published summary of international broadcasting activity.
- Buyer's Guide to portable and tabletop radios: The definitive consumer's guide, complete with prices and comparative ratings.
- Over a dozen articles designed to help you get the most enjoyment out of your listening moments.

Your copy of RADIO DATABASE INTERNATIONAL provides you, day after day, with a solid wealth of tools to master the exciting world of international radio. For more details, please see the table of contents on pages 18-19.

NOW HEAR THIS

TEN-TEC'S NEW RX-325 SHORT WAVE RECEIVER

TEN-TEC, America's premier producer of high quality amateur radio equipment, now brings the ultimate in design to short wave listening.

With continuous frequency coverage from 100 kHz to 30 MHz the RX-325 receives short wave, medium wave, and long wave frequencies, and detects AM, SSB, and CW signals.

The latest advances in low-noise circuitry, quality ceramic filters, phase-locked loop technology and microprocessor controls insure high sensitivity and freedom from adjacent channel interference. The RF stage employs a low noise bi-polar amplifier for excellent sensitivity and a diode quad first mixer for improved dynamic range.

Although this new receiver is highly sophisticated, all controls are user-friendly. Favorite frequencies, such as BBC, VOA, WWV plus local AM stations, are easily stored in a 25 memory bank for recall at the touch of a button. Memories not only store the frequencies, but the modes and the tuning rates. The tuning knob allows you to change tuning speed automatically — in 100 Hz, 500 Hz, 1kHz or 5kHz steps.

The TEN-TEC RX-325 combines ultimate performance and ease of operation for a lifetime of listening pleasure.

Consider these features. We think you'll agree the RX-325 incorporates every worthwhile feature for maximum short wave listening pleasure.

- Keyboard or tuning knob frequency entry.
- 25 high capacity memories.
- Mode switches select AM, LSB (cw), or USB (cw).
- Blue vacuum fluorescent display.
- "S" Meter with SINPO S-scale.
- Built-in quartz digital clock with timer.
- Communications type noise blanker.

- RF attenuator.
- Programmable band scan and memory scan.
- Two built-in ceramic i-f filters.
- Hi and Lo impedence antenna terminals.
- Switchable AGC, built-in speaker.
  Audio output is 2 watts at 10% distortion.
  Striking high-tech appearance finished in black.
  Durable, high quality epoxy-glass circuit boards.
  Dimensions (HWD) 3¼" x 9½" x 7". Weight 5 lbs. 5 oz.
  115 VAC adapter included, also 13.8 VDC capability.

Introductory factory price $549.

See your TEN-TEC dealer or write

TEN-TEC, INC.
SEVIERVILLE, TENNESSEE 37862

I'M UPSTAIRS, DEAR, TUNING IN THE WORLD

by
Arnold Hartley

Arnold Hartley has been active in radio since 1930, first as a writer and producer, then from the late Forties as owner of a number of successful broadcast properties. One of these — WOV, now WADO, in New York — was the first independent US station to have its own world radio listening post.

Arnold, President of Key Broadcast Management, Inc., currently serves as promotional consultant for independent stations. He is also writing a book on the development of foreign-language broadcasting in the United States, as well as preparing his personal memoirs for the Broadcast Pioneers Archive, Washington DC.

I've been listening to international broadcasts lo these many, many years — in fact, from about the time the Third Reich began attracting the nervous attention of the world with its ominous "Germany Calling" broadcasts. That's how long ago it was. But despite the endless fascination I've found in tuning about the world, I've had little success until recently in persuading others to sample the wonders of the medium.

Now change is in the air, thanks to the myriad advances brought about by high technology. I suspect that before long even my wife will be able to tell visitors, "He's upstairs listening to his radio," without that customary overtone of annoyance.

The biggest improvements are technical-
...but, paradoxically, with the result that listening has been made easier. In the past, even the most willing converts were bewildered by the difficulty in finding the channels they were looking for. Now it's as simple as punching up the numbers you want as you would on a calculator or a Touch-tone telephone. The age of digital radio is here and world broadcasting has taken it to heart.

Suppose, for example, you are curious to know what the Israelis are saying about the latest disaster in Lebanon, and it's 3:00 in the afternoon. Press the buttons to give you 9435 kHz on the screen of your receiver and there it is. If you miss that newscast, there will be others in English a little later on and throughout the evening.

That's also true with all the other major broadcasts you'll find on the international airwaves, whether from the BBC or Radio Moscow or the Deutsche Welle or the Netherlands, or Australia, Canada, or Tahiti. They and more than a hundred others have schedules and faithfully fulfill them. All you need is RADIO DATABASE INTERNATIONAL to tell you when and where to tune.

Another improvement is in the reception quality of modern receivers. Unless you have ambitions to pick up really weak and noisy signals just for the sport of it, you no longer need to string up an outside antenna of any kind. The telescoping antenna that comes with your radio is sufficient for everyone but the most dedicated aficionado.

So much for your radio — small in size, easy to carry around, simple to tune and — yes — not all that expensive. Now what?

To begin with, you must understand that you are entering a world of such fascinating variety that you cannot easily imagine it. There are more channels of entertainment and information via world radio than on all of cable and satellite TV combined. On shortwave, the air is filled with all the languages of civilized humanity and some others as well. And with the languages go the music and the verbal rites and literature and poetry.

Understand also that nearly all the major nations of the world take time each day to speak

Continued on page 22

25-1000MHz Plus!   IC-R7000

ICOM's commercial quality scanning receiver... Top quality at a gem of a price.

ICOM introduces the IC-R7000 advanced technology 25-2000MHz* continuous coverage communications receiver. With 99 owner programmable memories, the IC-R7000 covers low band, aircraft, marine, business, FM broadcast, amateur radio, emergency services, government and television bands.

Keyboard Entry. For simplified operation and quick tuning, the IC-R7000 features direct keyboard entry. Precise frequencies can be selected by pushing the digit keys in sequence of the frequency or by turning the main tuning knob.

99 Memories. The IC-R7000 has 99 memories available to store your favorite frequencies, including the operating mode. All memories may be called up by simply pressing the Memory switch, then rotating the memory channel knob, or by direct keyboard entry.

Scanning. A sophisticated scanning system provides instant access to most used frequencies. By depressing the Auto-M switch, the IC-R7000 automatically memorizes frequencies in use while the unit is in the scan mode. This allows you to recall frequencies that were in use.

Other Outstanding Features:
● Optional voice synthesizer

● FM wide/FM narrow/AM/ upper and lower SSB modes
● Six tuning speeds: 0.1, 1.0, 5, 10, 12.5 or 25KHz
● Dual color fluorescent display with memory channel readout and dimmer switch
● Compact Size: 4³/₈"H x 11¹/₄"W x 10⁷/₈"D
● Dial lock, noise blanker, combined S-meter and center meter
● Optional RC-12 infrared remote controller

* Specifications guaranteed from 25-1000MHz and 1260-1300MHz. No coverage from 1000-1025MHz. No additional module required for coverage to approximately 2.0GHz.

All this at a price you'll appreciate.

ICOM HF Receiver
IC-R71A

The World Class
World Receiver

ICOM introduces the IC-R71A 100KHz to 30MHz superior-grade general coverage HF receiver with innovative features including keyboard frequency entry and wireless remote control (optional).

This easy-to-use and versatile receiver is ideal for anyone wanting to listen in to worldwide communications.

With 32 programmable memory channels, SSB/AM/ RTTY/CW/FM (opt.), dual VFO's, scanning, selectable AGC and noise blanker, the IC-R71A's versatility is unmatched by any other commercial grade unit in its price range.

Superior Receiver Performance. Passband tuning, wide dynamic range (100dB) a deep IF notch filter, adjustable AGC (Automatic Gain Control) and noise blanker provide easy-to-adjust clear reception even in the presence of strong interference or high noise levels. A preamplifier allows improved reception of weak signals.

32 Tunable Memories. Thirty-two tunable memories, more than any other general coverage receiver on the market, offer instant recall of your favorite frequencies. Each memory stores frequency, VFO and operating mode, and is backed by an internal lithium memory battery.

Keyboard Entry. ICOM introduces a unique feature to shortwave receivers...direct keyboard entry for simplified operation. Precise frequencies can be easily selected by pushing the digit keys in sequence of frequency. The frequency will be automatically entered without changing the main tuning control.

Options. FM, RC-11 wireless remote controller, synthesized voice frequency readout, IC-CK70 DC adapter for 12 volt operation, MB-12 mobile mounting bracket, two CW filters, FL32-500Hz and FL63-250Hz, and high-grade 455KHz crystal filter, FL44A.

RADIO BEIJING: 40 YEARS OF OPENING CHINA'S DOOR

by
Larry Miller

This is XNCR, New China's Broadcasting Station, North Shensi. Today marks the premier broadcast of daily English language newscasts presented by the New China News Agency. We plan to bring to our radio audience the march of China — one fifth of all humanity — which profoundly affects the future course of world events.
— Radio Beijing's Inaugural Broadcast, September 11, 1947

The year was 1940. Manchuria, the coastal regions, the rich Yangtze River valley and the north of China were all under Japanese control. By World War II, the Chinese, a partner of the Western Allies in their struggle against Germany, Italy and Japan, were a nation economically prostrate and politically divided.

Even during the Occupation, however, the Nationalist government chose to devote much of its efforts to fighting the Communist forces which, by 1941, had taken over much of the Yangtze River valley. As the People's Liberation Army continued its march south through China, so did a small clandestine radio station called XNCR.

Broadcasting over antiquated equipment from caves along the Army's route, it signed on for the first time with an English transmission on September 11, 1947. The announcer for that first broadcast was a pig-tailed young woman named Wei Lin. "The studio was in a doorless cave with no proper equipment," says Ms. Wei, "and only a kerosene lantern for lighting. Whenever we started broadcasting, we had to hang up a coarse felt blanket to keep out the bleating of nearby sheep". There were no tape recorders then — the only music they could use was a phonograph recording of the Triumphal March from the opera *Aïda*. Other songs were simply sung into the microphone.

The station bounced around the countryside, following the army from place to place, until settling in the capital city, Peiping — now Beijing — in 1949.

"We were very busy and our lives were hard," recounts the veteran broadcaster, "but we were all in high spirits. I will never forget those days...". Neither will anyone else who tuned to those spartan programs on 7500 kHz during the heady days of revolutionary China.

Forty years after those first broadcasts, Radio Beijing has grown from tiny clandestine status to one of the largest, most established world radio broadcasters on the air.

Located on the second floor of the Broadcasting Building, some six kilometers west of Tian'anmen Square, the center of the nation's capital, is Radio Beijing's English Service. Three shifts of editors and announcers work around the clock to put

Radio Beijing English Service Staff. From left to right: Zhang Jian-xin, Wei Lin, Yuan Fang, Li Dan, Xiao Yong, Simo, Deng Jian and Tong.

Tian'anmen Square in the heart of Beijing

together 17 hours each day of English programs for audiences around the world.

And just as Radio Beijing has taken a great leap forward since it's cave-dwelling days, so has the programming. During the Cultural Revolution in the early 1970s, the station devoted entire programs to the recitation of the works of Chairman Mao Zedong.

Today, as the People's Republic of China actively pursues the policy of *duiwai kaifang,* or "open door", Radio Beijing concentrates on programs that help the listener understand this ancient culture. The station presents features on culture, history and people of China, among which are "China in Construction" and "Folk Tales and Across the Land". All broadcasts begin with news and commentary on both international and domestic affairs.

Unfortunately for listeners in Eastern North America, Radio Beijing's signal does not provide the best reception. The station has tried to arrange relays of its broadcasts to improve signal quality. The first of these was undertaken in cooperation with the Albanians from 1968-78. More recently, Radio Beijing fell victim to a change in government in France when, in the fall of 1976, conservative Prime Minister Jacques Chirac abruptly cancelled a briefly implemented transmitter swap between his government and that of the People's Republic of China.

But what the station lacks in reliable reception is more than made up for by the friendliness and helpfulness of the staff. Write a letter to Radio Beijing and you might well get a reply from staffer Chen Yu, along with a package of literature and small souveniers. Occasionally, the station even invites listeners to visit China as a guest of Radio Beijing.

Few countries offer such a broad range of world radio programming as does China. From a myriad of local and national domestic stations to the vast output of Radio Beijing, the world radio air-

waves crackle with the rich diversity of Chinese broadcasts. With your world radio, you can share with the Chinese their feelings, their songs, their way of life.

KEEPING TABS ON THE BBC'S 100 MILLION LISTENERS

by
Graham L. Mytton, BBC

For most of its 54 years, the BBC External Service — the United Kingdom's official world radio organization — has maintained an audience research department to measure and analyze its audience in different parts of the world, as well as to seek the opinion of listeners to the BBC's various world radio programs.

The BBC's International Broadcasting and Audience Research Department is the largest of its kind in the world. Surveys are carried out in a number of countries each year on behalf of the BBC by independent market or opinion research companies to obtain information about the size and characteristics of the audience for the BBC, as well as other broadcasters. The surveys are based on interviews — mainly personal, but occasionally by telephone — with carefully drawn samples of adults.

BBC Heard Weekly by 100 Million Adults

Audience surveys like this have enabled the BBC to estimate its global audience at around 100 million adults listening to one or another of the BBC's thirty-seven language broadcasts at least once a week. There may be more. We believe that it is a modest claim based on the best evidence available. In any event, it points to the continuing vigor of world radio broadcasting.

Facilities for carrying out such studies vary considerably. Western Europe, for example, presents few problems. However, in some less developed areas, there may be no resident research organization, so there may be difficulties in covering the rural population. In certain other countries, it is not possible for the BBC to carry out surveys at all.

However, in spite of these difficulties, over the past ten years survey results have been available for more than eighty countries. Some of the main findings from individual surveys are given below; they are, of course, subject to the margin of error inherent in all sampling procedures.

The figures show considerable differences between countries in the amount of listening to external broadcasters. The results must be assessed against a number of other factors, such as the number of hours of transmission, availability of mediumwave AM as well as shortwave, the quality of the BBC's signals, the local radio and television alternatives, world events, the state of the country's development and the languages understood by listeners in that country.

Wide Variation Among Broadcasters in Attracting Listeners

For example, a survey was carried out in Pakistan in June and July of 1982. Interviews among a representative sampling of the adult urban population indicated that 46.8% of these people listened regularly — at least once a week — to the BBC Urdu Service. This is equivalent to a regular adult urban audience of about 5.5 million in Pakistan. All India Radio had a somewhat larger Urdu audience (58.5%) but those for the other international broadcasters, on the other hand, were much smaller: Radio Tehran 11.1%, Radio Kabul 5.9%, Radio Moscow 2.9%, VOA 2.7%, Radio Peking 1.8% and Deutsche Welle 0.6%. The largest audience in Pakistan for English-language broadcasting was for the BBC, which was heard regularly by 4.8%, equivalent to about a quarter of a million adult listeners.

Interviews were also conducted in some of the more accessible rural areas of Punjab and Sind provinces. About a third of those respondents listened regularly to the BBC Urdu Service, whereas a somewhat higher proportion listened to All India Radio. If the rural listeners were added to the urban, it is estimated that the total audience in Pakistan for the BBC Urdu Service is of the order of 10 million adults.

In the first four months of 1981, a survey was also carried out in India among a representative sample of the urban and rural population of two northern states — Uttar Pradesh and Rajasthan — where Hindi is the main language. The survey confirmed previous evidence of a large audience for the BBC Hindi Service, with 24.2% of the sample tuning in regularly. A particularly high listening level was found to exist in Rajasthan, which is better served than Uttar Pradesh by mediumwave AM broadcasts from Masirah Island.

Based on this survey it is estimated that there are over 15 million regular listeners to the BBC Hindi Service in these two states of India alone. Further, taking into account varying reception conditions and population structures, it can be broadly estimated that the Hindi Service is heard regularly by some 35 million adults in the subcontinent as a whole. The survey also asked about six other foreign broadcasters in Hindi. Apart from the Sri Lanka Broadcasting Corporation, with 30.2% of the sample listening regularly, audiences were much smaller than for the BBC: Radio Pakistan 8.7%, Radio Moscow 3.8%, Voice of America 2.4%, Radio Peking 1.4% and Deutsche Welle 0.7%. BBC broadcasts in Urdu were regularly heard by 3.4% of the sample, equivalent to about 2,250,000 adults in the two states, and English broadcasts by 2.1%, about 1,250,000 adults.

Who Listens, and Why

But counting listeners is not the whole of audience research. Obviously, it is good to be able to know how many are listening. But we also like to know details about demographics — that is, specifics about just who the listeners are. There is too much complexity to cover much of this aspect here, as audiences vary from country to country. But some broad generalizations can be made.

In every case, men outnumber women. The audience is generally better educated, better housed, better off and younger than the population as a whole. But this point should not be misunderstood or exaggerated. In India, for example, although better educated and urban employed people form a disproportionately large section of the audience, peasants and illiterates are still the larger group.

In order to perform their functions as well as possible, programme makers need more information about the tastes and preferences of the audience in various parts of the world. Unfortunately, sample surveys are not often suitable for providing the kind of in-depth reaction to programming required by programme makers. This can be more readily acquired from an analysis of the substantial amount of mail received from listeners and by the use of postal questionnaire techniques. Naturally, the volume of correspondence gives no indication whatsoever of the audience size, which may fluctuate wildly in response to all kinds of stimuli both within and beyond the BBC's control.

Letters from Listeners Uniquely Helpful

Even so, letters from all parts of the world continue to be a valuable source of reaction to programme output, as well as providing extensive data on reception conditions and indicating the wide geographic spread of the audience. In 1985, the External Services received some 450,000 letters from around the world. Leading the way was the Arabic Service with 65,000, followed by the English language World Service with 54,000 and the Hindi Service with 49,000 letters. A major stimulant to letter writing in many languages is the "English by Radio" program series.

It is worth mentioning here that these English lessons on the BBC, now broadcast to all parts of the world and with commentaries provided in many languages, are very popular and attract new listeners anxious to learn or improve their English. These listeners often stay with the broadcasts to hear news and other programmes.

Postal questionnaire techniques provide an opportunity to question groups of listeners about all aspects of their BBC listening and general media usage. These questionnaires also eliminate the haphazard effects inherent in relying on listener correspondence for such information. This methodology is particularly appropriate for stimulating in-depth reaction to current programming, for testing ideas for the future, and for producing a wide range of very detailed information on listening habits, reception conditions and radio set ownership.

In 1985, over 27,000 questionnaires were returned by BBC listeners. Additionally, in 1984 there was a listening diary in the World Service magazine, *London Calling,* which prompted over 5,000 listeners to keep detailed hour by hour records of their World Service listening for a week. A similar exercise on a smaller scale was carried out with Arabic listeners.

Special Research for Measuring within Closed Societies

Some areas of the world are completely closed to research — either by surveys on the ground or by postal questionnaires. Much of the communist world is in this category, although some indication of the size of audiences in Eastern and Central Europe is obtained by special research carried out by Radio Liberty and Radio Free Europe (RFE/RL). Most of this information on radio listening in COMECON countries is obtained from visitors to Western Europe. It is not an ideal way to do research, but provides useful information in an otherwise barren field. Occasionally, it is possible to verify parts of this research by reference to what little radio audience research occasionally becomes available from these closed countries.

There are two bright features of BBC research in recent years relating to listening in the communist countries. In 1982, a successful postal survey was carried out of listeners in Yugoslavia. China provides an even more striking example of a change in atmosphere. Before 1979, almost no letters were ever received by the BBC Chinese Service from inside the People's Republic. Only 17 were received, for example, in 1978. With the removal of restrictions, mail shot up to nearly 18,000 in 1979 and to over 29,000 in 1980. This was followed by a postal survey in 1981 during which more than 2,000 questionnaires on radio reception were completed by listeners in mainland China and sent to the BBC. Such postal research in China continues to date. More recently, market research on the streets of China has become possible, so data on radio listening in some of the main cities will soon become available.

Research Allows Decisions to be Based on Facts

Research in world radio broadcasting helps the program makers and planners avoid mistakes and false assumptions that are all too easy to make from a position physically removed from the target audience. For example, it is often assumed that in the rich industrialized countries of North America, Europe and Japan, only shortwave enthusiasts like "DXers" listen to broadcasts from other countries.

This is a fallacy.

Take Europe, for example. First of all, there are many ordinary radio listeners who know little or nothing of kilohertz or frequency spectrums who listen regularly to radio stations transmitting from other countries. In most cases nowadays, however, such listening is on mediumwave AM, as shortwave listening in Western Europe has declined. The major world radio broadcasters in Europe, including the BBC, Deutschlandfunk, Radio Luxembourg and Radio Moscow now use frequencies in the mediumwave AM band for at least some of their transmissions directed at audiences in Europe.

It might be argued that in many cases, listeners to broadcasts emanating from other countries in Europe are really only "eavesdropping" on the domestic transmissions of neighboring countries. But the aforementioned four international broadcasters each uses mediumwave AM for transmissions in languages intended for other countries. Thus, the BBC broadcasts some of its programmes in English, French and German on mediumwave AM to Western Europe. So does Radio Moscow. Deutsch-

landfunk uses no shortwave at all, but directs its programmes in various East and West European languages to its target areas in both mediumwave AM and longwave frequencies. It now has plans to build a series of FM stations to increase its audience in East Germany. This will not be the only example of international broadcasting on FM. The BBC has broadcast for many years to Greater Berlin on FM. International broadcasters know that to be completely effective, especially in Northern and Western Europe, they need to develop and sustain services in frequencies alongside the domestic radio services.

Secondly, and despite these developments, shortwave listening survives in many developed countries and is by no means confined to enthusiasts. Indeed, enthusiasts form a minority of the listenership to world radio broadcasts. For example, in 1986, a survey conducted in Greece found a regular audience to the BBC Greek Service of over 2% of the adult population. A similar survey in 1982 in Finland found 1.5% of the adult population listening regularly to the BBC Finnish Service.

Two Million Hear BBC Regularly on Shortwave in US

In the United States, where it has been assumed that no one but radio buffs listen to shortwave, a survey for the BBC in 1981-1982 found a regular audience to the BBC World Service in English of 1.3% — equivalent to approximately two million adults. New digital sets, such as are reported on in this book, make tuning to world radio on shortwave very much simpler. The wide availability of these sets may increase listening to shortwave internationally.

We often ask listeners in our surveys why they tune to the BBC. The overwhelming reason given is that they want to hear news. In totalitarian states this is easy enough to understand. In other countries which are not dictatorial or totalitarian, government control of the main radio and TV stations nonetheless means very often that the news is colored by official attitudes. People often tune to the BBC to see if they can find out more. Thus, during an international crisis, there is plenty of evidence that listeners in the country concerned increase their listening to foreign stations, especially the major ones.

But even in countries, such as the US, where the local media are under no bureaucratic or political control, many listeners explain that they listen to the BBC or other major world radio broadcasts to hear world news not provided on their own stations. Commercial radio stations in the United States broadcast very little world news, it being a minority interest spread thinly around the country. But two million listeners is a handsome minority for the BBC World Service! This figure, by the way, is *in addition to* listening to rebroadcasts of the BBC on local US stations.

In Japan, shortwave listening survives. The BBC conducted a survey there in 1983. A previous survey in 1976 found a regular adult audience of about half a million listening to the BBC Japanese Service. The 1983 survey, on the other hand, showed a slightly smaller audience at just under

400,000. In the Middle East and North Africa there has been a move in recent years away from shortwave listening. This is because the major international broadcasters in the region have developed mediumwave AM facilities in order for their Arabic Services to compete with domestic stations and, more importantly, with the successful and popular commercial stations, such as Radio Monte Carlo, broadcasting from Cyprus — which, incidentally, is interesting in that it has recently added shortwave to its established mediumwave AM operation, rather than the customary *vice versa.*

Withal, there is ample evidence that large numbers of people in the Arab World continue to listen to the shortwave transmissions of major international broadcasters, especially in those areas where some mediumwave AM transmissions cannot reach. For example, in Morocco — which is well beyond the reach of any BBC mediumwave AM transmitters — the BBC's Arabic Services were listened to regularly in 1986 by no less than one in six urban adults every week.

The Future of World Broadcasting

The 1980s will probably be looked back on as a decade in which world radio broadcasters engaged in a major rethinking of their tactics with respect to technology.

Will direct broadcasting by satellite be feasible? Already the BBC is feeding most of its relay transmitters around the world by satellite, thus improving the technical quality. With the development of cable TV/radio in the rich industrialized nations, will international sound broadcasting be made available as one service among the others so that a high quality feed, perhaps even in stereo, may be provided direct to the homes of those who want it? Can jamming, which has so adversely affected shortwave listening in Poland and the USSR be overcome? Is direct radio broadcasting by satellite technically and politically feasible prospect?

Perhaps most important of all, what will be the impact of the 1987 World Administrative Radio Conference (WARC-87)? This crucial gathering is to decide on a number of fundamental aspects of how the shortwave spectrum is to be utilized for world radio broadcasting.

Whatever happens, shortwave broadcasting is certain to survive as a major element in world radio broadcasting for the rest of this century. The VOA, BBC, Deutsche Welle and Radio Nederland have shown their confidence that this is so by recent investments in new transmitters, and there are plans for others. Too, both Radio France International and Radio Japan have undertaken ambitious programs aiming at the improvement of their standing among world radio broadcasters.

Dr. Graham L. Mytton is the Head of International Broadcasting and Audience Research with the BBC External Services. His career with the BBC began in 1964, and has included duties with the African Service and Radio 4. He has published two books, including *Listening Looking and Learning* (Lusaka, 1975) and *Mass Communications in Africa* (London, 1983).

TABLE OF CONTENTS

HOW TO USE YOUR RADIO DATABASE INTERNATIONAL

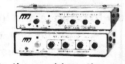

Indoor Tuned Active Antenna
MFJ's World Grabber

Here's what the "World Radio TV Handbook" said about the MFJ-1020: *"The MFJ-1020 is a fine value in flexibility ... the MFJ-1020 performs very well, indeed."*

"World Grabber." Put this handsome unit on your operating desk and listen to the world! Its performance rivals, often exceeds reception from outside long antennas.

Unique tuned circuitry minimizes intermodulation distortion, provides additional RF selectivity and reduces noise outside the tuned band.

Amplification also permits using the MFJ-1020 as a preselector with an external antenna, for added versatility.

Covers 300 KHz to 30 MHz in 5 bands. Switch selects .3-.7, .7-1.6, 1.6-4, 4-11, 11-30 MHz.

Adjustable telescoping antenna. Swivels for maximum signal, minimum noise.

MFJ-1020

NEW IMPROVED WITH HIGHER GAIN!

$**79**95

Full controls for tuning, band selection, gain and function (On-Off/Bypass). LED indicator. FET, bipolar circuitry. Phono jack provided for use with external antenna.

Universal power. Operates on 9 V battery (not included); any 9-18 VDC supply, or 110 VAC with optional AC adapter, MFJ-1312, $9.95.

Convenient size. The handsome beige and walnut grain plastic and metal cabinet easily fits on your desk for it measures just 5x2x6 inches.

Travel the World with your ears. Wherever you live, city apartment or country home, MFJ-1020 will grab the SWL world for you!

ACCESSORIES

RTTY/ASCII/CW RECEIVE ONLY SWL COMPUTER INTERFACE
MFJ-1225 $**69**95

FREE MFJ RTTY/ASCII/CW Software Tape and Cable for C-64 and VIC-20.

Receive commercial, military, and amateur RTTY/ASCII/CW using your personal computer.

The MFJ-1225 Computer interface plugs between your receiver & VIC-20, Apple, TRS-80C, Atari, TI-99, Commodore 64 and most other personal computers. Requires suitable software.

Copies all shifts (850, 425, 170 Hz shift and all others) and all speeds. Automatic noise limiter suppress static crashes for better copy. 2 LED tuning indicator makes tuning fast, easy, positive. 4½x1¼x4¼ in. 12-15 VDC or 110 VAC with optional adapter, MFJ-1312, $9.95.

In addition, MFJ-1225's unique general purpose socket provides RTTY out, RTTY inverted out, CW out, CW inverted out, ground and +5 VDC for interfacing to most any personal computer with the proper software.

DUAL TUNABLE SSB/CW FILTER
MFJ-752B $**99**95

The 752B is MFJ's most versatile filter. Zero in your SWL signal and notch out interfering signals at the same time. Primary filter has tunable peak, notch, lowpass and highpass. Auxiliary filter has peak, notch. Gives constant output as bandwidth is varied. Linear frequency control.

Switch for 2 receivers. Drives speaker. 10x2x6 in. 9-18 VDC or 110 VAC with MFJ-1312, $9.95.

DX'ers FILTER
MFJ-732 $**69**95

Uncover signals buried in the airways. Helps eliminate heterodyning and signal interference. Select lowpass and highpass cutoffs at 300, 500, 1500, 2200 and 3000 Hz for much improved copy.

Speaker, 2W amp. 9-18 VDC, 110 VAC with MFJ-1312, $9.95.

24 HOUR LCD CLOCKS
MFJ-108   MFJ-107
$**19**95 $**9**95

Huge 5/8 in. LCD numbers. Choose from dual clock with seperate UTC and Local time display or single unit with 24 Hour display. Both mounted in a brushed aluminum frame, easy to read. Both can be operated in alternating time-date display mode. Battery included. MFJ-108, 4½x1x2; MFJ-107, 2¼x1x2. Imported.

24/12 HOUR CLOCK WITH ID TIMER
MFJ-106 $**19**95

Switch to 24 hour UTC or 12 hour format! Battery backup. ID timer alerts every 9 minutes after reset. Red .6 in. LEDs. Synchronizable to WWV. Alarm, snooze functions. PM, alarm on indicators. Silver/Black cabinet. 5x2x3 in., 110 VAC, 60 Hz. Imported.

Order from MFJ and try it — no obligation!

- If not delighted, return it within 30 days for a prompt refund (less shipping).
- One year unconditional guarantee. • Made in U.S.A. • Add $5 each shipping/handling • Call or write for FREE Catalog. Over 100 products.

Continued from page 5

to you in English, to tell you how they view the life of man on earth and to sing and play and recite for you, bringing the best people to their microphones to get and hold your attention.

And that brings us to the subject of this book, because no matter what your listening pleasure, you've got to know where and when to tune.

In RADIO DATABASE INTERNATIONAL you'll find virtually all the information you need to let you open the shutters on this wondrous window to the world. RDI lets you know about the new generation of high-tech radios — how they perform, what they cost. It tells you also when and where to find the stations that broadcast such a rich diversity of programs: live coverage of unfolding events, concerts, world and local news, political commentary, drama, sports, and so much more.

So, even if you've never been more than fifty miles away from the family hearth, this book will give you something very special: the key to your world.

Today, I find — often in surprising ways — that more people are discovering the excitement of world radio for themselves. Take what happened one Saturday afternoon recently when I walked in on our local tailor and found him, amidst needle and thread, listening on his little Sony world-band radio to a station in West Africa. He had come upon the broadcast by pure accident. His use for world radio to that moment had lain in the soccer broadcasts from his home country. That Saturday, out of curiousity, he had tuned across the dial and discovered this West African program. He was intrigued, so I went home and got my copy of RADIO DATABASE INTERNATIONAL and lent it to him.

The next time I came in, he was full of information on the many other stations he had discovered, including a particularly powerful one that offered all sorts of music, from Arabic vocals to Paul Anka, and emanated from, of all places, Abu Dhabi.

Now, my friend the tailor has become an enthusiastic explorer of world radio. I think it was my copy of RDI that really did it. And he still has it, by the way. In view of the pleasure he's getting from it, I just don't have the heart to ask him for it. So I'll get another copy and set it down among good deeds done.

Rarely do good deeds cost so little!

WORLDWIDE BROADCASTS

You can tune in world radio broadcasts in either of two ways: by country or by frequency.

This quick-access "Worldwide Broadcasts" section tells you the year-around frequencies of major world broadcasts — those of at least 50 kW power — in English, French, German, Japanese and Spanish. It's perfect for getting right to the station you want.

Survey findings at International Broadcasting Services indicate that world radio listeners especially enjoy "traveling" around the bands...finding what they like to hear, rather than simply tuning directly to a given country. For that reason, the at-a-glance "Worldscan" section farther on in this book provides you with something special: the ability to scan up and down the over-1,100 channels of news and entertainment found within the world radio bands. This also serves to complement the "Worldwide Broadcasts" section by providing in one handy chapter a wealth of details concerning every station on each channel.

AFGHANISTAN
RADIO AFGHANISTAN
  English 6085 kHz

ALBANIA
RADIO TIRANA
  English 6200, 7065, 7075, 7080, 7120, 7300,
    9555, 9760, 11960, 11985, 15430 kHz
  French 7065, 7075, 7080, 11885, 11905, 11960,
    11985 kHz
  German 6076, 7310 kHz
  Spanish 6200, 7065, 7120, 7300, 9750, 9790,
    11985 kHz

ALGERIA
RTV ALGERIENNE
  English 9509, 9640, 15160, 17745 kHz
  French 9509, 9640, 15160, 17745 kHz
  Spanish 9509, 9640, 15160, 17745 kHz

ANGOLA
"VOICE OF NAMIBIA"
  Multilingual 7245 kHz
RADIO NACIONAL
  English 7245 kHz
  French 7245 kHz
  Spanish 7245 kHz

ARGENTINA
RADIODIFUSION ARGENTINA-RAE
  English 9690, 11710, 15345 kHz
  French 6060, 11710 kHz
  German 15345 kHz
  Spanish 6060, 9690, 11710, 15345 kHz
  Japanese 9690 kHz
RADIO NACIONAL
  Spanish 6060, 11710 kHz

AUSTRALIA
AUSTRALIAN BROADCASTING CORP
  English 15425 kHz
  Multilingual 4835, 4910, 5025 kHz
RADIO AUSTRALIA
  English 5995, 6035, 6060, 6080, 7205, 7215,
    9580, 9620, 9645, 9655, 9710, 9770, 11705,
    11720, 11800, 11910, 15160, 15165, 15180,
    15240, 15320, 15395, 15415, 17715, 17725,
    17750, 17795, 17830 kHz
  French 15140, 15160, 15320, 17750 kHz
  Japanese 9710, 11800 kHz

AUSTRIA
RADIO AUSTRIA INTERNATIONAL
  English 5945, 6000, 6155, 7170, 9635, 9770,
    11660, 11670, 11840, 11935, 12015, 12025,
    15185, 15270, 15315, 15320, 15410,
    15465 kHz
  French 5945, 6000, 6155, 9615, 9635, 11670,
    11840, 11860, 12015, 12025, 15185, 15315,
    15410 kHz
  German 5945, 6000, 6155, 7165, 7170, 9580,
    9590, 9615, 9635, 9760, 9770, 11660, 11670,
    11840, 11860, 11935, 12015, 12025, 15185,
    15270, 15315, 15320, 15410, 15465 kHz
  Spanish 5945, 6000, 6155, 7165, 9580, 9590,
    9615, 9760, 11660, 11670, 11860, 12015,
    15315 kHz

BANGLADESH
RADIO BANGLADESH
  English 6240, 7505, 9855, 11555, 11645, 12030,
    15525, 15585, 17653 kHz

BELGIUM
BELGISCHE RADIO TV
  English 5910, 9830, 9880, 9905, 9925, 11980,
    15510, 15515, 21810 kHz

German 5910 kHz
Spanish 5910, 9830, 9905, 9925, 11980 kHz

RADIO-TV BELGE FRANCAISE
  French 5965, 6040, 6050, 6075, 9900, 11850,
    11855, 15210, 15580, 17675, 17680, 17685,
    21460 kHz
  German 5965, 17680, 17685 kHz

BOTSWANA
RADIO BOTSWANA
  Multilingual 3356, 4820, 5955, 5965, 7255 kHz

BRAZIL
RADIO NACIONAL
  English 11745, 15155, 15335 kHz
  French 11765 kHz
  German 6065, 15155, 15335, 17860 kHz
  Spanish 9655, 11745 kHz

BULGARIA
RADIO SOFIA
  English 6070, 7115, 9560, 9595, 9665, 9700,
    9740, 11720, 11735, 11750, 11765, 11840,
    11880, 15140, 15215, 15310, 15330 kHz
  French 6070, 9560, 9595, 9700, 9740, 11720,
    11735, 11765, 11840, 11880, 15140, 15215,
    15310 kHz
  German 6035, 6070, 7155, 9700, 11720,
    15140 kHz
  Spanish 9560, 9745, 9755, 11765, 11850, 11870,
    11880, 15310, 15370 kHz

BURKINA FASO
RTV BURKINA
  English 7230 kHz
  French 4815 kHz
  Multilingual 7230 kHz

BURMA
BURMA BROADCASTING SERVICE
  English 5985, 7185, 9730 kHz

CAMEROON
R NATIONALE DU CAMEROUN
  English 7150 kHz
  French 7150 kHz
  Multilingual 4850, 7240, 9746 kHz
RADIO DOUALA
  English 4795 kHz
  French 4795 kHz
RADIO GAROUA
  English 5010 kHz
  French 5010 kHz
  Multilingual 5010 kHz

CANADA
BBC
  English 6120 kHz
CANADIAN BROADCASTING CORP
  English 6065, 6195, 9625, 11720 kHz
  French 6065, 6195, 9625, 11720 kHz
  Multilingual 6195, 9625, 11720 kHz
RADIO CANADA INTERNATIONAL
  English 5960, 6140, **6170**, **7130**, **7155**, **7275**,
    9535, **9555**, 9650, **9740**, 9750, 9755, 9760,
    11710, **11775**, 11825, **11840**, 11845, 11855,
    11925, 11940, 11945, 11955, 11960, 15150,

15180, 15190, **15235**, 15260, 15325, 15440,
17820, 17875 kHz
French 5960, 6140, **6170**, **7130**, **7155**, **7230**,
  7275, 9535, **9555**, **9650**, **9740**, 9750, 9755,
  9760, 11710, **11775**, 11825, **11840**, 11845,
  11855, 11940, 11945, 11955, 11960, 15150,
  15180, 15190, **15235**, 15260, 15325, 15440,
  17820, 17875 kHz
German **7235**, **9555**, 15325, 17820 kHz
Spanish 9535, 11845, 11940, 15190 kHz
Multilingual **9555**, **11915**, **11935**, **15160**,
  15325 kHz

CENTRAL AFRICAN REP
RTV CENTRAFRICAINE
  French 5035 kHz

CHAD
RADIODIFFUSION NATIONALE
  Multilingual 4904, 7120 kHz

CHINA (PR)
RADIO BEIJING
  English 4130, 4200, 4800, 5250, 6825, 7480,
    7590, 9290, 9440, 9550, 9570, 9700, 9860,
    11455, 11500, 11515, 11650, 11660, 11755,
    11860, 11905, 11970, 15165, 15195, 15280,
    15385, 15520, 17795 kHz
  French 3270, 4020, 7055, 7190, 7335, 7800,
    9880 kHz
  German 4130, 5250, 7590, 9860, 11500 kHz
  Spanish 4800, 6933, 7375, 9590, 9640, 9700,
    9860, 9945, 11445, 11650, 11685, 11970,
    11980, 15100, 15120, 15180, 15200, 15510,
    15520, 17650, 17680, 17775, 17795 kHz
  Japanese 4960, 7480, 11515 kHz

CHINA (TAIWAN)
VOICE OF FREE CHINA
  English **5985**, 9685, 9765, 9955, 15370 kHz
  French 9765 kHz
  Spanish 9765, 9955, **15130**, **15215**, **17805**,
    17845 kHz
  Japanese 7130 kHz
VOICE OF ASIA
  English 7285, 7445 kHz

COLOMBIA
RADIO SUTATENZA
  Spanish 5095 kHz

CONGO
RTV CONGOLAISE
  French 6115, 9715, 15190 kHz
  Multilingual 6115, 9715, 15190 kHz

COSTA RICA
FARO DEL CARIBE
  Spanish 9645 kHz

CUBA
RADIO HABANA
  English 6090, 6100, 6140, 9525, 9740, 11725,
    11850, 15300, 17750, 17885 kHz
  French 6090, 9730, 11710, 11795, 11850, 11950,
    15125, 17795, 17885 kHz
  Spanish 6060, 6090, 9550, 9655, 9730, 9770,

11710, 11760, 11950, 11970, 15125, 15230, 15300, 15340, 17750, 17795 kHz

CZECHOSLOVAKIA
RADIO PRAGUE
English 5930, 6055, 7345, 9540, 9605, 9630, 9740, 11855, 11990, 15110, 15205, 17705, 17840, 21505, 21705 kHz
French 5930, 6055, 7290, 7345, 9505, 9600, 11990, 15205 kHz
German 6055 kHz
Spanish 5930, 7345, 9540, 9630, 9740, 11990 kHz
Multilingual 6055, 7345, 9505, 9630 kHz 17840, 21505, 21705 kHz

DOMINICAN REPUBLIC
RADIO CLARIN
Spanish 11700 kHz

ECUADOR
HCJB-VOICE OF THE ANDES
English 6095, 6130, 6205, 6230, 9655, 9745, 9845, 9860, 9870, 11740, 11835, 11910, 11925, 15115, 15155, 15220, 15270, 17790, 17890 kHz
French 6095, 9860, 11835, 15155, 15220, 15270, 17790 kHz
German 6075, 6090, 6205, 9655, 9720, 9725, 9845, 9860, 11835, 15250, 15270, 17790 kHz
Spanish 6050, 9765, 9860, 11835, 11910, 11960, 15160, 15270, 17790, 17890 kHz
Japanese 6075, 9715, 11835, 15295 kHz
RADIO NACIONAL
Spanish 15270, 17790 kHz

EGYPT
RADIO CAIRO
English 9475, 9675, 9805, 15255, 15375, 17675 kHz
French 9805, 15335 kHz
German 9805 kHz
Spanish 9475, 9740, 11715 kHz

EQUATORIAL GUINEA
RADIO NACIONAL
English 9553 kHz
Multilingual 4925.6, 4926 kHz

ETHIOPIA
"RADIO FREEDOM"
English 9595 kHz
"VOICE OF NAMIBIA"
Multilingual 9595 kHz
VOICE OF REVOLUTIONARY ETHIOPIA
English 7165, 9560 kHz
French 7165, 9560 kHz

FINLAND
RADIO FINLAND
English 9530, 9535, 9540, 9605, 9655, 11715, 11755, 11935, 11945, 15115, 15265, 15400, 15430, 17785, 17800 kHz
German 9530, 9655, 11755, 11935, 15265 kHz

FRANCE
RADIO FRANCE INTERNATIONAL
English 6175, 7135, 9535, 9545, 9550, 9790,

9800, **11705**, 11880, 11995, 17620, 17795, 21685 kHz
French 5950, 5990, 6040, 6045, 6055, 6085, 6145, 6175, 7120, 7135, **7160**, 7280, 9535, 9545, 9550, 9575, **9715**, 9745, 9790, **9800**, 9805, 9810, 11660, 11670, 11695, 11700, 11705, 11790, 11800, 11805, 11845, 11880, 11930, 11955, 11965, **11995**, 15135, 15155, 15180, 15190, 15200, 15300, 15315, 15365, 15425, 15435, 17620, 17720, 17785, 17795, 17800, 17845, 17850, **17860**, 17875, 21580, 21620, 21685 kHz
German 6010, 6145, 7145 kHz
Spanish 5950, **5990**, 5995, 6055, 6085, 9535, **9715**, 9790, **9800**, 11670, 11955, 11965, **11995** kHz

GABON
ADVENTIST WORLD RADIO
French 9630 kHz
AFRIQUE NUMERO UN
English 17750 kHz
French 4830, 7200, 11940, 15200, 15475, 17820, 17870 kHz
Multilingual 7200, 15200 kHz
RTV GABONAISE
Multilingual 4777, 7270 kHz

GERMANY (DR)
RADIO BERLIN INTERNATIONAL
English 5965, 6010, 6040, 6070, 6080, 6115, 6125, 6165, 7185, 7260, 7295, 9505, 9560, 9620, 9645, 9665, 9730, 11705, 11750, 11785, 11810, 11890, 11960, 11970, 11975, 15105, 15145, 15170, 15240, 15255, 15390, 15440, 15445, 17700, 17705, 17755, 17765, 17880, 21465, 21540 kHz
French 5965, 6040, 6115, 7185, 7260, 7295, 9505, 9620, 9665, 9730, 9770, 11705, 11750, 11785, 11810, 11890, 11970, 15105, 15145, 15170, 15255, 15390, 17755 kHz
German 5965, 6010, 6040, 6070, 6080, 6105, 6115, 6125, 7185, 7295, 9505, 9560, 9600, 9620, 9635, 9645, 9665, 9730, 9770, 11700, 11705, 11750, 11785, 11810, 11825, 11890, 11960, 11970, 11975, 15105, 15170, 15240, 15445, 17700, 17705, 17755, 17765, 17880, 21540 kHz
Spanish 6010, 6040, 6070, 6125, 6165, 7185, 7260, 7295, 9505, 9600, 9620, 9645, 9730, 11785 kHz
STIMME DER DDR
German 6115 kHz

GERMANY (FR)
BAYERISCHER RUNDFUNK
German 6085 kHz
DEUTSCHE WELLE
English 5960, **5995**, 6010, 6035, **6040**, **6085**, **6120**, 6130, 6145, **6170**, **6185**, 7110, 7130, 7150, 7195, **7200**, **7225**, 7285, **9545**, **9565**, 9585, **9600**, 9610, **9615**, 9625, **9640**, **9650**, **9690**, **9700**, **9735**, 9745, 9765, 11765, **11785**, **11945**, **11965**, **15105**, 15135, 15150, 15160, **15185**, 15205, 15320, 15330, **15410**, 17765, 17780, **17800**, 17825, **21500**, **21560**, 21600, 21680 kHz

French 7150, 7195, **7225**, **9565**, 9610, 9625,
9700, **9735**, 9765, 11765, 11945, **11965**,
15135, 15185, **15410**, 17765, **17800**, 17825,
21600 kHz

German 3995, 6040, **6045**, **6065**, 6075, **6085**,
6100, 6145, **6160**, 7130, 7145, 7175, **7225**,
7285, **9545**, 9570, **9605**, 9615, **9640**, 9645,
9650, **9690**, 9700, 9715, **9735**, **11705**, 11720,
11730, **11765**, **11785**, **11795**, 11820, 11855,
11945, 11955, **15105**, **15210**, **15245**, 15260,
15270, **15275**, 15320, **15355**, **15410**, **17715**,
17810, 17845, **17860**, **17875**, 21560,
21680 kHz

Spanish 6010, 6045, 6120, 6130, 6145, 7235,
9545, **9565**, **9605**, **9690**, 9700, **9735**, **11705**,
11785, **11795**, 11810, **11865**, **15105**,
15295 kHz

Japanese **7170**, **7265**, **9505**, **9640**, 9670, 9680,
11805, 11810, **11845**, **11865**, 11910, 15185,
15400, 15405 kHz

R AMERICAN SECTOR
German 6005 kHz

GHANA
GHANA BROADCASTING CORPORATION
English 3366, 7295 kHz
Multilingual 4915 kHz

GREECE
FONI TIS HELLADAS
English 7395, 9420, 9860, 11645 kHz
French 9420 kHz
Spanish 7395, 9420, 9860 kHz
Multilingual 6205, 7370, 9860, 9905, 11645,
11915, 15405, 15630, 17565, 17770 kHz

GUAM
KTWR-TRANS WORLD RADIO
English 9510, 9820, 11840, 15350 kHz
Japanese 9820, 11765, 11840 kHz

GUINEA
RTV GUINEENNE
English 7125, 9650, 15310 kHz
French 7125, 9650, 15310 kHz
Multilingual 7125, 9650, 15310 kHz

HOLLAND
RADIO NEDERLAND
English 5955, **6020**, **6165**, 7175, **9515**, **9540**,
9590, **9630**, **9650**, **9715**, 9895, 11720, **11735**,
11740, 11930, 13770, 15560, **17575**, **17605**,
21480, **21485**, **21685** kHz
French **9540**, 9895, 11730, **11740**, 15280, 15560,
17605, **21685** kHz
Spanish 6020, 6110, **6165**, 7230, **9590**, 9610,
9895, 11930, **15315**, **17605** kHz

HUNGARY
RADIO BUDAPEST
English 6025, 6110, 7220, 7225, 9520, 9585,
9835, 11910, 15220, 17710 kHz
German 7155, 7220, 7225, 9585, 9835,
11910 kHz
Spanish 6025, 6110, 7220, 9520, 9585, 9835,
11910 kHz

INDIA
ALL INDIA RADIO
English 6035, 6050, 7150, 7215, 9545, 9550,
9595, 9665, 9755, 9910, 11620, 11715, 11765,
11795, 11810, 11845, 11865, 11870, 15110,
15130, 15175, 15230, 15265, 15320, 15335,
17387, 17705, 17875 kHz
French 9755, 11865, 15365, 17830 kHz
Multilingual 6045, 6050, 6145, 7110, 7150, 7160,
7265, 7280, 9545, 9610, 9615, 9675, 10335,
11620, 11730, 11815, 11830, 11850, 11895,
15160, 15245, 15250, 15305, 15320,
17705 kHz

INDONESIA
VOICE OF INDONESIA
English 11790, 15150 kHz
French 11790, 15150 kHz
German 11790, 15150 kHz
Spanish 11790, 15150 kHz
Japanese 11790, 15150 kHz

IRAN
VOICE OF THE ISLAMIC REPUBLIC
English 9022, 9765, 11930, 15084 kHz
French 9022, 9765, 11930, 15084 kHz
German 9022, 9765, 11930 kHz
Spanish 9022, 15084 kHz

IRAQ
RADIO BAGHDAD
English 7170, 11750 kHz

ISRAEL
KOL ISRAEL
English 7412, 9009, 9390, 9435, 9815, 11585,
11605, 11655, 12025, 12027.5, 15560, 15585,
17630 kHz
French 7412, 9009, 9390, 9435, 9815, 11585,
11605, 11655, 12025, 12027.5, 15560, 15585,
17630 kHz
Spanish 7412, 9009, 9435, 9815, 11585,
11655 kHz

ITALY
RTV ITALIANA
English 5990, 6165, 7235, 7275, 7290, 9575,
9710, 9775, 11800, 11905, 15330 kHz
French 5990, 7235, 7290, 9575, 9710, 11800,
11905 kHz
German 5990, 7275, 7290, 9575 kHz
Spanish 5990, 7275, 9575, 9710, 11800, 11905,
15245 kHz
Multilingual 6060 kHz

IVORY COAST
RTV IVOIRIENNE
English 11940 kHz
French 6015, 9620, 11920 kHz

JAPAN
NIHON SHORTWAVE BROADCASTING
Japanese 3925, 6055, 6115, 9595, 9760 kHz
RADIO CANADA INTL
Japanese 6055, 9595 kHz
RADIO JAPAN/NHK
English 5990, 6080, 7105, 9505, 9575, 9605,

9645, 11710, 11840, 11875, 11950, 15195,
15235, 15300, 17755, 17810, 17825, 21610,
21640 kHz
French 6080, 7105, 9645, 11840 kHz
German 6080, 7105 kHz
Spanish 5990, 9525, 11950, 15195, 17825,
21610, 21640 kHz
Japanese 5990, 9505, 9525, 9575, 9605, 9645,
11840, 11950, 15195, 15235, 17755, 17810,
17825, 21610, 21640 kHz

JORDAN
RADIO JORDAN
English 9560 kHz (irregular)

KAMPUCHEA (CAMBODIA)
VOICE OF THE PEOPLE
English 11938 kHz
French 11938 kHz

KENYA
VOICE OF KENYA
Multilingual 4885, 11800 kHz

KOREA (DPR)
"VOICE OF REUNIFICATION"
English 4556.8 kHz
RADIO PYONGYANG
English 6576, 7205, 9325, 9555, 9625, 9715,
9750, 9765, 11830, 11880, 12000, 13750,
15140, 15160, 15180, 15245, 15305,
15340 kHz
French 6165, 6576, 7205, 9325, 11830, 11880,
12000, 13750, 15340, 15415 kHz
German 6576, 7205, 9325 kHz
Spanish 6576, 7205, 9325, 9555, 9715, 9750,
11755, 15140, 15160 kHz
Japanese 3015, 6540, 9505, 9600, 11780,
11830 kHz

KOREA (REPUBLIC)
RADIO KOREA
English 6165, 6485, 7275, 7550, 9570, 9640,
9750, 9870, 11740, 11810, 13670, 15375,
15395, 15575 kHz
French 7275, 11805, 11810, 13670, 15575 kHz
German 6485, 7275, 7550, 9870, 13670,
15575 kHz
Spanish 6485, 7550, 9570, 9870, 11725, 11810,
15575 kHz
Japanese 6165, 6175, 7275, 9640, 15375 kHz

KUWAIT
RADIO KUWAIT
English 11675, 15345 kHz

LESOTHO
RADIO LESOTHO
English 4800 kHz
Multilingual 4800 kHz

LIBERIA
LIBERIAN BROADCASTING SYSTEM
Multilingual 3255, 6090 kHz
RADIO ELWA
English 11830 kHz
French 6070, 11830 kHz
Multilingual 9550, 11830 kHz

LIBYA
RADIO JAMAHIRIYA
English 11815, 15450 kHz (irregular)

LUXEMBOURG
RADIO LUXEMBOURG
English 6090 kHz
French 15350 kHz
German 6090 kHz

MADAGASCAR
RADIO MADAGASIKARA
French 5010 kHz
Multilingual 3288, 6135 kHz

MALAWI
MALAWI BROADCASTING CORP
English 5995 kHz
Multilingual 3380 kHz

MALAYSIA
RADIO MALAYSIA
English 7295 kHz
Multilingual 9665 kHz
VOICE OF MALAYSIA
English 6175, 9750, 15295 kHz

MALI
RTV MALIENNE
English 5995 kHz
Multilingual 5995 kHz

MALTA
IBRA RADIO
English 9515 kHz
French 9720 kHz
German 6110, 9515 kHz
RADIO MEDITERRANEAN
English 6110 kHz
French 6110 kHz
Arabic 6110 kHz

MAURITANIA
ORT DE MAURITANIE
French 4845 kHz
Spanish 4845 kHz
Multilingual 4845, 7245 kHz

MEXICO
RADIO MEXICO INTERNATIONAL
Spanish 15430 kHz (irregular)

MONACO
RADIO MONTE CARLO
Multilingual **9795**, **15465** kHz
TRANS WORLD RADIO
English 7160, 9495, 11695 kHz
French 7235 kHz
German 6220, 7205, 9805 kHz
Multilingual 9495, 9775, 11660 kHz

MONGOLIA
RADIO ULAN BATOR
English 7235, 9575, 9616, 12015, 15305 kHz

MOROCCO
RADIO MEDI UN
Multilingual 9575, 15390 kHz

NAMIBIA
RADIO SOUTH WEST AFRICA
  Multilingual 3295 kHz
SOUTH AFRICA BROADCASTING CORP
  Multilingual 4965 kHz

NEPAL
RADIO NEPAL
  English 5005, 7165 kHz (irregular)

NETHERLANDS ANTILLES
TRANS WORLD RADIO
  English 9535, 11815 kHz
  German 9535, 15355 kHz
  Spanish 9535, 9665, 11895, 15355 kHz
  Multilingual 11875 kHz

NICARAGUA
LA VOZ DE NICARAGUA
  English 6014.8 kHz
  Spanish 6014.8 kHz

NIGERIA
FEDERAL RADIO CORPORATION
  Multilingual 6050 kHz
RADIO NIGERIA
  Multilingual 3326, 4770, 4990, 6089, 7285 kHz
VOICE OF NIGERIA
  English 7255, 11770, 15120, 15185 kHz
  French 7255, 15120 kHz
  German 15120 kHz

NORTHERN MARIANA IS
KYOI/CSM WORLD RADIO (planned)
  Multilingual 9665, 9670, 11900, 15190,
    15405 kHz

NORWAY
RADIO NORWAY INTERNATIONAL
  English 6015, 6030, 6040, 9520, 9525, 9580,
    9590, 9605, 9650, 9655, 11860, 11870, 11925,
    11935, 15165, 15180, 15185, 15205, 15225,
    15230, 15245, 15265, 15300, 15305, 15310,
    17740, 17770, 17830, 17850 kHz
  Multilingual 6015, 6030, 6040, 9520, 9525, 9580,
    9590, 9605, 9650, 9655, 11860, 11870, 11925,
    11935, 15165, 15180, 15185, 15205, 15225,
    15230, 15245, 15265, 15300, 15305, 15310,
    17740, 17770, 17830, 17850 kHz

PAKISTAN
RADIO PAKISTAN
  English 7315, 9465, 9885, 11670, 11675, 11740,
    11810, 15115, 15420, 15595, 15605,
    17660 kHz
  French 9465, 11790, 12015 kHz
  Multilingual 15605, 17660 kHz

PAPUA NEW GUINEA
NATIONAL BROADCASTING COMM OF PNG
  Multilingual 3925 kHz

PHILIPPINES
FAR EAST BROADCASTING COMPANY
  English 6030, 9665, 11850, 11865, 15350,
    15430 kHz
  German 6120, 7240 kHz

RADIO VERITAS ASIA
  English 9540, 15195 kHz
  Japanese 9550, 9560 kHz

POLAND
RADIO POLONIA
  English 6095, 6135, 7125, 7145, 7270, 7285,
    9525, 9540, 9675, 11815, 11840, 15120 kHz
  French 6095, 6135, 7125, 7270, 7285, 9525,
    9540, 9675, 11840, 15120 kHz
  German 6095, 6135, 7125, 7270, 7285, 9540 kHz
  Spanish 6135, 7145, 7270, 9525, 9675, 11840,
    15120 kHz

PORTUGAL
ADVENTIST WORLD RADIO
  English 9670 kHz
  German 9670 kHz
RADIO PORTUGUESA
  English 6095, 7155, 7200, 9565, 9605, 9680,
    9705, 9740, 15105, 15250 kHz
  French 7155, 7200, 9605, 9740, 15250 kHz
  German 7155, 7200, 9605, 9740 kHz

ROMANIA
RADIO BUCHAREST
  English 5990, 6055, 6155, 7135, 7145, 7165,
    7195, 9510, 9570, 9640, 9685, 9690, 9750,
    11740, 11775, 11810, 11830, 11840, 11885,
    11940, 15250, 15335, 15380, 17790, 17805,
    21665 kHz
  French 5990, 6055, 6190, 7195, 9570, 9590,
    9685, 9690, 9750, 11775, 11790, 11810,
    11885, 11940, 15250, 15335, 15365 kHz
  German 5990, 7135, 7195, 9690, 11940,
    15250 kHz
  Spanish 5990, 6150, 6155, 7225, 9510, 9570,
    9690, 11810, 11940 kHz

RWANDA
RADIO DE LA REPUBLIQUE RWANDAISE
  Multilingual 6055 kHz

SAUDI ARABIA
BROADCASTING SERVICE OF THE KINGDOM
  English 9705, 9720 kHz
  French 9705, 9720 kHz

SENEGAL
ORT DU SENEGAL
  English 4890 kHz
  French 4890 kHz
  Multilingual 4890, 7173 kHz

SEYCHELLES
FAR EAST BROADCASTING ASS'N
  English 9590, 11865, 15120, 17780 kHz
  French 11900 kHz

SIERRA LEONE
SIERRA LEONE BROADCASTING SERVICE
  French 5980 kHz
  Multilingual 5980 kHz

SINGAPORE
SINGAPORE BROADCASTING CORP
  English 5010, 5052, 11940 kHz

SOMALIA
RADIO MOGADISHU
  English 6095 kHz

SOUTH AFRICA
RADIO RSA
  English 3230, 4810, 4990, 5980, 6010, 7270,
    9585, 9615, 11900, 15220, 21590 kHz
  French 4810, 7270, 9585, 11900, 15220,
    21590 kHz
  German 11880, 11900, 15185, 17850 kHz
  Spanish 6065, 6160, 9580 kHz
SOUTH AFRICAN BROADCASTING CORP
  English 3250, 4835, 7170, 11790 kHz
  Multilingual 3215, 4880, 7205 kHz

SPAIN
RADIO EXTERIOR DE ESPANA
  English 5900, 6055, 6125, 7105, 9630, 9780,
    11690, 11880 kHz
  French 5900, 7105, 9780, 11690 kHz
  Spanish 6020, 6055, 6125, 6140, 7450, 9360,
    9530, 9570, 9620, 9630, 9650, 11635, 11730,
    11790, 11880, 11890, 11920, 11940, 11945,
    15215, **15365**, 15395, 15535, 17770, 17845,
    17890, 21595 kHz

SRI LANKA
SRI LANKA BROADCASTING CORP
  English 9720, 11800 kHz

SURINAME
RADIO SURINAME INERNATIONAL
  Multilingual **17755** kHz

SWAZILAND
SWAZI COMMERCIAL RADIO
  Multilingual 4980 kHz
TRANS WORLD RADIO
  English 9550 kHz
  French 7195 kHz

SWEDEN
RADIO SWEDEN INTERNATIONAL
  English 6065, 9615, 9630, 9695, 9710, 9745,
    11705, 11785, 11845, 11940, 11950, 15110,
    15115, 15190, 15240, 15345, 15390, 15435,
    17840, 17845, 21570 kHz
  French 6065, 9615, 9630, 11805, 15345,
    21690 kHz
  German 6065, 9630, 9655, 9760, 11805 kHz
  Spanish 6065, 9605, 9695, 9710, 11705, 11955,
    15240 kHz

SWITZERLAND
RED CROSS BROADCASTING SERVICE
  English 7210, 9560, 9725, 11745, 11795, 11905,
    11955, 15305, 17785, 17830 kHz
  French 7210 kHz
  German 7210 kHz
  Spanish 6135, 7210, 9625, 9725, 11925 kHz
  Multilingual 11955, 15420, 17830 kHz
SWISS BROADCASTING CORPORATION
  French 3985, 6165, 9535 kHz
  German 3985, 6165, 9535 kHz
SWISS RADIO INTERNATIONAL
  English 3985, 6135, 6165, 6190, 9535, 9560,

9590, 9625, 9725, 11745, 11795, 11905,
    11925, 11935, 11955, 15305, 15430, 15570,
    17785, 17830 kHz
  French 3985, 5965, 6135, 6165, 9535, 9560,
    9590, 9625, 9725, 9885, 11745, 11795, 11905,
    11935, 11955, 15305, 15420, 15430, 15570,
    17785, 17830 kHz
  German 3985, 5965, 6135, 6165, 9535, 9560,
    9590, 9625, 9725, 9885, 11745, 11795, 11905,
    11925, 11955, 15305, 15420, 15430, 15570,
    17785, 17830 kHz
  Spanish 5965, 6035, 6135, 9590, 9625, 9680,
    9725, 9885, 15305 kHz

SYRIA
SYRIAN BROADCASTING SERVICE
  English 11625, 7455 kHz
  French 12085 kHz
  German 7455 kHz
  Spanish 9485, 11640 kHz

TANZANIA
RADIO TANZANIA
  English 9684 kHz

THAILAND
RADIO THAILAND
  English 9655, 11905 kHz
  French 9655, 11905 kHz
  Japanese 9655, 11905 kHz

TOGO
RADIO LOME
  English 5047, 7265 kHz
  Multilingual 5047, 7265 kHz

TURKEY
TURKISH RADIO-TV CORPORATION
  English 6105, 7205, 7215, 9560, 9730, 17725,
    17885 kHz
  French 7215 kHz
  German 7215 kHz

UNITED ARAB EMIRATES
UAE RADIO
  English 9550, 11730, 11955, 15300, 15320,
    17775, 17830, 21605, 21700 kHz

UNITED KINGDOM
BBC
  English **3915**, 3955, **5965**, 5975, **6005**, 6010,
    6015, 6045, 6050, 6125, 6150, 6195, **7105**,
    7130, **7135**, 7150, **7160**, 7165, 7170, 7185,
    7210, 7260, 7325, 9410, **9510, 9515, 9590,
    9600**, 9610, 9640, 9660, **9715**, 9750, 9760,
    9915, **11745, 11750, 11775**, 11780,
    11820, 11860, 11955, 12095, 15070,
    15105, 15205, 15215, **15260**, 15270, **15310**,
    15390, 15400, 17705, 17780, 17790, 17810,
    17880, 17885, 21470, 21550, 21630, **21660**,
    21710 kHz
  French 3955, 6120, 6125, 6195, **7105**, 7150,
    7165, 7210, 7295, **9600, 9610**, 11720, 11780,
    11825, **15105**, 15115, 15150, 17810,
    21640 kHz
  German 3955, 6195, 7130, 7260, 7295, 9530,
    9565, 9750 kHz
  Spanish **6055**, 6110, 7140, **9765, 11820, 17830**,
    21490 kHz

USA

AFRTS-US MILITARY (relays CBS, etc)
English 6030, 6125, 6140, 9530, 9590, **9700**, 11730, 11790, 11805, **15265**, 15330, 15345, 15355, **15400**, 15430, 17765, 21570 kHz

KCBI
English 11790 kHz

KGEI-VOICE OF FRIENDSHIP
English 15280 kHz
German 15280 kHz
Spanish 9615, 15280, 15355 kHz

KNLS-VOICE OF THE NEW LIFE
English 11850, 11960 kHz

KVOH-VOICE OF HOPE
English 6005, 9525, 9852.5, 11930, 12025, 15566, 17775 kHz

RADIO MARTI
Spanish 6075, 9525, 9570, 9590, 11815, 11930 kHz

VOICE OF AMERICA
English **3990**, 5745, **5955**, **5965**, **5995**, **6035**, **6040**, **6045**, **6060**, 6080, **6090**, **6095**, **6110**, 6125, 6130, **6190**, **7170**, 7195, **7200**, **7205**, **7260**, **7275**, **7280**, **7325**, 9350, 9455, 9530, **9540**, **9545**, **9550**, **9575**, **9635**, 9670, **9700**, **9715**, **9740**, **9760**, **9770**, 9775, 10234, 10869, 11090, 11580, 11680, **11715**, **11720**, 11740, **11760**, **11775**, **11805**, **11835**, **11840**, **11915**, **11920**, **11925**, 14398, **15160**, **15185**, **15205**, **15215**, **15260**, **15290**, 15315, 15375, 15410, 15415, **15425**, **15445**, 15580, **15600**, **17735**, **17740**, 17765, 17775, 17785, 17800, **17820**, 17830, 17865, **17870**, 18137.5, 19480, **21540**, 21545 kHz
French 6020, **6180**, **6190**, **7135**, **7265**, 9565, 10234, 10869, 11740, **11810**, **11850**, **11875**, 11890, **11920**, 15160, 15195, **15315**, **15400**, 17640, **17705**, **17730**, 19261.5, 19480, 21470, **21680** kHz
German 15715 kHz
Spanish 5745, 6040, 6140, 6155, 6190, 6873, 9505, 9525, 9540, 9565, **9580**, 9640, 9670, 9840, 11740, 11890, 11895, 11920, 11950, 15160, 15185, 15195, 15265, **15285**, **15385**, 15390, 15400, 17705, **17710**, 17715, 17730, 17740, 17765, 17810, **17830**, **17885**, 21560, 21580, 21590, 21610 kHz
Multilingual **7175**, 9575, **9750**, 10869, **11710**, 11915, **15600**, **17780**, **21500** kHz

VOICE OF THE OAS
Spanish 9565, 11830, 15160 kHz

WHRI-WORLD HARVEST RADIO
English 5995, 7355, 9620, 9690, 9770, 11770, 11790, 15105, 15310 kHz

WINB-WORLD INTL BROADCASTERS
English 15185, 17730 kHz
Multilingual 15145 kHz

WMLK-ASSEMBLIES OF YAWEH
English 9455, 15150 kHz

WRNO WORLDWIDE
English 6185, 7355, 9715, 9852.5, 11705, 11965, 15420 kHz
German 11965 kHz
Multilingual 6185 kHz

WYFR-FAMILY RADIO
English **6300**, 7355, 7365, **7845**, 9455, 9535,
9590, 9680, 9715, 9852.5, **11550**, 11830, **15055**, 15170, 15215, 15260, 15400, 15440, 15566, 17640, 17750, 17845, 21525, 21615 kHz
French 6175, 9535, 9605, 15375, 15440, 17750, 21525, 21615 kHz
German 7355, 7365, 15440, 15566, 17845, 21615 kHz
Spanish 6065, 6105, 6175, 9550, 9605, 9705, 9715, 11790, 11855, 15215, 15375, 15445, 17805, 17845 kHz

USSR

"RADIO MAGALLANES"
Spanish 7240, 7440, 9450, 9490, 9640, 9650, 9715, 9810, 11630, 11650, 11745, 11800, 11860, 11890, 11900, 12020, 12030, 12040 kHz

KAZAKH RADIO
German 5970 kHz

RADIO AFGHANISTAN
English 11880 kHz
German 11880 kHz

RADIO KIEV
English 6020, 6165, 7175, 7195, 7205, 7280, 7320, 9560, 9685, 9710, 9800, 9820, 11720, 11790, 11960, 13605, 15180 kHz
German 5980, 6020, 6165, 7175, 7320, 9560, 9650 kHz

RADIO MOSCOW/RP&P
English 4060, 4825, 4860, 5900, 5905, 5920, 5940, 5960, 5980, 6005, 6020, 6045, 6050, 6090, 6120, 6130, 6145, 6175, 7100, **7115**, 7130, 7135, 7140, 7150, 7160, 7165, 7175, 7185, 7195, 7245, 7260, 7265, 7290, 7295, 7300, 7305, 7310, 7315, 7320, 7335, 7355, 7360, 7390, 9450, 9470, 9480, 9490, 9520, 9530, 9550, 9560, 9575, 9580, 9600, 9610, 9625, 9635, 9640, 9645, 9650, 9655, 9685, **9700**, 9705, 9710, 9720, 9745, 9750, 9760, 9765, 9775, 9780, 9785, 9795, 9810, 9820, 9865, 11670, 11675, 11690, 11700, 11705, 11710, 11715, 11720, 11725, 11730, 11735, 11745, **11750**, 11755, 11765, 11770, 11775, 11780, 11785, 11790, 11800, 11805, 11810, 11820, 11830, **11840**, 11845, **11850**, 11860, 11890, 11900, 11950, 11955, 11975, 12000, 12005, 12010, 12015, 12030, 12040, 12045, 12050, 12055, 12060, 12065, 12075, 13605, 13635, 13645, 13655, 13665, 13680, 13705, 15110, 15125, 15140, 15150, 15155, 15170, 15175, 15195, 15210, 15220, 15245, 15260, 15265, 15280, 15285, 15295, 15320, 15330, 15370, 15405, 15420, 15425, 15440, 15455, 15480, 15490, 15500, 15510, 15515, 15530, 15535, 15540, 15585, 17555, 17680, 17720, 17730, 17775, 17815, 17820, 17835, 17850, 17860, 17875, 17880, 17885, 21450, 21465, 21505, 21530, 21545, 21585, 21670, 21690, 21725, 21740 kHz
French 5950, 6010, 6120, 7195, 7240, 7320, 7330, 7360, 7370, 7440, 9450, 9470, 9480, 9490, 9515, 9560, 9610, 9630, 9640, 9650, 9675, 9710, 9745, 9760, 9785, 9810, 11630, 11670, 11690, 11700, 11715, 11725, 11745, 11800, 11805, 11890, 11900, 11930, 11950, 11960, 11970, 11980, 11990, 12010, 12020,

12050, 12055, 13635, 15125, 15175, 15210,
15465, 15470, 15490, 15510, 15535, 15550,
15585, 17680, 17760, 17860 kHz
German 5920, 5950, 5960, 6145, 7360, 9450,
9580, 11870, 11960, 12020, 13635, 15125,
15420, 17840 kHz
Spanish 4825, 5920, 5960, 5975, 6130, 6145,
7135, 7240, 7250, 7280, 7335, 7340, 7360,
7370, 7420, 7440, 9450, 9490, 9520, 9580,
9610, 9640, 9650, **9665**, 9670, 9675, 9685,
9710, 9720, 9745, 9785, 9795, 9810, 11630,
11650, 11670, 11700, 11705, 11745, 11800,
11805, **11850**, 11860, 11870, 11890, 11900,
11920, 11930, 11960, 11980, 12010, 12020,
12030, 12040, 13660, 15140, 15480 kHz
Japanese 5940, 5950, 5960, 6020, 6050, 7170,
7245, 7260, 7280, 7340, 9520, 9540, 9565,
9795, 9865, 9895, 11730, 11915, 12030,
15245, 17885 kHz

RADIO TASHKENT
English 5945, 5985, 7325, 9540, 9600, 9650,
9715, 11785, 15460 kHz
RADIO TIKHIY OKEAN
English 3995, 4485, 5900, 5940, 5950, 5980,
6020, 6035, 6080, 6190, 7175, 7210, 7260,
7370, 9620, 9635, 9795, 9810, 11730, 11815,
11900, 11910, 11950, 12030, 12050, 12070,
15265, 17775, 17870, 21515, 21530 kHz
RADIO VILNIUS
English 6100, 9685, 11720, 11790, 11960,
13605, 15180 kHz
RADIO YEREVAN
English 11790, 13605, 15180 kHz
RS SOV BELORUSSIA
English 6175 kHz
German 5980, 6175, 6185, 7205, 9550,
11870 kHz

VATICAN STATE
VATICAN RADIO
English 6015, 6145, 6150, 6185, 6190, 6252,
7125, 7250, 9605, 9610, 9615, 9625, 9645,
9650, 11700, 11725, 11740, 11760, 11775,
11810, 11830, 11845, 11865, 15120, 15190,
17730, 17840, 17845, 17865, 21485 kHz
French 6015, 6150, 6185, 6190, 6252, 7250,
9605, 9625, 9645, 11700, 11725, 11740,
11760, 11810, 11845, 15120, 15190, 17730,
17840, 21485 kHz
German 6185, 6190, 6252, 7250, 9645,
11740 kHz
Spanish 6015, 6035, 6150, 6190, 6252, 7250,
9615, 9645, 9735, 11740, 11845, 11955,
15405, 17740, 17865, 21725 kHz
Japanese 6015, 9615, 11830, 15190, 17865 kHz
Multilingual 6190, 6252, 7250, 9625, 9645,
11700, 11740 kHz

VENEZUELA
RADIO NACIONAL
Spanish 9500, 9540 kHz

YUGOSLAVIA
RADIO LJUBLJANA
Multilingual 6100, 7240, 9620 kHz

RADIO YUGOSLAVIA
English 6100, 7240, 9620, 11735, 15240,
15415 kHz
French 6100, 7240, 9620, 15240 kHz
German 6100, 7240, 9620 kHz
Spanish 6100, 7240, 9620, 11735 kHz

ZAIRE
LA VOIX DU ZAIRE
Multilingual 15245 kHz

ZAMBIA
RADIO ZAMBIA
Multilingual 4910 kHz
RADIO ZAMBIA-ZBS
English 6060, 9505, 11880 kHz
Multilingual 3346, 6165, 7220, 7235 kHz

ZIMBABWE
ZIMBABWE BROADCASTING CORPORATION
English 7284.3 kHz
Multilingual 5975, 6045, 7121.4 kHz

NOTE: Frequencies in bold are via relay sites.

These often provide best reception.

NEWS OTHER SOURCES MISS

Henry Shapiro, United Press International's Moscow correspondent since the Forties, tells the story of a strange telephone call he got during World War II. It was early on the morning of June 22, 1941, four hours after Hitler attacked the Soviet Union along a 3,000-kilometer front. The phone call was from the foreign editor of Tass, the Soviet Union's sole news agency.

"Is it true," the editor asked Shapiro, "that the BBC reported that the Germans have invaded the Soviet Union?" It was. But the Soviet people were not to learn through their own media that they were at war until noon — a full eight hours after German troops began their drive into the heart of Mother Russia.

Much News Missed by Domestic Media

Today, it's easy to look at such an incident, shrug, and blame it on the lack of technology at the time or the philosophy of the Soviets. But despite mind-boggling advances in technology that allow instantaneous global communications, it's still not easy to find out what's going on around the world from the domestic media...and that applies not only to the Soviet Union.

Take Sweden, for example. A modern, internationally active nation of over eight million people, it is rarely reported on by the North American press. In fact, in 1986 only two major events caught the attention of the US press: the assasination of Prime Minister Olaf Palme and the detection of Chernobyl-generated radiation by a Swedish nuclear power group.

Naturally, there is a great deal more to Sweden than an isolated instance of political violence and the odd fallout from a nuclear reactor run amuck. How does one find out about it, or its even less-reported neighbors of Norway and Finland?

The answer is world radio. Radio Sweden International broadcasts a program called *Nordic Newsweek*, which focuses on events in the entire region, as well as Sweden. Radio Finland offers the excellent *Northern Report*, and Radio Norway International, though limited to Sunday-only programs in English, offers *Norway Today.*

Israel Radio's Sara Manobla

News from Specialized World Regions

In addition to the news, all three of these Nordic nations offer interesting, easy-to-hear programs that not only provide listeners local and regional news, but also give them an opportunity to enjoy a bit of Scandanavian culture and meet the Nordic people. In short, these stations provide a well-rounded and in-depth look at each country and region so as to provide us with an understanding as to *why* these events have taken place.

BBC: The Finest in Radio Journalism

But not all news on world radio is regional. The British Broadcasting Corporation (BBC), reknowned throughout the world — even in France, according to the Paris newspaper *Le Monde* — for its accuracy, timeliness and lack of bias, offers bulletins of world news unequaled in scope at the top of almost every hour. In addition, in-depth news programs, such as *Twenty-Four Hours*, provide analyses of the main news of the day. *Twenty-Four Hours* is heard four times daily, after the regular newscasts at 0500, 0700, 1300 and 2000 World Time, and is but one of several such programs.

BUUULLLSHIT!

James Vowden and Pam Creighton, newsreaders on the BBC World Service.

The BBC, like many other international broadcasters, goes yet one step further. On a typical day, you may hear a program on gardening hosted by the popular Margaret Howard, have a chance to pick up the phone and speak directly to the Prime Minister, or hear a stage version of George Bernard Shaw's *Pygmalion* featuring a galaxy of top-flight performers. Rock concerts, classical music, sports and inspiration are all a regular part of world radio's daily draw.

For nearly every country on this planet, there is an organization eager to present to you its peoples, events and ideas that you otherwise might never hear of. From the tiny islands of the South Pacific to the People's Republic of China, world radio offers an unparalleled view of your world.

THE
NEW JAPAN RADIO
NRD-525

UNPARALLELED PERFORMANCE AND SOPHISTICATED FEATURES!

Rated a full FIVE STARS by Larry Magne in RADIO DATABASE INTERNATIONAL Whitepaper.

"... it must be said that the NRD-525 is as close to the optimum shortwave listener's receiver as is in existence."

"Japan Radio has taken the features shortwave listeners have always sought ... and packaged the lot into what is unquestionably the best overall shortwave listener's receiver on the market today."

"The NRD-525 exemplifies once again that Japan Radio receivers are for the connoisseur."

Larry Magne, International Broadcast Services

The JRC NRD-525 truly stands alone in performance and features! Enjoy exceptional sensitivity and selectivity coupled with rock-solid stability. Continuous coverage from 90.00 to 34000.00 Khz with readout to 10 Hz! Razor-sharp notch filter and passband tuning for digging out that weak DX! All modes are standard including FM and FAX! 24 hour digital clock timer with relay contacts. Incredible 200 channel scanning sweeping memory stores frequency, mode, bandwidth, AGC and ATT settings for each channel. Other standard features include keypad, RIT, MONITOR, AGC, ATT, BFO and dual NB. Available options include VHF/UHF, RS-232, RTTY Demodulator and a wide variety of filters. Operates from 110/220 VAC or 13.8 VDC! Write today for your full color brochure!

Japan Radio Co., Ltd.

WORLD RADIO: WHAT IT'S ALL ABOUT
by
George Wood, Radio Sweden International

Right now, as you read this book, the air around you is filled with all manner of radio waves. The crackle of radar and space communications, police and fire departments, airlines and taxis. There's the local broadcast station humming away and the "ham" down the block. But amongst all of these invisible waves that constantly flow through our bodies are some very weak and fragile signals. They are weaker than the others because they have traveled around the world. These signals are known as "shortwave."

Radio Programs Heard Worldwide

Shortwave signals come from radio stations located in virtually every part of the globe. There are hundreds of stations in Africa, Asia, the Pacific and the Americas. And they broadcast programs of such variety that even the most ardent cable TV viewer — intoxicated with the number of channels available — would be boggled. There is news, sports, entertainment, history, commentary, talk shows, music and more music...each reflecting a different perspective, a different people.

By comparison, domestic radio, with its limited formats and local orientation, pales. As a result, the average shortwave listener is far more knowledgeable about what is going on in the world than someone who only reads, say, the *Kenosha News*.

Radios for Listening

To listen to these stations, you have to have a radio, specifically one that can pick up world radio signals. The 1950's pre-hifi sets and all their brothers and sisters are enough to get a person started, but they do have their limitations. You can hear a few stations — usually poorly — on such a receiver, but you're depriving yourself of much of the ease and enjoyment by not investing in what is, after all, the primary tool of the trade.

Quality shortwave receivers used to be big and expensive, with long antennas and earphones. No more. The same electronics revolution that brought us mini-calculators, home computers and video games has created a revolution in receiver design. A few years ago, the Japanese, after ensuring that every home in the country had a stereo, color TV and VCR, looked for the next product to make a profit on. They hit upon shortwave radio and, rather quickly, the competitive Japanese market was bombarded with new, small receivers filled with the latest technology. Almost overnight, millions of Japanese young people had begun to tune in the world via shortwave. The successful Japanese manufacturers turned their eyes to Western markets.

A good place to start looking for a new world-band radio is in the pages of RADIO DATABASE INTERNATIONAL. This book lists virtually every radio station in the world, as well as reviews of the latest radios on the market. Larry Magne's receiver reviews are considered the standard reference on new receivers.

There are a number of features to look for in a receiver. Cost is probably the most important and most obvious — you have to stick to something that matches your funds. Fortunately, the cost of good world radios has come down, and the frantic pace of technology often means that last year's model can be purchased inexpensively from specialty firms, discount houses or from other listeners who want this year's radio.

Size is also important. Do you want a radio that you can take with you while trekking across South America? Or is your radio going to become a permanent fixture on the living room desk?

Accuracy of tuning is another factor. If you want to hear the BBC on 9510 kHz, can you read "9510" on the dial, or is it just someplace between "9" and "10"? Today, with digital readout — like the display on your pocket calculator — finding an exact frequency is as easy as keying in a number on your Touch-tone phone. Punch in a frequency on the keypad, see it on the display, then sit back and listen. Otherwise, if you choose a radio without digital read-out you may find yourself spending more time looking for a station than listening to it.

Among the most important characteristics of a world-band radio are selectivty and sensitivity. Sensitivity indicates just how strong a signal must be before you can pick it up. A radio with good sensitivity will receive not only the high-powered stations but also the weaker ones. A radio with poor sensitivity will miss out on all but the strongest.

Unfortunately, many new radios that are sensitive lack proper selectivity. For example, if you're listening to a weak station on 9535 kHz, will the strong station alongside on 9530 kHz bleed over and overpower it? A selective radio will allow you to hear the signal on 9535 kHz while the one on 9530 kHz is attenuated. A poor receiver will have the station on 9530 kHz all over the dial.

Other factors include whether an ac power is required or if you can use batteries; if there is a built-in 24-hour clock for World Time; tone controls; the ability to change the bandwidth to eliminate interefence, and so on.

Radios Come with Built-in Antennas

After you've purchased your receiver, the next question concerns antennas. Most of the new radios are so good that they do very well with only the built-in whip antenna. In fact, if you try to put on an outside antenna, you may find that you're bringing in too many signals and that everything is just a mess. The radio might even "overload". So even if your radio has a connector for an external antenna, it may work so well that you won't even want to use it.

Another recent development is the active antenna. It's a small box with a whip antenna that can approach the level of performance of a long outside antenna. Some are, in fact, quite good. But, again, most receivers do very well with only the antenna that comes with it.

Where to Find Stations

Once you've decided on an antenna, you're all set to go exploring the world of radio. The first question is what to go looking for, and the possibilities are endless.

You know from listening to ordinary broadcasts that each station occupies a particular spot on the dial day-in-and-day-out. As you know from looking at any ordinary radio, the AM band runs from 540 to 1600 kHz. These frequencies are part of what is called the mediumwave spectrum. Below that is longwave and above it is shortwave.

On the shortwave bands, certain sections are reserved for domestic radio stations, whereas others are set aside for both domestic and international stations. Each group of frequencies is given a title — "meter bands" — based roughly on wavelength. With today's new world-band radios, you don't need to know meter bands, but this designation can be helpful in identifying the range of frequencies you're listening to. These meter bands are delineated in the "Lexicon" found towards the back of your RADIO DATABASE INTERNATIONAL.

The 120, 90 and 60 meter bands are restricted to use by stations in the tropics only. This is because shortwave is better at rejecting static than is mediumwave AM, plus shortwave is more cost effective than either mediumwave AM or FM for reaching local audiences. There are thousands of such stations throughout the Third World which broadcast programs generally intended for a local audience, but which can be heard up to thousands of kilometers away on good world-band radios. The

locations of the stations, the unusual music and unique programming make for some truly exotic listening.

Generally speaking, a good rule to note is that higher frequencies are easier to receive during hours of daylight, especially during the spring, summer and fall. The lower frequencies are usually better during hours of darkness, notably during the winter. One thing you'll notice is that when the higher frequencies are unusuable, more stations will crowd into the lower ones, making interference a problem.

Some stations, looking for interference-free channels, broadcast — as you'll see when perusing your RDI — outside the prescribed shortwave bands. For example, the BBC can be heard on 9410 kHz, below the present 31 meter band which starts at 9500 kHz, and on 15070, below the 19 meter band that commences at 15100 kHz. Some stations particularly active in out-of-band broadcasting include Radio Moscow, the Voice of America, Radio Beijing, Radio Nederland and Radio Tirana.

In between the shortwave bands, along with a handful of illegal clandestine broadcasters, are other radio services — "utility" stations — such as ships at sea, traffic with aircraft, and communications between embassies and diplomatic missions. Also, of course, there are radio amateurs and CBers. Unlike most broadcast stations, however, many of these services use a system called single sideband, or SSB. This is a way of imposing a speech signal on a radio wave that is more efficient than ordinary radio. If you hear an SSB signal on a conventional radio, it sounds a bit like Donald Duck. The only way to make sense of the transmission is to use a radio equipped to receive SSB signals.

Keeping Abreast of World-Radio Developments

There are many other aspects of shortwave listening you may want to become involved in. There are a number of good clubs in which members report the stations they have recently heard. And there are even programs on the world radio bands to help you through this maze of frequencies.

The longest running program of this type is "Sweden Calling DXers" ("DXers" being a term describing those who are interested in seeking out weak, distant signals), broadcast on Radio Sweden International. The program first went on the air in 1948, edited by "Mr. DX," Arne Skoog. Like the clubs, it is made up mostly of information sent in by listeners. Each month some 50 to 80 people write in with news about what they've been hearing. And each contributor goes on the mailing list for one year to receive the English scripts of the program, sent out free of charge (for more information write to

Sweden Calling DXers, Radio Sweden International, S-105 10 Stockholm, Sweden. Other excellent shortwave programs include "Media Network" on Radio Netherlands and "Shortwave Listener's Digest" on Radio Canada International. For those interested in the technical side of shortwave listening, try tuning in Swiss Radio International and the popular "Swiss Shortwave Merry-go-Round."

No matter what your reason for listening to shortwave — be it an in-depth view of world news, a glimpse of some culture far away, or as a pasttime — you're sure to find it a fascinating and informative use of your time. Without a doubt, world radio is your round-trip ticket to the world!

_____

George Wood grew up around Berkley, California in the 1950s, discovering world radio at the ripe age of ten. Visiting Sweden first as an exchange student and later as a draft resister and finally, in 1975, for reserach at Radio Sweden International, he never got around to returning to the States. Today, he hosts "Sweden Calling DXers" over Radio Sweden International and acts as a CBS News correspondent from Stockholm. He lives in a small apartment near Broadcasting House and continues to seek the answer to the Cosmic Question of Life.

Yaesu has serious listeners for the serious listener.

Yaesu's serious about giving you better ways to tune in the world around you.

And whether it's for local action or worldwide DX, you'll find our VHF/UHF and HF receivers are the superior match for all your listening needs.

The FRG-9600. A premium VHF/UHF scanning communications receiver. The 9600 is no typical scanner. And it's easy to see why.

You won't miss any local action with continuous coverage from 60 to 905 MHz.

You have more operating modes to listen in on: upper or lower sideband, CW, AM wide or narrow, and FM wide or narrow.

You can even watch television programs by plugging in a video monitor into the optional video output.

Scan in steps of 5, 10, 12½, 25 and 100 KHz. Store any frequency and

related operating mode into any of the 99 memories. Scan the memories. Or in between them. Or simply "dial up" any frequency with the frequency entry pad.

Plus there's more, including a 24-hour clock, multiplexed output, fluorescent readout, signal strength graph, and an AC power adapter.

The FRG-8800 HF communications receiver. A better way to listen to the world. If you want a complete communications package, the FRG-8800 is just right for you.

You get continuous worldwide coverage from 150 KHz to 30 MHz. And local coverage from 118 to 174 MHz with an optional VHF converter.

Listen in on any mode: upper and lower sideband, CW, AM wide or narrow, and FM.

Store frequencies and operating modes into any of the twelve channels for instant recall.

Scan the airwaves with a number of programmable scanning functions.

Plus you get keyboard frequency entry. An LCD display for easy readout. A SINPO signal graph. Computer interface capability for advanced listening functions. Two 24 hour clocks. Recording functions. And much more to make your listening station complete.

Listen in. When you want more from your VHF/UHF or HF receivers, just look to Yaesu. We take your listening seriously.

YAESU

Yaesu USA
17210 Edwards Road, Cerritos, CA 90701
(213) 404-2700

Yaesu Cincinnati Service Center
9070 Gold Park Drive, Hamilton, OH 45011
(513) 874-3100

Dealer inquiries invited.

Prices and specifications subject to change without notice.
FRG-9600 SSB coverage: 60 to 460 MHz.

YAESU FRG-8800　YAESU FRG-9600

150 KHz-30MHz
NEW PRICE
$519.95 +$6.00 UPS
LIST $599.95
SAVE $80

The FRG-7700 was a great receiver. Now the new generation FRG-8800 takes you a step forward.

- CAT computer compatible
- 12 memories—scan—RIT
- Keyboard frequency entry
- Dual 24 hour clock timer recorder control
- Optional FRV8800 VHF converter 118-174 MHz
- All mode AM–SSB–CW–FM
- Green LCD display
- 150 KHz to 30 MHz

EEB Exclusive Options

1. 24 hour bench test and complete realignment for optimum performance including double-extended warranty $40
2. 4 KHz ceramic filter replaces 6 KHz AM wide ceramic filter installed $50
3. 2.4 KHz mechanical filter replaces SSB ceramic filter Installed $95

60-905 MHz
NEW LOW PRICE
$499.95 +$6.00 UPS
LIST $579.95
SAVE $80

A premium VHF/UHF scanning communications receiver.

- You won't miss any local action with continuous coverage from 60 to 905 MHz.
- Cable T.V. "Analyser." Check out everything on your cable.
- You have more operating modes to listen in on: upper or lower sideband, CW, AM wide or narrow, and FM wide or narrow.
- You can even watch television programs by plugging in a video monitor into the optional video output. VU 9600 $25.
- Scan in steps of 5, 10, 12½, 25 and 100 KHz. Store any frequency and related operating mode into any of the 99 memories. Scan the memories. Or in between them. Or simply "dial up" any frequency with the frequency entry pad.
- Plus there's much more, including a 24-hour clock, multiplexed output, signal strength graph, and an AC power adapter (included.)
- CAT computer compatible.

Frequency (kHz)   Country / Station / Location   World Time   Power (kW): Network: Target   World Time

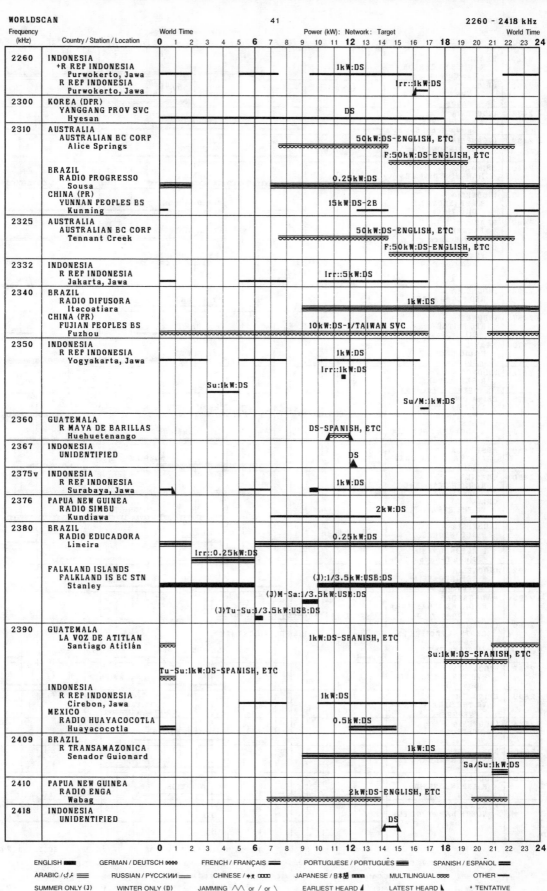

Frequency (kHz)	Country / Station / Location	Details
2260	INDONESIA +R REP INDONESIA Purwokerto, Jawa R REP INDONESIA Purwokerto, Jawa	1kW:DS Irr::1kW:DS
2300	KOREA (DPR) YANGGANG PROV SVC Hyesan	DS
2310	AUSTRALIA AUSTRALIAN BC CORP Alice Springs BRAZIL RADIO PROGRESSO Sousa CHINA (PR) YUNNAN PEOPLES BS Kunming	50kW:DS-ENGLISH, ETC F:50kW:DS-ENGLISH, ETC 0.25kW:DS 15kW:DS-2B
2325	AUSTRALIA AUSTRALIAN BC CORP Tennant Creek	50kW:DS-ENGLISH, ETC F:50kW:DS-ENGLISH, ETC
2332	INDONESIA R REP INDONESIA Jakarta, Jawa	Irr::5kW:DS
2340	BRAZIL RADIO DIFUSORA Itacoatiara CHINA (PR) FUJIAN PEOPLES BS Fuzhou	1kW:DS 10kW:DS-1/TAIWAN SVC
2350	INDONESIA R REP INDONESIA Yogyakarta, Jawa	1kW:DS Irr::1kW:DS Su:1kW:DS Su/M:1kW:DS
2360	GUATEMALA R MAYA DE BARILLAS Huehuetenango	DS-SPANISH, ETC
2367	INDONESIA UNIDENTIFIED	DS
2375v	INDONESIA R REP INDONESIA Surabaya, Jawa	1kW:DS
2376	PAPUA NEW GUINEA RADIO SIMBU Kundiawa	2kW:DS
2380	BRAZIL RADIO EDUCADORA Limeira FALKLAND ISLANDS FALKLAND IS BC STN Stanley	0.25kW:DS Irr::0.25kW:DS (J):1/3.5kW:USB:DS (J)M-Sa:1/3.5kW:USB:DS (J)Tu-Su:1/3.5kW:USB:DS
2390	GUATEMALA LA VOZ DE ATITLAN Santiago Atitlán Tu-Su:1kW:DS-SPANISH, ETC INDONESIA R REP INDONESIA Cirebon, Jawa MEXICO RADIO HUAYACOCOTLA Huayacocotla	1kW:DS-SPANISH, ETC Su:1kW:DS-SPANISH, ETC 1kW:DS 0.5kW:DS
2409	BRAZIL R TRANSAMAZONICA Senador Guiomard	1kW:DS Sa/Su:1kW:DS
2410	PAPUA NEW GUINEA RADIO ENGA Wabag	2kW:DS-ENGLISH, ETC
2418	INDONESIA UNIDENTIFIED	DS

0 1 2 3 4 5 6 7 8 9 10 11 12 13 14 15 16 17 18 19 20 21 22 23 24

ENGLISH ▬▬   GERMAN / DEUTSCH ◊◊◊◊   FRENCH / FRANÇAIS ≡≡≡   PORTUGUESE / PORTUGUÊS ≡≡≡   SPANISH / ESPAÑOL ≡≡≡

ARABIC / ﺏﺮﻋ ≡≡≡   RUSSIAN / РУССКИИ ≡≡≡   CHINESE / 中文 ◊◊◊◊   JAPANESE / 日本語 ▬▬▬   MULTILINGUAL ▭▭▭   OTHER ▬▬

SUMMER ONLY (J)   WINTER ONLY (D)   JAMMING ∧∧ or / or \   EARLIEST HEARD ◀   LATEST HEARD ▶   + TENTATIVE

Frequency (kHz)	Country / Station / Location	Power (kW) : Network : Target
2420	BRAZIL — RADIO SAO CARLOS — São Carlos	0.5kW:DS
2430	CHINA (PR) — VO THE STRAIT-PLA — Fuzhou	10kW:TAIWAN-2
2432.5	INDONESIA — R REP INDONESIA — Banda Aceh, Sumat'a	50kW:DS
2439.5	INDONESIA — R REP INDONESIA — Surakarta, Jawa	1kW:DS
2445	CHINA (PR) — JIANGXI PEOPLES BS — Nanchang	10kW:DS
2455.8	INDONESIA — R REP INDONESIA — Díli, Timur	Irr::0.3kW:DS
2460	BRAZIL — +PROGRESSO DO ACRE — Rio Branco	1kW:DS/PROJECTED
2460	CHINA (PR) — YUNNAN PEOPLES BS — Kunming	15kW:DS-CHINESE / Su:15kW:DS-CHINESE
2464v	INDONESIA — RPD PURWAKARTA — Purwakarta, Jawa	Irr::0.25kW:DS
2467	INDONESIA — RPD BLITAR — Blitar, Jawa	Irr::0.5kW:DS-2
2470	BRAZIL — RADIO CACIQUE — Sorocaba	Irr::1kW:DS
2472	INDONESIA — R REP INDONESIA — Purwokerto, Jawa	1kW:DS
2475	CHINA (PR) — ZHEJIANG PBS — Hangzhou	10kW:DS-CHINESE
2475	INDONESIA — R ANGKATAN BERSE'A — Jakarta, Jawa	Irr::0.5kW:DS
2485	AUSTRALIA — AUSTRALIAN BC CORP — Katherine	50kW:DS
2490	BRAZIL — RADIO 8 SETEMBRO — Descalvado	0.25kW:DS
2490	CHINA (PR) — VO THE STRAIT-PLA — Fuzhou	10kW:TAIWAN-1
2490	INDONESIA — R REP INDONESIA — Semarang, Jawa	1kW:DS
2490	R REP INDONESIA — Ujung Pandang, Su'i	0.5kW:DS
2492	INDONESIA — R REP INDONESIA — Mataram, Lombok	DS
2495v	MADAGASCAR — RADIO MADAGASIKARA — Antananarivo	Alternative Frequency to 5010vkHz
2560	CHINA (PR) — CENTRAL PEOPLES BS — Urümqi	15kW:DS-MINORITIES
2560	XINJIANG PBS — Urümqi	15kW:DS-UIGHUR
2582	INDONESIA — RPD TENGAH SELATAN — Soë, Timur	0.3kW:DS-2
2600	CHINA (PR) — VO THE STRAIT-PLA — Fuzhou	50kW:TAIWAN-2
2624	INDONESIA — +RPD BLORA — Blora, Jawa	0.3kW:DS-2
2670v	KOREA (DPR) — NORTH HWANGHAE PS — Sariwŏn	DS
2695v	INDONESIA — R REP INDONESIA — Ende, Flores	0.5kW:DS
2696	KOREA (DPR) — NORTH HAMGYONG PS — Ch'ŏngjin	Irr::DS

Frequency (kHz)	Country / Station / Location	World Time 0 ... 12 ... 18 ... 24 / Power (kW): Network: Target
2754	CHINA (PR) VO THE STRAIT-PLA Fuzhou	SPR:TAIWAN-2/2X1377KHZ
2776	KOREA (DPR) SOUTH HAMGYONG PS Hamhŭng	DS
2800	CHINA (PR) VO THE STRAIT-PLA Fuzhou	50kW:TAIWAN-2
2835v	INDONESIA RPD LUMAJANG Lumajang, Jawa	DS
2850v	KOREA (DPR) KOREAN CENTRAL BS Pyŏngyang	100kW:DS
2901	INDONESIA R REP INDONESIA Mataram, Lombok	Irr:::DS
2904v	INDONESIA RPD NGADA Bajawa, N Tenggara	0.5kW:DS-2
2950.3	BOLIVIA UNIDENTIFIED	DS
2952	USSR RADIO MOSCOW/RP&P Vladivostok	SPR:2X1476 KHZ
2963	INDONESIA RPD MANGGARAI Ruteng, Flores	0.3kW:DS-2
3000	INDONESIA RPD JAWA TIMUR Surabaya, Jawa	1kW:DS-1
3015	KOREA (DPR) RADIO PYONGYANG Pyŏngyang	100kW::EAS
3018v	INDONESIA +RPD KAMPAR Bangkinang, Sumat'a	DS
3060v	INTERNATIONAL WATERS VOICE OF PEACE	SPR:DS-2X1530V KHZ
3143	INDONESIA RPD BELITUNG Tanjung Pandan,Sum	DS
3171	INDONESIA RKP DAERAH TINGKAT Jember, Jawa	0.5kW:DS-2
3192v	LIBYA RADIO JAMAHIRIYA Tripoli	Irr::100kW::NAF/ME
3200	CHINA (PR) VO THE STRAIT-PLA Fuzhou SWAZILAND TRANS WORLD RADIO Manzini	10kW:TAIWAN-1 25kW::SAF (J):25kW::SAF (J)Sa/Su:25kW::SAF
3204.4	INDONESIA R REP INDONESIA Bandung, Jawa	Irr::10kW:DS
3205	BRAZIL R RIBEIRAO PRETO Ribeirão Prêto INDIA ALL INDIA RADIO Lucknow PAPUA NEW GUINEA RADIO WEST SEPIK Vanimo	1kW:DS 10kW:DS-ENGLISH, ETC 4kW:DS
3210v	MOZAMBIQUE RADIO MOCAMBIQUE Maputo	100kW:DS
3211v	ECUADOR RADIO FEDERACION Sucúa	Irr::10kW:DS
3215 (con'd)	CHINA (TAIWAN) CENTRAL BC SYSTEM Hsin-chu INDONESIA R REP INDONESIA Manado, Sulawesi SOUTH AFRICA SOUTH AFRICAN BC Meyerton	Irr::10kW:PRC-2 10kW:DS 100kW:DS-RADIO ORION

ENGLISH ▬▬   GERMAN / DEUTSCH ▨▨▨▨   FRENCH / FRANÇAIS ══   PORTUGUESE / PORTUGUÊS ▤▤▤   SPANISH / ESPAÑOL ══

ARABIC /ﻉﺭ ══   RUSSIAN / РУССКИИ ══   CHINESE / 中文 ▫▫▫▫   JAPANESE / 日本語 ▦▦▦   MULTILINGUAL ▩▩▩   OTHER ▬

SUMMER ONLY (J)   WINTER ONLY (D)   JAMMING ∧∧ or / or \   EARLIEST HEARD ◢   LATEST HEARD ◣   + TENTATIVE

| Frequency (kHz) | Country / Station / Location | World Time ... 0 1 2 3 4 5 6 7 8 9 10 11 12 13 14 15 16 17 18 19 20 21 22 23 24 | Power (kW): Network: Target | World Time |

3215 (con'd) — SOUTH AFRICA / SOUTH AFRICAN BC / Meyerton — 100kW:DS-RADIO ORANJE

3216v — VENEZUELA / ONDAS PANAMERICANA / El Vigía — Irr::1kW:DS

3220 — CHINA (PR) / CENTRAL PEOPLES BS — DS-1

3220 — ECUADOR / HCJB-VO THE ANDES / Quito — 10kW:DS

3220 — PAPUA NEW GUINEA / RADIO MOROBE / Lae — 2kW:DS

3220.5 — KOREA (DPR) / UNIDENTIFIED — DS

3222 — TOGO / RADIO KARA / Lama-Kara — 10kW:DS-FRENCH, ETC

3223 — INDIA / ALL INDIA RADIO / Simla — 2.5kW:DS-ENGLISH, ETC

3223v — INDONESIA / R REP INDONESIA / Mataram, Lombok — 5kW:DS

3225 — BRAZIL / LINS RADIO CLUBE / Lins — Irr::1kW:DS

3225 — INDONESIA / R REP INDONESIA / Tanjungpinang, Sum — 10kW:DS

3225v — VENEZUELA / RADIO OCCIDENTE / Tovar — 1kW:DS / Sa/Su:1kW:DS

3229.3 — PERU / R SOL DE LOS ANDES / Juliaca — 0.4kW:DS-SPANISH, ETC / Irr::0.4kW:DS

3230 — LIBERIA / RADIO ELWA / Monrovia — 10kW:DS / Sa-M:10kW:DS / Sa/Su:10kW:DS / Su:10kW:DS

3230 — NEPAL / RADIO NEPAL / Harriharpur — Alt 7165kHz:100kW::SAS / Alt 7165kHz:(D):100kW:DS / (D):100kW:DS

3230 — SOUTH AFRICA / RADIO RSA / Meyerton — 250kW::SAF/CAF

3230v — CLANDESTINE (ASIA) / 'VO AFGHANISTAN' / Pakistan — Irr::0.5kW:PRO-AFGHAN REBELS:SAS

3231.8 — INDONESIA / R REP INDONESIA / Bukittinggi, Sumat'a — Irr::10kW:DS / 10kW:DS

3232 — MADAGASCAR / +R MADAGASIKARA / Antananarivo — DS

3232.2 — CONGO / RTV CONGOLAISE / Brazzaville — Irr::4kW:DS-FRENCH, ETC

3235 — BRAZIL / RADIO CLUBE / Marilia — 0.5kW:DS

3235 — INDIA / ALL INDIA RADIO / Gauhati — 10kW:DS-B/ENGLISH, ETC

3235 — PAPUA NEW GUINEA / R WEST NEW BRITAIN / Kimbe — 2kW:DS

3239.6 — PERU / RADIO AMERICA / Lima — Irr::2.5kW:DS

ENGLISH ▪▪▪▪   GERMAN / DEUTSCH ◊◊◊◊   FRENCH / FRANÇAIS ▬▬   PORTUGUESE / PORTUGUÊS ▬▬   SPANISH / ESPAÑOL ▬▬

ARABIC / ﻉﺏ ▬▬   RUSSIAN / РУССКИИ ▬▬   CHINESE / 中文 ◊◊◊◊   JAPANESE / 日本語 ▪▪▪▪   MULTILINGUAL ▬▬▬   OTHER ▬▬

SUMMER ONLY (J)   WINTER ONLY (D)   JAMMING /\/\ or / or \   EARLIEST HEARD ◢   LATEST HEARD ◣   + TENTATIVE

Frequency (kHz)	Country / Station / Location	Power (kW): Network: Target / Schedule
3240	GHANA — GHANA BC CORP, Accra	DS-ENGLISH, ETC
	SWAZILAND — TRANS WORLD RADIO, Manzini	25kW::SAF
3240v	ECUADOR — R ANTENA LIBRE, Esmeraldas	1kW:DS
3240.5	INDONESIA — R REP INDONESIA, Ambon, Maluku	1kW:DS
3241	INDONESIA — R REP INDONESIA, Sibolga, Sumatera	Irr::5kW:DS
3245	BRAZIL — RADIO CLUBE, Varginha	1kW:DS / M-Sa:1kW:DS
	PAPUA NEW GUINEA — RADIO GULF, Kerema	10kW:DS
3249.5	HONDURAS — RADIO LUZ Y VIDA, Santa Bárbara	0.8kW:DS / Su:0.8kW:DS
3249.8	INDONESIA — R REP INDONESIA, Banjarmasin, Kali'n	10kW:DS-A
3250	PERU — RADIO QOLLYASUYO, Juliaca	Irr::1kW:DS
	SOUTH AFRICA — SOUTH AFRICAN BC, Meyerton	100kW:DS-RADIO FIVE
3253v	VENEZUELA — RADIO 980, El Tigre	1kW:DS
3255	BRAZIL — R EDUCADORA CARIRI, Crato	1kW:DS / Tu-Su:1kW:DS
	LIBERIA — LIBERIAN BC SYSTEM, Monrovia	50kW:DS-ENGLISH, ETC / M-F:50kW:DS-ENGLISH, ETC / M-Sa:50kW:DS-ENGLISH, ETC
3259	JAPAN — NIPPON HOSO KYOKAI, Sendai-Haramachi	Irr::0.3kW:DS-1(FEEDER)
3259.7	INDONESIA — R REP INDONESIA, Kupang, Timur	10kW:DS
3260	CHINA (PR) — GUIZHOU PEOPLES BS, Guiyang	10kW:DS
	NIGER — ORT DU NIGER, Niamey	4kW:DS / Sa:4kW:DS / Sa/Su:4kW:DS / Su:4kW:DS
	PAPUA NEW GUINEA — RADIO MADANG, Madang	2kW:DS
	PERU — LA VOZ DE OXAPAMPA, Oxapampa	2.5kW:DS / Irr::2.5kW:DS
3260.7	ECUADOR — LV DE RIO CARRIZAL, Calceta	3kW:DS
3264.8	INDONESIA — R REP INDONESIA, Bengkulu, Sumatera	10kW:DS
3265	INDONESIA — R REP INDONESIA, Gorontalo, Sulawesi	10kW:DS
3268 (con'd)	INDIA — ALL INDIA RADIO, Kohima	2kW:DS-ENGLISH, ETC

ENGLISH ▬▬ GERMAN / DEUTSCH ◊◊◊◊ FRENCH / FRANÇAIS ▬▬ PORTUGUESE / PORTUGUÊS ▬▬ SPANISH / ESPAÑOL ▬▬

ARABIC / عربى ▬▬ RUSSIAN / РУССКИИ ▬▬ CHINESE / 中文 ◻◻◻◻ JAPANESE / 日本語 ▬▬ MULTILINGUAL ▬▬ OTHER ▬▬

SUMMER ONLY (J)   WINTER ONLY (D)   JAMMING /\/\ or / or \   EARLIEST HEARD ◢   LATEST HEARD ◣   + TENTATIVE

Frequency (kHz)	Country / Station / Location	Power (kW): Network: Target	World Time

World Time scale: 0 1 2 3 4 5 **6** 7 8 9 10 11 **12** 13 14 15 16 17 **18** 19 20 21 22 23 **24**

3268 (con'd)	INDIA — ALL INDIA RADIO — Kohima	Irr::2kW:DS-ENGLISH, ETC
3270	CHINA (PR) — RADIO BEIJING — Beijing	Irr::50kW::AS / Irr::50kW::AF
	NAMIBIA — R SOUTHWEST AFRICA — Windhoek	100kW:DS-1
3275	BRAZIL — RADIO DIFUSORA — Cáceres	1kW:DS / M-Sa:1kW:DS
	PAPUA NEW GUINEA — R SOUTH HIGHLANDS — Mendi	2kW:DS
	SWAZILAND — TRANS WORLD RADIO — Manzini	25kW::SAF
	VENEZUELA — RADIO MARA — Maracaibo	1kW:DS
3277	INDIA — RADIO KASHMIR — Srinagar	7.5kW:DS-ENGLISH, ETC
3277v	INDONESIA — R REP INDONESIA — Jakarta, Jawa	1kW:DS / Su:1kW:DS
3280	PERU — +RADIO HUARI — Huari	DS
3280v	ECUADOR — LA VOZ DEL NAPO — Tena	2.5kW:DS-SPANISH, ETC / Su:2.5kW:DS-SPANISH, ETC
3285	BELIZE — RADIO BELIZE — Belmopan	1kW:DS-ENGLISH,SPANISH
	BRAZIL — RADIO BANDEIRANTES — Cachoeira Paulista	2.5kW:DS
3286	INDONESIA — R REP INDONESIA — Madiun, Jawa	Irr::1kW:DS
3286v	ECUADOR — RADIO RIO TARQUI — Cuenca	0.36kW:DS
3288v	MADAGASCAR — R MADAGASIKARA — Antananarivo	M-Sa:100kW:DS / 100kW:DS-FRENCH, ETC
3289.7	ECUADOR — R PANAMERICANA — Quero	1kW:DS
3289.8	ZAMBIA — RADIO ZAMBIA — Lusaka	Irr:::DS-ENGLISH, ETC
3290	CHINA (PR) — CENTRAL PEOPLES BS	DS-2
	PAPUA NEW GUINEA — RADIO CENTRAL — Port Moresby	2kW:DS-ENGLISH, ETC
	PERU — RADIO TAYABAMBA — Tayabamba	1kW:DS / Su:1kW:DS
	TRISTAN DA CUNHA — TRISTAN BC SERVICE — Edinburgh	M-F:0.04kW:DS / M/W/F:0.04kW:DS / Su:0.04kW:DS
3291v	INDONESIA — +RPDT KOTAMADYA — Pematangsiantar	Irr::0.5kW:DS-2
3295 (con'd)	INDIA — ALL INDIA RADIO — Delhi	10kW::SEA

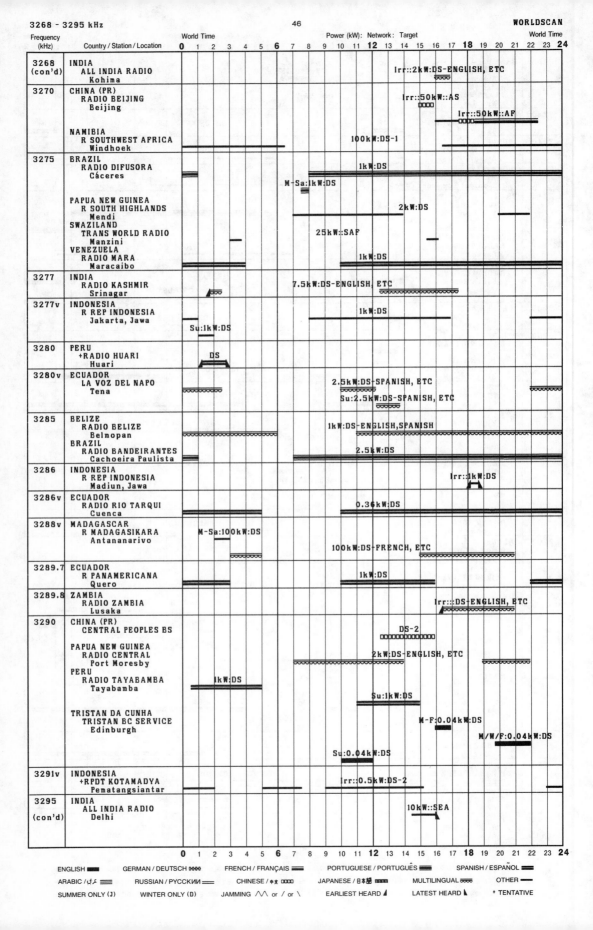

ENGLISH ▰▰▰   GERMAN / DEUTSCH ◊◊◊◊   FRENCH / FRANÇAIS ▭▭▭   PORTUGUESE / PORTUGUÊS ▰▰▰   SPANISH / ESPAÑOL ▰▰▰

ARABIC / ﻉﺭﺏ ▰▰▰   RUSSIAN / РУССКИИ ▭▭▭   CHINESE / 中文 ◊◊◊◊   JAPANESE / 日本語 ▰▰▰   MULTILINGUAL ∿∿∿   OTHER ▭▭▭

SUMMER ONLY (J)   WINTER ONLY (D)   JAMMING /\/\/\ or / or \   EARLIEST HEARD ◢   LATEST HEARD ◣   + TENTATIVE

Frequency (kHz)	Country / Station / Location	World Time	Power (kW): Network: Target	World Time

Scale: 0 1 2 3 4 5 6 7 8 9 10 11 12 13 14 15 16 17 18 19 20 21 22 23 24

Frequency (kHz)	Country / Station / Location	Details
3295 (con'd)	NAMIBIA — R SOUTHWEST AFRICA — Windhoek	100kW:DS-2/ENG, GER, ETC
3300	BURUNDI — LA VOIX DE LA REV — Bujumbura	25kW:DS / 25kW:DS-FRENCH, ETC / Su:25kW:DS-FRENCH, ETC
	CHINA (PR) — VO THE STRAIT-PLA — Fuzhou	10kW:TAIWAN-2
	GUATEMALA — RADIO CULTURAL — Guatemala City	10kW:DS / M:10kW:DS / M-Sa:10kW:DS / Su:10kW:DS / Tu-Su:10kW:DS
	INDONESIA — RPD LAMPUNG UTARA — Kotabumi, Sumatera	0.3kW:DS
3305	INDIA — ALL INDIA RADIO — Ranchi	2kW:DS-ENGLISH, ETC / Irr::2kW:DS-ENGLISH, ETC
	PAPUA NEW GUINEA — RADIO WESTERN — Daru	10kW:DS-ENGLISH, ETC
3305.7	ZIMBABWE — ZIMBABWE BC CORP — Gweru	Irr::10/100kW:DS-ENGLISH, ETC / Irr:Sa:10/100kW:DS-ENGLISH, ETC
3306	INDONESIA — R REP INDONESIA — Díli, Timur	10kW:DS
3310	CHINA (PR) — JILIN PEOPLES BS — Changchun	10kW:DS
	PERU — RADIO BAGUA — Bagua	1kW:DS
3310.3	BOLIVIA — RADIO SAN MIGUEL — Riberalta	0.5kW:DS / Su:0.5kW:DS / Irr:Su:0.5kW:DS
3315	INDIA — ALL INDIA RADIO — Bhopal	Irr::10kW:DS-ENGLISH, ETC / 10kW:DS-ENGLISH, ETC
	PAPUA NEW GUINEA — RADIO MANUS — Lorengau	2kW:DS-ENGLISH, ETC
3316.2	ECUADOR — RADIO PASTAZA — Puyo	2.5kW:DS / M-Sa:2.5kW
3320	KOREA (DPR) — RADIO PYONGYANG — Pyŏngyang	EAS
	SOUTH AFRICA — SOUTH AFRICAN BC — Meyerton	100kW:RADIO SUID-AFRIKA
3323v	ECUADOR — RADIO CHANGAY — Macas	DS
3324.8	GUATEMALA — R MAYA DE BARILLAS — Huehuetenango	1kW:DS-SPANISH, ETC
3325	BRAZIL — RDIF UNIVERSITARIA — Guarulhos	1kW:DS
	INDONESIA — R REP INDONESIA — Palangkaráya, Kali'n	10kW:DS
	PAPUA NEW GUINEA — R NORTH SOLOMONS — Kieta	10kW:DS

Scale: 0 1 2 3 4 5 6 7 8 9 10 11 12 13 14 15 16 17 18 19 20 21 22 23 24

ENGLISH ▬▬   GERMAN / DEUTSCH ◊◊◊◊   FRENCH / FRANÇAIS ═══   PORTUGUESE / PORTUGUÊS ▬▬   SPANISH / ESPAÑOL ▬▬

ARABIC / رب ═══   RUSSIAN / РУССКИЙ ═══   CHINESE / 中文 □□□□   JAPANESE / 日本語 ▤▤▤   MULTILINGUAL ▭▭▭   OTHER ▬▬

SUMMER ONLY (J)   WINTER ONLY (D)   JAMMING /\/\ or / or \   EARLIEST HEARD ◢   LATEST HEARD ◤   + TENTATIVE

Frequency (kHz)	Country / Station / Location	World Time 0 ... 6 ... 12 ... 18 ... 24	Power (kW): Network: Target

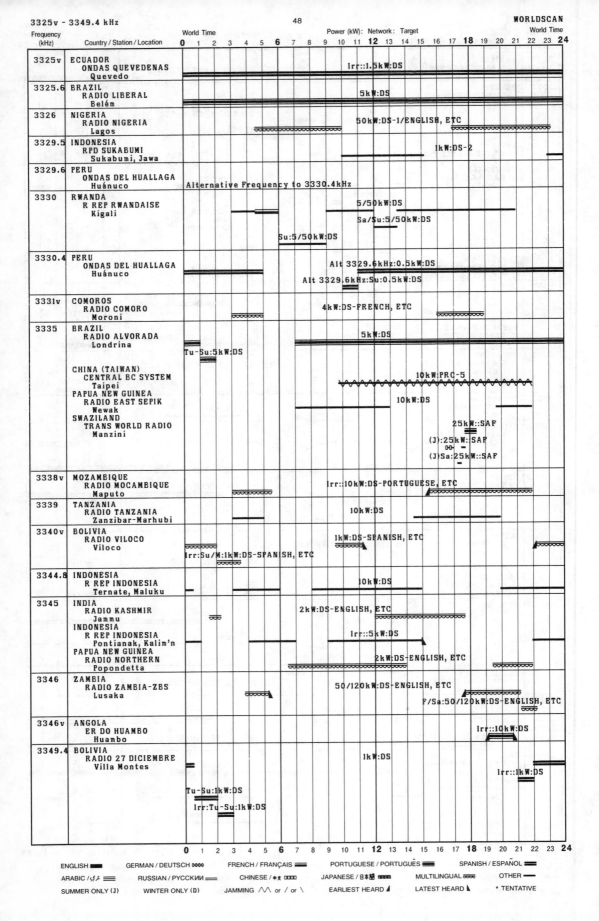

Frequency (kHz)	Country / Station / Location	Details
3325v	ECUADOR — ONDAS QUEVEDENAS — Quevedo	Irr:1.5kW:DS
3325.6	BRAZIL — RADIO LIBERAL — Belém	5kW:DS
3326	NIGERIA — RADIO NIGERIA — Lagos	50kW:DS-1/ENGLISH, ETC
3329.5	INDONESIA — RPD SUKABUMI — Sukabumi, Jawa	1kW:DS-2
3329.6	PERU — ONDAS DEL HUALLAGA — Huánuco	Alternative Frequency to 3330.4kHz
3330	RWANDA — R REP RWANDAISE — Kigali	5/50kW:DS — Sa/Su:5/50kW:DS — Su:5/50kW:DS
3330.4	PERU — ONDAS DEL HUALLAGA — Huánuco	Alt 3329.6kHz:0.5kW:DS — Alt 3329.6kHz:Su:0.5kW:DS
3331v	COMOROS — RADIO COMORO — Moroni	4kW:DS-FRENCH, ETC
3335	BRAZIL — RADIO ALVORADA — Londrina	5kW:DS — Tu-Su:5kW:DS
	CHINA (TAIWAN) — CENTRAL BC SYSTEM — Taipei	10kW:PRC-5
	PAPUA NEW GUINEA — RADIO EAST SEPIK — Wewak	10kW:DS
	SWAZILAND — TRANS WORLD RADIO — Manzini	25kW::SAF — (J):25kW::SAF — (J)Sa:25kW::SAF
3338v	MOZAMBIQUE — RADIO MOCAMBIQUE — Maputo	Irr::10kW:DS-PORTUGUESE, ETC
3339	TANZANIA — RADIO TANZANIA — Zanzibar-Marhubi	10kW:DS
3340v	BOLIVIA — RADIO VILOCO — Viloco	1kW:DS-SPANISH, ETC — Irr:Su/M:1kW:DS-SPANISH, ETC
3344.8	INDONESIA — R REP INDONESIA — Ternate, Maluku	10kW:DS
3345	INDIA — RADIO KASHMIR — Jammu	2kW:DS-ENGLISH, ETC
	INDONESIA — R REP INDONESIA — Pontianak, Kalim'n	Irr::5kW:DS
	PAPUA NEW GUINEA — RADIO NORTHERN — Popondetta	2kW:DS-ENGLISH, ETC
3346	ZAMBIA — RADIO ZAMBIA-ZBS — Lusaka	50/120kW:DS-ENGLISH, ETC — F/Sa:50/120kW:DS-ENGLISH, ETC
3346v	ANGOLA — ER DO HUAMBO — Huambo	Irr::10kW:DS
3349.4	BOLIVIA — RADIO 27 DICIEMBRE — Villa Montes	1kW:DS — Irr::1kW:DS — Tu-Su:1kW:DS — Irr:Tu-Su:1kW:DS

ENGLISH ▬▬ GERMAN / DEUTSCH ◊◊◊◊ FRENCH / FRANÇAIS ▬▬ PORTUGUESE / PORTUGUÊS ▬▬ SPANISH / ESPAÑOL ▬▬

ARABIC / العربية ▬▬ RUSSIAN / РУССКИИ ▬▬ CHINESE / 中文 ◊◊◊◊ JAPANESE / 日本語 ▬▬ MULTILINGUAL ▭▭▭ OTHER ▬

SUMMER ONLY (J) WINTER ONLY (D) JAMMING ∧∧ or / or \ EARLIEST HEARD ◢ LATEST HEARD ◣ + TENTATIVE

Frequency (kHz)	Country / Station / Location	World Time 0 1 2 3 4 5 6 7 8 9 10 11 12	Power (kW): Network: Target 13 14 15 16 17 18 19 20 21 22 23 24 World Time

Frequency (kHz)	Country / Station / Location	Details
3350	KOREA (DPR) SOUTH PYONGYANG PS Pyŏngsong	DS
3354.7	ANGOLA R NAC DE ANGOLA Luanda	10kW:DS-A/INACTIVE
3355	INDIA ALL INDIA RADIO Kurseong	20kW:DS-ENGLISH, ETC / Irr::20kW:DS-ENGLISH, ETC
	NEW CALEDONIA RFO-N CALEDONIE Nouméa	20kW:DS / M-Sa:20kW:DS
3355v	INDONESIA R REP INDONESIA Jambi, Sumatera	7.5kW:DS
3356	BOTSWANA RADIO BOTSWANA Gaborone	50kW:DS-ENGLISH, ETC
3360	CHINA (PR) CENTRAL PEOPLES BS	TAIWAN-2
	GUATEMALA LA VOZ DE NAHUALA Nahualá	0.5/1kW:DS-SPANISH, ETC / Su:0.5/1kW:DS-SPANISH, ETC
	PAPUA NEW GUINEA RADIO MILNE BAY Alotau	10kW:DS-ENGLISH, ETC
3365	BRAZIL RADIO CULTURA Araraquara	1kW:DS
	INDIA ALL INDIA RADIO Delhi	10kW:DS-ENGLISH, ETC
3366	GHANA GHANA BC CORP Accra	50kW:DS-2
3367v	BOLIVIA RADIO 16 DE MARZO Bolívar, Oruro	Irr::DS
3370	BOLIVIA RADIO FLORIDA Samaipata	1kW:DS / Su:1kW:DS / Tu-Su:1kW:DS
	GUATEMALA RADIO TEZULUTLAN Cobán	1/5kW:DS
3370v	MADAGASCAR R MADAGASAKIRA Antananarivo	DS
3375	BRAZIL RADIO DOURADOS Dourados	5kW:DS / M-Sa:5kW:DS
	RADIO EDUCADORA Guajará Mirim	5kW:DS
	RADIO EQUATORIAL Macapá	1kW:DS
	RADIO NACIONAL S Gabriel Cachoeira	5kW:DS
	INDIA ALL INDIA RADIO Gauhati	10kW:DS-A/ENGLISH, ETC
	INDONESIA R REP INDONESIA Medan, Sumatera	7.5kW:DS
	PAPUA NEW GUINEA R WESTERN HIGHLAND Mount Hagen	2kW:DS
3377.5	JAPAN NIPPON HOSO KYOKAI Osaka-Mihara	Irr::0.3kW:DS-2(FEEDER)
3378	AUSTRIA SCHULUNGSSENDER Vienna	M-F:10kW:DS-ARMY TRAINING
3380	GUATEMALA RADIO CHORTIS Jocotán	1kW:DS
(con'd)	MALAWI MALAWI BC CORP Limbe	100kW:DS-ENGLISH, ETC

World Time: 0 1 2 3 4 5 6 7 8 9 10 11 12 13 14 15 16 17 18 19 20 21 22 23 24

ENGLISH ▰▰▰   GERMAN / DEUTSCH ০০০০   FRENCH / FRANÇAIS ▬▬   PORTUGUESE / PORTUGUÊS ▬▬   SPANISH / ESPAÑOL ▬▬

ARABIC /ﻉﺏﺭ ≡≡≡   RUSSIAN / РУССКИИ ══   CHINESE / 中文 ০০০০   JAPANESE / 日本語 ▰▰▰   MULTILINGUAL ০০০০   OTHER ━━

SUMMER ONLY (J)   WINTER ONLY (D)   JAMMING /\/\ or / or \   EARLIEST HEARD ◢   LATEST HEARD ◣   + TENTATIVE

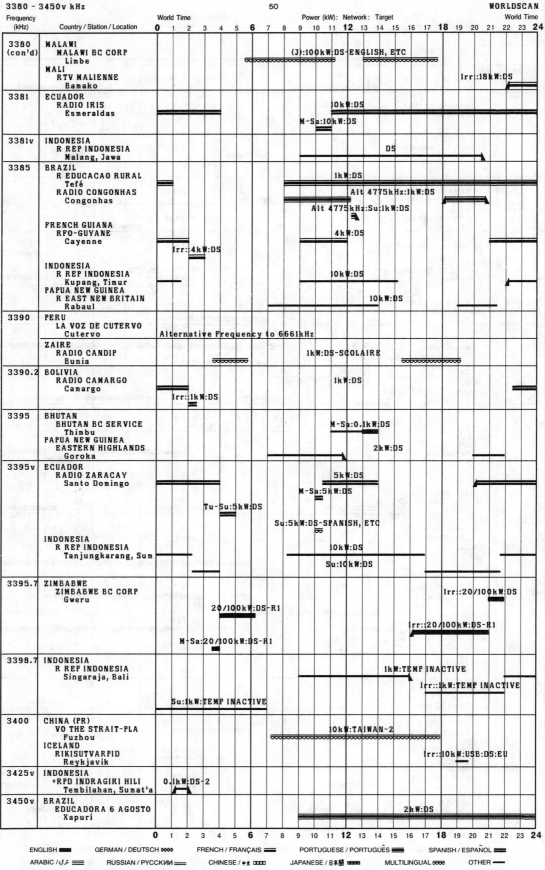

Frequency (kHz)	Country / Station / Location	Transmission details
3380 (con'd)	MALAWI MALAWI BC CORP Limbe	(J):100kW:DS-ENGLISH, ETC
	MALI RTV MALIENNE Bamako	Irr::18kW:DS
3381	ECUADOR RADIO IRIS Esmeraldas	10kW:DS M-Sa:10kW:DS
3381v	INDONESIA R REP INDONESIA Malang, Jawa	DS
3385	BRAZIL R EDUCACAO RURAL Tefé	1kW:DS
	RADIO CONGONHAS Congonhas	Alt 4775kHz:1kW:DS Alt 4775kHz:Su:1kW:DS
	FRENCH GUIANA RFO-GUYANE Cayenne	4kW:DS Irr::4kW:DS
	INDONESIA R REP INDONESIA Kupang, Timur	10kW:DS
	PAPUA NEW GUINEA R EAST NEW BRITAIN Rabaul	10kW:DS
3390	PERU LA VOZ DE CUTERVO Cutervo	Alternative Frequency to 6661kHz
	ZAIRE RADIO CANDIP Bunia	1kW:DS-SCOLAIRE
3390.2	BOLIVIA RADIO CAMARGO Camargo	1kW:DS Irr::1kW:DS
3395	BHUTAN BHUTAN BC SERVICE Thimbu	M-Sa:0.1kW:DS
	PAPUA NEW GUINEA EASTERN HIGHLANDS Goroka	2kW:DS
3395v	ECUADOR RADIO ZARACAY Santo Domingo	5kW:DS M-Sa:5kW:DS Tu-Su:5kW:DS Su:5kW:DS-SPANISH, ETC
	INDONESIA R REP INDONESIA Tanjungkarang, Sum	10kW:DS Su:10kW:DS
3395.7	ZIMBABWE ZIMBABWE BC CORP Gweru	Irr::20/100kW:DS 20/100kW:DS-R1 Irr::20/100kW:DS-R1 M-Sa:20/100kW:DS-R1
3398.7	INDONESIA R REP INDONESIA Singaraja, Bali	1kW:TEMP INACTIVE Irr::1kW:TEMP INACTIVE Su:1kW:TEMP INACTIVE
3400	CHINA (PR) VO THE STRAIT-PLA Fuzhou	10kW:TAIWAN-2
	ICELAND RIKISUTVARPID Reykjavik	Irr::10kW:USB:DS:EU
3425v	INDONESIA +RPD INDRAGIRI HILI Tembilahan, Sumat'a	0.1kW:DS-2
3450v	BRAZIL EDUCADORA 6 AGOSTO Xapurí	2kW:DS

ENGLISH ▬▬ GERMAN / DEUTSCH ০০০০ FRENCH / FRANÇAIS ▦▦▦ PORTUGUESE / PORTUGUÊS ▦▦▦ SPANISH / ESPAÑOL ▦▦▦

ARABIC / ﺍﻟﻌﺮﺑﻴﺔ ▦▦ RUSSIAN / РУССКИИ ▦▦ CHINESE / 中文 ০০০০ JAPANESE / 日本語 ▦▦▦ MULTILINGUAL ০০০০ OTHER ▬▬

SUMMER ONLY (J) WINTER ONLY (D) JAMMING ∧∧ or / or \ EARLIEST HEARD ◢ LATEST HEARD ◣ + TENTATIVE

Frequency (kHz)	Country / Station / Location	Power (kW): Network: Target (World Time 0–24)
3450v (con'd)	BRAZIL EDUCADORA 6 AGOSTO Xapurí	Tu-Su:2kW:DS
3452	INDONESIA RPD KOTA BARU Kota Baru, Kalim'n	Irr::DS-2
3458v	INDONESIA RPD LEBAK Lebak, Jawa	0.35kW:DS-2
3460v	INDONESIA RPD ACEH TIMUR Langsa, Sumatera	DS-2
3478v	INDONESIA RPD KETAPANG Ketapang, Kalim'n	0.5kW:DS-2
3480v	BOLIVIA RADIO PADILLA Padilla	0.5kW:DS/INACTIVE / Irr::0.5kW:DS/INACTIVE
3510v	CLANDESTINE (M EAST) 'VO THE CRUSADER' Near Iran	MOJAHEDIN-E KHALQ:ME
3535	CHINA (PR) VO THE STRAIT-PLA Fuzhou	10kW:TAIWAN-1
3569v	BRAZIL RADIO 3 DE JULHO Brasiléia	0.25kW:DS / Irr::0.25kW:DS
3579	INDONESIA RPD ASAHAN Kisaran, Sumatera	0.8kW:DS-2 / Irr::0.8kW:DS-2
3607.5 (con'd)	JAPAN NIPPON HOSO KYOKAI Hiroshima-Gion	Irr::0.6kW:DS-1(FEEDER)

World Time: 0 1 2 3 4 5 6 7 8 9 10 11 12 13 14 15 16 17 18 19 20 21 22 23 24

ENGLISH ▬▬ GERMAN / DEUTSCH ଡଡଡଡ FRENCH / FRANÇAIS ═══ PORTUGUESE / PORTUGUÊS ▬▬ SPANISH / ESPAÑOL ▬▬

ARABIC / ﻋﺮﺑﻲ ≡≡≡ RUSSIAN / РУССКИИ ═══ CHINESE / 中文 ଡଡଡଡ JAPANESE / 日本語 ▬▬ MULTILINGUAL ଡଡଡଡ OTHER ▬▬

SUMMER ONLY (J)   WINTER ONLY (D)   JAMMING /\/\ or / or \   EARLIEST HEARD ◢   LATEST HEARD ◣   + TENTATIVE

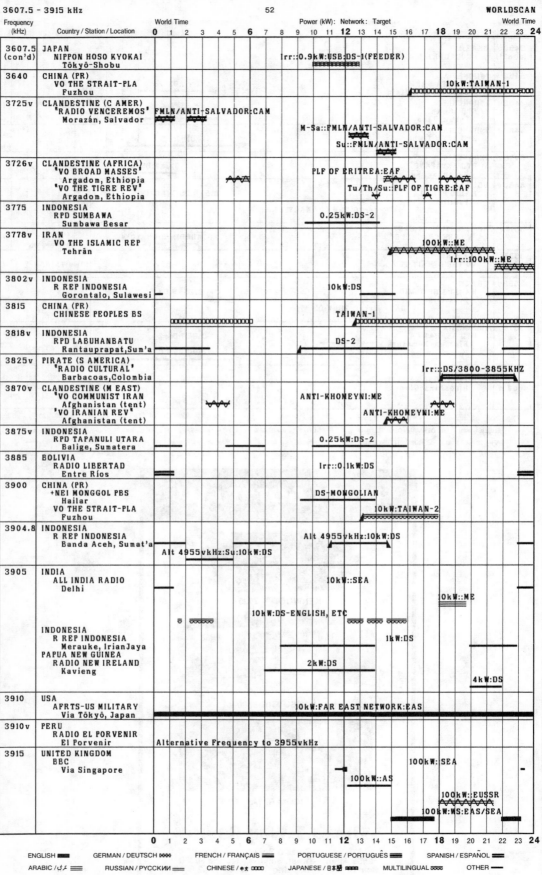

Frequency   World Time   Power (kW): Network: Target   World Time
(kHz)   Country / Station / Location

Time scale: 0 1 2 3 4 5 6 7 8 9 10 11 12 13 14 15 16 17 18 19 20 21 22 23 24

Frequency (kHz)	Country / Station / Location	Power (kW): Network: Target
3915v	CLANDESTINE (M EAST) 'VO THE CRUSADER' Near Iran	MOJAHEDIN-E KHALQ:ME (jamming)
3916v	INDONESIA R REP INDONESIA Ternate, Maluku	Alt 3946vkHz:10kW:DS
3920	KOREA (DPR) NORTH PYONGYANG PS Sinŭiju	DS
3925	INDIA ALL INDIA RADIO Delhi	10kW:DS-ENGLISH, ETC / Irr::10kW:DS-ENGLISH, ETC
	JAPAN NIHON SHORTWAVE BC Sapporo-Ebetsu	10kW:DS-1:EAS/PAC
	NIHON SHORTWAVE BC Tôkyô-Nagara	50kW:DS-1:EAS/PAC M-F:50kW:DS-1:EAS/PAC M-Sa:50kW:DS-1:EAS/PAC
	RADIO CANADA INTL Tôkyô/Sapporo	50/10kW::EAS/PAC
	PAPUA NEW GUINEA NATIONAL BC OF PNG Port Moresby	50kW:TEMP INACTIVE
3925v	PERU R NUEVO CAJAMARCA Nueva Cajamarca	Alternative Frequency to 3970vkHz
3929.8	SOUTH AFRICA CAPITAL RADIO Umtata	20kW:DS
	SOUTHERN SOUND Umtata	20kW:DS
3930	KOREA (REPUBLIC) KOREAN BC SYSTEM Suwŏn	5kW:DS-1
3931v	CAPE VERDE VOZ DE SAO VICENTE Mindelo-São Vicent	Irr:10kW:DS / 10kW:DS
3935	INDONESIA R REP INDONESIA Semarang, Jawa	10kW:DS
3935v	CLANDESTINE (M EAST) 'VO THE MARTYRS' Near Iran	Irr:::USB:ANTI-KHOMEYNI:ME
3940	CHINA (PR) HUBEI PEOPLES BS Wuhan	DS
	HONG KONG RTV HONG KONG Kowloon	Irr::2kW:SPECIAL EVENTS:EAS
3945	INDONESIA R REP INDONESIA Denpasar, Bali	10kW:DS
	R REP INDONESIA Tanjungkarang, Sum	Irr::2.5kW:DS
	JAPAN NIHON SHORTWAVE BC Tôkyô-Nagara	10kW:DS-2:EAS/PAC
	VANUATU RADIO VANUATU Vila, Efate Island	10kW:DS-ENGLISH,FR,ETC M-Sa:10kW:DS-ENGLISH,FR,ETC
3946v	INDONESIA R REP INDONESIA Ternate, Maluku	Alternative Frequency to 3916vkHz
3950	CHINA (PR) QINGHAI PEOPLES BS Xining	10kW:DS-CHINESE
3953	INDONESIA R REP INDONESIA Bogor, Jawa	Irr::1kW:DS
3955	UNITED KINGDOM BBC Daventry	100kW::EU
	BBC Multiple Locations	100kW:WS:EU 100/250kW:WS:EU/NAF
	BBC Skelton, Cumbria	100kW:WS:EU 100/250kW::WEU/NAF

Time scale: 0 1 2 3 4 5 6 7 8 9 10 11 12 13 14 15 16 17 18 19 20 21 22 23 24

| Frequency (kHz) | Country / Station / Location | World Time 0 ... 12 ... 24 | Power (kW): Network: Target | World Time |

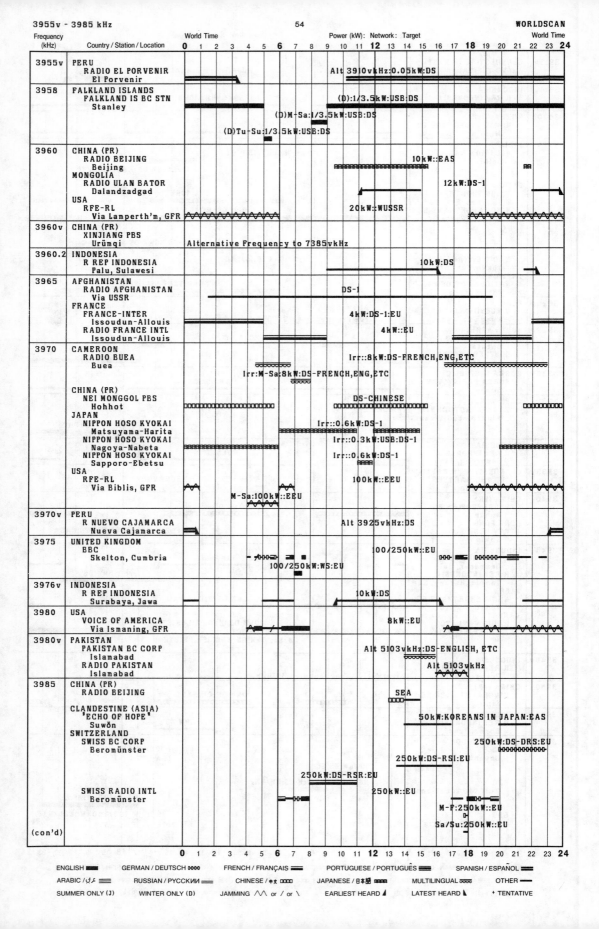

3955v — PERU — RADIO EL PORVENIR — El Porvenir — Alt 3910vkHz:0.05kW:DS

3958 — FALKLAND ISLANDS — FALKLAND IS BC STN — Stanley — (D):1/3.5kW:USB:DS — (D)M-Sa:1/3.5kW:USB:DS — (D)Tu-Su:1/3.5kW:USB:DS

3960 — CHINA (PR) — RADIO BEIJING — Beijing — 10kW::EAS
MONGOLIA — RADIO ULAN BATOR — Dalandzadgad — 12kW:DS-1
USA — RFE-RL — Via Lamperth'm, GFR — 20kW::WUSSR

3960v — CHINA (PR) — XINJIANG PBS — Urümqi — Alternative Frequency to 7385vkHz

3960.2 — INDONESIA — R REP INDONESIA — Palu, Sulawesi — 10kW:DS

3965 — AFGHANISTAN — RADIO AFGHANISTAN — Via USSR — DS-1
FRANCE — FRANCE-INTER — Issoudun-Allouis — 4kW:DS-1:EU
RADIO FRANCE INTL — Issoudun-Allouis — 4kW::EU

3970 — CAMEROON — RADIO BUEA — Buea — Irr::8kW:DS-FRENCH,ENG,ETC — Irr:M-Sa:8kW:DS-FRENCH,ENG,ETC
CHINA (PR) — NEI MONGGOL PBS — Hohhot — DS-CHINESE
JAPAN — NIPPON HOSO KYOKAI — Matsuyama-Harita — Irr::0.6kW:DS-1
NIPPON HOSO KYOKAI — Nagoya-Nabeta — Irr::0.3kW:USB:DS-1
NIPPON HOSO KYOKAI — Sapporo-Ebetsu — Irr::0.6kW:DS-1
USA — RFE-RL — Via Biblis, GFR — 100kW::EEU — M-Sa:100kW::EEU

3970v — PERU — R NUEVO CAJAMARCA — Nueva Cajamarca — Alt 3925vkHz:DS

3975 — UNITED KINGDOM — BBC — Skelton, Cumbria — 100/250kW::EU — 100/250kW:WS:EU

3976v — INDONESIA — R REP INDONESIA — Surabaya, Jawa — 10kW:DS

3980 — USA — VOICE OF AMERICA — Via Ismaning, GFR — 8kW::EU

3980v — PAKISTAN — PAKISTAN BC CORP — Islamabad — Alt 5103vkHz:DS-ENGLISH, ETC
RADIO PAKISTAN — Islamabad — Alt 5103vkHz

3985 — CHINA (PR) — RADIO BEIJING — SEA
CLANDESTINE (ASIA) — 'ECHO OF HOPE' — Suwŏn — 50kW:KOREANS IN JAPAN:EAS
SWITZERLAND — SWISS BC CORP — Beromünster — 250kW:DS-DRS:EU — 250kW:DS-RSI:EU — 250kW:DS-RSR:EU
SWISS RADIO INTL — Beromünster — 250kW::EU — M-F:250kW::EU — Sa/Su:250kW::EU

(con'd)

ENGLISH ▬▬ GERMAN / DEUTSCH ⬦⬦⬦⬦ FRENCH / FRANÇAIS ═══ PORTUGUESE / PORTUGUÊS ≣≣ SPANISH / ESPAÑOL ═══
ARABIC /ﻉﺏﻉ ≣≣ RUSSIAN / РУССКИИ ═══ CHINESE / 中文 ⬦⬦⬦⬦ JAPANESE / 日本語 ▦▦▦ MULTILINGUAL ⎓⎓⎓ OTHER ▬▬
SUMMER ONLY (J) WINTER ONLY (D) JAMMING ∧∧ or / or \ EARLIEST HEARD ◢ LATEST HEARD ◣ + TENTATIVE

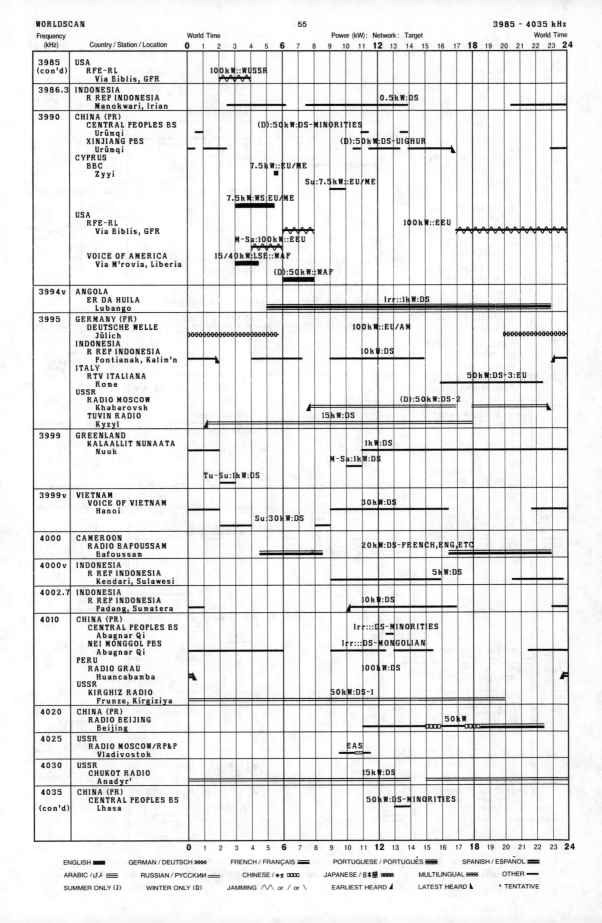

Frequency (kHz)	Country / Station / Location	Power (kW): Network: Target / World Time
3985 (con'd)	USA · RFE-RL · Via Biblis, GFR	100kW::WUSSR
3986.3	INDONESIA · R REP INDONESIA · Manokwari, Irian	0.5kW:DS
3990	CHINA (PR) · CENTRAL PEOPLES BS · Urümqi	(D):50kW:DS-MINORITIES
	XINJIANG PBS · Urümqi	(D):50kW:DS-UIGHUR
	CYPRUS · BBC · Zyyi	7.5kW::EU/ME · Su:7.5kW::EU/ME · 7.5kW:WS:EU/ME
	USA · RFE-RL · Via Biblis, GFR	100kW::EEU · M-Sa:100kW::EEU
	VOICE OF AMERICA · Via M'rovia, Liberia	15/40kW:LSB::WAF · (D):50kW::WAF
3994v	ANGOLA · ER DA HUILA · Lubango	Irr::1kW:DS
3995	GERMANY (FR) · DEUTSCHE WELLE · Jülich	100kW::EU/AM
	INDONESIA · R REP INDONESIA · Pontianak, Kalim'n	10kW:DS
	ITALY · RTV ITALIANA · Rome	50kW:DS-3:EU
	USSR · RADIO MOSCOW · Khabarovsk	(D):50kW:DS-2
	TUVIN RADIO · Kyzyl	15kW:DS
3999	GREENLAND · KALAALLIT NUNAATA · Nuuk	1kW:DS · M-Sa:1kW:DS · Tu-Su:1kW:DS
3999v	VIETNAM · VOICE OF VIETNAM · Hanoi	30kW:DS · Su:30kW:DS
4000	CAMEROON · RADIO BAFOUSSAM · Bafoussam	20kW:DS-FRENCH,ENG,ETC
4000v	INDONESIA · R REP INDONESIA · Kendari, Sulawesi	5kW:DS
4002.7	INDONESIA · R REP INDONESIA · Padang, Sumatera	10kW:DS
4010	CHINA (PR) · CENTRAL PEOPLES BS · Abagnar Qi	Irr:::DS-MINORITIES
	NEI MONGGOL PBS · Abagnar Qi	Irr:::DS-MONGOLIAN
	PERU · RADIO GRAU · Huancabamba	100kW:DS
	USSR · KIRGHIZ RADIO · Frunze, Kirgiziya	50kW:DS-1
4020	CHINA (PR) · RADIO BEIJING · Beijing	50kW
4025	USSR · RADIO MOSCOW/RP&P · Vladivostok	EAS
4030	USSR · CHUKOT RADIO · Anadyr'	15kW:DS
4035 (con'd)	CHINA (PR) · CENTRAL PEOPLES BS · Lhasa	50kW:DS-MINORITIES

ENGLISH ▆▆   GERMAN / DEUTSCH ∞∞   FRENCH / FRANÇAIS ▬▬   PORTUGUESE / PORTUGUÊS ▬▬   SPANISH / ESPAÑOL ▬▬

ARABIC /ぅ≠ ▬   RUSSIAN / PУCCКИИ ▬   CHINESE / ✦✗ ∞∞   JAPANESE / 日本語 ▬▬   MULTILINGUAL ∞∞   OTHER ▬

SUMMER ONLY (J)   WINTER ONLY (D)   JAMMING ∧∧ or / or \   EARLIEST HEARD ◢   LATEST HEARD ◣   + TENTATIVE

Frequency (kHz)	Country / Station / Location	World Time 0 ... Power (kW): Network: Target ... 24

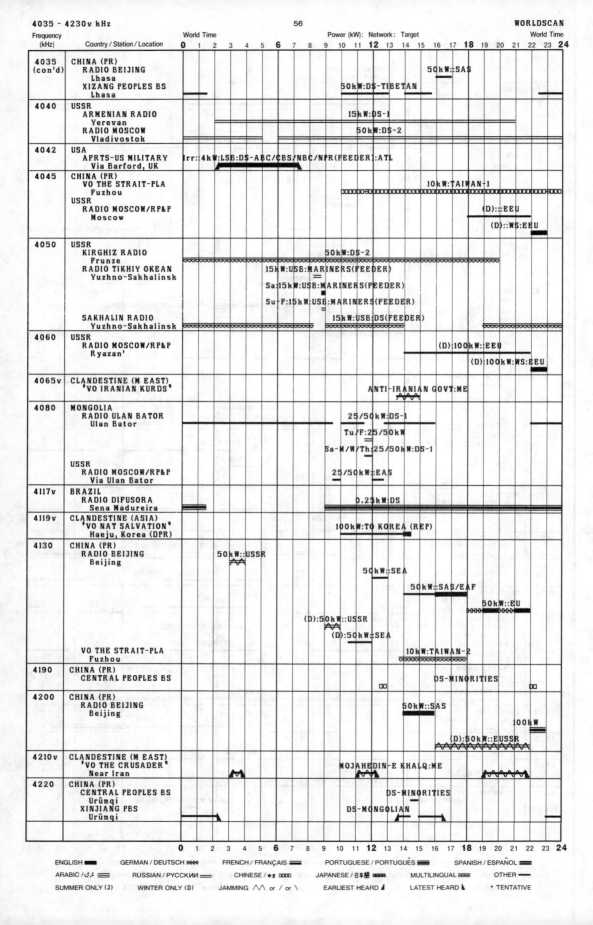

4035 (con'd) — CHINA (PR) RADIO BEIJING, Lhasa — 50kW::SAS
XIZANG PEOPLES BS, Lhasa — 50kW:DS-TIBETAN

4040 — USSR, ARMENIAN RADIO, Yerevan — 15kW:DS-1
RADIO MOSCOW, Vladivostok — 50kW:DS-2

4042 — USA, AFRTS-US MILITARY, Via Barford, UK — Irr::4kW:LSB:DS-ABC/CBS/NBC/NPR(FEEDER):ATL

4045 — CHINA (PR), VO THE STRAIT-PLA, Fuzhou — 10kW:TAIWAN-1
USSR, RADIO MOSCOW/RP&P, Moscow — (D)::EEU
(D)::WS:EEU

4050 — USSR, KIRGHIZ RADIO, Frunze — 50kW:DS-2
RADIO TIKHIY OKEAN, Yuzhno-Sakhalinsk — 15kW:USB:MARINERS(FEEDER)
Sa:15kW:USB:MARINERS(FEEDER)
Su-F:15kW:USB:MARINERS(FEEDER)
SAKHALIN RADIO, Yuzhno-Sakhalinsk — 15kW:USB:DS(FEEDER)

4060 — USSR, RADIO MOSCOW/RP&P, Ryazan' — (D):100kW:EEU
(D):100kW:WS:EEU

4065v — CLANDESTINE (M EAST), 'VO IRANIAN KURDS' — ANTI-IRANIAN GOVT:ME

4080 — MONGOLIA, RADIO ULAN BATOR, Ulan Bator — 25/50kW:DS-1
Tu/F:25/50kW
Sa-M/W/Th:25/50kW:DS-1
USSR, RADIO MOSCOW/RP&P, Via Ulan Bator — 25/50kW:EAS

4117v — BRAZIL, RADIO DIFUSORA, Sena Madureira — 0.25kW:DS

4119v — CLANDESTINE (ASIA), 'VO NAT SALVATION', Haeju, Korea (DPR) — 100kW:TO KOREA (REP)

4130 — CHINA (PR), RADIO BEIJING, Beijing — 50kW::USSR
50kW::SEA
50kW::SAS/EAF
50kW::EU
(D):50kW::USSR
(D):50kW::SEA
VO THE STRAIT-PLA, Fuzhou — 10kW:TAIWAN-2

4190 — CHINA (PR), CENTRAL PEOPLES BS — DS-MINORITIES

4200 — CHINA (PR), RADIO BEIJING, Beijing — 50kW::SAS
100kW
(D):50kW::EUSSR

4210v — CLANDESTINE (M EAST), 'VO THE CRUSADER', Near Iran — MOJAHEDIN-E KHALQ:ME

4220 — CHINA (PR), CENTRAL PEOPLES BS, Urūmqi — DS-MINORITIES
XINJIANG PBS, Urūmqi — DS-MONGOLIAN

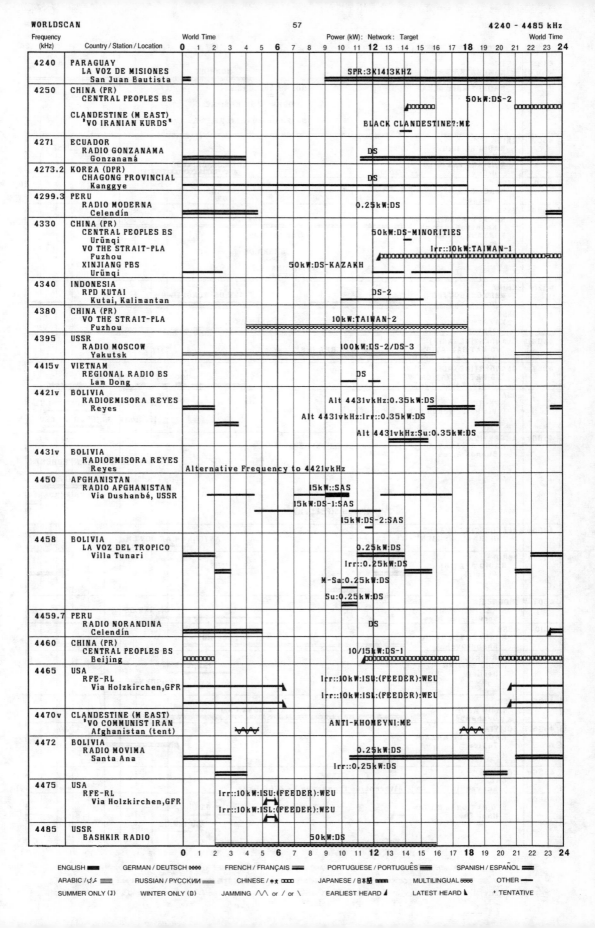

Frequency (kHz)	Country / Station / Location	World Time / Power (kW): Network: Target
4485 (con'd)	USSR KAMCHATKA RADIO Petropavlovsk	50kW:DS
	RADIO TIKHIY OKEAN Petropavlovsk	50kW:MARINERS:PAC
		Sa:50kW:MARINERS:PAC
		Su-F:50kW:MARINERS:PAC
4500	CHINA (PR) RADIO BEIJING Urümqi	(D):50kW::EUSSR
	XINJIANG PBS Urümqi	50kW:DS-CHINESE
4510	USSR UZBEK RADIO Fergana	15kW:DS
4520	USSR KHANTY-MANSIYSK R Khanty-Mansiysk	50kW:DS
	KORYASK RADIO Palana	Sa/Su:15kW:DS
		Su:15kW:DS
		Irr:W/F:15kW:DS
4525	CHINA (PR) NEI MONGGOL PBS Dongsheng	10kW:DS-MONGOLIAN
4545	USSR KAZAKH RADIO Alma-Ata	50kW:DS-1
4556.8	CLANDESTINE (ASIA) 'VO NAT SALVATION' Haeju, Korea (DPR)	100kW:TO KOREA (REP)
4557v	CLANDESTINE (ASIA) 'VO NAT SALVATION' Haeju, Korea (DPR)	100kW:TO KOREA (REP)
4565	USA RFE-RL Via Holzkirchen,GFR	Irr::10kW:ISL:(FEEDER):WEU
		Irr::10kW:ISU:(FEEDER):WEU
4588	ARGENTINA RADIO RIVADAVIA Buenos Aires	Irr:2.5kW:USB:DS(FEEDER)
		M-F:2.5kW:USB:DS(FEEDER)
		M-Sa:2.5kW:USB:DS(FEEDER)
		Sa:2.5kW:USB:DS(FEEDER)
		Su:2.5kW:USB:DS(FEEDER)
4605v	CLANDESTINE (M EAST) 'VO IRANIAN KURDS'	ANTI-IRANIAN GOVT:ME
4607v	PERU RADIO AYAVIRI Ayaviri	DS
		Irr:::DS
4607.4	INDONESIA R REP INDONESIA Serui, Irian Jaya	0.25kW:DS
4610	USSR KHABAROVSK RADIO Khabarovsk	50kW:DS
4620	CHINA (PR) RADIO BEIJING Beijing	10kW::EAS
		Irr::10kW
4635	USSR TAJIK RADIO Dushanbé	50kW:DS-1
4636.7	BOLIVIA RADIO 23 DE MARZO Tupiza	DS
		Irr:::DS
4656v	ECUADOR CRE Guayaquil	Alternative Frequency to 4766.6kHz
4660v	LAOS LAO NATIONAL RADIO Houa Phan	1kW:DS
		Su:1kW:DS

Frequency (kHz)	Country / Station / Location	World Time — Power (kW): Network: Target — World Time
4678v	VIETNAM REGIONAL RADIO BS Binh Tri Thien	DS
4679.6	ECUADOR R NACIONAL ESPEJO Quito	5kW:DS
4682	BOLIVIA RADIO PAITITI Guayaramerín	0.75kW:DS / Irr::0.75kW:DS
4699v	INDONESIA RK INFORMASI PER'N Surabaya, Jawa	2kW:DS / Irr::2kW:DS
4701	BOLIVIA RADIO RIBERALTA Riberalta	3kW:DS / Irr::3kW:DS
4701v	VIETNAM REGIONAL RADIO BS Gia Lai-Kon Tum	Alt 4730vkHz:DS
4718v	VIETNAM REGIONAL RADIO BS Son La	Alt 4755vkHz:DS
4719.3	INDONESIA R REP INDONESIA Ujung Pandang,Sul'i	Alt 4753kHz:50kW:DS
4720v	BOLIVIA RADIO ABAROA Riberalta	0.5kW:DS / Irr:M:0.5kW:DS / M-F:0.5kW:DS / Sa/Su:0.5kW:DS / Tu-Su:0.5kW:DS / Irr:Tu-Su:0.5kW:DS
4725v	BURMA BURMA BC SERVICE Rangoon	Sa:50kW:DS-BURMESE / 50kW:DS-MINORITIES
4730v	VIETNAM REGIONAL RADIO BS Gia Lai-Kon Tum	Alternative Frequency to 4701vkHz
4732v	PERU RADIO SAN JUAN Caraz	Irr::DS
4734v	MOZAMBIQUE RADIO MOCAMBIQUE Maputo	Alt 4743vkHz:25kW:DS
4735	CHINA (PR) CENTRAL PEOPLES BS Urümqi XINJIANG PBS Urümqi	50kW:DS-MINORITIES / 50kW:DS-UIGHUR / Irr::50kW:DS-UIGHUR
4739.5	BOLIVIA RADIO MAMORE Guayaramerín	0.5kW:DS / Irr::0.5kW:DS
4740	AFGHANISTAN RADIO AFGHANISTAN Via Ashkhabad,USSR	100kW:DS-1:ME/SAS
4743v	MOZAMBIQUE RADIO MOCAMBIQUE Maputo	Alternative Frequency to 4734vkHz
4749	BOLIVIA RADIO SANTA ANA Santa Ana	Alternative Frequency to 4804vkHz
4750	CHINA (PR) NEI MONGGOL PBS XIZANG PEOPLES BS Lhasa	15kW:DS-MONGOLIAN / 50kW:DS-CHINESE
4751v	ZAIRE LA VOIX DU ZAIRE Lubumbashi	Irr::10kW:DS
4753	INDONESIA R REP INDONESIA Ujung Pandang,Sul'i	Alternative Frequency to 4719.3kHz

World Time: 0 1 2 3 4 5 6 7 8 9 10 11 12 13 14 15 16 17 18 19 20 21 22 23 24

ENGLISH ▬▬ GERMAN / DEUTSCH ▭▭▭▭ FRENCH / FRANÇAIS ▬▬ PORTUGUESE / PORTUGUÊS ▬▬ SPANISH / ESPAÑOL ▬▬

ARABIC / ﻋﺮﺑﻲ ▬▬ RUSSIAN / РУССКИИ ▬▬ CHINESE / 中文 ▭▭▭▭ JAPANESE / 日本語 ▬▬ MULTILINGUAL ▭▭▭▭ OTHER ▬▬

SUMMER ONLY (J) WINTER ONLY (D) JAMMING ∧∧ or / or \ EARLIEST HEARD ◢ LATEST HEARD ◣ + TENTATIVE

Frequency (kHz)	Country / Station / Location	World Time: Power (kW): Network: Target

4755 BRAZIL
R EDUCACAO RURAL, Campo Grande — 10kW:DS; M-Sa:10kW:DS; Tu-Su:10kW:DS
RADIO DO MARANHAO, São Luís — 2kW:DS
HONDURAS
RADIO FAMILIA — DS

4755v VIETNAM
REGIONAL RADIO BS, Son La — Alternative Frequency to 4718vkHz

4756v VIETNAM
REGIONAL RADIO BS, Nghe Tinh — Irr:::DS

4760 CHINA (PR)
YUNNAN PEOPLES BS, Ziyun, Guizhou — 50kW:DS-CHINESE; Su:50kW:DS-CHINESE
LIBERIA
RADIO ELWA, Monrovia — 10kW:DS; F-Su:10kW:DS; M-Sa:10kW:DS; Sa/Su:10kW:DS
SWAZILAND
TRANS WORLD RADIO, Manzini — 100kW::EAF
+TRANS WORLD RADIO, Manzini — (D):25/100kW::EAF
VENEZUELA
RADIO FRONTERA, San Antonio — Irr:1kW:DS

4762 VIETNAM
UNIDENTIFIED — DS

4762v PERU
RADIO INCA, Lima — 1.8kW:DS

4764.2 INDONESIA
R REP INDONESIA, Medan, Sumatera — 50kW:DS; Su:50kW:DS

4765 BOLIVIA
RADIO HUANAY, Huanay — Irr:M-Sa:1kW:DS; M-Sa:1kW:DS
BRAZIL
RADIO NACIONAL, Cruzeiro do Sul — 10kW:DS; Tu-Su:10kW:DS
RADIO RURAL, Santarém — 10kW:DS

4765v CUBA
RADIO MOSCOW, Havana — 10kW::CA

4766.6 ECUADOR
CRE, Guayaquil — Alt 4656vkHz:5kW:DS; Alt 4656vkHz:M-Sa:5kW:DS; Alt 4656vkHz:Tu-Su:5kW:DS

4770 ANGOLA
ER LUNDA NORTE, Dundo-Luachimo — Irr::0.5kW:DS
CHINA (PR)
CENTRAL PEOPLES BS, Beijing — (D):15kW:TAIWAN-1
NIGERIA
RADIO NIGERIA, Kaduna — 50kW:DS-2/ENGLISH, ETC
VENEZUELA
RADIO MUNDIAL, Ciudad Bolívar — 1kW:DS

4770v VIETNAM
VOICE OF VIETNAM, Hanoi — 30kW:DS; Su:30kW:DS

World Time: 0 1 2 3 4 5 6 7 8 9 10 11 12 13 14 15 16 17 18 19 20 21 22 23 24

Frequency (kHz)	Country / Station / Location	World Time · Power (kW): Network: Target · World Time
4774.8	COLOMBIA RADIO SUPER Medellín	2kW:DS-SUPER
4775	BRAZIL R PORTAL DA AMAZ'A Cuiabá	1kW:DS Irr::1kW:DS
	RADIO CONGONHAS Congonhas	Alternative Frequency to 3385kHz
	INDIA ALL INDIA RADIO Gauhati	10kW:DS-B
	PERU RADIO TARMA Tarma	1kW:DS
4775v	BOLIVIA RADIO LOS ANDES Tarija	Irr::3kW:DS Irr:M-Sa:3kW:DS
	INDONESIA R REP INDONESIA Jakarta, Jawa	50kW:DS Irr::50kW:DS
4777	GABON RTV GABONAISE Libreville	100kW:DS-FRENCH, ETC M-Sa:100kW:DS-FRENCH, ETC
4780	USSR KARELIAN RADIO Petrozavodsk	50kW:DS
4780v	DJIBOUTI (JIBUTI) RTV DE DJIBOUTI Djibouti	20kW:DS Irr::20kW:DS F:20kW:DS Sa-Th:20kW:DS Irr:20kW:DS-RAMADAN
4780.2	VENEZUELA LV DE CARABOBO Valencia	1kW:DS M-Sa:1kW:DS
4782.8	MALI RTV MALIENNE Bamako	18kW:DS-FRENCH, ETC M-Sa:18kW:DS-FRENCH, ETC
4785	BOLIVIA RADIO BALLIVIAN San Borja	0.5kW:DS
	BRAZIL RADIO BRASIL Campinas	1kW:DS
	RADIO CAIARI Pôrto Velho	1kW:DS Irr::1kW:DS
	RADIO RIBAMAR São Luís	5kW:DS
	CHINA (PR) ZHEJIANG PBS Qu Xian	10kW:DS-CHINESE
	COLOMBIA ECOS DEL COMBEIMA Ibagué	5kW:DS-SUPER
	TANZANIA RADIO TANZANIA Dar es Salaam	50kW:DS-SWAHILI
	USSR AZERBAIJANI RADIO Baku	50kW:DS-1
4785v	PERU RADIO COOPERATIVA Satipo	1kW:DS
4790	PERU RADIO ATLANTIDA Iquitos	1kW:DS Irr:Tu-Su:1kW:DS
4790v	INDONESIA R REP INDONESIA Fak Fak, Irian Jaya	1kW:DS

World Time: 0 1 2 3 4 5 6 7 8 9 10 11 12 13 14 15 16 17 18 19 20 21 22 23 24

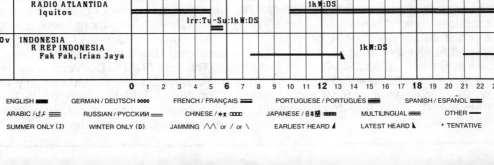

ENGLISH ▬▬   GERMAN / DEUTSCH ▯▯▯▯   FRENCH / FRANÇAIS ▬▬   PORTUGUESE / PORTUGUÊS ▬▬   SPANISH / ESPAÑOL ▬▬

ARABIC / عربى ▬   RUSSIAN / РУССКИИ ▬   CHINESE / 中文 ▯▯▯▯   JAPANESE / 日本語 ▬▬   MULTILINGUAL ▨▨▨   OTHER ▬

SUMMER ONLY (J)   WINTER ONLY (D)   JAMMING ∧∧ or / or \   EARLIEST HEARD ◢   LATEST HEARD ◣   + TENTATIVE

Frequency (kHz)	Country / Station / Location	World Time												Power (kW): Network: Target											World Time
		0	1	2	3	4	5	6	7	8	9	10	11	12	13	14	15	16	17	18	19	20	21	22	23	24

4790v (con'd) — PAKISTAN, AZAD KASHMIR RADIO, Islamabad — 100kW:DS

4792v — ECUADOR, EMISORA ATALAYA, Guayaquil — 5kW:DS; Irr:Sa/Su:5kW:DS; Tu-Su:5kW:DS

4795 — BRAZIL, RADIO AQUIDAUANA, Aquidauana — 2kW:DS; M-Sa:2kW:DS; Tu-Su:2kW:DS

CAMEROON, RADIO DOUALA, Douala — Irr:100kW:DS; Irr:M-F:100kW:DS; Irr:Sa/Su:100kW:DS; Irr::100kW:DS-FRENCH,ENG,ETC

ECUADOR, LV DE LOS CARAS, Bahía de Caráquez — 5kW:DS; Irr::5kW:DS

USSR, BURYAT RADIO, Ulan-Ude — 50kW:DS

4796.6 — BOLIVIA, R NUEVA AMERICA, La Paz — 10kW:DS; Irr:M-Sa:10kW:DS; Irr:Su:10kW:DS

(con'd)

| | | 0 | 1 | 2 | 3 | 4 | 5 | 6 | 7 | 8 | 9 | 10 | 11 | 12 | 13 | 14 | 15 | 16 | 17 | 18 | 19 | 20 | 21 | 22 | 23 | 24 |

ENGLISH ▬   GERMAN / DEUTSCH 0000   FRENCH / FRANÇAIS ▬   PORTUGUESE / PORTUGUÊS ▬   SPANISH / ESPAÑOL ▬

ARABIC /ﻉﺏﺝ ≡   RUSSIAN / РУССКИИ ═   CHINESE / ✦✗ 0000   JAPANESE / 日本語 ▦▦   MULTILINGUAL ₷₷₷   OTHER ▬

SUMMER ONLY (J)   WINTER ONLY (D)   JAMMING /\/\ or / or \   EARLIEST HEARD ◢   LATEST HEARD ◣   + TENTATIVE

Frequency (kHz) | Country / Station / Location | World Time ... Power (kW): Network: Target ... World Time

0 1 2 3 4 5 **6** 7 8 9 10 11 **12** 13 14 15 16 17 **18** 19 20 21 22 23 **24**

4796.6 (con'd)
BOLIVIA
R NUEVA AMERICA
La Paz
Su:10kW:DS
Tu-Su:10kW:DS

4797
VIETNAM
UNIDENTIFIED
DS

4799.8
CHINA (PR)
XINJIANG PBS
Urümqi
(D):50kW:DS-CHINESE

4800
INDIA
ALL INDIA RADIO
Hyderabad
10kW:DS-ENGLISH, ETC
Irr::10kW:DS-ENGLISH, ETC

LESOTHO
RADIO LESOTHO
Maseru
100kW:DS-ENGLISH, ETC.

USSR
YAKUT RADIO
Yakutsk
Alternative Frequency to 7100kHz

4800v
ECUADOR
RADIO POPULAR
Cuenca
5kW:DS
Irr::5kW:DS

4804
KENYA
VOICE OF KENYA
Nairobi
Irr::5kW:DS-GENERAL
Irr:M-F:5kW:DS-GENERAL
Irr:M-Sa:5kW:DS-GENERAL
Irr:Sa:5kW:DS-GENERAL

4804v
BOLIVIA
RADIO SANTA ANA
Santa Ana
Alt 4749kHz:0.25kW:DS
Alt 4749kHz:Irr::0.25kW:DS

4805
BRAZIL
RADIO ITATIAIA
Belo Horizonte
0.5kW:DS

4805v
BRAZIL
DIFUSORA AMAZONAS
Manaus
5kW:DS

4807
SAO TOME E PRINCIPE
RADIO NACIONAL
São Tomé
Irr::10kW:DS
Sa:10kW:DS

4810
SOUTH AFRICA
RADIO RSA
Meyerton
(J):250kW::WAF

USSR
ARMENIAN RADIO
Yerevan
50kW:DS-1
50kW:DS-2

KIRGHIZ RADIO
Frunze, Kirgiziya
50kW:DS-1

4810v
PERU
RADIO SAN MARTIN
Tarapoto
3kW:DS
M-Sa:3kW:DS

4810.4
BOLIVIA
RADIO LIBERTAD
Dist. Santa Fe
DS
M-Sa:DS

ECUADOR
LV DE GALAPAGOS
San Cristóbal
5kW:DS

4814.8
BRAZIL
R NAC TABATINGA
Benjamim Constant
10kW:DS

4815
BRAZIL
RADIO DIFUSORA
Londrina
0.5kW:DS

BURKINA FASO
RTV BURKINA
Ouagadougou
Irr::50kW
50kW:DS/ES

CHINA (PR)
RADIO BEIJING
Togtoh
10kW::EAS
Irr::10kW::EUSSR

(con'd)

0 1 2 3 4 5 **6** 7 8 9 10 11 **12** 13 14 15 16 17 **18** 19 20 21 22 23 **24**

ENGLISH ▬▬   GERMAN / DEUTSCH 0000   FRENCH / FRANÇAIS ═══   PORTUGUESE / PORTUGUÊS ▦▦▦   SPANISH / ESPAÑOL ▭▭▭

ARABIC / عربى ≡≡   RUSSIAN / РУССКИИ ═══   CHINESE / 中文 0000   JAPANESE / 日本語 ▦▦▦   MULTILINGUAL 6666   OTHER ▬▬

SUMMER ONLY (J)   WINTER ONLY (D)   JAMMING /\/\ or / or \   EARLIEST HEARD ◢   LATEST HEARD ◣   + TENTATIVE

Frequency (kHz)	Country / Station / Location	World Time 0 ... 12 ... 24 (Power (kW): Network: Target)
4815 (con'd)	**PAKISTAN** PAKISTAN BC CORP — Karachi	10kW:DS
4816.3	**BOLIVIA** RADIO NACIONAL — La Paz	DS-SPANISH, ETC
4819.6	**ECUADOR** RADIO PAZ Y BIEN — Ambato	2kW:DS-SPANISH, ETC / Tu-Su:2kW:DS-SPANISH, ETC
4820	**BOTSWANA** RADIO BOTSWANA — Gaborone	50kW:DS-ENGLISH, ETC
	HONDURAS LV EVANGELICA — Tegucigalpa	5kW:DS / Irr:5kW:DS / M:5kW:DS / Tu-Su:5kW:DS
	INDIA ALL INDIA RADIO — Calcutta	10kW:DS
	USSR KHANTY-MANSIYSK R — Khanty-Mansiysk	50kW:DS
4820v	**ANGOLA** +ER DA HUILA — Lubango	Irr::25kW:DS
4822v	**VIETNAM** REGIONAL RADIO BS — Ha Tuyen	Irr::DS
4825	**BRAZIL** RADIO EDUCADORA — Bragança	5kW:DS
	GUATEMALA RADIO MAM — Cabricán	1kW:DS/SPANISH, ETC
	MAURITANIA ORT DE MAURITANIE — Nouakchott	Alternative Frequency to 4845kHz
	PERU LV DE LA SELVA — Iquitos	10kW:DS
	USSR RADIO MOSCOW/RP&P — Star'obel'sk	(D):100kW::EU
	TURKMEN RADIO — Ashkhabad	50kW:DS-1
4826v	**PERU** RADIO SICUANI — Sicuani	0.35kW:DS-SPANISH, ETC / Tu-Su:0.35kW:DS
4827v	**BOLIVIA** RADIO GRIGOTA — Santa Cruz	Irr:1kW:DS / 1kW:DS / Irr:M-Sa:1kW:DS / Sa:1kW:DS / Su:1kW:DS / Su-F:1kW:DS
4830	**GABON** AFRIQUE NUMERO UN — Moanda-Moyabe	250kW::CAF
	THAILAND RADIO THAILAND — Pathum Thani	10kW:DS-1
	VENEZUELA RADIO TACHIRA — San Cristóbal	10kW:DS / Irr:Tu-Su:10kW:DS
4830v	**CHINA (PR)** LIAONING PBS — Shenyang	10kW:DS
4832	**COSTA RICA** RADIO RELOJ — San José	3kW:DS
4834.8 (con'd)	**MALI** RTV MALIENNE — Bamako	Irr:::DS-FRENCH, ETC

World Time: 0 1 2 3 4 5 6 7 8 9 10 11 12 13 14 15 16 17 18 19 20 21 22 23 24

ENGLISH ▬▬   GERMAN / DEUTSCH ◊◊◊◊   FRENCH / FRANÇAIS ═══   PORTUGUESE / PORTUGUÊS ▬▬   SPANISH / ESPAÑOL ▬▬

ARABIC / ﺏﺮﻋ ═══   RUSSIAN / РУССКИИ ═══   CHINESE / 中文 ◊◊◊◊   JAPANESE / 日本語 ▬▬▬   MULTILINGUAL ▭▭▭▭   OTHER ▬

SUMMER ONLY (J)   WINTER ONLY (D)   JAMMING ∧∧ or / or \   EARLIEST HEARD ◢   LATEST HEARD ◣   + TENTATIVE

Frequency (kHz)	Country / Station / Location	World Time	Power (kW): Network: Target	World Time

4834.8 (con'd) — MALI — RTV MALIENNE — Bamako — Irr:M-Sa::DS-FRENCH, ETC

4835 — AUSTRALIA — AUSTRALIAN BC CORP — Alice Springs — 50kW:DS-ENGLISH, ETC

BRAZIL — +RTV ACAUA — Teresina — 0.5kW:DS

GUATEMALA — RADIO TEZULUTLAN — Cobán — 2.5/3kW:DS

INDONESIA — R REP INDONESIA — Ambon, Maluku — 10kW:DS

MALAYSIA — RTM-SARAWAK — Kuching-Stapok — 10kW:DS-MALAY, MELANEU

4837v — MONGOLIA — RADIO ULAN BATOR — Altai — 12kW:DS

4837.5 — BRAZIL — RADIO ATALAIA — Corumbá — 5kW:DS

4839 — ZAIRE — RADIO BUKAVU — Bukavu — Irr::4kW:DS-FRENCH, ETC / Irr:Su:4kW:DS-FRENCH, ETC

4840 — CHINA (PR) — HEILONGJIANG PBS — Harbin — 50kW:DS-CHINESE

VO THE STRAIT-PLA — Fuzhou — 10kW:TAIWAN-2 / (D):10kW:TAIWAN-2

INDIA — ALL INDIA RADIO — Bombay — 10kW:DS / Irr::10kW:DS

PERU — RADIO ANDAHUAYLAS — Andahuaylas — 2kW:DS

VENEZUELA — RADIO VALERA — Valera — 1kW:DS

4845 — BOLIVIA — RADIO FIDES — La Paz — 10kW:DS / M-Sa:10kW:DS / Tu-Su:10kW:DS

BRAZIL — RADIO NACIONAL — Manaus — 250kW:DS / Tu-Sa:250kW:DS

MALAYSIA — RADIO MALAYSIA — Kajang — 50kW:DS-TAMIL / Sa/Su:50kW:DS-TAMIL / Su:50kW:DS-TAMIL

MAURITANIA — ORT DE MAURITANIE — Nouakchott — Alt 4825kHz:100kW:DS

4845v — COLOMBIA — RADIO BUCARAMANGA — Bucaramanga — Irr::1kW:DS

4850 — CAMEROON — RADIO NATIONALE — Yaoundé — 100kW:DS-ENGLISH, FRENCH

CHINA (PR) — UNIDENTIFIED

INDIA — ALL INDIA RADIO — Kohima — 2kW:DS

MONGOLIA — RADIO ULAN BATOR — Ulan Bator — 100kW:DS-1 / Tu/F:100kW::EUSSR / Sa-M/W/Th:100kW:DS-1

(con'd)

World Time: 0 1 2 3 4 5 6 7 8 9 10 11 12 13 14 15 16 17 18 19 20 21 22 23 24

ENGLISH ▬▬   GERMAN / DEUTSCH ००००   FRENCH / FRANÇAIS ═══   PORTUGUESE / PORTUGUÊS ▤▤   SPANISH / ESPAÑOL ▬▬

ARABIC / العربية ≡≡   RUSSIAN / РУССКИИ ══   CHINESE / 中文 ००००   JAPANESE / 日本語 ▦▦   MULTILINGUAL ०००००   OTHER ▬

SUMMER ONLY (J)   WINTER ONLY (D)   JAMMING ∧∧ or / or \   EARLIEST HEARD ◢   LATEST HEARD ◣   + TENTATIVE

Frequency (kHz)	Country / Station / Location	World Time 0–24 / Power (kW): Network: Target
4850 (con'd)	USSR RADIO MOSCOW/RP&P Via Ulan Bator	100kW::EAS
	UZBEK RADIO Tashkent	50kW:DS-2
	VENEZUELA RADIO CAPITAL Caracas	1kW:DS
4851v	ECUADOR RADIO LUZ Y VIDA Loja	5kW:DS / Irr::5kW:DS
4852.7	YEMEN (PDR) 'VO PALESTINE' Via Radio San'ā	100kW:PLO / Irr::100kW:PLO
	RADIO SAN'A San'ā	100kW:DS / F:100kW:DS
4855	BRAZIL R POR MUNDO MELHOR Gov Valadares	1kW:DS / M-Sa:1kW:DS
	RADIO ARUANA Barra do Garças	1kW:DS
4855v	MAURITIUS MAURITIUS BC CORP Curepipe	10kW:DS-FRENCH,ENG,ETC
4855.8	INDONESIA R REP INDONESIA Palembang,Sumatera	Irr::10kW:DS / Irr:Su:10kW:DS
4857v	BOLIVIA RADIO EL CONDOR Uyuni	DS
4860	INDIA ALL INDIA RADIO Delhi	10kW::SEA / 10kW:DS-ENGLISH, ETC / Irr::10kW:DS-ENGLISH, ETC / 10kW:DS-FORCES/ENG, ETC
	USSR CHITA RADIO Chita	15kW:DS
	CHITA RADIO Serpukhov	(D):100kW::EEU
	RADIO MOSCOW/RP&P Kalinin	(D):50kW:N AMERICAN
4860v	PERU R CHINCHAYCOCHA Junín	Irr::0.5kW:DS
4865	BRAZIL R VERDES FLORESTAS Cruzeiro do Sul	5kW:DS
	RADIO SOCIEDADE Feira de Santana	1kW:DS
	CHINA (PR) GANSU PEOPLES BS Lanzhou	50kW:DS-CHINESE
	COLOMBIA LV DEL CINARUCO Arauca	1kW:DS-CARACOL / Tu-Su:1kW:DS-CARACOL
	MONGOLIA RADIO ULAN BATOR Sainshand	12kW:DS-1 / Tu/F:12kW::EUSSR / Sa-M/W/Th:12kW:DS-1
	USSR RADIO MOSCOW/RP&P Via Sainshand,Mong	12kW::EAS
4867	INDONESIA R REP INDONESIA Wamena, IrianJaya	Alternative Frequency to 5043.7kHz
4870	BENIN ORT DU BENIN Cotonou	Irr::30kW:DS / 30kW:DS-FRENCH, ETC / M-Sa:30kW:DS-FRENCH, ETC
(con'd)		

World Time: 0 1 2 3 4 5 6 7 8 9 10 11 12 13 14 15 16 17 18 19 20 21 22 23 24

ENGLISH ▬▬ GERMAN / DEUTSCH ◊◊◊◊ FRENCH / FRANÇAIS ═══ PORTUGUESE / PORTUGUÊS ▬▬ SPANISH / ESPAÑOL ▬▬

ARABIC / ﻋﺮﺑﻰ ═══ RUSSIAN / РУССКИИ ═══ CHINESE / 中文 ◻◻◻◻ JAPANESE / 日本語 ▬▬▬ MULTILINGUAL ⌂⌂⌂⌂ OTHER ▬▬

SUMMER ONLY (J) WINTER ONLY (D) JAMMING /\/\ or / or \ EARLIEST HEARD ◢ LATEST HEARD ◣ + TENTATIVE

Frequency (kHz)	Country / Station / Location	Power (kW): Network: Target

4870 (con'd) — BENIN / ORT DU BENIN / Cotonou — Sa/Su:30kW:DS-FRENCH, ETC — Su:30kW:DS-FRENCH, ETC

ECUADOR / RADIO RIO AMAZONAS / Macuma — 5kW:DS-SPANISH, ETC — Tu-Su:5kW:DS-SPANISH, ETC — Irr:Tu-Su:5kW:DS-SPANISH, ETC

SRI LANKA / SRI LANKA BC CORP / Colombo-Ekala — 10kW:DS-SINHALA COMM'L

4871v — INDONESIA / R REP INDONESIA / Sorong, Irian Jaya — 10kW:DS

4872v C — MOZAMBIQUE / EP DA ZAMBEZIA / Quelimane — Alt 4902vkHz:Irr::0.25kW:DS-PORTUGUESE, ET

4875 — BRAZIL / R JORNAL DO BRASIL / Rio de Janeiro — 10kW:DS

RADIO NACIONAL / Boa Vista — 10kW:DS

INDONESIA / R REP INDONESIA / Sorong, Irian Jaya — 10kW:DS — Sa:10kW:DS — Su-F:10kW:DS

4875v — INDONESIA / R REP INDONESIA / Sorong, Irian Jaya — 10kW:DS — Sa:10kW:DS — Su-F:10kW:DS

4875.2 — COLOMBIA / RADIO SUPER / Medellín — 2kW:DS-SUPER

4876 — BOLIVIA / R LA CRUZ DEL SUR / La Paz — Irr::10kW:DS — 10kW:DS

4878.8 — PAKISTAN / PAKISTAN BC CORP / Quetta — 10kW:DS — Irr::10kW:DS — Sa-Th:10kW:DS

4879v — BANGLADESH / RADIO BANGLADESH / Dhaka — 10/100kW:DS

4880 — BRAZIL / R DIFUSORA ACREANA / Rio Branco — Alt 4885kHz:5kW:DS

SOUTH AFRICA / SOUTH AFRICAN BC / Meyerton — M-F:100kW:DS-AGRICULTURE RPT — 100kW:RADIO SUID-AFRIKA — Sa/Su:100kW:RADIO SUID-AFRIKA

4882v — VIETNAM / REGIONAL RADIO BS / Thanh Hoa — DS

4883 — CHINA (PR) / RADIO BEIJING / Hohhot — 50kW::EAS — Irr::50kW::EUSSR

4885 — ANGOLA / ER DO ZAIRE / M'banza Congo — 5kW:DS

BRAZIL / R CLUBE DO PARA / Belém — 5kW:DS

R DIFUSORA ACREANA / Rio Branco — Alternative Frequency to 4880kHz

COLOMBIA / ONDAS DEL META / Villavicencio — 5kW:DS-SUPER

KENYA / VOICE OF KENYA / Nairobi

ENGLISH ▬▬ GERMAN / DEUTSCH ∞∞∞ FRENCH / FRANÇAIS ═══ PORTUGUESE / PORTUGUÊS ▬▬ SPANISH / ESPAÑOL ═══

ARABIC / عربى ═══ RUSSIAN / РУССКИИ ═══ CHINESE / 中文 ∞∞∞ JAPANESE / 日本語 ▬▬▬ MULTILINGUAL ∞∞∞ OTHER ▬▬

SUMMER ONLY (J) WINTER ONLY (D) JAMMING ∧∧ or / or \ EARLIEST HEARD ◢ LATEST HEARD ◣ * TENTATIVE

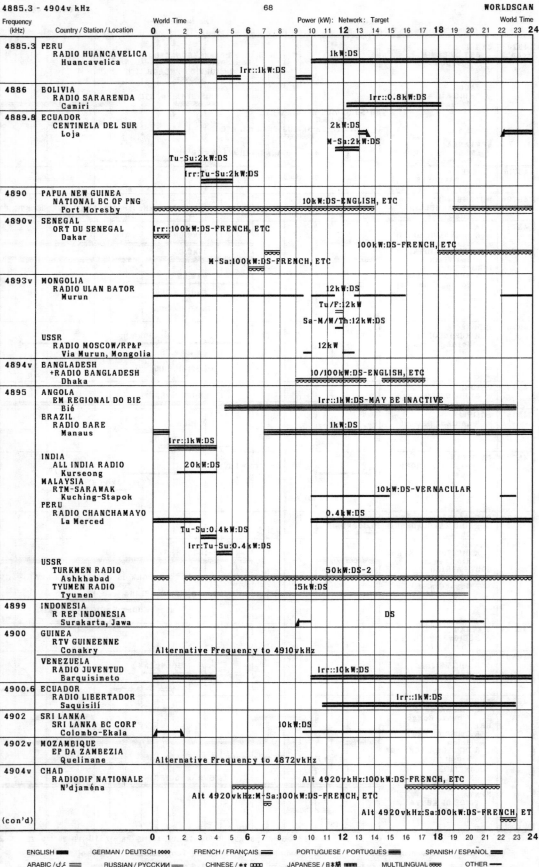

Frequency　　　　　　　　　　　　World Time　　　　　　　　Power (kW):　Network:　Target　　　　　　World Time
(kHz)　　Country / Station / Location　0　1　2　3　4　5　6　7　8　9　10　11　12　13　14　15　16　17　18　19　20　21　22　23　24

Frequency (kHz)	Country / Station / Location	Details
4885.3	PERU RADIO HUANCAVELICA Huancavelica	1kW:DS / Irr::1kW:DS
4886	BOLIVIA RADIO SARARENDA Camiri	Irr::0.8kW:DS
4889.8	ECUADOR CENTINELA DEL SUR Loja	2kW:DS / M-Sa:2kW:DS / Tu-Su:2kW:DS / Irr:Tu-Su:2kW:DS
4890	PAPUA NEW GUINEA NATIONAL BC OF PNG Port Moresby	10kW:DS-ENGLISH, ETC
4890v	SENEGAL ORT DU SENEGAL Dakar	Irr::100kW:DS-FRENCH, ETC / 100kW:DS-FRENCH, ETC / M-Sa:100kW:DS-FRENCH, ETC
4893v	MONGOLIA RADIO ULAN BATOR Murun	12kW:DS / Tu/F:12kW / Sa-M/W/Th:12kW:DS
	USSR RADIO MOSCOW/RP&P Via Murun, Mongolia	12kW
4894v	BANGLADESH +RADIO BANGLADESH Dhaka	10/100kW:DS-ENGLISH, ETC
4895	ANGOLA EM REGIONAL DO BIE Bié	Irr::1kW:DS-MAY BE INACTIVE
	BRAZIL RADIO BARE Manaus	1kW:DS / Irr::1kW:DS
	INDIA ALL INDIA RADIO Kurseong	20kW:DS
	MALAYSIA RTM-SARAWAK Kuching-Stapok	10kW:DS-VERNACULAR
	PERU RADIO CHANCHAMAYO La Merced	0.4kW:DS / Tu-Su:0.4kW:DS / Irr:Tu-Su:0.4kW:DS
	USSR TURKMEN RADIO Ashkhabad	50kW:DS-2
	TYUMEN RADIO Tyumen	15kW:DS
4899	INDONESIA R REP INDONESIA Surakarta, Jawa	DS
4900	GUINEA RTV GUINEENNE Conakry	Alternative Frequency to 4910vkHz
	VENEZUELA RADIO JUVENTUD Barquisimeto	Irr::10kW:DS
4900.6	ECUADOR RADIO LIBERTADOR Saquisilí	Irr::1kW:DS
4902	SRI LANKA SRI LANKA BC CORP Colombo-Ekala	10kW:DS
4902v	MOZAMBIQUE EP DA ZAMBEZIA Quelimane	Alternative Frequency to 4872vkHz
4904v	CHAD RADIODIF NATIONALE N'djaména	Alt 4920vkHz:100kW:DS-FRENCH, ETC / Alt 4920vkHz:M-Sa:100kW:DS-FRENCH, ETC / Alt 4920vkHz:Sa:100kW:DS-FRENCH, ET
(con'd)		

0　1　2　3　4　5　6　7　8　9　10　11　12　13　14　15　16　17　18　19　20　21　22　23　24

Frequency (kHz)	Country / Station / Location	World Time / Power (kW): Network: Target

4904v (con'd) — CHAD / RADIODIF NATIONALE / N'djaména — Alt 4920vkHz:Su:100kW:DS-FRENCH, ETC

4905 — BRAZIL
- R RELOGIO FEDERAL / Rio de Janeiro — 5kW:DS — Irr::5kW:DS
- RADIO ARAGUAIA / Araguaína — 1kW:DS

CHINA (PR) / CENTRAL PEOPLES BS / Beijing — 10kW:DS-1

UNITED ARAB EMIRATES / VOICE OF THE UAE / Abu Dhabi — Irr

4908v — PERU / RADIO COBRIZA 2000 / Pacaycasa — Alternative Frequency to 4927vkHz

4910 — AUSTRALIA / AUSTRALIAN BC CORP / Tennant Creek — 50kW:DS-ENGLISH, ETC

HONDURAS / LV DE LA MOSQUITIA / Puerto Lempira — 0.5kW:DS

4910v — GUINEA / RTV GUINEENNE / Conakry — Alt 4900kHz:18kW:DS-FRENCH, ETC — Alt 4900kHz:M-Sa:18kW:DS-FRENCH, ETC — Alt 4900kHz:Su:18kW:DS-FRENCH, ETC

INDONESIA / R REP INDONESIA / Bukittinggi, Sumat'a — 1kW:DS

ZAMBIA / RADIO ZAMBIA / Lusaka — 50kW:DS-ENGLISH, ETC — F/Sa:50kW:DS-ENGLISH, ETC

4910.2 — PERU / RADIO TAWANTINSUYO / Cuzco — 5kW:DS-SPANISH, ETC

4910.7 — PERU / RADIO LIBERTAD / Trujillo — Irr::1kW:DS

4911v — ECUADOR / EM GRAN COLOMBIA / Quito — Irr::10kW:DS

4915 — BRAZIL
- RADIO ANHANGUERA / Goiânia — 10kW:DS
- RADIO NACIONAL / Macapá — 10kW:DS

CHINA (PR) / GUANGXI PEOPLES BS / Nanning — 10kW:DS-1

GHANA / GHANA BC CORP / Accra — 50kW:DS-1/ENGLISH, ETC — Sa/Su:50kW:DS-1/ENGLISH, ETC

4915v — COLOMBIA / ARMONIAS CAQUETA / Florencia — 3kW:DS — M-Sa:3kW:DS — Tu-Su:3kW:DS

KENYA / VOICE OF KENYA / Nairobi — Alt 6075kHz:100kW:DS-SWAHILI — Alt 6075kHz:M-Sa:100kW:DS-SWAHILI — Alt 6075kHz:Sa:100kW:DS-SWAHILI

4920 — AUSTRALIA / AUSTRALIAN BC CORP / Brisbane — 10kW:DS — M-Sa:10kW:DS

INDIA / ALL INDIA RADIO / Madras — 10kW:DS-A/ENGLISH, ETC — Irr::10kW:DS-A/ENGLISH, ETC

USSR / YAKUT RADIO / Yakutsk — 50kW:DS

World Time scale: 0 1 2 3 4 5 6 7 8 9 10 11 12 13 14 15 16 17 18 19 20 21 22 23 24

ENGLISH ▬▬   GERMAN / DEUTSCH ◊◊◊◊   FRENCH / FRANÇAIS ═══   PORTUGUESE / PORTUGUÊS ▰▰▰   SPANISH / ESPAÑOL ▬▬

ARABIC /ﻉ ﻉ ≡≡   RUSSIAN / РУССКИИ ═══   CHINESE / ★☆ ◻◻◻◻   JAPANESE / 日本語 ▦▦▦   MULTILINGUAL ▒▒▒   OTHER ▬▬

SUMMER ONLY (J)   WINTER ONLY (D)   JAMMING /\/\ or / or \   EARLIEST HEARD ◢   LATEST HEARD ◣   + TENTATIVE

Frequency (kHz)	Country / Station / Location	World Time / Power (kW): Network: Target
4920v	**CHAD** RADIODIF NATIONALE N'djaména	Alternative Frequency to 4904vkHz
	INDONESIA R REP INDONESIA Tanjungpinang, Sum	Irr::10kW:DS
4920.4	**ECUADOR** RADIO QUITO Quito	5kW:DS M-Sa:5kW:DS Tu-Su:5kW:DS
4921v	**PERU** ONDAS DEL TITICACA Puno	1kW:DS-SPANISH, ETC Tu-Su:1kW:DS
4924.2	**BOLIVIA** RADIO COSMOS Cochabamba	Irr::1kW:DS Irr:M-Sa:1kW:DS
4925	**BRAZIL** RADIO DIFUSORA Taubaté	1kW:DS Irr:1kW:DS
	CHINA (PR) HEILONGJIANG PBS Harbin	50kW:DS-2
4925.6	**EQUATORIAL GUINEA** RADIO NACIONAL Batá	Alt 5004vkHz:100kW:DS-SPANISH, ETC
4927	**INDONESIA** R REP INDONESIA Jambi, Sumatera	7.5kW:DS Irr::7.5kW:DS
4927v	**PERU** RADIO COBRIZA 2000 Pacaycasa	Alt 4908vkHz:Irr:::DS
4930	**HAITI** RADIO STATION 4VEH Cap Haïtien	1.5kW:DS/FR,ENG,SP,ETC
	USSR RADIO MOSCOW Ashkabad	50kW:DS-2
	RADIO MOSCOW Tbilisi	50kW:DS-2
4931.6	**INDONESIA** R REP INDONESIA Surakarta, Jawa	Irr::0.5kW:DS
4934.7	**PERU** RADIO TROPICAL Tarapoto	1kW:DS
4935	**BOLIVIA** RADIO MONTEAGUDO Monteagudo	1kW:DS
	BRAZIL R JORNAL A CRITICA Manaus	5kW:DS
	RADIO DIFUSORA Jataí	2.5kW:DS
	CLANDESTINE (AFRICA) "AV DO GALO NEGRO"	UNITA/PORT,ETC:SAF
	NAMIBIA R SOUTHWEST AFRICA Windhoek	100kW:DS-1
4935v	**BRAZIL** RADIO CAPIXABA Vitória	Irr::1kW:DS
	PERU RADIO ABANCAY Abancay	1kW:DS
4939.8	**VENEZUELA** RADIO YARACUY San Felipe	10kW:DS
4940	**CHINA (PR)** QINGHAI PEOPLES BS Xining	10kW:DS-CHINESE
	SRI LANKA SRI LANKA BC CORP Colombo-Ekala	10kW:DS-ENGLISH
	USSR UKRAINIAN RADIO Kiev	50kW:DS-2

ENGLISH ▬▬   GERMAN / DEUTSCH ◊◊◊◊   FRENCH / FRANÇAIS ══   PORTUGUESE / PORTUGUÊS ▬   SPANISH / ESPAÑOL ══

ARABIC /ﻉﺭ ═   RUSSIAN / РУССКИИ ══   CHINESE / 中文 ◊◊◊◊   JAPANESE / 日本語 ▬▬   MULTILINGUAL ▦▦   OTHER ▬

SUMMER ONLY (J)   WINTER ONLY (D)   JAMMING /\/\ or / or \   EARLIEST HEARD ◢   LATEST HEARD ◣   + TENTATIVE

Frequency (kHz)	Country / Station / Location	World Time 0...24 / Power (kW): Network: Target
4945	BOLIVIA	
	RADIO ILLIMANI	Irr::10kW:DS
	La Paz	
	BRAZIL	
	RADIO DIFUSORA	1kW:DS
	Poços de Caldas	Tu-Su:1kW:DS
	RADIO NACIONAL	50kW:DS
	Pôrto Velho	Tu-Sa:50kW:DS
	VOZ SAO FRANCISCO	2kW:DS
	Petrolina	
	COLOMBIA	
	CARACOL NEIVA	2.5kW:DS-CARACOL
	Neiva	
	SOUTH AFRICA	
	RADIO RSA	250kW::SAF
	Meyerton	
4945v	URUGUAY	
	LA VOZ DE ARTIGAS	Irr:::FEEDER
	Artigas	
4945.8	INDONESIA	
	R REP INDONESIA	Irr::1.5kW:DS
	Bandung, Jawa	
4950	CLANDESTINE (AFRICA)	
	"A VOZ DA VERDADE"	5kW:ANTI-ANGOLA, CUBA
	Pietersburg, S Af	
	MALAYSIA	
	RTM-SARAWAK	10kW:DS
	Kuching-Stapok	
	PAKISTAN	
	PAKISTAN BC CORP	10kW:DS
	Peshawar	
	RADIO PAKISTAN	10kW::SAS
	Peshawar	
	PERU	
	R MADRE DE DIOS	5kW:DS
	Puerto Maldonado	
	RADIO UCAYALI	0.5kW:DS
	Contamana	
4952v	ANGOLA	
	ER DA HUILA	Irr::25kW:DS
	Lubango	
4954.7	BRAZIL	
	RADIO CLUBE	Irr::2.5kW:DS
	Rondonópolis	Irr:M-Sa:2.5kW:DS
		Irr:Tu-Su:2.5kW:DS
4955	BRAZIL	
	RADIO CULTURA	2.5kW:DS
	Campos	
	RADIO MARAJOARA	10kW:DS
	Belém	
4955v	INDONESIA	
	R REP INDONESIA	
	Banda Aceh, Sumat'a	Alternative Frequency to 3904.8kHz
	PERU	
	R CULTURAL AMAUTA	1kW:DS-SPANISH, ETC
	Huanta	
4957.5	USSR	
	AZERBAIJANI RADIO	50kW:DS-2
	Baku	
4960	CHINA (PR)	
	RADIO BEIJING	50kW::EAS
	Kunming	
	INDIA	
	ALL INDIA RADIO	10kW:DS
	Delhi	
	ALL INDIA RADIO	2kW:DS
	Ranchi	
4960v	ECUADOR	
	RADIO FEDERACION	5kW:DS-SPANISH, ETC
	Sucúa	M-W:5kW:DS-SPANISH, ETC
		Tu-Su:5kW:DS-SPANISH, ETC
4960.3	PERU	
	RADIO LA MERCED	Tu-Su:0.5kW:DS
	La Merced	0.5kW:DS
4965 (con'd)	BRAZIL	
	RADIO ALVORADA	5kW:DS
	Parintins	

World Time: 0 1 2 3 4 5 **6** 7 8 9 10 11 **12** 13 14 15 16 17 **18** 19 20 21 22 23 **24**

ENGLISH ▬▬   GERMAN / DEUTSCH ◘◘◘◘   FRENCH / FRANÇAIS ▭▭   PORTUGUESE / PORTUGUÊS ▭▭   SPANISH / ESPAÑOL ▬▬

ARABIC /ﻉﺮﺑ ▭▭   RUSSIAN / РУССКИИ ▬▬   CHINESE / 中文 ◘◘◘◘   JAPANESE / 日本語 ▭▭   MULTILINGUAL ▭▭   OTHER ▬▬

SUMMER ONLY (J)   WINTER ONLY (D)   JAMMING ∧∧ or / or \   EARLIEST HEARD ◢   LATEST HEARD ◣   + TENTATIVE

Frequency (kHz)	Country / Station / Location	World Time 0 1 2 3 4 5 6 7 8 9 10 11 12 13 14 15 16 17 18 19 20 21 22 23 24	World Time

Power (kW): Network: Target

4965 (con'd)
BRAZIL
 TRIANGULO MINEIRO
  Uberaba — Irr::5kW:DS
NAMIBIA
 SW AFRICA BC CORP
  Windhoek — 100kW:DS-2/ENG, GER, ETC

4965v
BOLIVIA
 RADIO JUAN XXIII
  San Ignacio Velasco — 3kW:DS
  Irr:M-Sa:3kW:DS
  M-Sa:3kW:DS
  Su:3kW:DS
  Irr:Su:3kW:DS
  Irr:Tu-Su:3kW:DS
BRAZIL
 RADIO POTI
  Natal — 1kW:DS

4966
PERU
 RADIO SAN MIGUEL
  Cuzco — 5kW:DS-SPANISH, ETC
  Tu-Su:5kW:DS

4968
SRI LANKA
 SRI LANKA BC CORP
  Colombo-Ekala — 10kW:DS

4969.8
ANGOLA
 ER DA CABINDA
  Cabinda — Irr::1kW:DS

4970
CHINA (PR)
 CENTRAL PEOPLES BS
  Urümqi — 50kW:DS-MINORITIES
 RADIO BEIJING
  Urümqi — (D):50kW::EUSSR
 XINJIANG PBS
  Urümqi — 50kW:DS-KAZAKH
MALAYSIA
 RTM-KOTA KINABALU
  Kota Kinabalu — 10kW:DS-MALAY/ENGLISH
VENEZUELA
 RADIO RUMBOS
  Caracas — 10kW:DS
  M-Sa:10kW:DS
  Tu-Su:10kW:SA

4970v
PERU
 RADIO IMAGEN
  Tarapoto — Alt 5199vkHz:Irr::1kW:DS
  Alt 5199vkHz:1kW:DS
  Alt 5199vkHz:Su:1kW:DS
  Alt 5199vkHz:Tu-Su:1kW:DS

4971v
CAMEROON
 RADIO NATIONALE
  Yaoundé — Irr:Sa/Su:30kW:DS
  Irr:30kW:DS-FRENCH,ENG,ETC

4973
CLANDESTINE (AFRICA)
 "AV DO GALO NEGRO" — Su/M/W/F::UNITA/PORT,ETC:SAF
  Tu/Th/Sa/Su::UNITA/PORT,ETC:SAF

4975
BOLIVIA
 MARIA AUXILIADORA
  Montero — 1kW:DS
BRAZIL
 RADIO TIMBIRA
  São Luís — 2.5kW:DS
CHINA (PR)
 FUJIAN PEOPLES BS
  Jianyang — 10kW:REG DS-1/TAIWAN SV
PERU
 RADIO DEL PACIFICO
  Lima — 4kW:DS
  M-Sa:4kW:DS
  Tu-Su:4kW:DS
USSR
 RADIO DUSHANBE
  Dushanbé — 50kW::ME/SAS
 RADIO MOSCOW/RP&P
(con'd) Dushanbé — 50kW::ME/SAS

0 1 2 3 4 5 6 7 8 9 10 11 12 13 14 15 16 17 18 19 20 21 22 23 24

ENGLISH ▬▬ GERMAN / DEUTSCH ◊◊◊◊ FRENCH / FRANÇAIS ▬▬ PORTUGUESE / PORTUGUÊS ▬▬ SPANISH / ESPAÑOL ▬▬

ARABIC / ﻉﺏﺭﻍ ▬▬ RUSSIAN / РУССКИИ ▬▬ CHINESE / 中文 ◊◊◊◊ JAPANESE / 日本語 ▬▬ MULTILINGUAL ▬▬ OTHER ▬▬

SUMMER ONLY (J) WINTER ONLY (D) JAMMING /\/\ or / or \ EARLIEST HEARD ◢ LATEST HEARD ◣ + TENTATIVE

Frequency (kHz)	Country / Station / Location	World Time / Power (kW): Network: Target
4975 (con'd)	USSR — TADZHIK RADIO — Dushanbé	50kW:DS-2
4975.2	COLOMBIA — ONDAS ORTEGUAZA — Florencia	Irr::1kW:DS-TODELAR · 1kW:DS-TODELAR
4976	BRAZIL — RADIO IGUATEMI — Osasco	Irr::1kW:DS · Irr:M-Sa:1kW:DS
4976v	UGANDA — RADIO UGANDA — Kampala	Irr::20kW:DS · Irr:M-F:20kW:DS · Irr:M-Sa:20kW:DS
4977v	CLANDESTINE (AFRICA) — 'VO BROAD MASSES' — Argadom, Ethiopia	Irr:::PLF OF ERITREA:EAF
	'VO THE TIGRE REV' — Argadom, Ethiopia	Irr:Tu/Th/Su::PLF OF TIGRE:EAF
	ECUADOR — RADIO TARQUI — Quito	Irr::3kW:DS
4977.2	PERU — RADIO LA HORA — Cuzco	DS
4980	BOLIVIA — R BATALLON TOPATER — Oruro	Irr::5kW:DS · Irr:M-Sa:5kW:DS · Irr:Tu-Su:5kW:DS
	CHINA (PR) — CENTRAL PEOPLES BS — Urümqi	DS-MINORITIES
	XINJIANG PBS — Urümqi	DS-MONGOLIAN
	SWAZILAND — SWAZI COMMERCIAL R — Sandlane	M-F:100kW::SAF · M-F:100kW:PARALELO 27:SAF
	VENEZUELA — ECOS DEL TORBES — San Cristóbal	10kW:DS
4980v	PAKISTAN — AZAD KASHMIR RADIO — Islamabad	Irr::10kW:DS
4980.6	ECUADOR — ONDAS AZUAYAS — Cuenca	Irr::10kW:DS
4985	BRAZIL — R BRASIL CENTRAL — Goiânia	10kW:DS
	MALAYSIA — RADIO MALAYSIA — Kajang	10kW:DS
4990	BOLIVIA — RADIO BENI — Magdalena	Irr::0.5kW:DS · 0.5kW:DS
	CHINA (PR) — HUNAN PEOPLES BS — Changsha	10kW:DS
	NIGERIA — RADIO NIGERIA — Lagos	50kW:DS-1/ENGLISH, ETC
	SOUTH AFRICA — RADIO RSA — Meyerton	250kW::SAF/CAF
	URUGUAY — RADIO PAYSANDU — Paysandú	Irr:::DS
	USSR — ARMENIAN RADIO — Yerevan	50kW:DS-1
	RADIO YEREVAN — Yerevan	50kW::ME
	VENEZUELA — RADIO BARQUISIMETO — Barquisimeto	15kW:DS-TEMP INACTIVE

ENGLISH · GERMAN/DEUTSCH · FRENCH/FRANÇAIS · PORTUGUESE/PORTUGUÊS · SPANISH/ESPAÑOL · ARABIC · RUSSIAN/РУССКИИ · CHINESE · JAPANESE/日本語 · MULTILINGUAL · OTHER · SUMMER ONLY (J) · WINTER ONLY (D) · JAMMING · EARLIEST HEARD · LATEST HEARD · TENTATIVE

Frequency (kHz)	Country / Station / Location	World Time / Power (kW): Network: Target

World Time: 0 1 2 3 4 5 6 7 8 9 10 11 12 13 14 15 16 17 18 19 20 21 22 23 24

Frequency (kHz)	Country / Station / Location	Details
4990v	IRAN VO THE ISLAMIC REP Tehrān	DS:ME
4991	BOLIVIA RADIO ANIMAS Chocaya	1kW:DS / M-Sa:1kW:DS / Irr:Su:1kW:DS / Tu-Su:1kW:DS
	ECUADOR RADIO BAHA'I Otavalo	5kW:DS
4991v	PERU RADIO ANCASH Huáraz	3/10kW:DS
4995v	MONGOLIA RADIO ULAN BATOR	12kW:DS-1 / Tu/F:12kW::EUSSR / Sa-M/W/Th:12kW:DS-1
	USSR RADIO MOSCOW/RP&P Via Mongolia	12kW::EAS
4995.8	PERU RADIO ANDINA Huancayo	1kW:DS / Irr::1kW:DS / Tu-Su:1kW:DS
5004v	EQUATORIAL GUINEA RADIO NACIONAL Batá	Alternative Frequency to 4925.6kHz
5005	MALAYSIA RTM-SARAWAK Sibu	Sa:10kW:DS-VERNACULAR / 10kW:DS-VERNACULAR
	NEPAL RADIO NEPAL Harriharpur	100kW::SAS / 100kW:DS
5005.5	BOLIVIA RADIO CRISTAL La Paz	1kW:DS / Irr::1kW:DS
5005.7	SURINAME STICHTING R OMROEP Paramaribo	0.35kW:DS / Tu-Su:0.35kW:DS
5007v	PAKISTAN PAKISTAN BC CORP Rawalpindi	Irr::10kW:DS / Irr:F:10kW:DS
5010	CAMEROON RADIO GAROUA Garoua	100kW:DS / 100kW:DS-FRENCH, ETC / Sa/Su:100kW:DS-FRENCH, ETC
	CHINA (PR) GUANGXI PEOPLES BS Nanning	10kW:DS-2
	COLOMBIA CULT SURCOLOMBIANA Neiva	Irr::2.5kW:DS-VERY IRR
	PERU RADIO ECO Iquitos	1kW:DS / M-Sa:1kW:DS
	SINGAPORE SINGAPORE BC CORP Jurong	50kW:DS-ENGLISH
5010v	MADAGASCAR RADIO MADAGASIKARA Antananarivo	Alt 2495vkHz:100kW:DS
5015 (con'd)	BRAZIL RADIO COPACABANA São Gonçalo	1kW:DS

World Time: 0 1 2 3 4 5 6 7 8 9 10 11 12 13 14 15 16 17 18 19 20 21 22 23 24

ENGLISH ▬▬ GERMAN / DEUTSCH ◊◊◊◊ FRENCH / FRANÇAIS ▦▦ PORTUGUESE / PORTUGUÊS ▤▤ SPANISH / ESPAÑOL ▬▬

ARABIC / عربى ▦▦ RUSSIAN / РУССКИИ ══ CHINESE / 中文 ▦▦ JAPANESE / 日本語 ▦▦ MULTILINGUAL ▬▬ OTHER ▬▬

SUMMER ONLY (J) WINTER ONLY (D) JAMMING /\/\ or / or \ EARLIEST HEARD ◢ LATEST HEARD ◣ + TENTATIVE

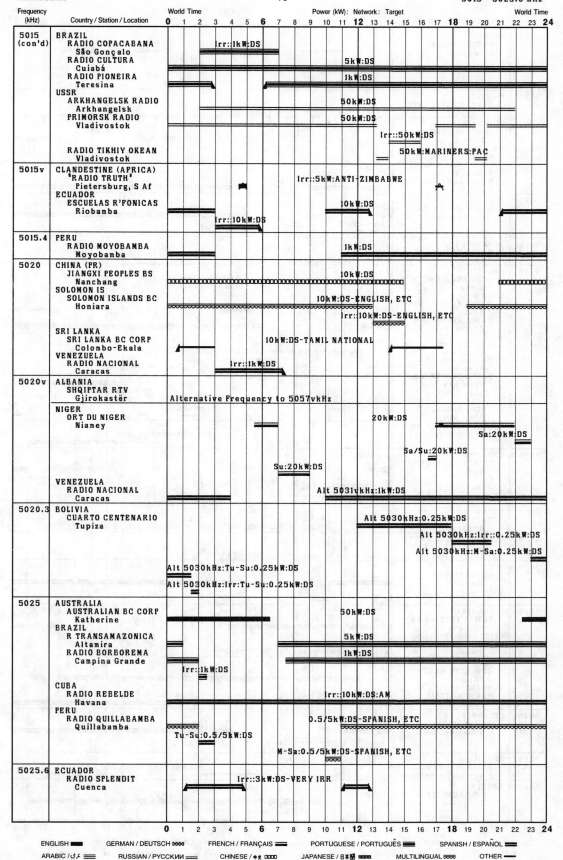

Frequency (kHz)	Country / Station / Location	World Time 0 ... 24
5015 (con'd)	**BRAZIL** RADIO COPACABANA / São Gonçalo	Irr::1kW:DS
	RADIO CULTURA / Cuiabá	5kW:DS
	RADIO PIONEIRA / Teresina	1kW:DS
	USSR ARKHANGELSK RADIO / Arkhangelsk	50kW:DS
	PRIMORSK RADIO / Vladivostok	50kW:DS / Irr::50kW:DS
	RADIO TIKHIY OKEAN / Vladivostok	50kW:MARINERS:PAC
5015v	**CLANDESTINE (AFRICA)** 'RADIO TRUTH' / Pietersburg, S Af	Irr::5kW:ANTI-ZIMBABWE
	ECUADOR ESCUELAS R'FONICAS / Riobamba	10kW:DS / Irr::10kW:DS
5015.4	**PERU** RADIO MOYOBAMBA / Moyobamba	1kW:DS
5020	**CHINA (PR)** JIANGXI PEOPLES BS / Nanchang	10kW:DS
	SOLOMON IS SOLOMON ISLANDS BC / Honiara	10kW:DS-ENGLISH, ETC / Irr::10kW:DS-ENGLISH, ETC
	SRI LANKA SRI LANKA BC CORP / Colombo-Ekala	10kW:DS-TAMIL NATIONAL
	VENEZUELA RADIO NACIONAL / Caracas	Irr::1kW:DS
5020v	**ALBANIA** SHQIPTAR RTV / Gjirokastër	Alternative Frequency to 5057vkHz
	NIGER ORT DU NIGER / Niamey	20kW:DS / Sa:20kW:DS / Sa/Su:20kW:DS / Su:20kW:DS
	VENEZUELA RADIO NACIONAL / Caracas	Alt 5031vkHz:1kW:DS
5020.3	**BOLIVIA** CUARTO CENTENARIO / Tupiza	Alt 5030kHz:0.25kW:DS / Alt 5030kHz:Irr::0.25kW:DS / Alt 5030kHz:M-Sa:0.25kW:DS / Alt 5030kHz:Tu-Su:0.25kW:DS / Alt 5030kHz:Irr:Tu-Su:0.25kW:DS
5025	**AUSTRALIA** AUSTRALIAN BC CORP / Katherine	50kW:DS
	BRAZIL R TRANSAMAZONICA / Altamira	5kW:DS
	RADIO BORBOREMA / Campina Grande	1kW:DS / Irr::1kW:DS
	CUBA RADIO REBELDE / Havana	Irr::10kW:DS:AM
	PERU RADIO QUILLABAMBA / Quillabamba	0.5/5kW:DS-SPANISH, ETC / Tu-Su:0.5/5kW:DS / M-Sa:0.5/5kW:DS-SPANISH, ETC
5025.6	**ECUADOR** RADIO SPLENDIT / Cuenca	Irr::3kW:DS-VERY IRR

World Time 0 1 2 3 4 5 6 7 8 9 10 11 12 13 14 15 16 17 18 19 20 21 22 23 24

ENGLISH ■■■   GERMAN / DEUTSCH ◊◊◊◊   FRENCH / FRANÇAIS ══   PORTUGUESE / PORTUGUÊS ▬▬   SPANISH / ESPAÑOL ▬▬

ARABIC / ٷٵ ≡   RUSSIAN / РУССКИИ ══   CHINESE / 中文 ▫▫▫▫   JAPANESE / 日本語 ▦▦▦   MULTILINGUAL ▨▨▨   OTHER ▬▬

SUMMER ONLY (J)   WINTER ONLY (D)   JAMMING /\/\ or / or \   EARLIEST HEARD ◢   LATEST HEARD ◣   + TENTATIVE

Frequency (kHz)	Country / Station / Location	World Time 0 1 2 3 4 5 **6** 7 8 9 10 11 **12** 13 14 15 16 17 **18** 19 20 21 22 23 **24**

Power (kW): Network: Target

5026v UGANDA
  RADIO UGANDA
  Kampala — 20kW:DS
  M-F:20kW:DS
  M-Sa:20kW:DS

5030 BOLIVIA
  CUARTO CENTENARIO
  Tupiza — Alternative Frequency to 5020.3kHz
  CHINA (PR)
  CENTRAL PEOPLES BS
  Xi'an — 10kW:DS-2
  MALAYSIA
  RTM-SARAWAK
  Kuching-Stapok — 10kW:DS-BIDAYUTH
  VENEZUELA
  RADIO CONTINENTE
  Caracas — Irr::15kW:DS

5030v PERU
  RADIO LOS ANDES
  Huamachuco — 1kW:DS
  Irr::1kW:DS

5031v VENEZUELA
  RADIO NACIONAL
  Caracas — Alternative Frequency to 5020vkHz

5035 AUSTRIA
  SCHULUNGSSENDER
  Vienna — 10kW:DS-ARMY TRAINING
  BRAZIL
  R EDUCACAO RURAL
  Coarí — 1kW:DS
  RADIO APARECIDA
  Aparecida — 2.5kW:DS
  USSR
  KAZAKH RADIO
  Alma-Ata — 50kW:DS-2
  RADIO ALMA-ATA
  Alma-Ata — 50kW::AS
  RADIO MOSCOW/RP&P
  Alma-Ata — 50kW::AS
  (J):50kW::AS
  RADIO TASHKENT
  Alma-Ata — 50kW::AS

5035v CENTRAL AFRICAN REP
  RTV CENTRAFRICAINE
  Bangui — 100kW:DS-FRENCH, ETC

5038.8 ECUADOR
  LA VOZ DEL UPANO
  Macas — DS
  Irr:::DS
  Su::DS
  SUDAN
  RADIO OF THE SUDAN
  Omdurman — 20kW:DS

5039v CLANDESTINE (C AMER)
  'LA VOZ DE LA UNO'
  Tegucigalpa — Alternative Frequency to 5890vkHz

5039.8 PERU
  RADIO LIBERTAD
  Junín — 1kW:DS
  Irr:1kW:DS

5040 CHINA (PR)
  FUJIAN PEOPLES BS
  Fuzhou — 10kW:DS-1/TAIWAN SVC
  GUINEA-BISSAU
  RADIO NACIONAL
  Bissau — Alternative Frequency to 5475.5kHz
  USSR
  GEORGIAN RADIO
  Tbilisi — 50kW:DS-1
  VENEZUELA
  RADIO MATURIN
  Maturín — Irr::10kW:DS

5040v COLOMBIA
  RADIO CINCO
  Villvicencio — Irr::2kW:DS
  Irr:Tu-Su:2kW:DS

5043.7 INDONESIA
  R REP INDONESIA
  Wamena, IrianJaya — Alt 4867kHz:0.5kW:DS

5043.8 ANGOLA
  ER DE BENGUELA
  Benguela — Irr::1kW:DS
  Irr:M-Sa:1kW:DS

World Time: **0** 1 2 3 4 5 **6** 7 8 9 10 11 **12** 13 14 15 16 17 **18** 19 20 21 22 23 **24**

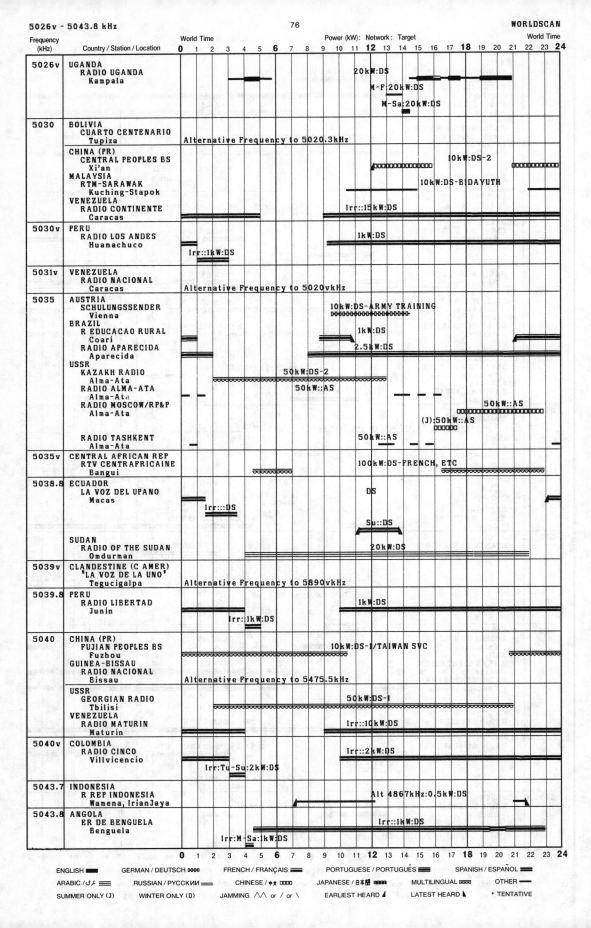

Frequency (kHz)	Country / Station / Location	Power (kW): Network: Target	World Time

5043.8 (con'd) ANGOLA — ER DE BENGUELA, Benguela — Irr:Sa:1kW:DS

5045 BRAZIL
- R CULTURA DO PARA, Belém — 10kW:DS
- RADIO DIFUSORA, Presidente Prudente — 0.5kW:DS / Tu-Su:0.5kW:DS

INDONESIA
- R REP INDONESIA, Jayapura, IrianJaya — DS

5045v PERU — RADIO MUNDO, Cuzco — Alt 5120vkHz:1kW:DS-SPANISH, ETC

5046 INDONESIA — R REP INDONESIA, Yogyakarta, Jawa — Irr::20kW:DS / 20kW:DS

5047 TOGO — RADIO LOME, Lomé-Togblekope — 100kW:DS / 100kW:DS-FRENCH, ETC

5049v PERU — RADIO RIOJA, Rioja — 1kW:DS

5049.7 CHINA (PR)
- GUANGXI RADIO, Guangzhou — 50kW::SEA
- RADIO BEIJING, Guangzhou — 50kW::SEA

5049.8 ECUADOR — R JESUS GRAN PODER, Quito — 5kW:DS

5050 INDIA — ALL INDIA RADIO, Aizawl — 10kW:DS-ENGLISH, ETC / Irr::10kW:DS-ENGLISH, ETC

TANZANIA — RADIO TANZANIA, Dar es Salaam — 10kW:DS-SWAHILI

5050v COLOMBIA — LA VOZ DE YOPAL, Yopal — 1kW:DS / Irr::1kW:DS

5050.3 PERU — RADIO CANGALLO, Cangallo — 0.5kW:DS

5052 SINGAPORE — SINGAPORE BC CORP, Jurong — 50kW:DS-1

5055 BRAZIL
- RADIO MAUA, Rio de Janeiro — 1/5kW:DS
- COSTA RICA — FARO DEL CARIBE, San José — 5kW:DS / Irr::5kW:DS

INDONESIA — R REP INDONESIA, Nabire, Irian Jaya — Alternative Frequency to 6127kHz

SWAZILAND — TRANS WORLD RADIO, Manzini — 25kW::SAF / (J)M-F:25kW::SAF

5055v ECUADOR — RADIO CATOLICA, Quito — 9kW:DS
FRENCH GUIANA — RFO-GUYANE, Cayenne — 10kW:DS / Irr::10kW:DS

5057v ALBANIA — SHQIPTAR RTV, Gjirokastër — Alt 5020vkHz:15kW:DS

5060 BURMA — BURMESE ARMY STN, Taunggyi — 0.05kW:DS
CHINA (PR) — CENTRAL PEOPLES BS, Changji — 10kW:DS-MINORITIES
(con'd)

ENGLISH ▆▆	GERMAN / DEUTSCH ▭▭▭	FRENCH / FRANÇAIS ▬▬	PORTUGUESE / PORTUGUÊS ▰▰	SPANISH / ESPAÑOL ▬▬
ARABIC / العربية ≣	RUSSIAN / РУССКИИ ▬	CHINESE / 中文 ▭▭▭	JAPANESE / 日本語 ▬▬▬	MULTILINGUAL ▭▭▭	OTHER ▬
SUMMER ONLY (J)	WINTER ONLY (D)	JAMMING ∧∧ or / or \	EARLIEST HEARD ◢	LATEST HEARD ◣	♦ TENTATIVE

Frequency (kHz)	Country / Station / Location	World Time 0-24 / Power (kW): Network: Target
5060 (con'd)	**CHINA (PR)** RADIO BEIJING Changji	Irr::10kW::EUSSR
	XINJIANG PBS Changji	10kW:DS-MONGOLIAN
5060v	**ICELAND** RIKISUTVARPID Reykjavik	Irr::10kW:USB:DS:EU
5060.3	**PERU** RADIO AMAZONAS Iquitos	1kW:DS Irr:M:1kW:DS Tu-Su:1kW:DS
5061v	**ANGOLA** ER DO HUAMBO Huambo	1kW:DS
5063v	**ECUADOR** R NAC PROGRESO Loja	5kW:DS Tu-Su:5kW:DS Irr:Tu-Su:5kW:DS
5066v	**ZAIRE** RADIO CANDIP Bunia	1kW:DS-SCOLAIRE Sa/Su:1kW:DS-SCOLAIRE Su:1kW:DS-SCOLAIRE
5068	**SAUDI ARABIA** BS OF THE KINGDOM	Irr:::DS
5070	**CHINA (PR)** FUJIAN PEOPLES BS Fuzhou	10kW:DS-1/TAIWAN SVC
5075	**CHINA (PR)** CENTRAL PEOPLES BS Urümqi	50kW:DS-2 Sa-Tu/Th:50kW:DS-2
	COLOMBIA RADIO SUTATENZA Bogotá	Irr::25kW:DS-STANDBY TX
5076v	**BOLIVIA** RADIO ICHILO Villa Busch	Irr::0.12kW:DS Irr:Sa/Su:0.12kW:DS Irr:Su-F:0.12kW:DS Irr:Tu-Su:0.12kW:DS
5084.7	**PERU** RADIO CELENDIN Celendín	DS Irr:::DS
5087.5	**CUBA** RADIO REBELDE	Irr::10kW:DS-SPORTS:CAM
5090	**CHINA (PR)** CENTRAL PEOPLES BS Xi'an	50kW:TAIWAN-2
5094v	**PAKISTAN** PAKISTAN BC CORP Islamabad	100kW:DS
5095	**COLOMBIA** RADIO SUTATENZA Bogotá	50kW:DS Irr:::50kW:DS
5103v	**PAKISTAN** PAKISTAN BC CORP Islamabad	Alternative Frequency to 3980vkHz
	RADIO PAKISTAN Islamabad	Alternative Frequency to 3980vkHz
5109	**CLANDESTINE (ASIA)** ⁺VO BURMESE PEOPLE	Tu-Su::BURMESE COMMUNIST:SEA
5120v	**PERU** RADIO MUNDO Cuzco	Alternative Frequency to 5045vkHz
	VIETNAM REGIONAL RADIO BS Nghia Binh	DS

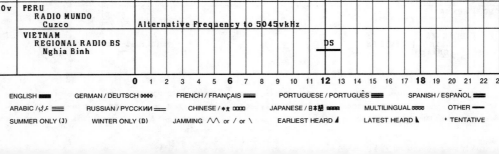

ENGLISH ▅▅▅   GERMAN / DEUTSCH ◧◧◧◧   FRENCH / FRANÇAIS ▬▬   PORTUGUESE / PORTUGUÊS ▤▤▤   SPANISH / ESPAÑOL ▰▰▰

ARABIC / ﺏﺮﻋ ≡≡   RUSSIAN / РУССКИИ ▭▭   CHINESE / 中文 ◫◫◫◫   JAPANESE / 日本語 ▦▦▦   MULTILINGUAL ◨◨◨   OTHER ▬

SUMMER ONLY (J)   WINTER ONLY (D)   JAMMING ∧∧ or / or \   EARLIEST HEARD ◢   LATEST HEARD ◣   ⁺ TENTATIVE

Frequency (kHz)	Country / Station / Location	Power (kW): Network: Target

5125 — CHINA (PR), CENTRAL PEOPLES BS, Beijing — (D):10kW:TAIWAN-1
USA, RFE-RL, Via Holzkirchen,GFR — Irr::10kW:ISL:(FEEDER):WEU / Irr::10kW:ISU:(FEEDER):WEU

5145v — CHINA (PR), RADIO BEIJING, Beijing — 120kW::EAS/EUSSR

5145.3 — PERU, LV TAWANTINSUYO, San Marcos — Irr::DS

5163 — CHINA (PR), CENTRAL PEOPLES BS, Xi'an — 50kW:DS-2

5170 — CHINA (PR), VO THE STRAIT-PLA, Fuzhou — (D):10kW:TAIWAN-2

5191v — ANGOLA, EP DO MOXICO, Luena — Irr::5kW:DS

5195 — GERMANY (FR), DEUTSCHE WELLE, Elmshorn — Irr::10kW:USB:(FEEDER):WEU

5199v — PERU, RADIO IMAGEN, Tarapoto — Alternative Frequency to 4970vkHz

5200v — CLANDESTINE (ASIA), 'VO NATIONAL ARMY', Southern Laos — KAMPUCHEAN REBELS:SEA

5220 — CHINA (PR), RADIO BEIJING, Beijing — (D):10kW::SEA / 10kW::SEA / (D):10kW

5230 — USA, AFRTS-US MILITARY, Via Barford, UK — Irr:4kW:LSB:DS-ABC/CBS/NBC/NPR(FEEDER):ATL

5240 — CHINA (PR), VO THE STRAIT-PLA, Fuzhou — 10kW:TAIWAN-1

5250 — CHINA (PR), RADIO BEIJING, Beijing — 50kW / (D):50kW
RADIO BEIJING, Urümqi — 100kW
CLANDESTINE (ASIA), 'VO DEM KAMPUCHEA', Beijing, China — 50kW:PRO-KHMER ROUGE:SEA

5257v — INDONESIA, R REP INDONESIA, Sibolga, Sumatera — 1kW:DS

5260 — USSR, KAZAKH RADIO, Alma-Ata — 50kW:DS-2

5274.4 — PERU, RADIO SAN JUAN, Chota — 1kW:DS / Irr:1kW:DS

5280 — GERMANY (FR), DEUTSCHE WELLE, Elmshorn — Irr::20kW:LSB:(FEEDER):ENA

5290 — USSR, KRASNOYARSK RADIO, Krasnoyarsk — 100kW:DS

5290v — CHAD, RADIO MOUNDOU, Moundou — 2.5kW:DS

5295 — CHINA (PR), RADIO BEIJING — (D)
RADIO BEIJING, Beijing — (D):15kW
USA, RFE-RL, Via Holzkirchen,GFR — Irr::10kW:ISL:(FEEDER):WEU / Irr::10kW:ISU:(FEEDER):WEU

5325v — PERU, RADIO ACOBAMBA, Acobamba — 1kW:DS

ENGLISH ▬　GERMAN / DEUTSCH ◊◊◊◊　FRENCH / FRANÇAIS ▬　PORTUGUESE / PORTUGUÊS ▬　SPANISH / ESPAÑOL ▬
ARABIC / ﺏﺮﻋ ▬　RUSSIAN / РУССКИИ ▬　CHINESE / 中文 ◊◊◊◊　JAPANESE / 日本語 ▬　MULTILINGUAL ▬　OTHER ▬
SUMMER ONLY (J)　WINTER ONLY (D)　JAMMING ∧∧ or / or \　EARLIEST HEARD ◢　LATEST HEARD ◣　+ TENTATIVE

Frequency (kHz)	Country / Station / Location	World Time 0 1 2 3 4 5 **6** 7 8 9 10 11 **12** 13 14 15 16 17 **18** 19 20 21 22 23 **24**
5340	PARAGUAY R 1 DE MARZO, ETC Asunción	Alternative Frequency to 5350kHz
5350	PARAGUAY R 1 DE MARZO, ETC Asunción	Alt 5340kHz:Irr::10kW:USB:DS-SPORTS(FEEDER):SA
5365.3	CLANDESTINE (C AMER) '15 DE SETIEMBRE' Honduras	Alternative Frequency to 7194.8kHz
5376.8	USA AFRTS-US MILITARY Via Barford, UK	Irr::4kW:LSB:DS-ABC/CBS/NBC/NPR(FEEDER):ATL
5405v	ANGOLA EP DE NAMIBE Moçâmedes	5kW:DS
5440	CHINA (PR) CENTRAL PEOPLES BS Urümqi XINJIANG PBS Urümqi	50kW:DS-MINORITIES 50kW:DS-KAZAKH
5450v	BOLIVIA RADIO MACHUPO San Ramón Ribera	Irr::DS
5451v	INDONESIA R REP INDONESIA Biak, Irian Jaya	Alt 5500vkHz:Irr::1kW:DS
5475.5	GUINEA-BISSAU RADIO NACIONAL Bissau	Alt 5040kHz:Irr::10kW:DS
5500v	INDONESIA R REP INDONESIA Biak, Irian Jaya	Alternative Frequency to 5451vkHz
5505	BOLIVIA RADIO 2 DE FEBRERO Rurrenabaque	0.5kW:DS Tu-Su:0.5kW:DS
5505v	BOLIVIA RADIO 2 DE FEBRERO Rurrenabaque	M-Sa:0.5kW:DS
5508	CHINA (PR) VO THE STRAIT-PLA Fuzhou	SPR:DS-2/6X918KHZ
5581v	BOLIVIA RADIO SAN JOSE San José Chiquitos	0.5kW:DS
5609v	VIETNAM REGIONAL RADIO BS Hoang Lien Son	DS
5617.5	PERU RADIO ILUCAN Cutervo	Irr::0.2kW:DS 0.2kW:DS
5660v	LAOS LAO NATIONAL RADIO Xieng Khouang	1kW:DS Irr::1kW:DS
5720v	PERU RADIO SAN MIGUEL S Miguel Pallaques	Irr::DS

World Time: 0 1 2 3 4 5 **6** 7 8 9 10 11 **12** 13 14 15 16 17 **18** 19 20 21 22 23 **24**

ENGLISH ▄▄▄   GERMAN / DEUTSCH ▭▭▭▭   FRENCH / FRANÇAIS ▬▬   PORTUGUESE / PORTUGUÊS ▬▬▬   SPANISH / ESPAÑOL ▬▬▬

ARABIC / ﺏﺮﻋ ≡≡   RUSSIAN / РУССКИЙ ▬▬   CHINESE / 中文 ▭▭▭▭   JAPANESE / 日本語 ▦▦▦   MULTILINGUAL ▧▧▧   OTHER ▬▬

SUMMER ONLY (J)   WINTER ONLY (D)   JAMMING ⋀⋀ or / or \   EARLIEST HEARD ◢   LATEST HEARD ◣   + TENTATIVE

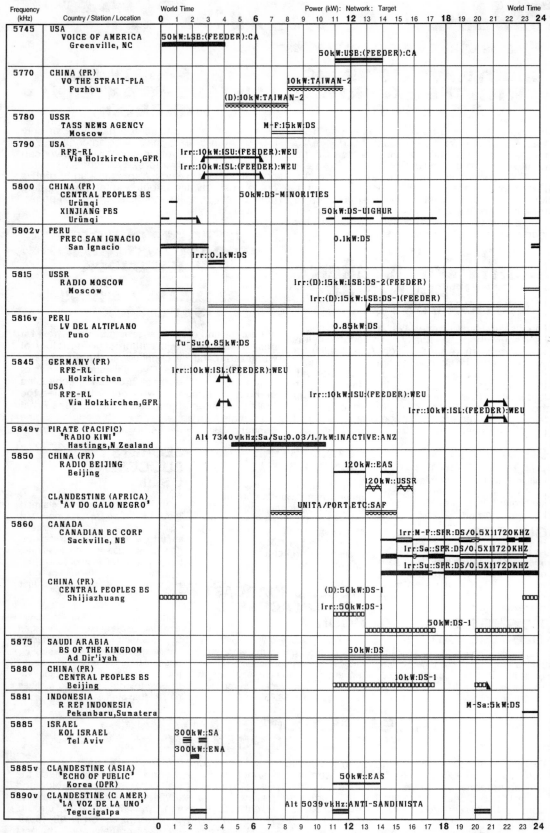

Frequency (kHz)	Country / Station / Location	Power (kW): Network: Target
5745	USA — VOICE OF AMERICA — Greenville, NC	50kW:LSB:(FEEDER):CA / 50kW:USB:(FEEDER):CA
5770	CHINA (PR) — VO THE STRAIT-PLA — Fuzhou	10kW:TAIWAN-2 / (D):10kW:TAIWAN-2
5780	USSR — TASS NEWS AGENCY — Moscow	M-F:15kW:DS
5790	USA — RFE-RL — Via Holzkirchen,GFR	Irr::10kW:ISU:(FEEDER):WEU / Irr::10kW:ISL:(FEEDER):WEU
5800	CHINA (PR) — CENTRAL PEOPLES BS — Urümqi / XINJIANG PBS — Urümqi	50kW:DS-MINORITIES / 50kW:DS-UIGHUR
5802v	PERU — FREC SAN IGNACIO — San Ignacio	0.1kW:DS / Irr::0.1kW:DS
5815	USSR — RADIO MOSCOW — Moscow	Irr:(D):15kW:LSB:DS-2(FEEDER) / Irr:(D):15kW:LSB:DS-1(FEEDER)
5816v	PERU — LV DEL ALTIPLANO — Puno	0.85kW:DS / Tu-Su:0.85kW:DS
5845	GERMANY (PR) — RFE-RL — Holzkirchen / USA — RFE-RL — Via Holzkirchen,GFR	Irr::10kW:ISL:(FEEDER):WEU / Irr::10kW:ISU:(FEEDER):WEU / Irr::10kW:ISL:(FEEDER):WEU
5849v	PIRATE (PACIFIC) — "RADIO KIWI" — Hastings,N Zealand	Alt 7340vkHz:Sa/Su:0.03/1.7kW:INACTIVE:ANZ
5850	CHINA (PR) — RADIO BEIJING — Beijing / CLANDESTINE (AFRICA) — "AV DO GALO NEGRO"	120kW::EAS / 120kW::USSR / UNITA/PORT.ETC:SAF
5860	CANADA — CANADIAN BC CORP — Sackville, NB / CHINA (PR) — CENTRAL PEOPLES BS — Shijiazhuang	Irr:M-F::SFR:DS/0.5X1720KHZ / Irr:Sa::SFR:DS/0.5X1720KHZ / Irr:Su::SFR:DS/0.5X1720KHZ / (D):50kW:DS-1 / Irr::50kW:DS-1 / 50kW:DS-1
5875	SAUDI ARABIA — BS OF THE KINGDOM — Ad Dir'iyah	50kW:DS
5880	CHINA (PR) — CENTRAL PEOPLES BS — Beijing	10kW:DS-1
5881	INDONESIA — R REP INDONESIA — Pekanbaru,Sumatera	M-Sa:5kW:DS
5885	ISRAEL — KOL ISRAEL — Tel Aviv	300kW::SA / 300kW::ENA
5885v	CLANDESTINE (ASIA) — "ECHO OF PUBLIC" — Korea (DPR)	50kW::EAS
5890v	CLANDESTINE (C AMER) — "LA VOZ DE LA UNO" — Tegucigalpa	Alt 5039vkHz:ANTI-SANDINISTA

World Time: 0 1 2 3 4 5 6 7 8 9 10 11 12 13 14 15 16 17 18 19 20 21 22 23 24

ENGLISH ▄▄▄   GERMAN / DEUTSCH ००००   FRENCH / FRANÇAIS ▬▬   PORTUGUESE / PORTUGUÊS ▬▬   SPANISH / ESPAÑOL ▬▬

ARABIC / ﻋﺮﺑﻲ ≡   RUSSIAN / PУССКИИ ▬   CHINESE / 中文 ००००   JAPANESE / 日本語 ▬▬   MULTILINGUAL ६६६६   OTHER ▬

SUMMER ONLY (J)   WINTER ONLY (D)   JAMMING ∧∧ or / or \   EARLIEST HEARD ◢   LATEST HEARD ◣   + TENTATIVE

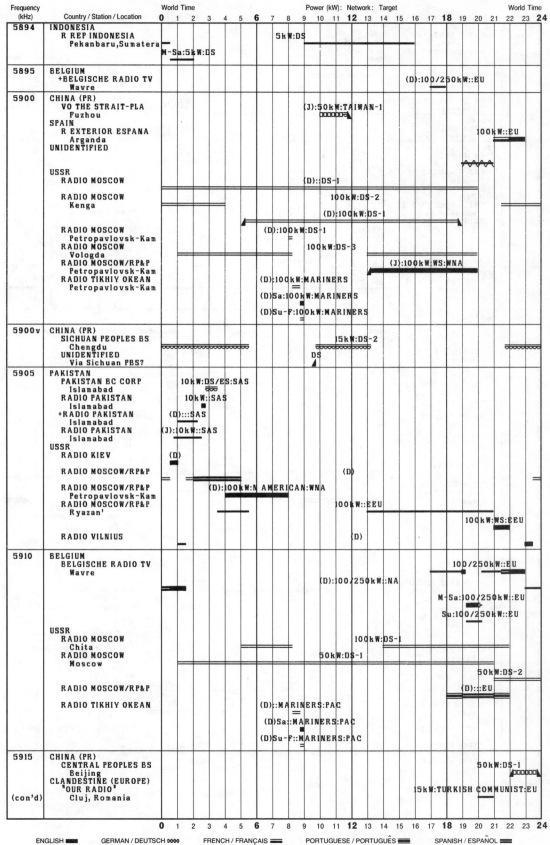

Frequency (kHz)	Country / Station / Location	Power (kW): Network: Target
5894	INDONESIA R REP INDONESIA Pekanbaru,Sumatera	5kW:DS M-Sa:5kW:DS
5895	BELGIUM +BELGISCHE RADIO TV Wavre	(D):100/250kW::EU
5900	CHINA (PR) VO THE STRAIT-PLA Fuzhou	(J):50kW:TAIWAN-1
	SPAIN R EXTERIOR ESPANA Arganda	100kW::EU
	UNIDENTIFIED	
	USSR RADIO MOSCOW	(D)::DS-1
	RADIO MOSCOW Kenga	100kW:DS-2 (D):100kW:DS-1
	RADIO MOSCOW Petropavlovsk-Kam	(D):100kW:DS-1
	RADIO MOSCOW Vologda	100kW:DS-3
	RADIO MOSCOW/RP&P Petropavlovsk-Kam	(J):100kW:WS:WNA
	RADIO TIKHIY OKEAN Petropavlovsk-Kam	(D):100kW:MARINERS (D)Sa:100kW:MARINERS (D)Su-F:100kW:MARINERS
5900v	CHINA (PR) SICHUAN PEOPLES BS Chengdu	15kW:DS-2
	UNIDENTIFIED Via Sichuan PBS?	DS
5905	PAKISTAN PAKISTAN BC CORP Islamabad	10kW:DS/ES:SAS
	RADIO PAKISTAN Islamabad	10kW::SAS
	+RADIO PAKISTAN Islamabad	(D):::SAS
	RADIO PAKISTAN Islamabad	(J):10kW::SAS
	USSR RADIO KIEV	(D)
	RADIO MOSCOW/RP&P	(D)
	RADIO MOSCOW/RP&P Petropavlovsk-Kam	(D):100kW:N AMERICAN:WNA
	RADIO MOSCOW/RP&P Ryazan'	100kW::EEU 100kW:WS:EEU
	RADIO VILNIUS	(D)
5910	BELGIUM BELGISCHE RADIO TV Wavre	100/250kW::EU (D):100/250kW::NA M-Sa:100/250kW::EU Su:100/250kW::EU
	USSR RADIO MOSCOW Chita	100kW:DS-1
	RADIO MOSCOW Moscow	50kW:DS-1 50kW:DS-2
	RADIO MOSCOW/RP&P	(D):::EU
	RADIO TIKHIY OKEAN	(D)::MARINERS:PAC (D)Sa::MARINERS:PAC (D)Su-F::MARINERS:PAC
5915	CHINA (PR) CENTRAL PEOPLES BS Beijing	50kW:DS-1
	CLANDESTINE (EUROPE) 'OUR RADIO'	15kW:TURKISH COMMUNIST:EU
(con'd)	Cluj, Romania	

ENGLISH ▬▬ GERMAN / DEUTSCH ∞∞∞ FRENCH / FRANÇAIS ═══ PORTUGUESE / PORTUGUÊS ▤▤▤ SPANISH / ESPAÑOL ▬▬

ARABIC / العربية ≡≡ RUSSIAN / РУССКИИ ═══ CHINESE / 中文 ▭▭▭ JAPANESE / 日本語 ▬▬ MULTILINGUAL ∞∞∞ OTHER ▬▬

SUMMER ONLY (J) WINTER ONLY (D) JAMMING /\/\ or / or \ EARLIEST HEARD ◢ LATEST HEARD ◣ + TENTATIVE

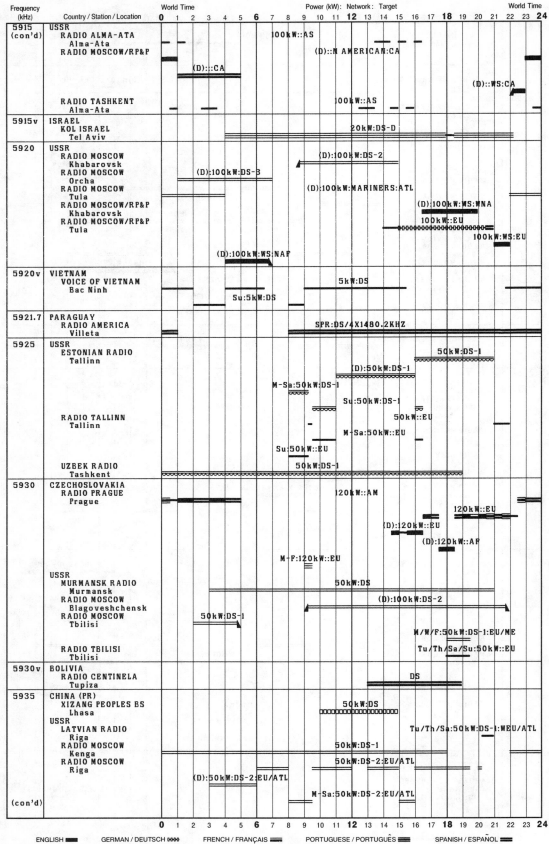

Frequency (kHz)	Country / Station / Location	Schedule
5915 (con'd)	USSR	
	RADIO ALMA-ATA — Alma-Ata	100kW::AS
	RADIO MOSCOW/RP&P	(D)::N AMERICAN:CA
		(D):::CA
		(D)::WS:CA
	RADIO TASHKENT — Alma-Ata	100kW::AS
5915v	ISRAEL	
	KOL ISRAEL — Tel Aviv	20kW:DS-D
5920	USSR	
	RADIO MOSCOW — Khabarovsk	(D):100kW:DS-2
	RADIO MOSCOW — Orcha	(D):100kW:DS-3
	RADIO MOSCOW — Tula	(D):100kW:MARINERS:ATL
	RADIO MOSCOW/RP&P — Khabarovsk	(D):100kW:WS:WNA
	RADIO MOSCOW/RP&P — Tula	100kW::EU / 100kW:WS:EU
		(D):100kW:WS:NAF
5920v	VIETNAM	
	VOICE OF VIETNAM — Bac Ninh	5kW:DS / Su:5kW:DS
5921.7	PARAGUAY	
	RADIO AMERICA — Villeta	SPR:DS/4X1480.2KHZ
5925	USSR	
	ESTONIAN RADIO — Tallinn	50kW:DS-1 / (D):50kW:DS-1 / M-Sa:50kW:DS-1 / Su:50kW:DS-1
	RADIO TALLINN — Tallinn	50kW::EU / M-Sa:50kW::EU / Su:50kW::EU
	UZBEK RADIO — Tashkent	50kW:DS-1
5930	CZECHOSLOVAKIA	
	RADIO PRAGUE — Prague	120kW::AM / 120kW::EU / (D):120kW::EU / (D):120kW::AF / M-F:120kW::EU
	USSR	
	MURMANSK RADIO — Murmansk	50kW:DS
	RADIO MOSCOW — Blagoveshchensk	(D):100kW:DS-2
	RADIO MOSCOW — Tbilisi	50kW:DS-1
	RADIO TBILISI — Tbilisi	M/W/F:50kW:DS-1:EU/ME / Tu/Th/Sa/Su:50kW::EU
5930v	BOLIVIA	
	RADIO CENTINELA — Tupiza	DS
5935	CHINA (PR)	
	XIZANG PEOPLES BS — Lhasa	50kW:DS
	USSR	
	LATVIAN RADIO — Riga	Tu/Th/Sa:50kW:DS-1:WEU/ATL
	RADIO MOSCOW — Kenga	50kW:DS-1
	RADIO MOSCOW — Riga	50kW:DS-2:EU/ATL / (D):50kW:DS-2:EU/ATL / M-Sa:50kW:DS-2:EU/ATL
(con'd)		

ENGLISH ■■■ GERMAN / DEUTSCH ◊◊◊◊ FRENCH / FRANÇAIS ≡≡≡ PORTUGUESE / PORTUGUÊS ≡≡≡ SPANISH / ESPAÑOL ≡≡≡

ARABIC / ﻉﺭﺏ ≡≡ RUSSIAN / РУССКИИ ═══ CHINESE / 中文 ▯▯▯▯ JAPANESE / 日本語 ■■■ MULTILINGUAL ▭▭▭▭ OTHER ───

SUMMER ONLY (J) WINTER ONLY (D) JAMMING ∧∧ or / or \ EARLIEST HEARD ◢ LATEST HEARD ◣ + TENTATIVE

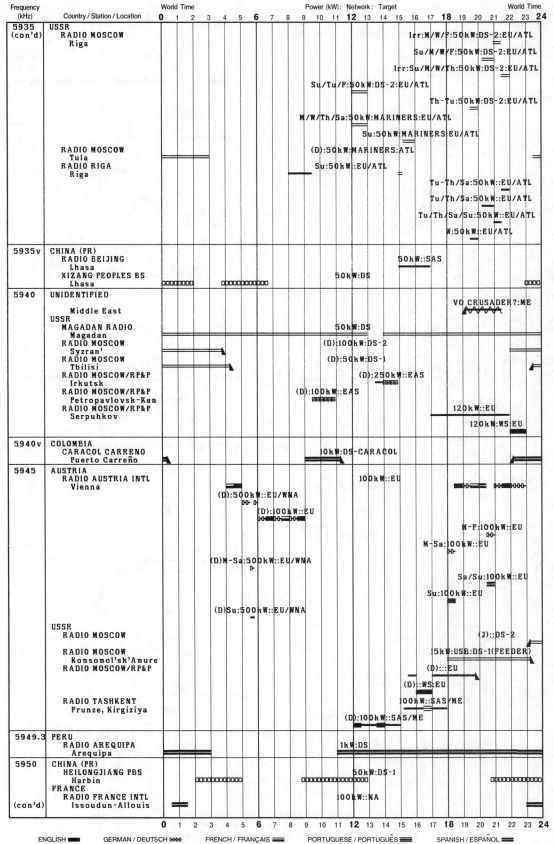

Frequency (kHz)	Country / Station / Location	Power (kW): Network: Target
5935 (con'd)	USSR RADIO MOSCOW Riga	Irr:M/W/F:50kW:DS-2:EU/ATL
		Su/M/W/F:50kW:DS-2:EU/ATL
		Irr:Su/M/W/Th:50kW:DS-2:EU/ATL
		Su/Tu/F:50kW:DS-2:EU/ATL
		Th-Tu:50kW:DS-2:EU/ATL
		M/W/Th/Sa:50kW:MARINERS:EU/ATL
		Su:50kW:MARINERS:EU/ATL
	RADIO MOSCOW Tula	(D):50kW:MARINERS:ATL
	RADIO RIGA Riga	Su:50kW::EU/ATL
		Tu-Th/Sa:50kW::EU/ATL
		Tu/Th/Sa:50kW::EU/ATL
		Tu/Th/Sa/Su:50kW::EU/ATL
		W:50kW::EU/ATL
5935v	CHINA (PR) RADIO BEIJING Lhasa	50kW::SAS
	XIZANG PEOPLES BS Lhasa	50kW:DS
5940	UNIDENTIFIED Middle East	VO CRUSADER?:ME
	USSR MAGADAN RADIO Magadan	50kW:DS
	RADIO MOSCOW Syzran'	(D):100kW:DS-2
	RADIO MOSCOW Tbilisi	(D):50kW:DS-1
	RADIO MOSCOW/RP&P Irkutsk	(D):250kW::EAS
	RADIO MOSCOW/RP&P Petropavlovsk-Kam	(D):100kW::EAS
	RADIO MOSCOW/RP&P Serpuhkov	120kW::EU
		120kW:WS:EU
5940v	COLOMBIA CARACOL CARRENO Puerto Carreño	10kW:DS-CARACOL
5945	AUSTRIA RADIO AUSTRIA INTL Vienna	100kW::EU
		(D):500kW::EU/WNA
		(D):100kW::EU
		M-F:100kW::EU
		M-Sa:100kW::EU
		(D)M-Sa:500kW::EU/WNA
		Sa/Su:100kW::EU
		Su:100kW::EU
		(D)Su:500kW::EU/WNA
	USSR RADIO MOSCOW	(J)::DS-2
	RADIO MOSCOW Komsomol'sk'Amure	15kW:USB:DS-1(FEEDER)
	RADIO MOSCOW/RP&P	(D):::EU
		(D)::WS:EU
	RADIO TASHKENT Frunze, Kirgiziya	100kW::SAS/ME
		(D):100kW::SAS/ME
5949.3	PERU RADIO AREQUIPA Arequipa	1kW:DS
5950	CHINA (PR) HEILONGJIANG PBS Harbin	50kW:DS-1
	FRANCE RADIO FRANCE INTL Issoudun-Allouis	100kW::NA
(con'd)		

0 1 2 3 4 5 6 7 8 9 10 11 12 13 14 15 16 17 18 19 20 21 22 23 24

ENGLISH ▬▬ GERMAN / DEUTSCH ◊◊◊◊ FRENCH / FRANÇAIS ═══ PORTUGUESE / PORTUGUÊS ▤▤ SPANISH / ESPAÑOL ▬▬

ARABIC / ﻉﺭﻑ ≡≡≡ RUSSIAN / РУССКИИ ══ CHINESE / 中文 ▫▫▫▫ JAPANESE / 日本語 ▦▦▦ MULTILINGUAL ▨▨▨ OTHER ▬

SUMMER ONLY (J) WINTER ONLY (D) JAMMING ∧∧ or / or \ EARLIEST HEARD ◢ LATEST HEARD ◣ + TENTATIVE

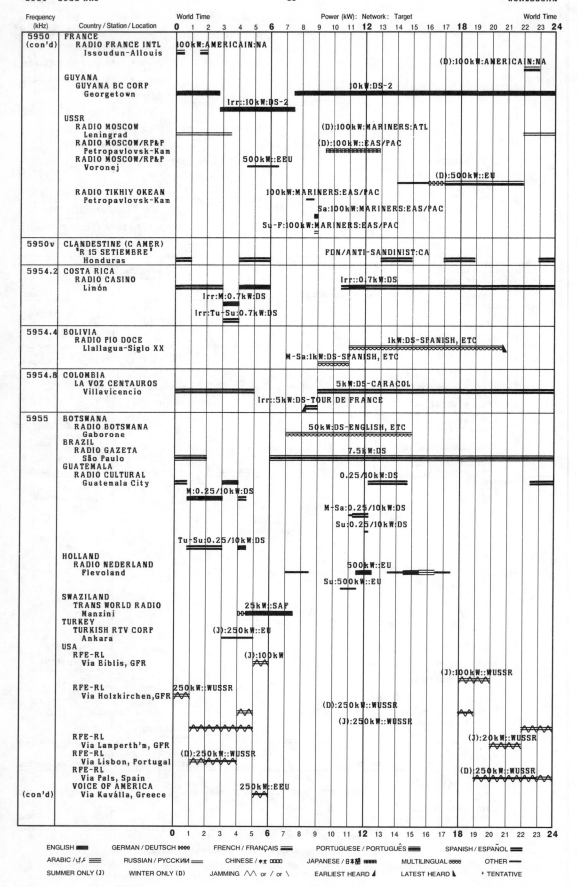

Frequency (kHz)	Country / Station / Location	Power (kW): Network: Target
5950 (con'd)	**FRANCE** RADIO FRANCE INTL — Issoudun-Allouis	100kW:AMERICAIN:NA (D):100kW:AMERICAIN:NA
	GUYANA GUYANA BC CORP — Georgetown	10kW:DS-2 Irr::10kW:DS-2
	USSR RADIO MOSCOW — Leningrad	(D):100kW:MARINERS:ATL
	RADIO MOSCOW/RP&P — Petropavlovsk-Kam	(D):100kW::EAS/PAC
	RADIO MOSCOW/RP&P — Voronej	500kW::EEU (D):500kW::EU
	RADIO TIKHIY OKEAN — Petropavlovsk-Kam	100kW:MARINERS:EAS/PAC Sa:100kW:MARINERS:EAS/PAC Su-F:100kW:MARINERS:EAS/PAC
5950v	**CLANDESTINE (C AMER)** 'R 15 SETIEMBRE' — Honduras	FDN/ANTI-SANDINIST:CA
5954.2	**COSTA RICA** RADIO CASINO — Limón	Irr::0.7kW:DS Irr:M:0.7kW:DS Irr:Tu-Su:0.7kW:DS
5954.4	**BOLIVIA** RADIO PIO DOCE — Llallagua-Siglo XX	1kW:DS-SPANISH, ETC M-Sa:1kW:DS-SPANISH, ETC
5954.8	**COLOMBIA** LA VOZ CENTAUROS — Villavicencio	5kW:DS-CARACOL Irr::5kW:DS-TOUR DE FRANCE
5955	**BOTSWANA** RADIO BOTSWANA — Gaborone	50kW:DS-ENGLISH, ETC
	BRAZIL RADIO GAZETA — São Paulo	7.5kW:DS
	GUATEMALA RADIO CULTURAL — Guatemala City	0.25/10kW:DS M:0.25/10kW:DS M-Sa:0.25/10kW:DS Su:0.25/10kW:DS Tu-Su:0.25/10kW:DS
	HOLLAND RADIO NEDERLAND — Flevoland	500kW::EU Su:500kW::EU
	SWAZILAND TRANS WORLD RADIO — Manzini	25kW::SAF
	TURKEY TURKISH RTV CORP — Ankara	(J):250kW::EU
	USA RFE-RL — Via Biblis, GFR	(J):100kW
	RFE-RL — Via Holzkirchen,GFR	250kW::WUSSR (J):100kW::WUSSR (D):250kW::WUSSR (J):250kW::WUSSR
	RFE-RL — Via Lamperth'm, GFR	(J):20kW::WUSSR
	RFE-RL — Via Lisbon, Portugal	(D):250kW::WUSSR
	RFE-RL — Via Pals, Spain	(D):250kW::WUSSR
(con'd)	VOICE OF AMERICA — Via Kaválla, Greece	250kW::EEU

ENGLISH ▬▬ GERMAN / DEUTSCH ◊◊◊◊ FRENCH / FRANÇAIS ▬▬ PORTUGUESE / PORTUGUÊS ▬▬ SPANISH / ESPAÑOL ▬▬

ARABIC / عربي ▬▬ RUSSIAN / РУССКИЙ ▬▬ CHINESE / 中文 ◊◊◊◊ JAPANESE / 日本語 ▬▬ MULTILINGUAL ▬▬ OTHER ▬

SUMMER ONLY (J) WINTER ONLY (D) JAMMING /\/\ or / or \ EARLIEST HEARD ◢ LATEST HEARD ◣ + TENTATIVE

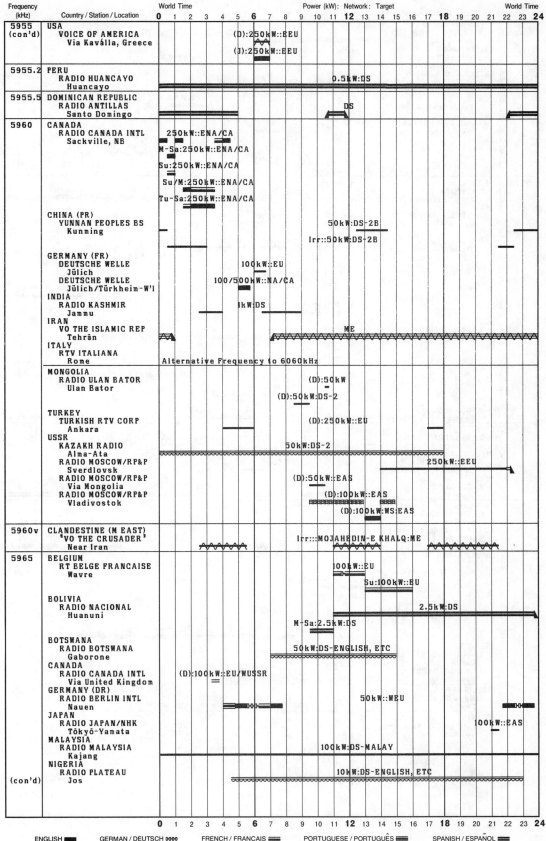

Frequency (kHz)	Country / Station / Location	Power (kW): Network: Target

5955 (con'd) USA — VOICE OF AMERICA, Via Kaválla, Greece — (D):250kW::EEU / (J):250kW::EEU

5955.2 PERU — RADIO HUANCAYO, Huancayo — 0.5kW:DS

5955.5 DOMINICAN REPUBLIC — RADIO ANTILLAS, Santo Domingo — DS

5960 CANADA — RADIO CANADA INTL, Sackville, NB — 250kW::ENA/CA; M-Sa:250kW::ENA/CA; Su:250kW::ENA/CA; Su/M:250kW::ENA/CA; Tu-Sa:250kW::ENA/CA

CHINA (PR) — YUNNAN PEOPLES BS, Kunming — 50kW:DS-2B; Irr::50kW:DS-2B

GERMANY (FR) — DEUTSCHE WELLE, Jülich — 100kW::EU; DEUTSCHE WELLE, Jülich/Türkheim-W'l — 100/500kW::NA/CA

INDIA — RADIO KASHMIR, Jammu — 1kW:DS

IRAN — VO THE ISLAMIC REP, Tehrān — ME

ITALY — RTV ITALIANA, Rome — Alternative Frequency to 6060kHz

MONGOLIA — RADIO ULAN BATOR, Ulan Bator — (D):50kW; (D):50kW:DS-2

TURKEY — TURKISH RTV CORP, Ankara — (D):250kW::EU

USSR — KAZAKH RADIO, Alma-Ata — 50kW:DS-2; RADIO MOSCOW/RP&P, Sverdlovsk — 250kW::EEU; RADIO MOSCOW/RP&P, Via Mongolia — (D):50kW::EAS; RADIO MOSCOW/RP&P, Vladivostok — (D):100kW::EAS; (D):100kW:WS:EAS

5960v CLANDESTINE (M EAST) — "VO THE CRUSADER", Near Iran — Irr:::MOJAHEDIN-E KHALQ:ME

5965 BELGIUM — RT BELGE FRANCAISE, Wavre — 100kW::EU; Su:100kW::EU

BOLIVIA — RADIO NACIONAL, Huanuni — 2.5kW:DS; M-Sa:2.5kW:DS

BOTSWANA — RADIO BOTSWANA, Gaborone — 50kW:DS-ENGLISH, ETC

CANADA — RADIO CANADA INTL, Via United Kingdom — (D):100kW::EU/WUSSR

GERMANY (DR) — RADIO BERLIN INTL, Nauen — 50kW::WEU

JAPAN — RADIO JAPAN/NHK, Tōkyō-Yamata — 100kW::EAS

MALAYSIA — RADIO MALAYSIA, Kajang — 100kW:DS-MALAY

NIGERIA — RADIO PLATEAU, Jos **(con'd)** — 10kW:DS-ENGLISH, ETC

ENGLISH ▬ GERMAN/DEUTSCH ◌◌◌◌ FRENCH/FRANÇAIS ═ PORTUGUESE/PORTUGUÊS ▬ SPANISH/ESPAÑOL ▬
ARABIC/ﺏﺮﻋ ═ RUSSIAN/РУССКИИ ═ CHINESE/中文 ◌◌◌◌ JAPANESE/日本語 ▬ MULTILINGUAL ▭▭ OTHER ▬
SUMMER ONLY (J) WINTER ONLY (D) JAMMING /\/\ or / or \ EARLIEST HEARD ◢ LATEST HEARD ◣ + TENTATIVE

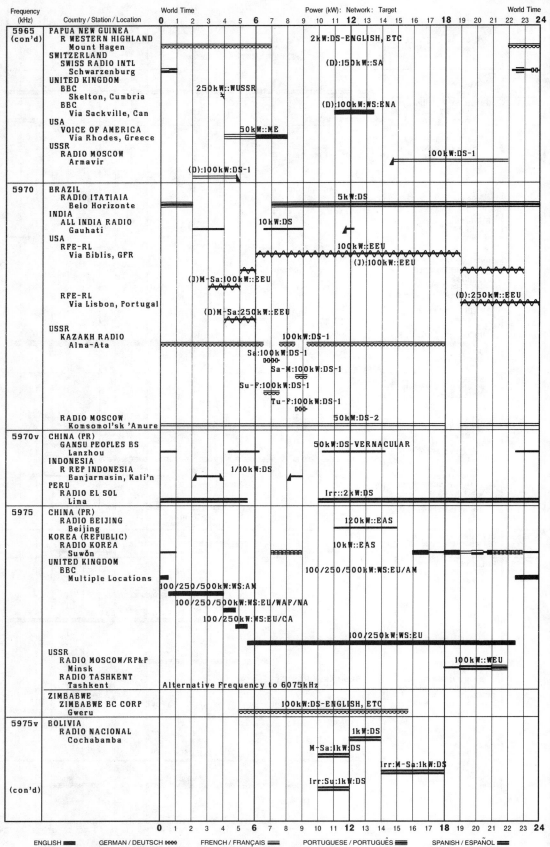

Frequency (kHz)	Country / Station / Location	Power (kW): Network: Target
5965 (con'd)	PAPUA NEW GUINEA	
	R WESTERN HIGHLAND, Mount Hagen	2kW:DS-ENGLISH, ETC
	SWITZERLAND	
	SWISS RADIO INTL, Schwarzenburg	(D):150kW::SA
	UNITED KINGDOM	
	BBC, Skelton, Cumbria	250kW::WUSSR
	BBC, Via Sackville, Can	(D):100kW:WS:ENA
	USA	
	VOICE OF AMERICA, Via Rhodes, Greece	50kW::ME
	USSR	
	RADIO MOSCOW, Armavir	100kW:DS-1
		(D):100kW:DS-1
5970	BRAZIL	
	RADIO ITATIAIA, Belo Horizonte	5kW:DS
	INDIA	
	ALL INDIA RADIO, Gauhati	10kW:DS
	USA	
	RFE-RL, Via Biblis, GFR	100kW::EEU
		(J):100kW::EEU
		(J)M-Sa:100kW::EEU
	RFE-RL, Via Lisbon, Portugal	(D):250kW::EEU
		(D)M-Sa:250kW::EEU
	USSR	
	KAZAKH RADIO, Alma-Ata	100kW:DS-1
		Sa:100kW:DS-1
		Sa-M:100kW:DS-1
		Su-F:100kW:DS-1
		Tu-F:100kW:DS-1
	RADIO MOSCOW, Komsomol'sk 'Amure	50kW:DS-2
5970v	CHINA (PR)	
	GANSU PEOPLES BS, Lanzhou	50kW:DS-VERNACULAR
	INDONESIA	
	R REP INDONESIA, Banjarmasin, Kali'n	1/10kW:DS
	PERU	
	RADIO EL SOL, Lima	Irr::2kW:DS
5975	CHINA (PR)	
	RADIO BEIJING, Beijing	120kW::EAS
	KOREA (REPUBLIC)	
	RADIO KOREA, Suwŏn	10kW::EAS
	UNITED KINGDOM	
	BBC, Multiple Locations	100/250/500kW:WS:EU/AM
		100/250/500kW:WS:AM
		100/250/500kW:WS:EU/WAF/NA
		100/250kW:WS:EU/CA
		100/250kW:WS:EU
	USSR	
	RADIO MOSCOW/RP&P, Minsk	100kW::WEU
	RADIO TASHKENT, Tashkent	Alternative Frequency to 6075kHz
	ZIMBABWE	
	ZIMBABWE BC CORP, Gweru	100kW:DS-ENGLISH, ETC
5975v	BOLIVIA	
	RADIO NACIONAL, Cochabamba	1kW:DS
		M-Sa:1kW:DS
		Irr:M-Sa:1kW:DS
		Irr:Su:1kW:DS
(con'd)		

World Time 0 1 2 3 4 5 6 7 8 9 10 11 12 13 14 15 16 17 18 19 20 21 22 23 24

ENGLISH · GERMAN / DEUTSCH · FRENCH / FRANÇAIS · PORTUGUESE / PORTUGUÊS · SPANISH / ESPAÑOL
ARABIC / عربي · RUSSIAN / РУССКИЙ · CHINESE / 中文 · JAPANESE / 日本語 · MULTILINGUAL · OTHER
SUMMER ONLY (J) · WINTER ONLY (D) · JAMMING /\/\ or / or \ · EARLIEST HEARD · LATEST HEARD · + TENTATIVE

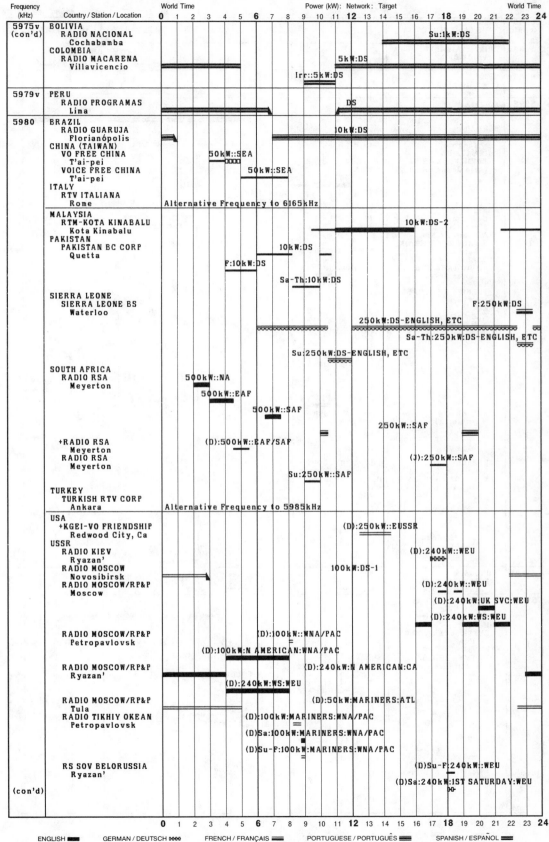

Frequency (kHz)	Country / Station / Location	World Time / Power (kW): Network: Target

5975v (con'd)	BOLIVIA
	  RADIO NACIONAL
	    Cochabamba
		Su:1kW:DS

	COLOMBIA
	  RADIO MACARENA
	    Villavicencio
		5kW:DS
		Irr::5kW:DS

5979v	PERU
	  RADIO PROGRAMAS
	    Lima
		DS

5980	BRAZIL
	  RADIO GUARUJA
	    Florianópolis
		10kW:DS

	CHINA (TAIWAN)
	  VO FREE CHINA
	    T'ai-pei
		50kW::SEA

	VOICE FREE CHINA T'ai-pei	50kW::SEA

	ITALY
	  RTV ITALIANA
	    Rome
		Alternative Frequency to 6165kHz

	MALAYSIA
	  RTM-KOTA KINABALU
	    Kota Kinabalu
		10kW:DS-2

	PAKISTAN
	  PAKISTAN BC CORP
	    Quetta
		10kW:DS
		F:10kW:DS
		Sa-Th:10kW:DS

	SIERRA LEONE
	  SIERRA LEONE BS
	    Waterloo
		F:250kW:DS
		250kW:DS-ENGLISH, ETC
		Sa-Th:250kW:DS-ENGLISH, ETC
		Su:250kW:DS-ENGLISH, ETC

	SOUTH AFRICA
	  RADIO RSA
	    Meyerton
		500kW::NA
		500kW::EAF
		500kW::SAF
		250kW::SAF

	+RADIO RSA Meyerton	(D):500kW::EAF/SAF
	RADIO RSA Meyerton	(J):250kW::SAF Su:250kW::SAF

	TURKEY
	  TURKISH RTV CORP
	    Ankara
		Alternative Frequency to 5985kHz

	USA
	  +KGEI-VO FRIENDSHIP
	    Redwood City, Ca
		(D):250kW::EUSSR

	USSR
	  RADIO KIEV
	    Ryazan'
		(D):240kW::WEU

	RADIO MOSCOW Novosibirsk	100kW:DS-1
	RADIO MOSCOW/RP&P Moscow	(D):240kW::WEU (D):240kW:UK SVC:WEU (D):240kW:WS:WEU
	RADIO MOSCOW/RP&P Petropavlovsk	(D):100kW::WNA/PAC (D):100kW:N AMERICAN:WNA/PAC
	RADIO MOSCOW/RP&P Ryazan'	(D):240kW:N AMERICAN:CA (D):240kW:WS:WEU
	RADIO MOSCOW/RP&P Tula	(D):50kW:MARINERS:ATL
	RADIO TIKHIY OKEAN Petropavlovsk	(D):100kW:MARINERS:WNA/PAC (D)Sa:100kW:MARINERS:WNA/PAC (D)Su-F:100kW:MARINERS:WNA/PAC
	RS SOV BELORUSSIA Ryazan'	(D)Su-F:240kW::WEU (D)Sa:240kW:1ST SATURDAY:WEU
(con'd)		

World Time: 0 1 2 3 4 5 6 7 8 9 10 11 12 13 14 15 16 17 18 19 20 21 22 23 24

ENGLISH ▰▰▰   GERMAN / DEUTSCH ⼝⼝⼝⼝   FRENCH / FRANÇAIS ══   PORTUGUESE / PORTUGUÊS ▰▰▰   SPANISH / ESPAÑOL ▰▰▰

ARABIC / ﺏﺭﻉ ══   RUSSIAN / РУССКИИ ══   CHINESE / ✦✦ ⼝⼝⼝⼝   JAPANESE / 日本語 ▰▰▰   MULTILINGUAL ⤫⤫⤫   OTHER ━━

SUMMER ONLY (J)   WINTER ONLY (D)   JAMMING ∧∧ or / or \   EARLIEST HEARD ◢   LATEST HEARD ◣   + TENTATIVE

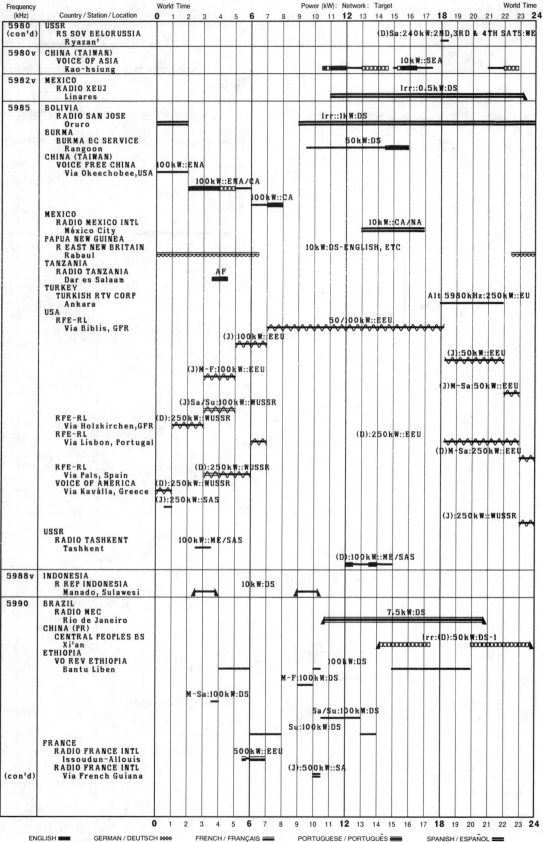

Frequency (kHz)	Country / Station / Location	World Time / Power (kW): Network: Target
5980 (con'd)	USSR RS SOV BELORUSSIA Ryazan'	(D)Sa:240kW:2ND,3RD & 4TH SATS:WE
5980v	CHINA (TAIWAN) VOICE OF ASIA Kao-hsiung	10kW::SEA
5982v	MEXICO RADIO XEUJ Linares	Irr::0.5kW:DS
5985	BOLIVIA RADIO SAN JOSE Oruro	Irr::1kW:DS
	BURMA BURMA BC SERVICE Rangoon	50kW:DS
	CHINA (TAIWAN) VOICE FREE CHINA Via Okeechobee,USA	100kW::ENA 100kW::ENA/CA 100kW::CA
	MEXICO RADIO MEXICO INTL México City	10kW::CA/NA
	PAPUA NEW GUINEA R EAST NEW BRITAIN Rabaul	10kW:DS-ENGLISH, ETC
	TANZANIA RADIO TANZANIA Dar es Salaam	AF
	TURKEY TURKISH RTV CORP Ankara	Alt 5980kHz:250kW::EU
	USA RFE-RL Via Biblis, GFR	50/100kW::EEU (J)100kW::EEU (J):50kW::EEU (J)M-F:100kW::EEU (J)M-Sa:50kW::EEU (J)Sa/Su:100kW::WUSSR
	RFE-RL Via Holzkirchen,GFR	(D):250kW::WUSSR
	RFE-RL Via Lisbon, Portugal	(D):250kW::EEU (D)M-Sa:250kW::EEU
	RFE-RL Via Pals, Spain	(D):250kW::WUSSR
	VOICE OF AMERICA Via Kaválla, Greece	(D):250kW::WUSSR (J):250kW::SAS (J):250kW::WUSSR
	USSR RADIO TASHKENT Tashkent	100kW::ME/SAS (D):100kW::ME/SAS
5988v	INDONESIA R REP INDONESIA Manado, Sulawesi	10kW:DS
5990	BRAZIL RADIO MEC Rio de Janeiro	7.5kW:DS
	CHINA (PR) CENTRAL PEOPLES BS Xi'an	Irr:(D):50kW:DS-1
	ETHIOPIA VO REV ETHIOPIA Bantu Liben	100kW:DS M-F:100kW:DS M-Sa:100kW:DS Sa/Su:100kW:DS Su:100kW:DS
	FRANCE RADIO FRANCE INTL Issoudun-Allouis	500kW::EEU
(con'd)	RADIO FRANCE INTL Via French Guiana	(J):500kW::SA

ENGLISH ■■■   GERMAN / DEUTSCH ◊◊◊◊   FRENCH / FRANÇAIS ≡≡≡   PORTUGUESE / PORTUGUÊS ≡≡≡   SPANISH / ESPAÑOL ≡≡≡

ARABIC / ٍٍٍ ≡≡≡   RUSSIAN / РУССКИИ ═══   CHINESE / 中文 ◊◊◊◊   JAPANESE / 日本語 ▬▬▬   MULTILINGUAL ▬▬▬   OTHER ——

SUMMER ONLY (J)   WINTER ONLY (D)   JAMMING /\/\ or / or \   EARLIEST HEARD ◢   LATEST HEARD ◣   + TENTATIVE

Frequency (kHz)	Country / Station / Location		World Time 0 ... Power (kW): Network: Target ... 24

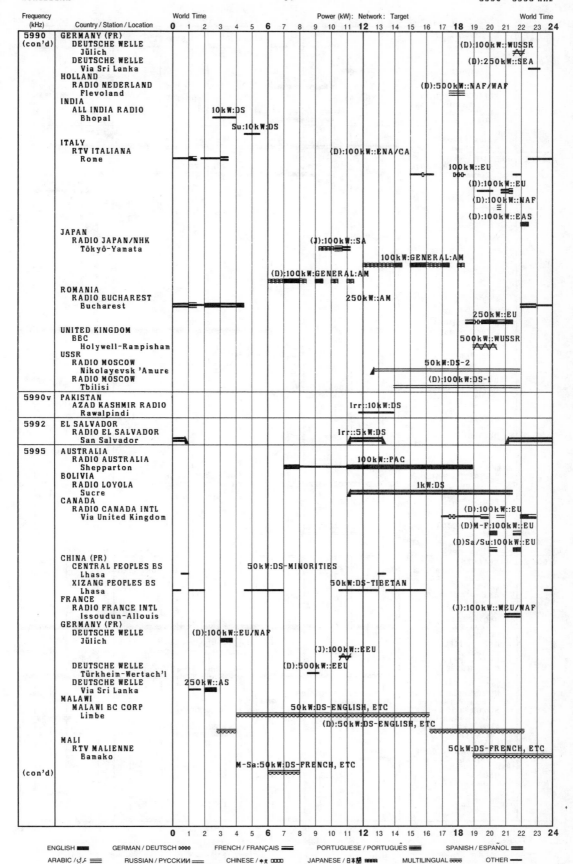

5990 (con'd) — **GERMANY (FR)**
DEUTSCHE WELLE — Jülich — (D):100kW::WUSSR
DEUTSCHE WELLE — Via Sri Lanka — (D):250kW::SEA
HOLLAND
RADIO NEDERLAND — Flevoland — (D):500kW::NAF/WAF
INDIA
ALL INDIA RADIO — Bhopal — 10kW:DS — Su:10kW:DS
ITALY
RTV ITALIANA — Rome — (D):100kW::ENA/CA — 100kW::EU — (D):100kW::EU — (D):100kW::NAF — (D):100kW::EAS
JAPAN
RADIO JAPAN/NHK — Tōkyō-Yamata — (J):100kW::SA — 100kW:GENERAL:AM — (D):100kW:GENERAL:AM
ROMANIA
RADIO BUCHAREST — Bucharest — 250kW::AM — 250kW::EU
UNITED KINGDOM
BBC — Holywell-Rampisham — 500kW::WUSSR
USSR
RADIO MOSCOW — Nikolayevsk 'Amure — 50kW:DS-2
RADIO MOSCOW — Tbilisi — (D):100kW:DS-1

5990v — **PAKISTAN**
AZAD KASHMIR RADIO — Rawalpindi — Irr::10kW:DS

5992 — **EL SALVADOR**
RADIO EL SALVADOR — San Salvador — Irr::5kW:DS

5995 — **AUSTRALIA**
RADIO AUSTRALIA — Shepparton — 100kW::PAC
BOLIVIA
RADIO LOYOLA — Sucre — 1kW:DS
CANADA
RADIO CANADA INTL — Via United Kingdom — (D):100kW::EU — (D)M-F:100kW::EU — (D)Sa/Su:100kW::EU
CHINA (PR)
CENTRAL PEOPLES BS — Lhasa — 50kW:DS-MINORITIES
XIZANG PEOPLES BS — Lhasa — 50kW:DS-TIBETAN
FRANCE
RADIO FRANCE INTL — Issoudun-Allouis — (J):100kW::WEU/WAF
GERMANY (FR)
DEUTSCHE WELLE — Jülich — (D):100kW::EU/NAF — (J):100kW::EEU
DEUTSCHE WELLE — Türkheim-Wertach'l — (D):500kW::EEU
DEUTSCHE WELLE — Via Sri Lanka — 250kW::AS
MALAWI
MALAWI BC CORP — Limbe — 50kW:DS-ENGLISH, ETC — (D):50kW:DS-ENGLISH, ETC
MALI
RTV MALIENNE — Bamako — 50kW:DS-FRENCH, ETC — M-Sa:50kW:DS-FRENCH, ETC

(con'd)

World Time: 0 1 2 3 4 5 6 7 8 9 10 11 12 13 14 15 16 17 18 19 20 21 22 23 24

ENGLISH ▬▬ GERMAN / DEUTSCH ◊◊◊◊ FRENCH / FRANÇAIS ══ PORTUGUESE / PORTUGUÊS ▭▭▭ SPANISH / ESPAÑOL ══
ARABIC / ﺏﺮﻋ ≡ RUSSIAN / РУССКИИ ═ CHINESE / 中文 ◊◊◊◊ JAPANESE / 日本語 ▭▭▭ MULTILINGUAL ▭▭▭ OTHER ▬
SUMMER ONLY (J) WINTER ONLY (D) JAMMING /\/\ or / or \ EARLIEST HEARD ◢ LATEST HEARD ◣ + TENTATIVE

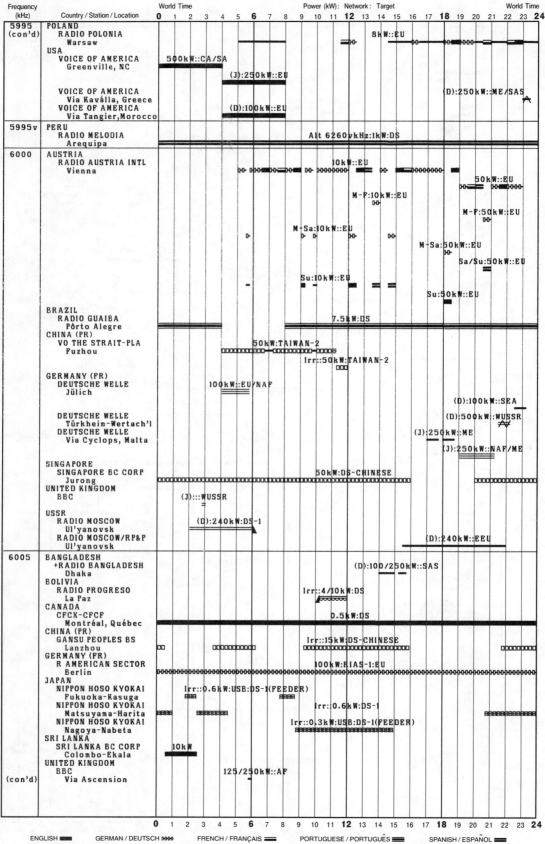

Frequency (kHz)	Country / Station / Location	World Time 0–24
5995 (con'd)	POLAND / RADIO POLONIA / Warsaw	8kW::EU
	USA / VOICE OF AMERICA / Greenville, NC	500kW::CA/SA
		(J):250kW::EU
	VOICE OF AMERICA / Via Kaválla, Greece	(D):250kW::ME/SAS
	VOICE OF AMERICA / Via Tangier, Morocco	(D):100kW::EU
5995v	PERU / RADIO MELODIA / Arequipa	Alt 6260vkHz:1kW:DS
6000	AUSTRIA / RADIO AUSTRIA INTL / Vienna	10kW::EU
		50kW::EU
		M-F:10kW::EU
		M-F:50kW::EU
		M-Sa:10kW::EU
		M-Sa:50kW::EU
		Sa/Su:50kW::EU
		Su:10kW::EU
		Su:50kW::EU
	BRAZIL / RADIO GUAIBA / Pôrto Alegre	7.5kW:DS
	CHINA (PR) / VO THE STRAIT-PLA / Fuzhou	50kW:TAIWAN-2
		Irr::50kW:TAIWAN-2
	GERMANY (FR) / DEUTSCHE WELLE / Jülich	100kW::EU/NAF
	DEUTSCHE WELLE / Türkheim-Wertach'l	(D):100kW::SEA
		(D):500kW::WUSSR
	DEUTSCHE WELLE / Via Cyclops, Malta	(J):250kW::ME
		(J):250kW::NAF/ME
	SINGAPORE / SINGAPORE BC CORP / Jurong	50kW:DS-CHINESE
	UNITED KINGDOM / BBC	(J):::WUSSR
	USSR / RADIO MOSCOW / Ul'yanovsk	(D):240kW:DS-1
	RADIO MOSCOW/RP&P / Ul'yanovsk	(D):240kW::EEU
6005	BANGLADESH / +RADIO BANGLADESH / Dhaka	(D):100/250kW::SAS
	BOLIVIA / RADIO PROGRESO / La Paz	Irr::4/10kW:DS
	CANADA / CFCX-CFCF / Montréal, Québec	0.5kW:DS
	CHINA (PR) / GANSU PEOPLES BS / Lanzhou	Irr::15kW:DS-CHINESE
	GERMANY (FR) / R AMERICAN SECTOR / Berlin	100kW:RIAS-1:EU
	JAPAN / NIPPON HOSO KYOKAI / Fukuoka-Kasuga	Irr::0.6kW:USB:DS-1(FEEDER)
	NIPPON HOSO KYOKAI / Matsuyama-Harita	Irr::0.6kW:DS-1
	NIPPON HOSO KYOKAI / Nagoya-Nabeta	Irr::0.3kW:USB:DS-1(FEEDER)
	SRI LANKA / SRI LANKA BC CORP / Colombo-Ekala	10kW
(con'd)	UNITED KINGDOM / BBC / Via Ascension	125/250kW::AF

World Time: 0 1 2 3 4 5 6 7 8 9 10 11 12 13 14 15 16 17 18 19 20 21 22 23 24

ENGLISH ▬▬ GERMAN / DEUTSCH ◇◇◇◇ FRENCH / FRANÇAIS ══ PORTUGUESE / PORTUGUÊS ▤▤ SPANISH / ESPAÑOL ▦▦

ARABIC /ﺀﺀ ═ RUSSIAN / РУССКИИ ══ CHINESE / 中文 ▢▢▢ JAPANESE / 日本語 ▨▨▨ MULTILINGUAL ▒▒▒▒ OTHER ──

SUMMER ONLY (J)   WINTER ONLY (D)   JAMMING /\/\ or / or \   EARLIEST HEARD ◢   LATEST HEARD ◣   + TENTATIVE

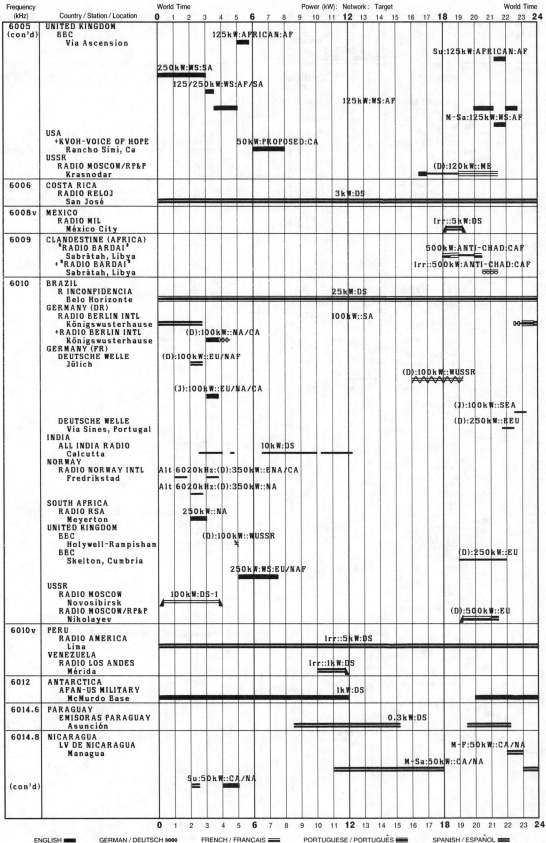

Frequency (kHz)	Country / Station / Location	World Time (0–24)
6005 (con'd)	**UNITED KINGDOM** BBC — Via Ascension	125kW:AFRICAN:AF; Su:125kW:AFRICAN:AF; 250kW:WS:SA; 125/250kW:WS:AF/SA; 125kW:WS:AF; M-Sa:125kW:WS:AF
	USA +KVOH-VOICE OF HOPE — Rancho Simi, Ca	50kW:PROPOSED:CA
	USSR RADIO MOSCOW/RP&P — Krasnodar	(D):120kW::ME
6006	**COSTA RICA** RADIO RELOJ — San José	3kW:DS
6008v	**MEXICO** RADIO MIL — México City	Irr::5kW:DS
6009	**CLANDESTINE (AFRICA)** "RADIO BARDAI" — Sabrâtah, Libya	500kW:ANTI-CHAD:CAF
	+"RADIO BARDAI" — Sabrâtah, Libya	Irr::500kW:ANTI-CHAD:CAF
6010	**BRAZIL** R INCONFIDENCIA — Belo Horizonte	25kW:DS
	GERMANY (DR) RADIO BERLIN INTL — Königswusterhause	100kW::SA
	+RADIO BERLIN INTL — Königswusterhause	(D):100kW::NA/CA
	GERMANY (FR) DEUTSCHE WELLE — Jülich	(D):100kW::EU/NAF; (D):100kW::WUSSR; (J):100kW::EU/NA/CA; (J):100kW::SEA; (D):250kW::EEU
	DEUTSCHE WELLE — Via Sines, Portugal	
	INDIA ALL INDIA RADIO — Calcutta	10kW:DS
	NORWAY RADIO NORWAY INTL — Fredrikstad	Alt 6020kHz:(D):350kW::ENA/CA; Alt 6020kHz:(D):350kW::NA
	SOUTH AFRICA RADIO RSA — Meyerton	250kW::NA
	UNITED KINGDOM BBC — Holywell-Rampisham	(D):100kW::WUSSR
	BBC — Skelton, Cumbria	(D):250kW::EU; 250kW:WS:EU/NAF
	USSR RADIO MOSCOW — Novosibirsk	100kW:DS-1
	RADIO MOSCOW/RP&P — Nikolayev	(D):500kW::EU
6010v	**PERU** RADIO AMERICA — Lima	Irr::5kW:DS
	VENEZUELA RADIO LOS ANDES — Mérida	Irr::1kW:DS
6012	**ANTARCTICA** AFAN-US MILITARY — McMurdo Base	1kW:DS
6014.6	**PARAGUAY** EMISORAS PARAGUAY — Asunción	0.3kW:DS
6014.8	**NICARAGUA** LV DE NICARAGUA — Managua	M-F:50kW::CA/NA; M-Sa:50kW::CA/NA; Su:50kW::CA/NA
(con'd)		

World Time: 0 1 2 3 4 5 6 7 8 9 10 11 12 13 14 15 16 17 18 19 20 21 22 23 24

ENGLISH ▰▰▰   GERMAN / DEUTSCH ◊◊◊◊   FRENCH / FRANÇAIS ▬▬▬   PORTUGUESE / PORTUGUÊS ▰▰▰   SPANISH / ESPAÑOL ▰▰▰

ARABIC /ﻉﺭﺏ ▬▬▬   RUSSIAN / РУССКИИ ▬▬▬   CHINESE / 中文 ◻◻◻◻   JAPANESE / 日本語 ▰▰▰▰   MULTILINGUAL ▭▭▭▭   OTHER ▬▬

SUMMER ONLY (J)   WINTER ONLY (D)   JAMMING /\/\ or / or \   EARLIEST HEARD ◢   LATEST HEARD ◣   + TENTATIVE

| Frequency (kHz) | Country / Station / Location | World Time | Power (kW): Network: Target | World Time |

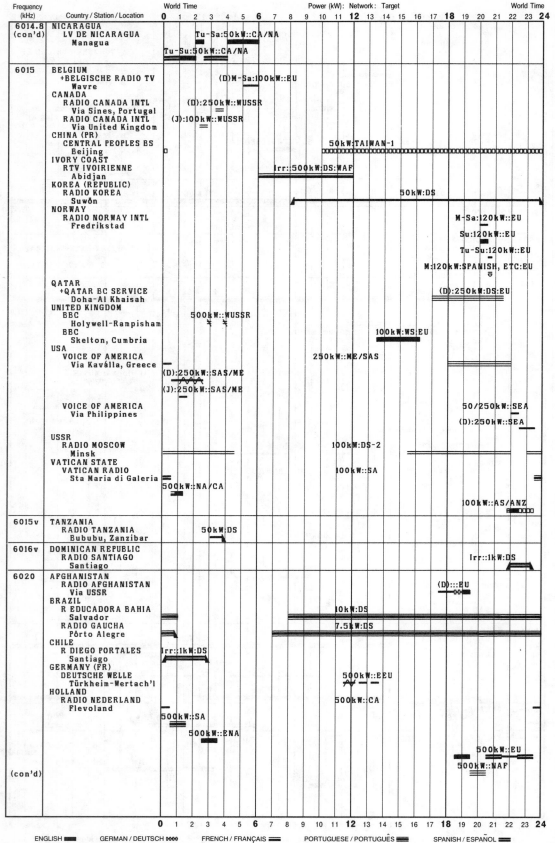

Frequency (kHz) — Country / Station / Location — World Time 0 1 2 3 4 5 6 7 8 9 10 11 12 13 14 15 16 17 18 19 20 21 22 23 24

6014.8 (con'd) NICARAGUA
LV DE NICARAGUA — Managua
Tu-Sa:50kW::CA/NA
Tu-Su:50kW::CA/NA

6015 BELGIUM
+BELGISCHE RADIO TV — Wavre
(D)M-Sa:100kW::EU
CANADA
RADIO CANADA INTL — Via Sines, Portugal
(D):250kW::WUSSR
RADIO CANADA INTL — Via United Kingdom
(J):100kW::WUSSR
CHINA (PR)
CENTRAL PEOPLES BS — Beijing
50kW:TAIWAN-1
IVORY COAST
RTV IVOIRIENNE — Abidjan
Irr::500kW:DS:WAF
KOREA (REPUBLIC)
RADIO KOREA — Suwŏn
50kW:DS
NORWAY
RADIO NORWAY INTL — Fredrikstad
M-Sa:120kW::EU
Su:120kW::EU
Tu-Su:120kW::EU
M:120kW:SPANISH, ETC:EU
QATAR
+QATAR BC SERVICE — Doha-Al Khaisah
(D):250kW:DS:EU
UNITED KINGDOM
BBC — Holywell-Rampisham
500kW::WUSSR
BBC — Skelton, Cumbria
100kW:WS:EU
USA
VOICE OF AMERICA — Via Kaválla, Greece
250kW::ME/SAS
(D):250kW::SAS/ME
(J):250kW::SAS/ME
VOICE OF AMERICA — Via Philippines
50/250kW::SEA
(D):250kW::SEA
USSR
RADIO MOSCOW — Minsk
100kW:DS-2
VATICAN STATE
VATICAN RADIO — Sta Maria di Galeria
100kW::SA
500kW::NA/CA
100kW::AS/ANZ

6015v TANZANIA
RADIO TANZANIA — Bububu, Zanzibar
50kW:DS

6016v DOMINICAN REPUBLIC
RADIO SANTIAGO — Santiago
Irr::1kW:DS

6020 AFGHANISTAN
RADIO AFGHANISTAN — Via USSR
(D):::EU
BRAZIL
R EDUCADORA BAHIA — Salvador
10kW:DS
RADIO GAUCHA — Pôrto Alegre
7.5kW:DS
CHILE
R DIEGO PORTALES — Santiago
Irr::1kW:DS
GERMANY (FR)
DEUTSCHE WELLE — Türkheim-Wertach'l
500kW::EEU
HOLLAND
RADIO NEDERLAND — Flevoland
500kW::CA
500kW::SA
500kW::ENA
500kW::EU
500kW::NAF

(con'd)

0 1 2 3 4 5 6 7 8 9 10 11 12 13 14 15 16 17 18 19 20 21 22 23 24

ENGLISH ▄▄▄   GERMAN / DEUTSCH 0000   FRENCH / FRANÇAIS ═══   PORTUGUESE / PORTUGUÊS ▄▄▄   SPANISH / ESPAÑOL ▄▄▄
ARABIC / ﻉﺏ ═══   RUSSIAN / РУССКИИ ═══   CHINESE / 中文 0000   JAPANESE / 日本語 ▄▄▄   MULTILINGUAL 0000   OTHER ▄▄▄
SUMMER ONLY (J)   WINTER ONLY (D)   JAMMING /\/\ or / or \   EARLIEST HEARD ◢   LATEST HEARD ◣   + TENTATIVE

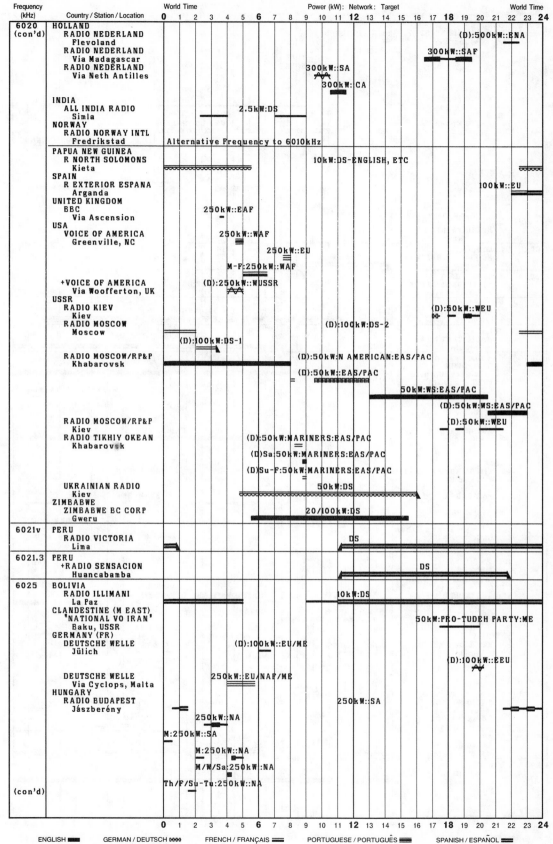

| Frequency (kHz) | Country / Station / Location | World Time | Power (kW): Network: Target | World Time |

6020 (con'd)

HOLLAND
- RADIO NEDERLAND, Flevoland — (D):500kW::ENA
- RADIO NEDERLAND, Via Madagascar — 300kW::SAF
- RADIO NEDERLAND, Via Neth Antilles — 300kW::SA / 300kW:CA

INDIA
- ALL INDIA RADIO, Simla — 2.5kW:DS

NORWAY
- RADIO NORWAY INTL, Fredrikstad — Alternative Frequency to 6010kHz

PAPUA NEW GUINEA
- R NORTH SOLOMONS, Kieta — 10kW:DS-ENGLISH, ETC

SPAIN
- R EXTERIOR ESPANA, Arganda — 100kW::EU

UNITED KINGDOM
- BBC, Via Ascension — 250kW::EAF

USA
- VOICE OF AMERICA, Greenville, NC — 250kW::WAF / 250kW::EU / M-F:250kW:WAF
- +VOICE OF AMERICA, Via Woofferton, UK — (D):250kW:WUSSR

USSR
- RADIO KIEV, Kiev — (D):50kW::WEU
- RADIO MOSCOW, Moscow — (D):100kW:DS-2 / (D):100kW:DS-1
- RADIO MOSCOW/RP&P, Khabarovsk — (D):50kW:N AMERICAN:EAS/PAC / (D):50kW::EAS/PAC / 50kW:WS:EAS/PAC / (D):50kW:WS:EAS/PAC
- RADIO MOSCOW/RP&P, Kiev — (D):50kW::WEU
- RADIO TIKHIY OKEAN, Khabarovsk — (D):50kW:MARINERS:EAS/PAC / (D)Sa:50kW:MARINERS:EAS/PAC / (D)Su-F:50kW:MARINERS:EAS/PAC
- UKRAINIAN RADIO, Kiev — 50kW:DS

ZIMBABWE
- ZIMBABWE BC CORP, Gweru — 20/100kW:DS

6021v

PERU
- RADIO VICTORIA, Lima — DS

6021.3

PERU
- +RADIO SENSACION, Huancabamba — DS

6025

BOLIVIA
- RADIO ILLIMANI, La Paz — 10kW:DS

CLANDESTINE (M EAST)
- "NATIONAL VO IRAN", Baku, USSR — 50kW:PRO-TUDEH PARTY:ME

GERMANY (FR)
- DEUTSCHE WELLE, Jülich — (D):100kW::EU/ME / (D):100kW::EEU
- DEUTSCHE WELLE, Via Cyclops, Malta — 250kW::EU/NAF/ME

HUNGARY
- RADIO BUDAPEST, Jászberény — 250kW::SA / 250kW::NA / M:250kW::SA / M:250kW::NA / M/W/Sa:250kW::NA / Th/F/Su-Tu:250kW::NA

(con'd)

ENGLISH ▬ GERMAN / DEUTSCH ◇◇◇◇ FRENCH / FRANÇAIS ▬▬ PORTUGUESE / PORTUGUÊS ▬▬ SPANISH / ESPAÑOL ▬▬

ARABIC / ﺏﺮﻋ ▬ RUSSIAN / РУССКИИ ▬ CHINESE / 中文 ▭▭▭▭ JAPANESE / 日本語 ▬▬▬ MULTILINGUAL ◇◇◇◇ OTHER ▬

SUMMER ONLY (J)   WINTER ONLY (D)   JAMMING /∧∧ or / or \   EARLIEST HEARD ◢   LATEST HEARD ◣   + TENTATIVE

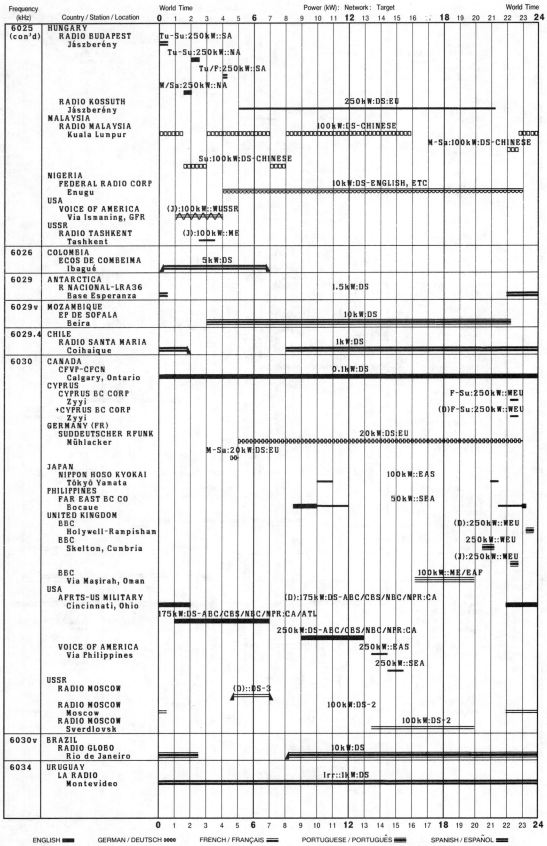

Frequency (kHz) / Country / Station / Location

- 6025 (con'd) HUNGARY — RADIO BUDAPEST, Jászberény — Tu-Su:250kW::SA; Tu-Su:250kW::NA; Tu/F:250kW:SA; W/Sa:250kW::NA
- RADIO KOSSUTH, Jászberény — 250kW:DS:EU
- MALAYSIA — RADIO MALAYSIA, Kuala Lumpur — 100kW:DS-CHINESE; M-Sa:100kW:DS-CHINESE; Su:100kW:DS-CHINESE
- NIGERIA — FEDERAL RADIO CORP, Enugu — 10kW:DS-ENGLISH, ETC
- USA — VOICE OF AMERICA, Via Ismaning, GFR — (J):100kW::WUSSR
- USSR — RADIO TASHKENT, Tashkent — (J):100kW::ME
- 6026 COLOMBIA — ECOS DE COMBEIMA, Ibagué — 5kW:DS
- 6029 ANTARCTICA — R NACIONAL-LRA36, Base Esperanza — 1.5kW:DS
- 6029v MOZAMBIQUE — EP DE SOFALA, Beira — 10kW:DS
- 6029.4 CHILE — RADIO SANTA MARIA, Coihaique — 1kW:DS
- 6030 CANADA — CFVP-CFCN, Calgary, Ontario — 0.1kW:DS
- CYPRUS — CYPRUS BC CORP, Zyyi — F-Su:250kW::WEU; +CYPRUS BC CORP, Zyyi — (D)F-Su:250kW::WEU
- GERMANY (FR) — SUDDEUTSCHER RFUNK, Mühlacker — 20kW:DS:EU; M-Sa:20kW:DS:EU
- JAPAN — NIPPON HOSO KYOKAI, Tōkyō Yamata — 100kW::EAS
- PHILIPPINES — FAR EAST BC CO, Bocaue — 50kW::SEA
- UNITED KINGDOM — BBC, Holywell-Rampisham — (D):250kW::WEU; BBC, Skelton, Cumbria — 250kW::WEU; (J):250kW::WEU; BBC, Via Maşirah, Oman — 100kW::ME/EAF
- USA — AFRTS-US MILITARY, Cincinnati, Ohio — (D):175kW:DS-ABC/CBS/NBC/NPR:CA; 175kW:DS-ABC/CBS/NBC/NPR:CA/ATL; 250kW:DS-ABC/CBS/NBC/NPR:CA
- VOICE OF AMERICA, Via Philippines — 250kW::EAS; 250kW::SEA
- USSR — RADIO MOSCOW — (D)::DS-3; RADIO MOSCOW, Moscow — 100kW:DS-2; RADIO MOSCOW, Sverdlovsk — 100kW:DS-2
- 6030v BRAZIL — RADIO GLOBO, Rio de Janeiro — 10kW:DS
- 6034 URUGUAY — LA RADIO, Montevideo — Irr::1kW:DS

ENGLISH ▬ GERMAN / DEUTSCH ◊◊◊◊ FRENCH / FRANÇAIS ═ PORTUGUESE / PORTUGUÊS ▰ SPANISH / ESPAÑOL ▭
ARABIC / ﺔﯾﺑرﻋ ≋ RUSSIAN / РУССКИЙ ─ CHINESE / 中文 ◻◻◻◻ JAPANESE / 日本語 ▰▰▰ MULTILINGUAL ▱▱▱ OTHER ─
SUMMER ONLY (J) WINTER ONLY (D) JAMMING ∧∧ or / or \ EARLIEST HEARD ◢ LATEST HEARD ◣ + TENTATIVE

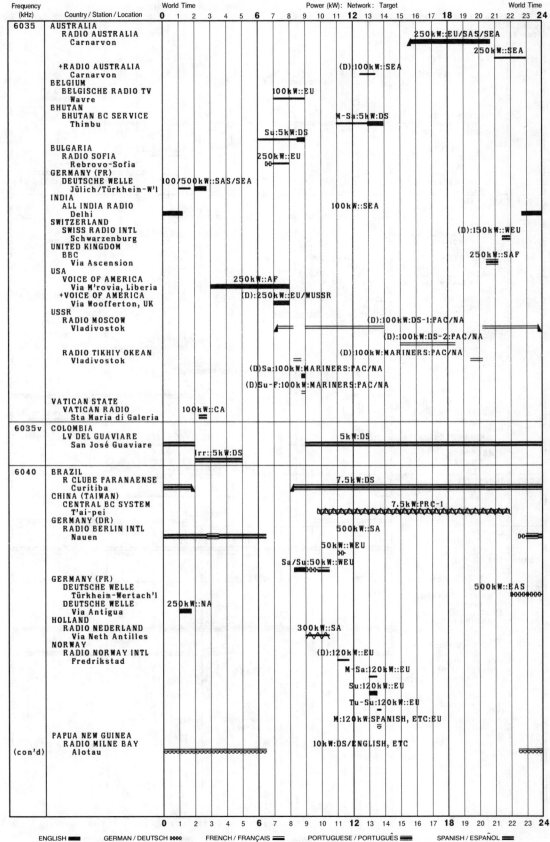

Frequency (kHz)	Country / Station / Location	World Time / Power (kW) : Network : Target
6035	AUSTRALIA	
	RADIO AUSTRALIA	250kW::EU/SAS/SEA
	Carnarvon	250kW::SEA
	+RADIO AUSTRALIA	(D):100kW::SEA
	Carnarvon	
	BELGIUM	
	BELGISCHE RADIO TV	100kW::EU
	Wavre	
	BHUTAN	
	BHUTAN BC SERVICE	M-Sa:5kW:DS
	Thimbu	Su:5kW:DS
	BULGARIA	
	RADIO SOFIA	250kW::EU
	Rebrovo-Sofia	
	GERMANY (FR)	
	DEUTSCHE WELLE	100/500kW::SAS/SEA
	Jülich/Türkheim-W'l	
	INDIA	
	ALL INDIA RADIO	100kW::SEA
	Delhi	
	SWITZERLAND	
	SWISS RADIO INTL	(D):150kW::WEU
	Schwarzenburg	
	UNITED KINGDOM	
	BBC	250kW::SAF
	Via Ascension	
	USA	
	VOICE OF AMERICA	250kW::AF
	Via M'rovia, Liberia	
	+VOICE OF AMERICA	(D):250kW::EU/WUSSR
	Via Woofferton, UK	
	USSR	
	RADIO MOSCOW	(D):100kW:DS-1:PAC/NA
	Vladivostok	(D):100kW:DS-2:PAC/NA
	RADIO TIKHIY OKEAN	(D):100kW:MARINERS:PAC/NA
	Vladivostok	(D)Sa:100kW:MARINERS:PAC/NA
		(D)Su-F:100kW:MARINERS:PAC/NA
	VATICAN STATE	
	VATICAN RADIO	100kW::CA
	Sta Maria di Galeria	
6035v	COLOMBIA	
	LV DEL GUAVIARE	5kW:DS
	San José Guaviare	Irr::5kW:DS
6040	BRAZIL	
	R CLUBE PARANAENSE	7.5kW:DS
	Curitiba	
	CHINA (TAIWAN)	
	CENTRAL BC SYSTEM	7.5kW:PRC-1
	T'ai-pei	
	GERMANY (DR)	
	RADIO BERLIN INTL	500kW::SA
	Nauen	50kW::WEU
		Sa/Su:50kW::WEU
	GERMANY (FR)	
	DEUTSCHE WELLE	500kW::EAS
	Türkheim-Wertach'l	
	DEUTSCHE WELLE	250kW::NA
	Via Antigua	
	HOLLAND	
	RADIO NEDERLAND	300kW::SA
	Via Neth Antilles	
	NORWAY	
	RADIO NORWAY INTL	(D):120kW::EU
	Fredrikstad	M-Sa:120kW::EU
		Su:120kW::EU
		Tu-Su:120kW::EU
		M:120kW:SPANISH, ETC:EU
	PAPUA NEW GUINEA	
	RADIO MILNE BAY	10kW:DS/ENGLISH, ETC
(con'd)	Alotau	

ENGLISH ▬▬ GERMAN / DEUTSCH ୦୦୦୦ FRENCH / FRANÇAIS ═══ PORTUGUESE / PORTUGUÊS ▭▭ SPANISH / ESPAÑOL ═══
ARABIC / ڒڒ ═══ RUSSIAN / РУССКИИ ═══ CHINESE / ✦✗ ୦୦୦୦ JAPANESE / 日本語 ▬▬▬ MULTILINGUAL ▬▬▬ OTHER ▬
SUMMER ONLY (J) WINTER ONLY (D) JAMMING ∧∧ or / or \ EARLIEST HEARD ◢ LATEST HEARD ◣ + TENTATIVE

Frequency (kHz)	Country / Station / Location	World Time / Power (kW) : Network : Target

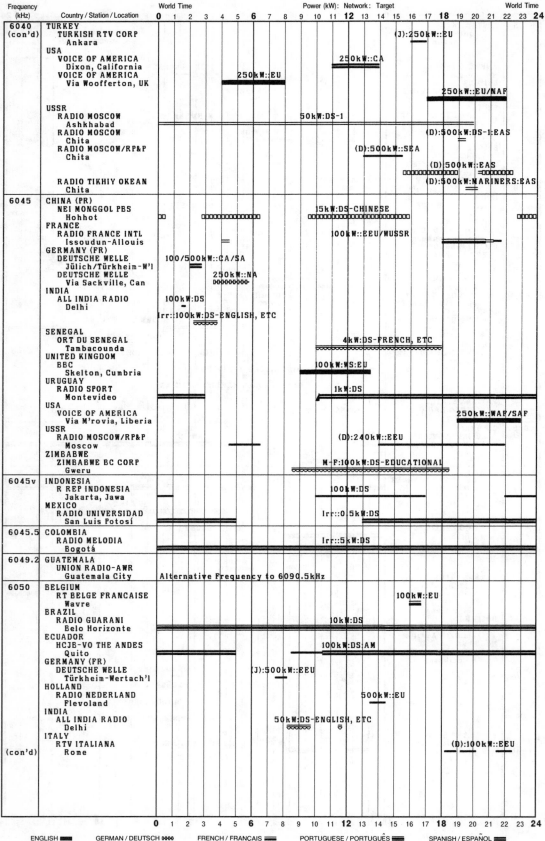

6040 (con'd)

TURKEY
TURKISH RTV CORP
Ankara — (J):250kW::EU

USA
VOICE OF AMERICA
Dixon, California — 250kW::CA
VOICE OF AMERICA
Via Woofferton, UK — 250kW::EU ; 250kW::EU/NAF

USSR
RADIO MOSCOW
Ashkhabad — 50kW:DS-1
RADIO MOSCOW
Chita — (D):500kW:DS-1:EAS
RADIO MOSCOW/RP&P
Chita — (D):500kW::SEA ; (D):500kW::EAS
RADIO TIKHIY OKEAN
Chita — (D):500kW:MARINERS:EAS

6045

CHINA (PR)
NEI MONGGOL PBS
Hohhot — 15kW:DS-CHINESE
FRANCE
RADIO FRANCE INTL
Issoudun-Allouis — 100kW::EEU/WUSSR
GERMANY (FR)
DEUTSCHE WELLE
Jülich/Türkheim-W'l — 100/500kW::CA/SA
DEUTSCHE WELLE
Via Sackville, Can — 250kW::NA
INDIA
ALL INDIA RADIO
Delhi — 100kW:DS ; Irr:100kW:DS-ENGLISH, ETC
SENEGAL
ORT DU SENEGAL
Tambacounda — 4kW:DS-FRENCH, ETC
UNITED KINGDOM
BBC
Skelton, Cumbria — 100kW:WS:EU
URUGUAY
RADIO SPORT
Montevideo — 1kW:DS
USA
VOICE OF AMERICA
Via M'rovia, Liberia — 250kW::WAF/SAF
USSR
RADIO MOSCOW/RP&P
Moscow — (D):240kW::EEU
ZIMBABWE
ZIMBABWE BC CORP
Gweru — M-F:100kW:DS-EDUCATIONAL

6045v

INDONESIA
R REP INDONESIA
Jakarta, Jawa — 100kW:DS
MEXICO
RADIO UNIVERSIDAD
San Luis Potosí — Irr::0.5kW:DS

6045.5

COLOMBIA
RADIO MELODIA
Bogotá — Irr::5kW:DS

6049.2

GUATEMALA
UNION RADIO-AWR
Guatemala City — Alternative Frequency to 6090.5kHz

6050

BELGIUM
RT BELGE FRANCAISE
Wavre — 100kW::EU
BRAZIL
RADIO GUARANI
Belo Horizonte — 10kW:DS
ECUADOR
HCJB-VO THE ANDES
Quito — 100kW:DS:AM
GERMANY (FR)
DEUTSCHE WELLE
Türkheim-Wertach'l — (J):500kW::EEU
HOLLAND
RADIO NEDERLAND
Flevoland — 500kW::EU
INDIA
ALL INDIA RADIO
Delhi — 50kW:DS-ENGLISH, ETC
ITALY
RTV ITALIANA
(con'd) Rome — (D):100kW::EEU

ENGLISH ▰▰▰   GERMAN / DEUTSCH ◊◊◊◊   FRENCH / FRANÇAIS ▭▭▭   PORTUGUESE / PORTUGUÊS ▰▰▰   SPANISH / ESPAÑOL ▭▭▭

ARABIC / العربية ▰▰▰   RUSSIAN / РУССКИИ ▭▭▭   CHINESE / 中文 ◊◊◊◊   JAPANESE / 日本語 ▰▰▰   MULTILINGUAL ◊◊◊◊   OTHER —

SUMMER ONLY (J)   WINTER ONLY (D)   JAMMING /\/\ or / or \   EARLIEST HEARD ◢   LATEST HEARD ◣   + TENTATIVE

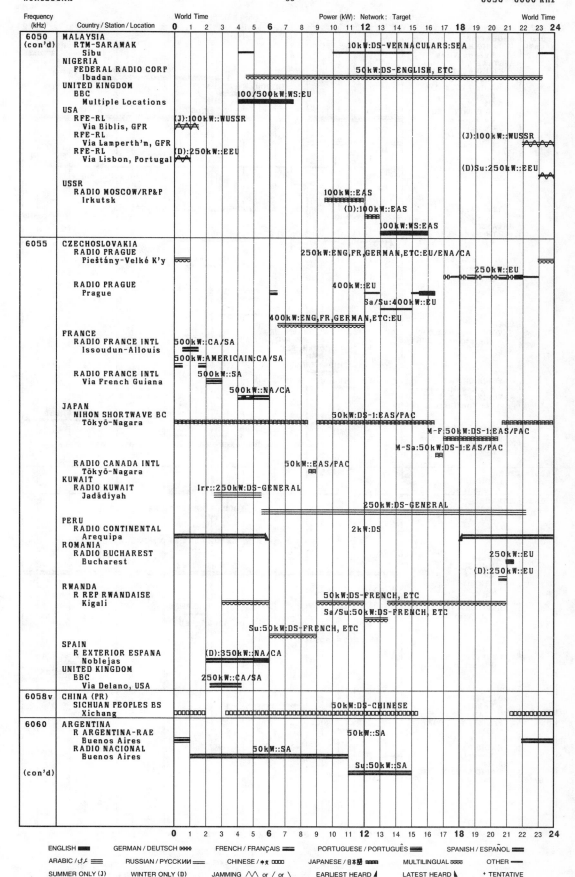

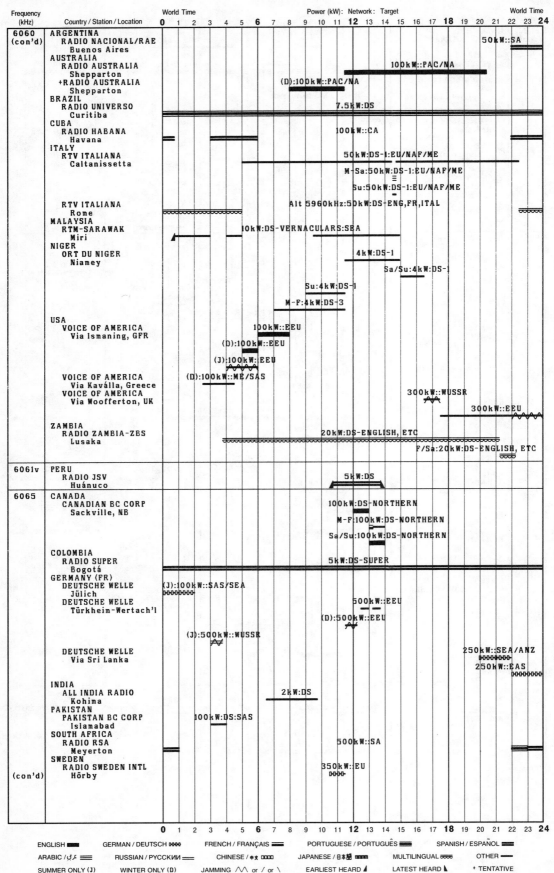

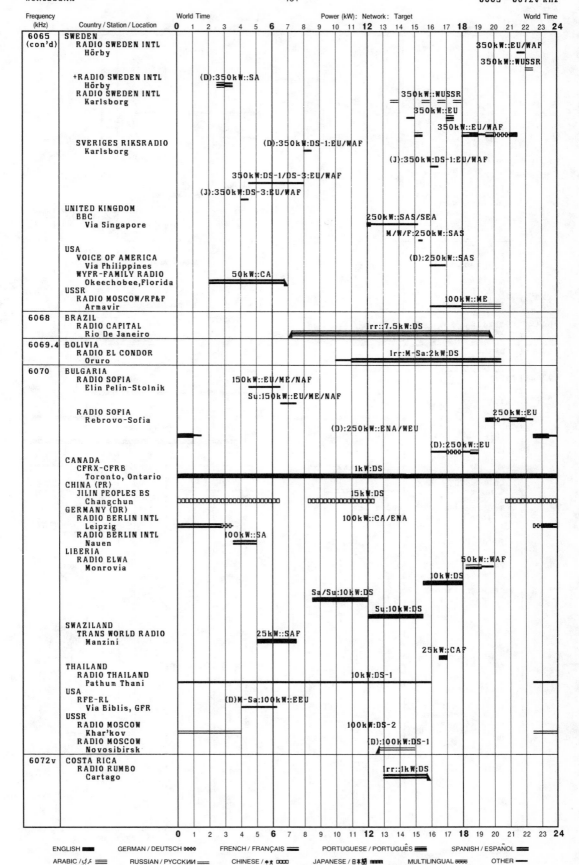

Frequency (kHz)	Country / Station / Location	Schedule (World Time) — Power (kW): Network: Target
6065 (con'd)	SWEDEN	
	RADIO SWEDEN INTL — Hörby	350kW::EU/WAF ; 350kW::WUSSR
	+RADIO SWEDEN INTL — Hörby	(D):350kW::SA
	RADIO SWEDEN INTL — Karlsborg	350kW::WUSSR ; 350kW::EU ; 350kW::EU/WAF
	SVERIGES RIKSRADIO — Karlsborg	(D):350kW:DS-1:EU/WAF ; (J):350kW:DS-1:EU/WAF ; 350kW:DS-1/DS-3:EU/WAF ; (J):350kW:DS-3:EU/WAF
	UNITED KINGDOM BBC — Via Singapore	250kW::SAS/SEA ; M/W/F:250kW::SAS
	USA VOICE OF AMERICA — Via Philippines	(D):250kW::SAS
	WYFR-FAMILY RADIO — Okeechobee,Florida	50kW::CA
	USSR RADIO MOSCOW/RP&P — Armavir	100kW::ME
6068	BRAZIL — RADIO CAPITAL — Rio De Janeiro	Irr::7.5kW:DS
6069.4	BOLIVIA — RADIO EL CONDOR — Oruro	Irr:M-Sa:2kW:DS
6070	BULGARIA	
	RADIO SOFIA — Elin Pelin-Stolnik	150kW::EU/ME/NAF ; Su:150kW::EU/ME/NAF
	RADIO SOFIA — Rebrovo-Sofia	250kW::EU ; (D):250kW::ENA/WEU ; (D):250kW::EU
	CANADA CFRX-CFRB — Toronto, Ontario	1kW:DS
	CHINA (PR) JILIN PEOPLES BS — Changchun	15kW:DS
	GERMANY (DR) RADIO BERLIN INTL — Leipzig	100kW::CA/ENA
	RADIO BERLIN INTL — Nauen	100kW::SA
	LIBERIA RADIO ELWA — Monrovia	50kW::WAF ; 10kW:DS ; Sa/Su:10kW:DS ; Su:10kW:DS
	SWAZILAND TRANS WORLD RADIO — Manzini	25kW::SAF ; 25kW::CAF
	THAILAND RADIO THAILAND — Pathum Thani	10kW:DS-1
	USA RFE-RL — Via Biblis, GFR	(D)M-Sa:100kW::EEU
	USSR RADIO MOSCOW — Khar'kov	100kW:DS-2
	RADIO MOSCOW — Novosibirsk	(D):100kW:DS-1
6072v	COSTA RICA RADIO RUMBO — Cartago	Irr::1kW:DS

ENGLISH ▬ GERMAN / DEUTSCH ◊◊◊◊ FRENCH / FRANÇAIS ═ PORTUGUESE / PORTUGUÊS ▤ SPANISH / ESPAÑOL ═

ARABIC / ﺏﺮﻋ ≡ RUSSIAN / РУССКИИ ═ CHINESE / ★★ ◻◻◻◻ JAPANESE / 日本語 ▦▦▦ MULTILINGUAL ▩▩▩ OTHER ▬

SUMMER ONLY (J) WINTER ONLY (D) JAMMING /\/\ or / or \ EARLIEST HEARD ◢ LATEST HEARD ◣ + TENTATIVE

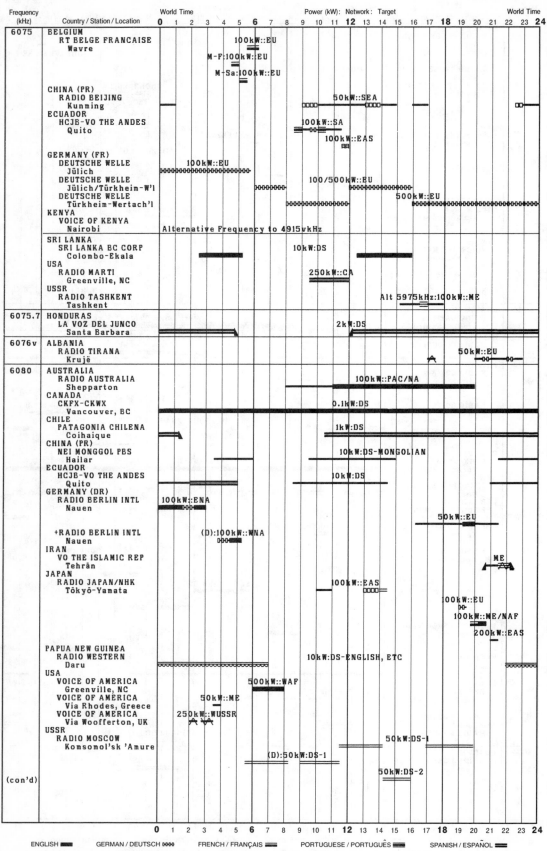

Frequency (kHz)	Country / Station / Location	Power (kW): Network: Target
6075	BELGIUM RT BELGE FRANCAISE Wavre	100kW::EU M-F:100kW::EU M-Sa:100kW::EU
	CHINA (PR) RADIO BEIJING Kunming	50kW::SEA
	ECUADOR HCJB-VO THE ANDES Quito	100kW::SA 100kW::EAS
	GERMANY (FR) DEUTSCHE WELLE Jülich	100kW::EU
	DEUTSCHE WELLE Jülich/Türkheim-W'l	100/500kW::EU
	DEUTSCHE WELLE Türkheim-Wertach'l	500kW::EU
	KENYA VOICE OF KENYA Nairobi	Alternative Frequency to 4915vkHz
	SRI LANKA SRI LANKA BC CORP Colombo-Ekala	10kW:DS
	USA RADIO MARTI Greenville, NC	250kW::CA
	USSR RADIO TASHKENT Tashkent	Alt 5975kHz:100kW::ME
6075.7	HONDURAS LA VOZ DEL JUNCO Santa Barbara	2kW:DS
6076v	ALBANIA RADIO TIRANA Krujë	50kW::EU
6080	AUSTRALIA RADIO AUSTRALIA Shepparton	100kW::PAC/NA
	CANADA CKFX-CKWX Vancouver, BC	0.1kW:DS
	CHILE PATAGONIA CHILENA Coihaique	1kW:DS
	CHINA (PR) NEI MONGGOL PBS Hailar	10kW:DS-MONGOLIAN
	ECUADOR HCJB-VO THE ANDES Quito	10kW:DS
	GERMANY (DR) RADIO BERLIN INTL Nauen	100kW::ENA 50kW::EU
	+RADIO BERLIN INTL Nauen	(D):100kW::WNA
	IRAN VO THE ISLAMIC REP Tehrān	ME
	JAPAN RADIO JAPAN/NHK Tōkyō-Yamata	100kW::EAS 100kW::EU 100kW::ME/NAF 200kW::EAS
	PAPUA NEW GUINEA RADIO WESTERN Daru	10kW:DS-ENGLISH, ETC
	USA VOICE OF AMERICA Greenville, NC	500kW::WAF
	VOICE OF AMERICA Via Rhodes, Greece	50kW::ME
	VOICE OF AMERICA Via Woofferton, UK	250kW::WUSSR
	USSR RADIO MOSCOW Komsomol'sk 'Amure	50kW:DS-1 (D):50kW:DS-1 50kW:DS-2
(con'd)		

World Time: 0 1 2 3 4 5 6 7 8 9 10 11 12 13 14 15 16 17 18 19 20 21 22 23 24

ENGLISH — GERMAN / DEUTSCH — FRENCH / FRANÇAIS — PORTUGUESE / PORTUGUÊS — SPANISH / ESPAÑOL — ARABIC / عربي — RUSSIAN / РУССКИЙ — CHINESE / 中文 — JAPANESE / 日本語 — MULTILINGUAL — OTHER — SUMMER ONLY (J) — WINTER ONLY (D) — JAMMING /\/\ or / or \ — EARLIEST HEARD — LATEST HEARD — + TENTATIVE

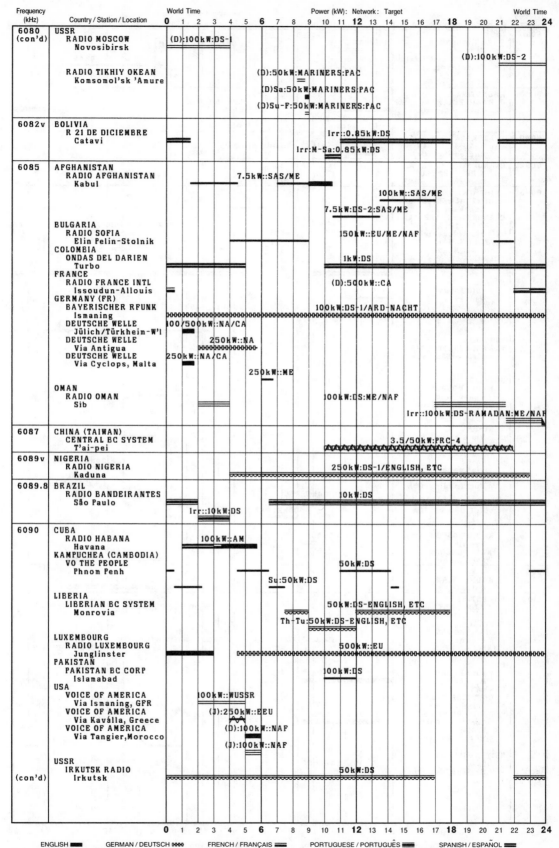

Frequency (kHz)	Country / Station / Location	World Time — Power (kW): Network: Target
6080 (con'd)	USSR — RADIO MOSCOW, Novosibirsk	(D):100kW:DS-1 / (D):100kW:DS-2
	RADIO TIKHIY OKEAN, Komsomol'sk 'Amure	(D):50kW:MARINERS:PAC / (D)Sa:50kW:MARINERS:PAC / (D)Su-F:50kW:MARINERS:PAC
6082v	BOLIVIA — R 21 DE DICIEMBRE, Catavi	Irr::0.85kW:DS / Irr:M-Sa:0.85kW:DS
6085	AFGHANISTAN — RADIO AFGHANISTAN, Kabul	7.5kW::SAS/ME / 100kW::SAS/ME / 7.5kW:DS-2:SAS/ME
	BULGARIA — RADIO SOFIA, Elin Pelin-Stolnik	150kW::EU/ME/NAF
	COLOMBIA — ONDAS DEL DARIEN, Turbo	1kW:DS
	FRANCE — RADIO FRANCE INTL, Issoudun-Allouis	(D):500kW::CA
	GERMANY (FR) — BAYERISCHER RFUNK, Ismaning	100kW:DS-1/ARD-NACHT
	DEUTSCHE WELLE, Jülich/Türkheim-W'l	100/500kW::NA/CA
	DEUTSCHE WELLE, Via Antigua	250kW::NA
	DEUTSCHE WELLE, Via Cyclops, Malta	250kW::NA/CA / 250kW::ME
	OMAN — RADIO OMAN, Sib	100kW:DS:ME/NAF / Irr::100kW:DS-RAMADAN:ME/NAF
6087	CHINA (TAIWAN) — CENTRAL BC SYSTEM, T'ai-pei	3.5/50kW:PRC-4
6089v	NIGERIA — RADIO NIGERIA, Kaduna	250kW:DS-1/ENGLISH, ETC
6089.8	BRAZIL — RADIO BANDEIRANTES, São Paulo	10kW:DS / Irr::10kW:DS
6090	CUBA — RADIO HABANA, Havana	100kW::AM
	KAMPUCHEA (CAMBODIA) — VO THE PEOPLE, Phnom Penh	50kW:DS / Su:50kW:DS
	LIBERIA — LIBERIAN BC SYSTEM, Monrovia	50kW:DS-ENGLISH, ETC / Th-Tu:50kW:DS-ENGLISH, ETC
	LUXEMBOURG — RADIO LUXEMBOURG, Junglinster	500kW::EU
	PAKISTAN — PAKISTAN BC CORP, Islamabad	100kW:DS
	USA — VOICE OF AMERICA, Via Ismaning, GFR	100kW::WUSSR
	VOICE OF AMERICA, Via Kaválla, Greece	(J):250kW::EEU
	VOICE OF AMERICA, Via Tangier, Morocco	(D):100kW::NAF / (J):100kW::NAF
(con'd)	USSR — IRKUTSK RADIO, Irkutsk	50kW:DS

0 1 2 3 4 5 6 7 8 9 10 11 12 13 14 15 16 17 18 19 20 21 22 23 24

ENGLISH ▬▬▬ GERMAN / DEUTSCH ∞∞∞ FRENCH / FRANÇAIS ═══ PORTUGUESE / PORTUGUÊS ▬▬ SPANISH / ESPAÑOL ═══

ARABIC /سڌ ═══ RUSSIAN / PYCCKИИ ═══ CHINESE / 中文 ∞∞∞ JAPANESE / 日本語 ▬▬▬ MULTILINGUAL ∞∞∞ OTHER ▬▬

SUMMER ONLY (J) WINTER ONLY (D) JAMMING /\/\ or / or \ EARLIEST HEARD ◢ LATEST HEARD ◣ + TENTATIVE

Frequency (kHz)	Country / Station / Location		Power (kW): Network: Target

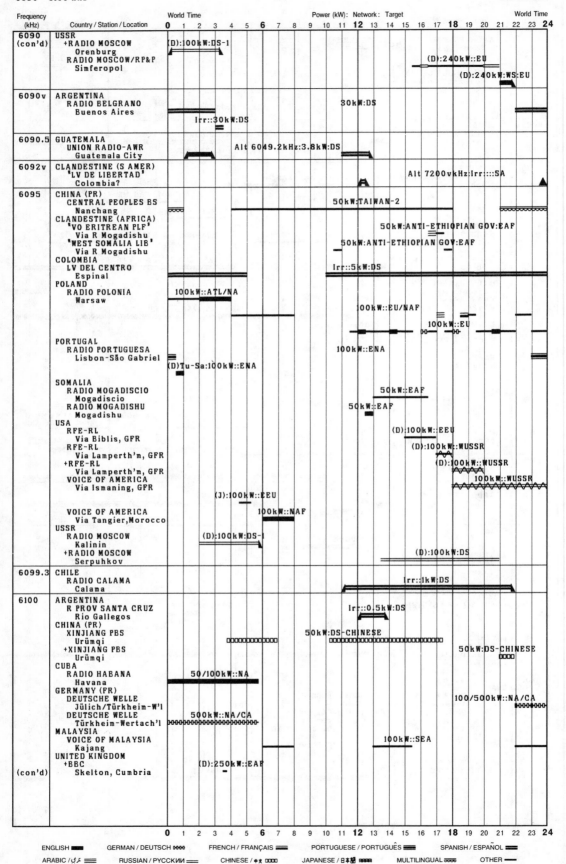

Content of the chart (by frequency):

6090 (con'd) — USSR
- +RADIO MOSCOW, Orenburg — (D):100kW:DS-1
- RADIO MOSCOW/RP&P, Simferopol — (D):240kW::EU / (D):240kW:WS:EU

6090v — ARGENTINA
- RADIO BELGRANO, Buenos Aires — 30kW:DS / Irr::30kW:DS

6090.5 — GUATEMALA
- UNION RADIO-AWR, Guatemala City — Alt 6049.2kHz:3.8kW:DS

6092v — CLANDESTINE (S AMER)
- 'LV DE LIBERTAD', Colombia? — Alt 7200vkHz:Irr::::SA

6095 — CHINA (PR)
- CENTRAL PEOPLES BS, Nanchang — 50kW:TAIWAN-2

CLANDESTINE (AFRICA)
- 'VO ERITREAN PLP', Via R Mogadishu — 50kW:ANTI-ETHIOPIAN GOV:EAF
- 'WEST SOMALIA LIB', Via R Mogadishu — 50kW:ANTI-ETHIOPIAN GOV:EAF

COLOMBIA
- LV DEL CENTRO, Espinal — Irr::5kW:DS

POLAND
- RADIO POLONIA, Warsaw — 100kW::ATL/NA / 100kW::EU/NAF / 100kW::EU

PORTUGAL
- RADIO PORTUGUESA, Lisbon-São Gabriel — 100kW::ENA / (D)Tu-Sa:100kW::ENA

SOMALIA
- RADIO MOGADISCIO, Mogadiscio — 50kW::EAF
- RADIO MOGADISHU, Mogadishu — 50kW::EAF

USA
- RFE-RL, Via Biblis, GFR — (D):100kW:EEU
- RFE-RL, Via Lamperth'm, GFR — (D):100kW::WUSSR
- +RFE-RL, Via Lamperth'm, GFR — (D):100kW::WUSSR
- VOICE OF AMERICA, Via Ismaning, GFR — 100kW::WUSSR
- VOICE OF AMERICA, Via Tangier, Morocco — (J):100kW:EEU / 100kW::NAF

USSR
- RADIO MOSCOW, Kalinin — (D):100kW:DS-1
- +RADIO MOSCOW, Serpuhkov — (D):100kW:DS

6099.3 — CHILE
- RADIO CALAMA, Calama — Irr::1kW:DS

6100 — ARGENTINA
- R PROV SANTA CRUZ, Rio Gallegos — Irr::0.5kW:DS

CHINA (PR)
- XINJIANG PBS, Urümqi — 50kW:DS-CHINESE
- +XINJIANG PBS, Urümqi — 50kW:DS-CHINESE

CUBA
- RADIO HABANA, Havana — 50/100kW::NA

GERMANY (FR)
- DEUTSCHE WELLE, Jülich/Türkheim-W'l — 100/500kW::NA/CA
- DEUTSCHE WELLE, Türkheim-Wertach'l — 500kW::NA/CA

MALAYSIA
- VOICE OF MALAYSIA, Kajang — 100kW::SEA

UNITED KINGDOM
- +BBC, (con'd) Skelton, Cumbria — (D):250kW::EAF

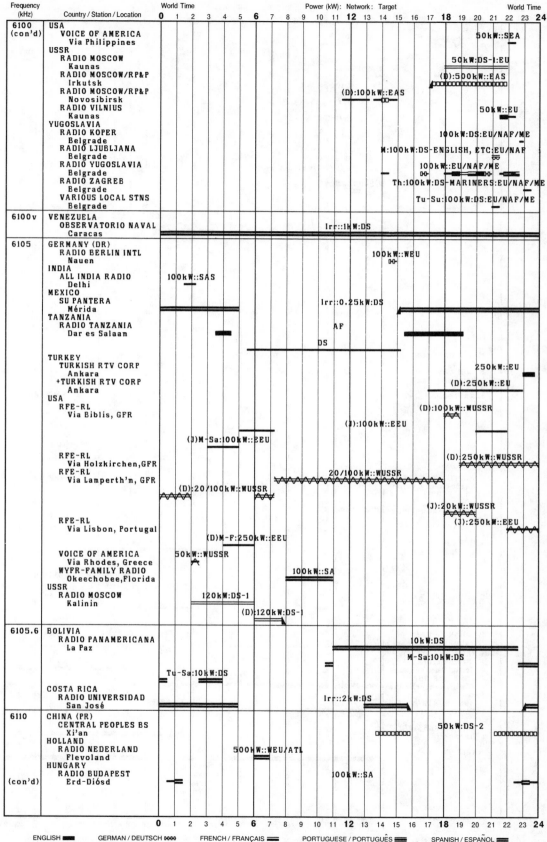

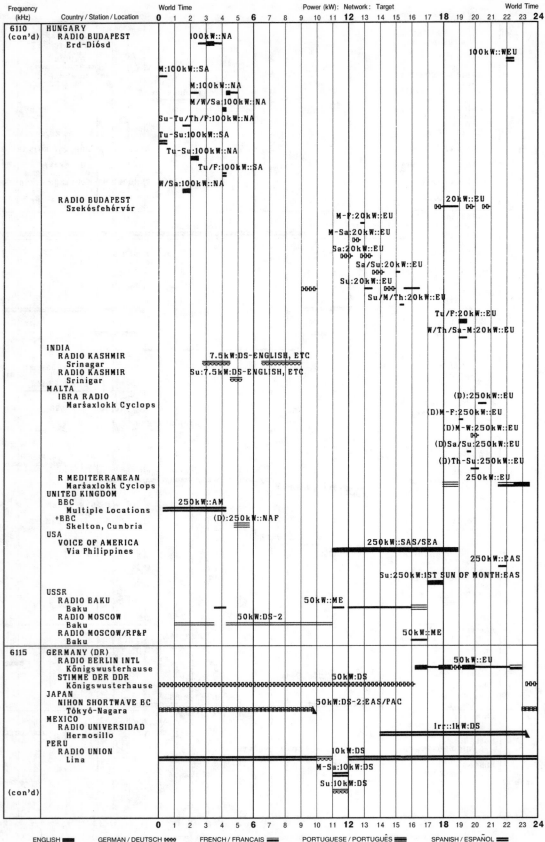

Frequency (kHz)   Country / Station / Location   World Time   Power (kW): Network: Target   World Time

0 1 2 3 4 5 6 7 8 9 10 11 12 13 14 15 16 17 18 19 20 21 22 23 24

6110 (con'd)

HUNGARY
RADIO BUDAPEST
Erd-Diósd
- 100kW::NA
- 100kW::WEU
- M:100kW::SA
- M:100kW::NA
- M/W/Sa:100kW::NA
- Su-Tu/Th/F:100kW::NA
- Tu-Su:100kW::SA
- Tu-Su:100kW::NA
- Tu/F:100kW::SA
- W/Sa:100kW::NA

RADIO BUDAPEST
Szekésfehérvár
- 20kW::EU
- M-F:20kW::EU
- M-Sa:20kW::EU
- Sa:20kW::EU
- Sa/Su:20kW::EU
- Su:20kW::EU
- Su/M/Th:20kW::EU
- Tu/F:20kW::EU
- W/Th/Sa-M:20kW::EU

INDIA
RADIO KASHMIR
Srinagar
- 7.5kW:DS-ENGLISH, ETC
RADIO KASHMIR
Srinigar
- Su:7.5kW:DS-ENGLISH, ETC

MALTA
IBRA RADIO
Marśaxlokk Cyclops
- (D):250kW::EU
- (D)M-F:250kW::EU
- (D)M-W:250kW::EU
- (D)Sa/Su:250kW::EU
- (D)Th-Su:250kW::EU

R MEDITERRANEAN
Marśaxlokk Cyclops
- 250kW::EU

UNITED KINGDOM
BBC
Multiple Locations
- 250kW::AM
+BBC
Skelton, Cumbria
- (D):250kW::NAF

USA
VOICE OF AMERICA
Via Philippines
- 250kW::SAS/SEA
- 250kW::EAS
- Su:250kW:1ST SUN OF MONTH:EAS

USSR
RADIO BAKU
Baku
- 50kW::ME
RADIO MOSCOW
Baku
- 50kW:DS-2
RADIO MOSCOW/RP&P
Baku
- 50kW::ME

6115

GERMANY (DR)
RADIO BERLIN INTL
Königswusterhause
- 50kW::EU
STIMME DER DDR
Königswusterhause
- 50kW:DS

JAPAN
NIHON SHORTWAVE BC
Tōkyō-Nagara
- 50kW:DS-2:EAS/PAC

MEXICO
RADIO UNIVERSIDAD
Hermosillo
- Irr::1kW:DS

PERU
RADIO UNION
Lima
- 10kW:DS
- M-Sa:10kW:DS
- Su:10kW:DS

(con'd)

0 1 2 3 4 5 6 7 8 9 10 11 12 13 14 15 16 17 18 19 20 21 22 23 24

ENGLISH ▬▬   GERMAN / DEUTSCH ◊◊◊◊   FRENCH / FRANÇAIS ▬▬   PORTUGUESE / PORTUGUÊS ▬▬   SPANISH / ESPAÑOL ▬▬

ARABIC /ﺏﺭﻉ ☰   RUSSIAN / РУССКИИ ═   CHINESE / ✦✪ ◻◻◻◻   JAPANESE / 日本語 ▰▰▰   MULTILINGUAL ▭▭▭   OTHER ▬

SUMMER ONLY (J)   WINTER ONLY (D)   JAMMING /\/\ or / or \   EARLIEST HEARD ◢   LATEST HEARD ◣   + TENTATIVE

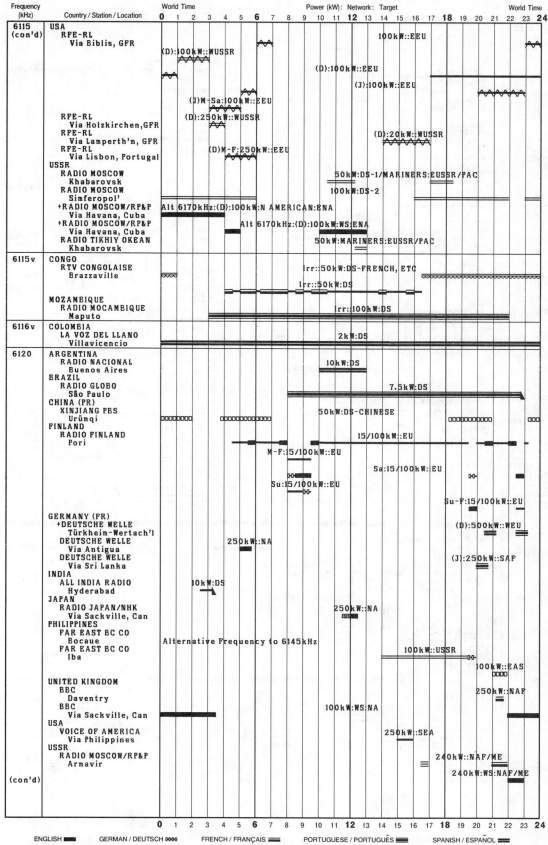

Frequency (kHz)	Country / Station / Location	Power (kW) : Network : Target
6115 (con'd)	USA	
	RFE-RL Via Biblis, GFR	100kW::EEU
		(D):100kW:WUSSR
		(D):100kW::EEU
		(J):100kW::EEU
		(J)M-Sa:100kW::EEU
	RFE-RL Via Holzkirchen, GFR	(D):250kW::WUSSR
	RFE-RL Via Lamperth'm, GFR	(D):20kW::WUSSR
	RFE-RL Via Lisbon, Portugal	(D)M-F:250kW::EEU
	USSR	
	RADIO MOSCOW Khabarovsk	50kW:DS-1/MARINERS:EUSSR/PAC
	RADIO MOSCOW Simferopol'	100kW:DS-2
	+RADIO MOSCOW/RP&P Via Havana, Cuba	Alt 6170kHz:(D):100kW:N AMERICAN:ENA
	+RADIO MOSCOW/RP&P Via Havana, Cuba	Alt 6170kHz:(D):100kW:WS:ENA
	RADIO TIKHIY OKEAN Khabarovsk	50kW:MARINERS:EUSSR/PAC
6115v	CONGO	
	RTV CONGOLAISE Brazzaville	Irr::50kW:DS-FRENCH, ETC
		Irr::50kW:DS
	MOZAMBIQUE	
	RADIO MOCAMBIQUE Maputo	Irr:100kW:DS
6116v	COLOMBIA	
	LA VOZ DEL LLANO Villavicencio	2kW:DS
6120	ARGENTINA	
	RADIO NACIONAL Buenos Aires	10kW:DS
	BRAZIL	
	RADIO GLOBO São Paulo	7.5kW:DS
	CHINA (PR)	
	XINJIANG PBS Urümqi	50kW:DS-CHINESE
	FINLAND	
	RADIO FINLAND Pori	15/100kW::EU
		M-F:15/100kW::EU
		Sa:15/100kW::EU
		Su:15/100kW::EU
		Su-F:15/100kW::EU
	GERMANY (FR)	
	+DEUTSCHE WELLE Türkheim-Wertach'l	(D):500kW::WEU
	DEUTSCHE WELLE Via Antigua	250kW::NA
	DEUTSCHE WELLE Via Sri Lanka	(J):250kW::SAF
	INDIA	
	ALL INDIA RADIO Hyderabad	10kW:DS
	JAPAN	
	RADIO JAPAN/NHK Via Sackville, Can	250kW::NA
	PHILIPPINES	
	FAR EAST BC CO Bocaue	Alternative Frequency to 6145kHz
	FAR EAST BC CO Iba	100kW::USSR
		100kW::EAS
	UNITED KINGDOM	
	BBC Daventry	250kW::NAF
	BBC Via Sackville, Can	100kW:WS:NA
	USA	
	VOICE OF AMERICA Via Philippines	250kW::SEA
	USSR	
	RADIO MOSCOW/RP&P Armavir	240kW::NAF/ME
(con'd)		240kW:WS:NAF/ME

ENGLISH ▬▬ GERMAN / DEUTSCH ▭▭▭ FRENCH / FRANÇAIS ▭▭▭ PORTUGUESE / PORTUGUÊS ▬▬▬ SPANISH / ESPAÑOL ▭▭▭

ARABIC / ﻉﺮﺑ ▬▬ RUSSIAN / РУССКИИ ▬▬ CHINESE / 中文 ▭▭▭▭ JAPANESE / 日本語 ▬▬▬ MULTILINGUAL ▭▭▭ OTHER ▬

SUMMER ONLY (J)   WINTER ONLY (D)   JAMMING /\/\ or / or \   EARLIEST HEARD ◢   LATEST HEARD ◣   + TENTATIVE

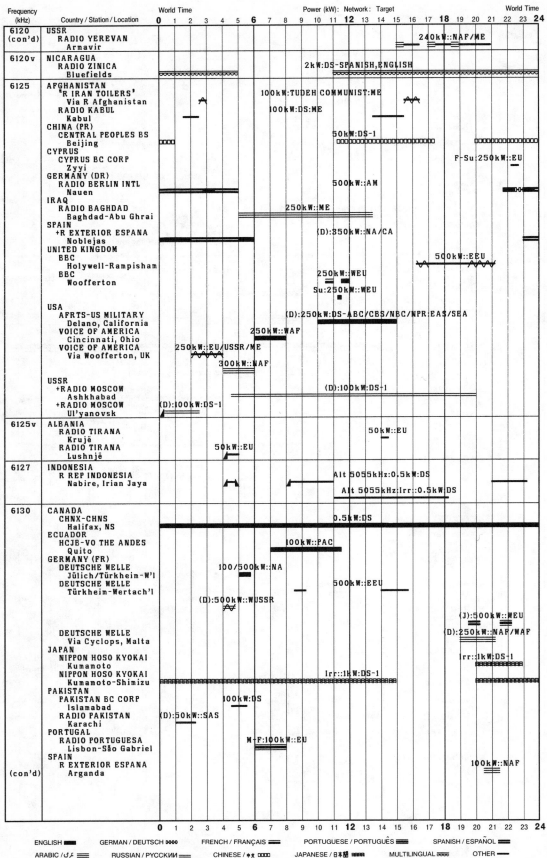

Frequency (kHz)	Country / Station / Location	World Time 0 1 2 3 4 5 6 7 8 9 10 11 12 13 14 15 16 17 18 19 20 21 22 23 24	Power (kW): Network: Target

6120 (con'd) — USSR — RADIO YEREVAN — Armavir — 240kW::NAF/ME

6120v — NICARAGUA — RADIO ZINICA — Bluefields — 2kW:DS-SPANISH,ENGLISH

6125 — AFGHANISTAN
'R IRAN TOILERS' — Via R Afghanistan — 100kW:TUDEH COMMUNIST:ME
RADIO KABUL — Kabul — 100kW:DS:ME
CHINA (PR)
CENTRAL PEOPLES BS — Beijing — 50kW:DS-1
CYPRUS
CYPRUS BC CORP — Zyyi — F-Su:250kW::EU
GERMANY (DR)
RADIO BERLIN INTL — Nauen — 500kW::AM
IRAQ
RADIO BAGHDAD — Baghdad-Abu Ghrai — 250kW::ME
SPAIN
+R EXTERIOR ESPANA — Noblejas — (D):350kW::NA/CA
UNITED KINGDOM
BBC — Holywell-Rampisham — 500kW::EEU
BBC — Woofferton — 250kW::WEU — Su:250kW::WEU
USA
AFRTS-US MILITARY — Delano, California — (D):250kW:DS-ABC/CBS/NBC/NPR:EAS/SEA
VOICE OF AMERICA — Cincinnati, Ohio — 250kW::WAF
VOICE OF AMERICA — Via Woofferton, UK — 250kW::EU/USSR/ME — 300kW::WAF
USSR
+RADIO MOSCOW — Ashkhabad — (D):100kW:DS-1
+RADIO MOSCOW — Ul'yanovsk — (D):100kW:DS-1

6125v — ALBANIA
RADIO TIRANA — Krujë — 50kW::EU
RADIO TIRANA — Lushnjë — 50kW::EU

6127 — INDONESIA
R REP INDONESIA — Nabire, Irian Jaya — Alt 5055kHz:0.5kW:DS — Alt 5055kHz:Irr:0.5kW:DS

6130 — CANADA
CHNX-CHNS — Halifax, NS — 0.5kW:DS
ECUADOR
HCJB-VO THE ANDES — Quito — 100kW::PAC
GERMANY (FR)
DEUTSCHE WELLE — Jülich/Türkheim-W'l — 100/500kW::NA
DEUTSCHE WELLE — Türkheim-Wertach'l — 500kW::EEU — (D):500kW::WUSSR — (J):500kW::WEU
DEUTSCHE WELLE — Via Cyclops, Malta — (D):250kW::NAF/WAF
JAPAN
NIPPON HOSO KYOKAI — Kumamoto — Irr::1kW:DS-1
NIPPON HOSO KYOKAI — Kumamoto-Shimizu — Irr::1kW:DS-1
PAKISTAN
PAKISTAN BC CORP — Islamabad — 100kW:DS
RADIO PAKISTAN — Karachi — (D):50kW::SAS
PORTUGAL
RADIO PORTUGUESA — Lisbon-São Gabriel — M-F:100kW::EU
SPAIN
(con'd) — R EXTERIOR ESPANA — Arganda — 100kW::NAF

| World Time 0 1 2 3 4 5 6 7 8 9 10 11 12 13 14 15 16 17 18 19 20 21 22 23 24 |

ENGLISH ▰▰▰   GERMAN / DEUTSCH ▨▨▨   FRENCH / FRANÇAIS ▤▤▤   PORTUGUESE / PORTUGUÊS ▤▤▤   SPANISH / ESPAÑOL ▰▰▰

ARABIC /ﻉﺭ ≡≡   RUSSIAN / РУССКИИ ▬▬   CHINESE / 中文 ▨▨▨   JAPANESE / 日本語 ▦▦▦   MULTILINGUAL ▨▨▨   OTHER ▬▬

SUMMER ONLY (J)   WINTER ONLY (D)   JAMMING ∧∧∧ or / or \   EARLIEST HEARD ◢   LATEST HEARD ◣   + TENTATIVE

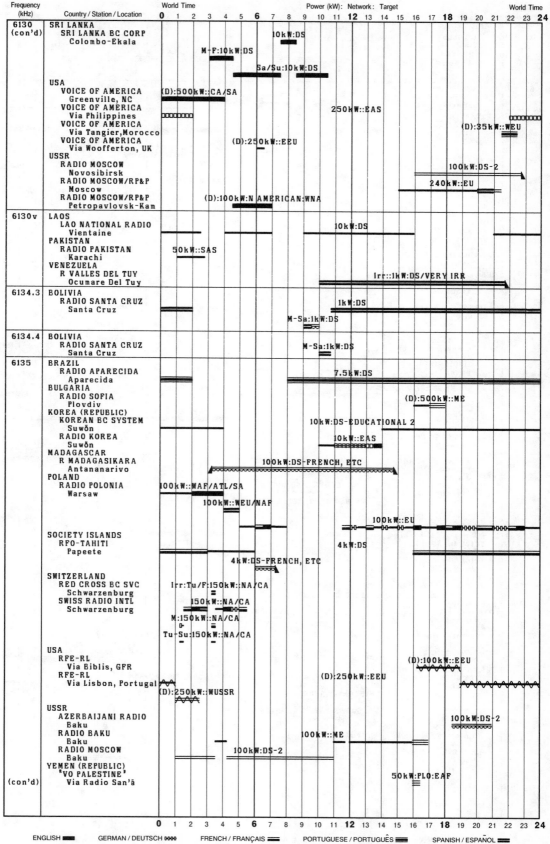

6130 (con'd) SRI LANKA — SRI LANKA BC CORP, Colombo-Ekala — 10kW:DS; M-F:10kW:DS; Sa/Su:10kW:DS

USA — VOICE OF AMERICA, Greenville, NC — (D):500kW::CA/SA

VOICE OF AMERICA, Via Philippines — 250kW::EAS

VOICE OF AMERICA, Via Tangier, Morocco — (D):35kW::WEU

VOICE OF AMERICA, Via Woofferton, UK — (D):250kW::EEU

USSR — RADIO MOSCOW, Novosibirsk — 100kW:DS-2

RADIO MOSCOW/RP&P, Moscow — 240kW::EU

RADIO MOSCOW/RP&P, Petropavlovsk-Kam — (D):100kW:N AMERICAN:WNA

6130v LAOS — LAO NATIONAL RADIO, Vientaine — 10kW:DS

PAKISTAN — RADIO PAKISTAN, Karachi — 50kW::SAS

VENEZUELA — R VALLES DEL TUY, Ocumare Del Tuy — Irr::1kW:DS/VERY IRR

6134.3 BOLIVIA — RADIO SANTA CRUZ, Santa Cruz — 1kW:DS; M-Sa:1kW:DS

6134.4 BOLIVIA — RADIO SANTA CRUZ, Santa Cruz — M-Sa:1kW:DS

6135 BRAZIL — RADIO APARECIDA, Aparecida — 7.5kW:DS

BULGARIA — RADIO SOFIA, Plovdiv — (D):500kW::ME

KOREA (REPUBLIC) — KOREAN BC SYSTEM, Suwŏn — 10kW:DS-EDUCATIONAL 2

RADIO KOREA, Suwŏn — 10kW::EAS

MADAGASCAR — R MADAGASIKARA, Antananarivo — 100kW:DS-FRENCH, ETC

POLAND — RADIO POLONIA, Warsaw — 100kW::WAF/ATL/SA; 100kW::WEU/NAF; 100kW::EU

SOCIETY ISLANDS — RFO-TAHITI, Papeete — 4kW:DS; 4kW:DS-FRENCH, ETC

SWITZERLAND — RED CROSS BC SVC, Schwarzenburg — Irr:Tu/F:150kW::NA/CA

SWISS RADIO INTL, Schwarzenburg — 150kW::NA/CA; M:150kW::NA/CA; Tu-Su:150kW::NA/CA

USA — RFE-RL, Via Biblis, GFR — (D):100kW::EEU

RFE-RL, Via Lisbon, Portugal — (D):250kW::EEU; (D):250kW::WUSSR

USSR — AZERBAIJANI RADIO, Baku — 100kW:DS-2

RADIO BAKU, Baku — 100kW::ME

RADIO MOSCOW, Baku — 100kW:DS-2

YEMEN (REPUBLIC) — "VO PALESTINE", Via Radio San'ā — 50kW:PLO:EAF

(con'd)

ENGLISH ▬▬	GERMAN / DEUTSCH ◊◊◊◊	FRENCH / FRANÇAIS ══
PORTUGUESE / PORTUGUÊS ▬▬	SPANISH / ESPAÑOL ══	
ARABIC / عربي ≣≣	RUSSIAN / РУССКИИ ══	CHINESE / 中文 ▢▢▢▢
JAPANESE / 日本語 ▬▬	MULTILINGUAL ▧▧▧	OTHER ▬▬
SUMMER ONLY (J)	WINTER ONLY (D)	JAMMING /\/\ or / or \
EARLIEST HEARD ◢	LATEST HEARD ◣	+ TENTATIVE

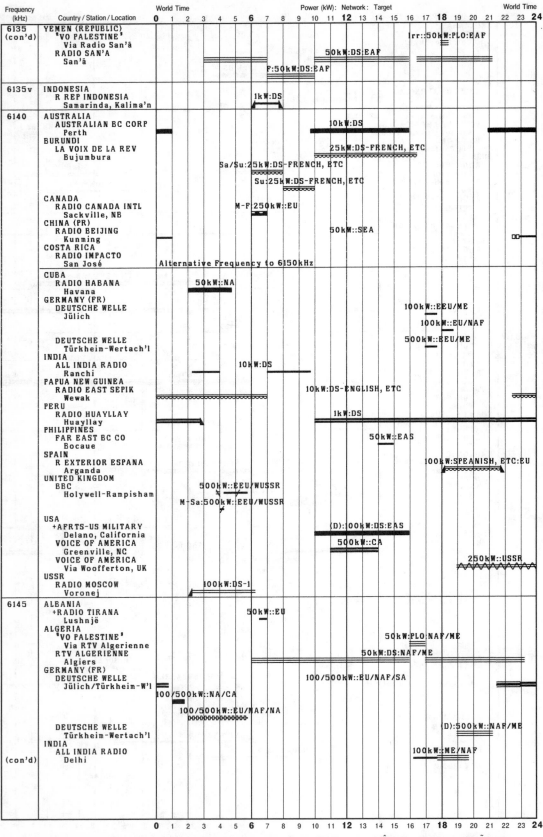

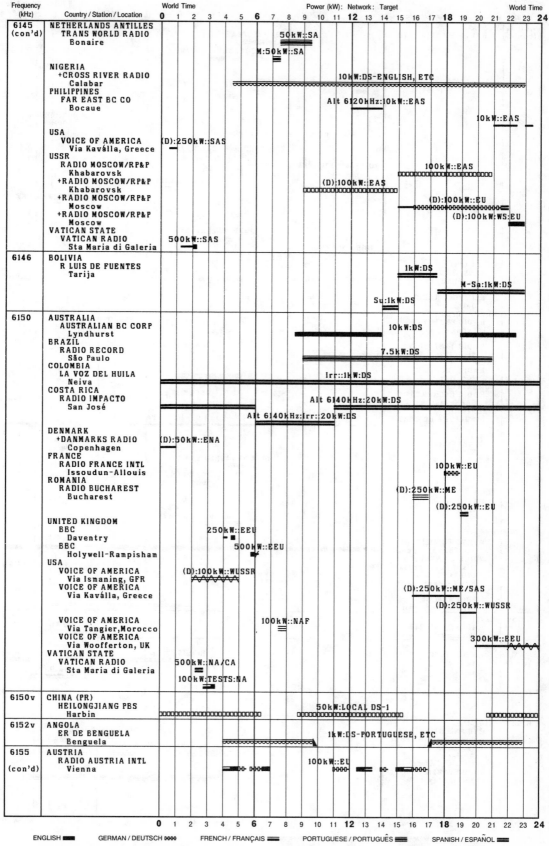

Frequency (kHz) / Country / Station / Location — World Time — Power (kW): Network: Target

- **6145 (con'd)** — NETHERLANDS ANTILLES, TRANS WORLD RADIO, Bonaire: 50kW::SA; M:50kW::SA
- NIGERIA, +CROSS RIVER RADIO, Calabar: 10kW:DS-ENGLISH, ETC
- PHILIPPINES, FAR EAST BC CO, Bocaue: Alt 6120kHz:10kW::EAS; 10kW::EAS
- USA, VOICE OF AMERICA, Via Kaválla, Greece: (D):250kW::SAS
- USSR, RADIO MOSCOW/RP&P, Khabarovsk: 100kW::EAS
- +RADIO MOSCOW/RP&P, Khabarovsk: (D):100kW::EAS
- +RADIO MOSCOW/RP&P, Moscow: (D):100kW::EU
- +RADIO MOSCOW/RP&P, Moscow: (D):100kW:WS:EU
- VATICAN STATE, VATICAN RADIO, Sta Maria di Galeria: 500kW::SAS
- **6146** — BOLIVIA, R LUIS DE FUENTES, Tarija: 1kW:DS; M-Sa:1kW:DS; Su:1kW:DS
- **6150** — AUSTRALIA, AUSTRALIAN BC CORP, Lyndhurst: 10kW:DS
- BRAZIL, RADIO RECORD, São Paulo: 7.5kW:DS
- COLOMBIA, LA VOZ DEL HUILA, Neiva: Irr::1kW:DS
- COSTA RICA, RADIO IMPACTO, San José: Alt 6140kHz:20kW:DS; Alt 6140kHz:Irr:20kW:DS
- DENMARK, +DANMARKS RADIO, Copenhagen: (D):50kW::ENA
- FRANCE, RADIO FRANCE INTL, Issoudun-Allouis: 100kW::EU
- ROMANIA, RADIO BUCHAREST, Bucharest: (D):250kW::ME; (D):250kW::EU
- UNITED KINGDOM, BBC, Daventry: 250kW::EEU
- BBC, Holywell-Rampisham: 500kW::EEU
- USA, VOICE OF AMERICA, Via Ismaning, GFR: (D):100kW::WUSSR
- VOICE OF AMERICA, Via Kaválla, Greece: (D):250kW::ME/SAS; (D):250kW::WUSSR
- VOICE OF AMERICA, Via Tangier, Morocco: 100kW::NAF
- VOICE OF AMERICA, Via Woofferton, UK: 300kW::EEU
- VATICAN STATE, VATICAN RADIO, Sta Maria di Galeria: 500kW:NA/CA; 100kW:TESTS:NA
- **6150v** — CHINA (PR), HEILONGJIANG PBS, Harbin: 50kW:LOCAL DS-1
- **6152v** — ANGOLA, ER DE BENGUELA, Benguela: 1kW:DS-PORTUGUESE, ETC
- **6155 (con'd)** — AUSTRIA, RADIO AUSTRIA INTL, Vienna: 100kW::EU

Frequency (kHz)	Country / Station / Location	World Time 0 1 2 3 4 5 **6** 7 8 9 10 11 **12** 13 14 15 16 17 **18** 19 20 21 22 23 **24**
6155 (con'd)	**AUSTRIA** RADIO AUSTRIA INTL Vienna	500kW::EU/NAF/ME
		300kW::EU/NAF/ME
		100kW::WEU/NAF
		(D):500kW::ENA
		M-F:100kW::EU
		M-Sa:100kW::EU
		M-F:100kW::WEU/NAF
		M-Sa:300kW::EU/NAF/ME
		(D)M-Sa:500kW::ENA
		Sa/Su:100kW::EU
		Sa/Su:100kW::WEU/NAF
		Su:100kW::EU
		Su:300kW::EU/NAF/ME
		(D)Su:500kW::ENA
	CHINA (PR) GANSU PEOPLES BS Lanzhou	15kW:DS-CHINESE
	INDIA ALL INDIA RADIO Delhi	100kW::SAS
	KOREA (DPR) RADIO PYONGYANG Pyŏngyang	200kW::ME/AF
	LIBYA RADIO JAMAHIRIYA Tripoli	500kW::NAF/WAF
	PERU RADIO PUCALLPA Pucallpa	1kW:DS
	ROMANIA RADIO BUCHAREST Bucharest	250kW::AM
	SINGAPORE SINGAPORE BC CORP Jurong	50kW:DS-2:SEA/PAC
	SWAZILAND SWAZI COMMERCIAL R Sandlane	M-F:10kW::SAF
		M-F:10kW:PARALELO 27:SAF
		Sa/Su:10kW:PARALELO 27:SAF
	TOGO RADIO KARA Lama-Kara	10kW:DS-FRENCH, ETC
		Sa/Su:10kW:DS-FRENCH, ETC
	USA AFRTS-US MILITARY Via Tôkyô, Japan	10kW:DS-FAR EAST NET:EAS
	VOICE OF AMERICA Dixon, California	(D):250kW::CA/SA
	WRNO WORLDWIDE New Orleans, La	Su:100kW::ENA
	USSR RADIO MOSCOW Nikolayevsk 'Amure	50kW:DS-2
6155v	**HAITI** RADIO CITADELLE Port-au-Prince	Irr::2kW:DS-FRENCH, ETC
6155.2	**BOLIVIA** RADIO FIDES La Paz	1kW:DS
		Irr::1kW:DS
		M-Sa:1kW:DS
		Tu-Su:1kW:DS
6160	**ALGERIA** 'VO PALESTINE' Via RTV Algerienne	50kW:PLO:EU/NAF
	RTV ALGERIENNE Algiers	50kW:DS-1:EU/NAF
	BRAZIL RADIO PAMPA	5kW:DS
(con'd)	Pôrto Alegre	

0 1 2 3 4 5 **6** 7 8 9 10 11 **12** 13 14 15 16 17 **18** 19 20 21 22 23 **24**

ENGLISH ▰▰▰   GERMAN / DEUTSCH ◊◊◊◊   FRENCH / FRANÇAIS ═══   PORTUGUESE / PORTUGUÊS ▰▰▰   SPANISH / ESPAÑOL ▰▰▰

ARABIC / ﻉﺭﺏ ═══   RUSSIAN / РУССКИИ   CHINESE / 中文 ◊◊◊◊   JAPANESE / 日本語 ▰▰▰   MULTILINGUAL ◊◊◊◊   OTHER ───

SUMMER ONLY (J)   WINTER ONLY (D)   JAMMING /\/\ or / or \   EARLIEST HEARD ◢   LATEST HEARD ◣   + TENTATIVE

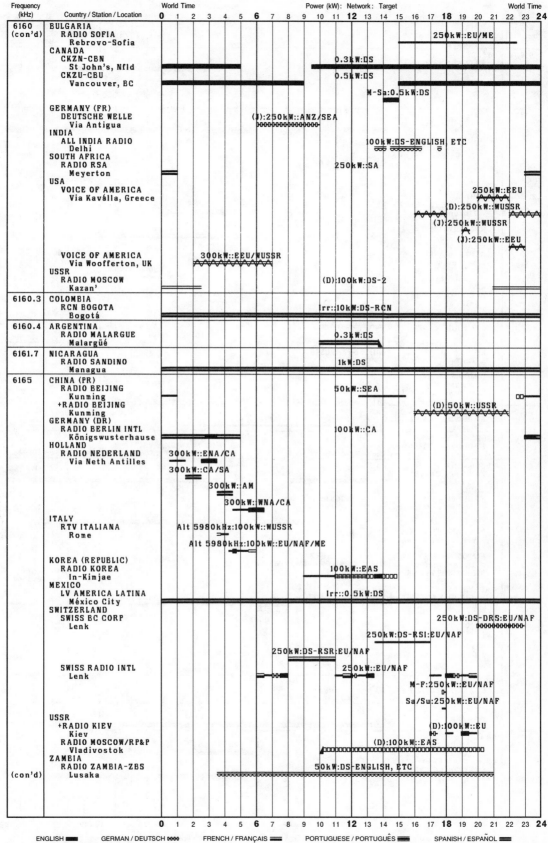

Frequency (kHz)	Country / Station / Location	Power (kW): Network: Target / Notes
6165 (con'd)	ZAMBIA — RADIO ZAMBIA-ZBS — Lusaka	F/Sa:50kW:DS-ENGLISH, ETC
6165v	CYPRUS — RADIO BAYRAK — Kato Dhikomo	7.5kW:DS-2 / Th-Tu:7.5kW:DS-2 / W:7.5kW:DS-2
6170	BRAZIL — RADIO CULTURA — São Paulo	7.5kW:DS
	CANADA — RADIO CANADA INTL — Via United Kingdom	100kW::EU / M-F:100kW::EU / Sa/Su:100kW::EU
	COLOMBIA — LA VOZ DE LA SELVA — Florencia	Irr::1kW:DS
	FRENCH GUIANA — RFO-GUYANE — Cayenne	4kW:DS
	GERMANY (PR) — DEUTSCHE WELLE — Türkheim-Wertach'l	(J):500kW::EEU
	DEUTSCHE WELLE — Via Sri Lanka	250kW::SAS/SEA
	PAKISTAN — PAKISTAN BC CORP — Islamabad	100kW:DS
	USA — RFE-RL — Via Biblis, GFR	(J):50/100kW::WUSSR
	RFE-RL — Via Lamperth'm, GFR	(D):100kW::WUSSR
	RFE-RL — Via Pals, Spain	(D):250kW::WUSSR
	USSR — RADIO MOSCOW — Armavir	100kW:DS-1
	+RADIO MOSCOW/RP&P — Via Havana, Cuba	Alternative Frequency to 6115kHz
6170v	PHILIPPINES — RADYO NG BAYAN — Marulas	10kW:DS
6174	PERU — RADIO TAWANTINSUYO — Cuzco	5kW:DS-SPANISH, ETC
6175	COSTA RICA — FARO DEL CARIBE — San José	2.5kW:DS
	FRANCE — RADIO FRANCE INTL — Issoudun-Allouis	100kW::NAF / 100kW::EU/NAF
	RADIO FRANCE INTL — Via French Guiana	500kW::CA
	JAPAN — NIPPON HOSO KYOKAI — Hiroshima-Gion	Irr::0.6kW:DS-1
	NIPPON HOSO KYOKAI — Tōkyō-Shōbu	Irr::0.9kW:USB:DS-1(FEEDER)
	MALAYSIA — VOICE OF MALAYSIA — Kajang	50kW::SEA
	PAKISTAN — RADIO PAKISTAN — Islamabad	100kW::SAS
	USA — WYFR-FAMILY RADIO — Okeechobee,Florida	100kW::SA / 100kW::CA
6176	CHINA (PR) — SHAANXI PEOPLES BS — Xi'an	15kW:DS
6179v	ARGENTINA — RADIO NACIONAL — Mendoza	1kW:DS
6180	BRAZIL — R NAC DA AMAZONIA — Brasília	250kW:DS
(con'd)	CHINA (TAIWAN) — CENTRAL BC SYSTEM — T'ai-pei	10/50kW:PRC-2

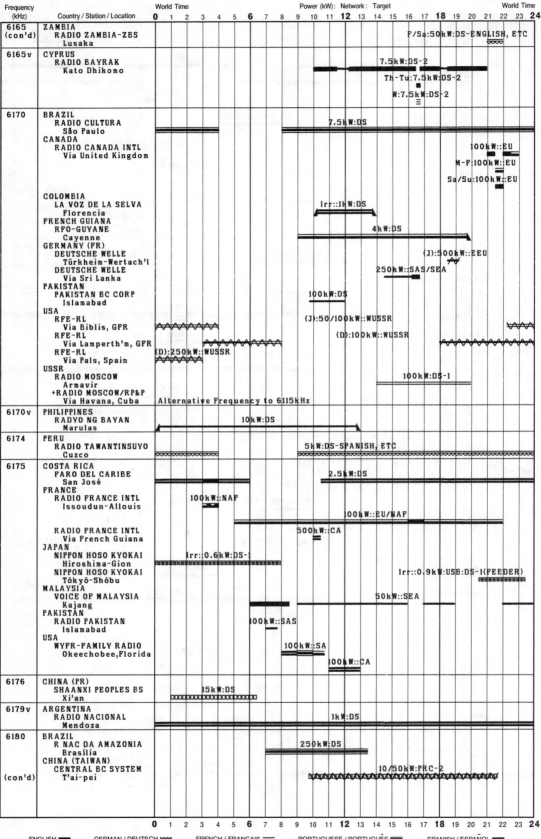

ENGLISH ▄▄ GERMAN / DEUTSCH ◊◊◊◊ FRENCH / FRANÇAIS ═══ PORTUGUESE / PORTUGUÊS ▬▬ SPANISH / ESPAÑOL ═══
ARABIC / عربى ═══ RUSSIAN / РУССКИИ ═══ CHINESE / 中文 □□□□ JAPANESE / 日本語 ▄▄▄ MULTILINGUAL ᴓᴓᴓ OTHER ▬▬
SUMMER ONLY (J) WINTER ONLY (D) JAMMING /\/\ or / or \ EARLIEST HEARD ◢ LATEST HEARD ◣ + TENTATIVE

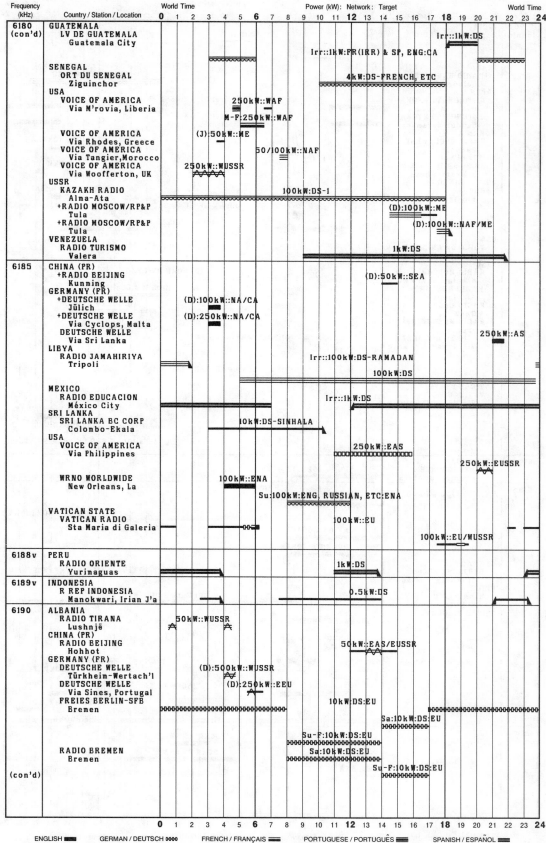

Frequency (kHz)	Country / Station / Location	Power (kW) : Network : Target
6180 (con'd)	**GUATEMALA**	
	LV DE GUATEMALA	Irr::1kW:DS
	Guatemala City	
		Irr::1kW:FR(IRR) & SP, ENG:CA
	SENEGAL	
	ORT DU SENEGAL	4kW:DS-FRENCH, ETC
	Ziguinchor	
	USA	
	VOICE OF AMERICA	250kW::WAF
	Via M'rovia, Liberia	
		M-F:250kW::WAF
	VOICE OF AMERICA	(J):50kW::ME
	Via Rhodes, Greece	
	VOICE OF AMERICA	50/100kW::NAF
	Via Tangier, Morocco	
	VOICE OF AMERICA	250kW::WUSSR
	Via Woofferton, UK	
	USSR	
	KAZAKH RADIO	100kW:DS-1
	Alma-Ata	
	+RADIO MOSCOW/RP&P	(D):100kW::ME
	Tula	
	+RADIO MOSCOW/RP&P	(D):100kW::NAF/ME
	Tula	
	VENEZUELA	
	RADIO TURISMO	1kW:DS
	Valera	
6185	**CHINA (PR)**	
	+RADIO BEIJING	(D):50kW::SEA
	Kunming	
	GERMANY (FR)	
	+DEUTSCHE WELLE	(D):100kW::NA/CA
	Jülich	
	+DEUTSCHE WELLE	(D):250kW::NA/CA
	Via Cyclops, Malta	
	DEUTSCHE WELLE	250kW::AS
	Via Sri Lanka	
	LIBYA	
	RADIO JAMAHIRIYA	Irr::100kW:DS-RAMADAN
	Tripoli	100kW:DS
	MEXICO	
	RADIO EDUCACION	Irr::1kW:DS
	México City	
	SRI LANKA	
	SRI LANKA BC CORP	10kW:DS-SINHALA
	Colombo-Ekala	
	USA	
	VOICE OF AMERICA	250kW::EAS
	Via Philippines	
		250kW::EUSSR
	WRNO WORLDWIDE	100kW::ENA
	New Orleans, La	
		Su:100kW:ENG, RUSSIAN, ETC:ENA
	VATICAN STATE	
	VATICAN RADIO	100kW::EU
	Sta Maria di Galeria	
		100kW::EU/WUSSR
6188v	**PERU**	
	RADIO ORIENTE	1kW:DS
	Yurimaguas	
6189v	**INDONESIA**	
	R REP INDONESIA	0.5kW:DS
	Manokwari, Irian J'a	
6190	**ALBANIA**	
	RADIO TIRANA	50kW::WUSSR
	Lushnjë	
	CHINA (PR)	
	RADIO BEIJING	50kW::EAS/EUSSR
	Hohhot	
	GERMANY (FR)	
	DEUTSCHE WELLE	(D):500kW::WUSSR
	Türkheim-Wertach'l	
	DEUTSCHE WELLE	(D):250kW::EEU
	Via Sines, Portugal	
	FREIES BERLIN-SFB	10kW:DS:EU
	Bremen	
		Sa:10kW:DS:EU
		Su-F:10kW:DS:EU
	RADIO BREMEN	Sa:10kW:DS:EU
	Bremen	
		Su-F:10kW:DS:EU
(con'd)		

6190 - 6195 kHz

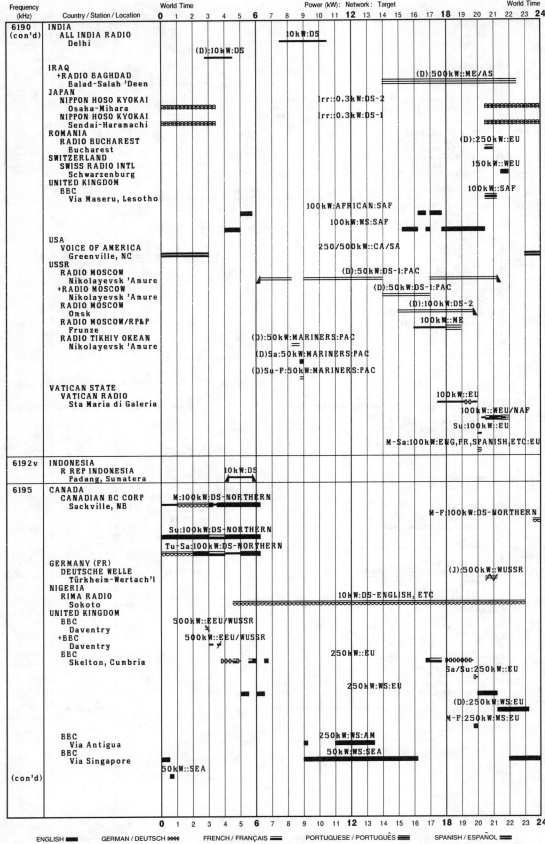

Frequency (kHz)	Country / Station / Location	Power (kW): Network: Target
6190 (con'd)	**INDIA**	
	ALL INDIA RADIO	10kW:DS
	Delhi	(D):10kW:DS
	IRAQ	
	+RADIO BAGHDAD	(D):500kW::ME/AS
	Balad-Salah 'Deen	
	JAPAN	
	NIPPON HOSO KYOKAI	Irr::0.3kW:DS-2
	Osaka-Mihara	
	NIPPON HOSO KYOKAI	Irr::0.3kW:DS-1
	Sendai-Haramachi	
	ROMANIA	
	RADIO BUCHAREST	(D):250kW::EU
	Bucharest	
	SWITZERLAND	
	SWISS RADIO INTL	150kW::WEU
	Schwarzenburg	
	UNITED KINGDOM	
	BBC	100kW::SAF
	Via Maseru, Lesotho	100kW:AFRICAN:SAF
		100kW:WS:SAF
	USA	
	VOICE OF AMERICA	250/500kW::CA/SA
	Greenville, NC	
	USSR	
	RADIO MOSCOW	(D):50kW:DS-1:PAC
	Nikolayevsk 'Amure	
	+RADIO MOSCOW	(D):50kW:DS-1:PAC
	Nikolayevsk 'Amure	
	RADIO MOSCOW	(D):100kW:DS-2
	Omsk	
	RADIO MOSCOW/RP&P	100kW::ME
	Frunze	
	RADIO TIKHIY OKEAN	(D):50kW:MARINERS:PAC
	Nikolayevsk 'Amure	(D)Sa:50kW:MARINERS:PAC
		(D)Su-F:50kW:MARINERS:PAC
	VATICAN STATE	
	VATICAN RADIO	100kW::EU
	Sta Maria di Galeria	100kW::WEU/NAF
		Su:100kW::EU
		M-Sa:100kW:ENG,FR,SPANISH,ETC:EU
6192v	**INDONESIA**	
	R REP INDONESIA	10kW:DS
	Padang, Sumatera	
6195	**CANADA**	
	CANADIAN BC CORP	M:100kW:DS-NORTHERN
	Sackville, NB	M-F:100kW:DS-NORTHERN
		Su:100kW:DS-NORTHERN
		Tu-Sa:100kW:DS-NORTHERN
	GERMANY (FR)	
	DEUTSCHE WELLE	(J):500kW::WUSSR
	Türkheim-Wertach'l	
	NIGERIA	
	RIMA RADIO	10kW:DS-ENGLISH, ETC
	Sokoto	
	UNITED KINGDOM	
	BBC	500kW::EEU/WUSSR
	Daventry	
	+BBC	500kW::EEU/WUSSR
	Daventry	
	BBC	250kW::EU
	Skelton, Cumbria	Sa/Su:250kW::EU
		250kW:WS:EU
		(D):250kW:WS:EU
		M-F:250kW:WS:EU
	BBC	250kW:WS:AM
	Via Antigua	
	BBC	50kW:WS:SEA
	Via Singapore	50kW::SEA
(con'd)		

ENGLISH ▄▄▄   GERMAN / DEUTSCH ०००   FRENCH / FRANÇAIS ▬▬   PORTUGUESE / PORTUGUÊS ▬▬   SPANISH / ESPAÑOL ▬▬

ARABIC /ﻋﺮﺑﻲ ▬▬   RUSSIAN / РУССКИИ ▬▬   CHINESE / 中文 ००००   JAPANESE / 日本語 ▄▄▄   MULTILINGUAL ▭▭▭▭   OTHER ▬▬▬

SUMMER ONLY (J)   WINTER ONLY (D)   JAMMING ⋀⋀ or / or \   EARLIEST HEARD ◢   LATEST HEARD ◣   + TENTATIVE

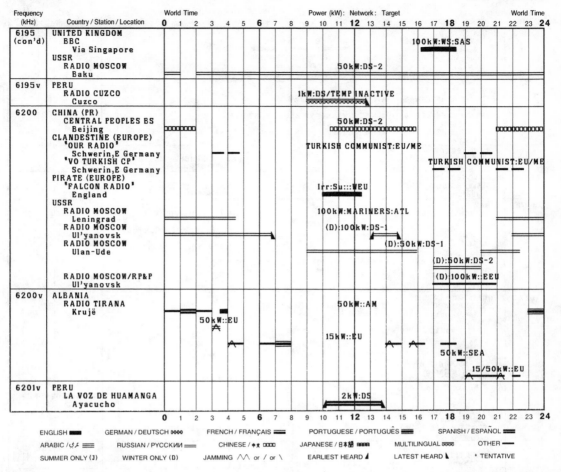

Frequency (kHz)	Country / Station / Location	World Time 0 1 2 3 4 5 6 7 8 9 10 11 12 13 14 15 16 17 18 19 20 21 22 23 24
6195 (con'd)	UNITED KINGDOM BBC Via Singapore	100kW:WS:SAS
	USSR RADIO MOSCOW Baku	50kW:DS-2
6195v	PERU RADIO CUZCO Cuzco	1kW:DS/TEMP INACTIVE
6200	CHINA (PR) CENTRAL PEOPLES BS Beijing	50kW:DS-2
	CLANDESTINE (EUROPE) 'OUR RADIO' Schwerin, E Germany	TURKISH COMMUNIST:EU/ME
	'VO TURKISH CP' Schwerin, E Germany	TURKISH COMMUNIST:EU/ME
	PIRATE (EUROPE) 'FALCON RADIO' England	Irr:Su:::WEU
	USSR RADIO MOSCOW Leningrad	100kW:MARINERS:ATL
	RADIO MOSCOW Ul'yanovsk	(D):100kW:DS-1
	RADIO MOSCOW Ulan-Ude	(D):50kW:DS-1
		(D):50kW:DS-2
	RADIO MOSCOW/RP&P Ul'yanovsk	(D):100kW:EEU
6200v	ALBANIA RADIO TIRANA Krujë	50kW::AM
		50kW::EU
		15kW::EU
		50kW::SEA
		15/50kW::EU
6201v	PERU LA VOZ DE HUAMANGA Ayacucho	2kW:DS

0 1 2 3 4 5 6 7 8 9 10 11 12 13 14 15 16 17 18 19 20 21 22 23 24

ENGLISH ■■■   GERMAN / DEUTSCH 0000   FRENCH / FRANÇAIS ■■■   PORTUGUESE / PORTUGUÊS ■■■   SPANISH / ESPAÑOL ■■■

ARABIC /ﻉﺭ ≡≡≡   RUSSIAN / РУССКИИ ===   CHINESE / ✦✗ 0000   JAPANESE / 日本語 ▧▧▧   MULTILINGUAL ▧▧▧   OTHER ——

SUMMER ONLY (J)   WINTER ONLY (D)   JAMMING ∧∧ or / or \   EARLIEST HEARD ◢   LATEST HEARD ◣   + TENTATIVE

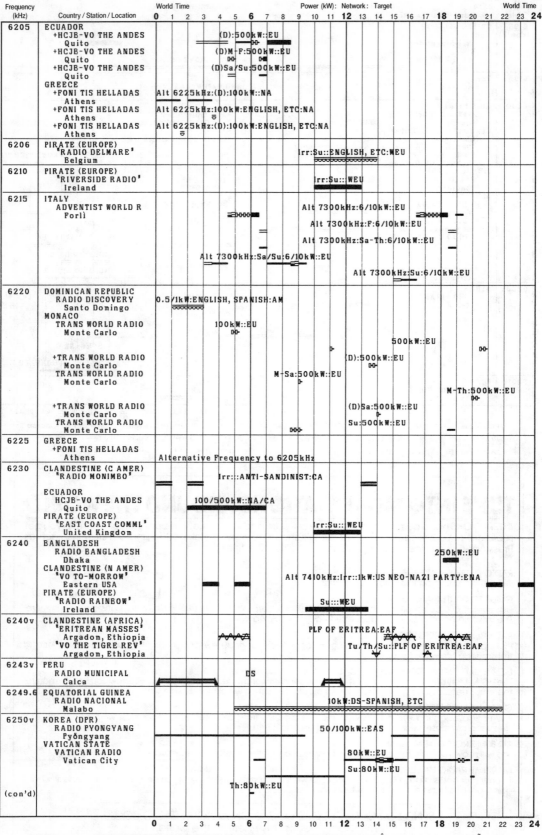

Frequency (kHz)	Country / Station / Location	World Time 0 ... 12 ... 24
6205	ECUADOR	
	+HCJB-VO THE ANDES Quito	(D):500kW::EU
	+HCJB-VO THE ANDES Quito	(D)M-F:500kW::EU
	+HCJB-VO THE ANDES Quito	(D)Sa/Su:500kW::EU
	GREECE	
	+FONI TIS HELLADAS Athens	Alt 6225kHz:(D):100kW::NA
	+FONI TIS HELLADAS Athens	Alt 6225kHz:100kW::ENGLISH, ETC:NA
	+FONI TIS HELLADAS Athens	Alt 6225kHz:(D):100kW::ENGLISH, ETC:NA
6206	PIRATE (EUROPE)	
	'RADIO DELMARE' Belgium	Irr:Su::ENGLISH, ETC:WEU
6210	PIRATE (EUROPE)	
	'RIVERSIDE RADIO' Ireland	Irr:Su:: WEU
6215	ITALY	
	ADVENTIST WORLD R Forlì	Alt 7300kHz:6/10kW::EU
		Alt 7300kHz:F:6/10kW::EU
		Alt 7300kHz:Sa-Th:6/10kW::EU
		Alt 7300kHz:Sa/Su:6/10kW::EU
		Alt 7300kHz:Su:6/10kW::EU
6220	DOMINICAN REPUBLIC	
	RADIO DISCOVERY Santo Domingo	0.5/1kW:ENGLISH, SPANISH:AM
	MONACO	
	TRANS WORLD RADIO Monte Carlo	100kW::EU
		500kW::EU
	+TRANS WORLD RADIO Monte Carlo	(D):500kW::EU
	TRANS WORLD RADIO Monte Carlo	M-Sa:500kW::EU
		M-Th:500kW::EU
	+TRANS WORLD RADIO Monte Carlo	(D)Sa:500kW::EU
	TRANS WORLD RADIO Monte Carlo	Su:500kW::EU
6225	GREECE	
	+FONI TIS HELLADAS Athens	Alternative Frequency to 6205kHz
6230	CLANDESTINE (C AMER)	
	'RADIO MONIMBO'	Irr:::ANTI-SANDINIST:CA
	ECUADOR	
	HCJB-VO THE ANDES Quito	100/500kW::NA/CA
	PIRATE (EUROPE)	
	'EAST COAST COMML' United Kingdom	Irr:Su:: WEU
6240	BANGLADESH	
	RADIO BANGLADESH Dhaka	250kW::EU
	CLANDESTINE (N AMER)	
	'VO TO-MORROW' Eastern USA	Alt 7410kHz:Irr::1kW:US NEO-NAZI PARTY:ENA
	PIRATE (EUROPE)	
	'RADIO RAINBOW' Ireland	Su:::WEU
6240v	CLANDESTINE (AFRICA)	
	'ERITREAN MASSES' Argadom, Ethiopia	PLF OF ERITREA:EAF
	'VO THE TIGRE REV' Argadom, Ethiopia	Tu/Th/Su:: PLF OF ERITREA:EAF
6243v	PERU	
	RADIO MUNICIPAL Calca	DS
6249.6	EQUATORIAL GUINEA	
	RADIO NACIONAL Malabo	10kW:DS-SPANISH, ETC
6250v	KOREA (DPR)	
	RADIO PYONGYANG Pyŏngyang	50/100kW::EAS
	VATICAN STATE	
	VATICAN RADIO Vatican City	80kW::EU
		Su:80kW::EU
(con'd)		Th:80kW::EU

ENGLISH ▮▮▮   GERMAN / DEUTSCH ◍◍◍◍   FRENCH / FRANÇAIS ═══   PORTUGUESE / PORTUGUÊS ▬▬▬   SPANISH / ESPAÑOL ▬▬▬
ARABIC / ﻉﺮﺑﻲ ≡≡≡   RUSSIAN / РУССКИИ ═══   CHINESE / 中文 ▯▯▯▯   JAPANESE / 日本語 ▬▬▬   MULTILINGUAL ▧▧▧   OTHER ▬▬
SUMMER ONLY (J)   WINTER ONLY (D)   JAMMING /\/\ or / or \   EARLIEST HEARD ◢   LATEST HEARD ◣   + TENTATIVE

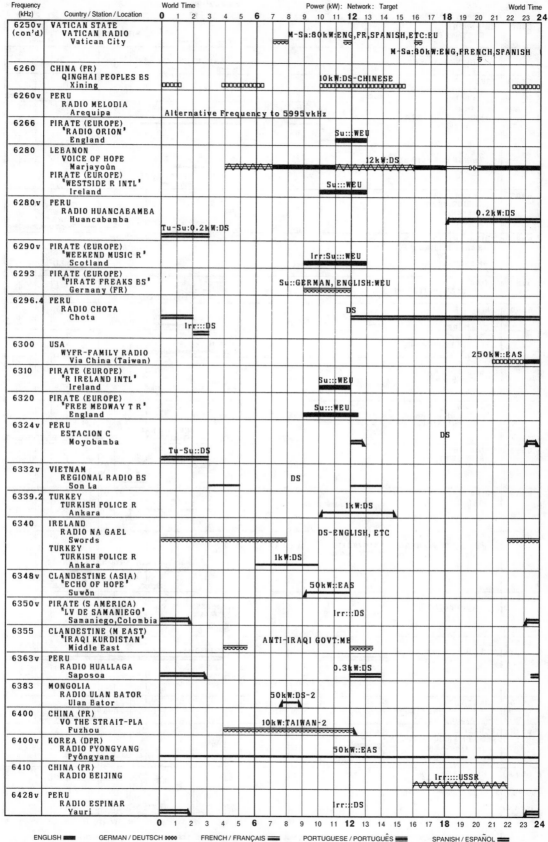

Frequency (kHz)	Country / Station / Location	Power (kW): Network: Target
6250v (con'd)	VATICAN STATE VATICAN RADIO Vatican City	M-Sa:80kW:ENG,FR,SPANISH,ETC:EU M-Sa:80kW:ENG,FRENCH,SPANISH
6260	CHINA (PR) QINGHAI PEOPLES BS Xining	10kW:DS-CHINESE
6260v	PERU RADIO MELODIA Arequipa	Alternative Frequency to 5995vkHz
6266	PIRATE (EUROPE) 'RADIO ORION' England	Su:::WEU
6280	LEBANON VOICE OF HOPE Marjayoûn	12kW:DS
	PIRATE (EUROPE) 'WESTSIDE R INTL' Ireland	Su:::WEU
6280v	PERU RADIO HUANCABAMBA Huancabamba	0.2kW:DS Tu-Su:0.2kW:DS
6290v	PIRATE (EUROPE) 'WEEKEND MUSIC R' Scotland	Irr:Su:::WEU
6293	PIRATE (EUROPE) 'PIRATE FREAKS BS' Germany (FR)	Su::GERMAN,ENGLISH:WEU
6296.4	PERU RADIO CHOTA Chota	DS Irr:::DS
6300	USA WYFR-FAMILY RADIO Via China (Taiwan)	250kW::EAS
6310	PIRATE (EUROPE) 'R IRELAND INTL' Ireland	Su:::WEU
6320	PIRATE (EUROPE) 'FREE MEDWAY T R' England	Su:::WEU
6324v	PERU ESTACION C Moyobamba	DS Tu-Su::DS
6332v	VIETNAM REGIONAL RADIO BS Son La	DS
6339.2	TURKEY TURKISH POLICE R Ankara	1kW:DS
6340	IRELAND RADIO NA GAEL Swords	DS-ENGLISH, ETC
	TURKEY TURKISH POLICE R Ankara	1kW:DS
6348v	CLANDESTINE (ASIA) 'ECHO OF HOPE' Suwŏn	50kW::EAS
6350v	PIRATE (S AMERICA) 'LV DE SAMANIEGO' Samaniego,Colombia	Irr:::DS
6355	CLANDESTINE (M EAST) 'IRAQI KURDISTAN' Middle East	ANTI-IRAQI GOVT:ME
6363v	PERU RADIO HUALLAGA Saposoa	0.3kW:DS
6383	MONGOLIA RADIO ULAN BATOR Ulan Bator	50kW:DS-2
6400	CHINA (PR) VO THE STRAIT-PLA Fuzhou	10kW:TAIWAN-2
6400v	KOREA (DPR) RADIO PYONGYANG Pyŏngyang	50kW::EAS
6410	CHINA (PR) RADIO BEIJING	Irr:::::USSR
6428v	PERU RADIO ESPINAR Yauri	Irr:::DS

World Time: 0 1 2 3 4 5 6 7 8 9 10 11 12 13 14 15 16 17 18 19 20 21 22 23 24

ENGLISH ■■■   GERMAN / DEUTSCH ₀₀₀₀   FRENCH / FRANÇAIS ═══   PORTUGUESE / PORTUGUÊS ═══   SPANISH / ESPAÑOL ■■■

ARABIC / ﻉﺭﻉ ═══   RUSSIAN / РУССКИИ ═══   CHINESE / 中文 □□□□   JAPANESE / 日本語 ▦▦▦   MULTILINGUAL ▦▦▦   OTHER ───

SUMMER ONLY (J)   WINTER ONLY (D)   JAMMING /\/\ or / or \   EARLIEST HEARD ◢   LATEST HEARD ◣   + TENTATIVE

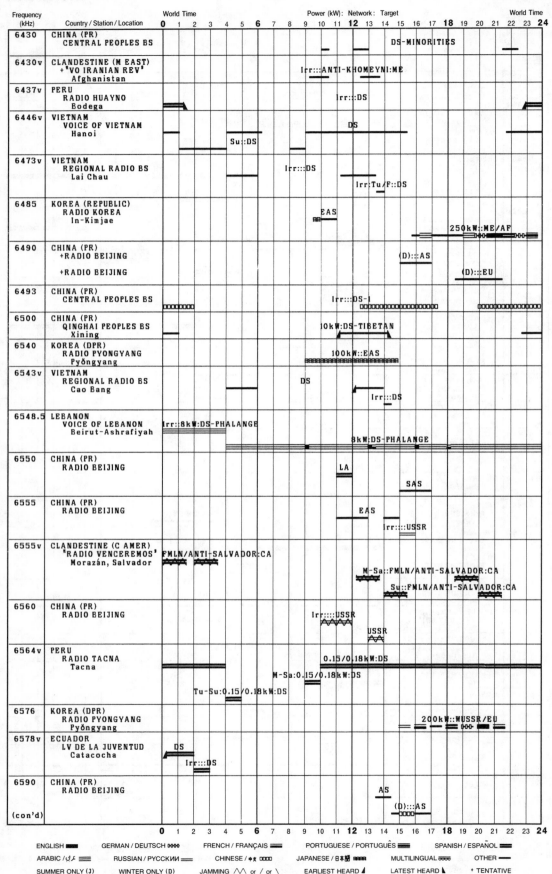

Frequency (kHz)	Country / Station / Location	World Time 0–24 / Power (kW): Network: Target
6430	CHINA (PR) CENTRAL PEOPLES BS	DS-MINORITIES
6430v	CLANDESTINE (M EAST) +"VO IRANIAN REV" Afghanistan	Irr:::ANTI-KHOMEYNI:ME
6437v	PERU RADIO HUAYNO Bodega	Irr:::DS
6446v	VIETNAM VOICE OF VIETNAM Hanoi	DS Su::DS
6473v	VIETNAM REGIONAL RADIO BS Lai Chau	Irr:::DS Irr:Tu/F::DS
6485	KOREA (REPUBLIC) RADIO KOREA In-Kimjae	EAS 250kW::ME/AF
6490	CHINA (PR) +RADIO BEIJING	(D):::AS
	+RADIO BEIJING	(D):::EU
6493	CHINA (PR) CENTRAL PEOPLES BS	Irr:::DS-1
6500	CHINA (PR) QINGHAI PEOPLES BS Xining	10kW:DS-TIBETAN
6540	KOREA (DPR) RADIO PYONGYANG Pyöngyang	100kW::EAS
6543v	VIETNAM REGIONAL RADIO BS Cao Bang	DS Irr:::DS
6548.5	LEBANON VOICE OF LEBANON Beirut-Ashrafiyah	Irr::8kW:DS-PHALANGE 8kW:DS-PHALANGE
6550	CHINA (PR) RADIO BEIJING	LA SAS
6555	CHINA (PR) RADIO BEIJING	EAS Irr::::USSR
6555v	CLANDESTINE (C AMER) "RADIO VENCEREMOS" Morazán, Salvador	FMLN/ANTI-SALVADOR:CA M-Sa::FMLN/ANTI-SALVADOR:CA Su::FMLN/ANTI-SALVADOR:CA
6560	CHINA (PR) RADIO BEIJING	Irr::::USSR USSR
6564v	PERU RADIO TACNA Tacna	0.15/0.18kW:DS M-Sa:0.15/0.18kW:DS Tu-Su:0.15/0.18kW:DS
6576	KOREA (DPR) RADIO PYONGYANG Pyöngyang	200kW::WUSSR/EU
6578v	ECUADOR LV DE LA JUVENTUD Catacocha	DS Irr:::DS
6590 (con'd)	CHINA (PR) RADIO BEIJING	AS (D):::AS

ENGLISH ▬   GERMAN / DEUTSCH ◊◊◊◊   FRENCH / FRANÇAIS ═   PORTUGUESE / PORTUGUÊS ≣   SPANISH / ESPAÑOL ▬

ARABIC /ﺀ ≣   RUSSIAN / РУССКИИ ═   CHINESE / 中文 ◻◻◻◻   JAPANESE / 日本語 ▩▩▩   MULTILINGUAL ▩▩▩   OTHER ▬

SUMMER ONLY (J)   WINTER ONLY (D)   JAMMING ∧∧ or / or \   EARLIEST HEARD ◢   LATEST HEARD ◣   + TENTATIVE

Frequency (kHz)	Country / Station / Location	World Time / Power (kW): Network: Target

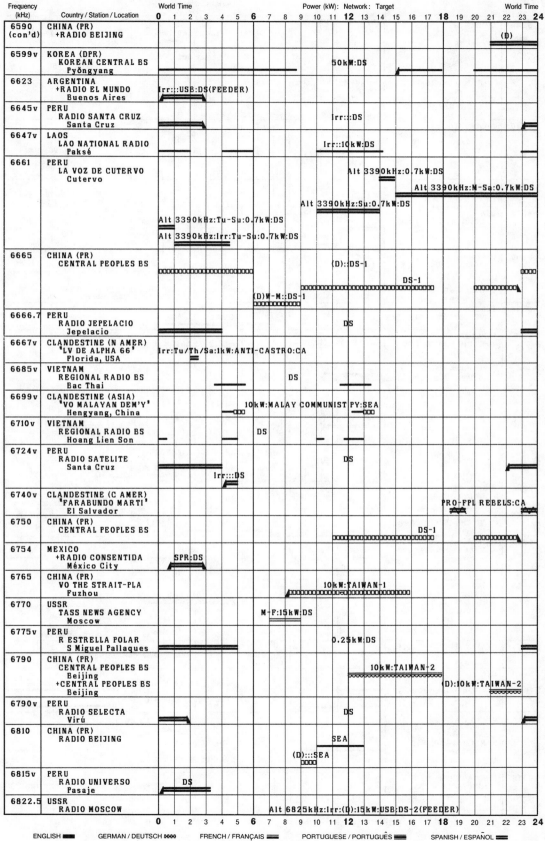

Frequency (kHz)	Country / Station / Location	Details
6590 (con'd)	CHINA (PR) +RADIO BEIJING	(D)
6599v	KOREA (DPR) KOREAN CENTRAL BS Pyŏngyang	50kW:DS
6623	ARGENTINA +RADIO EL MUNDO Buenos Aires	Irr:::USB:DS(FEEDER)
6645v	PERU RADIO SANTA CRUZ Santa Cruz	Irr:::DS
6647v	LAOS LAO NATIONAL RADIO Paksé	Irr::10kW:DS
6661	PERU LA VOZ DE CUTERVO Cutervo	Alt 3390kHz:0.7kW:DS / Alt 3390kHz:M-Sa:0.7kW:DS / Alt 3390kHz:Su:0.7kW:DS / Alt 3390kHz:Tu-Su:0.7kW:DS / Alt 3390kHz:Irr:Tu-Su:0.7kW:DS
6665	CHINA (PR) CENTRAL PEOPLES BS	(D)::DS-1 / DS-1 / (D)W-M::DS-1
6666.7	PERU RADIO JEPELACIO Jepelacio	DS
6667v	CLANDESTINE (N AMER) "LV DE ALPHA 66" Florida, USA	Irr:Tu/Th/Sa:1kW:ANTI-CASTRO:CA
6685v	VIETNAM REGIONAL RADIO BS Bac Thai	DS
6699v	CLANDESTINE (ASIA) "VO MALAYAN DEM'Y" Hengyang, China	10kW:MALAY COMMUNIST PY:SEA
6710v	VIETNAM REGIONAL RADIO BS Hoang Lien Son	DS
6724v	PERU RADIO SATELITE Santa Cruz	DS / Irr:::DS
6740v	CLANDESTINE (C AMER) "FARABUNDO MARTI" El Salvador	PRO-FPL REBELS:CA
6750	CHINA (PR) CENTRAL PEOPLES BS	DS-1
6754	MEXICO +RADIO CONSENTIDA México City	SPR:DS
6765	CHINA (PR) VO THE STRAIT-PLA Fuzhou	10kW:TAIWAN-1
6770	USSR TASS NEWS AGENCY Moscow	M-F:15kW:DS
6775v	PERU R ESTRELLA POLAR S Miguel Pallaques	0.25kW:DS
6790	CHINA (PR) CENTRAL PEOPLES BS Beijing +CENTRAL PEOPLES BS Beijing	10kW:TAIWAN-2 / (D):10kW:TAIWAN-2
6790v	PERU RADIO SELECTA Virú	DS
6810	CHINA (PR) RADIO BEIJING	SEA / (D):::SEA
6815v	PERU RADIO UNIVERSO Pasaje	DS
6822.5	USSR RADIO MOSCOW	Alt 6825kHz:Irr:(D):15kW:USB:DS-2(FEEDER)

ENGLISH ▬▬ GERMAN / DEUTSCH ◊◊◊◊ FRENCH / FRANÇAIS ═══ PORTUGUESE / PORTUGUÊS ▬▬ SPANISH / ESPAÑOL ▬▬
ARABIC / ﻋﺮﺑﻲ ═══ RUSSIAN / РУССКИИ ═══ CHINESE / 中文 ◊◊◊◊ JAPANESE / 日本語 ▬▬▬ MULTILINGUAL ▬▬▬ OTHER ▬▬
SUMMER ONLY (J) WINTER ONLY (D) JAMMING /\/\ or / or \ EARLIEST HEARD ◢ LATEST HEARD ◣ + TENTATIVE

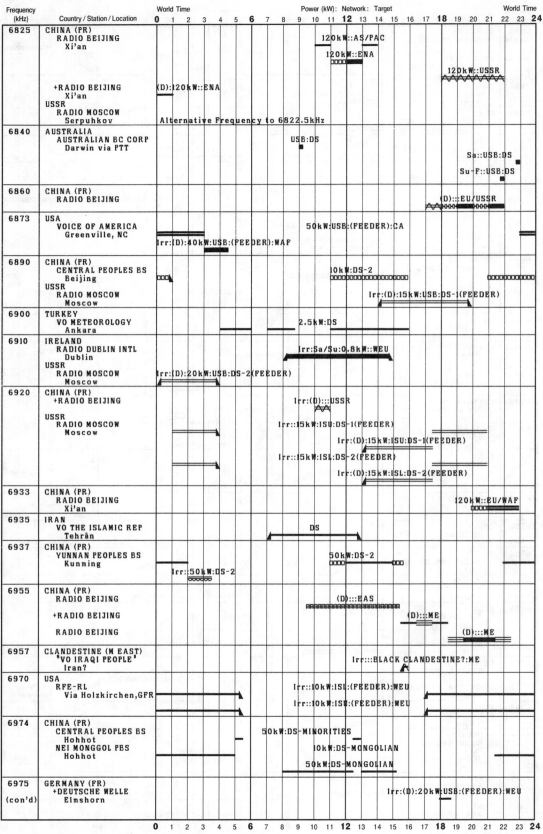

Frequency (kHz)	Country / Station / Location	Details
6825	CHINA (PR) RADIO BEIJING Xi'an	120kW::AS/PAC; 120kW::ENA; 120kW::USSR
	+RADIO BEIJING Xi'an	(D):120kW::ENA
	USSR RADIO MOSCOW Serpuhkov	Alternative Frequency to 6822.5kHz
6840	AUSTRALIA AUSTRALIAN BC CORP Darwin via PTT	USB:DS; Sa::USB:DS; Su-F::USB:DS
6860	CHINA (PR) RADIO BEIJING	(D):::EU/USSR
6873	USA VOICE OF AMERICA Greenville, NC	50kW:USB:(FEEDER):CA; Irr:(D):40kW:USB:(FEEDER):WAF
6890	CHINA (PR) CENTRAL PEOPLES BS Beijing	10kW:DS-2
	USSR RADIO MOSCOW Moscow	Irr:(D):15kW:USB:DS-1(FEEDER)
6900	TURKEY VO METEOROLOGY Ankara	2.5kW:DS
6910	IRELAND RADIO DUBLIN INTL Dublin	Irr:Sa/Su:0.8kW::WEU
	USSR RADIO MOSCOW Moscow	Irr:(D):20kW:USB:DS-2(FEEDER)
6920	CHINA (PR) +RADIO BEIJING	Irr:(D):::USSR
	USSR RADIO MOSCOW Moscow	Irr::15kW:ISU:DS-1(FEEDER); Irr:(D):15kW:ISU:DS-1(FEEDER); Irr::15kW:ISL:DS-2(FEEDER); Irr:(D):15kW:ISL:DS-2(FEEDER)
6933	CHINA (PR) RADIO BEIJING Xi'an	120kW::EU/WAF
6935	IRAN VO THE ISLAMIC REP Tehrân	DS
6937	CHINA (PR) YUNNAN PEOPLES BS Kunming	50kW:DS-2; Irr:50kW:DS-2
6955	CHINA (PR) RADIO BEIJING	(D):::EAS
	+RADIO BEIJING	(D):::ME
	RADIO BEIJING	(D):::ME
6957	CLANDESTINE (M EAST) "VO IRAQI PEOPLE" Iran?	Irr:::BLACK CLANDESTINE?:ME
6970	USA RFE-RL Via Holzkirchen,GFR	Irr::10kW:ISL:(FEEDER):WEU; Irr::10kW:ISU:(FEEDER):WEU
6974	CHINA (PR) CENTRAL PEOPLES BS Hohhot	50kW:DS-MINORITIES
	NEI MONGGOL PBS Hohhot	10kW:DS-MONGOLIAN; 50kW:DS-MONGOLIAN
6975 (con'd)	GERMANY (FR) +DEUTSCHE WELLE Elmshorn	Irr:(D):20kW:USB:(FEEDER):WEU

World Time: 0 1 2 3 4 5 6 7 8 9 10 11 12 13 14 15 16 17 18 19 20 21 22 23 24

Power (kW): Network: Target

ENGLISH ▰▰▰   GERMAN / DEUTSCH ০০০০   FRENCH / FRANÇAIS ▰▰▰   PORTUGUESE / PORTUGUÊS ▰▰▰   SPANISH / ESPAÑOL ▰▰▰
ARABIC /زيﺏ ▰▰▰   RUSSIAN / PУССКИИ ▰▰▰   CHINESE /◆☆ ০০০০   JAPANESE / 日本語 ▰▰▰   MULTILINGUAL ০০০০   OTHER ▬▬
SUMMER ONLY (J)   WINTER ONLY (D)   JAMMING ∧∧ or / or \   EARLIEST HEARD ◢   LATEST HEARD ◣   + TENTATIVE

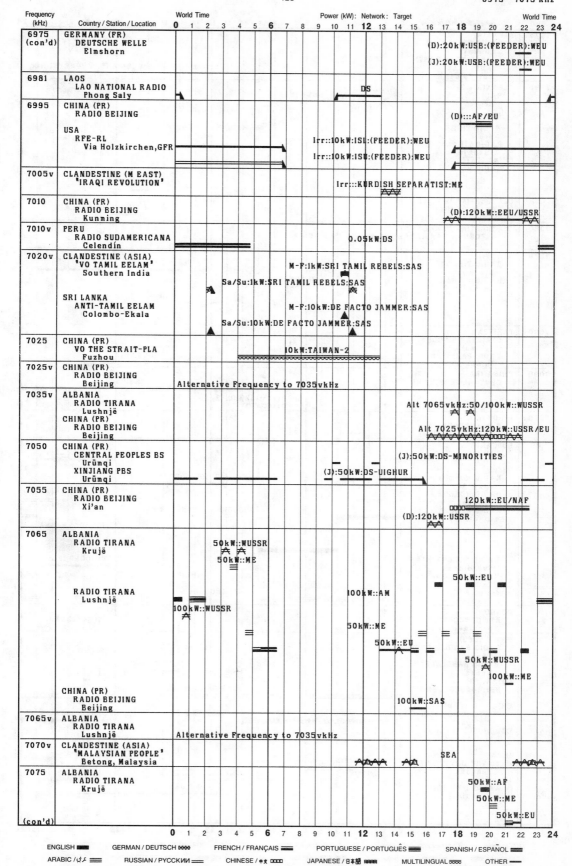

Frequency (kHz)	Country / Station / Location	World Time 0–24 / Power (kW) : Network : Target
6975 (con'd)	GERMANY (PR) DEUTSCHE WELLE Elmshorn	(D):20kW:USB:(FEEDER):WEU (J):20kW:USB:(FEEDER):WEU
6981	LAOS LAO NATIONAL RADIO Phong Saly	DS
6995	CHINA (PR) RADIO BEIJING	(D):::AF/EU
	USA RFE-RL Via Holzkirchen,GFR	Irr::10kW:ISL:(FEEDER):WEU Irr::10kW:ISU:(FEEDER):WEU
7005v	CLANDESTINE (M EAST) "IRAQI REVOLUTION"	Irr:::KURDISH SEPARATIST:ME
7010	CHINA (PR) RADIO BEIJING Kunming	(D):120kW::EEU/USSR
7010v	PERU RADIO SUDAMERICANA Celendín	0.05kW:DS
7020v	CLANDESTINE (ASIA) "VO TAMIL EELAM" Southern India	M-F:1kW:SRI TAMIL REBELS:SAS Sa/Su:1kW:SRI TAMIL REBELS:SAS
	SRI LANKA ANTI-TAMIL EELAM Colombo-Ekala	M-F:10kW:DE FACTO JAMMER:SAS Sa/Su:10kW:DE FACTO JAMMER:SAS
7025	CHINA (PR) VO THE STRAIT-PLA Fuzhou	10kW:TAIWAN-2
7025v	CHINA (PR) RADIO BEIJING Beijing	Alternative Frequency to 7035vkHz
7035v	ALBANIA RADIO TIRANA Lushnjë	Alt 7065vkHz:50/100kW::WUSSR
	CHINA (PR) RADIO BEIJING Beijing	Alt 7025vkHz:120kW::USSR/EU
7050	CHINA (PR) CENTRAL PEOPLES BS Urümqi	(J):50kW:DS-MINORITIES
	XINJIANG PBS Urümqi	(J):50kW:DS-UIGHUR
7055	CHINA (PR) RADIO BEIJING Xi'an	120kW::EU/NAF (D):120kW::USSR
7065	ALBANIA RADIO TIRANA Krujë	50kW::WUSSR 50kW::ME
	RADIO TIRANA Lushnjë	50kW::EU 100kW::AM 100kW::WUSSR 50kW::ME 50kW::EU 50kW::WUSSR 100kW::ME
	CHINA (PR) RADIO BEIJING Beijing	100kW::SAS
7065v	ALBANIA RADIO TIRANA Lushnjë	Alternative Frequency to 7035vkHz
7070v	CLANDESTINE (ASIA) "MALAYSIAN PEOPLE" Betong, Malaysia	SEA
7075	ALBANIA RADIO TIRANA Krujë	50kW::AF 50kW::ME 50kW::EU
(con'd)		

World Time: 0 1 2 3 4 5 6 7 8 9 10 11 12 13 14 15 16 17 18 19 20 21 22 23 24

ENGLISH ▬▬ GERMAN / DEUTSCH ◊◊◊◊ FRENCH / FRANÇAIS ≡≡ PORTUGUESE / PORTUGUÊS ≡≡ SPANISH / ESPAÑOL ▬

ARABIC /ﻉﺭﻉ ≡≡ RUSSIAN / РУССКИИ ≡≡ CHINESE / 中文 □□□□ JAPANESE / 日本語 ▬▬▬ MULTILINGUAL ▭▭▭ OTHER ▬

SUMMER ONLY (J) WINTER ONLY (D) JAMMING /\/\ or / or \ EARLIEST HEARD ◢ LATEST HEARD ◣ + TENTATIVE

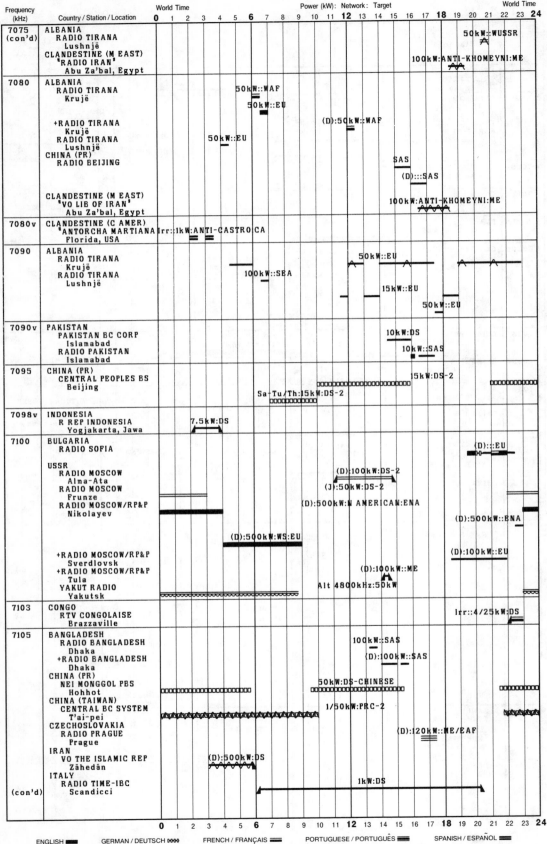

Frequency (kHz)	Country / Station / Location	Power (kW): Network: Target
7075 (con'd)	ALBANIA RADIO TIRANA Lushnjë	50kW::WUSSR
	CLANDESTINE (M EAST) 'RADIO IRAN' Abu Za'bal, Egypt	100kW:ANTI-KHOMEYNI:ME
7080	ALBANIA RADIO TIRANA Krujë	50kW::WAF / 50kW::EU
	+RADIO TIRANA Krujë	(D):50kW::WAF
	RADIO TIRANA Lushnjë	50kW::EU
	CHINA (PR) RADIO BEIJING	SAS / (D):::SAS
	CLANDESTINE (M EAST) 'VO LIB OF IRAN' Abu Za'bal, Egypt	100kW:ANTI-KHOMEYNI:ME
7080v	CLANDESTINE (C AMER) 'ANTORCHA MARTIANA' Florida, USA	Irr::1kW:ANTI-CASTRO:CA
7090	ALBANIA RADIO TIRANA Krujë	50kW::EU
	RADIO TIRANA Lushnjë	100kW::SEA / 15kW::EU / 50kW::EU
7090v	PAKISTAN PAKISTAN BC CORP Islamabad	10kW:DS
	RADIO PAKISTAN Islamabad	10kW::SAS
7095	CHINA (PR) CENTRAL PEOPLES BS Beijing	15kW:DS-2 / Sa-Tu/Th:15kW:DS-2
7098v	INDONESIA R REP INDONESIA Yogjakarta, Jawa	7.5kW:DS
7100	BULGARIA RADIO SOFIA	(D):::EU
	USSR RADIO MOSCOW Alma-Ata	(D):100kW:DS-2
	RADIO MOSCOW Frunze	(J):50kW:DS-2
	RADIO MOSCOW/RP&P Nikolayev	(D):500kW:N AMERICAN:ENA / (D):500kW::ENA
		(D):500kW:WS:EU
	+RADIO MOSCOW/RP&P Sverdlovsk	(D):100kW::EU
	+RADIO MOSCOW/RP&P Tula	(D):100kW::ME
	YAKUT RADIO Yakutsk	Alt 4800kHz:50kW
7103	CONGO RTV CONGOLAISE Brazzaville	Irr::4/25kW:DS
7105	BANGLADESH RADIO BANGLADESH Dhaka	100kW::SAS
	+RADIO BANGLADESH Dhaka	(D):100kW::SAS
	CHINA (PR) NEI MONGGOL PBS Hohhot	50kW:DS-CHINESE
	CHINA (TAIWAN) CENTRAL BC SYSTEM T'ai-pei	1/50kW:PRC-2
	CZECHOSLOVAKIA RADIO PRAGUE Prague	(D):120kW::ME/EAF
	IRAN VO THE ISLAMIC REP Zāhedān	(D):500kW:DS
(con'd)	ITALY RADIO TIME-IBC Scandicci	1kW:DS

ENGLISH ▬▬ GERMAN / DEUTSCH ◊◊◊◊ FRENCH / FRANÇAIS ▭▭ PORTUGUESE / PORTUGUÊS ▬▬ SPANISH / ESPAÑOL ▬▬

ARABIC / ✲ ≡ RUSSIAN / РУССКИИ ═ CHINESE / ✲✲ ▭▭ JAPANESE / 日本語 ▬▬ MULTILINGUAL ◊◊◊◊ OTHER ▬

SUMMER ONLY (J) WINTER ONLY (D) JAMMING /\/\ or / or \ EARLIEST HEARD ◢ LATEST HEARD ◣ + TENTATIVE

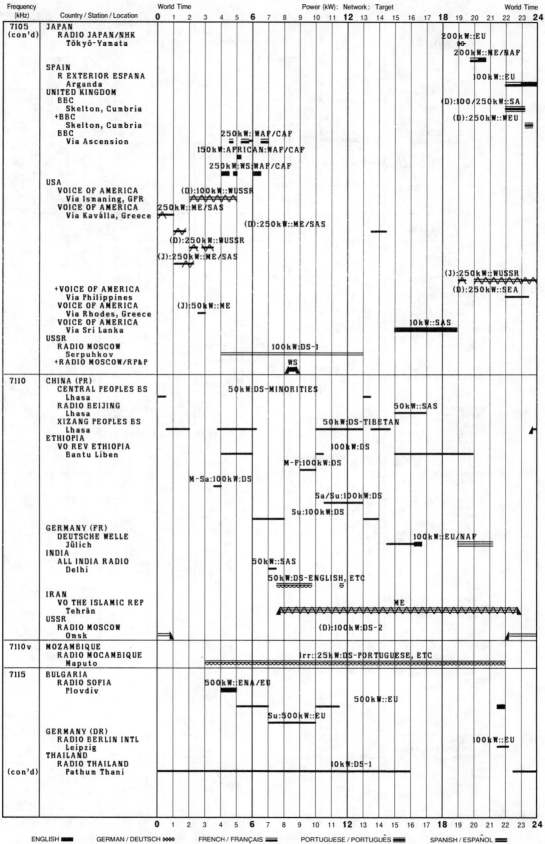

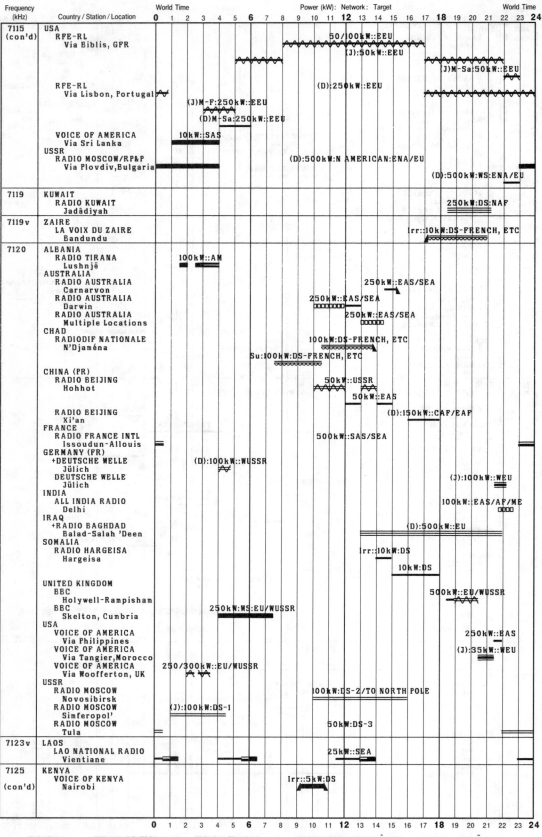

Frequency (kHz)	Country / Station / Location	World Time

7115 (con'd) — USA

RFE-RL Via Biblis, GFR
- 50/100kW::EEU
- (J):50kW::EEU
- (J)M-Sa:50kW::EEU

RFE-RL Via Lisbon, Portugal
- (D):250kW::EEU
- (J)M-F:250kW::EEU
- (D)M-Sa:250kW::EEU

VOICE OF AMERICA Via Sri Lanka — 10kW::SAS

USSR RADIO MOSCOW/RP&P Via Plovdiv,Bulgaria
- (D):500kW:N AMERICAN:ENA/EU
- (D):500kW:WS:ENA/EU

7119 — KUWAIT
RADIO KUWAIT Jadādiyah — 250kW:DS:NAF

7119 v — ZAIRE
LA VOIX DU ZAIRE Bandundu — Irr:10kW:DS-FRENCH, ETC

7120 — ALBANIA
RADIO TIRANA Lushnjë — 100kW::AM

AUSTRALIA
RADIO AUSTRALIA Carnarvon — 250kW::EAS/SEA
RADIO AUSTRALIA Darwin — 250kW::EAS/SEA
RADIO AUSTRALIA Multiple Locations — 250kW::EAS/SEA

CHAD
RADIODIF NATIONALE N'Djaména
- 100kW:DS-FRENCH, ETC
- Su:100kW:DS-FRENCH, ETC

CHINA (PR)
RADIO BEIJING Hohhot
- 50kW::USSR
- 50kW::EAS
RADIO BEIJING Xi'an — (D):150kW::CAF/EAF

FRANCE
RADIO FRANCE INTL Issoudun-Allouis — 500kW::SAS/SEA

GERMANY (FR)
+DEUTSCHE WELLE Jülich — (D):100kW::WUSSR
DEUTSCHE WELLE Jülich — (J):100kW::WEU

INDIA
ALL INDIA RADIO Delhi — 100kW::EAS/AF/ME

IRAQ
+RADIO BAGHDAD Balad-Salah 'Deen — (D):500kW::EU

SOMALIA
RADIO HARGEISA Hargeisa
- Irr::10kW:DS
- 10kW:DS

UNITED KINGDOM
BBC Holywell-Rampisham — 500kW::EU/WUSSR
BBC Skelton, Cumbria — 250kW:WS:EU/WUSSR

USA
VOICE OF AMERICA Via Philippines — 250kW::EAS
VOICE OF AMERICA Via Tangier,Morocco — (J):35kW::WEU
VOICE OF AMERICA Via Woofferton, UK — 250/300kW::EU/WUSSR

USSR
RADIO MOSCOW Novosibirsk — 100kW:DS-2/TO NORTH POLE
RADIO MOSCOW Simferopol' — (J):100kW:DS-1
RADIO MOSCOW Tula — 50kW:DS-3

7123 v — LAOS
LAO NATIONAL RADIO Vientiane — 25kW::SEA

7125 (con'd) — KENYA
VOICE OF KENYA Nairobi — Irr::5kW:DS

World Time: 0 1 2 3 4 5 6 7 8 9 10 11 12 13 14 15 16 17 18 19 20 21 22 23 24

Power (kW):   Network: Target

World Time: 0 1 2 3 4 5 6 7 8 9 10 11 12 13 14 15 16 17 18 19 20 21 22 23 24

ENGLISH ▬▬   GERMAN / DEUTSCH ◊◊◊◊   FRENCH / FRANÇAIS ▭▭   PORTUGUESE / PORTUGUÊS ▬▬   SPANISH / ESPAÑOL ▬▬

ARABIC / عربي ▭▭   RUSSIAN / РУССКИИ ▬▬   CHINESE / 中文 ◊◊◊◊   JAPANESE / 日本語 ▬▬   MULTILINGUAL ▭▭   OTHER ▬▬

SUMMER ONLY (J)   WINTER ONLY (D)   JAMMING ∧∧ or / or \   EARLIEST HEARD ◢   LATEST HEARD ◣   + TENTATIVE

Frequency (kHz)	Country / Station / Location

World Time / Power (kW) / Network / World Time
0 1 2 3 4 5 6 7 8 9 10 11 12 13 ... 17 18 19 20 21 22 23 24

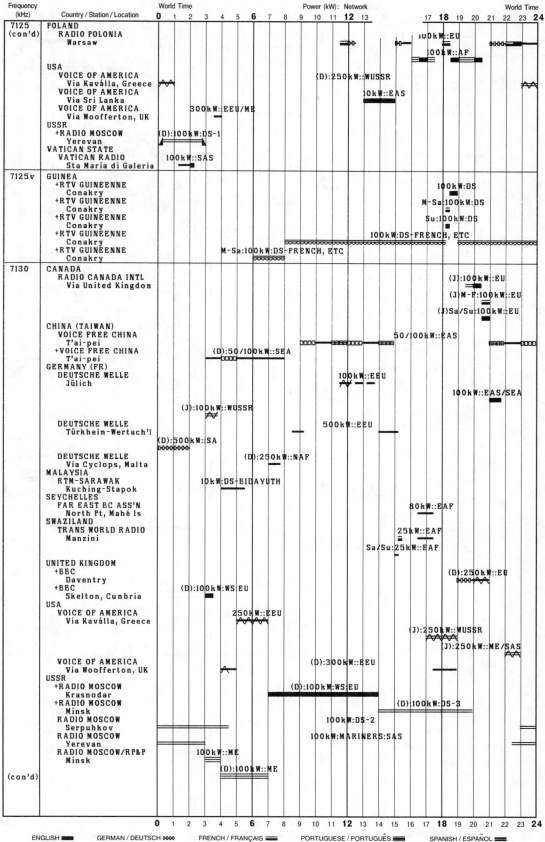

7125 (con'd)

POLAND
RADIO POLONIA
Warsaw
100kW::EU
100kW::AF

USA
VOICE OF AMERICA
Via Kaválla, Greece
(D):250kW::WUSSR
VOICE OF AMERICA
Via Sri Lanka
10kW::EAS
VOICE OF AMERICA
Via Woofferton, UK
300kW::EEU/ME
USSR
+RADIO MOSCOW
Yerevan
(D):100kW:DS-1
VATICAN STATE
VATICAN RADIO
Sta Maria di Galeria
100kW::SAS

7125v

GUINEA
+RTV GUINEENNE
Conakry
100kW:DS
+RTV GUINEENNE
Conakry
M-Sa:100kW:DS
+RTV GUINEENNE
Conakry
Su:100kW:DS
+RTV GUINEENNE
Conakry
100kW:DS-FRENCH, ETC
+RTV GUINEENNE
Conakry
M-Sa:100kW:DS-FRENCH, ETC

7130

CANADA
RADIO CANADA INTL
Via United Kingdom
(J):100kW::EU
(J)M-F:100kW::EU
(J)Sa/Su:100kW::EU

CHINA (TAIWAN)
VOICE FREE CHINA
T'ai-pei
50/100kW::EAS
+VOICE FREE CHINA
T'ai-pei
(D):50/100kW::SEA
GERMANY (FR)
DEUTSCHE WELLE
Jülich
100kW::EEU
100kW::EAS/SEA

DEUTSCHE WELLE
Türkheim-Wertach'l
(J):100kW::WUSSR
500kW::EEU
(D):500kW::SA

DEUTSCHE WELLE
Via Cyclops, Malta
(D):250kW::NAF
MALAYSIA
RTM-SARAWAK
Kuching-Stapok
10kW:DS-BIDAYUTH
SEYCHELLES
FAR EAST BC ASS'N
North Pt, Mahé Is
80kW::EAF
SWAZILAND
TRANS WORLD RADIO
Manzini
25kW::EAF
Sa/Su:25kW::EAF

UNITED KINGDOM
+BBC
Daventry
(D):250kW::EU
+BBC
Skelton, Cumbria
(D):100kW:WS:EU
USA
VOICE OF AMERICA
Via Kaválla, Greece
250kW::EEU
(J):250kW::WUSSR
(J):250kW::ME/SAS

VOICE OF AMERICA
Via Woofferton, UK
(D):300kW::EEU
USSR
+RADIO MOSCOW
Krasnodar
(D):100kW:WS:EU
+RADIO MOSCOW
Minsk
(D):100kW:DS-3
RADIO MOSCOW
Serpuhkov
100kW:DS-2
RADIO MOSCOW
Yerevan
100kW:MARINERS:SAS
RADIO MOSCOW/RP&P
Minsk
100kW::ME
(D):100kW::ME

(con'd)

0 1 2 3 4 5 6 7 8 9 10 11 12 13 14 15 16 17 18 19 20 21 22 23 24

ENGLISH ▬▬ GERMAN / DEUTSCH ০০০০ FRENCH / FRANÇAIS ▬▬ PORTUGUESE / PORTUGUÊS ▬▬ SPANISH / ESPAÑOL ▬▬

ARABIC / ىبرع ▬▬ RUSSIAN / РУССКИИ ▬▬ CHINESE / 中文 ০০০০ JAPANESE / 日本語 ▬▬ MULTILINGUAL ▬▬ OTHER ▬▬

SUMMER ONLY (J) WINTER ONLY (D) JAMMING /\/\ or / or \ EARLIEST HEARD ◢ LATEST HEARD ◣ + TENTATIVE

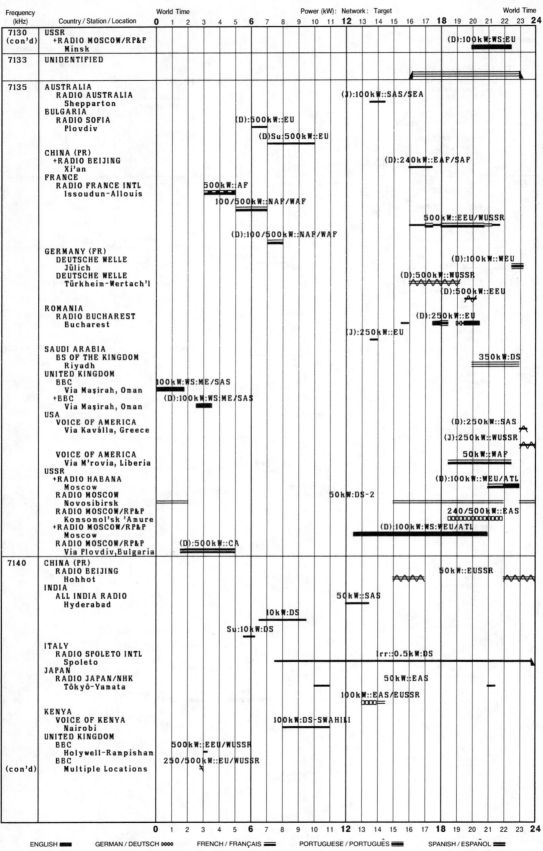

Frequency (kHz)	Country / Station / Location	Power (kW): Network: Target
7130 (con'd)	USSR +RADIO MOSCOW/RP&P Minsk	(D):100kW:WS:EU
7133	UNIDENTIFIED	
7135	AUSTRALIA RADIO AUSTRALIA Shepparton	(J):100kW::SAS/SEA
	BULGARIA RADIO SOFIA Plovdiv	(D):500kW::EU / (D)Su:500kW::EU
	CHINA (PR) +RADIO BEIJING Xi'an	(D):240kW::EAF/SAF
	FRANCE RADIO FRANCE INTL Issoudun-Allouis	500kW::AF / 100/500kW::NAF/WAF / 500kW::EEU/WUSSR / (D):100/500kW::NAF/WAF
	GERMANY (FR) DEUTSCHE WELLE Jülich	(D):100kW::WEU
	DEUTSCHE WELLE Türkheim-Wertach'l	(D):500kW::WUSSR / (D):500kW::EEU
	ROMANIA RADIO BUCHAREST Bucharest	(D):250kW::EU / (J):250kW::EU
	SAUDI ARABIA BS OF THE KINGDOM Riyadh	350kW:DS
	UNITED KINGDOM BBC Via Maşirah, Oman	100kW:WS:ME/SAS
	+BBC Via Maşirah, Oman	(D):100kW:WS:ME/SAS
	USA VOICE OF AMERICA Via Kaválla, Greece	(D):250kW::SAS / (J):250kW::WUSSR
	VOICE OF AMERICA Via M'rovia, Liberia	50kW::WAF
	USSR +RADIO HABANA Moscow	(D):100kW::WEU/ATL
	RADIO MOSCOW Novosibirsk	50kW:DS-2
	RADIO MOSCOW/RP&P Komsomol'sk 'Amure	240/500kW::EAS
	+RADIO MOSCOW/RP&P Moscow	(D):100kW:WS:WEU/ATL
	RADIO MOSCOW/RP&P Via Plovdiv,Bulgaria	(D):500kW::CA
7140	CHINA (PR) RADIO BEIJING Hohhot	50kW::EUSSR
	INDIA ALL INDIA RADIO Hyderabad	50kW::SAS
		10kW:DS / Su:10kW:DS
	ITALY RADIO SPOLETO INTL Spoleto	Irr::0.5kW:DS
	JAPAN RADIO JAPAN/NHK Tōkyō-Yamata	50kW::EAS / 100kW::EAS/EUSSR
	KENYA VOICE OF KENYA Nairobi	100kW:DS-SWAHILI
	UNITED KINGDOM BBC Holywell-Rampisham	500kW::EEU/WUSSR
(con'd)	BBC Multiple Locations	250/500kW::EU/WUSSR

ENGLISH ▬   GERMAN / DEUTSCH ▯▯▯▯   FRENCH / FRANÇAIS ≣   PORTUGUESE / PORTUGUÊS ≣   SPANISH / ESPAÑOL ≣

ARABIC / ‏جبر‎ ≣   RUSSIAN / РУССКИИ ▬   CHINESE / 中文 ▯▯▯▯   JAPANESE / 日本語 ▬▬   MULTILINGUAL ▭▭▭   OTHER ▬

SUMMER ONLY (J)   WINTER ONLY (D)   JAMMING /\/\ or / or \   EARLIEST HEARD ◢   LATEST HEARD ◣   + TENTATIVE

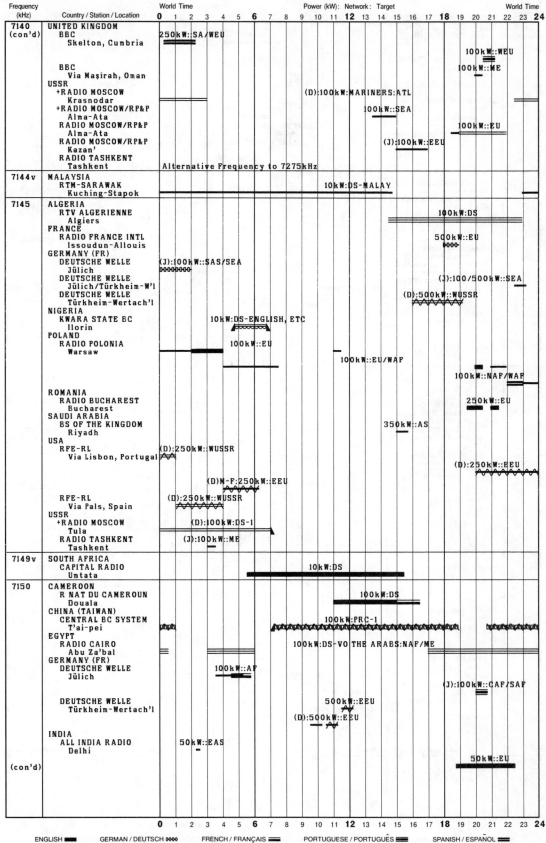

Frequency (kHz)	Country / Station / Location	Schedule notes
7140 (con'd)	UNITED KINGDOM	
	BBC — Skelton, Cumbria	250kW:SA/WEU
		100kW::WEU
	BBC — Via Maşirah, Oman	100kW::ME
	USSR	
	+RADIO MOSCOW — Krasnodar	(D):100kW:MARINERS:ATL
	+RADIO MOSCOW/RP&P — Alma-Ata	100kW::SEA
	RADIO MOSCOW/RP&P — Alma-Ata	100kW::EU
	RADIO MOSCOW/RP&P — Kazan'	(J):100kW::EEU
	RADIO TASHKENT — Tashkent	Alternative Frequency to 7275kHz
7144v	MALAYSIA	
	RTM-SARAWAK — Kuching-Stapok	10kW:DS-MALAY
7145	ALGERIA	
	RTV ALGERIENNE — Algiers	100kW:DS
	FRANCE	
	RADIO FRANCE INTL — Issoudun-Allouis	500kW::EU
	GERMANY (FR)	
	DEUTSCHE WELLE — Jülich	(J):100kW::SAS/SEA
	DEUTSCHE WELLE — Jülich/Türkheim-W'l	(J):100/500kW::SEA
	DEUTSCHE WELLE — Türkheim-Wertach'l	(D):500kW::WUSSR
	NIGERIA	
	KWARA STATE BC — Ilorin	10kW:DS-ENGLISH, ETC
	POLAND	
	RADIO POLONIA — Warsaw	100kW::EU / 100kW::EU/WAF / 100kW::NAF/WAF
	ROMANIA	
	RADIO BUCHAREST — Bucharest	250kW::EU
	SAUDI ARABIA	
	BS OF THE KINGDOM — Riyadh	350kW::AS
	USA	
	RFE-RL — Via Lisbon, Portugal	(D):250kW::WUSSR / (D):250kW::EEU
		(D)M-F:250kW::EEU
	RFE-RL — Via Pals, Spain	(D):250kW::WUSSR
	USSR	
	+RADIO MOSCOW — Tula	(D):100kW:DS-1
	RADIO TASHKENT — Tashkent	(J):100kW::ME
7149v	SOUTH AFRICA	
	CAPITAL RADIO — Umtata	10kW:DS
7150	CAMEROON	
	R NAT DU CAMEROUN — Douala	100kW:DS
	CHINA (TAIWAN)	
	CENTRAL BC SYSTEM — T'ai-pei	100kW:PRC-1
	EGYPT	
	RADIO CAIRO — Abu Za'bal	100kW:DS-VO THE ARABS:NAF/ME
	GERMANY (FR)	
	DEUTSCHE WELLE — Jülich	100kW::AF / (J):100kW::CAF/SAF
	DEUTSCHE WELLE — Türkheim-Wertach'l	500kW::EEU / (D):500kW::EEU
	INDIA	
	ALL INDIA RADIO — Delhi	50kW::EAS / 50kW::EU
(con'd)		

Legend:

ENGLISH ▬▬ GERMAN / DEUTSCH ◇◇◇◇ FRENCH / FRANÇAIS ═══ PORTUGUESE / PORTUGUÊS ═══ SPANISH / ESPAÑOL ═══

ARABIC / عربي ═══ RUSSIAN / РУССКИЙ ═══ CHINESE / 中文 ◇◇◇◇ JAPANESE / 日本語 ▬▬ MULTILINGUAL ▭▭ OTHER ▬▬

SUMMER ONLY (J)   WINTER ONLY (D)   JAMMING ∧∧ or / or \   EARLIEST HEARD ◢   LATEST HEARD ◣   + TENTATIVE

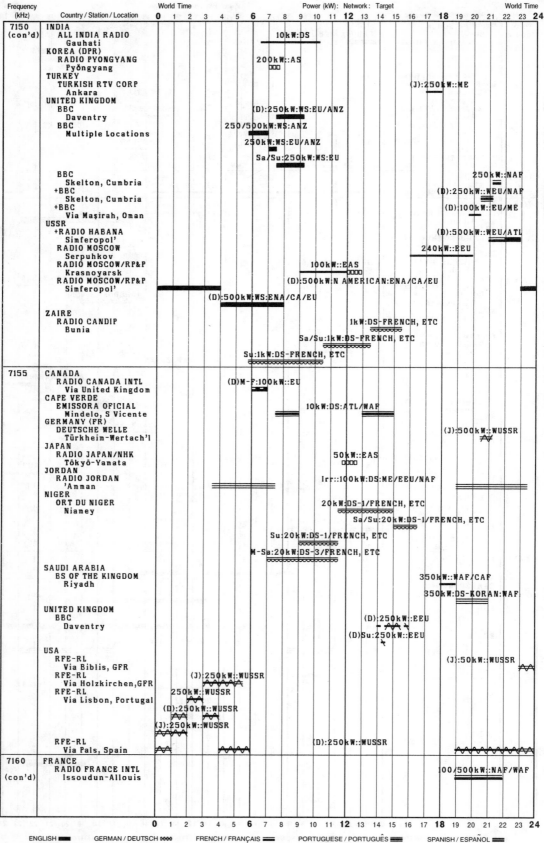

Frequency (kHz)	Country / Station / Location	World Time / Power (kW): Network: Target
7150 (con'd)	INDIA — ALL INDIA RADIO — Gauhati	10kW:DS
	KOREA (DPR) — RADIO PYONGYANG — Pyŏngyang	200kW::AS
	TURKEY — TURKISH RTV CORP — Ankara	(J):250kW::ME
	UNITED KINGDOM — BBC — Daventry	(D):250kW:WS:EU/ANZ
	BBC — Multiple Locations	250/500kW:WS:ANZ; 250kW:WS:EU/ANZ; Sa/Su:250kW:WS:EU
	BBC — Skelton, Cumbria	250kW::NAF
	+BBC — Skelton, Cumbria	(D):250kW::WEU/NAF
	+BBC — Via Maşirah, Oman	(D):100kW::EU/ME
	USSR — +RADIO HABANA — Simferopol'	(D):500kW::WEU/ATL
	RADIO MOSCOW — Serpuhkov	240kW::EEU
	RADIO MOSCOW/RP&P — Krasnoyarsk	100kW::EAS
	RADIO MOSCOW/RP&P — Simferopol'	(D):500kW:N AMERICAN:ENA/CA/EU; (D):500kW:WS:ENA/CA/EU
	ZAIRE — RADIO CANDIP — Bunia	1kW:DS-FRENCH, ETC; Sa/Su:1kW:DS-FRENCH, ETC; Su:1kW:DS-FRENCH, ETC
7155	CANADA — RADIO CANADA INTL — Via United Kingdom	(D)M-F:100kW::EU
	CAPE VERDE — EMISSORA OFICIAL — Mindelo, S Vicente	10kW:DS:ATL/WAF
	GERMANY (FR) — DEUTSCHE WELLE — Türkheim-Wertach'l	(J):500kW::WUSSR
	JAPAN — RADIO JAPAN/NHK — Tōkyō-Yamata	50kW::EAS
	JORDAN — RADIO JORDAN — 'Amman	Irr::100kW:DS:ME/EEU/NAF
	NIGER — ORT DU NIGER — Niamey	20kW:DS-1/FRENCH, ETC; Sa/Su:20kW:DS-1/FRENCH, ETC; Su:20kW:DS-1/FRENCH, ETC; M-Sa:20kW:DS-3/FRENCH, ETC
	SAUDI ARABIA — BS OF THE KINGDOM — Riyadh	350kW::WAF/CAF; 350kW:DS-KORAN:WAF
	UNITED KINGDOM — BBC — Daventry	(D):250kW::EEU; (D)Su:250kW::EEU
	USA — RFE-RL — Via Biblis, GFR	(J):50kW::WUSSR
	RFE-RL — Via Holzkirchen,GFR	(J):250kW::WUSSR
	RFE-RL — Via Lisbon, Portugal	250kW::WUSSR; (D):250kW::WUSSR; (J):250kW::WUSSR
	RFE-RL — Via Pals, Spain	(D):250kW::WUSSR
7160 (con'd)	FRANCE — RADIO FRANCE INTL — Issoudun-Allouis	100/500kW::NAF/WAF

ENGLISH ▬▬   GERMAN / DEUTSCH ✻✻✻✻   FRENCH / FRANÇAIS ═══   PORTUGUESE / PORTUGUÊS ▤▤▤   SPANISH / ESPAÑOL ═══

ARABIC / ﻉﺭﺏ ═══   RUSSIAN / РУССКИЙ ═══   CHINESE / ✻✻ ✻✻✻✻   JAPANESE / 日本語 ✻✻✻✻   MULTILINGUAL ✻✻✻✻   OTHER ▬▬

SUMMER ONLY (J)   WINTER ONLY (D)   JAMMING /\/\ or / or \   EARLIEST HEARD ◢   LATEST HEARD ◣   + TENTATIVE

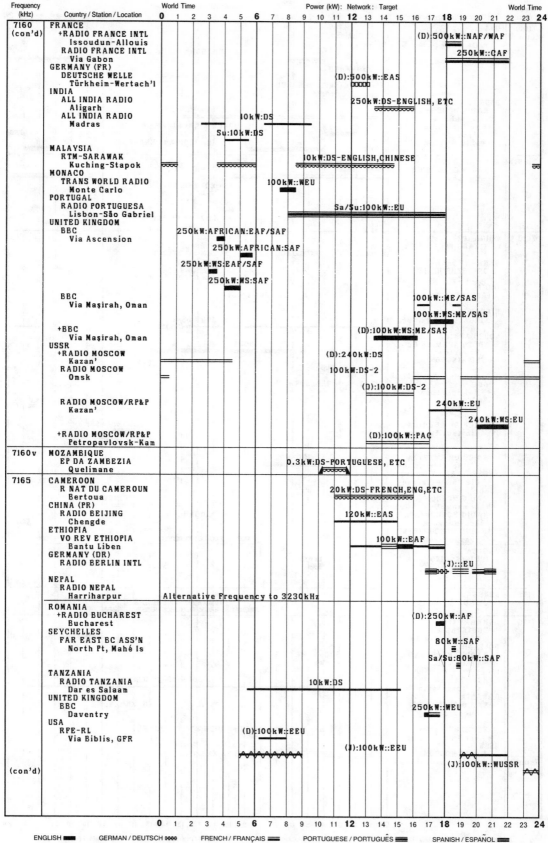

Frequency (kHz)	Country / Station / Location	Power (kW) : Network : Target — World Time (0–24)
7160 (con'd)	**FRANCE** +RADIO FRANCE INTL Issoudun-Allouis	(D):500kW::NAF/WAF
	RADIO FRANCE INTL Via Gabon	250kW::CAF
	GERMANY (FR) DEUTSCHE WELLE Türkheim-Wertach'l	(D):500kW::EAS
	INDIA ALL INDIA RADIO Aligarh	250kW:DS-ENGLISH, ETC
	ALL INDIA RADIO Madras	10kW:DS
		Su:10kW:DS
	MALAYSIA RTM-SARAWAK Kuching-Stapok	10kW:DS-ENGLISH,CHINESE
	MONACO TRANS WORLD RADIO Monte Carlo	100kW::WEU
	PORTUGAL RADIO PORTUGUESA Lisbon-São Gabriel	Sa/Su:100kW::EU
	UNITED KINGDOM BBC Via Ascension	250kW:AFRICAN:EAF/SAF
		250kW:AFRICAN:SAF
		250kW:WS:EAF/SAF
		250kW:WS:SAF
	BBC Via Maşirah, Oman	100kW::ME/SAS
		100kW:WS:ME/SAS
	+BBC Via Maşirah, Oman	(D):100kW:WS:ME/SAS
	USSR +RADIO MOSCOW Kazan'	(D):240kW:DS
	RADIO MOSCOW Omsk	100kW:DS-2
		(D):100kW:DS-2
	RADIO MOSCOW/RP&P Kazan'	240kW::EU
		240kW:WS:EU
	+RADIO MOSCOW/RP&P Petropavlovsk-Kam	(D):100kW::PAC
7160v	**MOZAMBIQUE** EP DA ZAMBEZIA Quelimane	0.3kW:DS-PORTUGUESE, ETC
7165	**CAMEROON** R NAT DU CAMEROUN Bertoua	20kW:DS-FRENCH,ENG,ETC
	CHINA (PR) RADIO BEIJING Chengde	120kW::EAS
	ETHIOPIA VO REV ETHIOPIA Bantu Liben	100kW::EAF
	GERMANY (DR) RADIO BERLIN INTL	(J):::EU
	NEPAL RADIO NEPAL Harriharpur	Alternative Frequency to 3230kHz
	ROMANIA +RADIO BUCHAREST Bucharest	(D):250kW::AF
	SEYCHELLES FAR EAST BC ASS'N North Pt, Mahé Is	80kW::SAF
		Sa/Su:80kW::SAF
	TANZANIA RADIO TANZANIA Dar es Salaam	10kW:DS
	UNITED KINGDOM BBC Daventry	250kW::WEU
	USA RFE-RL Via Biblis, GFR	(D):100kW::EEU
		(J):100kW::EEU
(con'd)		(J):100kW::WUSSR

ENGLISH ▬▬ GERMAN / DEUTSCH ◊◊◊◊ FRENCH / FRANÇAIS ▬▬ PORTUGUESE / PORTUGUÊS ▬▬ SPANISH / ESPAÑOL ▬▬
ARABIC / ﻉﺮﺑ ≡ RUSSIAN / РУССКИИ ▬ CHINESE / 中文 ◊◊◊◊ JAPANESE / 日本語 ▬▬▬ MULTILINGUAL ▭▭▭ OTHER ▬▬
SUMMER ONLY (J)   WINTER ONLY (D)   JAMMING /\/\ or / or \   EARLIEST HEARD ◢   LATEST HEARD ◣   + TENTATIVE

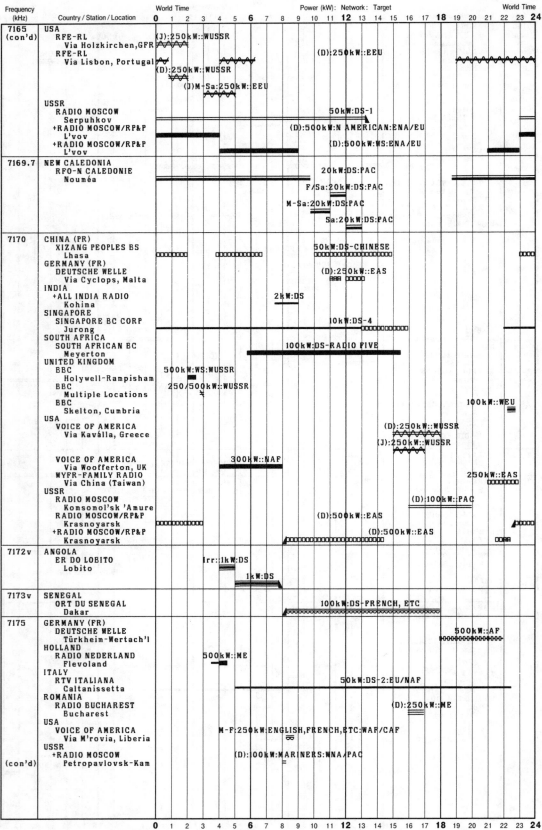

Frequency (kHz)	Country / Station / Location	Power (kW): Network: Target
7165 (con'd)	USA	
	RFE-RL Via Holzkirchen,GFR	(J):250kW::WUSSR
	RFE-RL Via Lisbon, Portugal	(D):250kW::EEU
		(D):250kW::WUSSR
		(J)M-Sa:250kW:EEU
	USSR	
	RADIO MOSCOW Serpuhkov	50kW:DS-1
	+RADIO MOSCOW/RP&P L'vov	(D):500kW:N AMERICAN:ENA/EU
	+RADIO MOSCOW/RP&P L'vov	(D):500kW:WS:ENA/EU
7169.7	NEW CALEDONIA	
	RFO-N CALEDONIE Nouméa	20kW:DS:PAC
		F/Sa:20kW:DS:PAC
		M-Sa:20kW:DS:PAC
		Sa:20kW:DS:PAC
7170	CHINA (PR)	
	XIZANG PEOPLES BS Lhasa	50kW:DS-CHINESE
	GERMANY (FR)	
	DEUTSCHE WELLE Via Cyclops, Malta	(D):250kW::EAS
	INDIA	
	+ALL INDIA RADIO Kohima	2kW:DS
	SINGAPORE	
	SINGAPORE BC CORP Jurong	10kW:DS-4
	SOUTH AFRICA	
	SOUTH AFRICAN BC Meyerton	100kW:DS-RADIO FIVE
	UNITED KINGDOM	
	BBC Holywell-Rampisham	500kW:WS:WUSSR
	BBC Multiple Locations	250/500kW::WUSSR
	BBC Skelton, Cumbria	100kW::WEU
	USA	
	VOICE OF AMERICA Via Kaválla, Greece	(D):250kW::WUSSR
		(J):250kW::WUSSR
	VOICE OF AMERICA Via Woofferton, UK	300kW::NAF
	WYFR-FAMILY RADIO Via China (Taiwan)	250kW::EAS
	USA	
	RADIO MOSCOW Komsomol'sk 'Amure	(D):100kW:PAC
	RADIO MOSCOW/RP&P Krasnoyarsk	(D):500kW::EAS
	+RADIO MOSCOW/RP&P Krasnoyarsk	(D):500kW::EAS
7172v	ANGOLA	
	ER DO LOBITO Lobito	Irr:1kW:DS
		1kW:DS
7173v	SENEGAL	
	ORT DU SENEGAL Dakar	100kW:DS-FRENCH, ETC
7175	GERMANY (FR)	
	DEUTSCHE WELLE Türkheim-Wertach'l	500kW::AF
	HOLLAND	
	RADIO NEDERLAND Flevoland	500kW::ME
	ITALY	
	RTV ITALIANA Caltanissetta	50kW:DS-2:EU/NAF
	ROMANIA	
	RADIO BUCHAREST Bucharest	(D):250kW::ME
	USA	
	VOICE OF AMERICA Via M'rovia, Liberia	M-F:250kW:ENGLISH,FRENCH,ETC:WAF/CAF
	USSR	
	+RADIO MOSCOW Petropavlovsk-Kam	(D):00kW:MARINERS:WNA/PAC
(con'd)		

ENGLISH ▰▰▰   GERMAN / DEUTSCH ◌◌◌◌   FRENCH / FRANÇAIS ▤▤▤   PORTUGUESE / PORTUGUÊS ▦▦▦   SPANISH / ESPAÑOL ▤▤▤

ARABIC / ﻉﺭﺏ ≡   RUSSIAN / РУССКИИ ═   CHINESE / ●✕ ◌◌◌◌   JAPANESE / 日本語 ▨▨▨   MULTILINGUAL ▩▩▩   OTHER ▬

SUMMER ONLY (J)   WINTER ONLY (D)   JAMMING /\/\ or / or \   EARLIEST HEARD ◢   LATEST HEARD ◣   + TENTATIVE

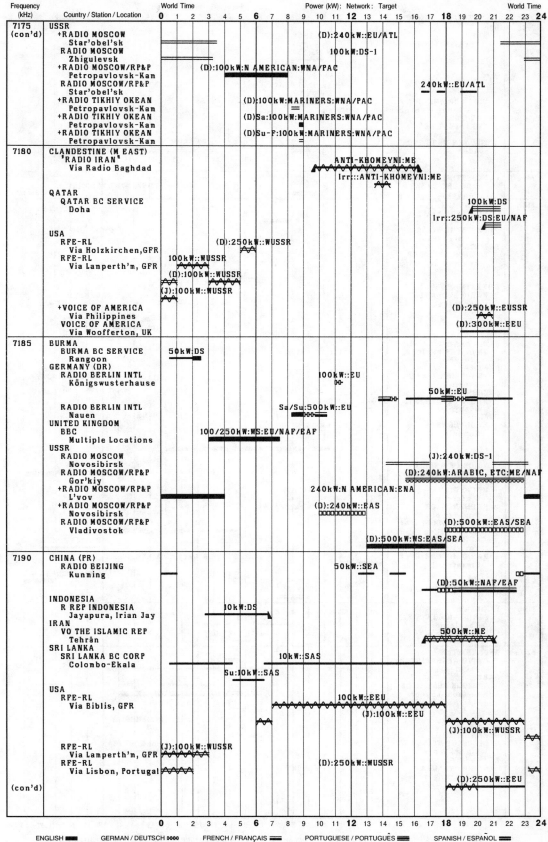

Frequency (kHz)	Country / Station / Location	Power (kW): Network: Target
7175 (con'd)	USSR +RADIO MOSCOW / Star'obel'sk	(D):240kW::EU/ATL
	RADIO MOSCOW / Zhigulevsk	100kW:DS-1
	+RADIO MOSCOW/RP&P / Petropavlovsk-Kam	(D):100kW:N AMERICAN:WNA/PAC
	RADIO MOSCOW/RP&P / Star'obel'sk	240kW::EU/ATL
	+RADIO TIKHIY OKEAN / Petropavlovsk-Kam	(D):100kW:MARINERS:WNA/PAC
	+RADIO TIKHIY OKEAN / Petropavlovsk-Kam	(D)Sa:100kW:MARINERS:WNA/PAC
	+RADIO TIKHIY OKEAN / Petropavlovsk-Kam	(D)Su-F:100kW:MARINERS:WNA/PAC
7180	CLANDESTINE (M EAST) "RADIO IRAN" / Via Radio Baghdad	ANTI-KHOMEYNI:ME / Irr::ANTI-KHOMEYNI:ME
	QATAR / QATAR BC SERVICE / Doha	100kW:DS / Irr::250kW:DS:EU/NAF
	USA / RFE-RL / Via Holzkirchen,GFR	(D):250kW::WUSSR
	RFE-RL / Via Lamperth'm, GFR	100kW::WUSSR / (D):100kW::WUSSR / (J):100kW::WUSSR
	+VOICE OF AMERICA / Via Philippines	(D):250kW::EUSSR
	VOICE OF AMERICA / Via Woofferton, UK	(D):300kW::EEU
7185	BURMA / BURMA BC SERVICE / Rangoon	50kW:DS
	GERMANY (DR) / RADIO BERLIN INTL / Königswusterhause	100kW::EU / 50kW::EU
	RADIO BERLIN INTL / Nauen	Sa/Su:500kW::EU
	UNITED KINGDOM / BBC / Multiple Locations	100/250kW:WS:EU/NAF/EAF
	USSR / RADIO MOSCOW / Novosibirsk	(J):240kW:DS-1
	RADIO MOSCOW/RP&P / Gor'kiy	(D):240kW:ARABIC, ETC:ME/NAF
	+RADIO MOSCOW/RP&P / L'vov	240kW:N AMERICAN:ENA
	+RADIO MOSCOW/RP&P / Novosibirsk	(D):240kW::EAS
	RADIO MOSCOW/RP&P / Vladivostok	(D):500kW::EAS/SEA / (D):500kW:WS:EAS/SEA
7190	CHINA (PR) / RADIO BEIJING / Kunming	50kW::SEA / (D):50kW::NAF/EAF
	INDONESIA / R REP INDONESIA / Jayapura, Irian Jay	10kW:DS
	IRAN / VO THE ISLAMIC REP / Tehrän	500kW::ME
	SRI LANKA / SRI LANKA BC CORP / Colombo-Ekala	10kW::SAS / Su:10kW::SAS
	USA / RFE-RL / Via Biblis, GFR	100kW::EEU / (J):100kW::EEU / (J):100kW::WUSSR
	RFE-RL / Via Lamperth'm, GFR	(J):100kW::WUSSR
	RFE-RL / Via Lisbon, Portugal	(D):250kW::WUSSR
(con'd)		(D):250kW::EEU

World Time: 0 1 2 3 4 5 6 7 8 9 10 11 12 13 14 15 16 17 18 19 20 21 22 23 24

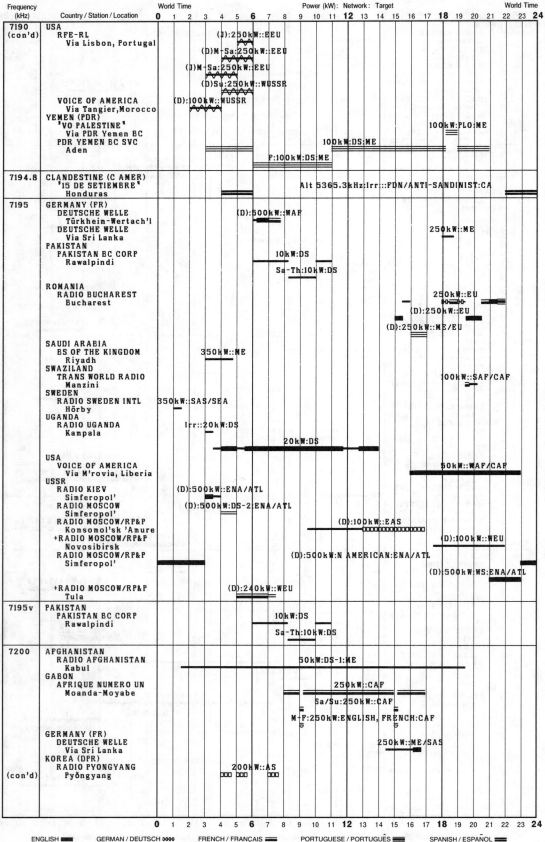

Frequency (kHz)	Country / Station / Location	0 1 2 3 4 5 6 7 8 9 10 11 **12** 13 14 15 16 17 **18** 19 20 21 22 23 **24**
7190 (con'd)	USA RFE-RL Via Lisbon, Portugal	(J):250kW::EEU / (D)M-Sa:250kW::EEU / (J)M-Sa:250kW::EEU / (D)Su:250kW::WUSSR
	VOICE OF AMERICA Via Tangier,Morocco	(D):100kW::WUSSR
	YEMEN (PDR) 'VO PALESTINE' Via PDR Yemen BC	100kW:PLO:ME
	PDR YEMEN BC SVC Aden	100kW:DS:ME / F:100kW:DS:ME
7194.8	CLANDESTINE (C AMER) '15 DE SETIEMBRE' Honduras	Alt 5365.3kHz:Irr::PDN/ANTI-SANDINIST:CA
7195	GERMANY (FR) DEUTSCHE WELLE Türkheim-Wertach'l	(D):500kW::WAF
	DEUTSCHE WELLE Via Sri Lanka	250kW::ME
	PAKISTAN PAKISTAN BC CORP Rawalpindi	10kW:DS / Sa-Th:10kW:DS
	ROMANIA RADIO BUCHAREST Bucharest	250kW::EU / (D):250kW::EU / (D):250kW::ME/EU
	SAUDI ARABIA BS OF THE KINGDOM Riyadh	350kW::ME
	SWAZILAND TRANS WORLD RADIO Manzini	100kW::SAF/CAF
	SWEDEN RADIO SWEDEN INTL Hörby	350kW::SAS/SEA
	UGANDA RADIO UGANDA Kampala	Irr::20kW:DS / 20kW:DS
	USA VOICE OF AMERICA Via M'rovia, Liberia	50kW::WAF/CAF
	USSR RADIO KIEV Simferopol'	(D):500kW::ENA/ATL
	RADIO MOSCOW Simferopol'	(D):500kW:DS-2:ENA/ATL
	RADIO MOSCOW/RP&P Komsomol'sk 'Amure	(D):100kW::EAS
	+RADIO MOSCOW/RP&P Novosibirsk	(D):100kW::WEU
	RADIO MOSCOW/RP&P Simferopol'	(D):500kW:N AMERICAN:ENA/ATL / (D):500kW:WS:ENA/ATL
	+RADIO MOSCOW/RP&P Tula	(D):240kW::WEU
7195v	PAKISTAN PAKISTAN BC CORP Rawalpindi	10kW:DS / Sa-Th:10kW:DS
7200	AFGHANISTAN RADIO AFGHANISTAN Kabul	50kW:DS-1:ME
	GABON AFRIQUE NUMERO UN Moanda-Moyabe	250kW::CAF / Sa/Su:250kW::CAF / M-F:250kW:ENGLISH, FRENCH:CAF
	GERMANY (FR) DEUTSCHE WELLE Via Sri Lanka	250kW::ME/SAS
(con'd)	KOREA (DPR) RADIO PYONGYANG Pyŏngyang	200kW::AS

0 1 2 3 4 5 **6** 7 8 9 10 11 **12** 13 14 15 16 17 **18** 19 20 21 22 23 **24**

ENGLISH ▬▬   GERMAN / DEUTSCH ◊◊◊◊   FRENCH / FRANÇAIS ═══   PORTUGUESE / PORTUGUÊS ▬▬   SPANISH / ESPAÑOL ▬▬

ARABIC / ﻲﺑﺮﻋ ═══   RUSSIAN / РУССКИИ ═══   CHINESE / 中文 ▭▭▭▭   JAPANESE / 日本語 ▬▬▬   MULTILINGUAL ▭▭▭   OTHER ▬▬

SUMMER ONLY (J)   WINTER ONLY (D)   JAMMING ∧∧ or / or \   EARLIEST HEARD ◢   LATEST HEARD ◣   + TENTATIVE

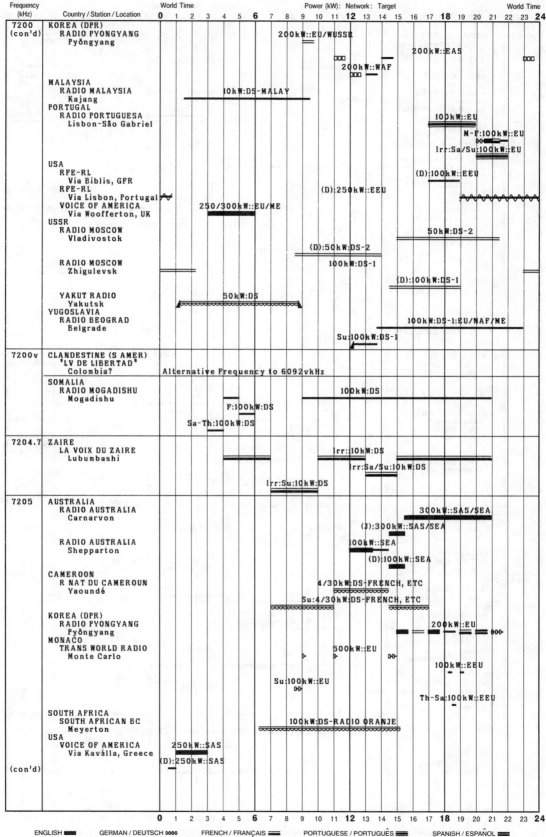

Frequency (kHz) | Country / Station / Location | World Time | Power (kW): Network: Target | World Time

7200 (con'd) — KOREA (DPR) RADIO PYONGYANG Pyŏngyang — 200kW::EU/WUSSR — 200kW::EAS — 200kW::WAF

MALAYSIA RADIO MALAYSIA Kajang — 10kW:DS-MALAY

PORTUGAL RADIO PORTUGUESA Lisbon-São Gabriel — 100kW::EU — M-F:100kW::EU — Irr:Sa/Su:100kW::EU

USA RFE-RL Via Biblis, GFR — (D):100kW::EEU
RFE-RL Via Lisbon, Portugal — (D):250kW::EEU
VOICE OF AMERICA Via Woofferton, UK — 250/300kW::EU/ME

USSR RADIO MOSCOW Vladivostok — 50kW:DS-2 — (D):50kW:DS-2
RADIO MOSCOW Zhigulevsk — 100kW:DS-1 — (D):100kW:DS-1
YAKUT RADIO Yakutsk — 50kW:DS

YUGOSLAVIA RADIO BEOGRAD Belgrade — 100kW:DS-1:EU/NAF/ME — Su:100kW:DS-1

7200v — CLANDESTINE (S AMER) "LV DE LIBERTAD" Colombia? — Alternative Frequency to 6092vkHz

SOMALIA RADIO MOGADISHU Mogadishu — 100kW:DS — F:100kW:DS — Sa-Th:100kW:DS

7204.7 — ZAIRE LA VOIX DU ZAIRE Lubumbashi — Irr:10kW:DS — Irr:Sa/Su:10kW:DS — Irr:Su:10kW:DS

7205 — AUSTRALIA RADIO AUSTRALIA Carnarvon — 300kW::SAS/SEA — (J):300kW::SAS/SEA
RADIO AUSTRALIA Shepparton — 100kW::SEA — (D):100kW::SEA

CAMEROON R NAT DU CAMEROUN Yaoundé — 4/30kW:DS-FRENCH, ETC — Su:4/30kW:DS-FRENCH, ETC

KOREA (DPR) RADIO PYONGYANG Pyŏngyang — 200kW::EU

MONACO TRANS WORLD RADIO Monte Carlo — 500kW::EU — 100kW::EEU — Su:100kW::EU — Th-Sa:100kW::EEU

SOUTH AFRICA SOUTH AFRICAN BC Meyerton — 100kW:DS-RADIO ORANJE

USA VOICE OF AMERICA Via Kaválla, Greece — 250kW::SAS — (D):250kW::SAS

(con'd)

ENGLISH ▪▪▪   GERMAN / DEUTSCH ०००   FRENCH / FRANÇAIS ══   PORTUGUESE / PORTUGUÊS ═══   SPANISH / ESPAÑOL ══

ARABIC / ‌ ‌ ‌ ≡   RUSSIAN / РУССКИИ ══   CHINESE / 中文 ००००   JAPANESE / 日本語 ▩▩▩   MULTILINGUAL ▩▩▩   OTHER ▬▬

SUMMER ONLY (J)   WINTER ONLY (D)   JAMMING /\/\ or / or \   EARLIEST HEARD ◢   LATEST HEARD ◣   + TENTATIVE

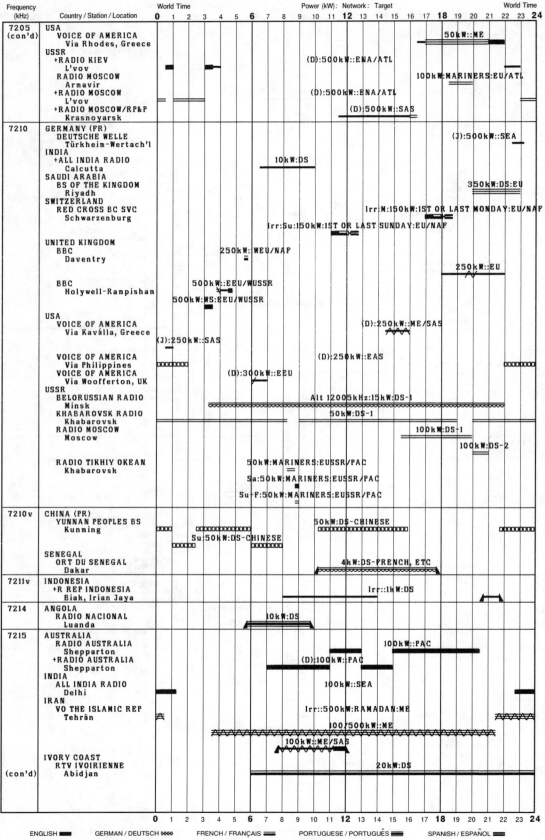

Frequency (kHz)   Country / Station / Location   World Time   Power (kW): Network: Target   World Time
0 1 2 3 4 5 6 7 8 9 10 11 12 13 14 15 16 17 18 19 20 21 22 23 24

7205 (con'd)
USA
VOICE OF AMERICA
Via Rhodes, Greece — 50kW::ME
USSR
+RADIO KIEV
L'vov — (D):500kW::ENA/ATL
RADIO MOSCOW
Armavir — 100kW:MARINERS:EU/ATL
+RADIO MOSCOW
L'vov — (D):500kW::ENA/ATL
+RADIO MOSCOW/RP&P
Krasnoyarsk — (D):500kW::SAS

7210
GERMANY (FR)
DEUTSCHE WELLE
Türkheim-Wertach'l — (J):500kW::SEA
INDIA
+ALL INDIA RADIO
Calcutta — 10kW:DS
SAUDI ARABIA
BS OF THE KINGDOM
Riyadh — 350kW:DS:EU
SWITZERLAND
RED CROSS BC SVC
Schwarzenburg — Irr:M:150kW:1ST OR LAST MONDAY:EU/NAF
— Irr:Su:150kW:1ST OR LAST SUNDAY:EU/NAF
UNITED KINGDOM
BBC
Daventry — 250kW::WEU/NAF
— 250kW::EU
BBC
Holywell-Rampisham — 500kW::EEU/WUSSR
— 500kW:WS:EEU/WUSSR
USA
VOICE OF AMERICA
Via Kaválla, Greece — (D):250kW::ME/SAS
— (J):250kW::SAS
VOICE OF AMERICA
Via Philippines — (D):250kW::EAS
VOICE OF AMERICA
Via Woofferton, UK — (D):300kW::EEU
USSR
BELORUSSIAN RADIO
Minsk — Alt 12005kHz:15kW:DS-1
KHABAROVSK RADIO
Khabarovsk — 50kW:DS-1
RADIO MOSCOW
Moscow — 100kW:DS-1
— 100kW:DS-2
RADIO TIKHIY OKEAN
Khabarovsk — 50kW:MARINERS:EUSSR/PAC
— Sa:50kW:MARINERS:EUSSR/PAC
— Su-F:50kW:MARINERS:EUSSR/PAC

7210v
CHINA (PR)
YUNNAN PEOPLES BS
Kunming — 50kW:DS-CHINESE
— Su:50kW:DS-CHINESE
SENEGAL
ORT DU SENEGAL
Dakar — 4kW:DS-FRENCH, ETC

7211v
INDONESIA
+R REP INDONESIA
Biak, Irian Jaya — Irr::1kW:DS

7214
ANGOLA
RADIO NACIONAL
Luanda — 10kW:DS

7215
AUSTRALIA
RADIO AUSTRALIA
Shepparton — 100kW::PAC
+RADIO AUSTRALIA
Shepparton — (D):100kW::PAC
INDIA
ALL INDIA RADIO
Delhi — 100kW::SEA
IRAN
VO THE ISLAMIC REP
Tehrän — Irr::500kW:RAMADAN:ME
— 100/500kW::ME
— 100kW::ME/SAS
IVORY COAST
RTV IVOIRIENNE
(con'd)   Abidjan — 20kW:DS

0 1 2 3 4 5 6 7 8 9 10 11 12 13 14 15 16 17 18 19 20 21 22 23 24

ENGLISH ▬▬   GERMAN / DEUTSCH ◊◊◊◊   FRENCH / FRANÇAIS ══   PORTUGUESE / PORTUGUÊS ▬   SPANISH / ESPAÑOL ═
ARABIC /ﻉﺭ ≡   RUSSIAN / РУССКИИ ═   CHINESE / 中文 ◻◻◻◻   JAPANESE / 日本語 ▤▤▤   MULTILINGUAL ▨▨▨   OTHER ▬
SUMMER ONLY (J)   WINTER ONLY (D)   JAMMING ∧∧ or / or \   EARLIEST HEARD ◢   LATEST HEARD ◣   + TENTATIVE

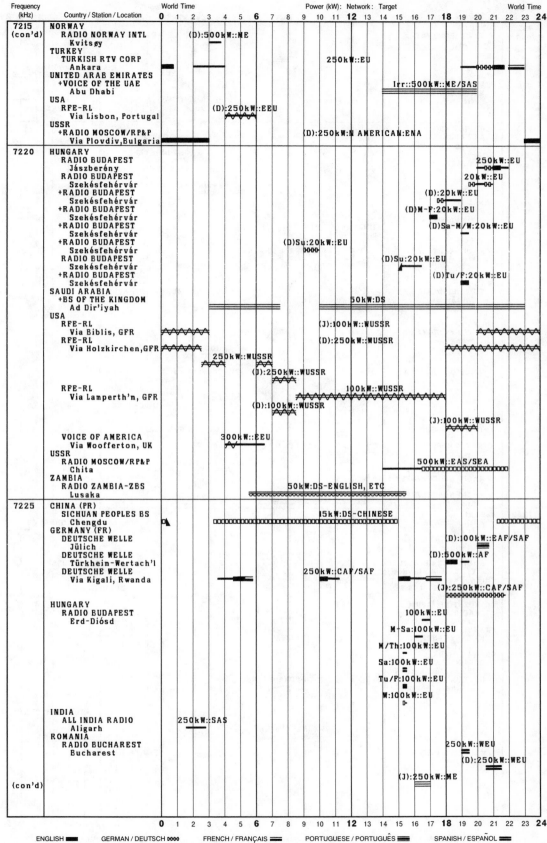

Frequency (kHz)	Country / Station / Location	Power (kW) : Network : Target
7215 (con'd)	NORWAY — RADIO NORWAY INTL, Kvitsøy	(D):500kW::ME
	TURKEY — TURKISH RTV CORP, Ankara	250kW::EU
	UNITED ARAB EMIRATES — +VOICE OF THE UAE, Abu Dhabi	Irr::500kW::ME/SAS
	USA — RFE-RL, Via Lisbon, Portugal	(D):250kW::EEU
	USSR — +RADIO MOSCOW/RP&P, Via Plovdiv, Bulgaria	(D):250kW:N AMERICAN:ENA
7220	HUNGARY — RADIO BUDAPEST, Jászberény	250kW::EU
	RADIO BUDAPEST, Székésfehérvár	20kW::EU
	+RADIO BUDAPEST, Székésfehérvár	(D):20kW::EU
	+RADIO BUDAPEST, Székésfehérvár	(D)M-F:20kW::EU
	+RADIO BUDAPEST, Székésfehérvár	(D)Sa-M/W:20kW::EU
	+RADIO BUDAPEST, Székésfehérvár	(D)Su:20kW::EU
	RADIO BUDAPEST, Székésfehérvár	(D)Su:20kW::EU
	+RADIO BUDAPEST, Székésfehérvár	(D)Tu/F:20kW::EU
	SAUDI ARABIA — +BS OF THE KINGDOM, Ad Dir'iyah	50kW:DS
	USA — RFE-RL, Via Biblis, GFR	(J):100kW::WUSSR
	RFE-RL, Via Holzkirchen,GFR	(D):250kW::WUSSR / 250kW::WUSSR / (J):250kW::WUSSR
	RFE-RL, Via Lamperth'm, GFR	100kW::WUSSR / (D):100kW::WUSSR / (J):100kW::WUSSR
	VOICE OF AMERICA, Via Woofferton, UK	300kW::EEU
	USSR — RADIO MOSCOW/RP&P, Chita	500kW::EAS/SEA
	ZAMBIA — RADIO ZAMBIA-ZBS, Lusaka	50kW:DS-ENGLISH, ETC
7225	CHINA (PR) — SICHUAN PEOPLES BS, Chengdu	15kW:DS-CHINESE
	GERMANY (FR) — DEUTSCHE WELLE, Jülich	(D):100kW::EAF/SAF
	DEUTSCHE WELLE, Türkheim-Wertach'l	(D):500kW::AF
	DEUTSCHE WELLE, Via Kigali, Rwanda	250kW::CAF/SAF / (J):250kW::CAF/SAF
	HUNGARY — RADIO BUDAPEST, Erd-Diósd	100kW::EU
		M-Sa:100kW::EU
		M/Th:100kW::EU
		Sa:100kW::EU
		Tu/F:100kW::EU
		W:100kW::EU
	INDIA — ALL INDIA RADIO, Aligarh	250kW::SAS
	ROMANIA — RADIO BUCHAREST, Bucharest	250kW::WEU / (D):250kW::WEU / (J):250kW::ME
(con'd)		

ENGLISH ▬ GERMAN / DEUTSCH ∞∞ FRENCH / FRANÇAIS ═ PORTUGUESE / PORTUGUÊS ▬ SPANISH / ESPAÑOL ═
ARABIC / ﻉﺭﺏ ═ RUSSIAN / РУССКИИ ═ CHINESE / ★★ ∞∞ JAPANESE / 日本語 ∞∞ MULTILINGUAL ∞∞ OTHER ▬
SUMMER ONLY (J) WINTER ONLY (D) JAMMING ∧∧ or / or \ EARLIEST HEARD ◢ LATEST HEARD ◣ + TENTATIVE

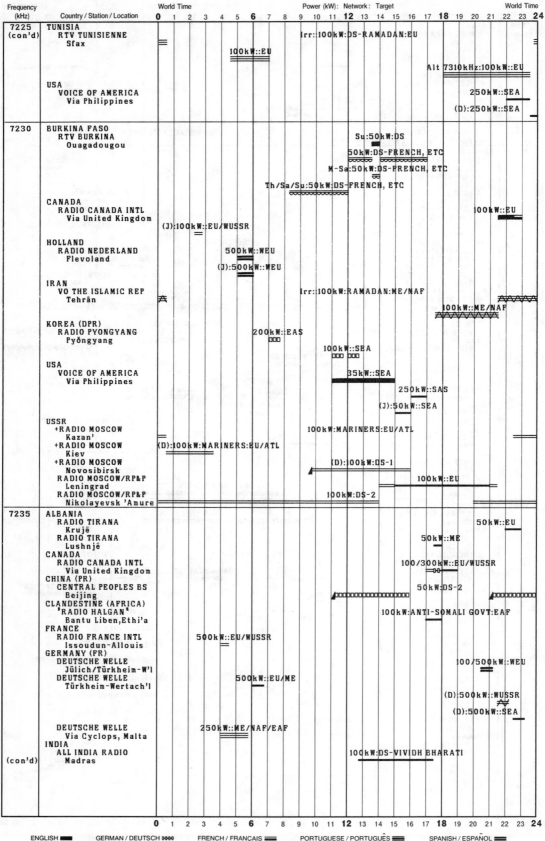

7225 (con'd)

TUNISIA
RTV TUNISIENNE
Sfax
— Irr::100kW:DS-RAMADAN:EU
— 100kW::EU
— Alt 7310kHz:100kW::EU

USA
VOICE OF AMERICA
Via Philippines
— 250kW::SEA
— (D):250kW::SEA

7230

BURKINA FASO
RTV BURKINA
Ouagadougou
— Su:50kW:DS
— 50kW:DS-FRENCH, ETC
— M-Sa:50kW:DS-FRENCH, ETC
— Th/Sa/Su:50kW:DS-FRENCH, ETC

CANADA
RADIO CANADA INTL
Via United Kingdom
— (J):100kW::EU/WUSSR
— 100kW::EU

HOLLAND
RADIO NEDERLAND
Flevoland
— 500kW::WEU
— (J):500kW::WEU

IRAN
VO THE ISLAMIC REP
Tehrān
— Irr::100kW:RAMADAN:ME/NAF
— 100kW::ME/NAF

KOREA (DPR)
RADIO PYONGYANG
Pyŏngyang
— 200kW::EAS

USA
VOICE OF AMERICA
Via Philippines
— 100kW::SEA
— 35kW::SEA
— 250kW::SAS
— (J):50kW::SEA

USSR
+RADIO MOSCOW
Kazan'
— 100kW:MARINERS:EU/ATL
+RADIO MOSCOW
Kiev
— (D):100kW:MARINERS:EU/ATL
+RADIO MOSCOW
Novosibirsk
— (D):100kW:DS-1
RADIO MOSCOW/RP&P
Leningrad
— 100kW::EU
RADIO MOSCOW/RP&P
Nikolayevsk 'Amure
— 100kW:DS-2

7235

ALBANIA
RADIO TIRANA
Krujë
— 50kW::EU
RADIO TIRANA
Lushnjë
— 50kW::ME
CANADA
RADIO CANADA INTL
Via United Kingdom
— 100/300kW::EU/WUSSR
CHINA (PR)
CENTRAL PEOPLES BS
Beijing
— 50kW:DS-2
CLANDESTINE (AFRICA)
'RADIO HALGAN'
Bantu Liben,Ethi'a
— 100kW:ANTI-SOMALI GOVT:EAF
FRANCE
RADIO FRANCE INTL
Issoudun-Allouis
— 500kW::EU/WUSSR
GERMANY (FR)
DEUTSCHE WELLE
Jülich/Türkheim-W'l
— 100/500kW::WEU
DEUTSCHE WELLE
Türkheim-Wertach'l
— 500kW::EU/ME
— (D):500kW::WUSSR
— (D):500kW::SEA

DEUTSCHE WELLE
Via Cyclops, Malta
— 250kW::ME/NAF/EAF
INDIA
ALL INDIA RADIO
Madras
— 100kW:DS-VIVIDH BHARATI

(con'd)

ENGLISH ▰ GERMAN / DEUTSCH ▨ FRENCH / FRANÇAIS ▤ PORTUGUESE / PORTUGUÊS ▤ SPANISH / ESPAÑOL ▭
ARABIC /ﻋﺮﺑﻰ ≡ RUSSIAN / РУССКИЙ ═ CHINESE / 中文 ▨ JAPANESE / 日本語 ▰ MULTILINGUAL ▨ OTHER ▬
SUMMER ONLY (J) WINTER ONLY (D) JAMMING ∧∧ or / or \ EARLIEST HEARD ◢ LATEST HEARD ◣ + TENTATIVE

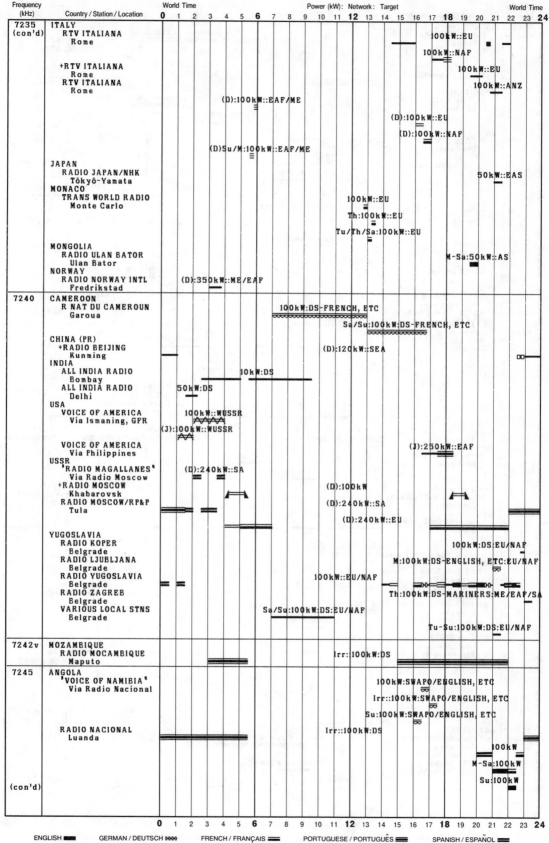

Frequency (kHz)	Country / Station / Location		World Time / Power (kW)::Network:Target

7235 (con'd)

ITALY
RTV ITALIANA — Rome — 100kW::EU / 100kW::NAF
+RTV ITALIANA — Rome — 100kW::EU
RTV ITALIANA — Rome — 100kW::ANZ
(D):100kW::EAF/ME
(D):100kW::EU
(D):100kW::NAF
(D)Su/M:100kW::EAF/ME

JAPAN
RADIO JAPAN/NHK — Tōkyō-Yamata — 50kW::EAS

MONACO
TRANS WORLD RADIO — Monte Carlo — 100kW::EU
Th:100kW::EU
Tu/Th/Sa:100kW::EU

MONGOLIA
RADIO ULAN BATOR — Ulan Bator — M-Sa:50kW::AS

NORWAY
RADIO NORWAY INTL — Fredrikstad — (D):350kW::ME/EAF

7240

CAMEROON
R NAT DU CAMEROUN — Garoua — 100kW:DS-FRENCH, ETC
Sa/Su:100kW:DS-FRENCH, ETC

CHINA (PR)
+RADIO BEIJING — Kunming — (D):120kW::SEA

INDIA
ALL INDIA RADIO — Bombay — 10kW:DS
ALL INDIA RADIO — Delhi — 50kW:DS

USA
VOICE OF AMERICA — Via Ismaning, GFR — 100kW::WUSSR
(J):100kW::WUSSR
VOICE OF AMERICA — Via Philippines — (J):250kW::EAF

USSR
"RADIO MAGALLANES" — Via Radio Moscow — (D):240kW::SA
+RADIO MOSCOW — Khabarovsk — (D):100kW
RADIO MOSCOW/RP&P — Tula — (D):240kW::SA
(D):240kW::EU

YUGOSLAVIA
RADIO KOPER — Belgrade — 100kW:DS:EU/NAF
RADIO LJUBLJANA — Belgrade — M:100kW:DS-ENGLISH, ETC:EU/NAF
RADIO YUGOSLAVIA — Belgrade — 100kW::EU/NAF
RADIO ZAGREB — Belgrade — Th:100kW:DS-MARINERS:ME/EAF/SA
VARIOUS LOCAL STNS — Belgrade — Sa/Su:100kW:DS:EU/NAF
Tu-Su:100kW:DS:EU/NAF

7242v

MOZAMBIQUE
RADIO MOCAMBIQUE — Maputo — Irr:100kW:DS

7245

ANGOLA
"VOICE OF NAMIBIA" — Via Radio Nacional — 100kW:SWAPO/ENGLISH, ETC
Irr::100kW:SWAPO/ENGLISH, ETC
Su:100kW:SWAPO/ENGLISH, ETC
RADIO NACIONAL — Luanda — Irr::100kW:DS
100kW
M-Sa:100kW
Su:100kW

(con'd)

World Time: 0 1 2 3 4 5 6 7 8 9 10 11 12 13 14 15 16 17 18 19 20 21 22 23 24

ENGLISH ▬ GERMAN / DEUTSCH ००० FRENCH / FRANÇAIS ═ PORTUGUESE / PORTUGUÊS ═ SPANISH / ESPAÑOL ▬
ARABIC / ═ RUSSIAN / РУССКИИ ═ CHINESE / 中文 ०००० JAPANESE / 日本語 ▬ MULTILINGUAL ▭▭▭▭ OTHER ▬
SUMMER ONLY (J)   WINTER ONLY (D)   JAMMING /\/\ or / or \   EARLIEST HEARD ◢   LATEST HEARD ◣   + TENTATIVE

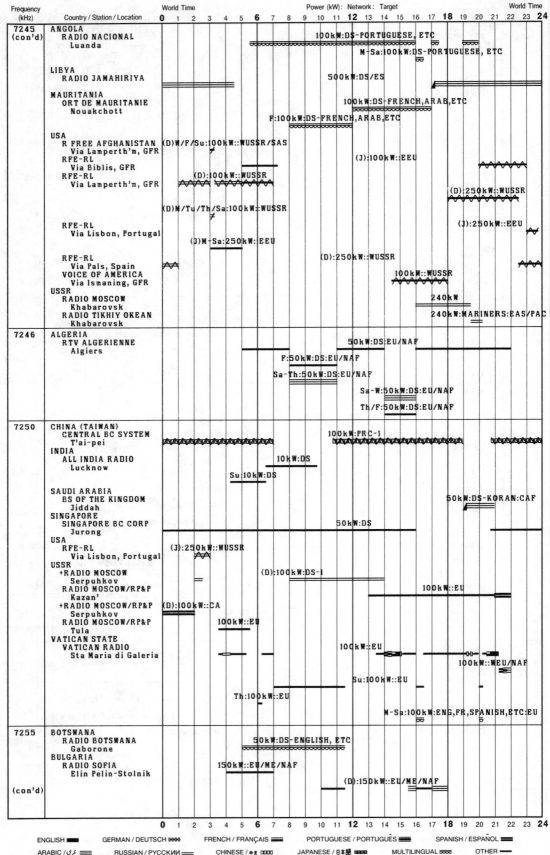

Frequency (kHz)	Country / Station / Location	Schedule
7245 (con'd)	**ANGOLA** RADIO NACIONAL Luanda	100kW:DS-PORTUGUESE, ETC / M-Sa:100kW:DS-PORTUGUESE, ETC
	LIBYA RADIO JAMAHIRIYA	500kW:DS/ES
	MAURITANIA ORT DE MAURITANIE Nouakchott	100kW:DS-FRENCH,ARAB,ETC / F:100kW:DS-FRENCH,ARAB,ETC
	USA R FREE AFGHANISTAN Via Lamperth'm, GFR	(D)W/F/Su:100kW::WUSSR/SAS
	RFE-RL Via Biblis, GFR	(J):100kW::EEU
	RFE-RL Via Lamperth'm, GFR	(D):100kW::WUSSR / (D):250kW::WUSSR / (D)M/Tu/Th/Sa:100kW::WUSSR
	RFE-RL Via Lisbon, Portugal	(J):250kW::EEU / (J)M-Sa:250kW::EEU
	RFE-RL Via Pals, Spain	(D):250kW::WUSSR
	VOICE OF AMERICA Via Ismaning, GFR	100kW::WUSSR
	USSR RADIO MOSCOW Khabarovsk	240kW
	RADIO TIKHIY OKEAN Khabarovsk	240kW:MARINERS:EAS/PAC
7246	**ALGERIA** RTV ALGERIENNE Algiers	50kW:DS:EU/NAF / F:50kW:DS:EU/NAF / Sa-Th:50kW:DS:EU/NAF / Sa-W:50kW:DS:EU/NAF / Th/F:50kW:DS:EU/NAF
7250	**CHINA (TAIWAN)** CENTRAL BC SYSTEM T'ai-pei	100kW:PRC-1
	INDIA ALL INDIA RADIO Lucknow	10kW:DS / Su:10kW:DS
	SAUDI ARABIA BS OF THE KINGDOM Jiddah	50kW:DS-KORAN:CAF
	SINGAPORE SINGAPORE BC CORP Jurong	50kW:DS
	USA RFE-RL Via Lisbon, Portugal	(J):250kW::WUSSR
	USSR +RADIO MOSCOW Serpuhkov	(D):100kW:DS-1
	RADIO MOSCOW/RP&P Kazan'	100kW::EU
	+RADIO MOSCOW/RP&P Serpuhkov	(D):100kW::CA
	RADIO MOSCOW/RP&P Tula	100kW::EU
	VATICAN STATE VATICAN RADIO Sta Maria di Galeria	100kW::EU / 100kW::WEU/NAF / Su:100kW::EU / Th:100kW::EU / M-Sa:100kW::ENG,FR,SPANISH,ETC:EU
7255	**BOTSWANA** RADIO BOTSWANA Gaborone	50kW:DS-ENGLISH, ETC
	BULGARIA RADIO SOFIA Elin Pelin-Stolnik	150kW::EU/ME/NAF / (D):150kW::EU/ME/NAF
(con'd)		

ENGLISH ▬ GERMAN / DEUTSCH ◊◊◊◊ FRENCH / FRANÇAIS ═══ PORTUGUESE / PORTUGUÊS ▬▬ SPANISH / ESPAÑOL ▬▬

ARABIC /ﻉﻝﺍ ═══ RUSSIAN / РУССКИИ ─── CHINESE /中文 □□□□ JAPANESE / 日本語 ▤▤▤▤ MULTILINGUAL ▨▨▨▨ OTHER ▬

SUMMER ONLY (J) WINTER ONLY (D) JAMMING ∧∧ or / or \ EARLIEST HEARD ◢ LATEST HEARD ◣ + TENTATIVE

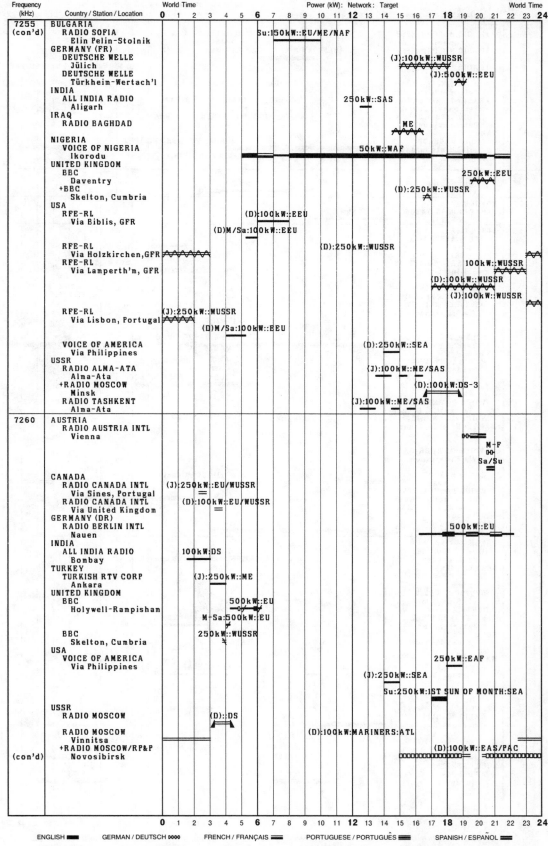

Frequency (kHz)	Country / Station / Location	World Time
7255 (con'd)	**BULGARIA**	
	RADIO SOFIA	Su:150kW::EU/ME/NAF
	Elin Pelin-Stolnik	
	GERMANY (FR)	
	DEUTSCHE WELLE	(J):100kW::WUSSR
	Jülich	
	DEUTSCHE WELLE	(J):500kW::EEU
	Türkheim-Wertach'l	
	INDIA	
	ALL INDIA RADIO	250kW::SAS
	Aligarh	
	IRAQ	
	RADIO BAGHDAD	ME
	NIGERIA	
	VOICE OF NIGERIA	50kW::WAF
	Ikorodu	
	UNITED KINGDOM	
	BBC	250kW::EEU
	Daventry	
	+BBC	(D):250kW::WUSSR
	Skelton, Cumbria	
	USA	
	RFE-RL	(D):100kW::EEU
	Via Biblis, GFR	
		(D)M/Sa:100kW::EEU
	RFE-RL	(D):250kW::WUSSR
	Via Holzkirchen,GFR	
	RFE-RL	100kW::WUSSR
	Via Lamperth'm, GFR	(D):100kW::WUSSR
		(J):100kW::WUSSR
	RFE-RL	(J):250kW::WUSSR
	Via Lisbon, Portugal	(D)M/Sa:100kW::EEU
	VOICE OF AMERICA	(D):250kW::SEA
	Via Philippines	
	USSR	
	RADIO ALMA-ATA	(J):100kW::ME/SAS
	Alma-Ata	
	+RADIO MOSCOW	(D):100kW:DS-3
	Minsk	
	RADIO TASHKENT	(J):100kW::ME/SAS
	Alma-Ata	
7260	**AUSTRIA**	
	RADIO AUSTRIA INTL	00 / M-F
	Vienna	00 / Sa/Su
	CANADA	
	RADIO CANADA INTL	(J):250kW::EU/WUSSR
	Via Sines, Portugal	
	RADIO CANADA INTL	(D):100kW::EU/WUSSR
	Via United Kingdom	
	GERMANY (DR)	
	RADIO BERLIN INTL	500kW::EU
	Nauen	
	INDIA	
	ALL INDIA RADIO	100kW:DS
	Bombay	
	TURKEY	
	TURKISH RTV CORP	(J):250kW::ME
	Ankara	
	UNITED KINGDOM	
	BBC	500kW::EU
	Holywell-Rampisham	M-Sa:500kW::EU
	BBC	250kW::WUSSR
	Skelton, Cumbria	
	USA	
	VOICE OF AMERICA	250kW::EAF
	Via Philippines	(J):250kW::SEA
		Su:250kW:1ST SUN OF MONTH:SEA
	USSR	
	RADIO MOSCOW	(D)::DS
	RADIO MOSCOW	(D):100kW:MARINERS:ATL
	Vinnitsa	
	+RADIO MOSCOW/RP&P	(D):100kW::EAS/PAC
(con'd)	Novosibirsk	

World Time scale: 0 1 2 3 4 5 6 7 8 9 10 11 12 13 14 15 16 17 18 19 20 21 22 23 24

Power (kW): Network: Target

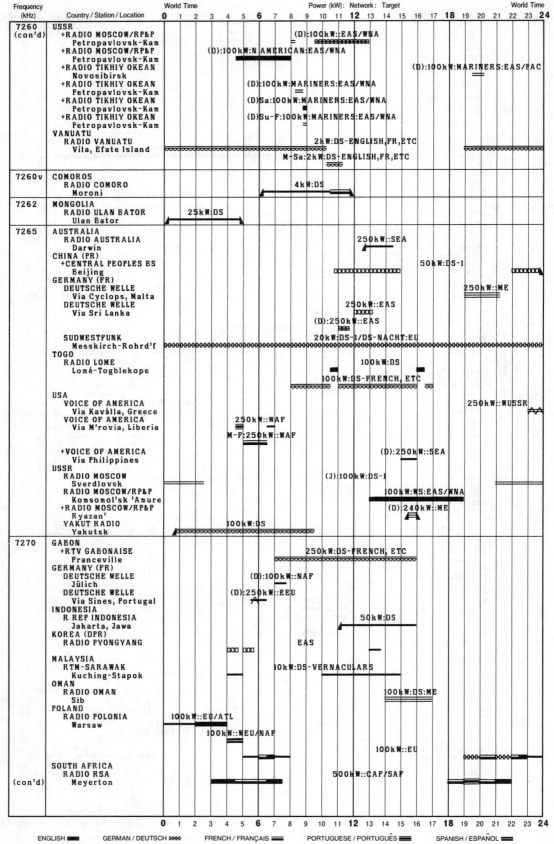

Frequency (kHz)	Country / Station / Location	World Time 0 ... 24
7260 (con'd)	USSR +RADIO MOSCOW/RP&P Petropavlovsk-Kam	(D):100kW::EAS/WNA
	+RADIO MOSCOW/RP&P Petropavlovsk-Kam	(D):100kW:N AMERICAN:EAS/WNA
	+RADIO TIKHIY OKEAN Novosibirsk	(D):100kW:MARINERS:EAS/PAC
	+RADIO TIKHIY OKEAN Petropavlovsk-Kam	(D):100kW:MARINERS:EAS/WNA
	+RADIO TIKHIY OKEAN Petropavlovsk-Kam	(D)Sa:100kW:MARINERS:EAS/WNA
	+RADIO TIKHIY OKEAN Petropavlovsk-Kam	(D)Su-F:100kW:MARINERS:EAS/WNA
	VANUATU RADIO VANUATU Vila, Efate Island	2kW:DS-ENGLISH,FR,ETC / M-Sa:2kW:DS-ENGLISH,FR,ETC
7260v	COMOROS RADIO COMORO Moroni	4kW:DS
7262	MONGOLIA RADIO ULAN BATOR Ulan Bator	25kW:DS
7265	AUSTRALIA RADIO AUSTRALIA Darwin	250kW::SEA
	CHINA (PR) +CENTRAL PEOPLES BS Beijing	50kW:DS-1
	GERMANY (FR) DEUTSCHE WELLE Via Cyclops, Malta	250kW::ME
	DEUTSCHE WELLE Via Sri Lanka	250kW::EAS
		(D):250kW::EAS
	SUDWESTFUNK Messkirch-Rohrd'f	20kW:DS-1/DS-NACHT:EU
	TOGO RADIO LOME Lomé-Togblekope	100kW:DS / 100kW:DS-FRENCH, ETC
	USA VOICE OF AMERICA Via Kaválla, Greece	250kW::WUSSR
	VOICE OF AMERICA Via M'rovia, Liberia	250kW::WAF / M-F:250kW::WAF
	+VOICE OF AMERICA Via Philippines	(D):250kW::SEA
	USSR RADIO MOSCOW Sverdlovsk	(J):100kW:DS-1
	RADIO MOSCOW/RP&P Komsomol'sk 'Amure	100kW:WS:EAS/WNA
	+RADIO MOSCOW/RP&P Ryazan'	(D):240kW::ME
	YAKUT RADIO Yakutsk	100kW:DS
7270	GABON +RTV GABONAISE Franceville	250kW:DS-FRENCH, ETC
	GERMANY (FR) DEUTSCHE WELLE Jülich	(D):100kW::NAF
	DEUTSCHE WELLE Via Sines, Portugal	(D):250kW::EEU
	INDONESIA R REP INDONESIA Jakarta, Jawa	50kW:DS
	KOREA (DPR) RADIO PYONGYANG	EAS
	MALAYSIA RTM-SARAWAK Kuching-Stapok	10kW:DS-VERNACULARS
	OMAN RADIO OMAN Sib	100kW:DS:ME
	POLAND RADIO POLONIA Warsaw	100kW::EU/ATL / 100kW::WEU/NAF / 100kW::EU
(con'd)	SOUTH AFRICA RADIO RSA Meyerton	500kW::CAF/SAF

ENGLISH ▬▬   GERMAN / DEUTSCH ◊◊◊◊   FRENCH / FRANÇAIS ══   PORTUGUESE / PORTUGUÊS ▬   SPANISH / ESPAÑOL ══

ARABIC /ﻉﺭ ≡   RUSSIAN / PУССКИИ ══   CHINESE / 中文 ◊◊◊◊   JAPANESE / 日本語 ▦▦▦   MULTILINGUAL ▩▩▩   OTHER ▬

SUMMER ONLY (J)   WINTER ONLY (D)   JAMMING ∧∧ or / or \   EARLIEST HEARD ◢   LATEST HEARD ◣   + TENTATIVE

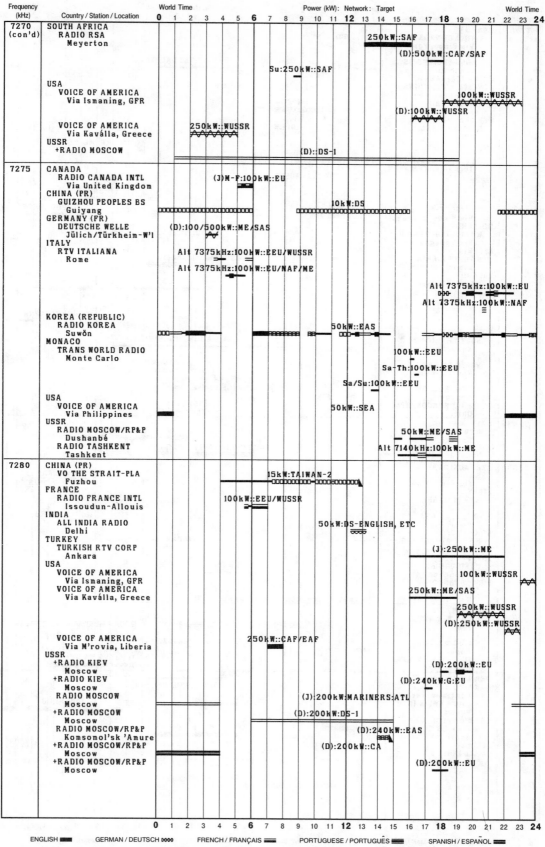

Frequency (kHz) — Country / Station / Location — World Time — Power (kW): Network: Target — World Time

Frequency (kHz)	Country / Station / Location	Schedule
7270 (con'd)	SOUTH AFRICA RADIO RSA Meyerton	250kW:SAF; (D):500kW:CAF/SAF; Su:250kW::SAF
	USA VOICE OF AMERICA Via Ismaning, GFR	100kW::WUSSR; (D):100kW::WUSSR
	VOICE OF AMERICA Via Kaválla, Greece	250kW:WUSSR
	USSR +RADIO MOSCOW	(D)::DS-1
7275	CANADA RADIO CANADA INTL Via United Kingdom	(J)M-F:100kW::EU
	CHINA (PR) GUIZHOU PEOPLES BS Guiyang	10kW:DS
	GERMANY (FR) DEUTSCHE WELLE Jülich/Türkheim-W'l	(D):100/500kW::ME/SAS
	ITALY RTV ITALIANA Rome	Alt 7375kHz:100kW::EEU/WUSSR; Alt 7375kHz:100kW::EU/NAF/ME; Alt 7375kHz:100kW::EU; Alt 7375kHz:100kW::NAF
	KOREA (REPUBLIC) RADIO KOREA Suwŏn	50kW::EAS
	MONACO TRANS WORLD RADIO Monte Carlo	100kW::EEU; Sa-Th:100kW::EEU; Sa/Su:100kW::EEU
	USA VOICE OF AMERICA Via Philippines	50kW::SEA
	USSR RADIO MOSCOW/RP&P Dushanbé	50kW::ME/SAS
	RADIO TASHKENT Tashkent	Alt 7140kHz:100kW::ME
7280	CHINA (PR) VO THE STRAIT-PLA Fuzhou	15kW:TAIWAN-2
	FRANCE RADIO FRANCE INTL Issoudun-Allouis	100kW::EEU/WUSSR
	INDIA ALL INDIA RADIO Delhi	50kW:DS-ENGLISH, ETC
	TURKEY TURKISH RTV CORP Ankara	(J):250kW::ME
	USA VOICE OF AMERICA Via Ismaning, GFR	100kW::WUSSR
	VOICE OF AMERICA Via Kaválla, Greece	250kW::ME/SAS; 250kW::WUSSR; (D):250kW::WUSSR
	VOICE OF AMERICA Via M'rovia, Liberia	250kW::CAF/EAF
	USSR +RADIO KIEV Moscow	(D):200kW::EU
	+RADIO KIEV Moscow	(D):240kW:G:EU
	RADIO MOSCOW Moscow	(J):200kW:MARINERS:ATL
	+RADIO MOSCOW Moscow	(D):200kW:DS-1
	RADIO MOSCOW/RP&P Komsomol'sk 'Amure	(D):240kW::EAS
	+RADIO MOSCOW/RP&P Moscow	(D):200kW::CA
	+RADIO MOSCOW/RP&P Moscow	(D):200kW::EU

ENGLISH ■■■   GERMAN / DEUTSCH ◊◊◊◊   FRENCH / FRANÇAIS ≡≡≡   PORTUGUESE / PORTUGUÊS ▬▬▬   SPANISH / ESPAÑOL ▬▬▬

ARABIC / ﻋﺮﺑﻰ ≡≡≡   RUSSIAN / РУССКИИ ══   CHINESE / 中文 ◻◻◻◻   JAPANESE / 日本語 ▦▦▦   MULTILINGUAL ◊◊◊◊   OTHER ——

SUMMER ONLY (J)   WINTER ONLY (D)   JAMMING ∧∧∧ or / or \   EARLIEST HEARD ◢   LATEST HEARD ◣   + TENTATIVE

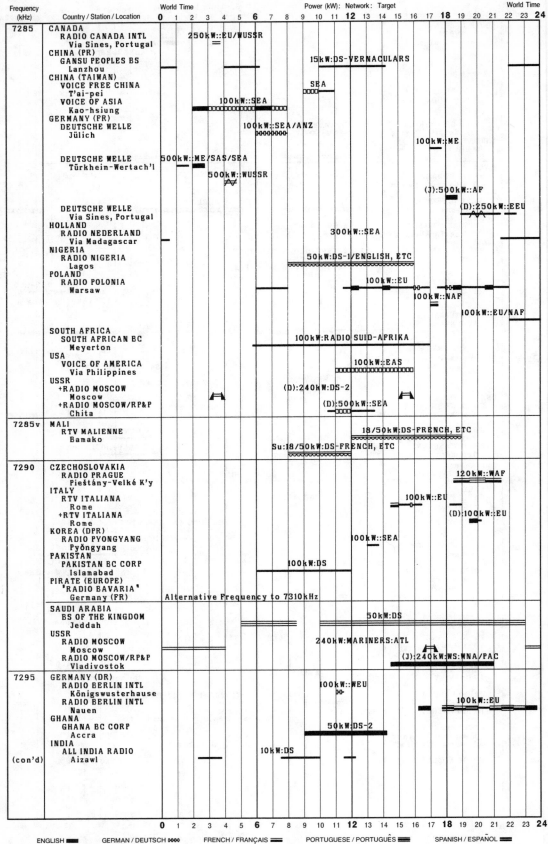

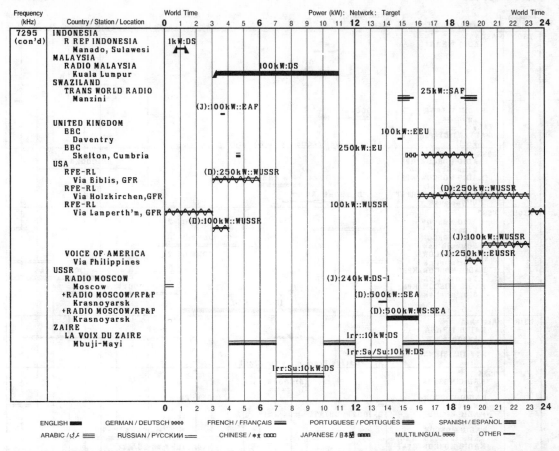

Frequency (kHz)	Country / Station / Location	Power (kW): Network: Target
7295 (con'd)	INDONESIA	
	R REP INDONESIA	
	Manado, Sulawesi	1kW:DS
	MALAYSIA	
	RADIO MALAYSIA	
	Kuala Lumpur	100kW:DS
	SWAZILAND	
	TRANS WORLD RADIO	
	Manzini	25kW::SAF
		(J):100kW::EAF
	UNITED KINGDOM	
	BBC	
	Daventry	100kW::EEU
	BBC	
	Skelton, Cumbria	250kW::EU
	USA	
	RFE-RL	
	Via Biblis, GFR	(D):250kW::WUSSR
	RFE-RL	
	Via Holzkirchen, GFR	(D):250kW::WUSSR
	RFE-RL	
	Via Lamperth'm, GFR	100kW::WUSSR (D):100kW::WUSSR
		(J):100kW::WUSSR
		(J):250kW::EUSSR
	VOICE OF AMERICA	
	Via Philippines	
	USSR	
	RADIO MOSCOW	
	Moscow	(J):240kW:DS-1
	+RADIO MOSCOW/RP&P	
	Krasnoyarsk	(D):500kW::SEA
	+RADIO MOSCOW/RP&P	
	Krasnoyarsk	(D):500kW:WS:SEA
	ZAIRE	
	LA VOIX DU ZAIRE	
	Mbuji-Mayi	Irr::10kW:DS
		Irr:Sa/Su:10kW:DS
		Irr:Su:10kW:DS

ENGLISH ▆▆▆   GERMAN / DEUTSCH ⊲⊲⊲⊲   FRENCH / FRANÇAIS ▬▬   PORTUGUESE / PORTUGUÊS ▬▬   SPANISH / ESPAÑOL ▬▬

ARABIC / ⸆⸇ ▬▬   RUSSIAN / РУССКИИ ▬▬   CHINESE / ⊕ ⊞ ⊲⊲⊲⊲   JAPANESE / 日本語 ▆▆▆   MULTILINGUAL ▬▬▬   OTHER —

Frequency (kHz)	Country / Station / Location	World Time / Power (kW): Network: Target

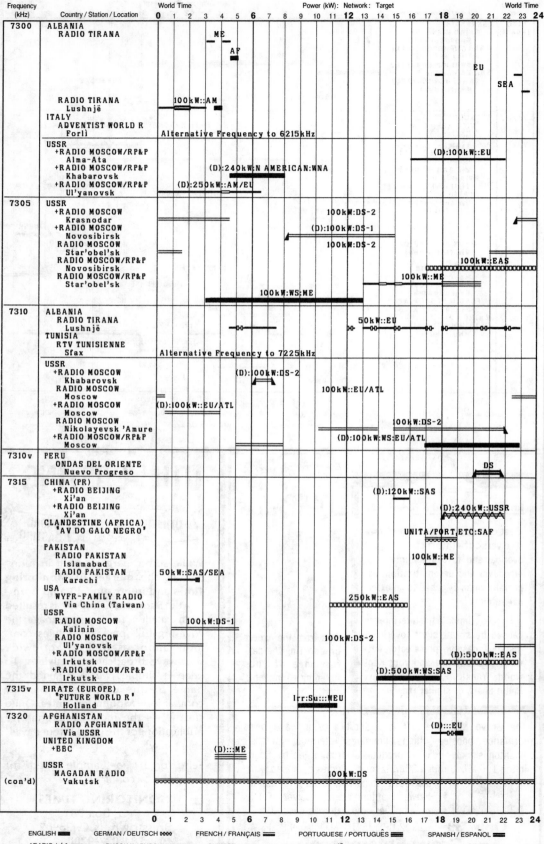

7300
ALBANIA
RADIO TIRANA — ME, AF, EU, SEA
RADIO TIRANA / Lushnjë — 100kW::AM
ITALY
ADVENTIST WORLD R / Forlì — Alternative Frequency to 6215kHz
USSR
+RADIO MOSCOW/RP&P / Alma-Ata — (D)::100kW::EU
+RADIO MOSCOW/RP&P / Khabarovsk — (D):240kW:N AMERICAN:WNA
+RADIO MOSCOW/RP&P / Ul'yanovsk — (D):250kW::AM/EU

7305
USSR
+RADIO MOSCOW / Krasnodar — 100kW:DS-2
+RADIO MOSCOW / Novosibirsk — (D):100kW:DS-1
RADIO MOSCOW / Star'obel'sk — 100kW:DS-2
RADIO MOSCOW/RP&P / Novosibirsk — 100kW::EAS
RADIO MOSCOW/RP&P / Star'obel'sk — 100kW::ME
— 100kW:WS:ME

7310
ALBANIA
RADIO TIRANA / Lushnjë — 50kW::EU
TUNISIA
RTV TUNISIENNE / Sfax — Alternative Frequency to 7225kHz
USSR
+RADIO MOSCOW / Khabarovsk — (D):100kW:DS-2
RADIO MOSCOW / Moscow — 100kW::EU/ATL
+RADIO MOSCOW / Moscow — (D):100kW::EU/ATL
RADIO MOSCOW / Nikolayevsk 'Amure — 100kW:DS-2
+RADIO MOSCOW/RP&P / Moscow — (D):100kW:WS:EU/ATL

7310v
PERU
ONDAS DEL ORIENTE / Nuevo Progreso — DS

7315
CHINA (PR)
+RADIO BEIJING / Xi'an — (D):120kW::SAS
+RADIO BEIJING / Xi'an — (D):240kW::USSR
CLANDESTINE (AFRICA)
'AV DO GALO NEGRO' — UNITA/PORT,ETC:SAF
PAKISTAN
RADIO PAKISTAN / Islamabad — 100kW::ME
RADIO PAKISTAN / Karachi — 50kW::SAS/SEA
USA
WYFR-FAMILY RADIO / Via China (Taiwan) — 250kW::EAS
USSR
RADIO MOSCOW / Kalinin — 100kW:DS-1
RADIO MOSCOW / Ul'yanovsk — 100kW:DS-2
+RADIO MOSCOW/RP&P / Irkutsk — (D):500kW::EAS
+RADIO MOSCOW/RP&P / Irkutsk — (D):500kW:WS:SAS

7315v
PIRATE (EUROPE)
'FUTURE WORLD R' / Holland — Irr:Su::WEU

7320
AFGHANISTAN
RADIO AFGHANISTAN / Via USSR — (D):::EU
UNITED KINGDOM
+BBC — (D):::ME
USSR
MAGADAN RADIO / Yakutsk — 100kW:DS
(con'd)

ENGLISH ▬ GERMAN / DEUTSCH ◇◇◇◇ FRENCH / FRANÇAIS ▬ PORTUGUESE / PORTUGUÊS ▬ SPANISH / ESPAÑOL ▬
ARABIC / ﺭﻉ ☰ RUSSIAN / РУССКИИ ▬ CHINESE / 中文 ◻◻◻◻ JAPANESE / 日本語 ▦▦▦ MULTILINGUAL ▦▦▦ OTHER ▬
SUMMER ONLY (J)   WINTER ONLY (D)   JAMMING ∧∧ or / or \   EARLIEST HEARD ◢   LATEST HEARD ◣   + TENTATIVE

Frequency (kHz)	Country / Station / Location	World Time / Power (kW): Network: Target

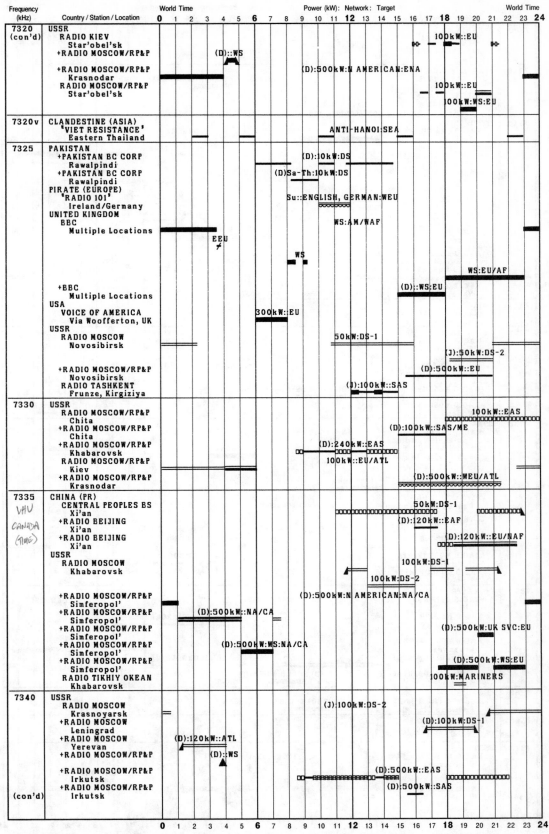

7320 (con'd) — USSR — RADIO KIEV, Star'obel'sk — 100kW::EU (18-19)
+RADIO MOSCOW/RP&P — (D)::WS (4-5)
+RADIO MOSCOW/RP&P, Krasnodar — (D):500kW:N AMERICAN:ENA (6-18)
RADIO MOSCOW/RP&P, Star'obel'sk — 100kW::EU (18)
— 100kW:WS:EU (20-21)

7320v — CLANDESTINE (ASIA) — "VIET RESISTANCE", Eastern Thailand — ANTI-HANOI:SEA

7325 — PAKISTAN
+PAKISTAN BC CORP, Rawalpindi — (D):10kW:DS
+PAKISTAN BC CORP, Rawalpindi — (D)Sa-Th:10kW:DS
PIRATE (EUROPE) "RADIO 101", Ireland/Germany — Su::ENGLISH, GERMAN:WEU
UNITED KINGDOM — BBC, Multiple Locations — WS:AM/WAF
— EEU — WS — WS:EU/AF
+BBC, Multiple Locations — (D)::WS:EU
USA — VOICE OF AMERICA, Via Woofferton, UK — 300kW::EU
USSR — RADIO MOSCOW, Novosibirsk — 50kW:DS-1
— (J):50kW:DS-2
+RADIO MOSCOW/RP&P, Novosibirsk — (D):500kW::EU
RADIO TASHKENT, Frunze, Kirgiziya — (J):100kW::SAS

7330 — USSR
RADIO MOSCOW/RP&P, Chita — 100kW::EAS
+RADIO MOSCOW/RP&P, Chita — (D):100kW::SAS/ME
+RADIO MOSCOW/RP&P, Khabarovsk — (D):240kW::EAS
RADIO MOSCOW/RP&P, Kiev — 100kW::EU/ATL
+RADIO MOSCOW/RP&P, Krasnodar — (D):500kW::WEU/ATL

7335 VHU CANADA (TIME) — CHINA (PR)
CENTRAL PEOPLES BS, Xi'an — 50kW:DS-1
+RADIO BEIJING, Xi'an — (D):120kW::EAF
+RADIO BEIJING, Xi'an — (D):120kW::EU/NAF
USSR — RADIO MOSCOW, Khabarovsk — 100kW:DS-1
— 100kW:DS-2
+RADIO MOSCOW/RP&P, Simferopol' — (D):500kW:N AMERICAN:NA/CA
+RADIO MOSCOW/RP&P, Simferopol' — (D):500kW::NA/CA
+RADIO MOSCOW/RP&P, Simferopol' — (D):500kW:UK SVC:EU
+RADIO MOSCOW/RP&P, Simferopol' — (D):500kW:WS:NA/CA
+RADIO MOSCOW/RP&P, Simferopol' — (D):500kW:WS:EU
RADIO TIKHIY OKEAN, Khabarovsk — 100kW::MARINERS

7340 — USSR
RADIO MOSCOW, Krasnoyarsk — (J):100kW:DS-2
+RADIO MOSCOW, Leningrad — (D):100kW:DS-1
+RADIO MOSCOW, Yerevan — (D):120kW::ATL
+RADIO MOSCOW/RP&P — (D)::WS
+RADIO MOSCOW/RP&P, Irkutsk — (D):500kW::EAS
+RADIO MOSCOW/RP&P, Irkutsk — (D):500kW::SAS
(con'd)

World Time scale: 0 1 2 3 4 5 6 7 8 9 10 11 12 13 14 15 16 17 18 19 20 21 22 23 24

ENGLISH ▬▬   GERMAN / DEUTSCH ◊◊◊◊   FRENCH / FRANÇAIS ═══   PORTUGUESE / PORTUGUÊS ▤▤▤   SPANISH / ESPAÑOL ═══
ARABIC / ﻉﻉ ≡≡≡   RUSSIAN / РУССКИИ ═══   CHINESE / ★☆ ▯▯▯▯   JAPANESE / 日本語 ▬▬▬   MULTILINGUAL ▨▨▨   OTHER ▬▬
SUMMER ONLY (J)   WINTER ONLY (D)   JAMMING ⋀⋀ or / or \   EARLIEST HEARD ◢   LATEST HEARD ◣   + TENTATIVE

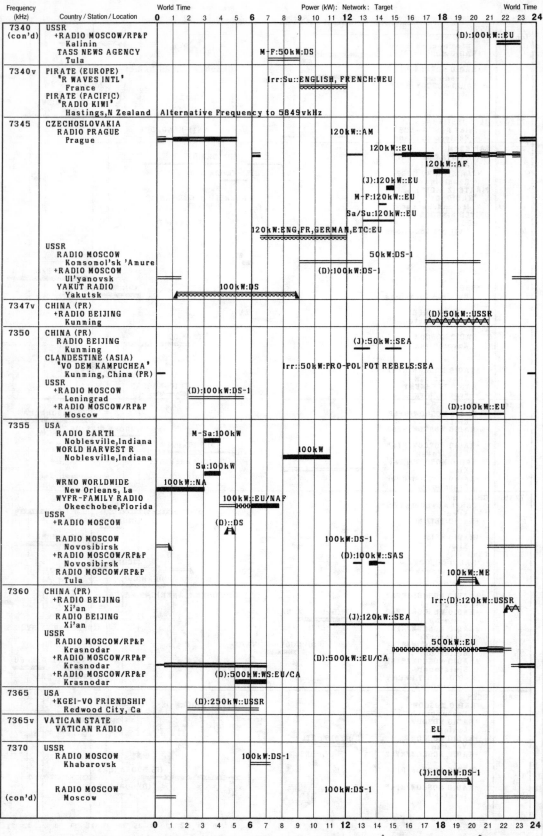

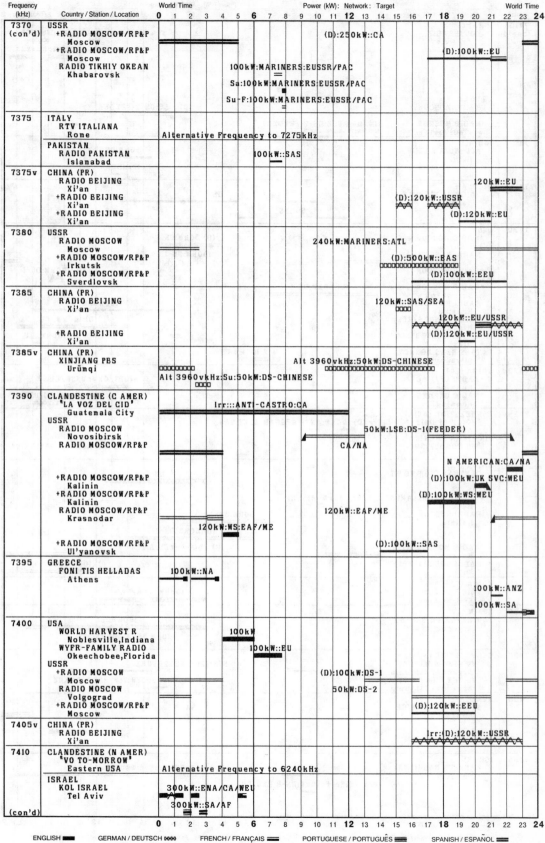

Frequency (kHz)	Country / Station / Location	World Time 0 — 24 / Power (kW): Network: Target
7370 (con'd)	USSR	
	+RADIO MOSCOW/RP&P Moscow	(D):250kW::CA
	+RADIO MOSCOW/RP&P Moscow	(D):100kW::EU
	RADIO TIKHIY OKEAN Khabarovsk	100kW:MARINERS:EUSSR/PAC
		Sa:100kW:MARINERS:EUSSR/PAC
		Su-F:100kW:MARINERS:EUSSR/PAC
7375	ITALY RTV ITALIANA Rome	Alternative Frequency to 7275kHz
	PAKISTAN RADIO PAKISTAN Islamabad	100kW::SAS
7375v	CHINA (PR) RADIO BEIJING Xi'an	120kW::EU
	+RADIO BEIJING Xi'an	(D):120kW::USSR
	+RADIO BEIJING Xi'an	(D):120kW::EU
7380	USSR RADIO MOSCOW Moscow	240kW:MARINERS:ATL
	+RADIO MOSCOW/RP&P Irkutsk	(D):500kW::EAS
	+RADIO MOSCOW/RP&P Sverdlovsk	(D):100kW::EEU
7385	CHINA (PR) RADIO BEIJING Xi'an	120kW::SAS/SEA
		120kW::EU/USSR
	+RADIO BEIJING Xi'an	(D):120kW::EU/USSR
7385v	CHINA (PR) XINJIANG PBS Urümqi	Alt 3960vkHz:50kW:DS-CHINESE
		Alt 3960vkHz:Su:50kW:DS-CHINESE
7390	CLANDESTINE (C AMER) 'LA VOZ DEL CID' Guatemala City	Irr:::ANTI-CASTRO:CA
	USSR RADIO MOSCOW Novosibirsk	50kW:LSB:DS-1(FEEDER)
	RADIO MOSCOW/RP&P	CA/NA
		N AMERICAN:CA/NA
	+RADIO MOSCOW/RP&P Kalinin	(D):100kW:UK SVC:WEU
	+RADIO MOSCOW/RP&P Kalinin	(D):100kW:WS:WEU
	RADIO MOSCOW/RP&P Krasnodar	120kW::EAF/ME
		120kW:WS:EAF/ME
	+RADIO MOSCOW/RP&P Ul'yanovsk	(D):100kW::SAS
7395	GREECE FONI TIS HELLADAS Athens	100kW::NA
		100kW::ANZ
		100kW::SA
7400	USA WORLD HARVEST R Noblesville,Indiana	100kW
	WYFR-FAMILY RADIO Okeechobee,Florida	100kW::EU
	USSR +RADIO MOSCOW Moscow	(D):100kW:DS-1
	RADIO MOSCOW Volgograd	50kW:DS-2
	+RADIO MOSCOW/RP&P Moscow	(D):120kW::EEU
7405v	CHINA (PR) RADIO BEIJING Xi'an	Irr:(D):120kW::USSR
7410	CLANDESTINE (N AMER) 'VO TO-MORROW' Eastern USA	Alternative Frequency to 6240kHz
	ISRAEL KOL ISRAEL Tel Aviv	300kW::ENA/CA/WEU
		300kW::SA/AF
(con'd)		

World Time: 0 1 2 3 4 5 6 7 8 9 10 11 12 13 14 15 16 17 18 19 20 21 22 23 24

ENGLISH ▆▆▆   GERMAN / DEUTSCH ০০০০   FRENCH / FRANÇAIS ═══   PORTUGUESE / PORTUGUÊS ▬▬▬   SPANISH / ESPAÑOL ▬▬▬

ARABIC / العربية ☰☰☰   RUSSIAN / РУССКИИ ═══   CHINESE / 中文 ০০০০   JAPANESE / 日本語 ▬▬▬   MULTILINGUAL ০০০০   OTHER ———

SUMMER ONLY (J)   WINTER ONLY (D)   JAMMING ∧∧ or / or \   EARLIEST HEARD ◢   LATEST HEARD ◣   + TENTATIVE

Frequency (kHz)	Country / Station / Location	World Time ... Power (kW): Network: Target ... World Time

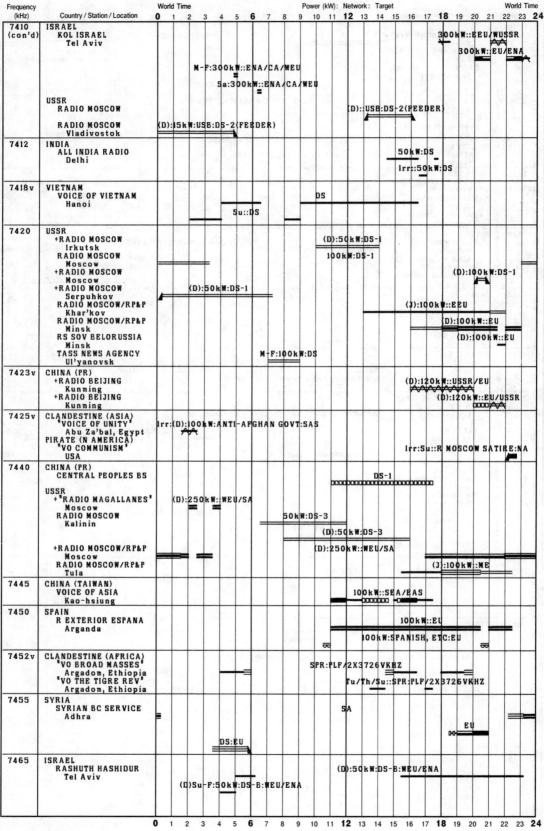

Frequency (kHz)	Country / Station / Location	
7410 (con'd)	ISRAEL KOL ISRAEL Tel Aviv	300kW::EEU/WUSSR / 300kW::EU/ENA / M-F:300kW::ENA/CA/WEU / Sa:300kW::ENA/CA/WEU
	USSR RADIO MOSCOW	(D)::USB:DS-2(FEEDER)
	RADIO MOSCOW Vladivostok	(D):15kW:USB:DS-2(FEEDER)
7412	INDIA ALL INDIA RADIO Delhi	50kW:DS / Irr::50kW:DS
7418v	VIETNAM VOICE OF VIETNAM Hanoi	DS / Su::DS
7420	USSR +RADIO MOSCOW Irkutsk	(D):50kW:DS-1
	RADIO MOSCOW Moscow	100kW:DS-1
	+RADIO MOSCOW Moscow	(D):100kW:DS-1
	+RADIO MOSCOW Serpuhkov	(D):50kW:DS-1
	RADIO MOSCOW/RP&P Khar'kov	(J):100kW::EEU
	RADIO MOSCOW/RP&P Minsk	(D):100kW::EU
	RS SOV BELORUSSIA Minsk	(D):100kW::EU
	TASS NEWS AGENCY Ul'yanovsk	M-F:100kW:DS
7423v	CHINA (PR) +RADIO BEIJING Kunming	(D):120kW::USSR/EU
	+RADIO BEIJING Kunming	(D):120kW::EU/USSR
7425v	CLANDESTINE (ASIA) "VOICE OF UNITY" Abu Za'bal, Egypt	Irr:(D):100kW:ANTI-AFGHAN GOVT:SAS
	PIRATE (N AMERICA) "VO COMMUNISM" USA	Irr:Su::R MOSCOW SATIRE:NA
7440	CHINA (PR) CENTRAL PEOPLES BS	DS-1
	USSR +"RADIO MAGALLANES" Moscow	(D):250kW:WEU/SA
	RADIO MOSCOW Kalinin	50kW:DS-3
		(D):50kW:DS-3
	+RADIO MOSCOW/RP&P Moscow	(D):250kW::WEU/SA
	RADIO MOSCOW/RP&P Tula	(J):100kW::NE
7445	CHINA (TAIWAN) VOICE OF ASIA Kao-hsiung	100kW::SEA/EAS
7450	SPAIN R EXTERIOR ESPANA Arganda	100kW::EU / 100kW:SPANISH, ETC:EU
7452v	CLANDESTINE (AFRICA) "VO BROAD MASSES" Argadom, Ethiopia	SPR:PLF/2X3726VKHZ
	"VO THE TIGRE REV" Argadom, Ethiopia	Tu/Th/Su::SPR:PLF/2X3726VKHZ
7455	SYRIA SYRIAN BC SERVICE Adhra	SA / EU / DS:EU
7465	ISRAEL RASHUTH HASHIDUR Tel Aviv	(D):50kW:DS-B:WEU/ENA / (D)Su-F:50kW:DS-B:WEU/ENA

World Time: 0 1 2 3 4 5 6 7 8 9 10 11 12 13 14 15 16 17 18 19 20 21 22 23 24

ENGLISH ▬▬   GERMAN / DEUTSCH ◊◊◊◊   FRENCH / FRANÇAIS ═══   PORTUGUESE / PORTUGUÊS ▬▬   SPANISH / ESPAÑOL ▬▬

ARABIC / ﻉﺏ ≡≡≡   RUSSIAN / РУССКИЙ ═══   CHINESE / 中文 ▭▭▭   JAPANESE / 日本語 ▬▬▬   MULTILINGUAL ∞∞∞   OTHER ▬▬

SUMMER ONLY (J)   WINTER ONLY (D)   JAMMING ∧∧ or / or \   EARLIEST HEARD ◢   LATEST HEARD ◣   + TENTATIVE

Frequency (kHz)	Country / Station / Location	Power (kW): Network: Target

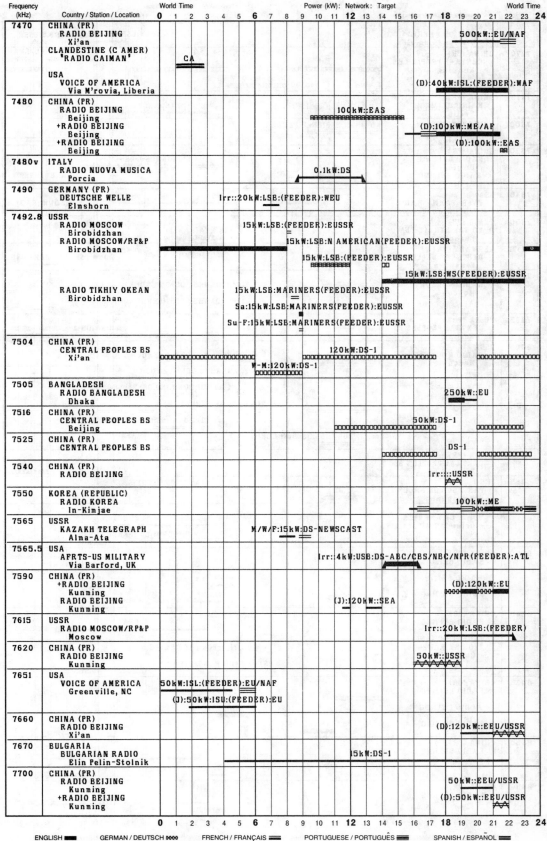

7470 CHINA (PR)
RADIO BEIJING
Xi'an — 500kW::EU/NAF
CLANDESTINE (C AMER)
'RADIO CAIMAN' — CA
USA
VOICE OF AMERICA
Via M'rovia, Liberia — (D):40kW:ISL:(FEEDER):WAF

7480 CHINA (PR)
RADIO BEIJING
Beijing — 100kW::EAS
+RADIO BEIJING
Beijing — (D):100kW::ME/AF
+RADIO BEIJING
Beijing — (D):100kW::EAS

7480v ITALY
RADIO NUOVA MUSICA
Porcia — 0.1kW:DS

7490 GERMANY (FR)
DEUTSCHE WELLE
Elmshorn — Irr::20kW:LSB:(FEEDER):WEU

7492.8 USSR
RADIO MOSCOW
Birobidzhan — 15kW:LSB:(FEEDER):EUSSR
RADIO MOSCOW/RP&P
Birobidzhan — 15kW:LSB:N AMERICAN(FEEDER):EUSSR
— 15kW:LSB:(FEEDER):EUSSR
— 15kW:LSB:WS(FEEDER):EUSSR
RADIO TIKHIY OKEAN
Birobidzhan — 15kW:LSB:MARINERS(FEEDER):EUSSR
— Sa:15kW:LSB:MARINERS(FEEDER):EUSSR
— Su-F:15kW:LSB:MARINERS(FEEDER):EUSSR

7504 CHINA (PR)
CENTRAL PEOPLES BS
Xi'an — 120kW:DS-1
— W-M:120kW:DS-1

7505 BANGLADESH
RADIO BANGLADESH
Dhaka — 250kW::EU

7516 CHINA (PR)
CENTRAL PEOPLES BS
Beijing — 50kW:DS-1

7525 CHINA (PR)
CENTRAL PEOPLES BS — DS-1

7540 CHINA (PR)
RADIO BEIJING — Irr:::USSR

7550 KOREA (REPUBLIC)
RADIO KOREA
In-Kimjae — 100kW::ME

7565 USSR
KAZAKH TELEGRAPH
Alma-Ata — M/W/F:15kW:DS-NEWSCAST

7565.5 USA
AFRTS-US MILITARY
Via Barford, UK — Irr::4kW:USB:DS-ABC/CBS/NBC/NPR(FEEDER):ATL

7590 CHINA (PR)
+RADIO BEIJING
Kunming — (D):120kW::EU
RADIO BEIJING
Kunming — (J):120kW::SEA

7615 USSR
RADIO MOSCOW/RP&P
Moscow — Irr::20kW:LSB:(FEEDER)

7620 CHINA (PR)
RADIO BEIJING
Kunming — 50kW::USSR

7651 USA
VOICE OF AMERICA
Greenville, NC — 50kW:ISL:(FEEDER):EU/NAF
— (J):50kW:ISU:(FEEDER):EU

7660 CHINA (PR)
RADIO BEIJING
Xi'an — (D):120kW::EEU/USSR

7670 BULGARIA
BULGARIAN RADIO
Elin Pelin-Stolnik — 15kW:DS-1

7700 CHINA (PR)
RADIO BEIJING
Kunming — 50kW::EEU/USSR
+RADIO BEIJING
Kunming — (D):50kW::EEU/USSR

ENGLISH ▬▬ GERMAN / DEUTSCH ◊◊◊◊ FRENCH / FRANÇAIS ═══ PORTUGUESE / PORTUGUÊS ▬▬ SPANISH / ESPAÑOL ▬▬
ARABIC / ﺏﺮﻋ ≡≡≡ RUSSIAN / РУССКИИ ═══ CHINESE / ✱✱ ◻◻◻◻ JAPANESE / 日本語 ▩▩▩▩ MULTILINGUAL ▦▦▦▦ OTHER ▬▬
SUMMER ONLY (J) WINTER ONLY (D) JAMMING /∨∨\ or / or \ EARLIEST HEARD ◢ LATEST HEARD ◣ + TENTATIVE

Frequency (kHz)	Country / Station / Location	World Time / Power (kW): Network: Target
7725	USA VOICE OF AMERICA Via Ismaning, GFR	40kW:USB:(FEEDER):EEU/ME
7770	CHINA (PR) CENTRAL PEOPLES BS Kunming	50kW:DS-2 / 1h/Sa-M:50kW:DS-2
7775	CHINA (PR) RADIO BEIJING Beijing	240kW::SEA
7800	CHINA (PR) RADIO BEIJING Kunming	50kW::EU/NAF
7820	CHINA (PR) RADIO BEIJING Beijing +RADIO BEIJING Beijing	120kW::EU/USSR / 120kW::EU/USSR
7845	USA WYFR-FAMILY RADIO Via China (Taiwan)	250kW::EAS
7850	CHINA (PR) VO THE STRAIT-PLA Fuzhou	10kW:TAIWAN-1
7917.5	GERMANY (FR) DEUTSCHE WELLE Elmshorn	20kW:USB:(FEEDER):WEU
7925	USSR RADIO MOSCOW Moscow	Irr::20kW:ISL:DS-3(FEEDER) / Irr::20kW:ISU:DS-1(FEEDER)
7935	CHINA (PR) CENTRAL PEOPLES BS Beijing	15kW:DS-1
8005	USSR RADIO MOSCOW Moscow	Irr::20kW:ISU:DS-1(FEEDER) / Irr::20kW:ISU:DS-2(FEEDER) / Irr:(D):20kW:ISU:DS-2(FEEDER) / Irr::20kW:ISL:DS-3(FEEDER) / Irr:(D):20kW:ISL:DS-3(FEEDER) / Irr:(J):20kW:ISL:DS-3(FEEDER)
8007	CHINA (PR) CENTRAL PEOPLES BS Xi'an	50kW:DS-2
8065v	PERU PARAISO LOS ANDES Moyobamba	DS
8110	USA VOICE OF AMERICA Delano, California	(D):50kW:ISL:(FEEDER):SEA / (D):50kW:ISU:(FEEDER):SEA
8300	CHINA (PR) RADIO BEIJING +RADIO BEIJING RADIO BEIJING	(D):::SEA/ANZ / (J):::SEA
8345	CHINA (PR) RADIO BEIJING CLANDESTINE (ASIA) 'VO DEM KAMPUCHEA' China (PR)	SEA / PRO-POL POT REBELS:SEA / PRO-KHMER ROUGE:SEA
8425	CHINA (PR) RADIO BEIJING +RADIO BEIJING RADIO BEIJING	(D) / N AMERICAN
8450	CHINA (PR) RADIO BEIJING	(D)
8490	CHINA (PR) RADIO BEIJING	

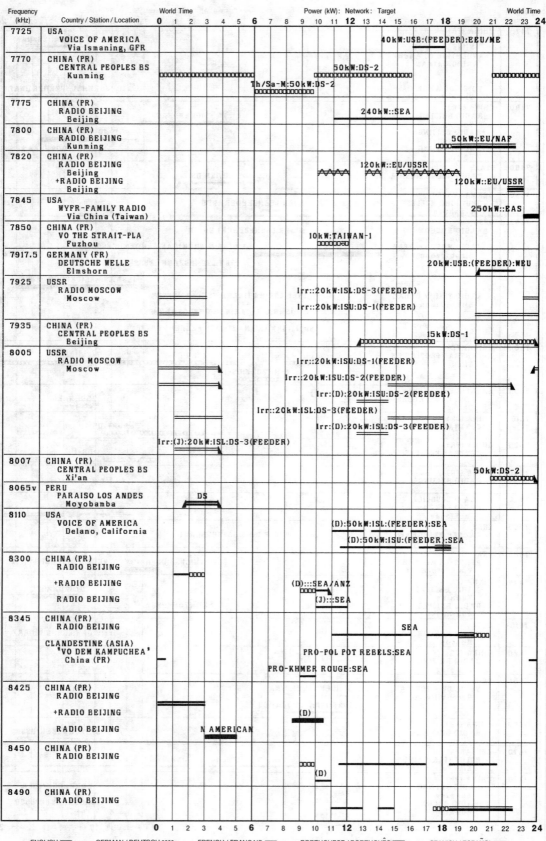

0 1 2 3 4 5 6 7 8 9 10 11 12 13 14 15 16 17 18 19 20 21 22 23 24

ENGLISH ▰▰▰   GERMAN / DEUTSCH ◦◦◦◦   FRENCH / FRANÇAIS ▬▬   PORTUGUESE / PORTUGUÊS ▤▤   SPANISH / ESPAÑOL ▬▬

ARABIC / ﻉﺮﺑ ▤▤   RUSSIAN / РУССКИЙ ▬▬   CHINESE / 中文 ◦◦◦◦   JAPANESE / 日本語 ▰▰▰   MULTILINGUAL ▭▭▭   OTHER ▬▬

SUMMER ONLY (J)   WINTER ONLY (D)   JAMMING /\/\ or / or \   EARLIEST HEARD ◢   LATEST HEARD ◣   + TENTATIVE

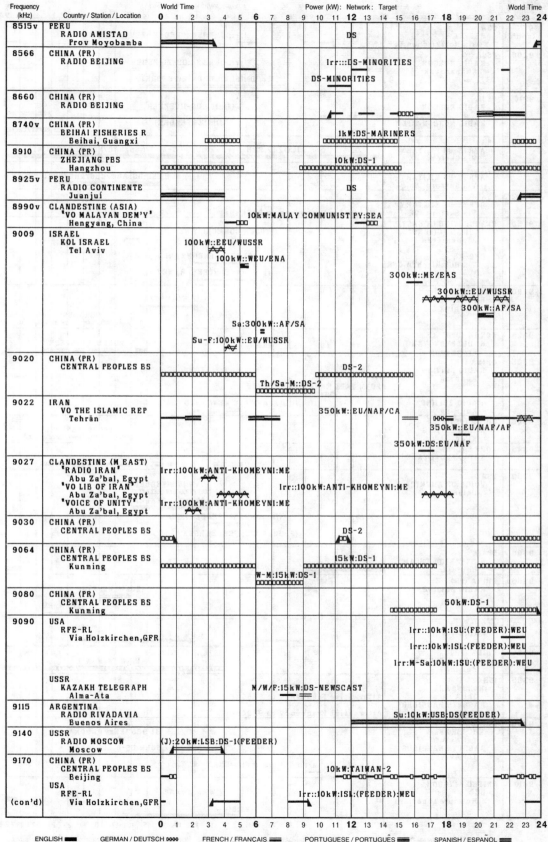

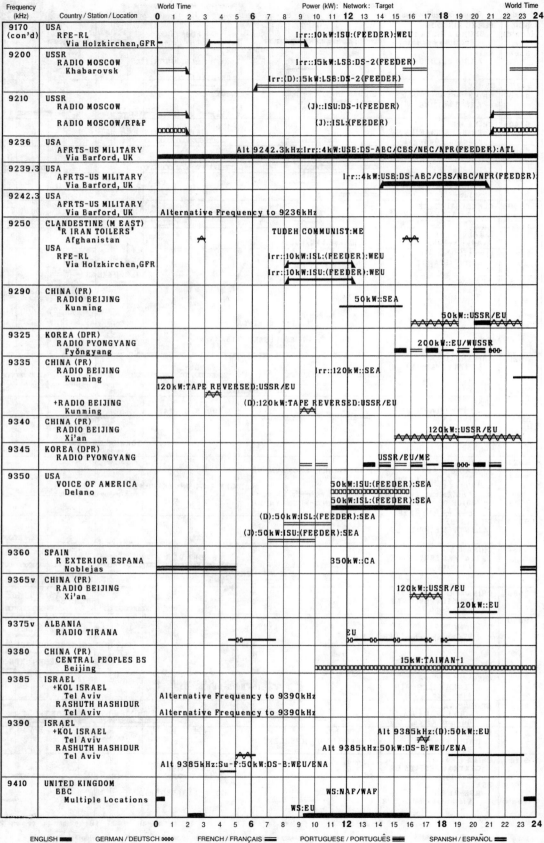

Frequency (kHz)	Country / Station / Location	World Time / Power (kW): Network: Target
9170 (con'd)	USA RFE-RL Via Holzkirchen,GFR	Irr::10kW:ISU:(FEEDER):WEU
9200	USSR RADIO MOSCOW Khabarovsk	Irr::15kW:LSB:DS-2(FEEDER) / Irr:(D):15kW:LSB:DS-2(FEEDER)
9210	USSR RADIO MOSCOW / RADIO MOSCOW/RP&P	(J)::ISU:DS-1(FEEDER) / (J)::ISL:(FEEDER)
9236	USA AFRTS-US MILITARY Via Barford, UK	Alt 9242.3kHz:Irr::4kW:USB:DS-ABC/CBS/NBC/NPR(FEEDER):ATL
9239.3	USA AFRTS-US MILITARY Via Barford, UK	Irr::4kW:USB:DS-ABC/CBS/NBC/NPR(FEEDER)
9242.3	USA AFRTS-US MILITARY Via Barford, UK	Alternative Frequency to 9236kHz
9250	CLANDESTINE (M EAST) 'R IRAN TOILERS' Afghanistan / USA RFE-RL Via Holzkirchen,GFR	TUDEH COMMUNIST:ME / Irr::10kW:ISL:(FEEDER):WEU / Irr::10kW:ISU:(FEEDER):WEU
9290	CHINA (PR) RADIO BEIJING Kunming	50kW::SEA / 50kW::USSR/EU
9325	KOREA (DPR) RADIO PYONGYANG Pyŏngyang	200kW::EU/WUSSR
9335	CHINA (PR) RADIO BEIJING Kunming / +RADIO BEIJING Kunming	Irr::120kW::SEA / 120kW:TAPE REVERSED:USSR/EU / (D):120kW:TAPE REVERSED:USSR/EU
9340	CHINA (PR) RADIO BEIJING Xi'an	120kW::USSR/EU
9345	KOREA (DPR) RADIO PYONGYANG	USSR/EU/ME
9350	USA VOICE OF AMERICA Delano	50kW:ISU:(FEEDER):SEA / 50kW:ISL:(FEEDER):SEA / (D):50kW:ISL:(FEEDER):SEA / (J):50kW:ISU:(FEEDER):SEA
9360	SPAIN R EXTERIOR ESPANA Noblejas	350kW::CA
9365v	CHINA (PR) RADIO BEIJING Xi'an	120kW::USSR/EU / 120kW::EU
9375v	ALBANIA RADIO TIRANA	EU
9380	CHINA (PR) CENTRAL PEOPLES BS Beijing	15kW:TAIWAN-1
9385	ISRAEL +KOL ISRAEL Tel Aviv / RASHUTH HASHIDUR Tel Aviv	Alternative Frequency to 9390kHz / Alternative Frequency to 9390kHz
9390	ISRAEL +KOL ISRAEL Tel Aviv / RASHUTH HASHIDUR Tel Aviv	Alt 9385kHz:(D):50kW::EU / Alt 9385kHz:50kW:DS-B:WEU/ENA / Alt 9385kHz:Su-F:50kW:DS-B:WEU/ENA
9410	UNITED KINGDOM BBC Multiple Locations	WS:NAF/WAF / WS:EU

World Time: 0 1 2 3 4 5 6 7 8 9 10 11 12 13 14 15 16 17 18 19 20 21 22 23 24

ENGLISH ▬ GERMAN / DEUTSCH ০০০০ FRENCH / FRANÇAIS ▬ PORTUGUESE / PORTUGUÊS ▬ SPANISH / ESPAÑOL ▬

ARABIC /ﺵﺵﺵ ▬ RUSSIAN / РУССКИИ ▬ CHINESE / 中文 ০০০০ JAPANESE / 日本語 ▬ MULTILINGUAL ০০০০ OTHER ▬

SUMMER ONLY (J)   WINTER ONLY (D)   JAMMING ∧∧ or / or \   EARLIEST HEARD ◢   LATEST HEARD ◣   + TENTATIVE

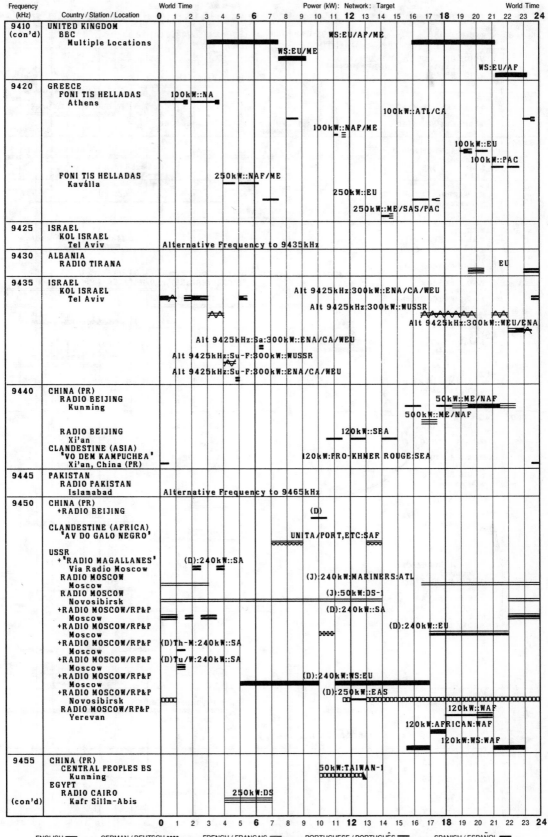

Frequency (kHz)	Country / Station / Location	World Time

9410 (con'd) UNITED KINGDOM
BBC
Multiple Locations
— WS:EU/AF/ME
— WS:EU/ME
— WS:EU/AF

9420 GREECE
FONI TIS HELLADAS
Athens
— 100kW::NA
— 100kW::ATL/CA
— 100kW::NAF/ME
— 100kW::EU
— 100kW::PAC
FONI TIS HELLADAS
Kaválla
— 250kW::NAF/ME
— 250kW::EU
— 250kW::ME/SAS/PAC

9425 ISRAEL
KOL ISRAEL
Tel Aviv
Alternative Frequency to 9435kHz

9430 ALBANIA
RADIO TIRANA
— EU

9435 ISRAEL
KOL ISRAEL
Tel Aviv
Alt 9425kHz:300kW::ENA/CA/WEU
Alt 9425kHz:300kW::WUSSR
Alt 9425kHz:300kW::WEU/ENA
Alt 9425kHz:Sa:300kW::ENA/CA/WEU
Alt 9425kHz:Su-F:300kW::WUSSR
Alt 9425kHz:Su-F:300kW::ENA/CA/WEU

9440 CHINA (PR)
RADIO BEIJING
Kunming
— 50kW::ME/NAF
— 500kW::ME/NAF
RADIO BEIJING
Xi'an
— 120kW::SEA
CLANDESTINE (ASIA)
'VO DEM KAMPUCHEA'
Xi'an, China (PR)
— 120kW:PRO-KHMER ROUGE:SEA

9445 PAKISTAN
RADIO PAKISTAN
Islamabad
Alternative Frequency to 9465kHz

9450 CHINA (PR)
+RADIO BEIJING
— (D)
CLANDESTINE (AFRICA)
'AV DO GALO NEGRO'
— UNITA/PORT,ETC:SAF
USSR
+'RADIO MAGALLANES'
Via Radio Moscow
— (D):240kW::SA
RADIO MOSCOW
Moscow
— (J):240kW:MARINERS:ATL
RADIO MOSCOW
Novosibirsk
— (J):50kW:DS-1
+RADIO MOSCOW/RP&P
Moscow
— (D):240kW::SA
+RADIO MOSCOW/RP&P
Moscow
— (D):240kW::EU
+RADIO MOSCOW/RP&P
Moscow
— (D)Th-M:240kW::SA
+RADIO MOSCOW/RP&P
Moscow
— (D)Tu/W:240kW::SA
+RADIO MOSCOW/RP&P
Moscow
— (D):240kW:WS:EU
+RADIO MOSCOW/RP&P
Novosibirsk
— (D):250kW::EAS
RADIO MOSCOW/RP&P
Yerevan
— 120kW:WAF
— 120kW:AFRICAN:WAF
— 120kW:WS:WAF

9455 CHINA (PR)
CENTRAL PEOPLES BS
Kunming
— 50kW:TAIWAN-1
EGYPT
RADIO CAIRO
(con'd) Kafr Silim-Abis
— 250kW:DS

| 0 | 1 | 2 | 3 | 4 | 5 | 6 | 7 | 8 | 9 | 10 | 11 | 12 | 13 | 14 | 15 | 16 | 17 | 18 | 19 | 20 | 21 | 22 | 23 | 24 |

ENGLISH ▬▬ GERMAN / DEUTSCH ▷◁◁◁ FRENCH / FRANÇAIS ≡≡≡ PORTUGUESE / PORTUGUÊS ≡≡≡ SPANISH / ESPAÑOL ≡≡

ARABIC / ﻉﺭﺐﻳ ≡≡≡ RUSSIAN / РУССКИЙ ═══ CHINESE / ◆✕ ◁◁◁◁ JAPANESE / 日本語 ▬▬▬ MULTILINGUAL ◶◶◶◶ OTHER ▬▬

SUMMER ONLY (J)   WINTER ONLY (D)   JAMMING /\/\ or / or \   EARLIEST HEARD ◢   LATEST HEARD ◣   ✦ TENTATIVE

Frequency (kHz)   Country / Station / Location   World Time   Power (kW) : Network : Target   World Time

0 1 2 3 4 5 6 7 8 9 10 11 12 13 14 15 16 17 18 19 20 21 22 23 24

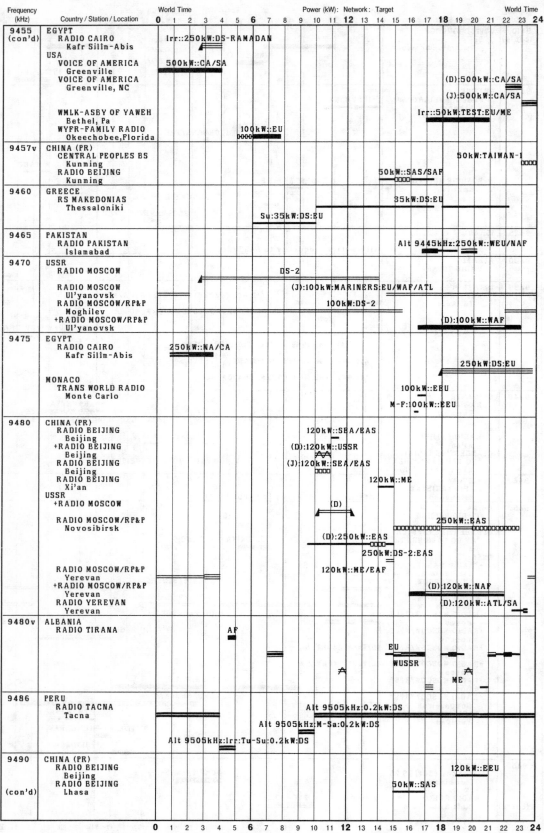

9455 (con'd)
EGYPT
  RADIO CAIRO — Kafr Silim-Abis — Irr::250kW:DS-RAMADAN
USA
  VOICE OF AMERICA — Greenville — 500kW::CA/SA
  VOICE OF AMERICA — Greenville, NC — (D):500kW::CA/SA
    (J):500kW::CA/SA
  WMLK-ASBY OF YAWEH — Bethel, Pa — Irr::50kW:TEST:EU/ME
  WYFR-FAMILY RADIO — Okeechobee, Florida — 100kW::EU

9457v
CHINA (PR)
  CENTRAL PEOPLES BS — Kunming — 50kW:TAIWAN-1
  RADIO BEIJING — Kunming — 50kW::SAS/SAF

9460
GREECE
  RS MAKEDONIAS — Thessaloniki — 35kW:DS:EU
  Su:35kW:DS:EU

9465
PAKISTAN
  RADIO PAKISTAN — Islamabad — Alt 9445kHz:250kW::WEU/NAF

9470
USSR
  RADIO MOSCOW — DS-2
  RADIO MOSCOW — Ul'yanovsk — (J):100kW:MARINERS:EU/WAF/ATL
  RADIO MOSCOW/RP&P — Moghilev — 100kW:DS-2
  +RADIO MOSCOW/RP&P — Ul'yanovsk — (D):100kW::WAF

9475
EGYPT
  RADIO CAIRO — Kafr Silim-Abis — 250kW::NA/CA
    250kW:DS:EU
MONACO
  TRANS WORLD RADIO — Monte Carlo — 100kW::EEU
  M-F:100kW::EEU

9480
CHINA (PR)
  RADIO BEIJING — Beijing — 120kW::SEA/EAS
  +RADIO BEIJING — Beijing — (D):120kW::USSR
  RADIO BEIJING — Beijing — (J):120kW::SEA/EAS
  RADIO BEIJING — Xi'an — 120kW::ME
USSR
  +RADIO MOSCOW — (D)
  RADIO MOSCOW/RP&P — Novosibirsk — 250kW::EAS
  (D):250kW::EAS
  250kW:DS-2:EAS
  RADIO MOSCOW/RP&P — Yerevan — 120kW::ME/EAF
  +RADIO MOSCOW/RP&P — Yerevan — (D):120kW::NAF
  RADIO YEREVAN — Yerevan — (D):120kW::ATL/SA

9480v
ALBANIA
  RADIO TIRANA — AF
  EU
  WUSSR
  ME

9486
PERU
  RADIO TACNA — Tacna — Alt 9505kHz:0.2kW:DS
  Alt 9505kHz:M-Sa:0.2kW:DS
  Alt 9505kHz:Irr:Tu-Su:0.2kW:DS

9490
CHINA (PR)
  RADIO BEIJING — Beijing — 120kW::EEU
(con'd)
  RADIO BEIJING — Lhasa — 50kW::SAS

0 1 2 3 4 5 6 7 8 9 10 11 12 13 14 15 16 17 18 19 20 21 22 23 24

ENGLISH ▬▬ GERMAN / DEUTSCH ⋈⋈⋈ FRENCH / FRANÇAIS ═══ PORTUGUESE / PORTUGUÊS ≡≡≡ SPANISH / ESPAÑOL ▭▭

ARABIC /ربي ≡≡ RUSSIAN / РУССКИИ ═══ CHINESE / 中文 ⋈⋈⋈ JAPANESE / 日本語 ▨▨▨ MULTILINGUAL ⋛⋛⋛ OTHER ▬▬

SUMMER ONLY (J) WINTER ONLY (D) JAMMING ∧∧ or / or \ EARLIEST HEARD ◢ LATEST HEARD ◥ + TENTATIVE

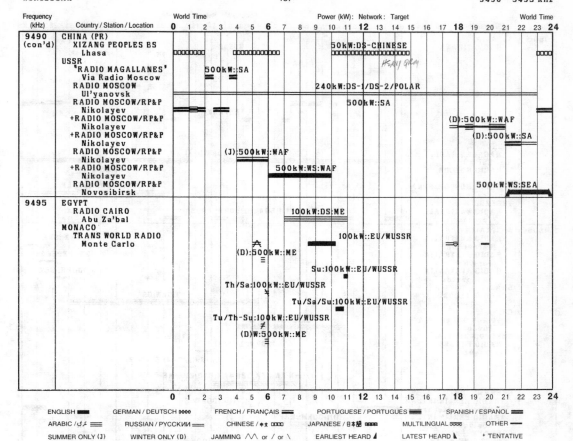

Frequency (kHz)	Country / Station / Location	Power (kW): Network: Target
9490 (con'd)	CHINA (PR)	
	XIZANG PEOPLES BS	
	Lhasa	50kW:DS-CHINESE
	USSR	
	'RADIO MAGALLANES'	500kW::SA
	Via Radio Moscow	
	RADIO MOSCOW	240kW:DS-1/DS-2/POLAR
	Ul'yanovsk	
	RADIO MOSCOW/RP&P	500kW::SA
	Nikolayev	
	+RADIO MOSCOW/RP&P	(D):500kW::WAF
	Nikolayev	
	+RADIO MOSCOW/RP&P	(D):500kW::SA
	Nikolayev	
	RADIO MOSCOW/RP&P	(J):500kW::WAF
	Nikolayev	
	+RADIO MOSCOW/RP&P	500kW:WS:WAF
	Nikolayev	
	RADIO MOSCOW/RP&P	500kW:WS:SEA
	Novosibirsk	
9495	EGYPT	
	RADIO CAIRO	100kW:DS:ME
	Abu Za'bal	
	MONACO	
	TRANS WORLD RADIO	100kW::EU/WUSSR
	Monte Carlo	(D):500kW::ME
		Su:100kW::EU/WUSSR
		Th/Sa:100kW::EU/WUSSR
		Tu/Sa/Su:100kW::EU/WUSSR
		Tu/Th-Su:100kW::EU/WUSSR
		(D)W:500kW::ME

ENGLISH ■■■　　GERMAN / DEUTSCH ◊◊◊◊　　FRENCH / FRANÇAIS ═══　　PORTUGUESE / PORTUGUÊS ▬▬▬　　SPANISH / ESPAÑOL ▬▬▬

ARABIC / عربى ═══　　RUSSIAN / РУССКИИ ═══　　CHINESE / 中文 ◻◻◻◻　　JAPANESE / 日本語 ▬▬▬▬　　MULTILINGUAL ▭▭▭▭　　OTHER ───

SUMMER ONLY (J)　　WINTER ONLY (D)　　JAMMING /\/\ or / or \　　EARLIEST HEARD ◢　　LATEST HEARD ◣　　+ TENTATIVE

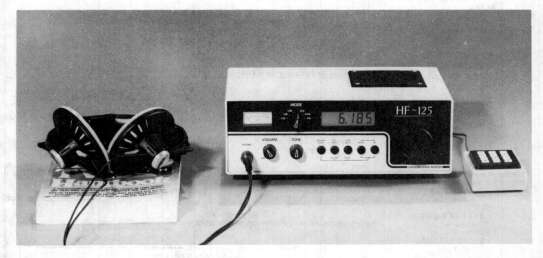

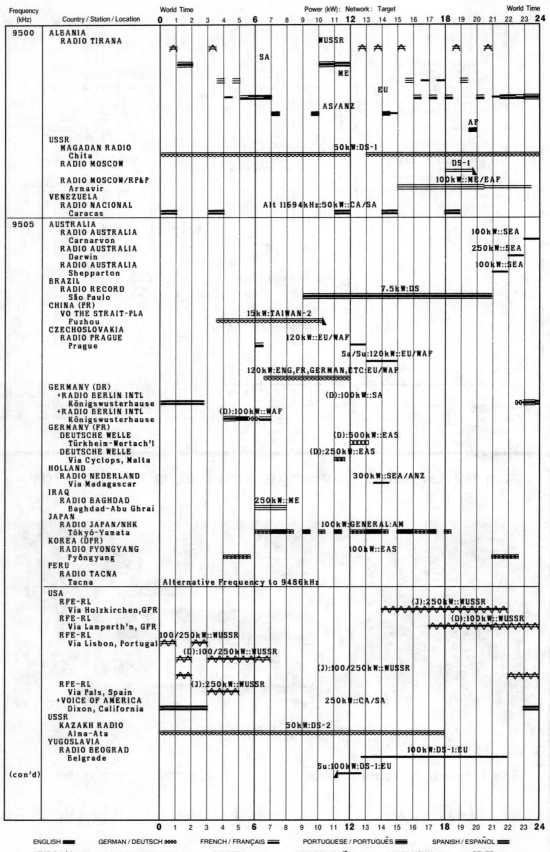

Frequency (kHz) / Country / Station / Location — World Time / Power (kW): Network: Target

9500

ALBANIA
  RADIO TIRANA — WUSSR, SA, ME, EU, AS/ANZ, AF
  USSR
  MAGADAN RADIO — 50kW:DS-1
    Chita
  RADIO MOSCOW — DS-1
  RADIO MOSCOW/RP&P — 100kW::ME/EAF
    Armavir
  VENEZUELA
  RADIO NACIONAL — Alt 11694kHz:50kW::CA/SA
    Caracas

9505

AUSTRALIA
  RADIO AUSTRALIA — 100kW::SEA
    Carnarvon
  RADIO AUSTRALIA — 250kW::SEA
    Darwin
  RADIO AUSTRALIA — 100kW::SEA
    Shepparton
BRAZIL
  RADIO RECORD — 7.5kW:DS
    São Paulo
CHINA (PR)
  VO THE STRAIT-PLA — 15kW:TAIWAN-2
    Fuzhou
CZECHOSLOVAKIA
  RADIO PRAGUE — 120kW::EU/WAF
    Prague — Sa/Su:120kW::EU/WAF
    120kW:ENG,FR,GERMAN,ETC:EU/WAF
GERMANY (DR)
  +RADIO BERLIN INTL — (D):100kW::SA
    Königswusterhause
  +RADIO BERLIN INTL — (D):100kW::WAF
    Königswusterhause
GERMANY (FR)
  DEUTSCHE WELLE — (D):500kW::EAS
    Türkheim-Wertach'l
  DEUTSCHE WELLE — (D):250kW::EAS
    Via Cyclops, Malta
HOLLAND
  RADIO NEDERLAND — 300kW::SEA/ANZ
    Via Madagascar
IRAQ
  RADIO BAGHDAD — 250kW:ME
    Baghdad-Abu Ghrai
JAPAN
  RADIO JAPAN/NHK — 100kW:GENERAL:AM
    Tōkyō-Yamata
KOREA (DPR)
  RADIO PYONGYANG — 100kW::EAS
    Pyŏngyang
PERU
  RADIO TACNA — Alternative Frequency to 9486kHz
    Tacna

USA
  RFE-RL — (J):250kW::WUSSR
    Via Holzkirchen,GFR
  RFE-RL — (D):100kW::WUSSR
    Via Lamperth'm, GFR
  RFE-RL — 100/250kW::WUSSR
    Via Lisbon, Portugal
    (D):100/250kW::WUSSR
    (J):100/250kW::WUSSR
  RFE-RL — (J):250kW::WUSSR
    Via Pals, Spain
  +VOICE OF AMERICA — 250kW::CA/SA
    Dixon, California
USSR
  KAZAKH RADIO — 50kW:DS-2
    Alma-Ata
YUGOSLAVIA
  RADIO BEOGRAD — 100kW:DS-1:EU
    Belgrade — Su:100kW:DS-1:EU

(con'd)

ENGLISH ▬ GERMAN / DEUTSCH ∞∞∞ FRENCH / FRANÇAIS ═ PORTUGUESE / PORTUGUÊS ▬ SPANISH / ESPAÑOL ═
ARABIC / عربي ≣ RUSSIAN / РУССКИИ ═ CHINESE / 中文 ▱▱▱▱ JAPANESE / 日本語 ▰▰▰ MULTILINGUAL ▱▱▱▱ OTHER ─
SUMMER ONLY (J) WINTER ONLY (D) JAMMING ∧∧ or / or \ EARLIEST HEARD ◢ LATEST HEARD ◣ + TENTATIVE

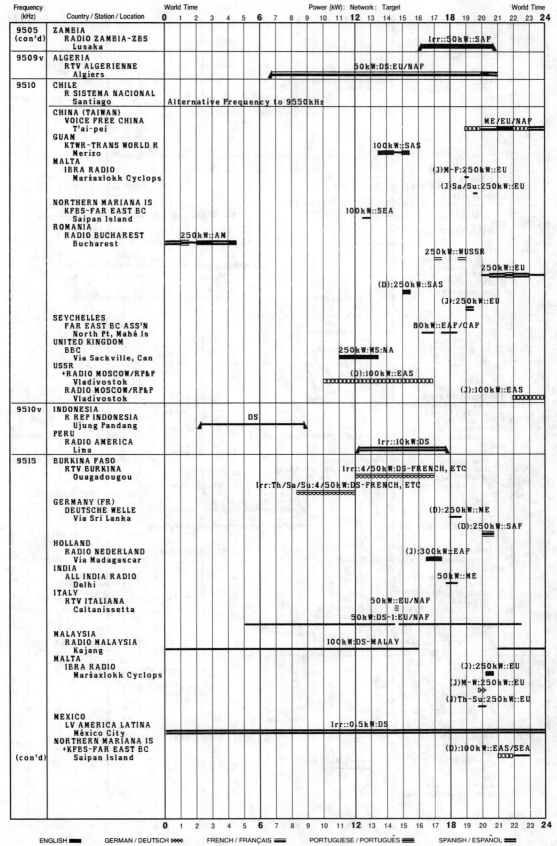

Frequency (kHz)	Country / Station / Location	Power (kW): Network: Target
9505 (con'd)	ZAMBIA RADIO ZAMBIA-ZBS Lusaka	Irr::50kW::SAF (16-18)
9509v	ALGERIA RTV ALGERIENNE Algiers	50kW:DS:EU/NAF
9510	CHILE R SISTEMA NACIONAL Santiago	Alternative Frequency to 9550kHz
	CHINA (TAIWAN) VOICE FREE CHINA T'ai-pei	ME/EU/NAF
	GUAM KTWR-TRANS WORLD R Merizo	100kW::SAS
	MALTA IBRA RADIO Maráaxlokk Cyclops	(J)M-F:250kW::EU / (J)Sa/Su:250kW::EU
	NORTHERN MARIANA IS KFBS-FAR EAST BC Saipan Island	100kW::SEA
	ROMANIA RADIO BUCHAREST Bucharest	250kW::AM / 250kW::WUSSR / 250kW::EU / (D):250kW::SAS / (J):250kW::EU
	SEYCHELLES FAR EAST BC ASS'N North Pt, Mahé Is	80kW::EAF/CAF
	UNITED KINGDOM BBC Via Sackville, Can	250kW:WS:NA
	USSR +RADIO MOSCOW/RP&P Vladivostok	(D):100kW::EAS
	RADIO MOSCOW/RP&P Vladivostok	(J):100kW::EAS
9510v	INDONESIA R REP INDONESIA Ujung Pandang	DS
	PERU RADIO AMERICA Lima	Irr::10kW:DS
9515	BURKINA FASO RTV BURKINA Ouagadougou	Irr::4/50kW:DS-FRENCH, ETC / Irr:Th/Sa/Su:4/50kW:DS-FRENCH, ETC
	GERMANY (FR) DEUTSCHE WELLE Via Sri Lanka	(D):250kW::ME / (D):250kW::SAF
	HOLLAND RADIO NEDERLAND Via Madagascar	(J):300kW::EAF
	INDIA ALL INDIA RADIO Delhi	50kW::ME
	ITALY RTV ITALIANA Caltanissetta	50kW::EU/NAF / 50kW:DS-1:EU/NAF
	MALAYSIA RADIO MALAYSIA Kajang	100kW:DS-MALAY
	MALTA IBRA RADIO Maráaxlokk Cyclops	(J):250kW::EU / (J)M-W:250kW::EU / (J)Th-Su:250kW::EU
	MEXICO LV AMERICA LATINA México City	Irr::0.5kW:DS
(con'd)	NORTHERN MARIANA IS +KFBS-FAR EAST BC Saipan Island	(D):100kW::EAS/SEA

ENGLISH ▬▬ GERMAN / DEUTSCH ◊◊◊◊ FRENCH / FRANÇAIS ▬▬ PORTUGUESE / PORTUGUÊS ▬▬ SPANISH / ESPAÑOL ▬▬

ARABIC /ڹﻟ ▬▬ RUSSIAN / РУССКИИ ▬▬ CHINESE / 中文 ◊◊◊◊ JAPANESE / 日本語 ▬▬ MULTILINGUAL ▬▬ OTHER ▬▬

SUMMER ONLY (J) WINTER ONLY (D) JAMMING ∧∧ or / or \ EARLIEST HEARD ◢ LATEST HEARD ◣ + TENTATIVE

Frequency (kHz)	Country / Station / Location	World Time 0 ... 12 ... 18 ... 24 — Power (kW): Network: Target

9515 (con'd)

TURKEY
  TURKISH RTV CORP
    Ankara — (J):250kW::ME
UNITED KINGDOM
  BBC
    Via Ascension — (J):250kW::SAF
  BBC
    Via Cincinnati, USA — 250kW:WS:ENA/CA/SA
  BBC
    Via Maseru, Lesotho — 100kW:WS:SAF / Sa/Su:100kW:WS:SAF
  +BBC
    Via Sackville, Can — 250kW:WS:NA
  +BBC
    Via Sackville, Can — Sa/Su:250kW:WS:NA
USSR
  RADIO MOSCOW
    Kazan' — (J):240kW:MARINERS:ME/EAF
  RADIO MOSCOW/RP&P
    Leningrad — (D):240kW::NAF/ME
  RADIO MOSCOW/RP&P
    Yerevan — (J):100kW::EAF

9519v

PERU
  RADIO LA CRONICA
    Lima — Irr::5kW:DS

9520

BRAZIL
  RADIO PAMPA
    Pôrto Alegre — Alt 9550kHz:10kW:DS
HUNGARY
  RADIO BUDAPEST
    Jászberény — 250kW::NA / M:250kW::NA / M/W/Sa:250kW:NA / Th/F/Su-Tu:250kW::NA / Tu-Su:250kW::NA / Tu/F:250kW::SA / W/Sa:250kW::NA
NORTHERN MARIANA IS
  KFBS-FAR EAST BC
    Saipan Island — (J):100kW::SEA
PAPUA NEW GUINEA
  NATIONAL BC OF PNG
    Port Moresby — 10kW:DS-ENGLISH, ETC
USA
  RFE-RL
    Via Biblis, GFR — (J):100kW::WUSSR
  RFE-RL
    Via Holzkirchen,GFR — 250kW::WUSSR / (D):250kW::WUSSR / (J):250kW::WUSSR
  RFE-RL
    Via Lamperth'm, GFR — (D):100kW::WUSSR / (J):100kW::WUSSR
  RFE-RL
    Via Lisbon, Portugal — (D):100/250kW::WUSSR
USSR
  RADIO MOSCOW
    Moscow — 240kW::ATL
  RADIO MOSCOW/RP&P
    Irkutsk — (J):240kW::EAS
  +RADIO MOSCOW/RP&P
    Krasnodar — (D):500kW::CA
  +RADIO MOSCOW/RP&P
    Krasnodar — (D):500kW:WS:CA/EU
  RADIO MOSCOW/RP&P
    Vladivostok — 250kW::EAS

9525 (con'd)

CLANDESTINE (M EAST)
  "FREE VO IRAN"
    Via Balad, Iraq — 500kW:ANTI-KHOMEYNI:ME
  "RADIO IRAN"
    Via Balad, Iraq — 500kW:ANTI-KHOMEYNI:ME
CUBA
  RADIO HABANA
    Havana — 50kW::NA
HOLLAND
  RADIO NEDERLAND
    Via Madagascar — 300kW::SEA
INDIA
  ALL INDIA RADIO
    Madras — 100kW:DS-VIVIDH BHARATI
IRAQ
  RADIO BAGHDAD
    Balad-Salah el Deen — 500kW

ENGLISH ▇▇▇   GERMAN / DEUTSCH ००००   FRENCH / FRANÇAIS ▬▬   PORTUGUESE / PORTUGUÊS ▬▬   SPANISH / ESPAÑOL ▬▬

ARABIC / ﻉﺭ ▬   RUSSIAN / РУССКИИ ▬   CHINESE / 中文 ००००   JAPANESE / 日本語 ▬▬   MULTILINGUAL ▬▬   OTHER ▬

SUMMER ONLY (J)   WINTER ONLY (D)   JAMMING /\/\ or / or \   EARLIEST HEARD ◢   LATEST HEARD ◣   + TENTATIVE

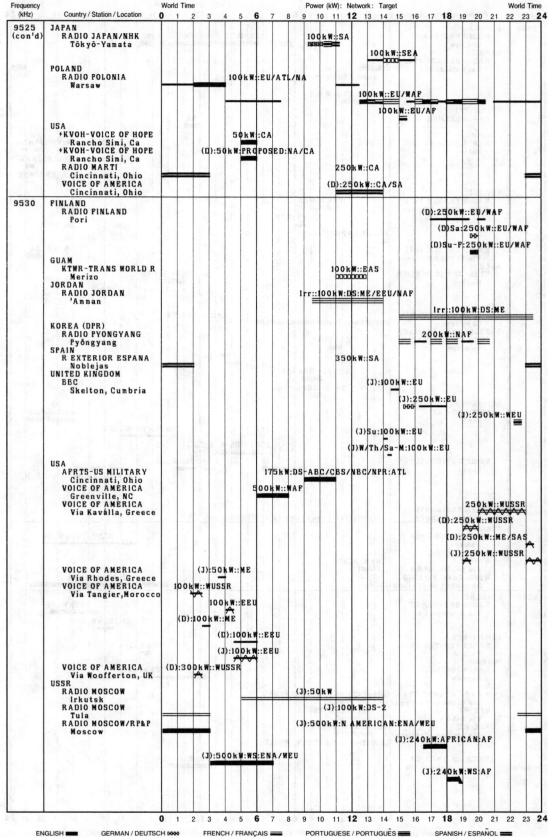

Frequency (kHz)	Country / Station / Location	World Time ... Power (kW): Network: Target ... World Time
9525 (con'd)	JAPAN	
	RADIO JAPAN/NHK Tōkyō-Yamata	100kW::SA
		100kW::SEA
	POLAND	
	RADIO POLONIA Warsaw	100kW::EU/ATL/NA
		100kW::EU/WAF
		100kW::EU/AF
	USA	
	+KVOH-VOICE OF HOPE Rancho Simi, Ca	50kW::CA
	+KVOH-VOICE OF HOPE Rancho Simi, Ca	(D):50kW:PROPOSED:NA/CA
	RADIO MARTI Cincinnati, Ohio	250kW::CA
	VOICE OF AMERICA Cincinnati, Ohio	(D):250kW::CA/SA
9530	FINLAND	
	RADIO FINLAND Pori	(D):250kW::EU/WAF
		(D)Sa:250kW::EU/WAF
		(D)Su-F:250kW::EU/WAF
	GUAM	
	KTWR-TRANS WORLD R Merizo	100kW::EAS
	JORDAN	
	RADIO JORDAN 'Amman	Irr::100kW:DS:ME/EEU/NAF
		Irr::100kW:DS:ME
	KOREA (DPR)	
	RADIO PYONGYANG Pyŏngyang	200kW::NAF
	SPAIN	
	R EXTERIOR ESPANA Noblejas	350kW::SA
	UNITED KINGDOM	
	BBC Skelton, Cumbria	(J):100kW::EU
		(J):250kW::EU
		(J):250kW::WEU
		(J)Su:100kW::EU
		(J)W/Th/Sa-M:100kW::EU
	USA	
	AFRTS-US MILITARY Cincinnati, Ohio	175kW:DS-ABC/CBS/NBC/NPR:ATL
	VOICE OF AMERICA Greenville, NC	500kW::WAF
	VOICE OF AMERICA Via Kaválla, Greece	250kW::WUSSR
		(D):250kW::WUSSR
		(D):250kW::ME/SAS
		(J):250kW::WUSSR
	VOICE OF AMERICA Via Rhodes, Greece	(J):50kW::ME
	VOICE OF AMERICA Via Tangier,Morocco	100kW::WUSSR
		100kW::EEU
		(D):100kW::ME
		(D):100kW::EEU
		(J):100kW::EEU
	VOICE OF AMERICA Via Woofferton, UK	(D):300kW::WUSSR
	USSR	
	RADIO MOSCOW Irkutsk	(J):50kW
	RADIO MOSCOW Tula	(J):100kW:DS-2
	RADIO MOSCOW/RP&P Moscow	(J):500kW:N AMERICAN:ENA/WEU
		(J):240kW:AFRICAN:AF
		(J):500kW:WS:ENA/WEU
		(J):240kW:WS:AF

ENGLISH ▬ GERMAN / DEUTSCH ◊◊◊ FRENCH / FRANÇAIS ═ PORTUGUESE / PORTUGUÊS ≡ SPANISH / ESPAÑOL ▬
ARABIC / ﻋﺭﺑﻲ ≡ RUSSIAN / РУССКИИ ═ CHINESE / 中文 □□□ JAPANESE / 日本語 ▬ MULTILINGUAL ▭▭ OTHER ▬
SUMMER ONLY (J) WINTER ONLY (D) JAMMING /\/\ or / or \ EARLIEST HEARD ◢ LATEST HEARD ◣ + TENTATIVE

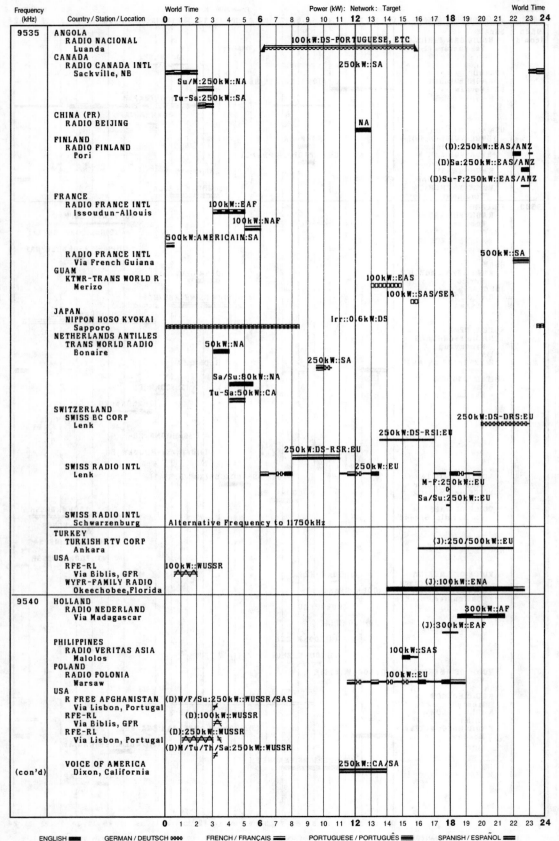

Frequency (kHz)	Country / Station / Location	World Time
9535	ANGOLA RADIO NACIONAL Luanda	100kW:DS-PORTUGUESE, ETC
	CANADA RADIO CANADA INTL Sackville, NB	250kW::SA / Su/M:250kW::NA / Tu-Sa:250kW::SA
	CHINA (PR) RADIO BEIJING	NA
	FINLAND RADIO FINLAND Pori	(D):250kW::EAS/ANZ / (D)Sa:250kW::EAS/ANZ / (D)Su-F:250kW::EAS/ANZ
	FRANCE RADIO FRANCE INTL Issoudun-Allouis	100kW::EAF / 100kW::NAF / 500kW:AMERICAIN:SA
	RADIO FRANCE INTL Via French Guiana	500kW::SA
	GUAM KTWR-TRANS WORLD R Merizo	100kW::EAS / 100kW::SAS/SEA
	JAPAN NIPPON HOSO KYOKAI Sapporo	Irr::0.6kW:DS
	NETHERLANDS ANTILLES TRANS WORLD RADIO Bonaire	50kW::NA / 250kW::SA / Sa/Su:80kW::NA / Tu-Sa:50kW::CA
	SWITZERLAND SWISS BC CORP Lenk	250kW:DS-DRS:EU / 250kW:DS-RSI:EU
	SWISS RADIO INTL Lenk	250kW:DS-RSR:EU / 250kW::EU / M-F:250kW::EU / Sa/Su:250kW::EU
	SWISS RADIO INTL Schwarzenburg	Alternative Frequency to 11750kHz
	TURKEY TURKISH RTV CORP Ankara	(J):250/500kW::EU
	USA RFE-RL Via Biblis, GFR	100kW::WUSSR
	WYFR-FAMILY RADIO Okeechobee, Florida	(J):100kW::ENA
9540	HOLLAND RADIO NEDERLAND Via Madagascar	300kW::AF / (J):300kW::EAF
	PHILIPPINES RADIO VERITAS ASIA Malolos	100kW::SAS
	POLAND RADIO POLONIA Warsaw	100kW::EU
	USA R FREE AFGHANISTAN Via Lisbon, Portugal	(D)W/F/Su:250kW::WUSSR/SAS
	RFE-RL Via Biblis, GFR	(D):100kW::WUSSR
	RFE-RL Via Lisbon, Portugal	(D):250kW::WUSSR
		(D)M/Tu/Th/Sa:250kW::WUSSR
(con'd)	VOICE OF AMERICA Dixon, California	250kW::CA/SA

ENGLISH ▬▬ GERMAN / DEUTSCH ◊◊◊◊ FRENCH / FRANÇAIS ▬▬ PORTUGUESE / PORTUGUÊS ▬▬ SPANISH / ESPAÑOL ▬▬

ARABIC / ﻲﺑﺮﻋ ▬▬ RUSSIAN / РУССКИЙ ▬▬ CHINESE / ◆★ ◻◻◻◻ JAPANESE / 日本語 ▬▬ MULTILINGUAL ▭▭▭ OTHER ▬

SUMMER ONLY (J) WINTER ONLY (D) JAMMING /\/\ or / or \ EARLIEST HEARD ◢ LATEST HEARD ◣ + TENTATIVE

Frequency (kHz)   Country / Station / Location   World Time   Power (kW): Network: Target   World Time

World Time scale: 0 1 2 3 4 5 6 7 8 9 10 11 12 13 14 15 16 17 18 19 20 21 22 23 24

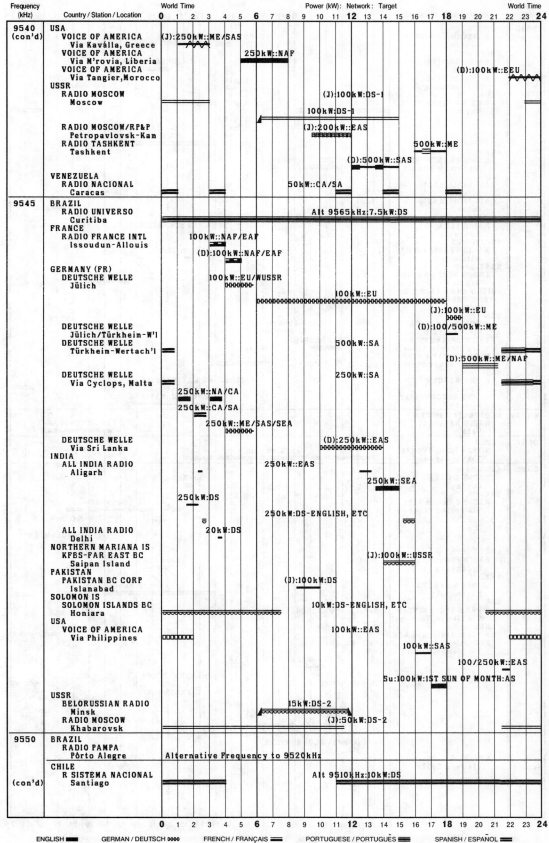

9540 (con'd) USA
- VOICE OF AMERICA, Via Kaválla, Greece — (J):250kW::ME/SAS
- VOICE OF AMERICA, Via M'rovia, Liberia — 250kW::NAF
- VOICE OF AMERICA, Via Tangier, Morocco — (D):100kW::EEU

USSR
- RADIO MOSCOW, Moscow — (J):100kW:DS-1 / 100kW:DS-1
- RADIO MOSCOW/RP&P, Petropavlovsk-Kam — (J):200kW::EAS
- RADIO TASHKENT, Tashkent — 500kW::ME / (D):500kW::SAS

VENEZUELA
- RADIO NACIONAL, Caracas — 50kW::CA/SA

9545 BRAZIL
- RADIO UNIVERSO, Curitiba — Alt 9565kHz:7.5kW:DS

FRANCE
- RADIO FRANCE INTL, Issoudun-Allouis — 100kW::NAF/EAF / (D):100kW::NAF/EAF

GERMANY (FR)
- DEUTSCHE WELLE, Jülich — 100kW::EU/WUSSR / 100kW::EU / (J):100kW::EU
- DEUTSCHE WELLE, Jülich/Türkheim-W'l — (D):100/500kW::ME
- DEUTSCHE WELLE, Türkheim-Wertach'l — 500kW::SA / (D):500kW::ME/NAF
- DEUTSCHE WELLE, Via Cyclops, Malta — 250kW::SA / 250kW::NA/CA / 250kW::CA/SA / 250kW::ME/SAS/SEA
- DEUTSCHE WELLE, Via Sri Lanka — (D):250kW::EAS

INDIA
- ALL INDIA RADIO, Aligarh — 250kW::EAS / 250kW::SEA / 250kW:DS / 250kW:DS-ENGLISH, ETC
- ALL INDIA RADIO, Delhi — 20kW:DS

NORTHERN MARIANA IS
- KFBS-FAR EAST BC, Saipan Island — (J):100kW::USSR

PAKISTAN
- PAKISTAN BC CORP, Islamabad — (J):100kW:DS

SOLOMON IS
- SOLOMON ISLANDS BC, Honiara — 10kW:DS-ENGLISH, ETC

USA
- VOICE OF AMERICA, Via Philippines — 100kW::EAS / 100kW::SAS / 100/250kW::EAS / Su:100kW:1ST SUN OF MONTH:AS

USSR
- BELORUSSIAN RADIO, Minsk — 15kW:DS-2
- RADIO MOSCOW, Khabarovsk — (J):50kW:DS-2

9550 BRAZIL
- RADIO PAMPA, Pôrto Alegre — Alternative Frequency to 9520kHz

CHILE
- R SISTEMA NACIONAL, Santiago — Alt 9510kHz:10kW:DS

(con'd)

World Time scale: 0 1 2 3 4 5 6 7 8 9 10 11 12 13 14 15 16 17 18 19 20 21 22 23 24

ENGLISH ▪▪▪   GERMAN / DEUTSCH ◊◊◊◊   FRENCH / FRANÇAIS ▤▤   PORTUGUESE / PORTUGUÊS ▨▨   SPANISH / ESPAÑOL ▤▤

ARABIC /ﺱﺏ▤   RUSSIAN / РУССКИИ ▭▭   CHINESE / 中文 ▨▨▨   JAPANESE / 日本語 ▨▨▨   MULTILINGUAL ▨▨▨   OTHER ▬

SUMMER ONLY (J)   WINTER ONLY (D)   JAMMING /\/\ or / or \   EARLIEST HEARD ◢   LATEST HEARD ◣   + TENTATIVE

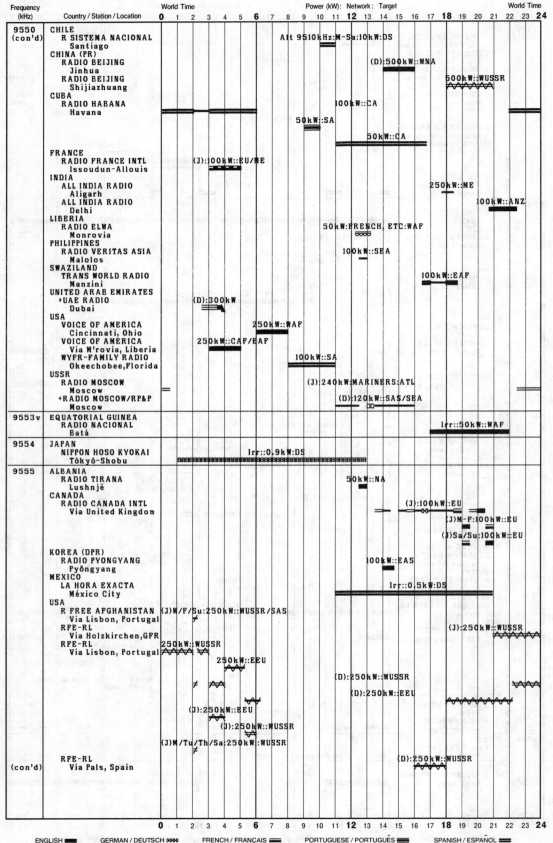

Frequency (kHz)	Country / Station / Location	World Time	Power (kW): Network: Target	World Time

9550 (con'd)

CHILE
R SISTEMA NACIONAL — Santiago — Alt 9510kHz:M-Sa:10kW:DS

CHINA (PR)
RADIO BEIJING — Jinhua — (D):500kW::WNA
RADIO BEIJING — Shijiazhuang — 500kW::WUSSR

CUBA
RADIO HABANA — Havana — 100kW::CA / 50kW::SA / 50kW::CA

FRANCE
RADIO FRANCE INTL — Issoudun-Allouis — (J):100kW::EU/ME

INDIA
ALL INDIA RADIO — Aligarh — 250kW::ME
ALL INDIA RADIO — Delhi — 100kW::ANZ

LIBERIA
RADIO ELWA — Monrovia — 50kW:FRENCH, ETC:WAF

PHILIPPINES
RADIO VERITAS ASIA — Malolos — 100kW::SEA

SWAZILAND
TRANS WORLD RADIO — Manzini — 100kW::EAF

UNITED ARAB EMIRATES
+UAE RADIO — Dubai — (D):300kW

USA
VOICE OF AMERICA — Cincinnati, Ohio — 250kW::WAF
VOICE OF AMERICA — Via M'rovia, Liberia — 250kW::CAF/EAF
WYFR-FAMILY RADIO — Okeechobee,Florida — 100kW::SA
USSR
RADIO MOSCOW — Moscow — (J):240kW:MARINERS:ATL
+RADIO MOSCOW/RP&P — Moscow — (D):120kW::SAS/SEA

9553v

EQUATORIAL GUINEA
RADIO NACIONAL — Batá — Irr::50kW::WAF

9554

JAPAN
NIPPON HOSO KYOKAI — Tōkyō-Shobu — Irr::0,9kW:DS

9555

ALBANIA
RADIO TIRANA — Lushnjë — 50kW::NA

CANADA
RADIO CANADA INTL — Via United Kingdom — (J):100kW::EU / (J)M-F:100kW::EU / (J)Sa/Su:100kW::EU

KOREA (DPR)
RADIO PYONGYANG — Pyŏngyang — 100kW::EAS

MEXICO
LA HORA EXACTA — México City — Irr::0,5kW:DS

USA
R FREE AFGHANISTAN — Via Lisbon, Portugal — (J)W/F/Su:250kW::WUSSR/SAS
RFE-RL — Via Holzkirchen,GFR — (J):250kW::WUSSR
RFE-RL — Via Lisbon, Portugal — 250kW::WUSSR / 250kW::EEU / (D):250kW::WUSSR / (D):250kW::EEU / (J):250kW::EEU / (J):250kW::WUSSR / (J)M/Tu/Th/Sa:250kW:WUSSR

(con'd)
RFE-RL — Via Pals, Spain — (D):250kW::WUSSR

ENGLISH ▆▆▆   GERMAN / DEUTSCH ◖◖◖◖   FRENCH / FRANÇAIS ▬▬   PORTUGUESE / PORTUGUÊS ▬▬   SPANISH / ESPAÑOL ▬▬

ARABIC / عربى ▬▬   RUSSIAN / РУССКИИ ▬▬   CHINESE / 中文 ◖◖◖◖   JAPANESE / 日本語 ▬▬   MULTILINGUAL ▬▬   OTHER ▬▬

SUMMER ONLY (J)   WINTER ONLY (D)   JAMMING ∧∧ or / or \   EARLIEST HEARD ◢   LATEST HEARD ◣   + TENTATIVE

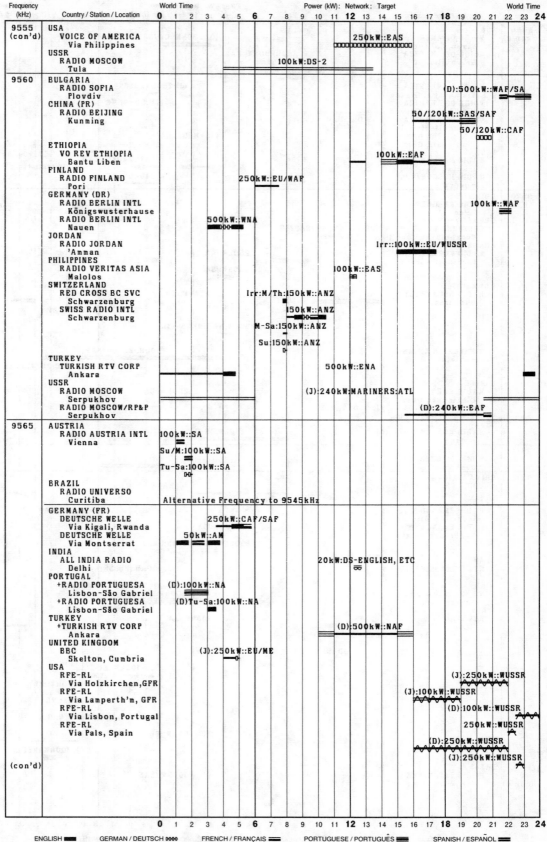

Frequency (kHz) | Country / Station / Location | World Time 0–24 | Power (kW): Network: Target

9555 (con'd)
- USA — VOICE OF AMERICA, Via Philippines — 250kW::EAS
- USSR — RADIO MOSCOW, Tula — 100kW:DS-2

9560
- BULGARIA — RADIO SOFIA, Plovdiv — (D):500kW::WAF/SA
- CHINA (PR) — RADIO BEIJING, Kunming — 50/120kW::SAS/SAF ; 50/120kW::CAF
- ETHIOPIA — VO REV ETHIOPIA, Bantu Liben — 100kW::EAF
- FINLAND — RADIO FINLAND, Pori — 250kW:EU/WAF
- GERMANY (DR) — RADIO BERLIN INTL, Königswusterhause — 100kW::WAF
- RADIO BERLIN INTL, Nauen — 500kW::WNA
- JORDAN — RADIO JORDAN, 'Amman — Irr::100kW::EU/WUSSR
- PHILIPPINES — RADIO VERITAS ASIA, Malolos — 100kW::EAS
- SWITZERLAND — RED CROSS BC SVC, Schwarzenburg — Irr:M/Th:150kW::ANZ
- SWISS RADIO INTL, Schwarzenburg — 150kW::ANZ ; M-Sa:150kW::ANZ ; Su:150kW::ANZ
- TURKEY — TURKISH RTV CORP, Ankara — 500kW::ENA
- USSR — RADIO MOSCOW, Serpukhov — (J):240kW:MARINERS:ATL
- RADIO MOSCOW/RP&P, Serpukhov — (D):240kW::EAF

9565
- AUSTRIA — RADIO AUSTRIA INTL, Vienna — 100kW::SA ; Su/M:100kW::SA ; Tu-Sa:100kW::SA
- BRAZIL — RADIO UNIVERSO, Curitiba — Alternative Frequency to 9545kHz
- GERMANY (FR) — DEUTSCHE WELLE, Via Kigali, Rwanda — 250kW::CAF/SAF
- DEUTSCHE WELLE, Via Montserrat — 50kW::AM
- INDIA — ALL INDIA RADIO, Delhi — 20kW:DS-ENGLISH, ETC
- PORTUGAL — +RADIO PORTUGUESA, Lisbon-São Gabriel — (D):100kW::NA
- +RADIO PORTUGUESA, Lisbon-São Gabriel — (D)Tu-Sa:100kW::NA
- TURKEY — +TURKISH RTV CORP, Ankara — (D):500kW::NAF
- UNITED KINGDOM — BBC, Skelton, Cumbria — (J):250kW::EU/ME
- USA — RFE-RL, Via Holzkirchen,GFR — (J):250kW::WUSSR
- RFE-RL, Via Lamperth'm, GFR — (J):100kW::WUSSR
- RFE-RL, Via Lisbon, Portugal — (D):100kW::WUSSR
- RFE-RL, Via Pals, Spain — 250kW::WUSSR ; (D):250kW::WUSSR ; (J):250kW::WUSSR

(con'd)

World Time: 0 1 2 3 4 5 6 7 8 9 10 11 12 13 14 15 16 17 18 19 20 21 22 23 24

| Frequency (kHz) | Country / Station / Location | World Time 0 1 2 3 4 5 6 7 8 9 10 11 12 13 14 15 16 17 18 19 20 21 22 23 24 | Power (kW): Network: Target | World Time |

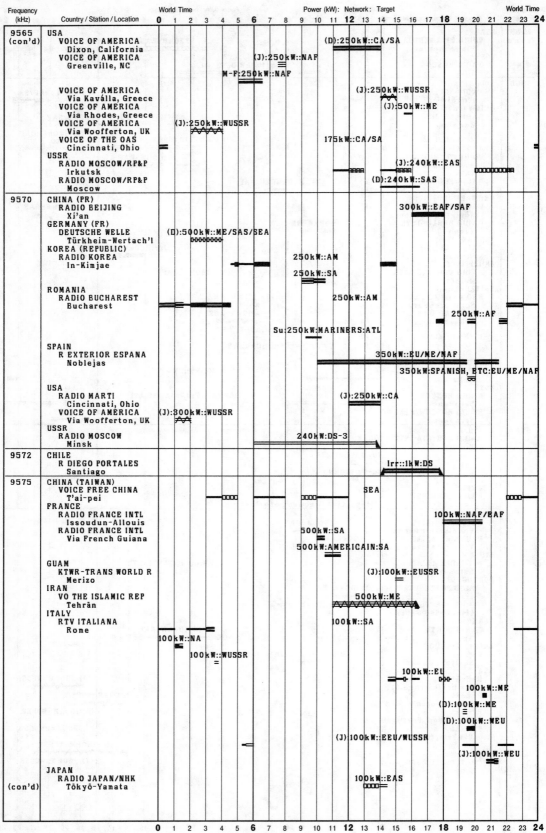

9565 (con'd)

USA
  VOICE OF AMERICA
  Dixon, California — (D):250kW::CA/SA
  VOICE OF AMERICA
  Greenville, NC — (J):250kW::NAF ; M-F:250kW::NAF
  VOICE OF AMERICA
  Via Kaválla, Greece — (J):250kW::WUSSR
  VOICE OF AMERICA
  Via Rhodes, Greece — (J):50kW::ME
  VOICE OF AMERICA
  Via Woofferton, UK — (J):250kW::WUSSR
  VOICE OF THE OAS
  Cincinnati, Ohio — 175kW::CA/SA
USSR
  RADIO MOSCOW/RP&P
  Irkutsk — (J):240kW::EAS
  RADIO MOSCOW/RP&P
  Moscow — (D):240kW::SAS

9570

CHINA (PR)
  RADIO BEIJING
  Xi'an — 300kW::EAF/SAF
GERMANY (FR)
  DEUTSCHE WELLE
  Türkheim-Wertach'l — (D):500kW::ME/SAS/SEA
KOREA (REPUBLIC)
  RADIO KOREA
  In-Kimjae — 250kW::AM ; 250kW::SA
ROMANIA
  RADIO BUCHAREST
  Bucharest — 250kW::AM ; 250kW::AF ; Su:250kW:MARINERS:ATL
SPAIN
  R EXTERIOR ESPANA
  Noblejas — 350kW::EU/ME/NAF ; 350kW:SPANISH, ETC:EU/ME/NAF
USA
  RADIO MARTI
  Cincinnati, Ohio — (J):250kW::CA
  VOICE OF AMERICA
  Via Woofferton, UK — (J):300kW::WUSSR
USSR
  RADIO MOSCOW
  Minsk — 240kW:DS-3

9572

CHILE
  R DIEGO PORTALES
  Santiago — Irr::1kW:DS

9575

CHINA (TAIWAN)
  VOICE FREE CHINA
  T'ai-pei — SEA
FRANCE
  RADIO FRANCE INTL
  Issoudun-Allouis — 100kW::NAF/EAF
  RADIO FRANCE INTL
  Via French Guiana — 500kW::SA ; 500kW:AMERICAIN:SA
GUAM
  KTWR-TRANS WORLD R
  Merizo — (J):100kW::EUSSR
IRAN
  VO THE ISLAMIC REP
  Tehrān — 500kW::ME
ITALY
  RTV ITALIANA
  Rome — 100kW::SA ; 100kW::NA ; 100kW::WUSSR ; 100kW::EU ; 100kW::ME ; (D):100kW::ME ; (D):100kW::WEU ; (J)100kW::EEU/WUSSR ; (J):100kW::WEU
JAPAN
  RADIO JAPAN/NHK
  Tōkyō-Yamata **(con'd)** — 100kW::EAS

World Time: 0 1 2 3 4 5 6 7 8 9 10 11 12 13 14 15 16 17 18 19 20 21 22 23 24

ENGLISH ▄▄▄   GERMAN / DEUTSCH ▮▮▮   FRENCH / FRANÇAIS ▬▬   PORTUGUESE / PORTUGUÊS ▬▬   SPANISH / ESPAÑOL ▬
ARABIC / ﻉﺮﺑﻲ ▬   RUSSIAN / РУССКИЙ ▬   CHINESE / 中文 ▮▮▮   JAPANESE / 日本語 ▮▮▮   MULTILINGUAL ▮▮▮   OTHER ▬
SUMMER ONLY (J)   WINTER ONLY (D)   JAMMING /\/\ or / or \   EARLIEST HEARD ◢   LATEST HEARD ◣   + TENTATIVE

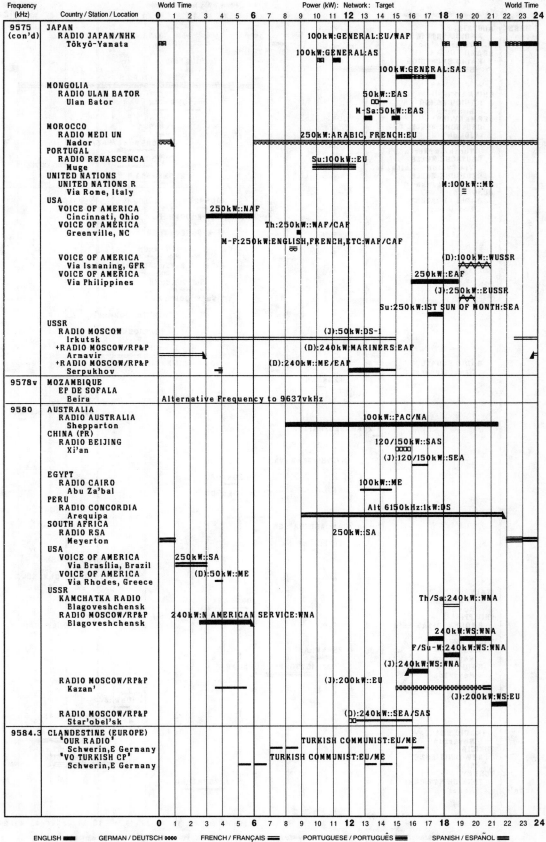

Frequency (kHz)	Country / Station / Location	World Time
9575 (con'd)	**JAPAN**	
	RADIO JAPAN/NHK Tōkyō-Yamata	100kW:GENERAL:EU/WAF
		100kW:GENERAL:AS
		100kW:GENERAL:SAS
	MONGOLIA	
	RADIO ULAN BATOR Ulan Bator	50kW::EAS
		M-Sa:50kW::EAS
	MOROCCO	
	RADIO MEDI UN Nador	250kW:ARABIC, FRENCH:EU
	PORTUGAL	
	RADIO RENASCENCA Muge	Su:100kW::EU
	UNITED NATIONS	
	UNITED NATIONS R Via Rome, Italy	M:100kW::ME
	USA	
	VOICE OF AMERICA Cincinnati, Ohio	250kW::NAF
	VOICE OF AMERICA Greenville, NC	Th:250kW::WAF/CAF
		M-F:250kW:ENGLISH,FRENCH,ETC:WAF/CAF
	VOICE OF AMERICA Via Ismaning, GFR	(D):100kW:WUSSR
	VOICE OF AMERICA Via Philippines	250kW::EAF
		(J):250kW::EUSSR
		Su:250kW:1ST SUN OF MONTH:SEA
	USSR	
	RADIO MOSCOW Irkutsk	(J):50kW:DS-1
	+RADIO MOSCOW/RP&P Armavir	(D):240kW:MARINERS:EAF
	+RADIO MOSCOW/RP&P Serpukhov	(D):240kW::ME/EAF
9578v	**MOZAMBIQUE**	
	EP DE SOFALA Beira	Alternative Frequency to 9637vkHz
9580	**AUSTRALIA**	
	RADIO AUSTRALIA Shepparton	100kW::PAC/NA
	CHINA (PR)	
	RADIO BEIJING Xi'an	120/150kW::SAS
		(J):120/150kW::SEA
	EGYPT	
	RADIO CAIRO Abu Za'bal	100kW::ME
	PERU	
	RADIO CONCORDIA Arequipa	Alt 6150kHz:1kW:DS
	SOUTH AFRICA	
	RADIO RSA Meyerton	250kW::SA
	USA	
	VOICE OF AMERICA Via Brasília, Brazil	250kW::SA
	VOICE OF AMERICA Via Rhodes, Greece	(D):50kW::ME
	USSR	
	KAMCHATKA RADIO Blagoveshchensk	Th/Sa:240kW::WNA
	RADIO MOSCOW/RP&P Blagoveshchensk	240kW:N AMERICAN SERVICE:WNA
		240kW:WS:WNA
		F/Su-W:240kW:WS:WNA
		(J):240kW:WS:WNA
	RADIO MOSCOW/RP&P Kazan'	(J):200kW::EU
		(J):200kW:WS:EU
	RADIO MOSCOW/RP&P Star'obel'sk	(D):240kW::SEA/SAS
9584.3	**CLANDESTINE (EUROPE)**	
	"OUR RADIO" Schwerin,E Germany	TURKISH COMMUNIST:EU/ME
	"VO TURKISH CP" Schwerin,E Germany	TURKISH COMMUNIST:EU/ME

World Time scale: 0 1 2 3 4 5 6 7 8 9 10 11 12 13 14 15 16 17 18 19 20 21 22 23 24

Power (kW): Network: Target

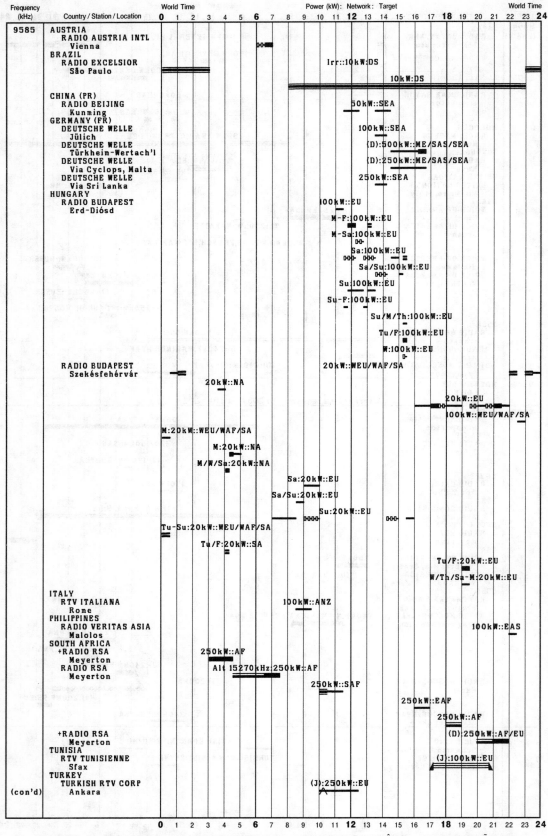

| Frequency (kHz) | Country / Station / Location | World Time | Power (kW): Network: Target | World Time |

9585

AUSTRIA
RADIO AUSTRIA INTL
  Vienna
BRAZIL
RADIO EXCELSIOR — Irr::10kW:DS
  São Paulo
      10kW:DS

CHINA (PR)
RADIO BEIJING — 50kW::SEA
  Kunming
GERMANY (FR)
DEUTSCHE WELLE — 100kW::SEA
  Jülich
DEUTSCHE WELLE — (D):500kW::ME/SAS/SEA
  Türkheim-Wertach'l
DEUTSCHE WELLE — (D):250kW::ME/SAS/SEA
  Via Cyclops, Malta
DEUTSCHE WELLE — 250kW::SEA
  Via Sri Lanka
HUNGARY
RADIO BUDAPEST — 100kW::EU
  Erd-Diósd
    M-F:100kW::EU
    M-Sa:100kW::EU
    Sa:100kW::EU
    Sa/Su:100kW::EU
    Su:100kW::EU
    Su-F:100kW::EU
    Su/M/Th:100kW::EU
    Tu/F:100kW::EU
    W:100kW::EU

RADIO BUDAPEST — 20kW::WEU/WAF/SA
  Szekésfehérvár
    20kW::NA
    20kW::EU
    100kW::WEU/WAF/SA
    M:20kW::WEU/WAF/SA
    M:20kW::NA
    M/W/Sa:20kW::NA
    Sa:20kW::EU
    Sa/Su:20kW::EU
    Su:20kW::EU
    Tu-Su:20kW::WEU/WAF/SA
    Tu/F:20kW::SA
    Tu/F:20kW::EU
    W/Th/Sa-M:20kW::EU

ITALY
RTV ITALIANA — 100kW::ANZ
  Rome
PHILIPPINES
RADIO VERITAS ASIA — 100kW::EAS
  Malolos
SOUTH AFRICA
+RADIO RSA — 250kW::AF
  Meyerton
RADIO RSA — Alt 15270kHz:250kW::AF
  Meyerton
    250kW::SAF
    250kW::EAF
    250kW::AF

+RADIO RSA — (D):250kW::AF/EU
  Meyerton
TUNISIA
RTV TUNISIENNE — (J):100kW::EU
  Sfax
TURKEY
TURKISH RTV CORP — (J):250kW::EU
(con'd) Ankara

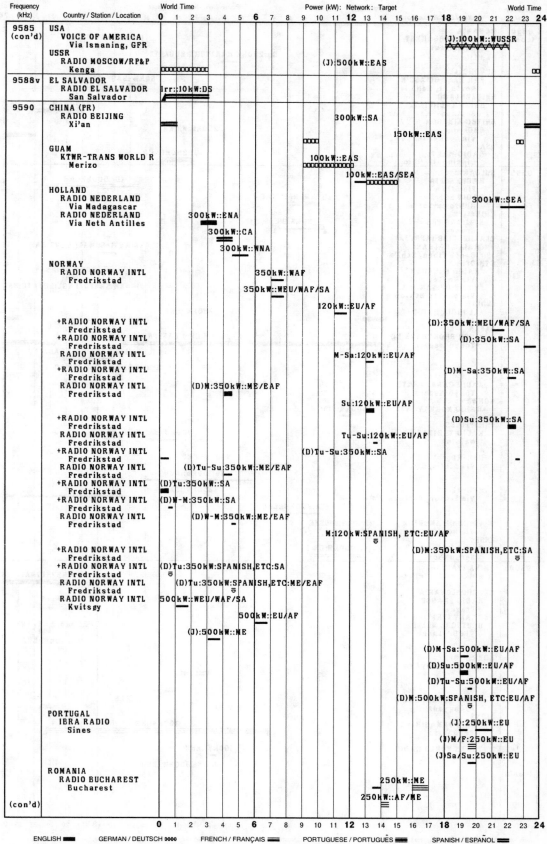

Frequency (kHz)	Country / Station / Location	World Time / Power (kW): Network: Target
9585 (con'd)	**USA** **VOICE OF AMERICA** Via Ismaning, GFR	(J):100kW::WUSSR
	USSR **RADIO MOSCOW/RP&P** Kenga	(J):500kW::EAS
9588v	**EL SALVADOR** **RADIO EL SALVADOR** San Salvador	Irr::10kW:DS
9590	**CHINA (PR)** **RADIO BEIJING** Xi'an	300kW::SA / 150kW::EAS
	GUAM **KTWR-TRANS WORLD R** Merizo	100kW::EAS / 100kW::EAS/SEA
	HOLLAND **RADIO NEDERLAND** Via Madagascar	300kW::SEA
	RADIO NEDERLAND Via Neth Antilles	300kW::ENA / 300kW::CA / 300kW::WNA
	NORWAY **RADIO NORWAY INTL** Fredrikstad	350kW::WAF / 350kW::WEU/WAF/SA / 120kW::EU/AF
	+**RADIO NORWAY INTL** Fredrikstad	(D):350kW::WEU/WAF/SA
	+**RADIO NORWAY INTL** Fredrikstad	(D):350kW::SA
	RADIO NORWAY INTL Fredrikstad	M-Sa:120kW::EU/AF
	+**RADIO NORWAY INTL** Fredrikstad	(D)M-Sa:350kW::SA
	RADIO NORWAY INTL Fredrikstad	(D)M:350kW::ME/EAF
	+**RADIO NORWAY INTL** Fredrikstad	Su:120kW::EU/AF
	RADIO NORWAY INTL Fredrikstad	(D)Su:350kW::SA
	RADIO NORWAY INTL Fredrikstad	Tu-Su:120kW::EU/AF
	+**RADIO NORWAY INTL** Fredrikstad	(D)Tu-Su:350kW::SA
	RADIO NORWAY INTL Fredrikstad	(D)Tu-Su:350kW::ME/EAF
	+**RADIO NORWAY INTL** Fredrikstad	(D)Tu:350kW::SA
	+**RADIO NORWAY INTL** Fredrikstad	(D)W-M:350kW::SA
	RADIO NORWAY INTL Fredrikstad	(D)W-M:350kW::ME/EAF
		M:120kW:SPANISH, ETC:EU/AF
	+**RADIO NORWAY INTL** Fredrikstad	(D)M:350kW:SPANISH,ETC:SA
	+**RADIO NORWAY INTL** Fredrikstad	(D)Tu:350kW:SPANISH,ETC:SA
	RADIO NORWAY INTL Fredrikstad	(D)Tu:350kW:SPANISH,ETC:ME/EAF
	RADIO NORWAY INTL Kvitsøy	500kW::WEU/WAF/SA / 500kW::EU/AF / (J):500kW::ME
		(D)M-Sa:500kW::EU/AF
		(D)Su:500kW::EU/AF
		(D)Tu-Su:500kW::EU/AF
		(D)M:500kW:SPANISH, ETC:EU/AF
	PORTUGAL **IBRA RADIO** Sines	(J):250kW::EU / (J)M/F:250kW::EU / (J)Sa/Su:250kW::EU
	ROMANIA **RADIO BUCHAREST** Bucharest	250kW::ME / 250kW::AF/ME
(con'd)		

World Time 0 1 2 3 4 5 6 7 8 9 10 11 12 13 14 15 16 17 18 19 20 21 22 23 24

ENGLISH ▬▬ GERMAN / DEUTSCH ০০০০ FRENCH / FRANÇAIS ═══ PORTUGUESE / PORTUGUÊS ▬▬ SPANISH / ESPAÑOL ▬▬

ARABIC / ﻉﺭﺏ ═══ RUSSIAN / РУССКИИ ═══ CHINESE / 中文 ০০০০ JAPANESE / 日本語 ▬▬ MULTILINGUAL ৪৪৪৪ OTHER ▬▬

SUMMER ONLY (J) WINTER ONLY (D) JAMMING /\/\ or / or \ EARLIEST HEARD ◢ LATEST HEARD ◣ + TENTATIVE

Frequency (kHz)	Country / Station / Location	World Time 0-24 (Power (kW): Network: Target)

9590 (con'd)

ROMANIA
RADIO BUCHAREST
Bucharest
- (D):250kW::WUSSR
- Su:250kW:MARINERS:WEU/ATL

SEYCHELLES
FAR EAST BC ASS'N
North Pt, Mahé Is
- 80kW::SAS

SWITZERLAND
SWISS RADIO INTL
Sottens
- 500kW::WAF

UNITED KINGDOM
BBC
Via Sackville, Can
- 250kW:WS:NA

USA
RADIO MARTI
Cincinnati, Ohio
- (D):250kW::CA

9595

BULGARIA
RADIO SOFIA
Plovdiv
- (D):500kW::ME
RADIO SOFIA
Rebrovo-Sofia
- 250kW::NAF/WAF

CHINA (PR)
XINJIANG PBS
Urümqi
- 50kW:DS

CLANDESTINE (AFRICA)
"RADIO HALGAN"
Bantu Liben, Ethi'a
- 100kW:ANTI-SOMALI GOVT:EAF

ETHIOPIA
"RADIO FREEDOM"
Via Vo Rev Ethiopia
- 100kW:ANC:SAF
"VOICE OF NAMIBIA"
Via Vo Rev Ethiopia
- 100kW:SWAPO/ENGLISH, ETC:SAF

INDIA
ALL INDIA RADIO
Aligarh
- 250kW::SEA

JAPAN
NIHON SHORTWAVE BC
Tōkyō-Nagara
- 50kW:DS-1:EAS/PAC
- M-F:50kW:DS-1:EAS/PAC
- M-Sa:50kW:DS-1:EAS/PAC

RADIO CANADA INTL
Tōkyō-Nagara
- 50kW::EAS/PAC

NORWAY
+RADIO NORWAY INTL
Kvitsøy
- 500kW::SAS

PHILIPPINES
RADIO VERITAS ASIA
Malolos
- 100kW:SAS/SEA

USA
RFE-RL
Via Biblis, GFR
- 100kW::EEU
- Su:100kW::EEU

RFE-RL
Via Lisbon, Portugal
- 250kW::EEU
- M-Sa:250kW::EEU

VOICE OF AMERICA
Via Woofferton, UK
- (J):250kW::WUSSR

USSR
RADIO MOSCOW
Serpukhov
- (J):100kW:DS-1

9600

CHINA (TAIWAN)
VOICE FREE CHINA
T'ai-pei
- ME/EU/NAF

CZECHOSLOVAKIA
RADIO PRAGUE
Prague
- 120kW::AF

GERMANY (FR)
DEUTSCHE WELLE
Via Sri Lanka
- (D):250kW::SEA/ANZ
- (D):250kW::SEA

KOREA (DPR)
RADIO PYONGYANG
- CA

RADIO PYONGYANG
Pyŏngyang
- 100kW::EAS

LIBYA
RADIO JAMAHIRIYA
Benghazi
- 100kW::ME

MONACO
TRANS WORLD RADIO
Monte Carlo
- 100kW::EEU
- Sa/Su:100kW::EEU

(con'd)

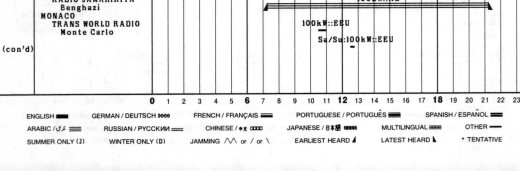

ENGLISH ▬▬ GERMAN / DEUTSCH ▨▨ FRENCH / FRANÇAIS ▬▬ PORTUGUESE / PORTUGUÊS ▬▬ SPANISH / ESPAÑOL ▬▬
ARABIC / العربية ≡≡ RUSSIAN / РУССКИИ ▬▬ CHINESE / 中文 ▨▨ JAPANESE / 日本語 ▨▨ MULTILINGUAL ▨▨ OTHER ▬▬
SUMMER ONLY (J) WINTER ONLY (D) JAMMING /\/\ or / or \ EARLIEST HEARD ◢ LATEST HEARD ◣ + TENTATIVE

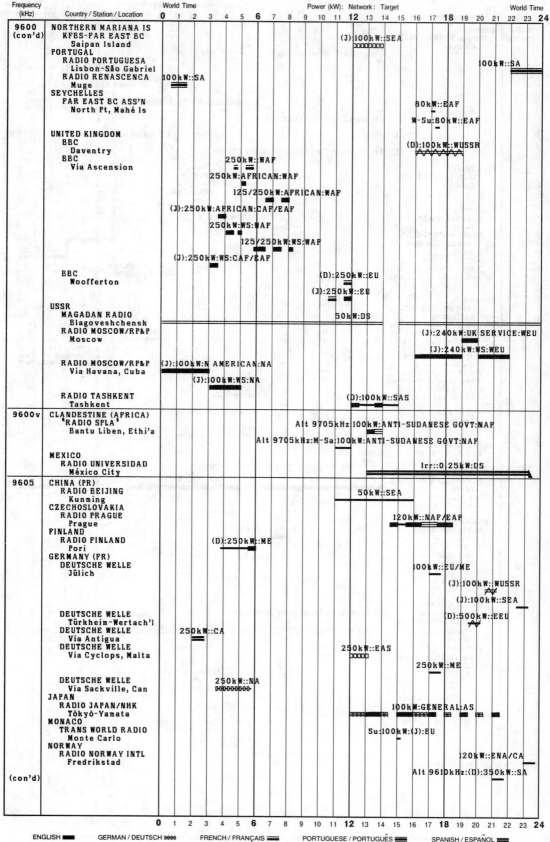

Frequency (kHz)	Country / Station / Location	World Time	Power (kW): Network: Target
9600 (con'd)	NORTHERN MARIANA IS		
	KFBS-FAR EAST BC		(J):100kW::SEA
	Saipan Island		
	PORTUGAL		
	RADIO PORTUGUESA		100kW::SA
	Lisbon-São Gabriel		
	RADIO RENASCENCA	100kW::SA	
	Muge		
	SEYCHELLES		
	FAR EAST BC ASS'N		80kW::EAF
	North Pt, Mahé Is		W-Su:80kW::EAF
	UNITED KINGDOM		
	BBC		(D):100kW::WUSSR
	Daventry		
	BBC		
	Via Ascension	250kW:WAF	
		250kW:AFRICAN:WAF	
		125/250kW:AFRICAN:WAF	
		(J):250kW:AFRICAN:CAF/EAF	
		250kW:WS:WAF	
		125/250kW:WS:WAF	
		(J):250kW:WS:CAF/EAF	
	BBC		(D):250kW::EU
	Woofferton		(J):250kW::EU
	USSR		
	MAGADAN RADIO	50kW:DS	
	Blagoveshchensk		
	RADIO MOSCOW/RP&P		(J):240kW:UK SERVICE:WEU
	Moscow		(J):240kW:WS:WEU
	RADIO MOSCOW/RP&P	(J):100kW:N AMERICAN:NA	
	Via Havana, Cuba	(J):100kW:WS:NA	
	RADIO TASHKENT		(D):100kW::SAS
	Tashkent		
9600v	CLANDESTINE (AFRICA)		
	"RADIO SPLA"	Alt 9705kHz 100kW:ANTI-SUDANESE GOVT:NAF	
	Bantu Liben, Ethi'a	Alt 9705kHz:M-Sa:100kW:ANTI-SUDANESE GOVT:NAF	
	MEXICO		
	RADIO UNIVERSIDAD	Irr::0.25kW:DS	
	México City		
9605	CHINA (PR)		
	RADIO BEIJING	50kW::SEA	
	Kunming		
	CZECHOSLOVAKIA		
	RADIO PRAGUE		120kW::NAF/EAF
	Prague		
	FINLAND		
	RADIO FINLAND	(D):250kW::ME	
	Pori		
	GERMANY (FR)		
	DEUTSCHE WELLE		100kW::EU/ME
	Jülich		(J):100kW::WUSSR
			(J):100kW::SEA
	DEUTSCHE WELLE		(D):500kW::EEU
	Türkheim-Wertach'l		
	DEUTSCHE WELLE	250kW::CA	
	Via Antigua		
	DEUTSCHE WELLE		250kW::EAS
	Via Cyclops, Malta		250kW::ME
	DEUTSCHE WELLE	250kW::NA	
	Via Sackville, Can		
	JAPAN		
	RADIO JAPAN/NHK		100kW:GENERAL:AS
	Tōkyō-Yamata		
	MONACO		
	TRANS WORLD RADIO		Su:100kW:(J):EU
	Monte Carlo		
	NORWAY		
	RADIO NORWAY INTL		120kW::ENA/CA
	Fredrikstad		Alt 9610kHz:(D):350kW::SA
(con'd)			

ENGLISH ▬ GERMAN / DEUTSCH ∞∞ FRENCH / FRANÇAIS ▬ PORTUGUESE / PORTUGUÊS ▬ SPANISH / ESPAÑOL ▬
ARABIC / ئبر ≡ RUSSIAN / РУССКИИ ═ CHINESE / 中文 □□□□ JAPANESE / 日本語 ▤▤▤ MULTILINGUAL ▨▨▨ OTHER ▬
SUMMER ONLY (J)   WINTER ONLY (D)   JAMMING /\/\ or / or \   EARLIEST HEARD ◢   LATEST HEARD ◣   + TENTATIVE

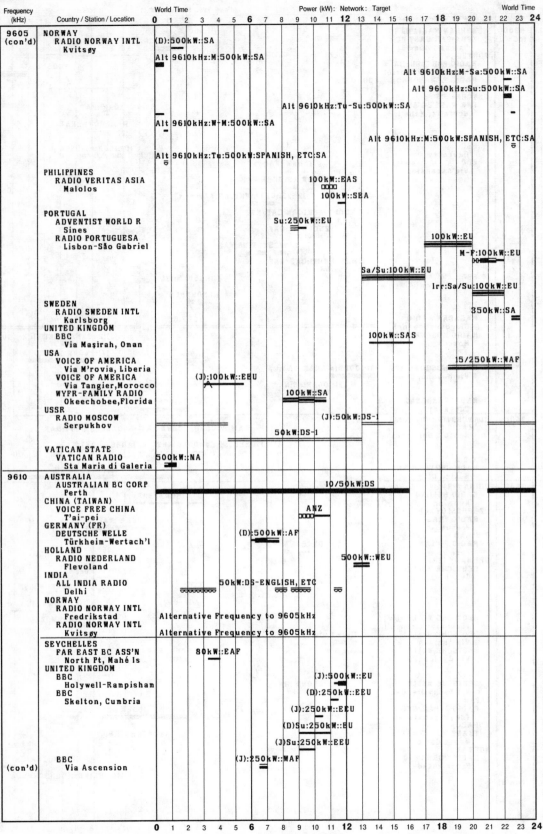

Frequency (kHz)	Country / Station / Location	World Time 0 – 24
9605 (con'd)	**NORWAY**	
	RADIO NORWAY INTL	(D):500kW::SA
	Kvitsøy	Alt 9610kHz:M:500kW::SA
		Alt 9610kHz:M-Sa:500kW::SA
		Alt 9610kHz:Su:500kW::SA
		Alt 9610kHz:Tu-Su:500kW:SA
		Alt 9610kHz:W-M:500kW::SA
		Alt 9610kHz:M:500kW:SPANISH, ETC:SA
		Alt 9610kHz:Tu:500kW:SPANISH, ETC:SA
	PHILIPPINES	
	RADIO VERITAS ASIA	100kW::EAS
	Malolos	100kW::SEA
	PORTUGAL	
	ADVENTIST WORLD R	Su:250kW::EU
	Sines	
	RADIO PORTUGUESA	100kW::EU
	Lisbon-São Gabriel	M-F:100kW::EU
		Sa/Su:100kW::EU
		Irr:Sa/Su:100kW::EU
	SWEDEN	
	RADIO SWEDEN INTL	350kW::SA
	Karlsborg	
	UNITED KINGDOM	
	BBC	100kW::SAS
	Via Maşirah, Oman	
	USA	
	VOICE OF AMERICA	15/250kW::WAF
	Via M'rovia, Liberia	
	VOICE OF AMERICA	(J):100kW::EEU
	Via Tangier, Morocco	
	WYFR-FAMILY RADIO	100kW::SA
	Okeechobee, Florida	
	USSR	
	RADIO MOSCOW	(J):50kW:DS-1
	Serpukhov	50kW:DS-1
	VATICAN STATE	
	VATICAN RADIO	500kW::NA
	Sta Maria di Galeria	
9610	**AUSTRALIA**	
	AUSTRALIAN BC CORP	10/50kW:DS
	Perth	
	CHINA (TAIWAN)	
	VOICE FREE CHINA	ANZ
	T'ai-pei	
	GERMANY (FR)	
	DEUTSCHE WELLE	(D):500kW::AF
	Türkheim-Wertach'l	
	HOLLAND	
	RADIO NEDERLAND	500kW::WEU
	Flevoland	
	INDIA	
	ALL INDIA RADIO	50kW:DS-ENGLISH, ETC
	Delhi	
	NORWAY	
	RADIO NORWAY INTL	Alternative Frequency to 9605kHz
	Fredrikstad	
	RADIO NORWAY INTL	Alternative Frequency to 9605kHz
	Kvitsøy	
	SEYCHELLES	
	FAR EAST BC ASS'N	80kW::EAF
	North Pt, Mahé Is	
	UNITED KINGDOM	
	BBC	(J):500kW::EU
	Holywell-Rampisham	
	BBC	(D):250kW::EEU
	Skelton, Cumbria	(J):250kW::EEU
		(D)Su:250kW::EU
		(J)Su:250kW::EEU
(con'd)	BBC	(J):250kW::WAF
	Via Ascension	

	0	1	2	3	4	5	6	7	8	9	10	11	12	13	14	15	16	17	18	19	20	21	22	23	24

ENGLISH ▅▅▅   GERMAN / DEUTSCH ◊◊◊◊   FRENCH / FRANÇAIS ▬▬▬   PORTUGUESE / PORTUGUÊS ▬▬   SPANISH / ESPAÑOL ▬▬

ARABIC / ﺍﻟﻌﺮﺑﻴﺔ ▬▬   RUSSIAN / РУССКИИ ▬▬   CHINESE / 中文 ◊◊◊◊   JAPANESE / 日本語 ▓▓▓   MULTILINGUAL ▓▓▓   OTHER ▬

SUMMER ONLY (J)   WINTER ONLY (D)   JAMMING ⋀⋀ or / or \   EARLIEST HEARD ◢   LATEST HEARD ◣   + TENTATIVE

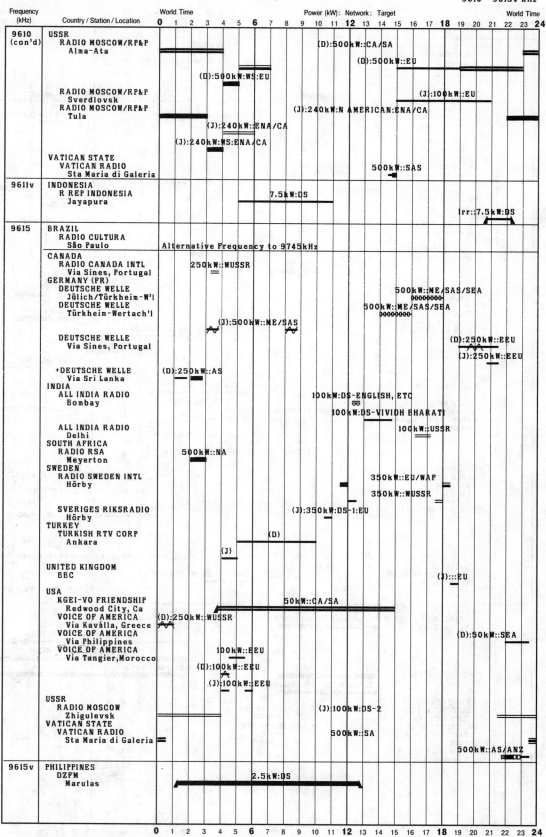

Frequency (kHz)	Country / Station / Location	World Time / Power (kW) : Network : Target
9610 (con'd)	USSR RADIO MOSCOW/RP&P Alma-Ata	(D):500kW::CA/SA · (D):500kW::EU · (D):500kW:WS:EU
	RADIO MOSCOW/RP&P Sverdlovsk	(J):100kW::EU
	RADIO MOSCOW/RP&P Tula	(J):240kW::N AMERICAN:ENA/CA · (J):240kW::ENA/CA · (J):240kW:WS:ENA/CA
	VATICAN STATE VATICAN RADIO Sta Maria di Galeria	500kW::SAS
9611v	INDONESIA R REP INDONESIA Jayapura	7.5kW:DS · Irr::7.5kW:DS
9615	BRAZIL RADIO CULTURA São Paulo	Alternative Frequency to 9745kHz
	CANADA RADIO CANADA INTL Via Sines, Portugal	250kW::WUSSR
	GERMANY (FR) DEUTSCHE WELLE Jülich/Türkheim-W'l	500kW::ME/SAS/SEA
	DEUTSCHE WELLE Türkheim-Wertach'l	500kW::ME/SAS/SEA · (J):500kW::ME/SAS
	DEUTSCHE WELLE Via Sines, Portugal	(D):250kW::EEU · (J):250kW::EEU
	+DEUTSCHE WELLE Via Sri Lanka	(D):250kW::AS
	INDIA ALL INDIA RADIO Bombay	100kW:DS-ENGLISH, ETC · 100kW:DS-VIVIDH BHARATI
	ALL INDIA RADIO Delhi	100kW::USSR
	SOUTH AFRICA RADIO RSA Meyerton	500kW::NA
	SWEDEN RADIO SWEDEN INTL Hörby	350kW::EU/WAF · 350kW::WUSSR
	SVERIGES RIKSRADIO Hörby	(J):350kW:DS-1:EU
	TURKEY TURKISH RTV CORP Ankara	(D) · (J)
	UNITED KINGDOM BBC	(J):::EU
	USA KGEI-VO FRIENDSHIP Redwood City, Ca	50kW::CA/SA
	VOICE OF AMERICA Via Kaválla, Greece	(D):250kW::WUSSR
	VOICE OF AMERICA Via Philippines	(D):50kW::SEA
	VOICE OF AMERICA Via Tangier, Morocco	100kW::EEU · (D):100kW::EEU · (J):100kW::EEU
	USSR RADIO MOSCOW Zhigulevsk	(J):100kW:DS-2
	VATICAN STATE VATICAN RADIO Sta Maria di Galeria	500kW::SA · 500kW::AS/ANZ
9615v	PHILIPPINES DZFM Marulas	2.5kW:DS

Frequency (kHz)	Country / Station / Location	World Time / Power (kW): Network: Target
9616v	**MONGOLIA** RADIO ULAN BATOR Ulan Bator	50kW::EAS M-Sa:50kW::EAS
9618	**MOZAMBIQUE** RADIO MOCAMBIQUE Maputo	120kW:DS
9620	**AUSTRALIA** RADIO AUSTRALIA Shepparton	100kW::EAS/PAC
	EGYPT RADIO CAIRO Abu Za'bal	100kW:DS-GENERAL:NAF
	GERMANY (DR) RADIO BERLIN INTL Königswusterhause	(J):100kW::NA
	+RADIO BERLIN INTL Nauen	(D):500kW::SA
	RADIO BERLIN INTL Nauen	500kW::NAF/WAF
	IVORY COAST RTV IVOIRIENNE Abidjan	DS:WAF
	NEW ZEALAND RADIO NEW ZEALAND Wellington	7.5kW:DS:PAC 7.5kW:DS-ENGLISH, ETC:PAC
	SPAIN R EXTERIOR ESPANA Arganda	(J):100kW::EU
	USA VOICE OF AMERICA Via M'rovia, Liberia	15kW::WAF
	VOICE OF AMERICA Via Philippines	50/250kW::SEA (D):250kW::EAF (J):250kW::SEA
	USSR RADIO MOSCOW Moscow	240kW:DS-2
	RADIO MOSCOW Vladivostok	(J):100kW:DS-1
	RADIO TIKHIY OKEAN Vladivostok	(J):100kW:MARINERS:PAC/WNA (J)Sa:100kW:MARINERS:PAC/WNA (J)Su-F:100kW:MARINERS:PAC/WNA
	YUGOSLAVIA RADIO KOPER Belgrade	100kW:DS:EU/ME/AF
	RADIO LJUBLJANA Belgrade	M:100kW:DS-ENGLISH, ETC:EU/ME
	RADIO YUGOSLAVIA Belgrade	100kW::EU/ME/NAF 100kW::WAF 100kW::ME/EAF
	RADIO ZAGREB Belgrade	Th:100kW:DS-MARINERS:ME
	VARIOUS LOCAL STNS Belgrade	Sa/Su:100kW:DS:EU/ME/AF Tu-Su:100kW:DS:EU/ME/NAF
9625	**CANADA** CANADIAN BC CORP Sackville, NB	M:100kW:DS-NORTHERN M-F:100kW:DS-NORTHERN Sa:100kW:DS-NORTHERN Su:100kW:DS-NORTHERN Tu-Sa:100kW:DS-NORTHERN
	GERMANY (FR) DEUTSCHE WELLE Türkheim-Wertach'l	(J):500kW::WAF
	DEUTSCHE WELLE Via Cyclops, Malta	(D):250kW::ME
	ROMANIA RADIO BUCHAREST Bucharest	250kW::EU 250kW::ME (J):250kW::WUSSR
(con'd)		

ENGLISH ▬▬▬ GERMAN / DEUTSCH ০০০০ FRENCH / FRANÇAIS ▭▭▭ PORTUGUESE / PORTUGUÊS ▬▬▬ SPANISH / ESPAÑOL ▬▬▬

ARABIC /ぅ ▬▬▬ RUSSIAN / РУССКИИ ▬▬▬ CHINESE / ☀☀ ০০০০ JAPANESE / 日本語 ▬▬▬ MULTILINGUAL ▩▩▩ OTHER ▬▬

SUMMER ONLY (J) WINTER ONLY (D) JAMMING ／\／\ or / or \ EARLIEST HEARD ◢ LATEST HEARD ◣ + TENTATIVE

Frequency (kHz)	Country / Station / Location	World Time 0 ... 24 (Power (kW): Network: Target)

9625 (con'd)

SWITZERLAND
RED CROSS BC SVC
Schwarzenburg — Irr:(D)Tu/F:150kW::CA — Irr:M/Th:150kW::SA

SWISS RADIO INTL
Schwarzenburg — 150kW::CA/SA
+SWISS RADIO INTL
Schwarzenburg — (D):150kW::CA
+SWISS RADIO INTL
Schwarzenburg — (D)M:150kW::CA
+SWISS RADIO INTL
Schwarzenburg — (D)Tu-Su:150kW::CA

UNITED KINGDOM
BBC — (J)::EU
— (J)Sa/Su:::EU

USA
RFE-RL
Via Biblis, GFR — (D):100kW::WUSSR
RFE-RL
Via Holzkirchen,GFR — (D):250kW::WUSSR
RFE-RL
Via Lisbon, Portugal — (J):100/250kW::WUSSR
— (D):100kW::WUSSR
RFE-RL
Via Pals, Spain — (D):250kW::WUSSR
— (J):250kW::WUSSR

VOICE OF AMERICA
Via Kaválla, Greece — (J):250kW::WUSSR
USSR
RADIO MOSCOW/RP&P
Chita — (D):500kW::EAS
— (D):500kW:WS:EAS/ANZ

VATICAN STATE
VATICAN RADIO
Sta Maria di Galeria — 500kW::AF
— Su:500kW::AF
— M-Sa:500kW:ENG,FRENCH,SPANISH

9630

BRAZIL
RADIO APARECIDA
Aparecida — Alternative Frequency to 9635kHz

CHINA (TAIWAN)
CENTRAL BC SYSTEM
T'ai-pei — PRC-3:EAS
CZECHOSLOVAKIA
RADIO PRAGUE
Piešťany-Velké K'y — 250kW:ENG,FR,GERMAN,ETC:AM
— 250kW::AM
— 250kW::SA

GABON
ADVENTIST WORLD R
Moanda-Moyabe — M-Sa:250kW:VIA AFRIQUE NR UN:WAF
HOLLAND
RADIO NEDERLAND
Via Neth Antilles — 300kW::ANZ
INDIA
ALL INDIA RADIO
Aligarh — 250kW::SAS/ME
SPAIN
R EXTERIOR ESPANA
Noblejas — 350kW::NA/CA
— (J):350kW::NA/CA

SWEDEN
RADIO SWEDEN INTL
Karlsborg — 350kW::EU/WAF
— 350kW::EU

TURKEY
TURKISH RTV CORP
Ankara — (J):250/500kW
USA
VOICE OF AMERICA
Greenville, NC — (D):500kW::SA
— (J):500kW::SA

VOICE OF AMERICA
Via Philippines — 50/250kW::SEA
— 50kW::SEA

USSR
RADIO MOSCOW
Kazan' — (J):100kW:DS-1

(con'd)

World Time: 0 1 2 3 4 5 6 7 8 9 10 11 12 13 14 15 16 17 18 19 20 21 22 23 24

ENGLISH ▬▬ GERMAN / DEUTSCH ▫▫▫ FRENCH / FRANÇAIS ▭▭ PORTUGUESE / PORTUGUÊS ▭▭ SPANISH / ESPAÑOL ▭▭
ARABIC / عربى ▭ RUSSIAN / РУССКИИ ▬ CHINESE / 中文 ▫▫▫ JAPANESE / 日本語 ▬▬ MULTILINGUAL ▫▫▫ OTHER ▬
SUMMER ONLY (J)   WINTER ONLY (D)   JAMMING ∧∧ or / or \   EARLIEST HEARD ◢   LATEST HEARD ◣   + TENTATIVE

Frequency (kHz)	Country / Station / Location	World Time / Power (kW) / Network / Target

9630 (con'd)

USSR
RADIO MOSCOW/RP&P
Serpukhov
- (D):100kW::WAF
- (J):240kW::EU/WAF

9630v

CHILE
RADIO AGRICULTURA
Santiago
- Irr::10kW:DS-TEMP INACTIVE
- 10kW:DS-TEMP INACTIVE
- M-Sa:10kW:DS-TEMP INACTIVE

9635

BRAZIL
RADIO APARECIDA
Aparecida
- Alt 9630kHz:10kW:DS

COLOMBIA
RADIO NACIONAL
Bogotá
- 25kW:DS

CYPRUS
CYPRUS BC CORP
Zyyi
- (J)F-Su:250kW::EU

IRAQ
RADIO BAGHDAD
Balad-Salah 'Deen
- 500kW

MALI
RTV MALIENNE
Bamako
- 18kW:DS-FRENCH, ETC
- Su:18kW:DS-FRENCH, ETC

SINGAPORE
SINGAPORE BC CORP
Jurong
- 50kW:DS-3

TURKEY
TURKISH RTV CORP
Ankara
- (J):500kW::EAS

UNITED KINGDOM
BBC
Skelton, Cumbria
- (D):100/250kW::EU
- (J):100/250kW::EU
- (J):::EU
- (D)Sa-M/W/Th:100/250kW::EU
- (D)Su:100/250kW::EU
- (J)Su:100/250kW::EU

USA
VOICE OF AMERICA
Via Kaválla, Greece
- 250kW::SAS/ME
- (D):250kW::SAS/ME
- (D):250kW::WUSSR
- (J):250kW::SAS/ME

VOICE OF AMERICA
Via Tangier, Morocco
- 100kW::EEU/WUSSR

+VOICE OF AMERICA
Via Tangier, Morocco
- (D):100kW::EEU

VOICE OF AMERICA
Via Tangier, Morocco
- (J):100kW::EEU/WUSSR

VOICE OF AMERICA
Via Woofferton, UK
- (J):250kW::WUSSR

USSR
RADIO MOSCOW
Vladivostok
- 50kW::WNA

RADIO MOSCOW/RP&P
Vladivostok
- 50kW:N AMERICAN:WNA
- 50kW:WS:WNA

RADIO TIKHIY OKEAN
Vladivostok
- 50kW:MARINERS:PAC/WNA
- Sa:50kW:MARINERS:PAC/WNA
- Su-F:50kW:MARINERS:PAC/WNA

9637v

MOZAMBIQUE
EP DE SOFALA
Beira
- Alt 9578vkHz:100kW:DS-2

9640

ALGERIA
RTV ALGERIENNE
Algiers
- 50kW:DS

BANGLADESH
RADIO BANGLADESH
Dhaka
- (J):100kW::SAS

CHINA (PR)
RADIO BEIJING
Kunming
- 120kW::EU/WAF
- (D):120kW::WUSSR

(con'd)

ENGLISH ▄▄▄   GERMAN / DEUTSCH ००००   FRENCH / FRANÇAIS ▬▬   PORTUGUESE / PORTUGUÊS ▬▬   SPANISH / ESPAÑOL ▬▬

ARABIC / عربى ▬▬   RUSSIAN / РУССКИИ ▬▬   CHINESE / ★★ ००००   JAPANESE / 日本語 ▬▬   MULTILINGUAL ०००   OTHER ▬▬

SUMMER ONLY (J)   WINTER ONLY (D)   JAMMING ∧∧ or / or \   EARLIEST HEARD ◢   LATEST HEARD ◣   + TENTATIVE

Frequency (kHz)	Country / Station / Location	World Time → Power (kW): Network: Target → World Time

9640 (con'd)

CUBA
RADIO HABANA
Havana — 100kW::CA (at ~11-12)

GERMANY (FR)
DEUTSCHE WELLE
Jülich — 100kW::SAS/SEA (at ~19-20)
DEUTSCHE WELLE
Türkheim-Wertach'l — (D):500kW::ME (at ~4-6), (J):500kW::NAF/ME (at ~4-7)
DEUTSCHE WELLE
Via Antigua — 250kW::NA (at ~3)
DEUTSCHE WELLE
Via Kigali, Rwanda — 250kW::AM (at ~1-3)
DEUTSCHE WELLE
Via Sri Lanka — 250kW::EAS (at ~11-12)

ICELAND
RIKISUTVARPID
Reykjavik — Irr::10kW:USB:DS:EU (at ~12-13)

KOREA (REPUBLIC)
RADIO KOREA
In-Kimjae — 100kW::EAS (at ~1-2), 100kW::SEA (at ~16-17), (at ~22-23)

SAUDI ARABIA
BS OF THE KINGDOM
Riyadh — Alternative Frequency to 9730kHz

SEYCHELLES
FAR EAST BC ASS'N
North Pt, Mahé Is — 25kW::SAS (at ~2)

UNITED KINGDOM
BBC
Daventry — 250kW:WS:CA/ANZ (at ~4-7)

USA
RFE-RL
Via Lisbon, Portugal — 250kW::EEU (at ~17-18)
VOICE OF AMERICA
Greenville, NC — M-F:250kW:FEED:CA (at ~18-19)

USSR
"RADIO MAGALLANES"
Via Radio Moscow — (D):500kW::SA (at ~2-4)
RADIO MOSCOW/RP&P
Moscow — (D):500kW::SA (at ~12-13), (D):240kW::WAF (at ~4-6), (J):240kW::EU (at ~14-17), (J):240kW:WS:EU (at ~18-20)

9645

AUSTRALIA
RADIO AUSTRALIA — (J):::SEA (at ~12-13)
RADIO AUSTRALIA
Carnarvon — 100kW::SEA (at ~9-11)

BRAZIL
RADIO BANDEIRANTES
São Paulo — 7.5kW:DS (at ~6-22), Irr::7.5kW:DS (at ~2-3)

COSTA RICA
FARO DEL CARIBE
San José — 50kW:DS (at ~11-13)

GERMANY (DR)
RADIO BERLIN INTL
Königswusterhause — (J):100kW::WAF/CA/SA (at ~11-12), (J):100kW::WAF (at ~3-4), (at ~22)

GERMANY (FR)
DEUTSCHE WELLE
Jülich — (D):100kW::EU/NAF (at ~19-20)

JAPAN
RADIO JAPAN/NHK
Tōkyō-Yamata — 200kW::SAS/EAF (at ~16-18), (D):100kW::NA (at ~0-1), (D):100kW:GENERAL:PAC/SA (at ~3-4)

PHILIPPINES
FAR EAST BC CO
Iba — 100kW::EAS (at ~9-11)

USA
VOICE OF AMERICA
Via Sri Lanka — 35kW::SAS (at ~13-16)
VOICE OF AMERICA
Via Tangier, Morocco — (D):100kW::EEU (at ~21-23)

USSR
BELORUSSIAN RADIO
Minsk — 50kW:DS-1 (at ~0-24)
RADIO MOSCOW/RP&P
Chita — (J):500kW::EAS (at ~19-21), (J):500kW:WS:EAS (at ~16-18)

(con'd)

ENGLISH ▄▄▄   GERMAN / DEUTSCH ◊◊◊◊   FRENCH / FRANÇAIS ═══   PORTUGUESE / PORTUGUÊS ▬▬▬   SPANISH / ESPAÑOL ▬▬▬

ARABIC / عربية ≡≡≡   RUSSIAN / РУССКИИ ═══   CHINESE / 中文 ◊◊◊◊   JAPANESE / 日本語 ▨▨▨   MULTILINGUAL ▨▨▨   OTHER ▬▬

SUMMER ONLY (J)   WINTER ONLY (D)   JAMMING /\/\ or / or \   EARLIEST HEARD ◢   LATEST HEARD ◣   + TENTATIVE

Frequency (kHz)	Country / Station / Location	Power (kW) : Network : Target

World Time scale: 0 1 2 3 4 5 6 7 8 9 10 11 12 13 14 15 16 17 18 19 20 21 22 23 24

9645 (con'd) — VATICAN STATE, VATICAN RADIO, Sta Maria di Galeria
- 100kW::CA
- 100kW::EU
- 100kW::EU/NAF
- Su:100kW::EU
- Su:100kW::EU/NAF
- M-Sa:100kW:ENG,FR,SPANISH,ETC:EU
- M-Sa:100kW:ENG,FR,SPANISH,ETC:EU/NAF

9650 — CANADA, RADIO CANADA INTL, Sackville, NB
- M-F:250kW::ENA/CA

GERMANY (FR), DEUTSCHE WELLE, Jülich
- 100kW::EAS
- (J):100kW::ME/SAS

DEUTSCHE WELLE, Jülich/Türkheim-W'l
- 100/500kW::USSR/AF
- 100/500kW::ME/AF

DEUTSCHE WELLE, Türkheim-Wertach'l
- 500kW::WUSSR
- (D):500kW::USSR
- 500kW::ME

DEUTSCHE WELLE, Via Cyclops, Malta
- 250kW::NAF
- (J):250kW::ME

DEUTSCHE WELLE, Via Sines, Portugal
- (J):250kW::EEU

DEUTSCHE WELLE, Via Sri Lanka
- (J):250kW::AS
- (J):250kW::SEA/ANZ

GUINEA, RTV GUINEENNE, Conakry
- 100kW:DS
- M-Sa:100kW:DS
- Su:100kW:DS
- 100kW:DS-FRENCH, ETC
- M-Sa:100kW:DS-FRENCH, ETC

HOLLAND, RADIO NEDERLAND, Via Neth Antilles
- 300kW::CA/ANZ

NORWAY, RADIO NORWAY INTL, Kvitsøy
- Alternative Frequency to 9655kHz

USA, VOICE OF AMERICA, Via Tangier, Morocco
- (D):100kW::EEU

USSR, 'RADIO MAGALLANES', Via Radio Moscow
- (D):500kW::SA

RADIO MOSCOW/RP&P, Frunze
- (D):500kW::SA
- (D):500kW::WAF
- (D):500kW:AFRICAN:EAF/SAF
- (D):500kW:WS:EAF/SAF

RADIO MOSCOW/RP&P, Moscow
- (J):100kW::EU

VATICAN STATE, VATICAN RADIO, Sta Maria di Galeria
- 100kW::SAS

9650v — ALBANIA, RADIO TIRANA, Lushnjë
- 100kW::SA

9654v — PERU, RADIO NORPERUANA, Chachapoyas
- 1kW:DS

9655 — AUSTRALIA, RADIO AUSTRALIA, Shepparton
- (J):100kW::PAC/EU

BRAZIL, RADIO NACIONAL, Brasília **(con'd)**
- 250kW::SA

World Time scale: 0 1 2 3 4 5 6 7 8 9 10 11 12 13 14 15 16 17 18 19 20 21 22 23 24

ENGLISH ▬▬ GERMAN / DEUTSCH ◊◊◊◊ FRENCH / FRANÇAIS ▬▬ PORTUGUESE / PORTUGUÊS ▬▬ SPANISH / ESPAÑOL ▬▬
ARABIC / عربي ▬▬ RUSSIAN / РУССКИЙ ▬▬ CHINESE / ◆☆ ◊◊◊◊ JAPANESE / 日本語 ▬▬ MULTILINGUAL ▬▬ OTHER ▬▬
SUMMER ONLY (J) WINTER ONLY (D) JAMMING ∧∧ or / or \ EARLIEST HEARD ◢ LATEST HEARD ◣ + TENTATIVE

Frequency (kHz)	Country / Station / Location	Power (kW) : Network : Target
9655 (con'd)	**CUBA**	
	RADIO HABANA	50kW::CA
	Havana	
	FINLAND	
	RADIO FINLAND	250kW::WUSSR
	Pori	(J):250kW::EU
		(J)Sa:250kW::EU
		(J)Su-F:250kW::EU
	MONACO	
	TRANS WORLD RADIO	W-F:100kW::EU
	Monte Carlo	
	NORWAY	
	RADIO NORWAY INTL	Alt 9650kHz:500kW::EU
	Kvitsøy	M-Sa:500kW::EU/AF
	+RADIO NORWAY INTL	(D)M-Sa:500kW::ME/SAS
	Kvitsøy	
	RADIO NORWAY INTL	Su:500kW::EU/AF
	Kvitsøy	
	+RADIO NORWAY INTL	(D)Su:500kW::ME/SAS
	Kvitsøy	
	RADIO NORWAY INTL	Tu-Su:500kW::EU/AF
	Kvitsøy	
	+RADIO NORWAY INTL	(D)Tu-Su:500kW::ME/SAS
	Kvitsøy	
	RADIO NORWAY INTL	M:500kW:SPANISH, ETC:EU/AF
	Kvitsøy	
	+RADIO NORWAY INTL	(D)M:500kW:SPANISH, ETC:ME/SAS
	Kvitsøy	
	PORTUGAL	
	IBRA RADIO	(J):250kW::EU/WUSSR
	Sines	
	SOUTH AFRICA	
	SOUTH AFRICAN BC	100kW:RADIO SUID-AFRIKA
	Meyerton	
	SWEDEN	
	RADIO SWEDEN INTL	(J):350kW::EU
	Karlsborg	
	THAILAND	
	RADIO THAILAND	100kW::SEA/EU
	Pathum Thani	100kW::AS
		100kW::EAS/SEA
		Sa/Su:100kW::SEA/EU
	USSR	
	RADIO MOSCOW	(J):100kW:MARINERS:ENA/CA
	Orcha	
	RADIO MOSCOW/RP&P	(D):100kW::ME/SAS
	Kazan'	
	RADIO MOSCOW/RP&P	(D):100kW::EAS
	Komsomol'sk 'Amure	
		(J):240kW:WS:WNA
9660	**ANGOLA**	
	RADIO NACIONAL	100kW:DS-PORTUGUESE, ETC
	Luanda	
	AUSTRALIA	
	AUSTRALIAN BC CORP	10kW:DS
	Brisbane	M-Sa:10kW:DS
	AUSTRIA	
	RADIO AUSTRIA INTL	100kW::CA
	Vienna	Su/M:100kW::CA
		Tu-Sa:100kW::CA
	TURKEY	
	+TURKISH RTV CORP	(D):250kW::NAF
	Ankara	
	UNITED KINGDOM	
	BBC	(D):250kW::EU
	Skelton, Cumbria	
	BBC	(D):250kW::EU
	Woofferton	
	USA	
	RFE-RL	(D):100kW::WUSSR
	Via Biblis, GFR	
	RFE-RL	250kW::WUSSR
	Via Holzkirchen,GFR	
(con'd)	RFE-RL	(J):100kW::WUSSR
	Via Lamperth'm, GFR	

ENGLISH ▬▬   GERMAN / DEUTSCH ০০০০   FRENCH / FRANÇAIS ▭▭   PORTUGUESE / PORTUGUÊS ▬   SPANISH / ESPAÑOL ▬

ARABIC / ﻉﺏﺭ ▬   RUSSIAN / РУССКИИ ▬   CHINESE / 中文 ০০০০   JAPANESE / 日本語 ▩▩▩   MULTILINGUAL ▩▩   OTHER ▬

SUMMER ONLY (J)   WINTER ONLY (D)   JAMMING /\/\ or / or \   EARLIEST HEARD ◢   LATEST HEARD ◣   + TENTATIVE

Frequency (kHz)	Country / Station / Location	Schedule (World Time 0–24) / Power (kW): Network: Target
9660 (con'd)	**USA** RFE-RL Via Lisbon, Portugal	(J):250kW::WUSSR
	RFE-RL Via Pals, Spain	(J):250kW::WUSSR
	VOICE OF AMERICA Via Ismaning, GFR	(J):100kW::WUSSR
	VOICE OF AMERICA Via Kavála, Greece	(J):250kW::ME
	VOICE OF AMERICA Via Philippines	100kW::EAS
	VENEZUELA RADIO RUMBOS Caracas	10kW:DS
9665	**AFGHANISTAN** RADIO AFGHANISTAN Via USSR	(J):::EU
	GERMANY (DR) RADIO BERLIN INTL Königswusterhause	100kW::EAF/SAF
	RADIO BERLIN INTL Nauen	500kW:NAF/WAF · 100kW::WAF · 100kW::NAF/WAF
	INDIA ALL INDIA RADIO Delhi	100kW::EU
	IRAQ RADIO BAGHDAD Balad-Salah el Deen	500kW · 500kW::NAF
	MALAYSIA RADIO MALAYSIA Kajang	100kW:DS-ENGLISH,CHI,ETC · Sa/Su:100kW:DS-ENGLISH,CHI,ETC · Su:100kW:DS-ENGLISH,CHI,ETC
	MONACO TRANS WORLD RADIO Monte Carlo	100kW::EU
	NETHERLANDS ANTILLES TRANS WORLD RADIO Bonaire	50kW::SA
	NORTHERN MARIANA IS KYOI Saipan Island	100kW:JAPANESE,ENGLISH:EAS
	PHILIPPINES FAR EAST BC CO Bocaue	50kW::SEA/SAS
	FAR EAST BC CO Iba	100kW::EAS
	ROMANIA RADIO BUCHAREST Bucharest	Su:250kW:MARINERS:ATL
9665v	**BRAZIL** RADIO MARUMBI Florianópolis	10kW:DS · Su-F:10kW:DS · Sa:10kW:DS-GERMAN,PORT
9670	**AUSTRIA** RADIO AUSTRIA INTL Vienna	500kW::SAS/SEA · 100kW::WEU/WAF
	CHINA (PR) CENTRAL PEOPLES BS Xi'an	50kW:DS-2
	RADIO BEIJING Xi'an	150kW::WUSSR
	GERMANY (FR) DEUTSCHE WELLE Jülich	(D):100kW::EU/NAF · (D):100kW::WAF
	DEUTSCHE WELLE Jülich/Türkheim-W'l	(D):100/500kW::EU/NAF/EAS
	DEUTSCHE WELLE Via Cyclops, Malta	(D):250kW::ME
	IRAN VO THE ISLAMIC REP	
(con'd)	**NORTHERN MARIANA IS** KYOI Saipan Island	100kW:JAPANESE,ENGLISH:EAS

World Time: 0 1 2 3 4 5 6 7 8 9 10 11 12 13 14 15 16 17 18 19 20 21 22 23 24

ENGLISH ▬▬   GERMAN / DEUTSCH ◊◊◊◊   FRENCH / FRANÇAIS ═══   PORTUGUESE / PORTUGUÊS ▬▬   SPANISH / ESPAÑOL ▬▬

ARABIC / بربي ≡≡≡   RUSSIAN / РУССКИИ ═══   CHINESE / 中文 ◊◊◊◊   JAPANESE / 日本語 ▓▓▓   MULTILINGUAL ▒▒▒   OTHER ▬▬

SUMMER ONLY (J)   WINTER ONLY (D)   JAMMING ∧∧ or / or \   EARLIEST HEARD ◢   LATEST HEARD ◣   + TENTATIVE

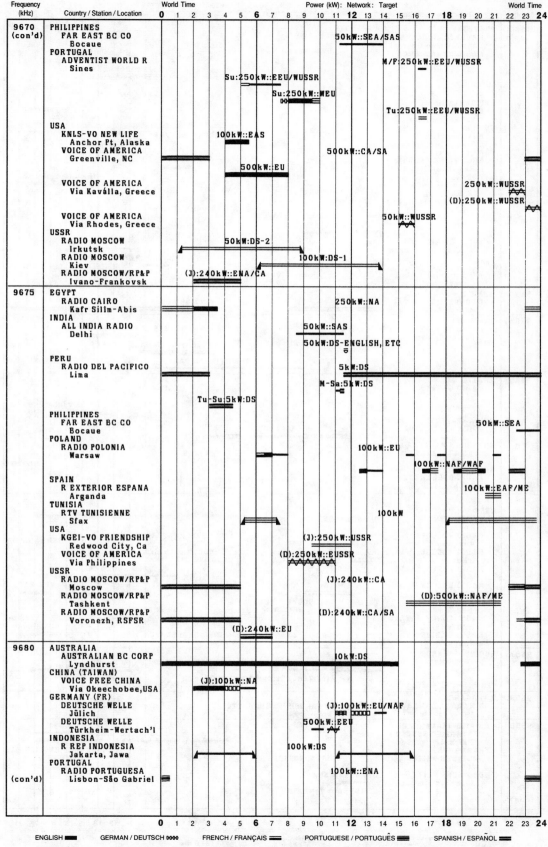

| Frequency (kHz) | Country / Station / Location | World Time | Power (kW): Network: Target | World Time |

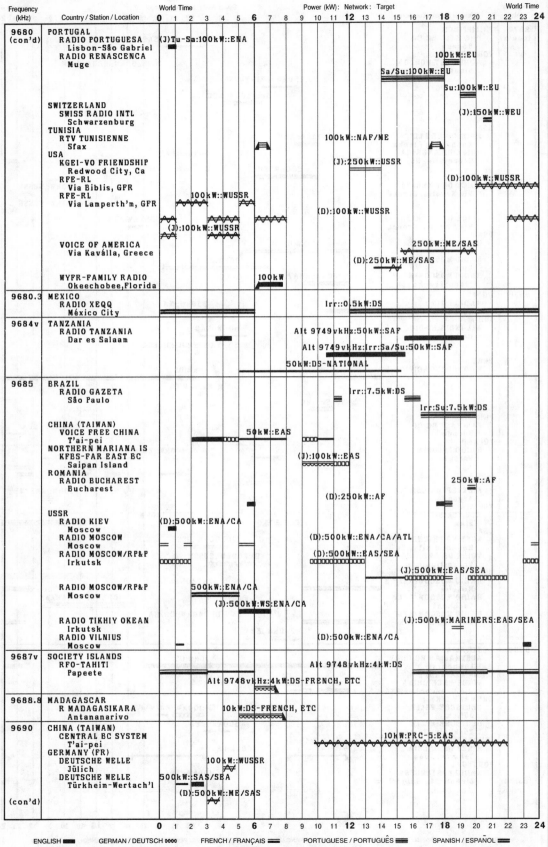

9680 (con'd)

PORTUGAL
RADIO PORTUGUESA
Lisbon-São Gabriel — (J)Tu-Sa:100kW::ENA
RADIO RENASCENCA
Muge — 100kW::EU / Sa/Su:100kW::EU / Su:100kW::EU

SWITZERLAND
SWISS RADIO INTL
Schwarzenburg — (J):150kW::WEU

TUNISIA
RTV TUNISIENNE
Sfax — 100kW::NAF/ME

USA
KGEI-VO FRIENDSHIP
Redwood City, Ca — (J):250kW::USSR
RFE-RL
Via Biblis, GFR — (D):100kW::WUSSR
RFE-RL
Via Lamperth'm, GFR — 100kW::WUSSR / (D):100kW::WUSSR
— (J):100kW::WUSSR
VOICE OF AMERICA
Via Kaválla, Greece — 250kW::ME/SAS / (D):250kW::ME/SAS
WYFR-FAMILY RADIO
Okeechobee,Florida — 100kW

9680.3

MEXICO
RADIO XEQQ
México City — Irr::0.5kW:DS

9684v

TANZANIA
RADIO TANZANIA
Dar es Salaam — Alt 9749vkHz:50kW::SAF / Alt 9749vkHz:Irr:Sa/Su:50kW::SAF / 50kW:DS-NATIONAL

9685

BRAZIL
RADIO GAZETA
São Paulo — Irr::7.5kW:DS / Irr:Su:7.5kW:DS

CHINA (TAIWAN)
VOICE FREE CHINA
T'ai-pei — 50kW::EAS
NORTHERN MARIANA IS
KFBS-FAR EAST BC
Saipan Island — (J):100kW::EAS

ROMANIA
RADIO BUCHAREST
Bucharest — 250kW::AF / (D):250kW::AF

USSR
RADIO KIEV
Moscow — (D):500kW::ENA/CA
RADIO MOSCOW
Moscow — (D):500kW::ENA/CA/ATL
RADIO MOSCOW/RP&P
Irkutsk — (D):500kW::EAS/SEA / (J):500kW::EAS/SEA
RADIO MOSCOW/RP&P
Moscow — 500kW::ENA/CA / (J):500kW:WS:ENA/CA
RADIO TIKHIY OKEAN
Irkutsk — (J):500kW:MARINERS:EAS/SEA
RADIO VILNIUS
Moscow — (D):500kW::ENA/CA

9687v

SOCIETY ISLANDS
RFO-TAHITI
Papeete — Alt 9748vkHz:4kW:DS / Alt 9748vkHz:4kW:DS-FRENCH, ETC

9688.8

MADAGASCAR
R MADAGASIKARA
Antananarivo — 10kW:DS-FRENCH, ETC

9690

CHINA (TAIWAN)
CENTRAL BC SYSTEM
T'ai-pei — 10kW:PRC-5:EAS
GERMANY (FR)
DEUTSCHE WELLE
Jülich — 100kW::WUSSR
DEUTSCHE WELLE
Türkheim-Wertach'l — 500kW:SAS/SEA / (D):500kW::ME/SAS

(con'd)

| 0 1 2 3 4 5 **6** 7 8 9 10 11 **12** 13 14 15 16 17 **18** 19 20 21 22 23 **24** |

ENGLISH ▬ GERMAN / DEUTSCH ∞∞ FRENCH / FRANÇAIS ═ PORTUGUESE / PORTUGUÊS ▤ SPANISH / ESPAÑOL ▤

ARABIC /ﻉﺏﻉ ═ RUSSIAN / РУССКИЙ ═ CHINESE / 中文 ∞∞ JAPANESE / 日本語 ▬ MULTILINGUAL ∞∞ OTHER ━

SUMMER ONLY (J)   WINTER ONLY (D)   JAMMING ∧∧ or / or \   EARLIEST HEARD ◢   LATEST HEARD ◣   + TENTATIVE

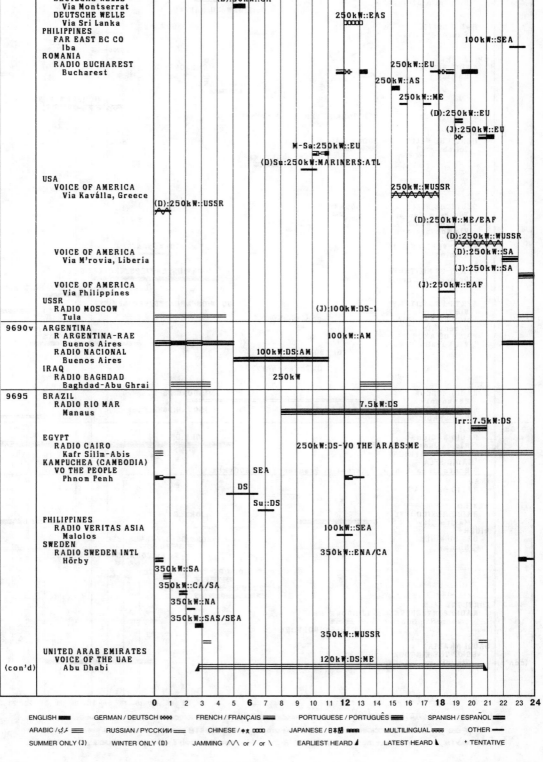

Frequency (kHz)	Country / Station / Location
9690 (con'd)	GERMANY (FR)
	DEUTSCHE WELLE
	Türkheim-Wertach'l — (J):500kW::NAF/ME
	DEUTSCHE WELLE
	Via Antigua — 250kW:CA/SEA/ANZ
	— 250kW::SA
	DEUTSCHE WELLE
	Via Cyclops, Malta — (J):250kW::NAF/ME
	DEUTSCHE WELLE
	Via Kigali, Rwanda — (D):250kW::SEA/ANZ
	DEUTSCHE WELLE
	Via Montserrat — (D):50kW::CA
	DEUTSCHE WELLE
	Via Sri Lanka — 250kW::EAS
	PHILIPPINES
	FAR EAST BC CO
	Iba — 100kW::SEA
	ROMANIA
	RADIO BUCHAREST
	Bucharest — 250kW::EU / 250kW::AS / 250kW::ME / (D):250kW::EU / (J):250kW::EU / M-Sa:250kW::EU / (D)Su:250kW:MARINERS:ATL
	USA
	VOICE OF AMERICA
	Via Kaválla, Greece — (D):250kW::USSR / 250kW::WUSSR / (D):250kW::ME/EAF
	VOICE OF AMERICA
	Via M'rovia, Liberia — (D):250kW::WUSSR / (D):250kW::SA / (J):250kW::SA
	VOICE OF AMERICA
	Via Philippines — (J):250kW::EAF
	USSR
	RADIO MOSCOW
	Tula — (J):100kW:DS-1
9690v	ARGENTINA
	R ARGENTINA-RAE
	Buenos Aires — 100kW::AM
	RADIO NACIONAL
	Buenos Aires — 100kW:DS:AM
	IRAQ
	RADIO BAGHDAD
	Baghdad-Abu Ghrai — 250kW
9695	BRAZIL
	RADIO RIO MAR
	Manaus — 7.5kW:DS / Irr::7.5kW:DS
	EGYPT
	RADIO CAIRO
	Kafr Silim-Abis — 250kW:DS-VO THE ARABS:ME
	KAMPUCHEA (CAMBODIA)
	VO THE PEOPLE
	Phnom Penh — SEA / DS / Su::DS
	PHILIPPINES
	RADIO VERITAS ASIA
	Malolos — 100kW::SEA
	SWEDEN
	RADIO SWEDEN INTL
	Hörby — 350kW::ENA/CA / 350kW::SA / 350kW::CA/SA / 350kW::NA / 350kW::SAS/SEA / 350kW::WUSSR
	UNITED ARAB EMIRATES
	VOICE OF THE UAE
(con'd)	Abu Dhabi — 120kW:DS:ME

ENGLISH ▰▰▰   GERMAN / DEUTSCH ◊◊◊◊   FRENCH / FRANÇAIS ═══   PORTUGUESE / PORTUGUÊS ▦▦▦   SPANISH / ESPAÑOL ▰▰▰

ARABIC /ﻉﺭﻉ ≡≡≡   RUSSIAN / РУССКИИ ═══   CHINESE / 中文 ◊◊◊◊   JAPANESE / 日本語 ▰▰▰   MULTILINGUAL ▩▩▩   OTHER ▬▬▬

SUMMER ONLY (J)   WINTER ONLY (D)   JAMMING /\/\ or / or \   EARLIEST HEARD ◢   LATEST HEARD ◣   + TENTATIVE

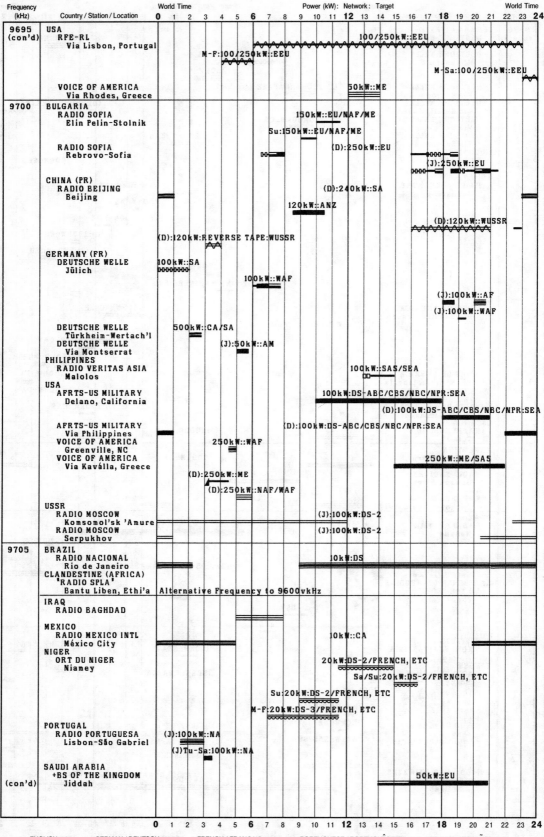

Frequency (kHz)	Country / Station / Location	Details
9695 (con'd)	**USA** RFE-RL Via Lisbon, Portugal	100/250kW::EEU / M-F:100/250kW::EEU / M-Sa:100/250kW::EEU
	VOICE OF AMERICA Via Rhodes, Greece	50kW::ME
9700	**BULGARIA** RADIO SOFIA Elin Pelin-Stolnik	150kW::EU/NAF/ME / Su:150kW::EU/NAF/ME
	RADIO SOFIA Rebrovo-Sofia	(D):250kW::EU / (J):250kW::EU
	CHINA (PR) RADIO BEIJING Beijing	(D):240kW::SA / 120kW::ANZ / (D):120kW::WUSSR / (D):120kW:REVERSE TAPE:WUSSR
	GERMANY (FR) DEUTSCHE WELLE Jülich	100kW::SA / 100kW::WAF / (J):100kW::AF / (J):100kW::WAF
	DEUTSCHE WELLE Türkheim-Wertach'l	500kW::CA/SA
	DEUTSCHE WELLE Via Montserrat	(J):50kW::AM
	PHILIPPINES RADIO VERITAS ASIA Malolos	100kW::SAS/SEA
	USA AFRTS-US MILITARY Delano, California	100kW:DS-ABC/CBS/NBC/NPR:SEA / (D):100kW:DS-ABC/CBS/NBC/NPR:SEA
	AFRTS-US MILITARY Via Philippines	(D):100kW:DS-ABC/CBS/NBC/NPR:SEA
	VOICE OF AMERICA Greenville, NC	250kW::WAF
	VOICE OF AMERICA Via Kaválla, Greece	250kW::ME/SAS / (D):250kW::ME / (D):250kW::NAF/WAF
	USSR RADIO MOSCOW Komsomol'sk 'Amure	(J):100kW:DS-2
	RADIO MOSCOW Serpukhov	(J):100kW:DS-2
9705	**BRAZIL** RADIO NACIONAL Rio de Janeiro	10kW:DS
	CLANDESTINE (AFRICA) "RADIO SPLA" Bantu Liben, Ethi'a	Alternative Frequency to 9600vkHz
	IRAQ RADIO BAGHDAD	
	MEXICO RADIO MEXICO INTL México City	10kW::CA
	NIGER ORT DU NIGER Niamey	20kW:DS-2/FRENCH, ETC / Sa/Su:20kW:DS-2/FRENCH, ETC / Su:20kW:DS-2/FRENCH, ETC / M-F:20kW:DS-3/FRENCH, ETC
	PORTUGAL RADIO PORTUGUESA Lisbon-São Gabriel	(J):100kW::NA / (J)Tu-Sa:100kW::NA
(con'd)	**SAUDI ARABIA** +BS OF THE KINGDOM Jiddah	50kW::EU

World Time: 0 1 2 3 4 5 6 7 8 9 10 11 12 13 14 15 16 17 18 19 20 21 22 23 24

Power (kW): Network: Target

ENGLISH ▄▄▄   GERMAN / DEUTSCH ◊◊◊◊   FRENCH / FRANÇAIS ▬▬   PORTUGUESE / PORTUGUÊS ▤▤   SPANISH / ESPAÑOL ▬▬

ARABIC /ﺵﻑ ▤▤   RUSSIAN / РУССКИИ ▬▬   CHINESE / 中文 ◊◊◊◊   JAPANESE / 日本語 ▬▬▬   MULTILINGUAL ▭▭▭   OTHER ▬▬

SUMMER ONLY (J)   WINTER ONLY (D)   JAMMING ∧∧ or / or \   EARLIEST HEARD ◢   LATEST HEARD ◣   + TENTATIVE

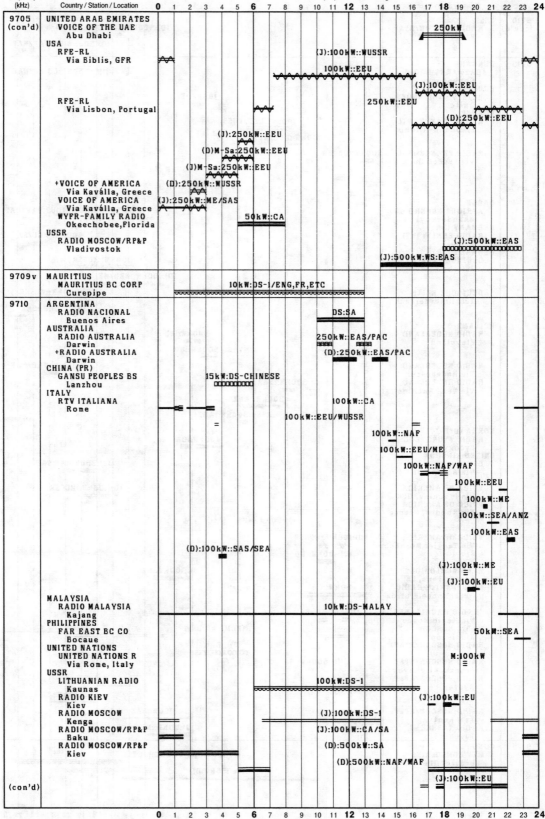

Frequency (kHz)	Country / Station / Location		World Time / Power (kW) : Network : Target
9705 (con'd)	UNITED ARAB EMIRATES		
	VOICE OF THE UAE	Abu Dhabi	250kW
	USA		
	RFE-RL	Via Biblis, GFR	(J):100kW::WUSSR / 100kW::EEU / (J):100kW::EEU
	RFE-RL	Via Lisbon, Portugal	250kW::EEU / (D):250kW::EEU
			(J):250kW::EEU
			(D)M-Sa:250kW::EEU
			(J)M-Sa:250kW::EEU
	+VOICE OF AMERICA	Via Kaválla, Greece	(D):250kW::WUSSR
	VOICE OF AMERICA	Via Kaválla, Greece	(J):250kW::ME/SAS
	WYFR-FAMILY RADIO	Okeechobee, Florida	50kW::CA
	USSR		
	RADIO MOSCOW/RP&P	Vladivostok	(J):500kW::EAS
			(J):500kW:WS:EAS
9709v	MAURITIUS		
	MAURITIUS BC CORP	Curepipe	10kW:DS-1/ENG,FR,ETC
9710	ARGENTINA		
	RADIO NACIONAL	Buenos Aires	DS:SA
	AUSTRALIA		
	RADIO AUSTRALIA	Darwin	250kW::EAS/PAC
	+RADIO AUSTRALIA	Darwin	(D):250kW::EAS/PAC
	CHINA (PR)		
	GANSU PEOPLES BS	Lanzhou	15kW:DS-CHINESE
	ITALY		
	RTV ITALIANA	Rome	100kW::CA
			100kW::EEU/WUSSR
			100kW::NAF
			100kW::EEU/ME
			100kW::NAF/WAF
			100kW::EEU
			100kW::ME
			100kW::SEA/ANZ
			100kW::EAS
			(D):100kW::SAS/SEA
			(J):100kW::ME
			(J):100kW::EU
	MALAYSIA		
	RADIO MALAYSIA	Kajang	10kW:DS-MALAY
	PHILIPPINES		
	FAR EAST BC CO	Bocaue	50kW::SEA
	UNITED NATIONS		
	UNITED NATIONS R	Via Rome, Italy	M:100kW
	USSR		
	LITHUANIAN RADIO	Kaunas	100kW:DS-1
	RADIO KIEV	Kiev	(J):100kW::EU
	RADIO MOSCOW	Kenga	(J):100kW:DS-1
	RADIO MOSCOW/RP&P	Baku	(J):100kW::CA/SA
	RADIO MOSCOW/RP&P	Kiev	(D):500kW::SA
			(D):500kW::NAF/WAF
(con'd)			(J):100kW::EU

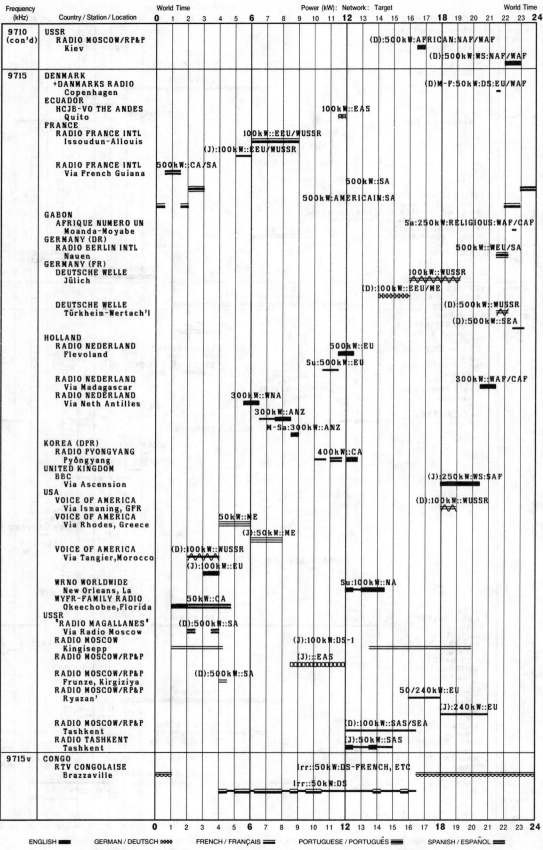

Frequency (kHz)	Country / Station / Location	World Time 0-24	Power (kW): Network: Target
9710 (con'd)	**USSR** RADIO MOSCOW/RP&P Kiev		(D):500kW:AFRICAN:NAF/WAF
			(D):500kW:WS:NAF/WAF
9715	**DENMARK** +DANMARKS RADIO Copenhagen		(D)M-F:50kW:DS:EU/WAF
	ECUADOR HCJB-VO THE ANDES Quito		100kW::EAS
	FRANCE RADIO FRANCE INTL Issoudun-Allouis		100kW::EEU/WUSSR
			(J):100kW::EEU/WUSSR
	RADIO FRANCE INTL Via French Guiana		500kW::CA/SA
			500kW::SA
			500kW:AMERICAIN:SA
	GABON AFRIQUE NUMERO UN Moanda-Moyabe		Sa:250kW:RELIGIOUS:WAF/CAF
	GERMANY (DR) RADIO BERLIN INTL Nauen		500kW::WEU/SA
	GERMANY (FR) DEUTSCHE WELLE Jülich		100kW::WUSSR
			(D):100kW::EEU/ME
	DEUTSCHE WELLE Türkheim-Wertach'l		(D):500kW::WUSSR
			(D):500kW::SEA
	HOLLAND RADIO NEDERLAND Flevoland		500kW::EU
			Su:500kW::EU
	RADIO NEDERLAND Via Madagascar		300kW::WAF/CAF
	RADIO NEDERLAND Via Neth Antilles		300kW::WNA
			300kW::ANZ
			M-Sa:300kW::ANZ
	KOREA (DPR) RADIO PYONGYANG Pyŏngyang		400kW::CA
	UNITED KINGDOM BBC Via Ascension		(J):250kW:WS:SAF
	USA VOICE OF AMERICA Via Ismaning, GFR		(D):100kW::WUSSR
	VOICE OF AMERICA Via Rhodes, Greece		50kW::ME
			(J):50kW::ME
	VOICE OF AMERICA Via Tangier, Morocco		(D):100kW::WUSSR
			(J):100kW::EU
	WRNO WORLDWIDE New Orleans, La		Su:100kW::NA
	WYFR-FAMILY RADIO Okeechobee, Florida		50kW::CA
	USSR 'RADIO MAGALLANES' Via Radio Moscow		(D):500kW::SA
	RADIO MOSCOW Kingisepp		(J):100kW:DS-1
	RADIO MOSCOW/RP&P		(J):::EAS
	RADIO MOSCOW/RP&P Frunze, Kirgiziya		(D):500kW::SA
	RADIO MOSCOW/RP&P Ryazan'		50/240kW::EU
			(J):240kW::EU
	RADIO MOSCOW/RP&P Tashkent		(D):100kW::SAS/SEA
	RADIO TASHKENT Tashkent		(J):50kW::SAS
9715v	**CONGO** RTV CONGOLAISE Brazzaville		Irr:50kW:DS-FRENCH, ETC
			Irr::50kW:DS

World Time: 0 1 2 3 4 5 6 7 8 9 10 11 12 13 14 15 16 17 18 19 20 21 22 23 24

ENGLISH ▬▬ GERMAN / DEUTSCH ᴅᴅᴅᴅ FRENCH / FRANÇAIS ═══ PORTUGUESE / PORTUGUÊS ▤▤▤ SPANISH / ESPAÑOL ▤▤▤
ARABIC /ﻉﺮﺑ ══ RUSSIAN / РУССКИИ ══ CHINESE / 中文 ᴅᴅᴅᴅ JAPANESE / 日本語 ▦▦▦ MULTILINGUAL ▨▨▨ OTHER ▬
SUMMER ONLY (J) WINTER ONLY (D) JAMMING ∧∧ or / or \ EARLIEST HEARD ◢ LATEST HEARD ◣ + TENTATIVE

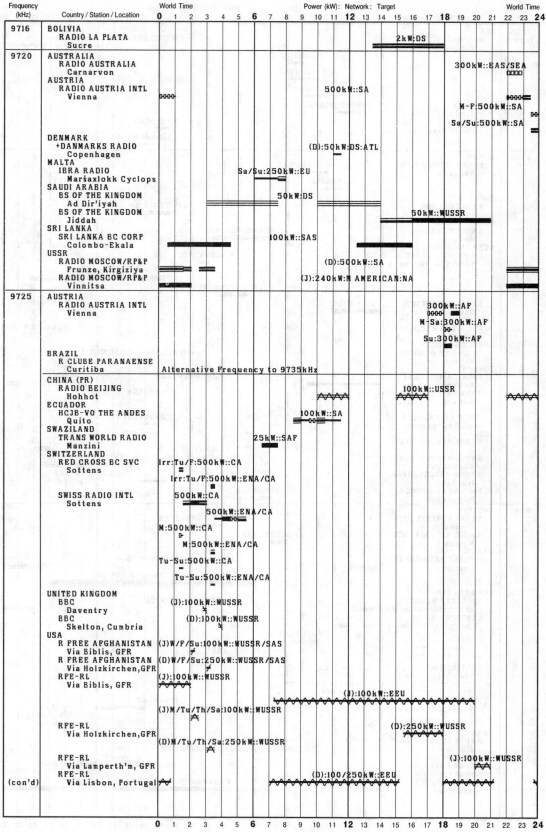

Frequency (kHz)	Country / Station / Location	Power (kW)::Network:Target (World Time 0–24)
9716	BOLIVIA — RADIO LA PLATA — Sucre	2kW:DS
9720	AUSTRALIA — RADIO AUSTRALIA — Carnarvon	300kW::EAS/SEA
	AUSTRIA — RADIO AUSTRIA INTL — Vienna	500kW::SA; M-F:500kW::SA; Sa/Su:500kW::SA
	DENMARK — +DANMARKS RADIO — Copenhagen	(D):50kW:DS:ATL
	MALTA — IBRA RADIO — Marsaxlokk Cyclops	Sa/Su:250kW::EU
	SAUDI ARABIA — BS OF THE KINGDOM — Ad Dir'iyah	50kW:DS
	SAUDI ARABIA — BS OF THE KINGDOM — Jiddah	50kW::WUSSR
	SRI LANKA — SRI LANKA BC CORP — Colombo-Ekala	100kW::SAS
	USSR — RADIO MOSCOW/RP&P — Frunze, Kirgiziya	(D):500kW::SA
	USSR — RADIO MOSCOW/RP&P — Vinnitsa	(J):240kW:N AMERICAN:NA
9725	AUSTRIA — RADIO AUSTRIA INTL — Vienna	300kW::AF; M-Sa:300kW::AF; Su:300kW::AF
	BRAZIL — R CLUBE PARANAENSE — Curitiba	Alternative Frequency to 9735kHz
	CHINA (PR) — RADIO BEIJING — Hohhot	100kW::USSR
	ECUADOR — HCJB-VO THE ANDES — Quito	100kW::SA
	SWAZILAND — TRANS WORLD RADIO — Manzini	25kW::SAF
	SWITZERLAND — RED CROSS BC SVC — Sottens	Irr:Tu/F:500kW::CA; Irr:Tu/F:500kW::ENA/CA
	SWITZERLAND — SWISS RADIO INTL — Sottens	500kW::CA; 500kW::ENA/CA; M:500kW::CA; M:500kW::ENA/CA; Tu-Su:500kW::CA; Tu-Su:500kW::ENA/CA
	UNITED KINGDOM — BBC — Daventry	(J):100kW::WUSSR
	BBC — Skelton, Cumbria	(D):100kW::WUSSR
	USA — R FREE AFGHANISTAN — Via Biblis, GFR	(J)W/F/Su:100kW::WUSSR/SAS
	R FREE AFGHANISTAN — Via Holzkirchen, GFR	(D)W/F/Su:250kW::WUSSR/SAS
	RFE-RL — Via Biblis, GFR	(J):100kW::WUSSR; (J):100kW::EEU
	RFE-RL — Via Holzkirchen, GFR	(J)M/Tu/Th/Sa:100kW::WUSSR; (D)M/Tu/Th/Sa:250kW::WUSSR; (D):250kW::WUSSR
	RFE-RL — Via Lamperth'm, GFR	(J):100kW::WUSSR
(con'd)	RFE-RL — Via Lisbon, Portugal	(D):100/250kW::EEU

ENGLISH ▬▬ GERMAN / DEUTSCH ◇◇◇◇ FRENCH / FRANÇAIS ══ PORTUGUESE / PORTUGUÊS ▬ SPANISH / ESPAÑOL ▬

ARABIC / ﻋﺮﺑﻲ ≣ RUSSIAN / РУССКИИ ══ CHINESE / ＊✕ ◇◇◇◇ JAPANESE / 日本語 ▬▬ MULTILINGUAL ▨▨ OTHER ▬

SUMMER ONLY (J) WINTER ONLY (D) JAMMING ∧∧ or / or \ EARLIEST HEARD ◢ LATEST HEARD ◣ + TENTATIVE

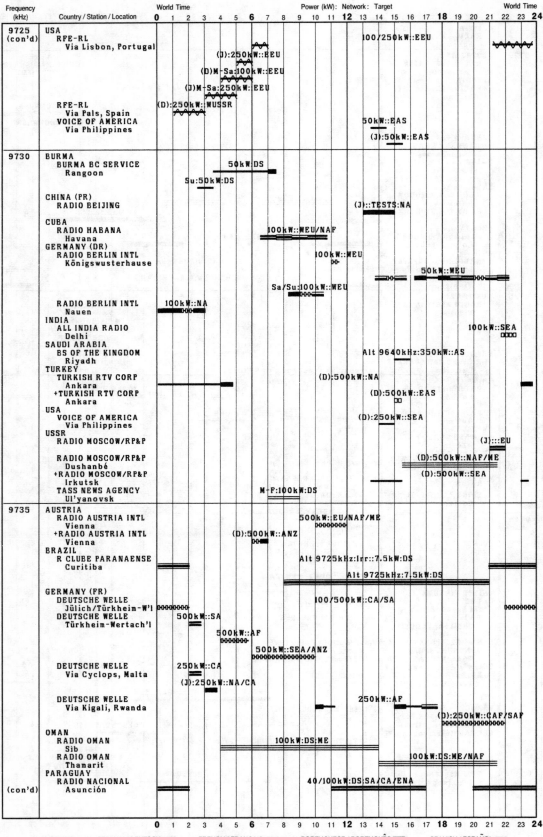

Frequency (kHz)	Country / Station / Location	World Time details
9725 (con'd)	USA — RFE-RL — Via Lisbon, Portugal	(J):250kW::EEU; (D)M-Sa:100kW::EEU; (J)M-Sa:250kW::EEU; 100/250kW::EEU
	RFE-RL — Via Pals, Spain	(D):250kW::WUSSR
	VOICE OF AMERICA — Via Philippines	50kW::EAS; (J):50kW::EAS
9730	BURMA — BURMA BC SERVICE — Rangoon	50kW:DS; Su:50kW:DS
	CHINA (PR) — RADIO BEIJING	(J)::TESTS:NA
	CUBA — RADIO HABANA — Havana	100kW::WEU/NAF
	GERMANY (DR) — RADIO BERLIN INTL — Königswusterhause	100kW::WEU; 50kW::WEU; Sa/Su:100kW::WEU
	RADIO BERLIN INTL — Nauen	100kW::NA
	INDIA — ALL INDIA RADIO — Delhi	100kW::SEA
	SAUDI ARABIA — BS OF THE KINGDOM — Riyadh	Alt 9640kHz:350kW::AS
	TURKEY — TURKISH RTV CORP — Ankara	(D):500kW::NA
	+TURKISH RTV CORP — Ankara	(D):500kW::EAS
	USA — VOICE OF AMERICA — Via Philippines	(D):250kW::SEA
	USSR — RADIO MOSCOW/RP&P	(J):::EU
	RADIO MOSCOW/RP&P — Dushanbé	(D):500kW::NAF/ME
	+RADIO MOSCOW/RP&P — Irkutsk	(D):500kW::SEA
	TASS NEWS AGENCY — Ul'yanovsk	M-F:100kW:DS
9735	AUSTRIA — RADIO AUSTRIA INTL — Vienna	500kW::EU/NAF/ME
	+RADIO AUSTRIA INTL — Vienna	(D):500kW::ANZ
	BRAZIL — R CLUBE PARANAENSE — Curitiba	Alt 9725kHz:Irr:7.5kW:DS; Alt 9725kHz:7.5kW:DS
	GERMANY (FR) — DEUTSCHE WELLE — Jülich/Türkheim-W'l	100/500kW::CA/SA
	DEUTSCHE WELLE — Türkheim-Wertach'l	500kW::SA; 500kW::AF; 500kW::SEA/ANZ
	DEUTSCHE WELLE — Via Cyclops, Malta	250kW::CA; (J):250kW::NA/CA
	DEUTSCHE WELLE — Via Kigali, Rwanda	250kW::AF; (D):250kW::CAF/SAF
	OMAN — RADIO OMAN — Sib	100kW:DS:ME
	RADIO OMAN — Thamarit	100kW:DS:ME/NAF
(con'd)	PARAGUAY — RADIO NACIONAL — Asunción	40/100kW:DS:SA/CA/ENA

ENGLISH ▬   GERMAN / DEUTSCH ◊◊◊◊   FRENCH / FRANÇAIS ══   PORTUGUESE / PORTUGUÊS ▦▦   SPANISH / ESPAÑOL ▬▬

ARABIC / العربية ≡≡   RUSSIAN / РУССКИЙ ══   CHINESE / 中文 ◌◌◌◌   JAPANESE / 日本語 ▦▦   MULTILINGUAL ▦▦▦   OTHER ▬

SUMMER ONLY (J)   WINTER ONLY (D)   JAMMING /\/\ or / or \   EARLIEST HEARD ◢   LATEST HEARD ◣   + TENTATIVE

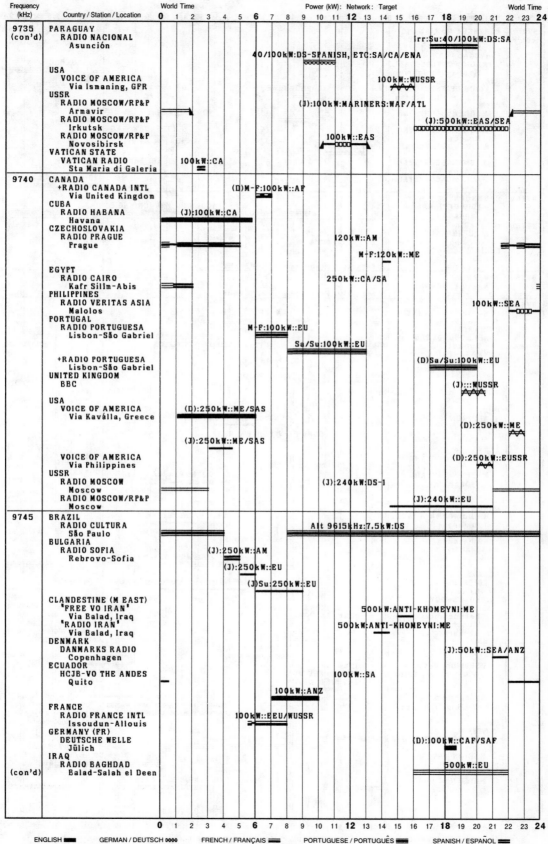

9735 (con'd) — PARAGUAY
RADIO NACIONAL, Asunción — Irr:Su:40/100kW:DS:SA / 40/100kW:DS-SPANISH, ETC:SA/CA/ENA

USA
VOICE OF AMERICA, Via Ismaning, GFR — 100kW::WUSSR

USSR
RADIO MOSCOW/RP&P, Armavir — (J):100kW:MARINERS:WAF/ATL
RADIO MOSCOW/RP&P, Irkutsk — (J):500kW::EAS/SEA
RADIO MOSCOW/RP&P, Novosibirsk — 100kW::EAS

VATICAN STATE
VATICAN RADIO, Sta Maria di Galeria — 100kW:CA

9740 — CANADA
+RADIO CANADA INTL, Via United Kingdom — (D)M-F:100kW::AF

CUBA
RADIO HABANA, Havana — (J):100kW::CA

CZECHOSLOVAKIA
RADIO PRAGUE, Prague — 120kW::AM / M-F:120kW::ME

EGYPT
RADIO CAIRO, Kafr Silîm-Abis — 250kW::CA/SA

PHILIPPINES
RADIO VERITAS ASIA, Malolos — 100kW::SEA

PORTUGAL
RADIO PORTUGUESA, Lisbon-São Gabriel — M-F:100kW::EU / Sa/Su:100kW::EU
+RADIO PORTUGUESA, Lisbon-São Gabriel — (D)Sa/Su:100kW::EU

UNITED KINGDOM
BBC — (J):::WUSSR

USA
VOICE OF AMERICA, Via Kaválla, Greece — (D):250kW::ME/SAS / (J):250kW::ME/SAS / (D):250kW::ME
VOICE OF AMERICA, Via Philippines — (D):250kW::EUSSR

USSR
RADIO MOSCOW, Moscow — (J):240kW:DS-1
RADIO MOSCOW/RP&P, Moscow — (J):240kW::EU

9745 — BRAZIL
RADIO CULTURA, São Paulo — Alt 9615kHz:7.5kW:DS

BULGARIA
RADIO SOFIA, Rebrovo-Sofia — (J):250kW::AM / (J):250kW::EU / (J)Su:250kW::EU

CLANDESTINE (M EAST)
"FREE VO IRAN", Via Balad, Iraq — 500kW:ANTI-KHOMEYNI:ME
"RADIO IRAN", Via Balad, Iraq — 500kW:ANTI-KHOMEYNI:ME

DENMARK
DANMARKS RADIO, Copenhagen — (J):50kW::SEA/ANZ

ECUADOR
HCJB-VO THE ANDES, Quito — 100kW::SA / 100kW::ANZ

FRANCE
RADIO FRANCE INTL, Issoudun-Allouis — 100kW::EEU/WUSSR

GERMANY (FR)
DEUTSCHE WELLE, Jülich — (D):100kW::CAF/SAF

IRAQ
RADIO BAGHDAD, Balad-Salah el Deen — 500kW::EU

(con'd)

ENGLISH ■■■   GERMAN / DEUTSCH ০০০০   FRENCH / FRANÇAIS ≡≡   PORTUGUESE / PORTUGUÊS ≣≣   SPANISH / ESPAÑOL ≡≡

ARABIC / ركاع ≡   RUSSIAN / РУССКИИ ═   CHINESE / 中文 ০০০০   JAPANESE / 日本語 ▄▄▄   MULTILINGUAL ▨▨▨   OTHER ▬

SUMMER ONLY (J)   WINTER ONLY (D)   JAMMING ∧∧ or / or \   EARLIEST HEARD ◢   LATEST HEARD ◣   + TENTATIVE

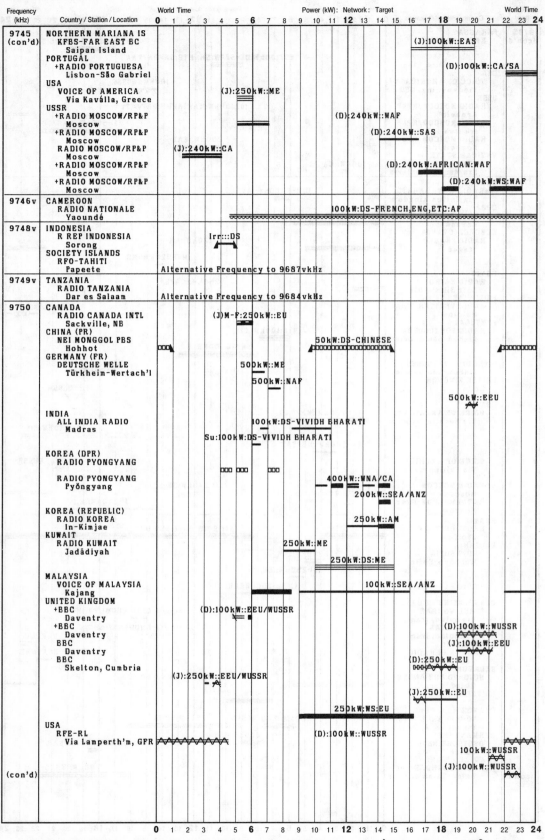

Frequency (kHz)	Country / Station / Location	World Time	Power (kW): Network: Target	World Time

9745 (con'd)
NORTHERN MARIANA IS
KFBS-FAR EAST BC
Saipan Island — (J):100kW::EAS
PORTUGAL
+RADIO PORTUGUESA
Lisbon-São Gabriel — (D):100kW::CA/SA
USA
VOICE OF AMERICA
Via Kaválla, Greece — (J):250kW::ME
USSR
+RADIO MOSCOW/RP&P
Moscow — (D):240kW::WAF
+RADIO MOSCOW/RP&P
Moscow — (D):240kW::SAS
RADIO MOSCOW/RP&P
Moscow — (J):240kW::CA
+RADIO MOSCOW/RP&P
Moscow — (D):240kW:AFRICAN:WAF
+RADIO MOSCOW/RP&P
Moscow — (D):240kW:WS:WAF

9746v
CAMEROON
RADIO NATIONALE
Yaoundé — 100kW:DS-FRENCH,ENG,ETC:AF

9748v
INDONESIA
R REP INDONESIA
Sorong — Irr::::DS
SOCIETY ISLANDS
RFO-TAHITI
Papeete — Alternative Frequency to 9687vkHz

9749v
TANZANIA
RADIO TANZANIA
Dar es Salaam — Alternative Frequency to 9684vkHz

9750
CANADA
RADIO CANADA INTL
Sackville, NB — (J)M-F:250kW::EU
CHINA (PR)
NEI MONGGOL PBS
Hohhot — 50kW:DS-CHINESE
GERMANY (FR)
DEUTSCHE WELLE
Türkheim-Wertach'l — 500kW::ME
500kW::NAF
500kW::EEU
INDIA
ALL INDIA RADIO
Madras — 100kW:DS-VIVIDH BHARATI
Su:100kW:DS-VIVIDH BHARATI
KOREA (DPR)
RADIO PYONGYANG
RADIO PYONGYANG
Pyŏngyang — 400kW::WNA/CA
200kW::SEA/ANZ
KOREA (REPUBLIC)
RADIO KOREA
In-Kimjae — 250kW::AM
KUWAIT
RADIO KUWAIT
Jadādiyah — 250kW::ME
250kW:DS:ME
MALAYSIA
VOICE OF MALAYSIA
Kajang — 100kW::SEA/ANZ
UNITED KINGDOM
+BBC
Daventry — (D):100kW::EEU/WUSSR
+BBC
Daventry — (D):100kW::WUSSR
BBC
Daventry — (J):100kW::EEU
BBC
Skelton, Cumbria — (D):250kW::EU
(J):250kW::EEU/WUSSR
(J):250kW::EU
250kW:WS:EU
USA
RFE-RL
Via Lamperth'm, GFR — (D):100kW::WUSSR
100kW::WUSSR
(J):100kW::WUSSR

(con'd)

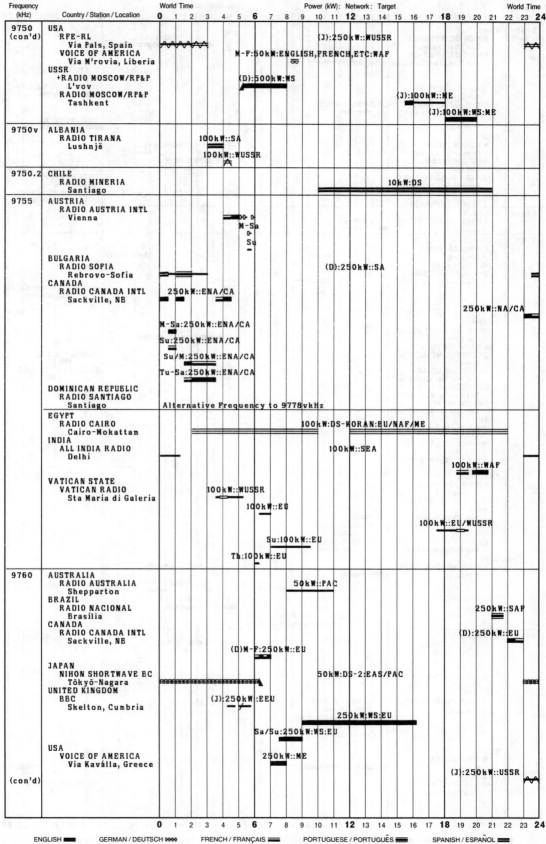

Frequency (kHz)	Country / Station / Location	Schedule (World Time 0–24) — Power (kW): Network: Target
9750 (con'd)	**USA** RFE-RL, Via Pals, Spain	(J):250kW::WUSSR
	VOICE OF AMERICA, Via M'rovia, Liberia	M-F:50kW:ENGLISH,FRENCH,ETC:WAF
	USSR +RADIO MOSCOW/RP&P, L'vov	(D):500kW:WS
	RADIO MOSCOW/RP&P, Tashkent	(J):100kW::ME / (J):100kW:WS:ME
9750v	**ALBANIA** RADIO TIRANA, Lushnjë	100kW::SA / 100kW::WUSSR
9750.2	**CHILE** RADIO MINERIA, Santiago	10kW:DS
9755	**AUSTRIA** RADIO AUSTRIA INTL, Vienna	M-Sa / Su
	BULGARIA RADIO SOFIA, Rebrovo-Sofia	(D):250kW::SA
	CANADA RADIO CANADA INTL, Sackville, NB	250kW::ENA/CA / 250kW::NA/CA / M-Sa:250kW::ENA/CA / Su:250kW::ENA/CA / Su/M:250kW::ENA/CA / Tu-Sa:250kW::ENA/CA
	DOMINICAN REPUBLIC RADIO SANTIAGO, Santiago	Alternative Frequency to 9778vkHz
	EGYPT RADIO CAIRO, Cairo-Mokattam	100kW:DS-KORAN:EU/NAF/ME
	INDIA ALL INDIA RADIO, Delhi	100kW::SEA / 100kW::WAF
	VATICAN STATE VATICAN RADIO, Sta Maria di Galeria	100kW::WUSSR / 100kW::EU / 100kW::EU/WUSSR / Su:100kW::EU / Th:100kW::EU
9760	**AUSTRALIA** RADIO AUSTRALIA, Shepparton	50kW::PAC
	BRAZIL RADIO NACIONAL, Brasília	250kW::SAF
	CANADA RADIO CANADA INTL, Sackville, NB	(D):250kW::EU / (D)M-F:250kW::EU
	JAPAN NIHON SHORTWAVE BC, Tōkyō-Nagara	50kW:DS-2:EAS/PAC
	UNITED KINGDOM BBC, Skelton, Cumbria	(J):250kW::EEU / 250kW:WS:EU / Sa/Su:250kW:WS:EU
(con'd)	**USA** VOICE OF AMERICA, Via Kaválla, Greece	250kW::ME / (J):250kW::USSR

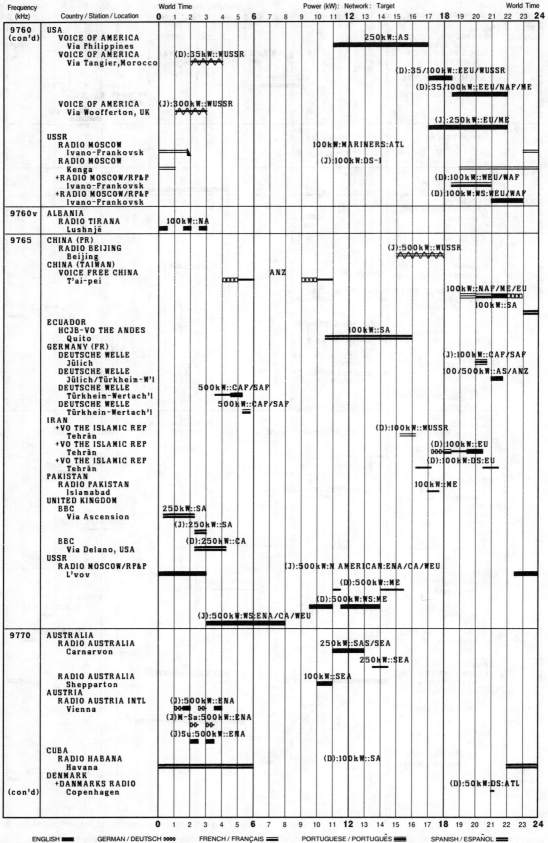

Frequency (kHz)	Country / Station / Location	World Time

9760 (con'd) USA

VOICE OF AMERICA — Via Philippines — 250kW::AS

VOICE OF AMERICA — Via Tangier, Morocco — (D):35kW::WUSSR; (D):35/100kW::EEU/WUSSR; (D):35/100kW::EEU/NAF/ME

VOICE OF AMERICA — Via Woofferton, UK — (J):300kW::WUSSR; (J):250kW::EU/ME

USSR

RADIO MOSCOW — Ivano-Frankovsk — 100kW:MARINERS:ATL

RADIO MOSCOW — Kenga — (J):100kW:DS-1

+RADIO MOSCOW/RP&P — Ivano-Frankovsk — (D):100kW::WEU/WAF

+RADIO MOSCOW/RP&P — Ivano-Frankovsk — (D):100kW:WS:WEU/WAF

9760v ALBANIA

RADIO TIRANA — Lushnjë — 100kW::NA

9765 CHINA (PR)

RADIO BEIJING — Beijing — (J):500kW::WUSSR

CHINA (TAIWAN)

VOICE FREE CHINA — T'ai-pei — ANZ; 100kW::NAF/ME/EU; 100kW::SA

ECUADOR

HCJB-VO THE ANDES — Quito — 100kW::SA

GERMANY (FR)

DEUTSCHE WELLE — Jülich — (J):100kW::CAF/SAF

DEUTSCHE WELLE — Jülich/Türkheim-W'l — 100/500kW::AS/ANZ

DEUTSCHE WELLE — Türkheim-Wertach'l — 500kW::CAF/SAF

DEUTSCHE WELLE — Türkhein-Wertach'l — 500kW::CAF/SAF

IRAN

+VO THE ISLAMIC REP — Tehrän — (D):100kW::WUSSR

+VO THE ISLAMIC REP — Tehrän — (D):100kW::EU

+VO THE ISLAMIC REP — Tehrän — (D):100kW:DS:EU

PAKISTAN

RADIO PAKISTAN — Islamabad — 100kW::ME

UNITED KINGDOM

BBC — Via Ascension — 250kW::SA; (J):250kW::SA; (D):250kW::CA

BBC — Via Delano, USA

USSR

RADIO MOSCOW/RP&P — L'vov — (J):500kW:N AMERICAN:ENA/CA/WEU; (D):500kW::ME; (D):500kW:WS:ME; (J):500kW:WS:ENA/CA/WEU

9770 AUSTRALIA

RADIO AUSTRALIA — Carnarvon — 250kW::SAS/SEA; 250kW::SEA

RADIO AUSTRALIA — Shepparton — 100kW::SEA

AUSTRIA

RADIO AUSTRIA INTL — Vienna — (J):500kW::ENA; (J)M-Sa:500kW::ENA; (J)Su:500kW::ENA

CUBA

RADIO HABANA — Havana — (D):100kW::SA

DENMARK

+DANMARKS RADIO — Copenhagen — (D):50kW:DS:ATL

(con'd)

ENGLISH ▰▰   GERMAN / DEUTSCH ㅁㅁㅁ   FRENCH / FRANÇAIS ▬▬   PORTUGUESE / PORTUGUÊS ▤▤   SPANISH / ESPAÑOL ▭▭
ARABIC / العربية ▱▱   RUSSIAN / РУССКИИ ══   CHINESE / 中文 ㅁㅁㅁ   JAPANESE / 日本語 ▨▨   MULTILINGUAL ▩▩   OTHER ▬
SUMMER ONLY (J)   WINTER ONLY (D)   JAMMING /\/\ or / or \   EARLIEST HEARD ◢   LATEST HEARD ◣   + TENTATIVE

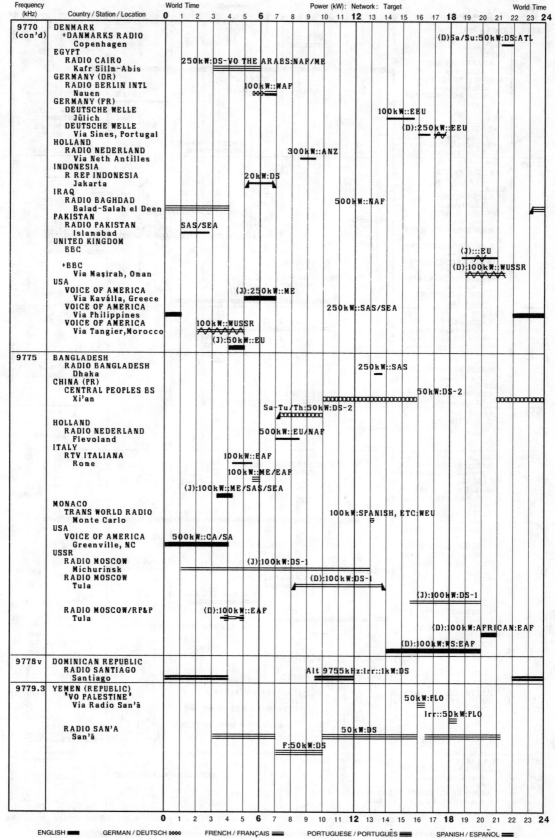

Frequency (kHz)	Country / Station / Location		World Time / Power (kW): Network: Target

9770 (con'd) — DENMARK
  +DANMARKS RADIO — Copenhagen — (D)Sa/Su:50kW:DS:ATL
EGYPT
  RADIO CAIRO — Kafr Silim-Abis — 250kW:DS-VO THE ARABS:NAF/ME
GERMANY (DR)
  RADIO BERLIN INTL — Nauen — 100kW::WAF
GERMANY (FR)
  DEUTSCHE WELLE — Jülich — 100kW::EEU
  DEUTSCHE WELLE — Via Sines, Portugal — (D):250kW::EEU
HOLLAND
  RADIO NEDERLAND — Via Neth Antilles — 300kW::ANZ
INDONESIA
  R REP INDONESIA — Jakarta — 20kW:DS
IRAQ
  RADIO BAGHDAD — Balad-Salah el Deen — 500kW::NAF
PAKISTAN
  RADIO PAKISTAN — Islamabad — SAS/SEA
UNITED KINGDOM
  BBC — (J):::EU
  +BBC — Via Maşirah, Oman — (D):100kW::WUSSR
USA
  VOICE OF AMERICA — Via Kaválla, Greece — (J):250kW::ME
  VOICE OF AMERICA — Via Philippines — 250kW::SAS/SEA
  VOICE OF AMERICA — Via Tangier, Morocco — 100kW::WUSSR / (J):50kW::EU

9775 — BANGLADESH
  RADIO BANGLADESH — Dhaka — 250kW::SAS
CHINA (PR)
  CENTRAL PEOPLES BS — Xi'an — 50kW:DS-2 / Sa-Tu/Th:50kW:DS-2
HOLLAND
  RADIO NEDERLAND — Flevoland — 500kW::EU/NAF
ITALY
  RTV ITALIANA — Rome — 100kW::EAF / 100kW::ME/EAF / (J):100kW::ME/SAS/SEA
MONACO
  TRANS WORLD RADIO — Monte Carlo — 100kW:SPANISH, ETC:WEU
USA
  VOICE OF AMERICA — Greenville, NC — 500kW::CA/SA
USSR
  RADIO MOSCOW — Michurinsk — (J):100kW:DS-1
  RADIO MOSCOW — Tula — (D):100kW:DS-1 / (J):100kW:DS-1
  RADIO MOSCOW/RP&P — Tula — (D):100kW::EAF / (D):100kW:AFRICAN:EAF / (D):100kW:WS:EAF

9778v — DOMINICAN REPUBLIC
  RADIO SANTIAGO — Santiago — Alt 9755kHz:Irr::1kW:DS

9779.3 — YEMEN (REPUBLIC)
  'VO PALESTINE' — Via Radio San'ā — 50kW:PLO / Irr::50kW:PLO
  RADIO SAN'A — San'ā — 50kW:DS / F:50kW:DS

World Time: 0 1 2 3 4 5 6 7 8 9 10 11 12 13 14 15 16 17 18 19 20 21 22 23 24

ENGLISH ▬▬   GERMAN / DEUTSCH ٥٥٥٥   FRENCH / FRANÇAIS ═══   PORTUGUESE / PORTUGUÊS ▬▬▬   SPANISH / ESPAÑOL ▬▬
ARABIC / ﻉﺭﺏ ═══   RUSSIAN / РУССКИЙ ═══   CHINESE / 中文 ٥٥٥٥   JAPANESE / 日本語 ▬▬▬   MULTILINGUAL ▬▬▬   OTHER ▬▬
SUMMER ONLY (J)   WINTER ONLY (D)   JAMMING /\/\ or / or \   EARLIEST HEARD ◢   LATEST HEARD ◣   + TENTATIVE

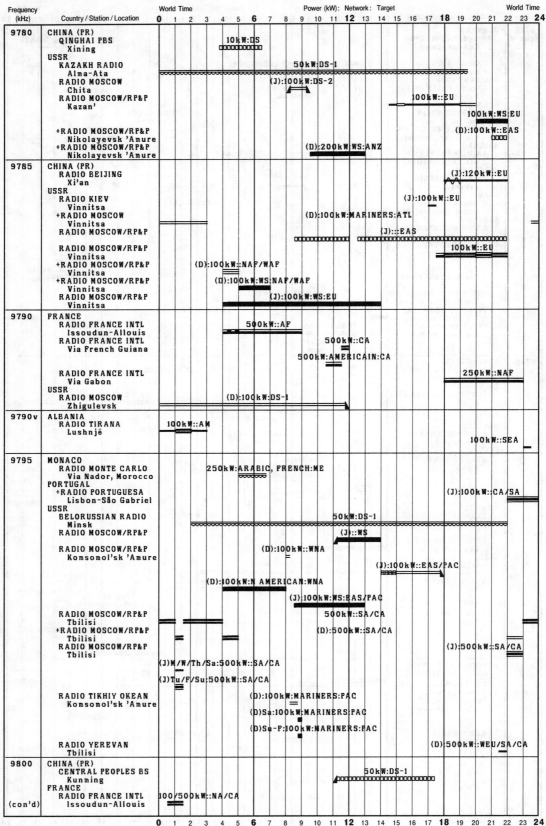

Frequency (kHz)	Country / Station / Location	World Time 0 ... 24 / Power (kW): Network: Target

9780 — CHINA (PR)
- QINGHAI PBS / Xining — 10kW:DS
- USSR — KAZAKH RADIO / Alma-Ata — 50kW:DS-1
- RADIO MOSCOW / Chita — (J):100kW:DS-2
- RADIO MOSCOW/RP&P / Kazan' — 100kW::EU
- — 100kW:WS:EU
- +RADIO MOSCOW/RP&P / Nikolayevsk 'Amure — (D):100kW::EAS
- +RADIO MOSCOW/RP&P / Nikolayevsk 'Amure — (D):200kW:WS:ANZ

9785 — CHINA (PR)
- RADIO BEIJING / Xi'an — (J):120kW::EU
- USSR — RADIO KIEV / Vinnitsa — (J):100kW::EU
- +RADIO MOSCOW / Vinnitsa — (D):100kW:MARINERS:ATL
- RADIO MOSCOW/RP&P — (J):::EAS
- RADIO MOSCOW/RP&P / Vinnitsa — 100kW::EU
- +RADIO MOSCOW/RP&P / Vinnitsa — (D):100kW::NAF/WAF
- +RADIO MOSCOW/RP&P / Vinnitsa — (D):100kW:WS:NAF/WAF
- RADIO MOSCOW/RP&P / Vinnitsa — (J):100kW:WS:EU

9790 — FRANCE
- RADIO FRANCE INTL / Issoudun-Allouis — 500kW:AF
- RADIO FRANCE INTL / Via French Guiana — 500kW::CA
- — 500kW:AMERICAIN:CA
- RADIO FRANCE INTL / Via Gabon — 250kW::NAF
- USSR — RADIO MOSCOW / Zhigulevsk — (D):100kW:DS-1

9790v — ALBANIA
- RADIO TIRANA / Lushnjë — 100kW::AM
- — 100kW::SEA

9795 — MONACO
- RADIO MONTE CARLO / Via Nador, Morocco — 250kW:ARABIC, FRENCH:ME
- PORTUGAL — +RADIO PORTUGUESA / Lisbon-São Gabriel — (J):100kW::CA/SA
- USSR — BELORUSSIAN RADIO / Minsk — 50kW:DS-1
- RADIO MOSCOW/RP&P — (J)::WS
- RADIO MOSCOW/RP&P / Komsomol'sk 'Amure — (D):100kW::WNA
- — (J):100kW::EAS/PAC
- — (D):100kW:N AMERICAN:WNA
- — (J):100kW:WS:EAS/PAC
- RADIO MOSCOW/RP&P / Tbilisi — 500kW::SA/CA
- +RADIO MOSCOW/RP&P / Tbilisi — (D):500kW::SA/CA
- RADIO MOSCOW/RP&P / Tbilisi — (J):500kW::SA/CA
- — (J)M/W/Th/Sa:500kW:SA/CA
- — (J)Tu/F/Su:500kW::SA/CA
- RADIO TIKHIY OKEAN / Komsomol'sk 'Amure — (D):100kW:MARINERS:PAC
- — (D)Sa:100kW:MARINERS:PAC
- — (D)Su-F:100kW:MARINERS:PAC
- RADIO YEREVAN / Tbilisi — (D):500kW:WEU/SA/CA

9800 — CHINA (PR)
- CENTRAL PEOPLES BS / Kunming — 50kW:DS-1
- FRANCE — RADIO FRANCE INTL / Issoudun-Allouis — 100/500kW::NA/CA

(con'd)

ENGLISH ▰▰▰   GERMAN / DEUTSCH ◊◊◊◊   FRENCH / FRANÇAIS ▤▤▤   PORTUGUESE / PORTUGUÊS ▦▦▦   SPANISH / ESPAÑOL ▤▤▤

ARABIC / عربي ▤▤▤   RUSSIAN / РУССКИИ ▤▤▤   CHINESE / 中文 ▱▱▱▱   JAPANESE / 日本語 ▰▰▰   MULTILINGUAL ▱▱▱▱   OTHER ▬▬▬

SUMMER ONLY (J)   WINTER ONLY (D)   JAMMING /\/\ or / or \   EARLIEST HEARD ◢   LATEST HEARD ◣   + TENTATIVE

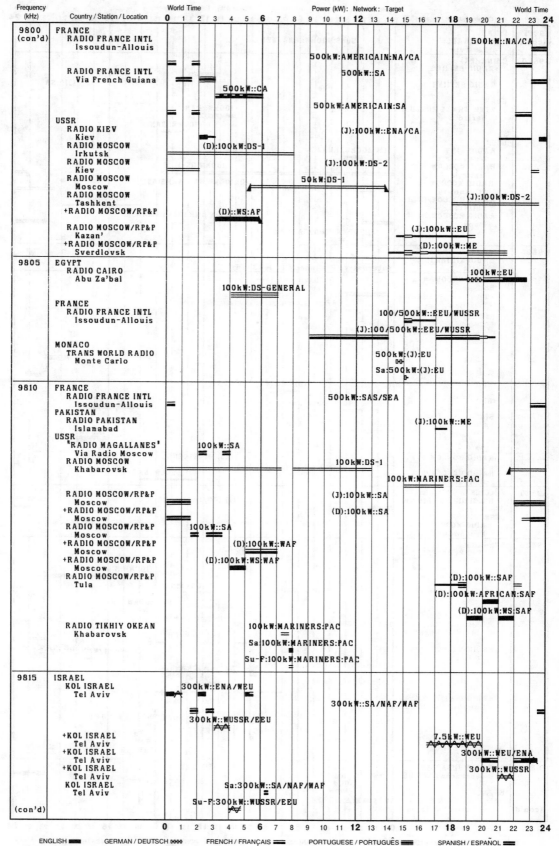

Frequency (kHz)	Country / Station / Location	World Time

9800 (con'd) — FRANCE, RADIO FRANCE INTL, Issoudun-Allouis — 500kW::NA/CA; 500kW:AMERICAIN:NA/CA

RADIO FRANCE INTL, Via French Guiana — 500kW:SA; 500kW::CA; 500kW:AMERICAIN:SA

USSR
RADIO KIEV, Kiev — (J):100kW:ENA/CA
RADIO MOSCOW, Irkutsk — (D):100kW:DS-1
RADIO MOSCOW, Kiev — (J):100kW:DS-2
RADIO MOSCOW, Moscow — 50kW:DS-1
RADIO MOSCOW, Tashkent — (J):100kW:DS-2
+RADIO MOSCOW/RP&P — (D)::WS:AF
RADIO MOSCOW/RP&P, Kazan' — (J):100kW::EU
+RADIO MOSCOW/RP&P, Sverdlovsk — (D):100kW::ME

9805 — EGYPT, RADIO CAIRO, Abu Za'bal — 100kW::EU; 100kW:DS-GENERAL

FRANCE, RADIO FRANCE INTL, Issoudun-Allouis — 100/500kW::EEU/WUSSR; (J):100/500kW::EEU/WUSSR

MONACO, TRANS WORLD RADIO, Monte Carlo — 500kW:(J):EU; Sa:500kW:(J):EU

9810 — FRANCE, RADIO FRANCE INTL, Issoudun-Allouis — 500kW::SAS/SEA
PAKISTAN, RADIO PAKISTAN, Islamabad — (J):100kW::ME
USSR, "RADIO MAGALLANES", Via Radio Moscow — 100kW::SA
RADIO MOSCOW, Khabarovsk — 100kW:DS-1; 100kW:MARINERS:PAC
RADIO MOSCOW/RP&P, Moscow — (J):100kW::SA
+RADIO MOSCOW/RP&P, Moscow — (D):100kW::SA
RADIO MOSCOW/RP&P, Moscow — 100kW::SA
+RADIO MOSCOW/RP&P, Moscow — (D):100kW::WAF
+RADIO MOSCOW/RP&P, Moscow — (D):100kW:WS:WAF
RADIO MOSCOW/RP&P, Tula — (D):100kW::SAF; (D):100kW:AFRICAN:SAF; (D):100kW:WS:SAF
RADIO TIKHIY OKEAN, Khabarovsk — 100kW:MARINERS:PAC; Sa:100kW:MARINERS:PAC; Su-F:100kW:MARINERS:PAC

9815 — ISRAEL, KOL ISRAEL, Tel Aviv — 300kW::ENA/WEU; 300kW::SA/NAF/WAF; 300kW::WUSSR/EEU
+KOL ISRAEL, Tel Aviv — 7.5kW::WEU
+KOL ISRAEL, Tel Aviv — 300kW::WEU/ENA
+KOL ISRAEL, Tel Aviv — 300kW::WUSSR
KOL ISRAEL, Tel Aviv — Sa:300kW::SA/NAF/WAF; Su-F:300kW::WUSSR/EEU

(con'd)

ENGLISH ▰▰▰   GERMAN / DEUTSCH ◊◊◊◊   FRENCH / FRANÇAIS ▰▰▰   PORTUGUESE / PORTUGUÊS ▰▰▰   SPANISH / ESPAÑOL ▰▰▰

ARABIC / ﻋﺮﺑﻲ ▰▰▰   RUSSIAN / РУССКИИ ▰▰▰   CHINESE / 中文 ◊◊◊◊   JAPANESE / 日本語 ▰▰▰   MULTILINGUAL ◊◊◊◊   OTHER ▬▬

SUMMER ONLY (J)   WINTER ONLY (D)   JAMMING ∧∧ or / or \   EARLIEST HEARD ◢   LATEST HEARD ◣   + TENTATIVE

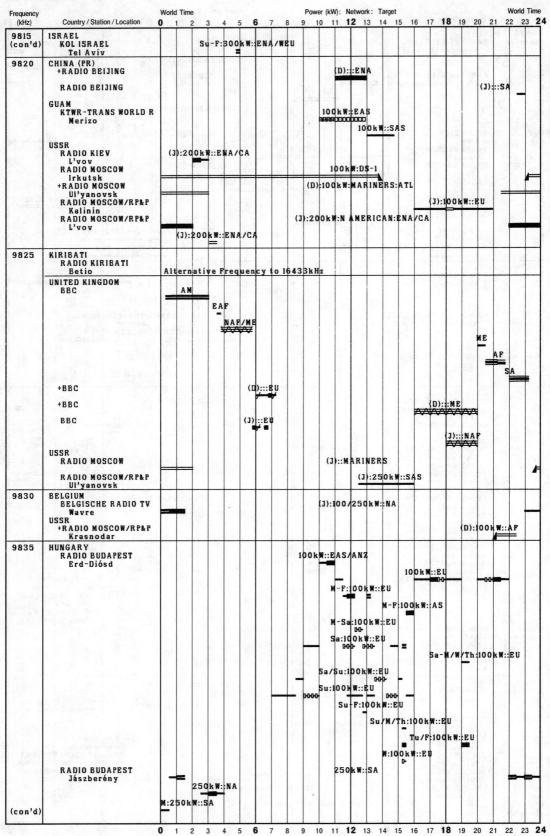

Frequency (kHz)	Country / Station / Location	World Time
9815 (con'd)	**ISRAEL** KOL ISRAEL Tel Aviv	Su-F:300kW::ENA/WEU
9820	**CHINA (PR)** +RADIO BEIJING	(D):::ENA
	RADIO BEIJING	(J):::SA
	GUAM KTWR-TRANS WORLD R Merizo	100kW::EAS / 100kW::SAS
	USSR RADIO KIEV L'vov	(J):200kW::ENA/CA
	RADIO MOSCOW Irkutsk	100kW:DS-1
	+RADIO MOSCOW Ul'yanovsk	(D):100kW:MARINERS:ATL
	RADIO MOSCOW/RP&P Kalinin	(J):100kW::EU
	RADIO MOSCOW/RP&P L'vov	(J):200kW:N AMERICAN:ENA/CA / (J):200kW::ENA/CA
9825	**KIRIBATI** RADIO KIRIBATI Betio	Alternative Frequency to 16433kHz
	UNITED KINGDOM BBC	AM / EAF / NAF/ME / ME / AF / SA
	+BBC	(D):::EU
	+BBC	(D):::ME
	BBC	(J):::EU / (J):::NAF
	USSR RADIO MOSCOW	(J)::MARINERS
	RADIO MOSCOW/RP&P Ul'yanovsk	(J):250kW::SAS
9830	**BELGIUM** BELGISCHE RADIO TV Wavre	(J):100/250kW::NA
	USSR +RADIO MOSCOW/RP&P Krasnodar	(D):100kW::AF
9835	**HUNGARY** RADIO BUDAPEST Erd-Diósd	100kW::EAS/ANZ / 100kW::EU / M-F:100kW::EU / M-F:100kW::AS / M-Sa:100kW::EU / Sa:100kW::EU / Sa-M/W/Th:100kW::EU / Sa/Su:100kW::EU / Su:100kW::EU / Su-F:100kW::EU / Su/M/Th:100kW::EU / Tu/F:100kW::EU / W:100kW::EU
	RADIO BUDAPEST Jászberény	250kW::SA / 250kW::NA / M:250kW::SA
(con'd)		

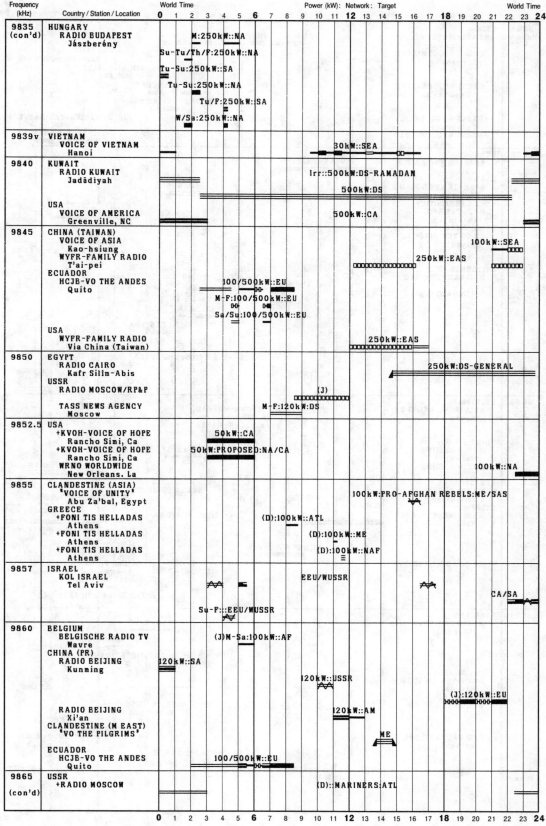

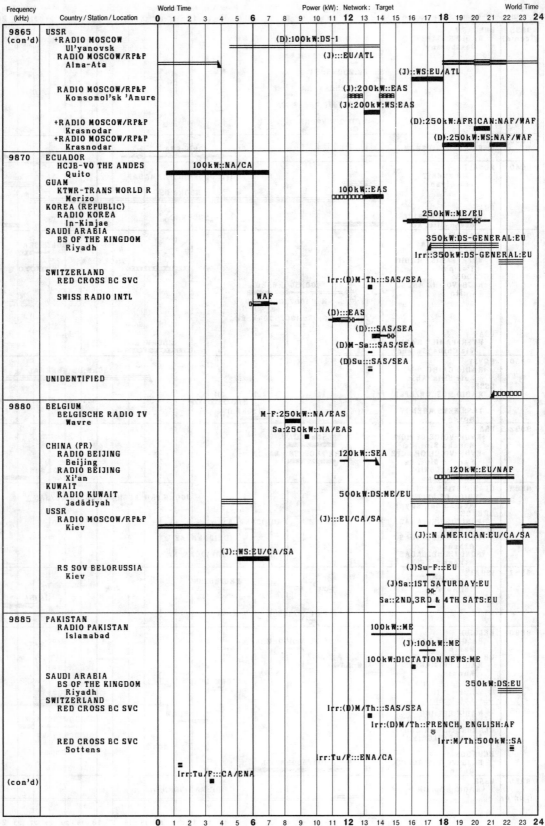

Frequency (kHz)	Country / Station / Location	World Time / Power (kW): Network: Target

9865 (con'd)

USSR
+RADIO MOSCOW — Ul'yanovsk — (D):100kW:DS-1
RADIO MOSCOW/RP&P — Alma-Ata — (J):::EU/ATL — (J)::WS:EU/ATL
RADIO MOSCOW/RP&P — Komsomol'sk 'Amure — (J):200kW::EAS — (J):200kW:WS:EAS
+RADIO MOSCOW/RP&P — Krasnodar — (D):250kW:AFRICAN:NAF/WAF
+RADIO MOSCOW/RP&P — Krasnodar — (D):250kW:WS:NAF/WAF

9870

ECUADOR
HCJB-VO THE ANDES — Quito — 100kW::NA/CA
GUAM
KTWR-TRANS WORLD R — Merizo — 100kW::EAS
KOREA (REPUBLIC)
RADIO KOREA — In-Kimjae — 250kW::ME/EU
SAUDI ARABIA
BS OF THE KINGDOM — Riyadh — 350kW:DS-GENERAL:EU — Irr:350kW:DS-GENERAL:EU
SWITZERLAND
RED CROSS BC SVC — Irr:(D)M-Th:::SAS/SEA
SWISS RADIO INTL — WAF — (D):::EAS — (D):::SAS/SEA — (D)M-Sa:::SAS/SEA — (D)Su:::SAS/SEA
UNIDENTIFIED

9880

BELGIUM
BELGISCHE RADIO TV — Wavre — M-F:250kW::NA/EAS — Sa:250kW::NA/EAS
CHINA (PR)
RADIO BEIJING — Beijing — 120kW::SEA
RADIO BEIJING — Xi'an — 120kW::EU/NAF
KUWAIT
RADIO KUWAIT — Jadâdiyah — 500kW:DS:ME/EU
USSR
RADIO MOSCOW/RP&P — Kiev — (J):::EU/CA/SA — (J)::N AMERICAN:EU/CA/SA
(J)::WS:EU/CA/SA
RS SOV BELORUSSIA — Kiev — (J)Su-F:::EU — (J)Sa::1ST SATURDAY:EU — Sa::2ND,3RD & 4TH SATS:EU

9885

PAKISTAN
RADIO PAKISTAN — Islamabad — 100kW::ME — (J):100kW::ME — 100kW:DICTATION NEWS:ME
SAUDI ARABIA
BS OF THE KINGDOM — Riyadh — 350kW:DS:EU
SWITZERLAND
RED CROSS BC SVC — Irr:(D)M/Th:::SAS/SEA — Irr:(D)M/Th::FRENCH, ENGLISH:AF
RED CROSS BC SVC — Sottens — Irr:M/Th:500kW::SA — Irr:Tu/F:::ENA/CA
Irr:Tu/F:::CA/ENA

(con'd)

ENGLISH ▬▬ GERMAN / DEUTSCH ◊◊◊◊ FRENCH / FRANÇAIS ≡≡≡ PORTUGUESE / PORTUGUÊS ▤▤ SPANISH / ESPAÑOL ▬▬

ARABIC / ﻉﺭﺑ ≡≡≡ RUSSIAN / РУССКИИ ≡≡≡ CHINESE / ★★ ◊◊◊◊ JAPANESE / 日本語 ▦▦▦ MULTILINGUAL ▨▨▨ OTHER ▬▬

SUMMER ONLY (J) WINTER ONLY (D) JAMMING ∧∧ or / or \ EARLIEST HEARD ◢ LATEST HEARD ◣ + TENTATIVE

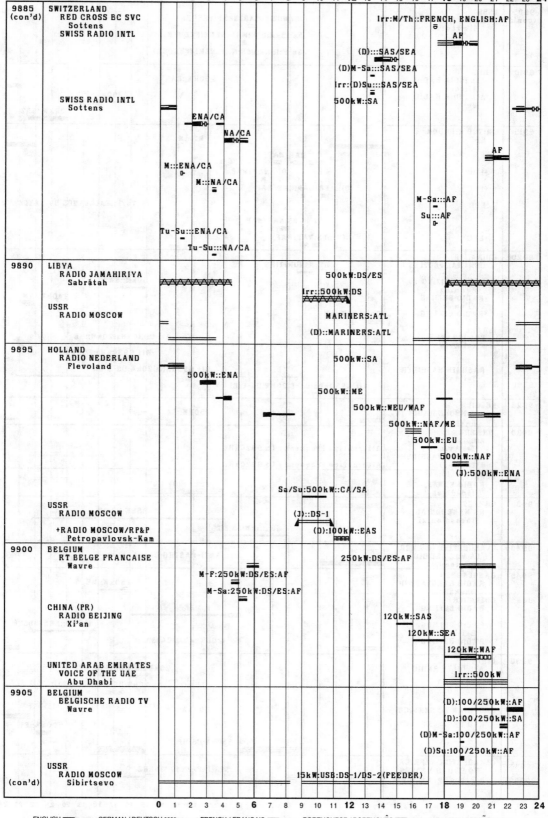

Frequency (kHz)	Country / Station / Location	Power (kW): Network: Target
9885 (con'd)	SWITZERLAND RED CROSS BC SVC Sottens	Irr:M/Th::FRENCH, ENGLISH:AF
	SWISS RADIO INTL	AF
		(D):::SAS/SEA
		(D)M-Sa:::SAS/SEA
		Irr:(D)Su:::SAS/SEA
		500kW::SA
	SWISS RADIO INTL Sottens	
		ENA/CA
		NA/CA
		AF
		M:::ENA/CA
		M:::NA/CA
		M-Sa:::AF
		Su:::AF
		Tu-Su:::ENA/CA
		Tu-Su:::NA/CA
9890	LIBYA RADIO JAMAHIRIYA Sabrātah	500kW:DS/ES
		Irr:500kW:DS
	USSR RADIO MOSCOW	MARINERS:ATL
		(D)::MARINERS:ATL
9895	HOLLAND RADIO NEDERLAND Flevoland	500kW::SA
		500kW::ENA
		500kW::ME
		500kW::WEU/WAF
		500kW::NAF/ME
		500kW::EU
		500kW::NAF
		(J):500kW::ENA
		Sa/Su:500kW::CA/SA
	USSR RADIO MOSCOW	(J)::DS-1
	+RADIO MOSCOW/RP&P Petropavlovsk-Kam	(D):100kW::EAS
9900	BELGIUM RT BELGE FRANCAISE Wavre	250kW:DS/ES:AF
		M-F:250kW:DS/ES:AF
		M-Sa:250kW:DS/ES:AF
	CHINA (PR) RADIO BEIJING Xi'an	120kW::SAS
		120kW::SEA
		120kW::WAF
	UNITED ARAB EMIRATES VOICE OF THE UAE Abu Dhabi	Irr::500kW
9905	BELGIUM BELGISCHE RADIO TV Wavre	(D):100/250kW::AF
		(D):100/250kW::SA
		(D)M-Sa:100/250kW::AF
		(D)Su:100/250kW::AF
(con'd)	USSR RADIO MOSCOW Sibirtsevo	15kW:USB:DS-1/DS-2(FEEDER)

World Time: 0 1 2 3 4 5 6 7 8 9 10 11 12 13 14 15 16 17 18 19 20 21 22 23 24

ENGLISH ▬   GERMAN / DEUTSCH ∞∞∞   FRENCH / FRANÇAIS ▭▭   PORTUGUESE / PORTUGUÊS ▬   SPANISH / ESPAÑOL ▬

ARABIC / ﻉ ﺭ ﺏ ≡   RUSSIAN / РУССКИИ ▬   CHINESE / 中文 ▭▭▭   JAPANESE / 日本語 ▬▬▬   MULTILINGUAL ▭▭▭   OTHER ▬

SUMMER ONLY (J)   WINTER ONLY (D)   JAMMING ∧∧ or / or \   EARLIEST HEARD ◢   LATEST HEARD ◣   + TENTATIVE

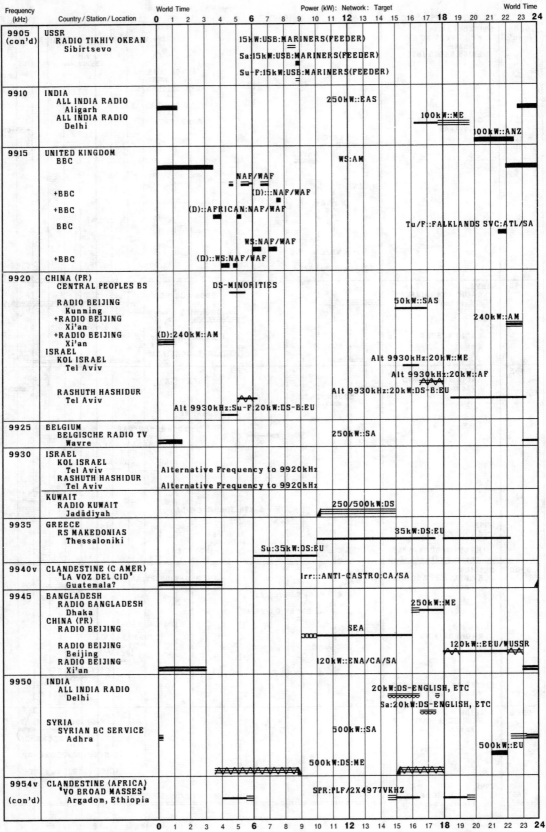

Frequency (kHz)	Country / Station / Location	Power (kW): Network: Target
9905 (con'd)	USSR RADIO TIKHIY OKEAN Sibirtsevo	15kW:USB:MARINERS(FEEDER) Sa:15kW:USB:MARINERS(FEEDER) Su-F:15kW:USB:MARINERS(FEEDER)
9910	INDIA ALL INDIA RADIO Aligarh ALL INDIA RADIO Delhi	250kW::EAS 100kW::ME 100kW::ANZ
9915	UNITED KINGDOM BBC +BBC +BBC BBC +BBC	WS:AM NAF/WAF (D):::NAF/WAF (D)::AFRICAN:NAF/WAF Tu/F::FALKLANDS SVC:ATL/SA WS:NAF/WAF (D)::WS:NAF/WAF
9920	CHINA (PR) CENTRAL PEOPLES BS RADIO BEIJING Kunming +RADIO BEIJING Xi'an +RADIO BEIJING Xi'an ISRAEL KOL ISRAEL Tel Aviv RASHUTH HASHIDUR Tel Aviv	DS-MINORITIES 50kW::SAS 240kW::AM (D):240kW::AM Alt 9930kHz:20kW::ME Alt 9930kHz:20kW::AF Alt 9930kHz:20kW:DS-B:EU Alt 9930kHz:Su-F:20kW:DS-B:EU
9925	BELGIUM BELGISCHE RADIO TV Wavre	250kW::SA
9930	ISRAEL KOL ISRAEL Tel Aviv RASHUTH HASHIDUR Tel Aviv KUWAIT RADIO KUWAIT Jadādiyah	Alternative Frequency to 9920kHz Alternative Frequency to 9920kHz 250/500kW:DS
9935	GREECE RS MAKEDONIAS Thessaloniki	35kW:DS:EU Su:35kW:DS:EU
9940v	CLANDESTINE (C AMER) 'LA VOZ DEL CID' Guatemala?	Irr:::ANTI-CASTRO:CA/SA
9945	BANGLADESH RADIO BANGLADESH Dhaka CHINA (PR) RADIO BEIJING RADIO BEIJING Beijing RADIO BEIJING Xi'an	250kW::ME SEA 120kW::EEU/WUSSR 120kW::ENA/CA/SA
9950	INDIA ALL INDIA RADIO Delhi SYRIA SYRIAN BC SERVICE Adhra	20kW:DS-ENGLISH, ETC Sa:20kW:DS-ENGLISH, ETC 500kW::SA 500kW::EU 500kW:DS:ME
9954v (con'd)	CLANDESTINE (AFRICA) 'VO BROAD MASSES' Argadom, Ethiopia	SPR:PLF:2X4977VKHZ

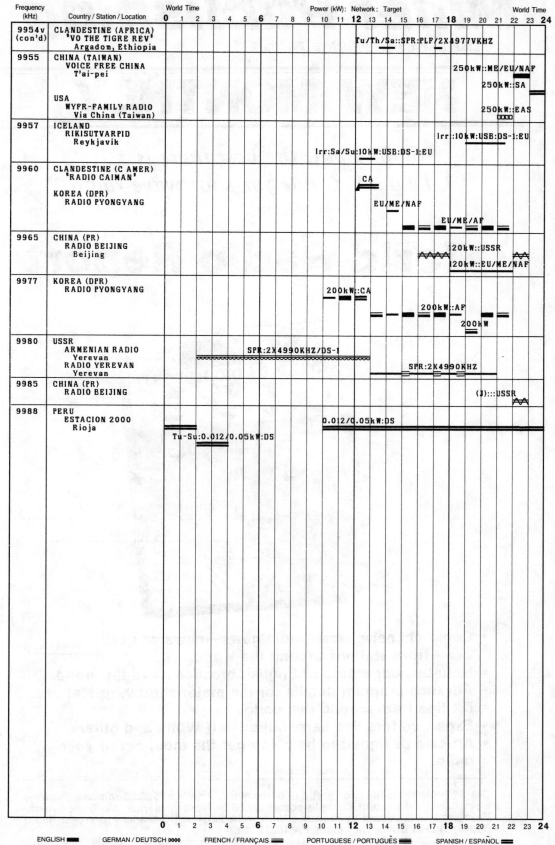

Frequency (kHz)	Country / Station / Location	Power (kW): Network: Target

9954v (con'd) — CLANDESTINE (AFRICA) "VO THE TIGRE REV" Argadom, Ethiopia — Tu/Th/Sa::SPR:PLF/2X4977VKHZ

9955 — CHINA (TAIWAN) VOICE FREE CHINA T'ai-pei — 250kW::ME/EU/NAF ; 250kW::SA
USA WYFR-FAMILY RADIO Via China (Taiwan) — 250kW::EAS

9957 — ICELAND RIKISUTVARPID Reykjavik — Irr::10kW:USB:DS-1:EU ; Irr:Sa/Su:10kW:USB:DS-1:EU

9960 — CLANDESTINE (C AMER) "RADIO CAIMAN" — CA
KOREA (DPR) RADIO PYONGYANG — EU/ME/NAF ; EU/ME/AF

9965 — CHINA (PR) RADIO BEIJING Beijing — 120kW::USSR ; 120kW::EU/ME/NAF

9977 — KOREA (DPR) RADIO PYONGYANG — 200kW::CA ; 200kW::AF ; 200kW

9980 — USSR ARMENIAN RADIO Yerevan — SPR:2X4990KHZ/DS-1
RADIO YEREVAN Yerevan — SPR:2X4990KHZ

9985 — CHINA (PR) RADIO BEIJING — (J):::USSR

9988 — PERU ESTACION 2000 Rioja — 0.012/0.05kW:DS ; Tu-Su:0.012/0.05kW:DS

ENGLISH ▰▰▰   GERMAN / DEUTSCH ▷◁▷◁   FRENCH / FRANÇAIS ≡≡≡   PORTUGUESE / PORTUGUÊS ≡≡≡   SPANISH / ESPAÑOL ▰▰▰
ARABIC / ﻋﺮﺑﻲ ≡≡   RUSSIAN / РУССКИЙ ══   CHINESE / 中文 ▭▭▭▭   JAPANESE / 日本語 ▰▰▰   MULTILINGUAL ◇◇◇◇   OTHER ▬▬
SUMMER ONLY (J)   WINTER ONLY (D)   JAMMING ∧∧ or / or \   EARLIEST HEARD ◢   LATEST HEARD ◣   † TENTATIVE

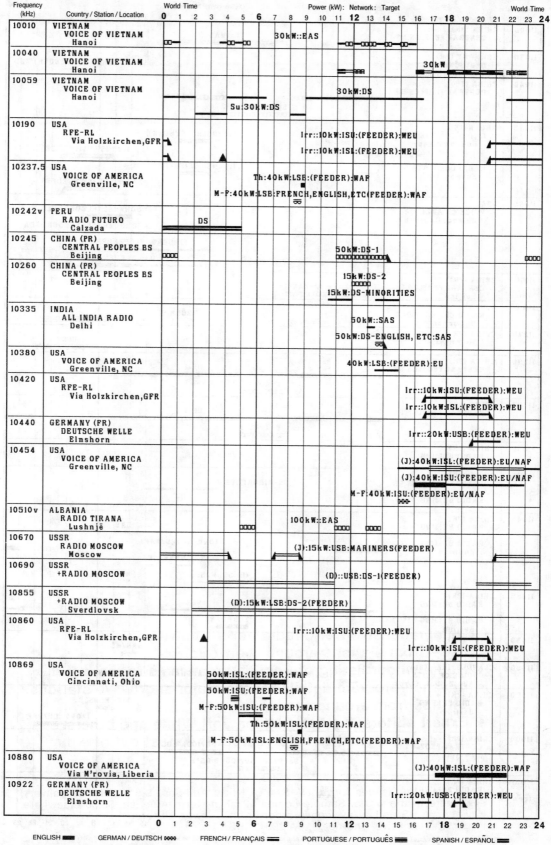

Frequency (kHz)	Country / Station / Location	Notes
10010	VIETNAM VOICE OF VIETNAM Hanoi	30kW::EAS
10040	VIETNAM VOICE OF VIETNAM Hanoi	30kW
10059	VIETNAM VOICE OF VIETNAM Hanoi	30kW:DS / Su:30kW:DS
10190	USA RFE-RL Via Holzkirchen,GFR	Irr::10kW:ISU:(FEEDER):WEU / Irr::10kW:ISL:(FEEDER):WEU
10237.5	USA VOICE OF AMERICA Greenville, NC	Th:40kW:LSB:(FEEDER):WAF / M-F:40kW:LSB:FRENCH,ENGLISH,ETC(FEEDER):WAF
10242v	PERU RADIO FUTURO Calzada	DS
10245	CHINA (PR) CENTRAL PEOPLES BS Beijing	50kW:DS-1
10260	CHINA (PR) CENTRAL PEOPLES BS Beijing	15kW:DS-2 / 15kW:DS-MINORITIES
10335	INDIA ALL INDIA RADIO Delhi	50kW::SAS / 50kW:DS-ENGLISH, ETC:SAS
10380	USA VOICE OF AMERICA Greenville, NC	40kW:LSB:(FEEDER):EU
10420	USA RFE-RL Via Holzkirchen,GFR	Irr::10kW:ISU:(FEEDER):WEU / Irr::10kW:ISL:(FEEDER):WEU
10440	GERMANY (FR) DEUTSCHE WELLE Elmshorn	Irr::20kW:USB:(FEEDER):WEU
10454	USA VOICE OF AMERICA Greenville, NC	(J):40kW:ISL:(FEEDER):EU/NAF / (J):40kW:ISU:(FEEDER):EU/NAF / M-F:40kW:ISU:(FEEDER):EU/NAF
10510v	ALBANIA RADIO TIRANA Lushnjë	100kW::EAS
10670	USSR RADIO MOSCOW Moscow	(J):15kW:USB:MARINERS(FEEDER)
10690	USSR +RADIO MOSCOW	(D)::USB:DS-1(FEEDER)
10855	USSR +RADIO MOSCOW Sverdlovsk	(D):15kW:LSB:DS-2(FEEDER)
10860	USA RFE-RL Via Holzkirchen,GFR	Irr::10kW:ISU:(FEEDER):WEU / Irr::10kW:ISL:(FEEDER):WEU
10869	USA VOICE OF AMERICA Cincinnati, Ohio	50kW:ISL:(FEEDER):WAF / 50kW:ISU:(FEEDER):WAF / M-F:50kW:ISU:(FEEDER):WAF / Th:50kW:ISL:(FEEDER):WAF / M-F:50kW:ISL:ENGLISH,FRENCH,ETC(FEEDER):WAF
10880	USA VOICE OF AMERICA Via M'rovia, Liberia	(J):40kW:ISL:(FEEDER):WAF
10922	GERMANY (FR) DEUTSCHE WELLE Elmshorn	Irr::20kW:USB:(FEEDER):WEU

World Time: 0 1 2 3 4 5 6 7 8 9 10 11 12 13 14 15 16 17 18 19 20 21 22 23 24

ENGLISH ▄▄▄   GERMAN / DEUTSCH ◊◊◊◊   FRENCH / FRANÇAIS ▬▬▬   PORTUGUESE / PORTUGUÊS ▬▬▬   SPANISH / ESPAÑOL ▬▬▬

ARABIC / ﻉﺮﺑﻲ ≡   RUSSIAN / РУССКИЙ ▬▬▬   CHINESE / 中文 ◻◻◻◻   JAPANESE / 日本語 ▒▒▒▒   MULTILINGUAL ▒▒▒▒   OTHER ▬▬

SUMMER ONLY (J)   WINTER ONLY (D)   JAMMING ∧∧ or / or \   EARLIEST HEARD ◢   LATEST HEARD ◣   + TENTATIVE

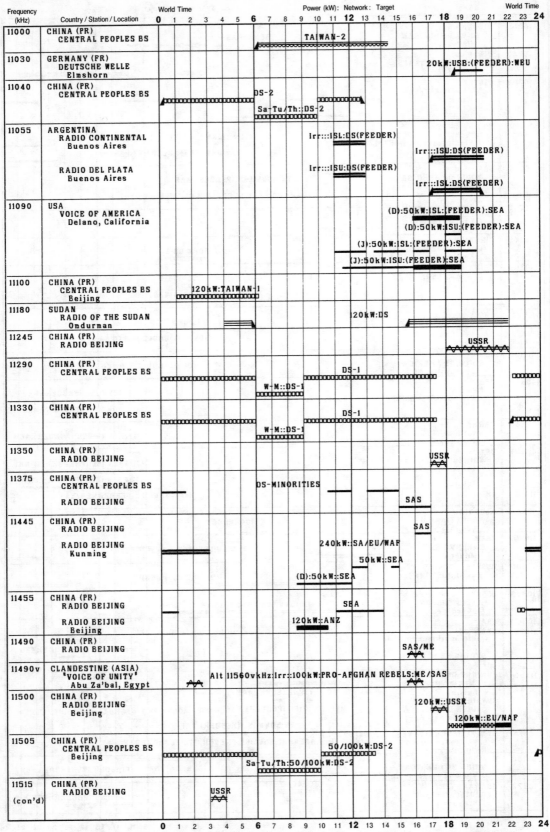

Frequency (kHz)	Country / Station / Location		World Time / Power (kW): Network: Target
11000	CHINA (PR) CENTRAL PEOPLES BS		TAIWAN-2
11030	GERMANY (FR) DEUTSCHE WELLE Elmshorn		20kW:USB:(FEEDER):WEU
11040	CHINA (PR) CENTRAL PEOPLES BS		DS-2 / Sa-Tu/Th::DS-2
11055	ARGENTINA RADIO CONTINENTAL Buenos Aires / RADIO DEL PLATA Buenos Aires		Irr:::ISL:DS(FEEDER) / Irr:::ISU:DS(FEEDER) / Irr:::ISU:DS(FEEDER) / Irr:::ISL:DS(FEEDER)
11090	USA VOICE OF AMERICA Delano, California		(D):50kW:ISL:(FEEDER):SEA / (D):50kW:ISU:(FEEDER):SEA / (J):50kW:ISL:(FEEDER):SEA / (J):50kW:ISU:(FEEDER):SEA
11100	CHINA (PR) CENTRAL PEOPLES BS Beijing		120kW:TAIWAN-1
11180	SUDAN RADIO OF THE SUDAN Omdurman		20kW:DS
11245	CHINA (PR) RADIO BEIJING		USSR
11290	CHINA (PR) CENTRAL PEOPLES BS		DS-1 / W-M::DS-1
11330	CHINA (PR) CENTRAL PEOPLES BS		DS-1 / W-M::DS-1
11350	CHINA (PR) RADIO BEIJING		USSR
11375	CHINA (PR) CENTRAL PEOPLES BS / RADIO BEIJING		DS-MINORITIES / SAS
11445	CHINA (PR) RADIO BEIJING / RADIO BEIJING Kunming		SAS / 240kW::SA/EU/WAF / 50kW::SEA / (D):50kW::SEA
11455	CHINA (PR) RADIO BEIJING / RADIO BEIJING Beijing		SEA / 120kW::ANZ
11490	CHINA (PR) RADIO BEIJING		SAS/ME
11490v	CLANDESTINE (ASIA) 'VOICE OF UNITY' Abu Za'bal, Egypt		Alt 11560vkHz:Irr::100kW:PRO-AFGHAN REBELS:ME/SAS
11500	CHINA (PR) RADIO BEIJING Beijing		120kW::USSR / 120kW::EU/NAF
11505	CHINA (PR) CENTRAL PEOPLES BS Beijing		50/100kW:DS-2 / Sa-Tu/Th:50/100kW:DS-2
11515 (con'd)	CHINA (PR) RADIO BEIJING		USSR

World Time
0 1 2 3 4 5 6 7 8 9 10 11 12 13 14 15 16 17 18 19 20 21 22 23 24

ENGLISH ▬▬   GERMAN / DEUTSCH ◊◊◊◊   FRENCH / FRANÇAIS ▬▬   PORTUGUESE / PORTUGUÊS ▬▬   SPANISH / ESPAÑOL ▬▬
ARABIC /ﻉﺭﻱ ▬▬   RUSSIAN / РУССКИИ ▬▬   CHINESE /⚫✱ ◊◊◊◊   JAPANESE / 日本語 ▬▬   MULTILINGUAL ◊◊◊◊   OTHER ▬▬
SUMMER ONLY (J)   WINTER ONLY (D)   JAMMING ∧∧ or / or \   EARLIEST HEARD ◢   LATEST HEARD ◣   + TENTATIVE

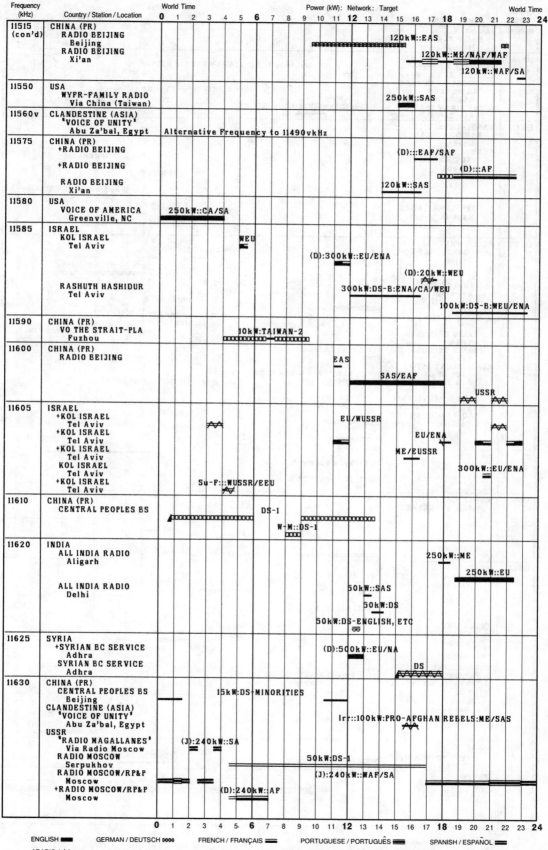

Frequency (kHz)	Country / Station / Location	World Time / Power (kW) / Network / Target
11515 (con'd)	CHINA (PR) RADIO BEIJING Beijing	120kW::EAS
	RADIO BEIJING Xi'an	120kW::ME/NAF/WAF / 120kW::WAF/SA
11550	USA WYFR-FAMILY RADIO Via China (Taiwan)	250kW::SAS
11560v	CLANDESTINE (ASIA) 'VOICE OF UNITY' Abu Za'bal, Egypt	Alternative Frequency to 11490vkHz
11575	CHINA (PR) +RADIO BEIJING	(D):::EAF/SAF
	+RADIO BEIJING	(D):::AF
	RADIO BEIJING Xi'an	120kW::SAS
11580	USA VOICE OF AMERICA Greenville, NC	250kW::CA/SA
11585	ISRAEL KOL ISRAEL Tel Aviv	WEU / (D):300kW::EU/ENA / (D):20kW::WEU
	RASHUTH HASHIDUR Tel Aviv	300kW:DS-B:ENA/CA/WEU / 100kW:DS-B:WEU/ENA
11590	CHINA (PR) VO THE STRAIT-PLA Fuzhou	10kW:TAIWAN-2
11600	CHINA (PR) RADIO BEIJING	EAS / SAS/EAF / USSR
11605	ISRAEL +KOL ISRAEL Tel Aviv	EU/WUSSR
	+KOL ISRAEL Tel Aviv	EU/ENA
	+KOL ISRAEL Tel Aviv	ME/EUSSR
	KOL ISRAEL Tel Aviv	300kW::EU/ENA
	+KOL ISRAEL Tel Aviv	Su-F::WUSSR/EEU
11610	CHINA (PR) CENTRAL PEOPLES BS	DS-1 / W-M::DS-1
11620	INDIA ALL INDIA RADIO Aligarh	250kW::ME / 250kW::EU
	ALL INDIA RADIO Delhi	50kW::SAS / 50kW:DS / 50kW:DS-ENGLISH, ETC
11625	SYRIA +SYRIAN BC SERVICE Adhra	(D):500kW::EU/NA
	SYRIAN BC SERVICE Adhra	DS
11630	CHINA (PR) CENTRAL PEOPLES BS Beijing	15kW:DS-MINORITIES
	CLANDESTINE (ASIA) 'VOICE OF UNITY' Abu Za'bal, Egypt	Irr::100kW:PRO-AFGHAN REBELS:ME/SAS
	USSR 'RADIO MAGALLANES' Via Radio Moscow	(J):240kW::SA
	RADIO MOSCOW Serpukhov	50kW:DS-1
	RADIO MOSCOW/RP&P Moscow	(J):240kW::WAF/SA
	+RADIO MOSCOW/RP&P Moscow	(D):240kW::AF

ENGLISH ▬ GERMAN / DEUTSCH ▨ FRENCH / FRANÇAIS ═ PORTUGUESE / PORTUGUÊS ▤ SPANISH / ESPAÑOL ▬

ARABIC / ﺔﻴﺑﺮﻋ ▤ RUSSIAN / PУССКИЙ ═ CHINESE / 中文 ▨ JAPANESE / 日本語 ▨ MULTILINGUAL ▨ OTHER ▬

SUMMER ONLY (J)   WINTER ONLY (D)   JAMMING ∧∧ or / or \   EARLIEST HEARD ◢   LATEST HEARD ◣   + TENTATIVE

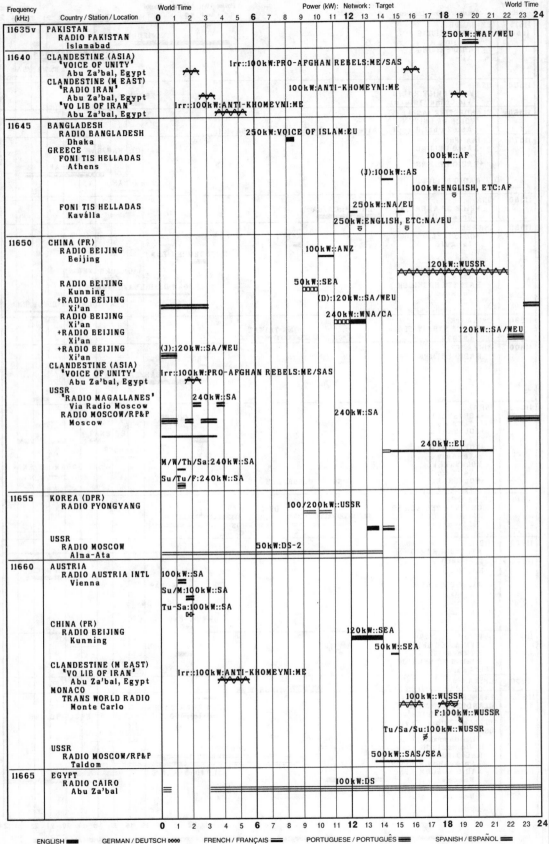

Frequency (kHz)	Country / Station / Location	World Time 0 1 2 3 4 5 **6** 7 8 9 10 11 **12** 13 14 15 16 17 **18** 19 20 21 22 23 **24**

Power (kW): Network : Target

11635v — PAKISTAN / RADIO PAKISTAN / Islamabad — 250kW::WAF/WEU

11640 — CLANDESTINE (ASIA) / 'VOICE OF UNITY' / Abu Za'bal, Egypt — Irr::100kW:PRO-AFGHAN REBELS:ME/SAS

CLANDESTINE (M EAST) / 'RADIO IRAN' / Abu Za'bal, Egypt — 100kW:ANTI-KHOMEYNI:ME

'VO LIB OF IRAN' / Abu Za'bal, Egypt — Irr::100kW:ANTI-KHOMEYNI:ME

11645 — BANGLADESH / RADIO BANGLADESH / Dhaka — 250kW:VOICE OF ISLAM:EU

GREECE / FONI TIS HELLADAS / Athens — 100kW::AF ; (J):100kW::AS ; 100kW::ENGLISH, ETC:AF

FONI TIS HELLADAS / Kaválla — 250kW::NA/EU ; 250kW:ENGLISH, ETC:NA/EU

11650 — CHINA (PR) / RADIO BEIJING / Beijing — 100kW::ANZ ; 120kW::WUSSR

RADIO BEIJING / Kunming — 50kW::SEA

+RADIO BEIJING / Xi'an — (D):120kW::SA/WEU

RADIO BEIJING / Xi'an — 240kW::WNA/CA ; 120kW::SA/WEU

+RADIO BEIJING / Xi'an —

+RADIO BEIJING / Xi'an — (J):120kW::SA/WEU

CLANDESTINE (ASIA) / 'VOICE OF UNITY' / Abu Za'bal, Egypt — Irr::100kW:PRO-AFGHAN REBELS:ME/SAS

USSR / 'RADIO MAGALLANES' / Via Radio Moscow — 240kW::SA

RADIO MOSCOW/RP&P / Moscow — 240kW::SA ; 240kW::EU

M/W/Th/Sa:240kW::SA

Su/Tu/F:240kW::SA

11655 — KOREA (DPR) / RADIO PYONGYANG — 100/200kW::USSR

USSR / RADIO MOSCOW / Alma-Ata — 50kW:DS-2

11660 — AUSTRIA / RADIO AUSTRIA INTL / Vienna — 100kW::SA

Su/M:100kW::SA

Tu-Sa:100kW::SA

CHINA (PR) / RADIO BEIJING / Kunming — 120kW::SEA ; 50kW::SEA

CLANDESTINE (M EAST) / 'VO LIB OF IRAN' / Abu Za'bal, Egypt — Irr::100kW:ANTI-KHOMEYNI:ME

MONACO / TRANS WORLD RADIO / Monte Carlo — 100kW::WUSSR ; F:100kW::WUSSR

Tu/Sa/Su:100kW::WUSSR

USSR / RADIO MOSCOW/RP&P / Taldom — 500kW::SAS/SEA

11665 — EGYPT / RADIO CAIRO / Abu Za'bal — 100kW:DS

World Time: 0 1 2 3 4 5 **6** 7 8 9 10 11 **12** 13 14 15 16 17 **18** 19 20 21 22 23 **24**

ENGLISH ▪▪▪▪ GERMAN / DEUTSCH 0000 FRENCH / FRANÇAIS ▬▬ PORTUGUESE / PORTUGUÊS ▬▬ SPANISH / ESPAÑOL ▬▬

ARABIC / عربى ≡≡ RUSSIAN / РУССКИИ ▬▬ CHINESE / 中文 0000 JAPANESE / 日本語 ▬▬ MULTILINGUAL 6666 OTHER ▬▬

SUMMER ONLY (J) WINTER ONLY (D) JAMMING ∧∧ or / or \ EARLIEST HEARD ◢ LATEST HEARD ◣ + TENTATIVE

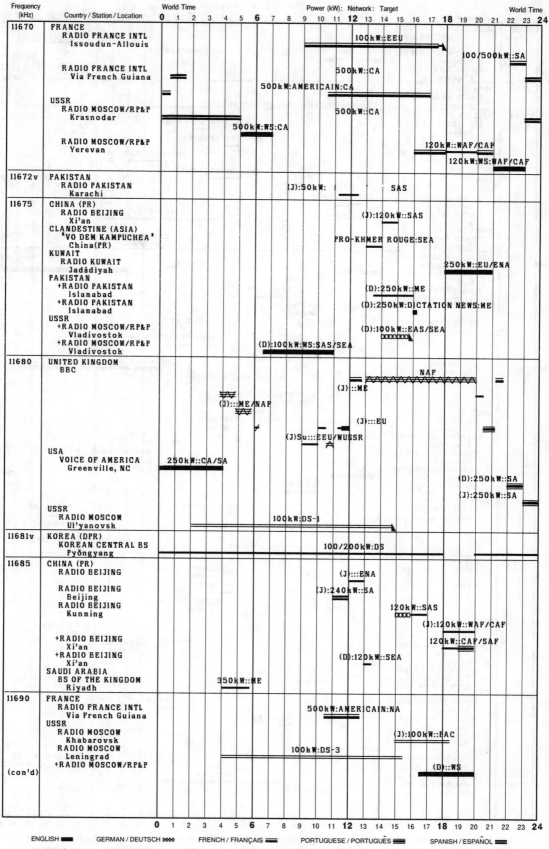

Frequency (kHz)	Country / Station / Location	Notes
11670	FRANCE RADIO FRANCE INTL Issoudun-Allouis	100kW::EEU 100/500kW::SA
	RADIO FRANCE INTL Via French Guiana	500kW::CA 500kW:AMERICAIN:CA
	USSR RADIO MOSCOW/RP&P Krasnodar	500kW::CA 500kW:WS:CA
	RADIO MOSCOW/RP&P Yerevan	120kW::WAF/CAF 120kW:WS:WAF/CAF
11672v	PAKISTAN RADIO PAKISTAN Karachi	(J):50kW: SAS
11675	CHINA (PR) RADIO BEIJING Xi'an	(J):120kW::SAS
	CLANDESTINE (ASIA) 'VO DEM KAMPUCHEA' China(PR)	PRO-KHMER ROUGE:SEA
	KUWAIT RADIO KUWAIT Jadādiyah	250kW::EU/ENA
	PAKISTAN +RADIO PAKISTAN Islamabad	(D):250kW::ME
	+RADIO PAKISTAN Islamabad	(D):250kW:DICTATION NEWS:ME
	USSR +RADIO MOSCOW/RP&P Vladivostok	(D):100kW::EAS/SEA
	+RADIO MOSCOW/RP&P Vladivostok	(D):100kW:WS:SAS/SEA
11680	UNITED KINGDOM BBC	NAF (J)::ME (J):::ME/NAF (J):::EU (J)Su:::EEU/WUSSR
	USA VOICE OF AMERICA Greenville, NC	250kW::CA/SA (D):250kW::SA (J):250kW::SA
	USSR RADIO MOSCOW Ul'yanovsk	100kW:DS-1
11681v	KOREA (DPR) KOREAN CENTRAL BS Pyŏngyang	100/200kW:DS
11685	CHINA (PR) RADIO BEIJING	(J):::ENA
	RADIO BEIJING Beijing	(J):240kW::SA
	RADIO BEIJING Kunming	120kW::SAS (J):120kW::WAF/CAF
	+RADIO BEIJING Xi'an	120kW::CAF/SAF
	+RADIO BEIJING Xi'an	(D):120kW::SEA
	SAUDI ARABIA BS OF THE KINGDOM Riyadh	350kW::ME
11690	FRANCE RADIO FRANCE INTL Via French Guiana	500kW:AMERICAIN:NA
	USSR RADIO MOSCOW Khabarovsk	(J):100kW::EAC
	RADIO MOSCOW Leningrad	100kW:DS-3
(con'd)	+RADIO MOSCOW/RP&P	(D)::WS

ENGLISH ▬▬ GERMAN / DEUTSCH ◊◊◊◊ FRENCH / FRANÇAIS ═══ PORTUGUESE / PORTUGUÊS ▬▬ SPANISH / ESPAÑOL ▬▬

ARABIC / العربية ═══ RUSSIAN / РУССКИИ ═══ CHINESE / 中文 □□□□ JAPANESE / 日本語 ▬▬▬▬ MULTILINGUAL ▭▭▭▭ OTHER ▬▬

SUMMER ONLY (J) WINTER ONLY (D) JAMMING /\/\ or / or \ EARLIEST HEARD ◢ LATEST HEARD ◣ + TENTATIVE

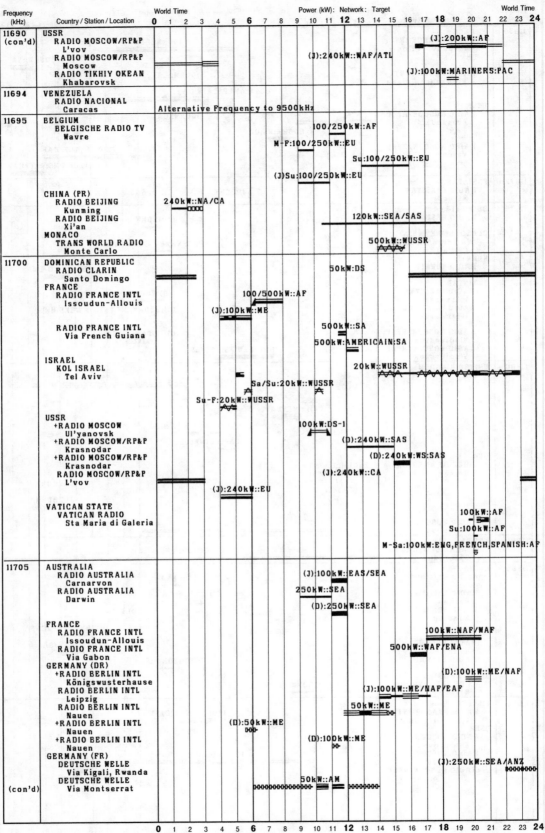

Frequency (kHz)	Country / Station / Location		Power (kW): Network: Target

World Time: 0 1 2 3 4 5 6 7 8 9 10 11 12 13 14 15 16 17 18 19 20 21 22 23 24

11690 (con'd) — USSR
- RADIO MOSCOW/RP&P L'vov — (J):200kW::AF
- RADIO MOSCOW/RP&P Moscow — (J):240kW::WAF/ATL
- RADIO TIKHIY OKEAN Khabarovsk — (J):100kW:MARINERS:PAC

11694 — VENEZUELA
- RADIO NACIONAL Caracas — Alternative Frequency to 9500kHz

11695 — BELGIUM
- BELGISCHE RADIO TV Wavre — 100/250kW:AF ; M-F:100/250kW::EU ; Su:100/250kW::EU ; (J)Su:100/250kW::EU
- CHINA (PR)
  - RADIO BEIJING Kunming — 240kW::NA/CA
  - RADIO BEIJING Xi'an — 120kW::SEA/SAS
- MONACO
  - TRANS WORLD RADIO Monte Carlo — 500kW::WUSSR

11700 — DOMINICAN REPUBLIC
- RADIO CLARIN Santo Domingo — 50kW:DS
- FRANCE
  - RADIO FRANCE INTL Issoudun-Allouis — 100/500kW::AF ; (J):100kW::ME
  - RADIO FRANCE INTL Via French Guiana — 500kW::SA ; 500kW:AMERICAIN:SA
- ISRAEL
  - KOL ISRAEL Tel Aviv — 20kW::WUSSR ; Sa/Su:20kW::WUSSR ; Su-F:20kW::WUSSR
- USSR
  - +RADIO MOSCOW Ul'yanovsk — 100kW:DS-1
  - +RADIO MOSCOW/RP&P Krasnodar — (D):240kW::SAS
  - +RADIO MOSCOW/RP&P Krasnodar — (D):240kW:WS:SAS
  - RADIO MOSCOW/RP&P L'vov — (J):240kW::CA ; (J):240kW::EU
- VATICAN STATE
  - VATICAN RADIO Sta Maria di Galeria — 100kW::AF ; Su:100kW:AF ; M-Sa:100kW:ENG,FRENCH,SPANISH:AF

11705 — AUSTRALIA
- RADIO AUSTRALIA Carnarvon — (J):100kW:EAS/SEA
- RADIO AUSTRALIA Darwin — 250kW::SEA ; (D):250kW::SEA
- FRANCE
  - RADIO FRANCE INTL Issoudun-Allouis — 100kW::NAF/WAF
  - RADIO FRANCE INTL Via Gabon — 500kW::WAF/ENA
- GERMANY (DR)
  - +RADIO BERLIN INTL Königswusterhause — (D):100kW::ME/NAF
  - RADIO BERLIN INTL Leipzig — (J):100kW::ME/NAF/EAF
  - RADIO BERLIN INTL Nauen — 50kW::ME
  - +RADIO BERLIN INTL Nauen — (D):50kW::ME
  - +RADIO BERLIN INTL Nauen — (D):100kW::ME
- GERMANY (FR)
  - DEUTSCHE WELLE Via Kigali, Rwanda — (J):250kW::SEA/ANZ
  - DEUTSCHE WELLE Via Montserrat — 50kW::AM

(con'd)

World Time: 0 1 2 3 4 5 6 7 8 9 10 11 12 13 14 15 16 17 18 19 20 21 22 23 24

ENGLISH ▬▬   GERMAN / DEUTSCH ◊◊◊◊   FRENCH / FRANÇAIS ▬▬   PORTUGUESE / PORTUGUÊS ▬▬   SPANISH / ESPAÑOL ▬▬

ARABIC / ﺍﻟﻌﺮﺑﻴﺔ ▬▬   RUSSIAN / РУССКИИ ▬▬   CHINESE / 中文 ◊◊◊◊   JAPANESE / 日本語 ▬▬   MULTILINGUAL ◊◊◊◊   OTHER ▬▬

SUMMER ONLY (J)   WINTER ONLY (D)   JAMMING ∧∧ or / or \   EARLIEST HEARD ◢   LATEST HEARD ◣   + TENTATIVE

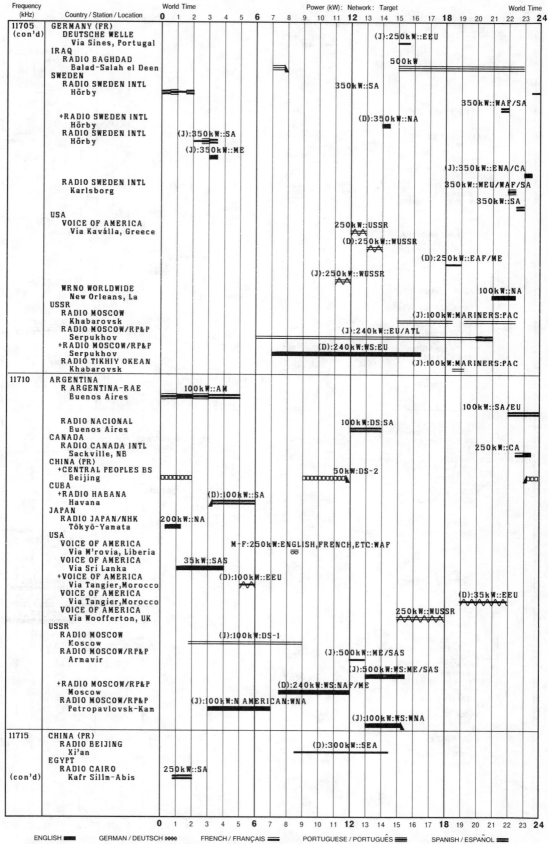

Frequency (kHz)	Country / Station / Location	Power (kW): Network: Target
11705 (con'd)	GERMANY (FR) DEUTSCHE WELLE Via Sines, Portugal	(J):250kW::EEU
	IRAQ RADIO BAGHDAD Balad-Salah el Deen	500kW
	SWEDEN RADIO SWEDEN INTL Hörby	350kW::SA
		350kW::WAF/SA
	+RADIO SWEDEN INTL Hörby	(D):350kW::NA
	RADIO SWEDEN INTL Hörby	(J):350kW::SA
		(J):350kW::ME
		(J):350kW::ENA/CA
	RADIO SWEDEN INTL Karlsborg	350kW::WEU/WAF/SA
		350kW::SA
	USA VOICE OF AMERICA Via Kaválla, Greece	250kW::USSR
		(D):250kW::WUSSR
		(D):250kW::EAF/ME
		(J):250kW::WUSSR
	WRNO WORLDWIDE New Orleans, La	100kW::NA
	USSR RADIO MOSCOW Khabarovsk	(J):100kW:MARINERS:PAC
	RADIO MOSCOW/RP&P Serpukhov	(J):240kW::EU/ATL
	+RADIO MOSCOW/RP&P Serpukhov	(D):240kW:WS:EU
	RADIO TIKHIY OKEAN Khabarovsk	(J):100kW:MARINERS:PAC
11710	ARGENTINA R ARGENTINA-RAE Buenos Aires	100kW::AM
		100kW::SA/EU
	RADIO NACIONAL Buenos Aires	100kW:DS:SA
	CANADA RADIO CANADA INTL Sackville, NB	250kW::CA
	CHINA (PR) +CENTRAL PEOPLES BS Beijing	50kW:DS-2
	CUBA +RADIO HABANA Havana	(D):100kW::SA
	JAPAN RADIO JAPAN/NHK Tôkyô-Yamata	200kW::NA
	USA VOICE OF AMERICA Via M'rovia, Liberia	M-F:250kW:ENGLISH,FRENCH,ETC:WAF
	VOICE OF AMERICA Via Sri Lanka	35kW:SAS
	+VOICE OF AMERICA Via Tangier,Morocco	(D):100kW::EEU
	VOICE OF AMERICA Via Tangier,Morocco	(D):35kW::EEU
	VOICE OF AMERICA Via Woofferton, UK	250kW::WUSSR
	USSR RADIO MOSCOW Moscow	(J):100kW:DS-1
	RADIO MOSCOW/RP&P Armavir	(J):500kW::ME/SAS
		(J):500kW:WS:ME/SAS
	+RADIO MOSCOW/RP&P Moscow	(D):240kW:WS:NAF/ME
	RADIO MOSCOW/RP&P Petropavlovsk-Kam	(J):100kW:N AMERICAN:WNA
		(J):100kW:WS:WNA
11715 (con'd)	CHINA (PR) RADIO BEIJING Xi'an	(D):300kW::SEA
	EGYPT RADIO CAIRO Kafr Silim-Abis	250kW::SA

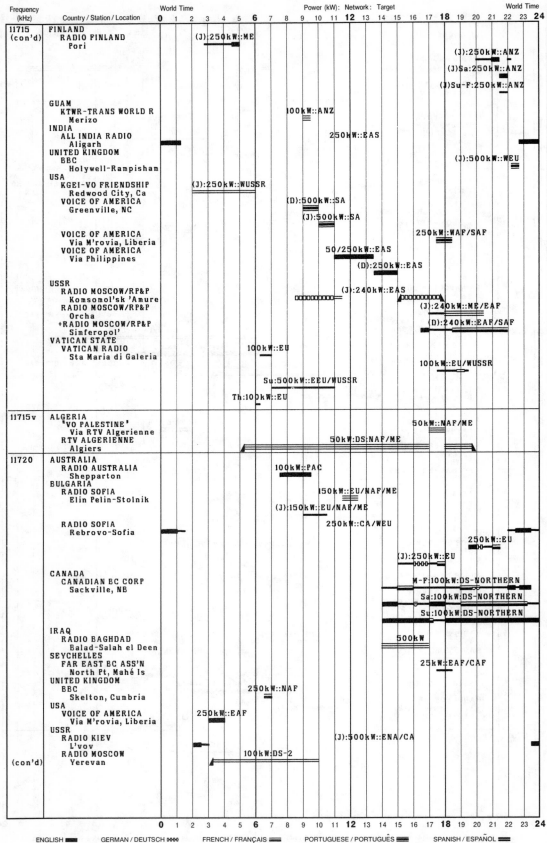

Frequency (kHz)	Country / Station / Location		Power (kW):: Network: Target	

World Time: 0 1 2 3 4 5 6 7 8 9 10 11 12 13 14 15 16 17 18 19 20 21 22 23 24

11715 (con'd)

FINLAND
- RADIO FINLAND, Pori — (J):250kW::ME; (J):250kW::ANZ; (J)Sa:250kW::ANZ; (J)Su-F:250kW::ANZ

GUAM
- KTWR-TRANS WORLD R, Merizo — 100kW::ANZ

INDIA
- ALL INDIA RADIO, Aligarh — 250kW::EAS

UNITED KINGDOM
- BBC, Holywell-Rampisham — (J):500kW::WEU

USA
- KGEI-VO FRIENDSHIP, Redwood City, Ca — (J):250kW::WUSSR
- VOICE OF AMERICA, Greenville, NC — (D):500kW::SA; (J):500kW::SA
- VOICE OF AMERICA, Via M'rovia, Liberia — 250kW:WAF/SAF
- VOICE OF AMERICA, Via Philippines — 50/250kW::EAS; (D):250kW::EAS

USSR
- RADIO MOSCOW/RP&P, Komsomol'sk 'Amure — (J):240kW::EAS
- RADIO MOSCOW/RP&P, Orcha — (J):240kW::ME/EAF
- +RADIO MOSCOW/RP&P, Simferopol' — (D):240kW::EAF/SAF

VATICAN STATE
- VATICAN RADIO, Sta Maria di Galeria — 100kW::EU; 100kW::EU/WUSSR; Su:500kW::EEU/WUSSR; Th:100kW::EU

11715v

ALGERIA
- "VO PALESTINE" Via RTV Algerienne — 50kW::NAF/ME
- RTV ALGERIENNE, Algiers — 50kW:DS:NAF/ME

11720

AUSTRALIA
- RADIO AUSTRALIA, Shepparton — 100kW::PAC

BULGARIA
- RADIO SOFIA, Elin Pelin-Stolnik — 150kW::EU/NAF/ME; (J):150kW::EU/NAF/ME
- RADIO SOFIA, Rebrovo-Sofia — 250kW::CA/WEU; 250kW::EU; (J):250kW::EU

CANADA
- CANADIAN BC CORP, Sackville, NB — M-F:100kW:DS-NORTHERN; Sa:100kW:DS-NORTHERN; Su:100kW:DS-NORTHERN

IRAQ
- RADIO BAGHDAD, Balad-Salah el Deen — 500kW

SEYCHELLES
- FAR EAST BC ASS'N, North Pt, Mahé Is — 25kW::EAF/CAF

UNITED KINGDOM
- BBC, Skelton, Cumbria — 250kW::NAF

USA
- VOICE OF AMERICA, Via M'rovia, Liberia — 250kW::EAF

USSR
- RADIO KIEV, L'vov — (J):500kW::ENA/CA
- RADIO MOSCOW, Yerevan — 100kW:DS-2

(con'd)

World Time: 0 1 2 3 4 5 6 7 8 9 10 11 12 13 14 15 16 17 18 19 20 21 22 23 24

ENGLISH ▬▬   GERMAN / DEUTSCH 0000   FRENCH / FRANÇAIS ▬▬   PORTUGUESE / PORTUGUÊS ▬▬   SPANISH / ESPAÑOL ▬▬

ARABIC /ئ ≡   RUSSIAN / РУССКИИ ═   CHINESE / 中文 0000   JAPANESE / 日本語 ▬▬   MULTILINGUAL ▭▭   OTHER ▬

SUMMER ONLY (J)   WINTER ONLY (D)   JAMMING /\/\ or / or \   EARLIEST HEARD ◢   LATEST HEARD ◣   + TENTATIVE

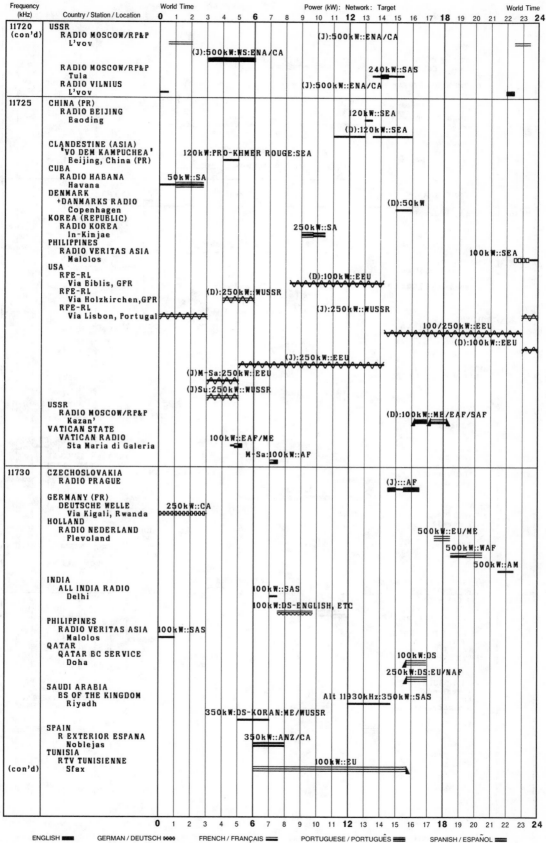

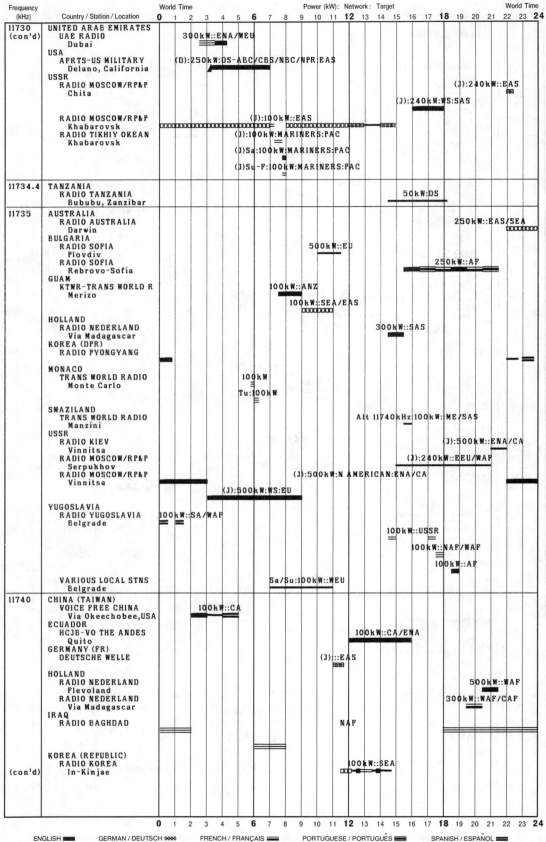

Frequency (kHz)	Country / Station / Location	Schedule (World Time)
11730 (con'd)	**UNITED ARAB EMIRATES** UAE RADIO — Dubai	300kW::ENA/WEU
	USA AFRTS-US MILITARY — Delano, California	(D):250kW:DS-ABC/CBS/NBC/NPR:EAS
	USSR RADIO MOSCOW/RP&P — Chita	(J):240kW::EAS (J):240kW:WS:SAS
	RADIO MOSCOW/RP&P — Khabarovsk	(J):100kW:EAS
	RADIO TIKHIY OKEAN — Khabarovsk	(J):100kW:MARINERS:PAC (J)Sa:100kW:MARINERS:PAC (J)Su-F:100kW:MARINERS:PAC
11734.4	**TANZANIA** RADIO TANZANIA — Bububu, Zanzibar	50kW:DS
11735	**AUSTRALIA** RADIO AUSTRALIA — Darwin	250kW::EAS/SEA
	BULGARIA RADIO SOFIA — Plovdiv	500kW::EU
	RADIO SOFIA — Rebrovo-Sofia	250kW::AF
	GUAM KTWR-TRANS WORLD R — Merizo	100kW::ANZ 100kW::SEA/EAS
	HOLLAND RADIO NEDERLAND — Via Madagascar	300kW::SAS
	KOREA (DPR) RADIO PYONGYANG	
	MONACO TRANS WORLD RADIO — Monte Carlo	100kW Tu:100kW
	SWAZILAND TRANS WORLD RADIO — Manzini	Alt 11740kHz:100kW:ME/SAS
	USSR RADIO KIEV — Vinnitsa	(J):500kW::ENA/CA
	RADIO MOSCOW/RP&P — Serpukhov	(J):240kW::EEU/WAF
	RADIO MOSCOW/RP&P — Vinnitsa	(J):500kW:N AMERICAN:ENA/CA (J):500kW:WS:EU
	YUGOSLAVIA RADIO YUGOSLAVIA — Belgrade	100kW::SA/WAF 100kW::USSR 100kW::NAF/WAF 100kW::AF
	VARIOUS LOCAL STNS — Belgrade	Sa/Su:100kW::WEU
11740	**CHINA (TAIWAN)** VOICE FREE CHINA — Via Okeechobee, USA	100kW::CA
	ECUADOR HCJB-VO THE ANDES — Quito	100kW::CA/ENA
	GERMANY (FR) DEUTSCHE WELLE	(J):::EAS
	HOLLAND RADIO NEDERLAND — Flevoland	500kW::WAF
	RADIO NEDERLAND — Via Madagascar	300kW::WAF/CAF
	IRAQ RADIO BAGHDAD	NAF
(con'd)	**KOREA (REPUBLIC)** RADIO KOREA — In-Kimjae	100kW::SEA

World Time: 0 1 2 3 4 5 6 7 8 9 10 11 12 13 14 15 16 17 18 19 20 21 22 23 24

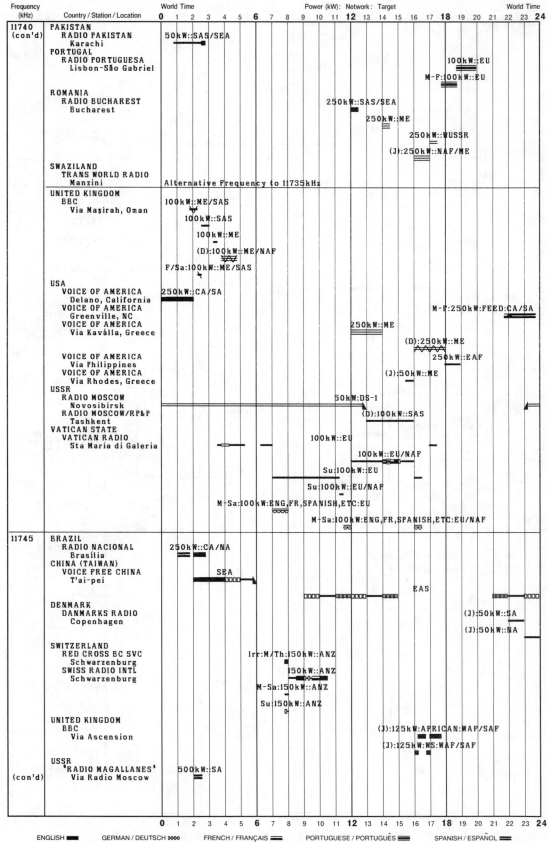

Frequency (kHz) | Country / Station / Location | World Time | Power (kW) : Network : Target | World Time

11740 (con'd)

PAKISTAN
RADIO PAKISTAN
Karachi — 50kW::SAS/SEA

PORTUGAL
RADIO PORTUGUESA
Lisbon-São Gabriel — 100kW::EU / M-F:100kW::EU

ROMANIA
RADIO BUCHAREST
Bucharest — 250kW::SAS/SEA / 250kW::ME / 250kW::WUSSR / (J):250kW::NAF/ME

SWAZILAND
TRANS WORLD RADIO
Manzini — Alternative Frequency to 11735kHz

UNITED KINGDOM
BBC
Via Maşirah, Oman — 100kW::ME/SAS / 100kW::SAS / 100kW::ME / (D):100kW::ME/NAF / F/Sa:100kW::ME/SAS

USA
VOICE OF AMERICA
Delano, California — 250kW::CA/SA
VOICE OF AMERICA
Greenville, NC — M-F:250kW:FEED:CA/SA
VOICE OF AMERICA
Via Kaválla, Greece — 250kW::ME / (D):250kW::ME / 250kW::EAF
VOICE OF AMERICA
Via Philippines
VOICE OF AMERICA
Via Rhodes, Greece — (J):50kW::ME

USSR
RADIO MOSCOW
Novosibirsk — 50kW:DS-1
RADIO MOSCOW/RP&P
Tashkent — (D):100kW::SAS

VATICAN STATE
VATICAN RADIO
Sta Maria di Galeria — 100kW::EU / 100kW::EU/NAF / Su:100kW::EU / Su:100kW::EU/NAF / M-Sa:100kW:ENG,FR,SPANISH,ETC:EU / M-Sa:100kW:ENG,FR,SPANISH,ETC:EU/NAF

11745

BRAZIL
RADIO NACIONAL
Brasília — 250kW::CA/NA

CHINA (TAIWAN)
VOICE FREE CHINA
T'ai-pei — SEA / EAS

DENMARK
DANMARKS RADIO
Copenhagen — (J):50kW::SA / (J):50kW::NA

SWITZERLAND
RED CROSS BC SVC
Schwarzenburg — Irr:M/Th:150kW::ANZ
SWISS RADIO INTL
Schwarzenburg — 150kW::ANZ / M-Sa:150kW::ANZ / Su:150kW::ANZ

UNITED KINGDOM
BBC
Via Ascension — (J):125kW:AFRICAN:WAF/SAF / (J):125kW:WS:WAF/SAF

USSR
'RADIO MAGALLANES'
Via Radio Moscow — 500kW::SA

(con'd)

ENGLISH ▬▬ GERMAN / DEUTSCH ▧▧▧ FRENCH / FRANÇAIS ≡≡≡ PORTUGUESE / PORTUGUÊS ▬▬▬ SPANISH / ESPAÑOL ▬▬

ARABIC / عربي ≡≡≡ RUSSIAN / РУССКИИ ═══ CHINESE / 中文 ▭▭▭▭ JAPANESE / 日本語 ▧▧▧ MULTILINGUAL ▭▭▭▭ OTHER ▬▬

SUMMER ONLY (J) WINTER ONLY (D) JAMMING /\/\ or / or \ EARLIEST HEARD ◢ LATEST HEARD ◣ + TENTATIVE

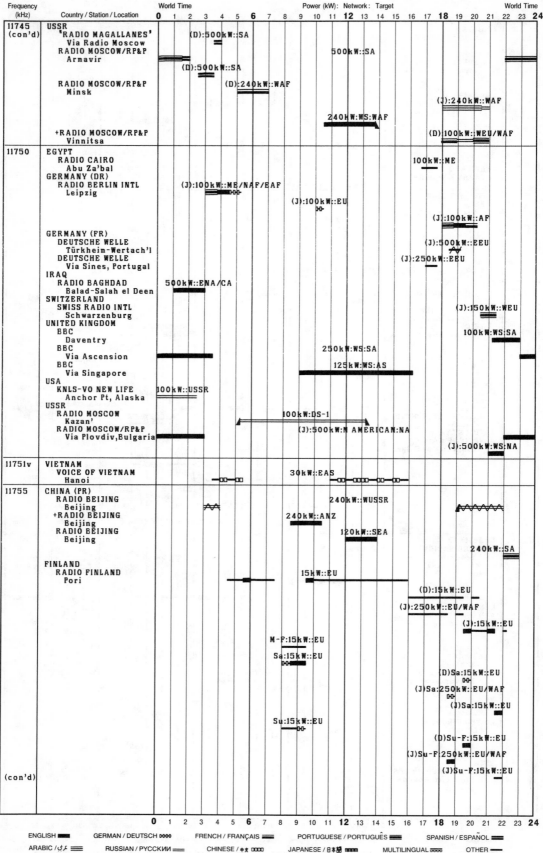

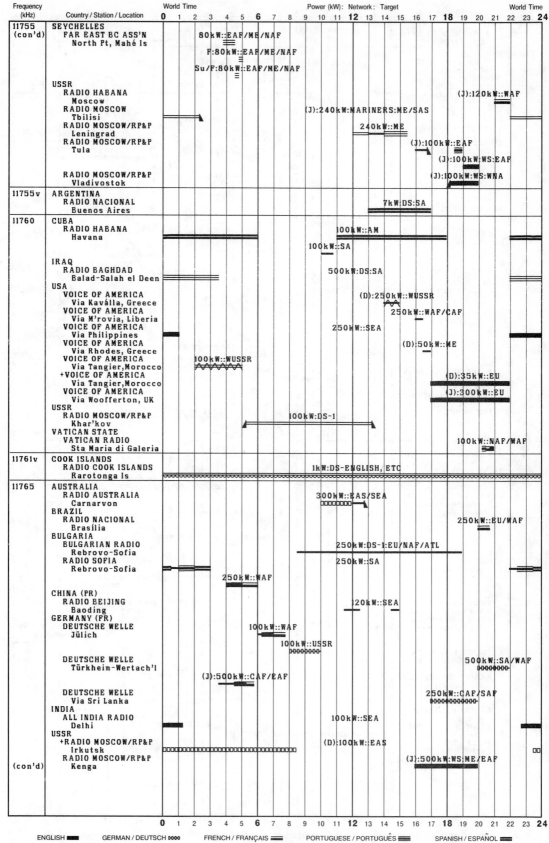

Frequency (kHz) — Country / Station / Location — World Time 0–24 — Power (kW): Network: Target

11755 (con'd)
- SEYCHELLES — FAR EAST BC ASS'N, North Pt, Mahé Is — 80kW::EAF/ME/NAF; F:80kW::EAF/ME/NAF; Su/F:80kW::EAF/ME/NAF
- USSR — RADIO HABANA, Moscow — (J):120kW::WAF
- RADIO MOSCOW, Tbilisi — (J):240kW:MARINERS:ME/SAS
- RADIO MOSCOW/RP&P, Leningrad — 240kW::ME
- RADIO MOSCOW/RP&P, Tula — (J):100kW::EAF; (J):100kW:WS:EAF
- RADIO MOSCOW/RP&P, Vladivostok — (J):100kW:WS:WNA

11755v
- ARGENTINA — RADIO NACIONAL, Buenos Aires — 7kW:DS:SA

11760
- CUBA — RADIO HABANA, Havana — 100kW::AM; 100kW::SA
- IRAQ — RADIO BAGHDAD, Balad-Salah el Deen — 500kW:DS:SA
- USA — VOICE OF AMERICA, Via Kaválla, Greece — (D):250kW::WUSSR
- VOICE OF AMERICA, Via M'rovia, Liberia — 250kW::WAF/CAF
- VOICE OF AMERICA, Via Philippines — 250kW::SEA
- VOICE OF AMERICA, Via Rhodes, Greece — (D):50kW::ME
- VOICE OF AMERICA, Via Tangier, Morocco — 100kW:WUSSR
- +VOICE OF AMERICA, Via Tangier, Morocco — (D):35kW::EU
- VOICE OF AMERICA, Via Woofferton, UK — (J):300kW::EU
- USSR — RADIO MOSCOW/RP&P, Khar'kov — 100kW:DS-1
- VATICAN STATE — VATICAN RADIO, Sta Maria di Galeria — 100kW::NAF/WAF

11761v
- COOK ISLANDS — RADIO COOK ISLANDS, Rarotonga Is — 1kW:DS-ENGLISH, ETC

11765
- AUSTRALIA — RADIO AUSTRALIA, Carnarvon — 300kW::EAS/SEA
- BRAZIL — RADIO NACIONAL, Brasília — 250kW::EU/WAF
- BULGARIA — BULGARIAN RADIO, Rebrovo-Sofia — 250kW:DS-1:EU/NAF/ATL
- RADIO SOFIA, Rebrovo-Sofia — 250kW::SA; 250kW::WAF
- CHINA (PR) — RADIO BEIJING, Baoding — 120kW::SEA
- GERMANY (FR) — DEUTSCHE WELLE, Jülich — 100kW::WAF; 100kW::USSR
- DEUTSCHE WELLE, Türkheim-Wertach'l — 500kW::SA/WAF
- DEUTSCHE WELLE, Via Sri Lanka — (J):500kW::CAF/EAF; 250kW::CAF/SAF
- INDIA — ALL INDIA RADIO, Delhi — 100kW::SEA
- USSR — +RADIO MOSCOW/RP&P, Irkutsk — (D):100kW::EAS
- RADIO MOSCOW/RP&P, Kenga (con'd) — (J):500kW:WS:ME/EAF

ENGLISH ▄▄▄ GERMAN / DEUTSCH ◊◊◊◊ FRENCH / FRANÇAIS ▬▬ PORTUGUESE / PORTUGUÊS ▬▬ SPANISH / ESPAÑOL ▬▬
ARABIC /ﻉﺮﻋ ≣ RUSSIAN / РУССКИИ ▬ CHINESE / 中文 ◊◊◊◊ JAPANESE / 日本語 ▄▄▄ MULTILINGUAL ◊◊◊ OTHER ▬
SUMMER ONLY (J) WINTER ONLY (D) JAMMING ∧∧ or / or \ EARLIEST HEARD ◢ LATEST HEARD ◣ + TENTATIVE

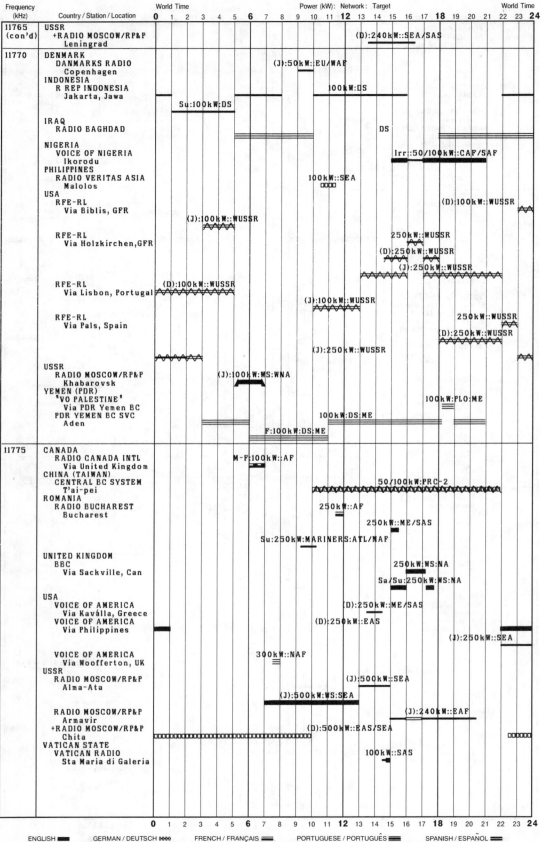

Frequency (kHz)	Country / Station / Location	World Time 0–24 schedule
11765 (con'd)	USSR +RADIO MOSCOW/RP&P Leningrad	(D):240kW::SEA/SAS
11770	DENMARK DANMARKS RADIO Copenhagen	(J):50kW::EU/WAF
	INDONESIA R REP INDONESIA Jakarta, Jawa	100kW:DS / Su:100kW:DS
	IRAQ RADIO BAGHDAD	DS
	NIGERIA VOICE OF NIGERIA Ikorodu	Irr::50/100kW::CAF/SAF
	PHILIPPINES RADIO VERITAS ASIA Malolos	100kW::SEA
	USA RFE-RL Via Biblis, GFR	(D):100kW::WUSSR / (J):100kW::WUSSR
	RFE-RL Via Holzkirchen,GFR	250kW::WUSSR / (D):250kW::WUSSR / (J):250kW::WUSSR
	RFE-RL Via Lisbon, Portugal	(D):100kW::WUSSR / (J):100kW::WUSSR
	RFE-RL Via Pals, Spain	250kW::WUSSR / (D):250kW::WUSSR / (J):250kW::WUSSR
	USSR RADIO MOSCOW/RP&P Khabarovsk	(J):100kW:WS:WNA
	YEMEN (PDR) "VO PALESTINE" Via PDR Yemen BC	100kW:PLO:ME
	PDR YEMEN BC SVC Aden	100kW:DS:ME / F:100kW:DS:ME
11775	CANADA RADIO CANADA INTL Via United Kingdom	M-F:100kW::AF
	CHINA (TAIWAN) CENTRAL BC SYSTEM T'ai-pei	50/100kW:PRC-2
	ROMANIA RADIO BUCHAREST Bucharest	250kW::AF / 250kW::ME/SAS / Su:250kW:MARINERS:ATL/NAF
	UNITED KINGDOM BBC Via Sackville, Can	250kW:WS:NA / Sa/Su:250kW:WS:NA
	USA VOICE OF AMERICA Via Kaválla, Greece	(D):250kW::ME/SAS
	VOICE OF AMERICA Via Philippines	(D):250kW::EAS / (J):250kW::SEA
	VOICE OF AMERICA Via Woofferton, UK	300kW::NAF
	USSR RADIO MOSCOW/RP&P Alma-Ata	(J):500kW::SEA / (J):500kW:WS:SEA
	RADIO MOSCOW/RP&P Armavir	(J):240kW::EAF
	+RADIO MOSCOW/RP&P Chita	(D):500kW::EAS/SEA
	VATICAN STATE VATICAN RADIO Sta Maria di Galeria	100kW::SAS

ENGLISH ▅▅▅ GERMAN / DEUTSCH ◊◊◊◊ FRENCH / FRANÇAIS ═══ PORTUGUESE / PORTUGUÊS ▭▭▭ SPANISH / ESPAÑOL ━━━

ARABIC / ﻉﺏ ≡≡ RUSSIAN / РУССКИИ ═══ CHINESE / ✳✳ ◊◊◊◊ JAPANESE / 日本語 ▬▬▬ MULTILINGUAL ◊◊◊◊ OTHER ▬▬▬

SUMMER ONLY (J) WINTER ONLY (D) JAMMING ∧∧ or / or \ EARLIEST HEARD ◢ LATEST HEARD ◣ + TENTATIVE

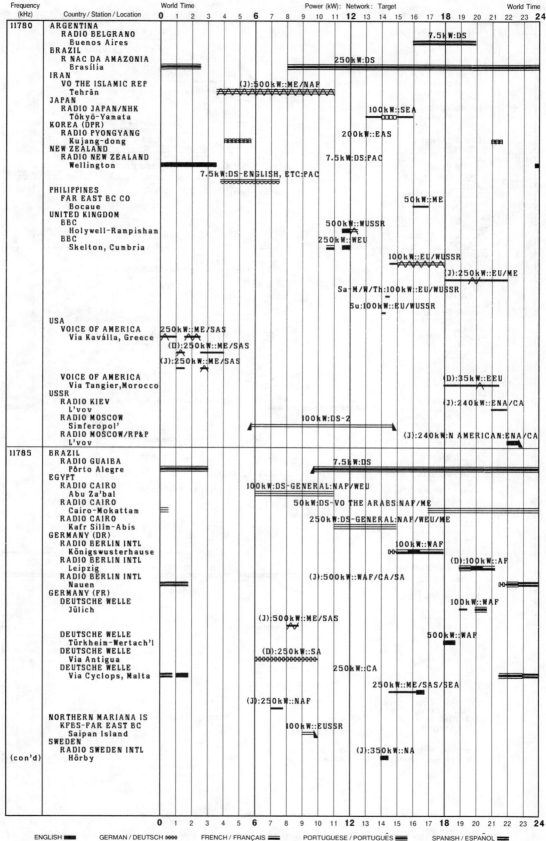

Frequency (kHz)	Country / Station / Location	Schedule (World Time / Power (kW): Network: Target)
11780	ARGENTINA	
	RADIO BELGRANO — Buenos Aires	7.5kW:DS
	BRAZIL	
	R NAC DA AMAZONIA — Brasília	250kW:DS
	IRAN	
	VO THE ISLAMIC REP — Tehrān	(J):500kW::ME/NAF
	JAPAN	
	RADIO JAPAN/NHK — Tōkyō-Yamata	100kW::SEA
	KOREA (DPR)	
	RADIO PYONGYANG — Kujang-dong	200kW::EAS
	NEW ZEALAND	
	RADIO NEW ZEALAND — Wellington	7.5kW:DS:PAC
		7.5kW:DS-ENGLISH, ETC:PAC
	PHILIPPINES	
	FAR EAST BC CO — Bocaue	50kW::ME
	UNITED KINGDOM	
	BBC — Holywell-Rampisham	500kW::WUSSR
	BBC — Skelton, Cumbria	250kW::WEU
		100kW::EU/WUSSR
		(J):250kW::EU/ME
		Sa-M/W/Th:100kW::EU/WUSSR
		Su:100kW::EU/WUSSR
	USA	
	VOICE OF AMERICA — Via Kaválla, Greece	250kW::ME/SAS
		(D):250kW::ME/SAS
		(J):250kW::ME/SAS
	VOICE OF AMERICA — Via Tangier, Morocco	(D):35kW::EEU
	USSR	
	RADIO KIEV — L'vov	(J):240kW::ENA/CA
	RADIO MOSCOW — Simferopol'	100kW:DS-2
	RADIO MOSCOW/RP&P — L'vov	(J):240kW:N AMERICAN:ENA/CA
11785	BRAZIL	
	RADIO GUAIBA — Pôrto Alegre	7.5kW:DS
	EGYPT	
	RADIO CAIRO — Abu Za'bal	100kW:DS-GENERAL:NAF/WEU
	RADIO CAIRO — Cairo-Mokattam	50kW:DS-VO THE ARABS:NAF/ME
	RADIO CAIRO — Kafr Silīm-Abis	250kW:DS-GENERAL:NAF/WEU/ME
	GERMANY (DR)	
	RADIO BERLIN INTL — Königswusterhause	100kW::WAF
	RADIO BERLIN INTL — Leipzig	(D):100kW::AF
	RADIO BERLIN INTL — Nauen	(J):500kW::WAF/CA/SA
	GERMANY (FR)	
	DEUTSCHE WELLE — Jülich	100kW::WAF
	DEUTSCHE WELLE — Türkheim-Wertach'l	(J):500kW::ME/SAS 500kW::WAF
	DEUTSCHE WELLE — Via Antigua	(D):250kW::SA
	DEUTSCHE WELLE — Via Cyclops, Malta	250kW::CA 250kW::ME/SAS/SEA
		(J):250kW::NAF
	NORTHERN MARIANA IS	
	KFBS-FAR EAST BC — Saipan Island	100kW::EUSSR
	SWEDEN	
(con'd)	RADIO SWEDEN INTL — Hörby	(J):350kW::NA

World Time: 0 1 2 3 4 5 6 7 8 9 10 11 12 13 14 15 16 17 18 19 20 21 22 23 24

ENGLISH ▬▬▬   GERMAN / DEUTSCH ◊◊◊◊   FRENCH / FRANÇAIS ≡≡≡   PORTUGUESE / PORTUGUÊS ≡≡≡   SPANISH / ESPAÑOL ≡≡≡

ARABIC / جمع ≡≡≡   RUSSIAN / РУССКИИ ═══   CHINESE / 中文 ◊◊◊◊   JAPANESE / 日本語 ▬▬▬   MULTILINGUAL ◦◦◦◦   OTHER ▬▬

SUMMER ONLY (J)   WINTER ONLY (D)   JAMMING ∧∧∧ or / or \   EARLIEST HEARD ◢   LATEST HEARD ◣   + TENTATIVE

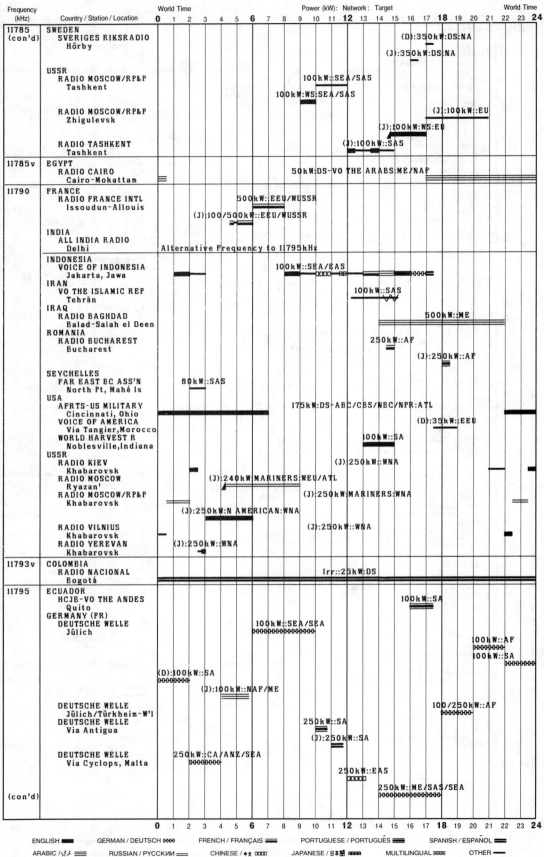

Frequency (kHz)	Country / Station / Location	Power (kW) : Network : Target
11785 (con'd)	SWEDEN — SVERIGES RIKSRADIO, Hörby	(D):350kW:DS:NA; (J):350kW:DS:NA
	USSR — RADIO MOSCOW/RP&P, Tashkent	100kW::SEA/SAS; 100kW:WS:SEA/SAS
	RADIO MOSCOW/RP&P, Zhigulevsk	(J):100kW::EU; (J):100kW:WS:EU
	RADIO TASHKENT, Tashkent	(J):100kW::SAS
11785v	EGYPT — RADIO CAIRO, Cairo-Mokattam	50kW:DS-VO THE ARABS:ME/NAF
11790	FRANCE — RADIO FRANCE INTL, Issoudun-Allouis	500kW::EEU/WUSSR; (J):100/500kW::EEU/WUSSR
	INDIA — ALL INDIA RADIO, Delhi	Alternative Frequency to 11795kHz
	INDONESIA — VOICE OF INDONESIA, Jakarta, Jawa	100kW::SEA/EAS
	IRAN — VO THE ISLAMIC REP, Tehrän	100kW::SAS
	IRAQ — RADIO BAGHDAD, Balad-Salah el Deen	500kW::ME
	ROMANIA — RADIO BUCHAREST, Bucharest	250kW::AF; (J):250kW::AF
	SEYCHELLES — FAR EAST BC ASS'N, North Pt, Mahé Is	80kW::SAS
	USA — AFRTS-US MILITARY, Cincinnati, Ohio	175kW:DS-ABC/CBS/NBC/NPR:ATL
	VOICE OF AMERICA, Via Tangier, Morocco	(D):35kW::EEU
	WORLD HARVEST R, Noblesville, Indiana	100kW::SA
	USSR — RADIO KIEV, Khabarovsk	(J):250kW::WNA
	RADIO MOSCOW, Ryazan'	(J):240kW:MARINERS:WEU/ATL
	RADIO MOSCOW/RP&P, Khabarovsk	(J):250kW:MARINERS:WNA; (J):250kW:N AMERICAN:WNA
	RADIO VILNIUS, Khabarovsk	(J):250kW::WNA
	RADIO YEREVAN, Khabarovsk	(J):250kW::WNA
11793v	COLOMBIA — RADIO NACIONAL, Bogotá	Irr::25kW:DS
11795	ECUADOR — HCJB-VO THE ANDES, Quito	100kW::SA
	GERMANY (FR) — DEUTSCHE WELLE, Jülich	100kW::SEA/SEA; 100kW::AF; 100kW::SA; (D):100kW::SA; (J):100kW::NAF/ME
	DEUTSCHE WELLE, Jülich/Türkheim-W'l	100/250kW::AF
	DEUTSCHE WELLE, Via Antigua	250kW::SA; (J):250kW::SA
	DEUTSCHE WELLE, Via Cyclops, Malta	250kW::CA/ANZ/SEA; 250kW::EAS; 250kW::ME/SAS/SEA
(con'd)		

ENGLISH ■■■   GERMAN / DEUTSCH ০০০০   FRENCH / FRANÇAIS ≡≡   PORTUGUESE / PORTUGUÊS ■■   SPANISH / ESPAÑOL ═══

ARABIC / العربية ≡≡≡   RUSSIAN / РУССКИИ ═══   CHINESE / 中文 ০০০০   JAPANESE / 日本語 ▨▨▨   MULTILINGUAL ০০০০   OTHER ▬▬

SUMMER ONLY (J)   WINTER ONLY (D)   JAMMING /\/\ or / or \   EARLIEST HEARD ◢   LATEST HEARD ◣   + TENTATIVE

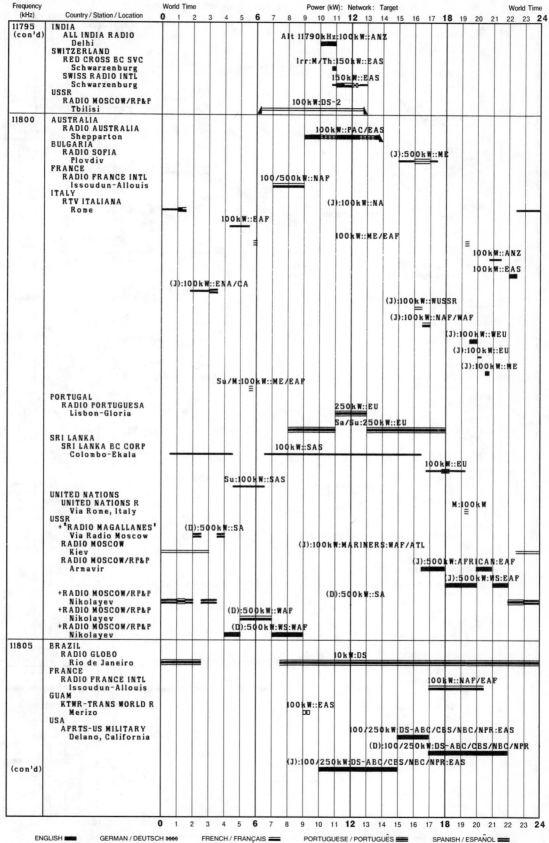

11795 (con'd)

INDIA
  ALL INDIA RADIO
    Delhi — Alt 11790kHz:100kW::ANZ
SWITZERLAND
  RED CROSS BC SVC
    Schwarzenburg — Irr:M/Th:150kW::EAS
  SWISS RADIO INTL
    Schwarzenburg — 150kW::EAS
USSR
  RADIO MOSCOW/RP&P
    Tbilisi — 100kW:DS-2

11800

AUSTRALIA
  RADIO AUSTRALIA
    Shepparton — 100kW::PAC/EAS
BULGARIA
  RADIO SOFIA
    Plovdiv — (J):500kW::ME
FRANCE
  RADIO FRANCE INTL
    Issoudun-Allouis — 100/500kW::NAF
ITALY
  RTV ITALIANA
    Rome — (J):100kW::NA
            100kW::EAF
            100kW::ME/EAF
            100kW::ANZ
            100kW::EAS
            (J):100kW::ENA/CA
            (J):100kW::WUSSR
            (J):100kW::NAF/WAF
            (J):100kW::WEU
            (J):100kW::EU
            (J):100kW::ME
            Su/M:100kW::ME/EAF
PORTUGAL
  RADIO PORTUGUESA
    Lisbon-Gloria — 250kW::EU
            Sa/Su:250kW::EU
SRI LANKA
  SRI LANKA BC CORP
    Colombo-Ekala — 100kW::SAS
            100kW::EU
            Su:100kW::SAS
UNITED NATIONS
  UNITED NATIONS R
    Via Rome, Italy — M:100kW
USSR
  +"RADIO MAGALLANES"
    Via Radio Moscow — (D):500kW::SA
  RADIO MOSCOW
    Kiev — (J):100kW:MARINERS:WAF/ATL
  RADIO MOSCOW/RP&P
    Armavir — (J):500kW:AFRICAN:EAF
            (J):500kW:WS:EAF
  +RADIO MOSCOW/RP&P
    Nikolayev — (D):500kW::SA
  +RADIO MOSCOW/RP&P
    Nikolayev — (D):500kW::WAF
  +RADIO MOSCOW/RP&P
    Nikolayev — (D):500kW:WS:WAF

11805

BRAZIL
  RADIO GLOBO
    Rio de Janeiro — 10kW:DS
FRANCE
  RADIO FRANCE INTL
    Issoudun-Allouis — 100kW::NAF/EAF
GUAM
  KTWR-TRANS WORLD R
    Merizo — 100kW::EAS
USA
  AFRTS-US MILITARY
    Delano, California — 100/250kW:DS-ABC/CBS/NBC/NPR:EAS
            (D):100/250kW:DS-ABC/CBS/NBC/NPR
            (J):100/250kW:DS-ABC/CBS/NBC/NPR:EAS

(con'd)

ENGLISH ▬▬ GERMAN / DEUTSCH ᴅᴅᴅᴅ FRENCH / FRANÇAIS ▬▬ PORTUGUESE / PORTUGUÊS ▬▬ SPANISH / ESPAÑOL ▬▬
ARABIC / ابى ≡ RUSSIAN / РУССКИИ ══ CHINESE / ✳☆ ᴅᴅᴅᴅ JAPANESE / 日本語 ▬▬ MULTILINGUAL ᴅᴅᴅᴅ OTHER ▬▬
SUMMER ONLY (J) WINTER ONLY (D) JAMMING /\/\ or / or \ EARLIEST HEARD ◢ LATEST HEARD ◣ + TENTATIVE

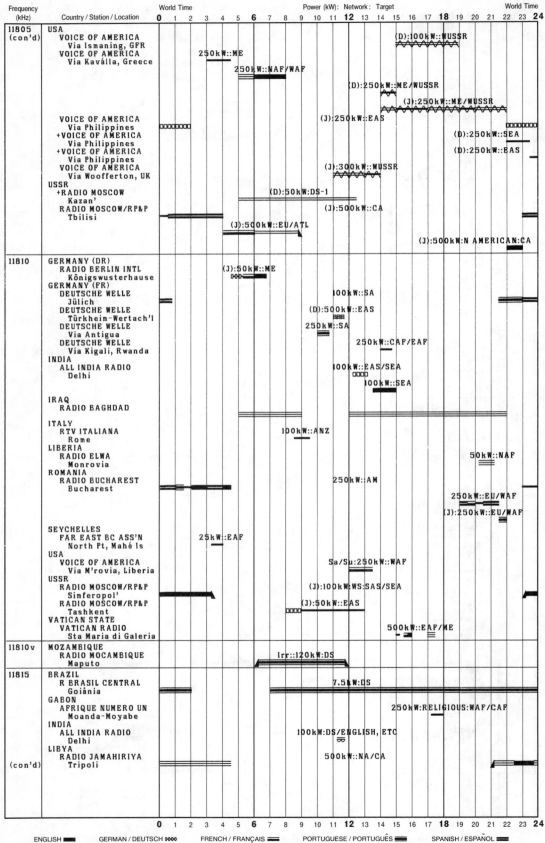

Frequency (kHz) | Country / Station / Location | World Time 0–24 | Power (kW): Network: Target

11805 (con'd)
USA
VOICE OF AMERICA — Via Ismaning, GFR — (D):100kW::WUSSR
VOICE OF AMERICA — Via Kaválla, Greece — 250kW::ME / 250kW::NAF/WAF — (D):250kW::ME/WUSSR — (J):250kW::ME/WUSSR — (J):250kW::EAS
VOICE OF AMERICA — Via Philippines
+VOICE OF AMERICA — Via Philippines — (D):250kW::SEA
+VOICE OF AMERICA — Via Philippines — (D):250kW::EAS
VOICE OF AMERICA — Via Woofferton, UK — (J):300kW::WUSSR
USSR
+RADIO MOSCOW — Kazan' — (D):50kW::DS-1
RADIO MOSCOW/RP&P — Tbilisi — (J):500kW::CA / (J):500kW::EU/ATL / (J):500kW:N AMERICAN:CA

11810
GERMANY (DR)
RADIO BERLIN INTL — Königswusterhause — (J):50kW::ME
GERMANY (FR)
DEUTSCHE WELLE — Jülich — 100kW::SA
DEUTSCHE WELLE — Türkheim-Wertach'l — (D):500kW::EAS
DEUTSCHE WELLE — Via Antigua — 250kW::SA
DEUTSCHE WELLE — Via Kigali, Rwanda — 250kW::CAF/EAF
INDIA
ALL INDIA RADIO — Delhi — 100kW::EAS/SEA / 100kW::SEA
IRAQ
RADIO BAGHDAD
ITALY
RTV ITALIANA — Rome — 100kW::ANZ
LIBERIA
RADIO ELWA — Monrovia — 50kW::NAF
ROMANIA
RADIO BUCHAREST — Bucharest — 250kW::AM / 250kW::EU/WAF / (J):250kW::EU/WAF
SEYCHELLES
FAR EAST BC ASS'N — North Pt, Mahé Is — 25kW::EAF
USA
VOICE OF AMERICA — Via M'rovia, Liberia — Sa/Su:250kW::WAF
USSR
RADIO MOSCOW/RP&P — Simferopol' — (J):100kW:WS:SAS/SEA
RADIO MOSCOW/RP&P — Tashkent — (J):50kW::EAS
VATICAN STATE
VATICAN RADIO — Sta Maria di Galeria — 500kW::EAF/ME

11810v
MOZAMBIQUE
RADIO MOCAMBIQUE — Maputo — Irr::120kW:DS

11815
BRAZIL
R BRASIL CENTRAL — Goiânia — 7.5kW:DS
GABON
AFRIQUE NUMERO UN — Moanda-Moyabe — 250kW:RELIGIOUS:WAF/CAF
INDIA
ALL INDIA RADIO — Delhi — 100kW:DS/ENGLISH, ETC
LIBYA
(con'd) RADIO JAMAHIRIYA — Tripoli — 500kW::NA/CA

ENGLISH ■■■ GERMAN / DEUTSCH ▨▨▨ FRENCH / FRANÇAIS ▤▤ PORTUGUESE / PORTUGUÊS ▦▦ SPANISH / ESPAÑOL ▬
ARABIC /عربي ≣ RUSSIAN / РУССКИИ ═ CHINESE / 中文 ▯▯▯ JAPANESE / 日本語 ▨▨ MULTILINGUAL ▨▨ OTHER ─
SUMMER ONLY (J)   WINTER ONLY (D)   JAMMING ∧∧ or / or \   EARLIEST HEARD ◢   LATEST HEARD ◣   + TENTATIVE

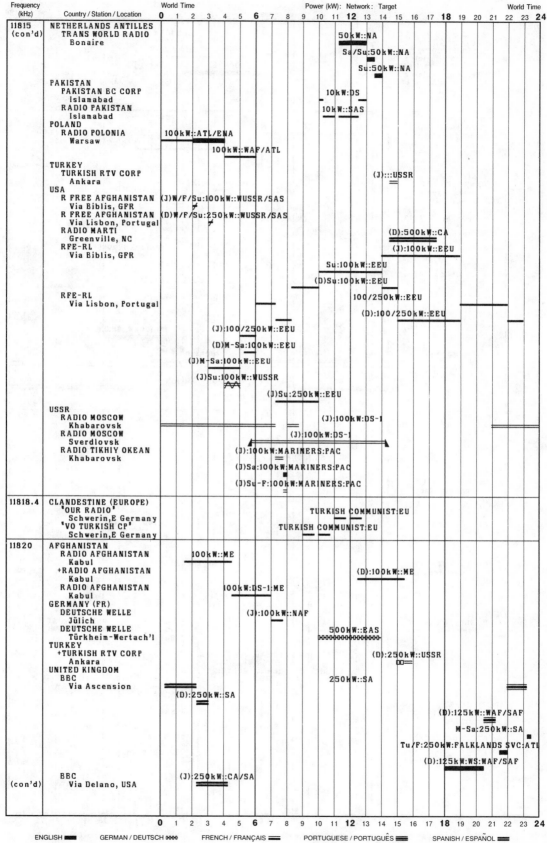

Frequency (kHz)	Country / Station / Location	World Time 0 ... 24 — Power (kW): Network: Target

11815 (con'd)

NETHERLANDS ANTILLES
TRANS WORLD RADIO
Bonaire
— 50kW::NA
— Sa/Su:50kW::NA
— Su:50kW::NA

PAKISTAN
PAKISTAN BC CORP
Islamabad — 10kW:DS
RADIO PAKISTAN
Islamabad — 10kW::SAS
POLAND
RADIO POLONIA
Warsaw — 100kW::ATL/ENA
— 100kW::WAF/ATL

TURKEY
TURKISH RTV CORP
Ankara — (J):::USSR
USA
R FREE AFGHANISTAN
Via Biblis, GFR — (J)W/F/Su:100kW::WUSSR/SAS
R FREE AFGHANISTAN
Via Lisbon, Portugal — (D)W/F/Su:250kW::WUSSR/SAS
RADIO MARTI
Greenville, NC — (D):500kW::CA
RFE-RL
Via Biblis, GFR — (J):100kW::EEU
— Su:100kW:EEU
— (D)Su:100kW::EEU
RFE-RL
Via Lisbon, Portugal — 100/250kW::EEU
— (D):100/250kW::EEU
— (J):100/250kW::EEU
— (D)M-Sa:100kW::EEU
— (J)M-Sa:100kW::EEU
— (J)Su:100kW::WUSSR
— (J)Su:250kW::EEU

USSR
RADIO MOSCOW
Khabarovsk — (J):100kW:DS-1
RADIO MOSCOW
Sverdlovsk — (J):100kW:DS-1
RADIO TIKHIY OKEAN
Khabarovsk — (J):100kW:MARINERS:PAC
— (J)Sa:100kW:MARINERS:PAC
— (J)Su-F:100kW:MARINERS:PAC

11818.4

CLANDESTINE (EUROPE)
'OUR RADIO'
Schwerin,E Germany — TURKISH COMMUNIST:EU
'VO TURKISH CP'
Schwerin,E Germany — TURKISH COMMUNIST:EU

11820

AFGHANISTAN
RADIO AFGHANISTAN
Kabul — 100kW::ME
+RADIO AFGHANISTAN
Kabul — (D):100kW::ME
RADIO AFGHANISTAN
Kabul — 100kW:DS-1:ME
GERMANY (FR)
DEUTSCHE WELLE
Jülich — (J):100kW::NAF
DEUTSCHE WELLE
Türkheim-Wertach'l — 500kW::EAS
TURKEY
+TURKISH RTV CORP
Ankara — (D):250kW::USSR
UNITED KINGDOM
BBC
Via Ascension — 250kW::SA
— (D):250kW::SA
— (D):125kW::WAF/SAF
— M-Sa:250kW::SA
— Tu/F:250kW:FALKLANDS SVC:ATL
— (D):125kW:WS:WAF/SAF
BBC
(con'd) Via Delano, USA — (J):250kW::CA/SA

0 1 2 3 4 5 6 7 8 9 10 11 12 13 14 15 16 17 18 19 20 21 22 23 24

ENGLISH ▬▬ GERMAN / DEUTSCH ◇◇◇◇ FRENCH / FRANÇAIS ═══ PORTUGUESE / PORTUGUÊS ▬▬ SPANISH / ESPAÑOL ▬▬
ARABIC / عربي ═══ RUSSIAN / PУССКИИ ═══ CHINESE / 中文 �□�□�□ JAPANESE / 日本語 ▬▬ MULTILINGUAL ◦◦◦◦ OTHER ▬▬
SUMMER ONLY (J) WINTER ONLY (D) JAMMING ∧∧ or / or \ EARLIEST HEARD ◢ LATEST HEARD ◣ + TENTATIVE

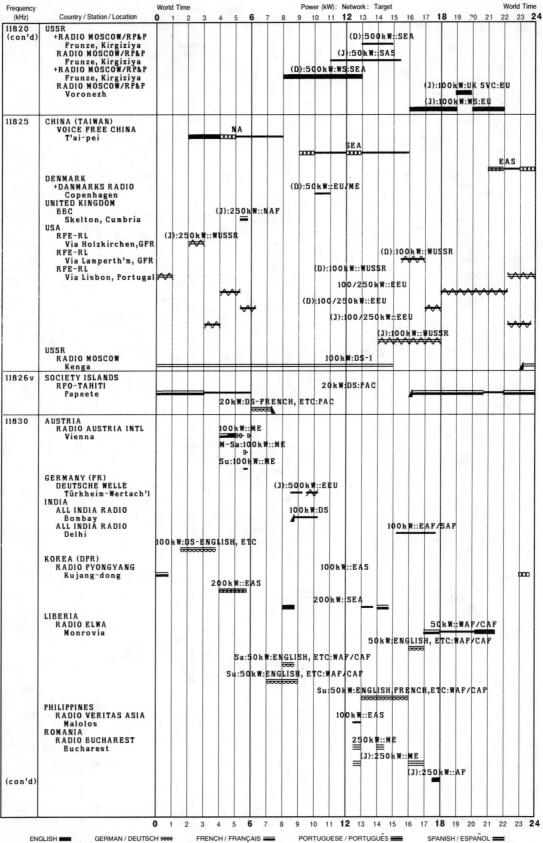

Frequency (kHz)	Country / Station / Location		World Time	Power (kW): Network: Target		World Time

11820 (con'd) — USSR
- +RADIO MOSCOW/RP&P, Frunze, Kirgiziya — (D):500kW::SEA
- RADIO MOSCOW/RP&P, Frunze, Kirgiziya — (J):50kW::SAS
- +RADIO MOSCOW/RP&P, Frunze, Kirgiziya — (D):500kW:WS:SEA
- RADIO MOSCOW/RP&P, Voronezh — (J):100kW:UK SVC:EU
- — (J):100kW:WS:EU

11825 — CHINA (TAIWAN)
- VOICE FREE CHINA, T'ai-pei — NA
- — SEA
- — EAS

DENMARK
- +DANMARKS RADIO, Copenhagen — (D):50kW::EU/ME

UNITED KINGDOM
- BBC, Skelton, Cumbria — (J):250kW::NAF

USA
- RFE-RL, Via Holzkirchen, GFR — (J):250kW::WUSSR
- RFE-RL, Via Lamperth'm, GFR — (D):100kW::WUSSR
- RFE-RL, Via Lisbon, Portugal — (D):100kW::WUSSR
- — 100/250kW::EEU
- — (D):100/250kW::EEU
- — (J):100/250kW::EEU
- — (J):100kW::WUSSR

USSR
- RADIO MOSCOW, Kenga — 100kW:DS-1

11826v — SOCIETY ISLANDS
- RFO-TAHITI, Papeete — 20kW:DS:PAC
- — 20kW:DS-FRENCH, ETC:PAC

11830 — AUSTRIA
- RADIO AUSTRIA INTL, Vienna — 100kW::ME
- — M-Sa:100kW::ME
- — Su:100kW::ME

GERMANY (FR)
- DEUTSCHE WELLE, Türkheim-Wertach'l — (J):500kW::EEU

INDIA
- ALL INDIA RADIO, Bombay — 100kW:DS
- ALL INDIA RADIO, Delhi — 100kW::EAF/SAF
- — 100kW:DS-ENGLISH, ETC

KOREA (DPR)
- RADIO PYONGYANG, Kujang-dong — 100kW::EAS
- — 200kW::EAS
- — 200kW:SEA

LIBERIA
- RADIO ELWA, Monrovia — 50kW::WAF/CAF
- — 50kW:ENGLISH, ETC:WAF/CAF
- — Sa:50kW:ENGLISH, ETC:WAF/CAF
- — Su:50kW:ENGLISH, ETC:WAF/CAF
- — Su:50kW:ENGLISH,FRENCH,ETC:WAF/CAF

PHILIPPINES
- RADIO VERITAS ASIA, Malolos — 100kW::EAS

ROMANIA
- RADIO BUCHAREST, Bucharest — 250kW::ME
- — (J):250kW::ME
- — (J):250kW::AF

(con'd)

| 0 | 1 | 2 | 3 | 4 | 5 | 6 | 7 | 8 | 9 | 10 | 11 | 12 | 13 | 14 | 15 | 16 | 17 | 18 | 19 | 20 | 21 | 22 | 23 | 24 |

ENGLISH ▄▄▄   GERMAN / DEUTSCH 0000   FRENCH / FRANÇAIS ═══   PORTUGUESE / PORTUGUÊS ▆▆▆   SPANISH / ESPAÑOL ══

ARABIC /ﻉﺭﺏ ═══   RUSSIAN / РУССКИИ ═══   CHINESE / 中文 0000   JAPANESE / 日本語 ▅▅▅   MULTILINGUAL ▅▅▅   OTHER ▬▬

SUMMER ONLY (J)   WINTER ONLY (D)   JAMMING /\/\ or / or \   EARLIEST HEARD ◢   LATEST HEARD ◣   + TENTATIVE

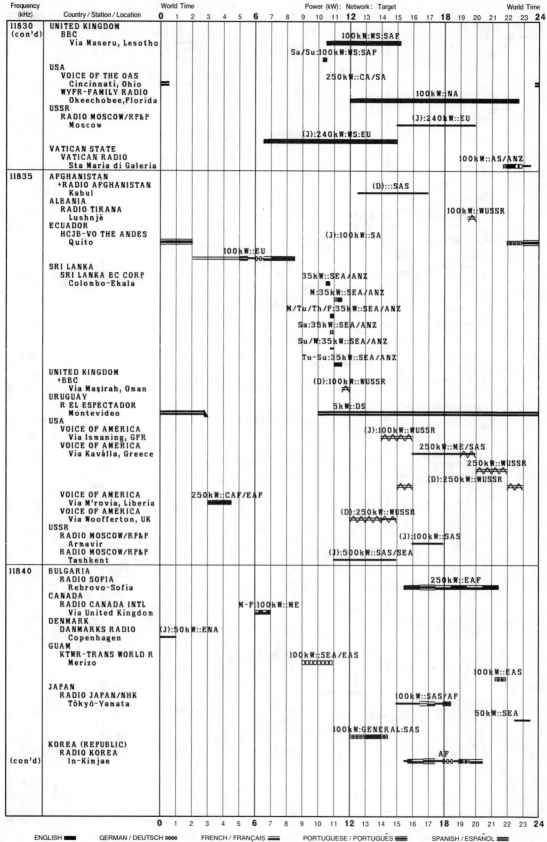

Frequency (kHz)	Country / Station / Location	Schedule
11830 (con'd)	**UNITED KINGDOM** BBC — Via Maseru, Lesotho	100kW:WS:SAF ; Sa/Su:100kW:WS:SAF
	USA VOICE OF THE OAS — Cincinnati, Ohio	250kW::CA/SA
	WYFR-FAMILY RADIO — Okeechobee, Florida	100kW::NA
	USSR RADIO MOSCOW/RP&P — Moscow	(J):240kW::EU ; (J):240kW:WS:EU
	VATICAN STATE VATICAN RADIO — Sta Maria di Galeria	100kW::AS/ANZ
11835	**AFGHANISTAN** +RADIO AFGHANISTAN — Kabul	(D):::SAS
	ALBANIA RADIO TIRANA — Lushnjë	100kW::WUSSR
	ECUADOR HCJB-VO THE ANDES — Quito	(J):100kW::SA ; 100kW::EU
	SRI LANKA SRI LANKA BC CORP — Colombo-Ekala	35kW::SEA/ANZ ; M:35kW::SEA/ANZ ; M/Tu/Th/F:35kW::SEA/ANZ ; Sa:35kW::SEA/ANZ ; Su/W:35kW::SEA/ANZ ; Tu-Su:35kW::SEA/ANZ
	UNITED KINGDOM +BBC — Via Maşirah, Oman	(D):100kW::WUSSR
	URUGUAY R EL ESPECTADOR — Montevideo	5kW::DS
	USA VOICE OF AMERICA — Via Ismaning, GFR	(J):100kW::WUSSR
	VOICE OF AMERICA — Via Kaválla, Greece	250kW::ME/SAS ; 250kW::WUSSR ; (D):250kW::WUSSR
	VOICE OF AMERICA — Via M'rovia, Liberia	250kW::CAF/EAF
	VOICE OF AMERICA — Via Woofferton, UK	(D):250kW::WUSSR
	USSR RADIO MOSCOW/RP&P — Armavir	(J):100kW::SAS
	RADIO MOSCOW/RP&P — Tashkent	(J):500kW::SAS/SEA
11840	**BULGARIA** RADIO SOFIA — Rebrovo-Sofia	250kW::EAF
	CANADA RADIO CANADA INTL — Via United Kingdom	M-F:100kW::ME
	DENMARK DANMARKS RADIO — Copenhagen	(J):50kW::ENA
	GUAM KTWR-TRANS WORLD R — Merizo	100kW::SEA/EAS ; 100kW::EAS
	JAPAN RADIO JAPAN/NHK — Tōkyō-Yamata	100kW::SAS/AF ; 50kW::SEA ; 100kW:GENERAL:SAS
	KOREA (REPUBLIC) RADIO KOREA — In-Kimjae	AF
(con'd)		

0 1 2 3 4 5 6 7 8 9 10 11 12 13 14 15 16 17 18 19 20 21 22 23 24

ENGLISH ▬▬ GERMAN / DEUTSCH ◗◖◗◖ FRENCH / FRANÇAIS ══ PORTUGUESE / PORTUGUÊS ≡≡ SPANISH / ESPAÑOL ═══

ARABIC /ﻉﺭﺏ ≡≡ RUSSIAN / PУССКИИ ═══ CHINESE / 中文 ▭▭▭ JAPANESE / 日本語 ▨▨▨ MULTILINGUAL ◷◷◷ OTHER ▬▬

SUMMER ONLY (J)   WINTER ONLY (D)   JAMMING ∧∧ or / or \   EARLIEST HEARD ◢   LATEST HEARD ◣   + TENTATIVE

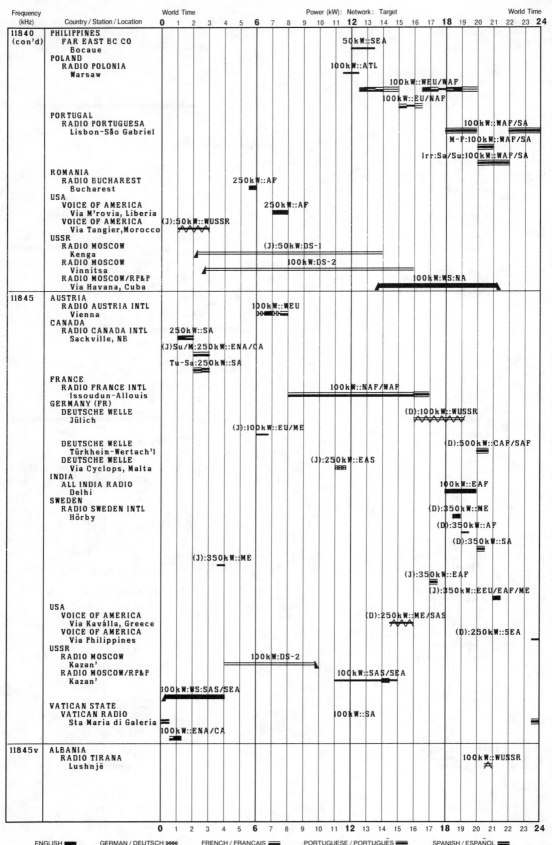

Frequency (kHz)	Country / Station / Location	World Time 0 ... Power (kW) : Network : Target ... 24

11840 (con'd)

PHILIPPINES
 FAR EAST BC CO — 50kW::SEA
  Bocaue
POLAND
 RADIO POLONIA — 100kW::ATL
  Warsaw
  100kW::WEU/WAF
  100kW::EU/NAF

PORTUGAL
 RADIO PORTUGUESA — 100kW::WAF/SA
  Lisbon-São Gabriel — M-F:100kW::WAF/SA
  Irr:Sa/Su:100kW::WAF/SA

ROMANIA
 RADIO BUCHAREST — 250kW::AF
  Bucharest
USA
 VOICE OF AMERICA — 250kW::AF
  Via M'rovia, Liberia
 VOICE OF AMERICA — (J):50kW::WUSSR
  Via Tangier, Morocco
USSR
 RADIO MOSCOW — (J):50kW:DS-1
  Kenga
 RADIO MOSCOW — 100kW:DS-2
  Vinnitsa
 RADIO MOSCOW/RP&P — 100kW:WS:NA
  Via Havana, Cuba

11845

AUSTRIA
 RADIO AUSTRIA INTL — 100kW::WEU
  Vienna
CANADA
 RADIO CANADA INTL — 250kW::SA
  Sackville, NB — (J)Su/M:250kW::ENA/CA
  Tu-Sa:250kW::SA

FRANCE
 RADIO FRANCE INTL — 100kW::NAF/WAF
  Issoudun-Allouis
GERMANY (FR)
 DEUTSCHE WELLE — (D):100kW::WUSSR
  Jülich — (J):100kW::EU/ME

 DEUTSCHE WELLE — (D):500kW::CAF/SAF
  Türkheim-Wertach'l
 DEUTSCHE WELLE — (J):250kW::EAS
  Via Cyclops, Malta
INDIA
 ALL INDIA RADIO — 100kW::EAF
  Delhi
SWEDEN
 RADIO SWEDEN INTL — (D):350kW::ME
  Hörby — (D):350kW::AF
  (D):350kW::SA

  (J):350kW::ME

  (J):350kW::EAF

  (J):350kW::EEU/EAF/ME

USA
 VOICE OF AMERICA — (D):250kW::ME/SAS
  Via Kaválla, Greece
 VOICE OF AMERICA — (D):250kW::SEA
  Via Philippines
USSR
 RADIO MOSCOW — 100kW:DS-2
  Kazan'
 RADIO MOSCOW/RP&P — 100kW::SAS/SEA
  Kazan'
  100kW:WS:SAS/SEA

VATICAN STATE
 VATICAN RADIO — 100kW::SA
  Sta Maria di Galeria
  100kW::ENA/CA

11845v

ALBANIA
 RADIO TIRANA — 100kW::WUSSR
  Lushnjë

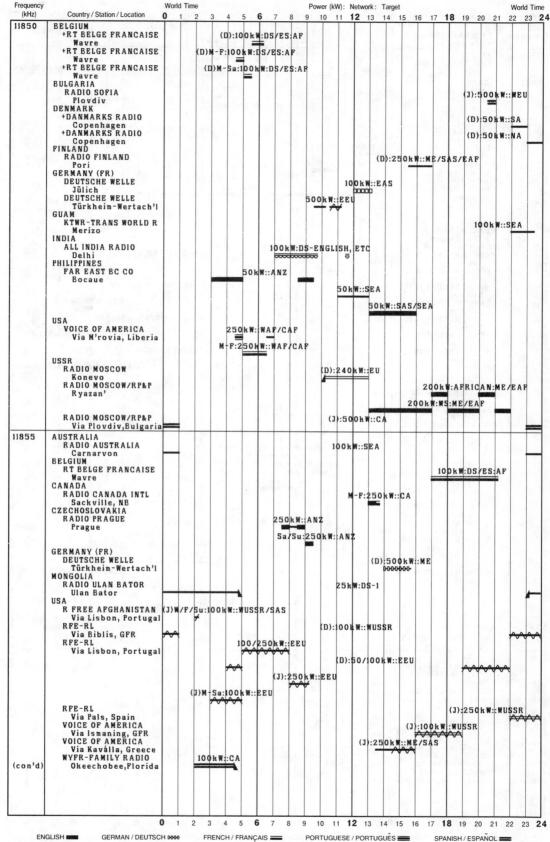

11850 BELGIUM
+RT BELGE FRANCAISE — (D):100kW:DS/ES:AF
Wavre
+RT BELGE FRANCAISE — (D)M-F:100kW:DS/ES:AF
Wavre
+RT BELGE FRANCAISE — (D)M-Sa:100kW:DS/ES:AF
Wavre
BULGARIA
RADIO SOFIA — (J):500kW::WEU
Plovdiv
DENMARK
+DANMARKS RADIO — (D):50kW::SA
Copenhagen
+DANMARKS RADIO — (D):50kW::NA
Copenhagen
FINLAND
RADIO FINLAND — (D):250kW::ME/SAS/EAF
Pori
GERMANY (FR)
DEUTSCHE WELLE — 100kW::EAS
Jülich
DEUTSCHE WELLE — 500kW::EEU
Türkheim-Wertach'l
GUAM
KTWR-TRANS WORLD R — 100kW::SEA
Merizo
INDIA
ALL INDIA RADIO — 100kW:DS-ENGLISH, ETC
Delhi
PHILIPPINES
FAR EAST BC CO — 50kW::ANZ
Bocaue
— 50kW::SEA
— 50kW::SAS/SEA
USA
VOICE OF AMERICA — 250kW: WAF/CAF
Via M'rovia, Liberia
— M-F:250kW::WAF/CAF
USSR
RADIO MOSCOW — (D):240kW::EU
Konevo
RADIO MOSCOW/RP&P — 200kW:AFRICAN:ME/EAF
Ryazan'
— 200kW:WS:ME/EAF
RADIO MOSCOW/RP&P — (J):500kW::CA
Via Plovdiv,Bulgaria

11855 AUSTRALIA
RADIO AUSTRALIA — 100kW::SEA
Carnarvon
BELGIUM
RT BELGE FRANCAISE — 100kW:DS/ES:AF
Wavre
CANADA
RADIO CANADA INTL — M-F:250kW::CA
Sackville, NB
CZECHOSLOVAKIA
RADIO PRAGUE — 250kW::ANZ
Prague
— Sa/Su:250kW::ANZ
GERMANY (FR)
DEUTSCHE WELLE — (D):500kW::ME
Türkheim-Wertach'l
MONGOLIA
RADIO ULAN BATOR — 25kW:DS-1
Ulan Bator
USA
R FREE AFGHANISTAN — (J)W/F/Su:100kW::WUSSR/SAS
Via Lisbon, Portugal
RFE-RL — (D):100kW::WUSSR
Via Biblis, GFR
RFE-RL — 100/250kW::EEU
Via Lisbon, Portugal
— (D):50/100kW::EEU
— (J):250kW::EEU
— (J)M-Sa:100kW::EEU
RFE-RL — (J):250kW::WUSSR
Via Pals, Spain
VOICE OF AMERICA — (J):100kW::WUSSR
Via Ismaning, GFR
VOICE OF AMERICA — (J):250kW::ME/SAS
Via Kaválla, Greece
WYFR-FAMILY RADIO — 100kW::CA
(con'd)   Okeechobee,Florida

ENGLISH ▬▬   GERMAN / DEUTSCH ◊◊◊◊   FRENCH / FRANÇAIS ══   PORTUGUESE / PORTUGUÊS ▦▦   SPANISH / ESPAÑOL ▱▱

ARABIC / عر ≡≡   RUSSIAN / РУССКИИ ══   CHINESE / ✦✶ ◻◻◻◻   JAPANESE / 日本語 ▥▥▥   MULTILINGUAL ▨▨▨   OTHER ▬

SUMMER ONLY (J)   WINTER ONLY (D)   JAMMING /\/\ or / or \   EARLIEST HEARD ◢   LATEST HEARD ◣   + TENTATIVE

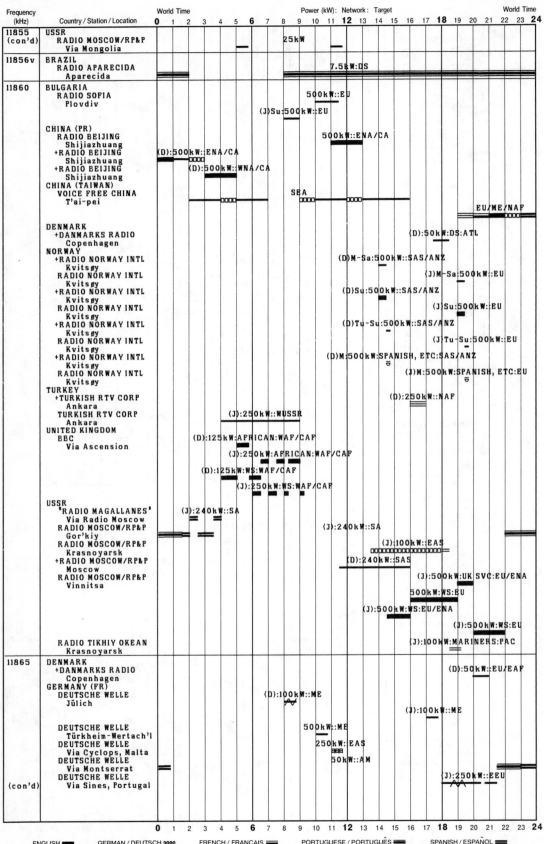

Frequency (kHz)	Country / Station / Location	World Time ... Power (kW): Network: Target ... World Time

11855 (con'd) — USSR — RADIO MOSCOW/RP&P — Via Mongolia — 25kW

11856v — BRAZIL — RADIO APARECIDA — Aparecida — 7.5kW:DS

11860 — BULGARIA — RADIO SOFIA — Plovdiv — 500kW::EU
— (J)Su:500kW::EU
— CHINA (PR) — RADIO BEIJING — Shijiazhuang — 500kW::ENA/CA
— +RADIO BEIJING — Shijiazhuang — (D):500kW::ENA/CA
— +RADIO BEIJING — Shijiazhuang — (D):500kW::WNA/CA
— CHINA (TAIWAN) — VOICE FREE CHINA — T'ai-pei — SEA — EU/ME/NAF
— DENMARK — +DANMARKS RADIO — Copenhagen — (D):50kW:DS:ATL
— NORWAY — +RADIO NORWAY INTL — Kvitsøy — (D)M-Sa:500kW::SAS/ANZ
— RADIO NORWAY INTL — Kvitsøy — (J)M-Sa:500kW::EU
— +RADIO NORWAY INTL — Kvitsøy — (D)Su:500kW::SAS/ANZ
— RADIO NORWAY INTL — Kvitsøy — (J)Su:500kW::EU
— +RADIO NORWAY INTL — Kvitsøy — (D)Tu-Su:500kW::SAS/ANZ
— RADIO NORWAY INTL — Kvitsøy — (J)Tu-Su:500kW::EU
— +RADIO NORWAY INTL — Kvitsøy — (D)M:500kW:SPANISH, ETC:SAS/ANZ
— RADIO NORWAY INTL — Kvitsøy — (J)M:500kW:SPANISH, ETC:EU
— TURKEY — +TURKISH RTV CORP — Ankara — (D):250kW::NAF
— TURKISH RTV CORP — Ankara — (J):250kW::WUSSR
— UNITED KINGDOM — BBC — Via Ascension — (D):125kW:AFRICAN:WAF/CAF
— (J):250kW:AFRICAN:WAF/CAF
— (D):125kW:WS:WAF/CAF
— (J):250kW:WS:WAF/CAF
— USSR — 'RADIO MAGALLANES' — Via Radio Moscow — (J):240kW::SA
— RADIO MOSCOW/RP&P — Gor'kiy — (J):240kW::SA
— RADIO MOSCOW/RP&P — Krasnoyarsk — (J):100kW::EAS
— +RADIO MOSCOW/RP&P — Moscow — (D):240kW::SAS
— RADIO MOSCOW/RP&P — Vinnitsa — (J):500kW:UK SVC:EU/ENA
— 500kW:WS:EU
— (J):500kW:WS:EU/ENA
— (J):500kW:WS:EU
— RADIO TIKHIY OKEAN — Krasnoyarsk — (J):100kW:MARINERS:PAC

11865 — DENMARK — +DANMARKS RADIO — Copenhagen — (D):50kW::EU/EAF
— GERMANY (FR) — DEUTSCHE WELLE — Jülich — (D):100kW::ME
— (J):100kW::ME
— DEUTSCHE WELLE — Türkheim-Wertach'l — 500kW::ME
— DEUTSCHE WELLE — Via Cyclops, Malta — 250kW::EAS
— DEUTSCHE WELLE — Via Montserrat — 50kW::AM
(con'd) — DEUTSCHE WELLE — Via Sines, Portugal — (J):250kW::EEU

ENGLISH ▮▮▮   GERMAN / DEUTSCH ◊◊◊◊   FRENCH / FRANÇAIS ═══   PORTUGUESE / PORTUGUÊS ═══   SPANISH / ESPAÑOL ═══

ARABIC / ﻉﺮﺑ ≡≡≡   RUSSIAN / PYCCKИИ ═══   CHINESE / ✹★ ◻◻◻◻   JAPANESE / 日本語 ▰▰▰   MULTILINGUAL ◘◘◘◘   OTHER ▬▬▬

SUMMER ONLY (J)   WINTER ONLY (D)   JAMMING /\/\ or / or \   EARLIEST HEARD ◢   LATEST HEARD ◣   + TENTATIVE

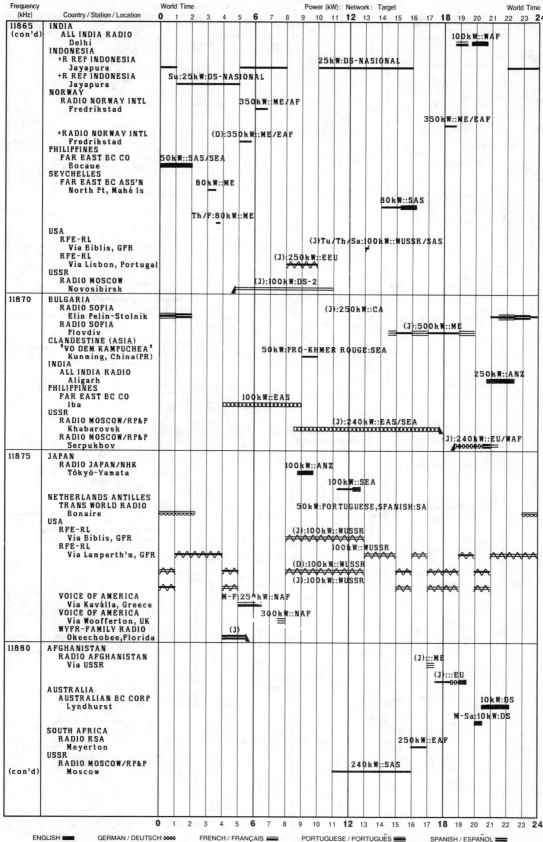

Frequency (kHz)	Country / Station / Location	Power (kW): Network : Target

World Time: 0 1 2 3 4 5 6 7 8 9 10 11 12 13 14 15 16 17 18 19 20 21 22 23 24

11865 (con'd)

INDIA
ALL INDIA RADIO, Delhi — 100kW::WAF

INDONESIA
+R REP INDONESIA, Jayapura — 25kW:DS-NASIONAL
+R REP INDONESIA, Jayapura — Su:25kW:DS-NASIONAL

NORWAY
RADIO NORWAY INTL, Fredrikstad — 350kW::ME/AF
— 350kW::ME/EAF
+RADIO NORWAY INTL, Fredrikstad — (D):350kW::ME/EAF

PHILIPPINES
FAR EAST BC CO, Bocaue — 50kW::SAS/SEA

SEYCHELLES
FAR EAST BC ASS'N, North Pt, Mahé Is — 80kW::ME
— 80kW::SAS
— Th/F:80kW::ME

USA
RFE-RL, Via Biblis, GFR — (J)Tu/Th/Sa:100kW::WUSSR/SAS
RFE-RL, Via Lisbon, Portugal — (J):250kW::EEU

USSR
RADIO MOSCOW, Novosibirsk — (J):100kW:DS-2

11870

BULGARIA
RADIO SOFIA, Elin Pelin-Stolnik — (J):250kW::CA
RADIO SOFIA, Plovdiv — (J):500kW::ME

CLANDESTINE (ASIA)
'VO DEM KAMPUCHEA', Kunming, China(PR) — 50kW:PRO-KHMER ROUGE:SEA

INDIA
ALL INDIA RADIO, Aligarh — 250kW::ANZ

PHILIPPINES
FAR EAST BC CO, Iba — 100kW::EAS

USSR
RADIO MOSCOW/RP&P, Khabarovsk — (J):240kW::EAS/SEA
RADIO MOSCOW/RP&P, Serpukhov — (J):240kW::EU/WAF

11875

JAPAN
RADIO JAPAN/NHK, Tōkyō-Yamata — 100kW::ANZ
— 100kW::SEA

NETHERLANDS ANTILLES
TRANS WORLD RADIO, Bonaire — 50kW:PORTUGUESE,SPANISH:SA

USA
RFE-RL, Via Biblis, GFR — (J):100kW::WUSSR
RFE-RL, Via Lamperth'm, GFR — 100kW::WUSSR
— (D):100kW::WUSSR
— (J):100kW::WUSSR

VOICE OF AMERICA, Via Kaválla, Greece — M-F:25kW::NAF
VOICE OF AMERICA, Via Woofferton, UK — 300kW::NAF
WYFR-FAMILY RADIO, Okeechobee, Florida — (J)

11880

AFGHANISTAN
RADIO AFGHANISTAN, Via USSR — (J):::ME
— (J):::EU

AUSTRALIA
AUSTRALIAN BC CORP, Lyndhurst — 10kW:DS
— M-Sa:10kW:DS

SOUTH AFRICA
RADIO RSA, Meyerton — 250kW::EAF

USSR
RADIO MOSCOW/RP&P, Moscow **(con'd)** — 240kW::SAS

World Time: 0 1 2 3 4 5 6 7 8 9 10 11 12 13 14 15 16 17 18 19 20 21 22 23 24

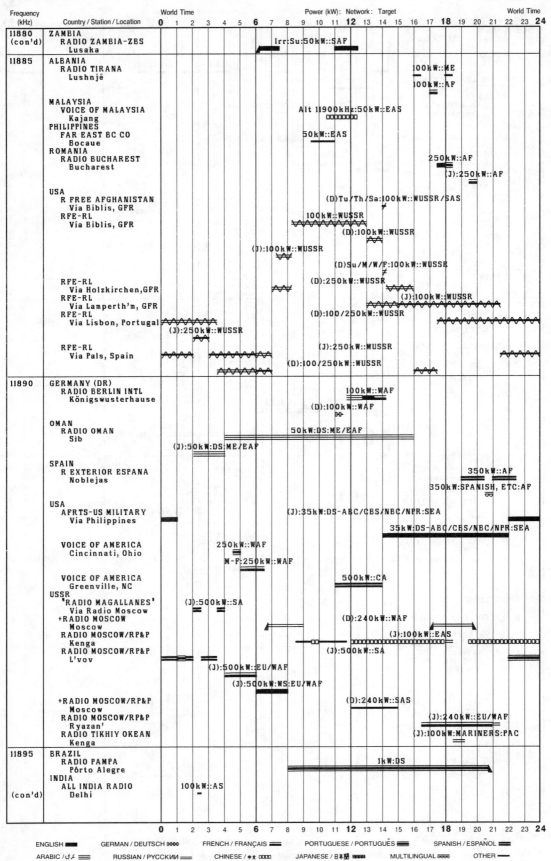

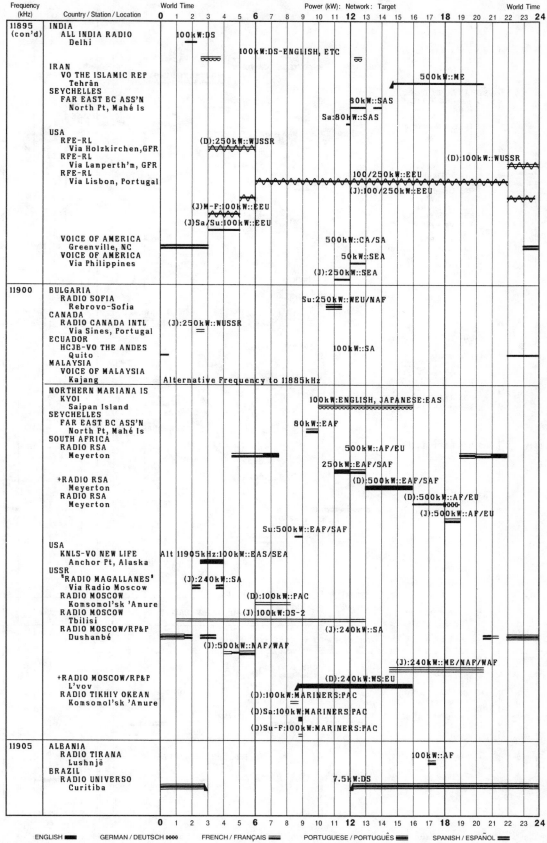

ENGLISH ▬ GERMAN / DEUTSCH ০০০০ FRENCH / FRANÇAIS ▬ PORTUGUESE / PORTUGUÊS ▬ SPANISH / ESPAÑOL ▬

ARABIC / عربى ▬ RUSSIAN / РУССКИИ ▬ CHINESE / ◆x ০০০০ JAPANESE / 日本語 ▬ MULTILINGUAL ০০০০ OTHER ▬

SUMMER ONLY (J) WINTER ONLY (D) JAMMING ∧∧ or / or \ EARLIEST HEARD ◢ LATEST HEARD ◣ + TENTATIVE

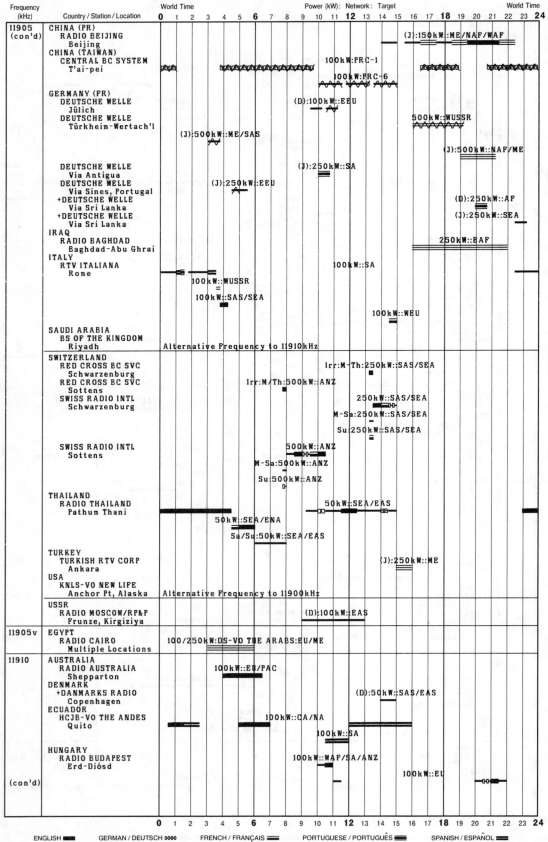

Frequency
(kHz)   Country / Station / Location   World Time   Power (kW): Network : Target   World Time

11905   CHINA (PR)
(con'd)   RADIO BEIJING   (J):150kW::ME/NAF/WAF
             Beijing
        CHINA (TAIWAN)
           CENTRAL BC SYSTEM   100kW:PRC-1
             T'ai-pei
                                                          100kW:PRC-6

        GERMANY (FR)
           DEUTSCHE WELLE   (D):100kW::EEU
             Jülich
           DEUTSCHE WELLE   500kW::WUSSR
             Türkheim-Wertach'l
        (J):500kW::ME/SAS
                                                                                (J):500kW::NAF/ME

           DEUTSCHE WELLE   (J):250kW::SA
             Via Antigua
           DEUTSCHE WELLE   (J):250kW::EEU
             Via Sines, Portugal
          +DEUTSCHE WELLE   (D):250kW::AF
             Via Sri Lanka
          +DEUTSCHE WELLE   (J):250kW::SEA
             Via Sri Lanka
        IRAQ
           RADIO BAGHDAD   250kW::EAF
             Baghdad-Abu Ghrai
        ITALY
           RTV ITALIANA   100kW::SA
             Rome   100kW::WUSSR
                                             100kW::SAS/SEA
                                                                  100kW::WEU

        SAUDI ARABIA
           BS OF THE KINGDOM
             Riyadh   Alternative Frequency to 11910 kHz
        SWITZERLAND
           RED CROSS BC SVC   Irr:M-Th:250kW::SAS/SEA
             Schwarzenburg
           RED CROSS BC SVC   Irr:M/Th:500kW::ANZ
             Sottens
           SWISS RADIO INTL   250kW:SAS/SEA
             Schwarzenburg
                                                M-Sa:250kW::SAS/SEA
                                                Su:250kW::SAS/SEA

           SWISS RADIO INTL   500kW::ANZ
             Sottens   M-Sa:500kW::ANZ
                                  Su:500kW::ANZ

        THAILAND
           RADIO THAILAND   50kW::SEA/EAS
             Pathum Thani   50kW::SEA/ENA
                                 Sa/Su:50kW::SEA/EAS

        TURKEY
           TURKISH RTV CORP   (J):250kW::ME
             Ankara
        USA
           KNLS-VO NEW LIFE
             Anchor Pt, Alaska   Alternative Frequency to 11900 kHz
        USSR
           RADIO MOSCOW/RP&P   (D):100kW::EAS
             Frunze, Kirgiziya

11905v EGYPT
           RADIO CAIRO   100/250kW:DS-VO THE ARABS:EU/ME
             Multiple Locations

11910   AUSTRALIA
           RADIO AUSTRALIA   100kW::EU/PAC
             Shepparton
        DENMARK
          +DANMARKS RADIO   (D):50kW::SAS/EAS
             Copenhagen
        ECUADOR
           HCJB-VO THE ANDES   100kW::CA/NA
             Quito   100kW::SA

        HUNGARY
           RADIO BUDAPEST   100kW::WAF/SA/ANZ
             Erd-Diósd   100kW::EU
(con'd)

        0   1   2   3   4   5   6   7   8   9   10 11 12 13 14 15 16 17 18 19 20 21 22 23 24

ENGLISH ▓▓▓   GERMAN / DEUTSCH ◊◊◊◊   FRENCH / FRANÇAIS ▤▤▤   PORTUGUESE / PORTUGUÊS ▦▦▦   SPANISH / ESPAÑOL ▨▨▨
ARABIC / ﻉﺭﺏ ▤▤   RUSSIAN / РУССКИИ ▭▭   CHINESE / 中文 ◊◊◊◊   JAPANESE / 日本語 ▨▨▨   MULTILINGUAL ▨▨▨   OTHER ▬▬
SUMMER ONLY (J)   WINTER ONLY (D)   JAMMING /\/\ or / or \   EARLIEST HEARD ◢   LATEST HEARD ◣   + TENTATIVE

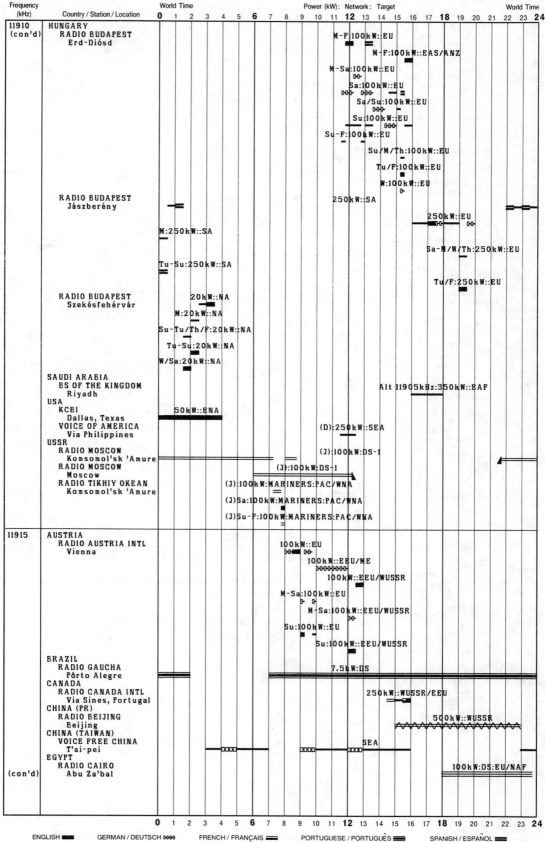

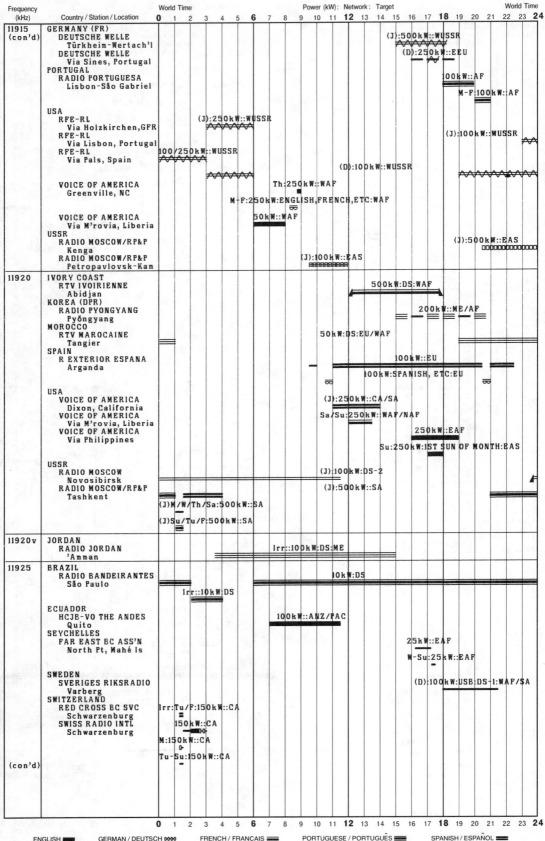

11915 (con'd) **GERMANY (FR)**
DEUTSCHE WELLE
Türkheim-Wertach'l — (J):500kW::WUSSR
DEUTSCHE WELLE
Via Sines, Portugal — (D):250kW::EEU
PORTUGAL
RADIO PORTUGUESA
Lisbon-São Gabriel — 100kW::AF / M-F:100kW::AF

USA
RFE-RL
Via Holzkirchen,GFR — (J):250kW::WUSSR
RFE-RL
Via Lisbon, Portugal — (J):100kW::WUSSR
RFE-RL
Via Pals, Spain — 100/250kW::WUSSR / (D):100kW::WUSSR
VOICE OF AMERICA
Greenville, NC — Th:250kW::WAF / M-F:250kW:ENGLISH,FRENCH,ETC:WAF
VOICE OF AMERICA
Via M'rovia, Liberia — 50kW::WAF
USSR
RADIO MOSCOW/RP&P
Kenga — (J):500kW::EAS
RADIO MOSCOW/RP&P
Petropavlovsk-Kam — (J):100kW::EAS

11920 **IVORY COAST**
RTV IVOIRIENNE
Abidjan — 500kW:DS:WAF
KOREA (DPR)
RADIO PYONGYANG
Pyŏngyang — 200kW::ME/AF
MOROCCO
RTV MAROCAINE
Tangier — 50kW:DS:EU/WAF
SPAIN
R EXTERIOR ESPANA
Arganda — 100kW::EU / 100kW:SPANISH, ETC:EU

USA
VOICE OF AMERICA
Dixon, California — (J):250kW::CA/SA
VOICE OF AMERICA
Via M'rovia, Liberia — Sa/Su:250kW::WAF/NAF
VOICE OF AMERICA
Via Philippines — 250kW::EAF / Su:250kW:1ST SUN OF MONTH:EAS
USSR
RADIO MOSCOW
Novosibirsk — (J):100kW:DS-2
RADIO MOSCOW/RP&P
Tashkent — (J):500kW::SA
(J)M/W/Th/Sa:500kW::SA
(J)Su/Tu/F:500kW::SA

11920v **JORDAN**
RADIO JORDAN
'Amman — Irr::100kW:DS:ME

11925 **BRAZIL**
RADIO BANDEIRANTES
São Paulo — 10kW:DS / Irr::10kW:DS

ECUADOR
HCJB-VO THE ANDES
Quito — 100kW::ANZ/PAC
SEYCHELLES
FAR EAST BC ASS'N
North Pt, Mahé Is — 25kW::EAF / W-Su:25kW::EAF

SWEDEN
SVERIGES RIKSRADIO
Varberg — (D):100kW:USB:DS-1:WAF/SA
SWITZERLAND
RED CROSS BC SVC
Schwarzenburg — Irr:Tu/F:150kW::CA
SWISS RADIO INTL
Schwarzenburg — 150kW::CA / M:150kW::CA / Tu-Su:150kW::CA

(con'd)

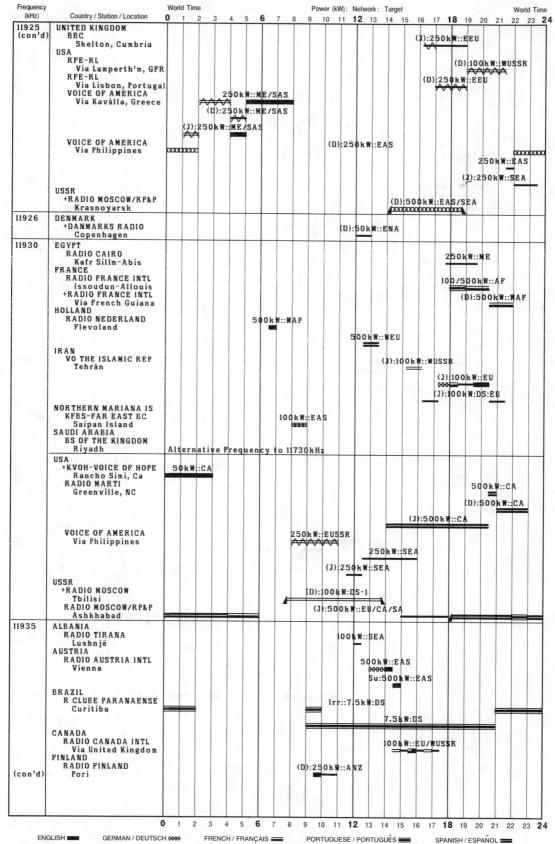

Frequency (kHz)	Country / Station / Location	Power (kW): Network: Target
11925 (con'd)	UNITED KINGDOM	
	BBC	
	Skelton, Cumbria	(J):250kW::EEU
	USA	
	RFE-RL	
	Via Lamperth'm, GFR	(D):100kW::WUSSR
	RFE-RL	
	Via Lisbon, Portugal	(D):250kW::EEU
	VOICE OF AMERICA	250kW::ME/SAS
	Via Kaválla, Greece	(D):250kW::ME/SAS
		(J):250kW::ME/SAS
	VOICE OF AMERICA	
	Via Philippines	(D):250kW::EAS
		250kW::EAS
		(J):250kW::SEA
	USSR	
	+RADIO MOSCOW/RP&P	(D):500kW::EAS/SEA
	Krasnoyarsk	
11926	DENMARK	
	+DANMARKS RADIO	(D):50kW::ENA
	Copenhagen	
11930	EGYPT	
	RADIO CAIRO	250kW::ME
	Kafr Silim-Abis	
	FRANCE	
	RADIO FRANCE INTL	100/500kW::AF
	Issoudun-Allouis	
	+RADIO FRANCE INTL	(D):500kW::WAF
	Via French Guiana	
	HOLLAND	
	RADIO NEDERLAND	500kW::WAF
	Flevoland	
		500kW::WEU
	IRAN	
	VO THE ISLAMIC REP	(J):100kW::WUSSR
	Tehrän	(J):100kW::EU
		(J):100kW:DS:EU
	NORTHERN MARIANA IS	
	KFBS-FAR EAST BC	100kW::EAS
	Saipan Island	
	SAUDI ARABIA	
	BS OF THE KINGDOM	Alternative Frequency to 11730kHz
	Riyadh	
	USA	
	+KVOH-VOICE OF HOPE	50kW::CA
	Rancho Simi, Ca	
	RADIO MARTI	500kW::CA
	Greenville, NC	(D):500kW::CA
		(J):500kW::CA
	VOICE OF AMERICA	
	Via Philippines	250kW::EUSSR
		250kW::SEA
		(J):250kW::SEA
	USSR	
	+RADIO MOSCOW	(D):100kW:DS-1
	Tbilisi	
	RADIO MOSCOW/RP&P	(J):500kW::EU/CA/SA
	Ashkhabad	
11935	ALBANIA	
	RADIO TIRANA	100kW::SEA
	Lushnjë	
	AUSTRIA	
	RADIO AUSTRIA INTL	500kW::EAS
	Vienna	Su:500kW::EAS
	BRAZIL	
	R CLUBE PARANAENSE	Irr::7.5kW:DS
	Curitiba	7.5kW:DS
	CANADA	
	RADIO CANADA INTL	100kW::EU/WUSSR
	Via United Kingdom	
	FINLAND	
	RADIO FINLAND	(D):250kW::ANZ
(con'd)	Pori	

World Time
0 1 2 3 4 5 6 7 8 9 10 11 12 13 14 15 16 17 18 19 20 21 22 23 24

ENGLISH ▬ GERMAN / DEUTSCH ∞∞∞ FRENCH / FRANÇAIS ═ PORTUGUESE / PORTUGUÊS ▬ SPANISH / ESPAÑOL ▬
ARABIC /ﻉﺵﻉ ≡ RUSSIAN / РУССКИИ ═ CHINESE / ＊＊ ∞∞∞ JAPANESE / 日本語 ▦ MULTILINGUAL ▨ OTHER ▬
SUMMER ONLY (J) WINTER ONLY (D) JAMMING /\/\ or / or \ EARLIEST HEARD ◢ LATEST HEARD ◣ + TENTATIVE

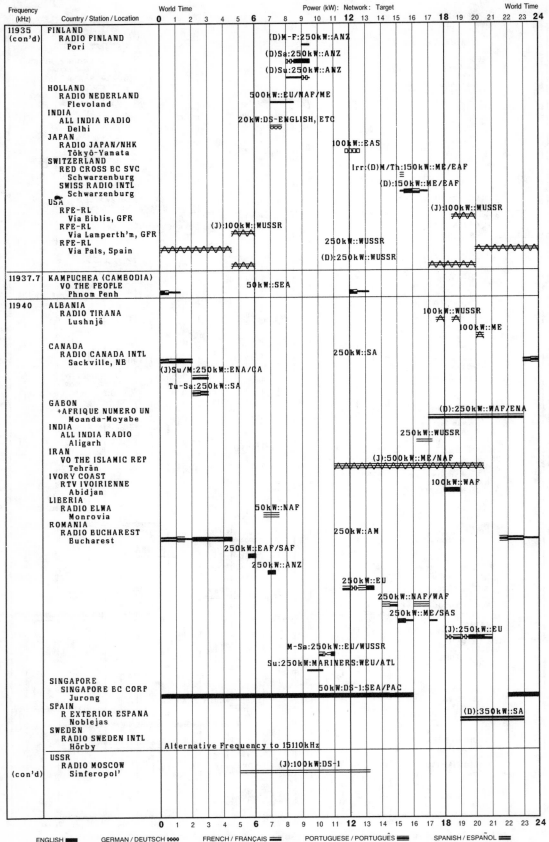

Frequency (kHz)	Country / Station / Location	World Time / Power (kW): Network: Target
11935 (con'd)	FINLAND — RADIO FINLAND, Pori	(D)M-F:250kW::ANZ / (D)Sa:250kW::ANZ / (D)Su:250kW::ANZ
	HOLLAND — RADIO NEDERLAND, Flevoland	500kW::EU/NAF/ME
	INDIA — ALL INDIA RADIO, Delhi	20kW:DS-ENGLISH, ETC
	JAPAN — RADIO JAPAN/NHK, Tōkyō-Yamata	100kW::EAS
	SWITZERLAND — RED CROSS BC SVC, Schwarzenburg	Irr:(D)M/Th:150kW::ME/EAF
	SWISS RADIO INTL, Schwarzenburg	(D):150kW::ME/EAF
	USA — RFE-RL, Via Biblis, GFR	(J):100kW::WUSSR
	RFE-RL, Via Lamperth'm, GFR	(J):100kW::WUSSR
	RFE-RL, Via Pals, Spain	250kW::WUSSR / (D):250kW::WUSSR
11937.7	KAMPUCHEA (CAMBODIA) — VO THE PEOPLE, Phnom Penh	50kW::SEA
11940	ALBANIA — RADIO TIRANA, Lushnjë	100kW::WUSSR / 100kW::ME
	CANADA — RADIO CANADA INTL, Sackville, NB	250kW::SA / (J)Su/M:250kW::ENA/CA / Tu-Sa:250kW::SA
	GABON — +AFRIQUE NUMERO UN, Moanda-Moyabe	(D):250kW::WAF/ENA
	INDIA — ALL INDIA RADIO, Aligarh	250kW::WUSSR
	IRAN — VO THE ISLAMIC REP, Tehrān	(J):500kW::ME/NAF
	IVORY COAST — RTV IVOIRIENNE, Abidjan	100kW::WAF
	LIBERIA — RADIO ELWA, Monrovia	50kW::NAF
	ROMANIA — RADIO BUCHAREST, Bucharest	250kW::AM / 250kW::EAF/SAF / 250kW::ANZ / 250kW::EU / 250kW::NAF/WAF / 250kW::ME/SAS / (J):250kW::EU / M-Sa:250kW::EU/WUSSR / Su:250kW:MARINERS:WEU/ATL
	SINGAPORE — SINGAPORE BC CORP, Jurong	50kW:DS-1:SEA/PAC
	SPAIN — R EXTERIOR ESPANA, Noblejas	(D):350kW::SA
	SWEDEN — RADIO SWEDEN INTL, Hörby	Alternative Frequency to 15110kHz
(con'd)	USSR — RADIO MOSCOW, Simferopol'	(J):100kW:DS-1

ENGLISH ▅ GERMAN / DEUTSCH ▨ FRENCH / FRANÇAIS ▤ PORTUGUESE / PORTUGUÊS ▤ SPANISH / ESPAÑOL ▤
ARABIC /عربى ▤ RUSSIAN / PYCCKИИ ▤ CHINESE / 中文 ▨ JAPANESE / 日本語 ▨ MULTILINGUAL ▨ OTHER ▬
SUMMER ONLY (J) WINTER ONLY (D) JAMMING ∧∧ or / or \ EARLIEST HEARD ◢ LATEST HEARD ◣ + TENTATIVE

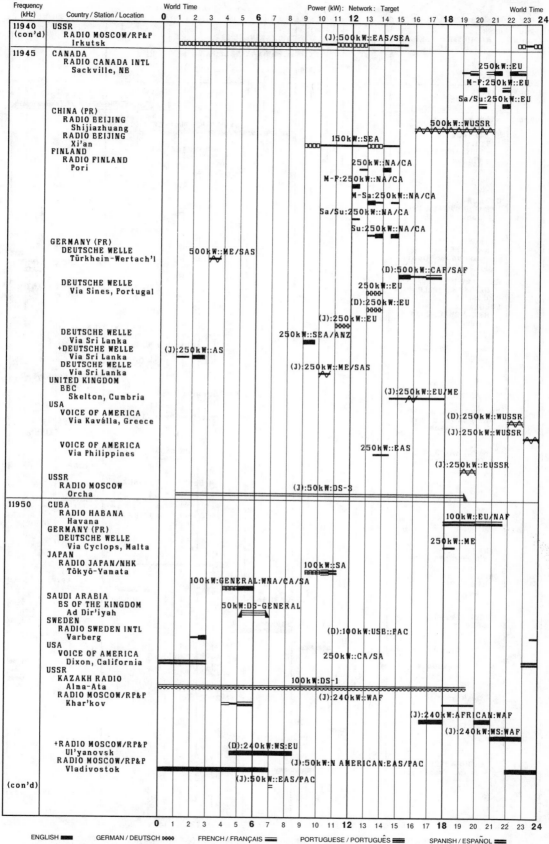

Frequency (kHz)	Country / Station / Location	World Time / Power (kW): Network: Target
11940 (con'd)	USSR RADIO MOSCOW/RP&P Irkutsk	(J):500kW::EAS/SEA
11945	CANADA RADIO CANADA INTL Sackville, NB	250kW::EU M-F:250kW::EU Sa/Su:250kW::EU
	CHINA (PR) RADIO BEIJING Shijiazhuang	500kW::WUSSR
	RADIO BEIJING Xi'an	150kW::SEA
	FINLAND RADIO FINLAND Pori	250kW::NA/CA M-F:250kW::NA/CA M-Sa:250kW::NA/CA Sa/Su:250kW::NA/CA Su:250kW::NA/CA
	GERMANY (FR) DEUTSCHE WELLE Türkheim-Wertach'l	500kW::ME/SAS
	DEUTSCHE WELLE Via Sines, Portugal	(D):500kW::CAF/SAF 250kW::EU (D):250kW::EU (J):250kW::EU
	DEUTSCHE WELLE Via Sri Lanka	250kW::SEA/ANZ
	+DEUTSCHE WELLE Via Sri Lanka	(J):250kW:AS
	DEUTSCHE WELLE Via Sri Lanka	(J):250kW::ME/SAS
	UNITED KINGDOM BBC Skelton, Cumbria	(J):250kW::EU/ME
	USA VOICE OF AMERICA Via Kaválla, Greece	(D):250kW::WUSSR (J):250kW::WUSSR
	VOICE OF AMERICA Via Philippines	250kW::EAS (J):250kW::EUSSR
	USSR RADIO MOSCOW Orcha	(J):50kW:DS-3
11950	CUBA RADIO HABANA Havana	100kW::EU/NAF
	GERMANY (FR) DEUTSCHE WELLE Via Cyclops, Malta	250kW::ME
	JAPAN RADIO JAPAN/NHK Tōkyō-Yamata	100kW::SA 100kW:GENERAL:WNA/CA/SA
	SAUDI ARABIA BS OF THE KINGDOM Ad Dir'iyah	50kW:DS-GENERAL
	SWEDEN RADIO SWEDEN INTL Varberg	(D):100kW:USB::PAC
	USA VOICE OF AMERICA Dixon, California	250kW::CA/SA
	USSR KAZAKH RADIO Alma-Ata	100kW:DS-1
	RADIO MOSCOW/RP&P Khar'kov	(J):240kW::WAF (J):240kW:AFRICAN:WAF (J):240kW:WS:WAF
	+RADIO MOSCOW/RP&P Ul'yanovsk	(D):240kW:WS:EU
	RADIO MOSCOW/RP&P Vladivostok	(J):50kW:N AMERICAN:EAS/PAC (J):50kW::EAS/PAC
(con'd)		

ENGLISH ▬▬ GERMAN / DEUTSCH ▭▭▭ FRENCH / FRANÇAIS ▬▬ PORTUGUESE / PORTUGUÊS ▬▬ SPANISH / ESPAÑOL ▬▬

ARABIC /بﺮﻋ ▬▬ RUSSIAN / РУССКИИ ▬▬ CHINESE / 中文 ▭▭▭ JAPANESE / 日本語 ▬▬▬ MULTILINGUAL ▭▭▭ OTHER ▬▬

SUMMER ONLY (J)   WINTER ONLY (D)   JAMMING ∧∧ or / or \   EARLIEST HEARD ◢   LATEST HEARD ◣   + TENTATIVE

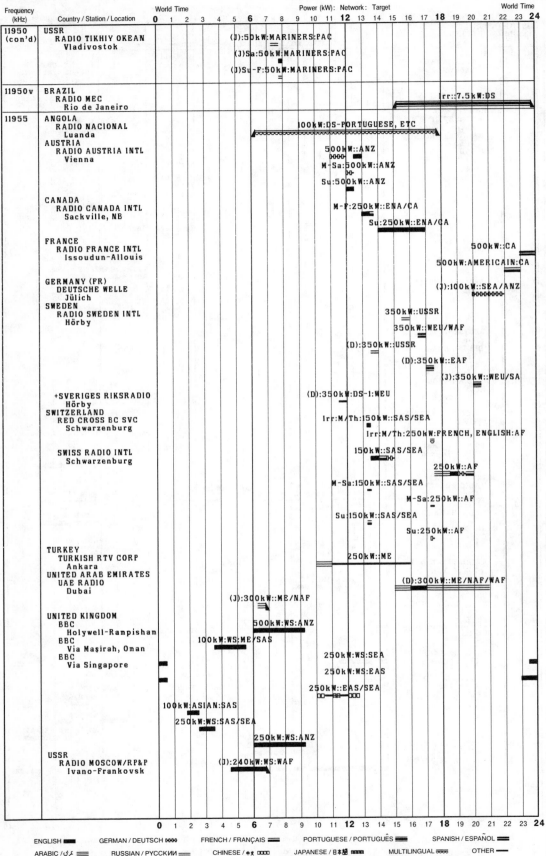

Frequency (kHz)	Country / Station / Location		
11950 (con'd)	USSR RADIO TIKHIY OKEAN Vladivostok	(J):50kW:MARINERS:PAC (J)Sa:50kW:MARINERS:PAC (J)Su-F:50kW:MARINERS:PAC	
11950v	BRAZIL RADIO MEC Rio de Janeiro	Irr::7.5kW:DS	
11955	ANGOLA RADIO NACIONAL Luanda	100kW:DS-PORTUGUESE, ETC	
	AUSTRIA RADIO AUSTRIA INTL Vienna	500kW::ANZ M-Sa:500kW::ANZ Su:500kW::ANZ	
	CANADA RADIO CANADA INTL Sackville, NB	M-F:250kW::ENA/CA Su:250kW::ENA/CA	
	FRANCE RADIO FRANCE INTL Issoudun-Allouis	500kW::CA 500kW::AMERICAIN:CA	
	GERMANY (FR) DEUTSCHE WELLE Jülich	(J):100kW::SEA/ANZ	
	SWEDEN RADIO SWEDEN INTL Hörby	350kW::USSR 350kW::WEU/WAF (D):350kW::USSR (D):350kW::EAF (J):350kW::WEU/SA	
	+SVERIGES RIKSRADIO Hörby	(D):350kW::DS-1:WEU	
	SWITZERLAND RED CROSS BC SVC Schwarzenburg	Irr:M/Th:150kW::SAS/SEA Irr:M/Th:250kW:FRENCH, ENGLISH:AF	
	SWISS RADIO INTL Schwarzenburg	150kW::SAS/SEA 250kW::AF M-Sa:150kW::SAS/SEA M-Sa:250kW::AF Su:150kW::SAS/SEA Su:250kW::AF	
	TURKEY TURKISH RTV CORP Ankara	250kW::ME	
	UNITED ARAB EMIRATES UAE RADIO Dubai	(D):300kW::ME/NAF/WAF (J):300kW::ME/NAF	
	UNITED KINGDOM BBC Holywell-Rampisham	500kW:WS:ANZ	
	BBC Via Maşirah, Oman	100kW:WS:ME/SAS	
	BBC Via Singapore	250kW:WS:SEA 250kW:WS:EAS 250kW::EAS/SEA 100kW:ASIAN:SAS 250kW:WS:SAS/SEA 250kW:WS:ANZ	
	USSR RADIO MOSCOW/RP&P Ivano-Frankovsk	(J):240kW:WS:WAF	

ENGLISH ▬▬   GERMAN / DEUTSCH ◊◊◊◊   FRENCH / FRANÇAIS ≡≡   PORTUGUESE / PORTUGUÊS ≡≡   SPANISH / ESPAÑOL ≡≡

ARABIC /‫عربى‬ ≡≡   RUSSIAN / РУССКИИ ≡≡   CHINESE /中文 ◻◻◻◻   JAPANESE / 日本語 ◙◙◙◙   MULTILINGUAL ◙◙◙◙   OTHER ▬▬

SUMMER ONLY (J)   WINTER ONLY (D)   JAMMING ∧∧ or / or \   EARLIEST HEARD ◢   LATEST HEARD ◣   + TENTATIVE

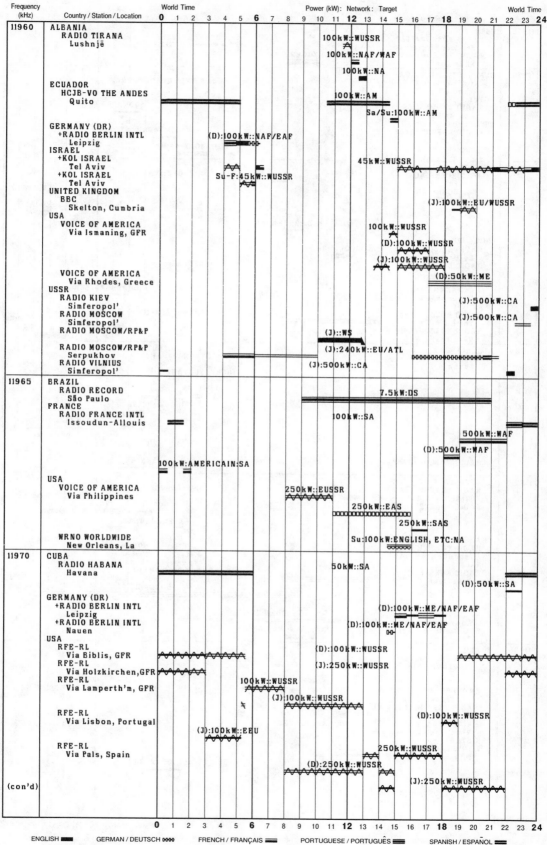

Frequency (kHz)	Country / Station / Location	Details
11960	ALBANIA RADIO TIRANA Lushnjë	100kW::WUSSR / 100kW::NAF/WAF / 100kW::NA
	ECUADOR HCJB-VO THE ANDES Quito	100kW::AM / Sa/Su:100kW::AM
	GERMANY (DR) +RADIO BERLIN INTL Leipzig	(D):100kW::NAF/EAF
	ISRAEL +KOL ISRAEL Tel Aviv	45kW::WUSSR
	+KOL ISRAEL Tel Aviv	Su-F:45kW::WUSSR
	UNITED KINGDOM BBC Skelton, Cumbria	(J):100kW::EU/WUSSR
	USA VOICE OF AMERICA Via Ismaning, GFR	100kW::WUSSR / (D):100kW::WUSSR / (J):100kW::WUSSR
	VOICE OF AMERICA Via Rhodes, Greece	(D):50kW::ME
	USSR RADIO KIEV Simferopol'	(J):500kW::CA
	RADIO MOSCOW Simferopol'	(J):500kW::CA
	RADIO MOSCOW/RP&P	(J)::WS
	RADIO MOSCOW/RP&P Serpukhov	(J):240kW::EU/ATL
	RADIO VILNIUS Simferopol'	(J):500kW::CA
11965	BRAZIL RADIO RECORD São Paulo	7.5kW:DS
	FRANCE RADIO FRANCE INTL Issoudun-Allouis	100kW::SA / 500kW::WAF / (D):500kW::WAF / 100kW:AMERICAIN:SA
	USA VOICE OF AMERICA Via Philippines	250kW::EUSSR / 250kW::EAS / 250kW::SAS
	WRNO WORLDWIDE New Orleans, La	Su:100kW:ENGLISH, ETC:NA
11970	CUBA RADIO HABANA Havana	50kW::SA / (D):50kW::SA
	GERMANY (DR) +RADIO BERLIN INTL Leipzig	(D):100kW::ME/NAF/EAF
	+RADIO BERLIN INTL Nauen	(D):100kW::ME/NAF/EAF
	USA RFE-RL Via Biblis, GFR	(D):100kW::WUSSR
	RFE-RL Via Holzkirchen,GFR	(J):250kW::WUSSR
	RFE-RL Via Lamperth'm, GFR	100kW::WUSSR / (J):100kW::WUSSR
	RFE-RL Via Lisbon, Portugal	(D):100kW::WUSSR
	RFE-RL Via Pals, Spain	(J):100kW::EEU / 250kW::WUSSR / (D):250kW::WUSSR / (J):250kW::WUSSR
(con'd)		

ENGLISH ▬▬ GERMAN / DEUTSCH ◘◘◘◘ FRENCH / FRANÇAIS ▬▬ PORTUGUESE / PORTUGUÊS ▬▬ SPANISH / ESPAÑOL ▬▬

ARABIC / عربى ▬▬ RUSSIAN / РУССКИИ ▬▬ CHINESE / 中文 ◘◘◘◘ JAPANESE / 日本語 ▬▬ MULTILINGUAL ◘◘◘◘ OTHER ▬▬

SUMMER ONLY (J)   WINTER ONLY (D)   JAMMING /\/\ or / or \   EARLIEST HEARD ◢   LATEST HEARD ◣   + TENTATIVE

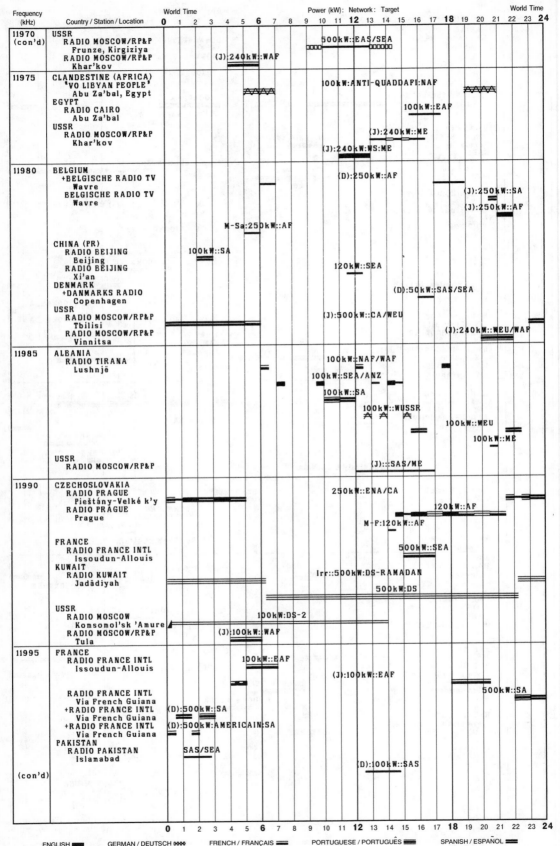

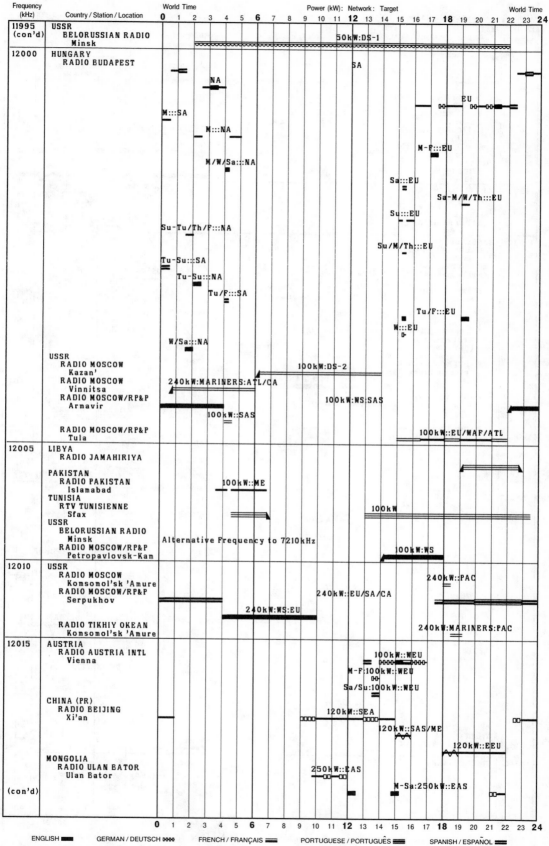

Frequency (kHz)	Country / Station / Location		0 1 2 3 4 5 6 7 8 9 10 11 12 13 14 15 16 17 18 19 20 21 22 23 24

Power (kW): Network: Target

11995 (con'd) — USSR — BELORUSSIAN RADIO — Minsk — 50kW:DS-1

12000 — HUNGARY — RADIO BUDAPEST
- SA
- NA
- M:::SA
- M:::NA
- M/W/Sa:::NA
- M-F:::EU
- Sa:::EU
- Sa-M/W/Th:::EU
- Su:::EU
- Su-Tu/Th/F:::NA
- Su/M/Th:::EU
- Tu-Su:::SA
- Tu-Su:::NA
- Tu/F:::SA
- Tu/F:::EU
- W:::EU
- W/Sa:::NA
- EU

USSR
- RADIO MOSCOW — Kazan' — 100kW:DS-2
- RADIO MOSCOW — Vinnitsa — 240kW:MARINERS:ATL/CA
- RADIO MOSCOW/RP&P — Armavir — 100kW:WS:SAS
- 100kW::SAS
- RADIO MOSCOW/RP&P — Tula — 100kW::EU/WAF/ATL

12005 — LIBYA — RADIO JAMAHIRIYA

PAKISTAN — RADIO PAKISTAN — Islamabad — 100kW::ME

TUNISIA — RTV TUNISIENNE — Sfax — 100kW

USSR — BELORUSSIAN RADIO — Minsk — Alternative Frequency to 7210kHz

RADIO MOSCOW/RP&P — Petropavlovsk-Kam — 100kW:WS

12010 — USSR
- RADIO MOSCOW — Komsomol'sk 'Amure — 240kW::PAC
- RADIO MOSCOW/RP&P — Serpukhov — 240kW::EU/SA/CA
- 240kW:WS:EU
- RADIO TIKHIY OKEAN — Komsomol'sk 'Amure — 240kW:MARINERS:PAC

12015 — AUSTRIA — RADIO AUSTRIA INTL — Vienna
- 100kW::WEU
- M-F:100kW::WEU
- Sa/Su:100kW::WEU

CHINA (PR) — RADIO BEIJING — Xi'an
- 120kW::SEA
- 120kW::SAS/ME
- 120kW::EEU

MONGOLIA — RADIO ULAN BATOR — Ulan Bator
- 250kW::CAS
- M-Sa:250kW::EAS

(con'd)

	0 1 2 3 4 5 6 7 8 9 10 11 12 13 14 15 16 17 18 19 20 21 22 23 24

ENGLISH ▬▬   GERMAN / DEUTSCH ◊◊◊◊   FRENCH / FRANÇAIS ▬▬   PORTUGUESE / PORTUGUÊS ▬▬   SPANISH / ESPAÑOL ▬▬

ARABIC / ‮عربى‬ ≡≡   RUSSIAN / РУССКИИ ═══   CHINESE / 中文 □□□□   JAPANESE / 日本語 ▨▨▨▨   MULTILINGUAL ▭▭▭▭   OTHER ▬▬

SUMMER ONLY (J)   WINTER ONLY (D)   JAMMING /\/\ or / or \   EARLIEST HEARD ◢   LATEST HEARD ◣   + TENTATIVE

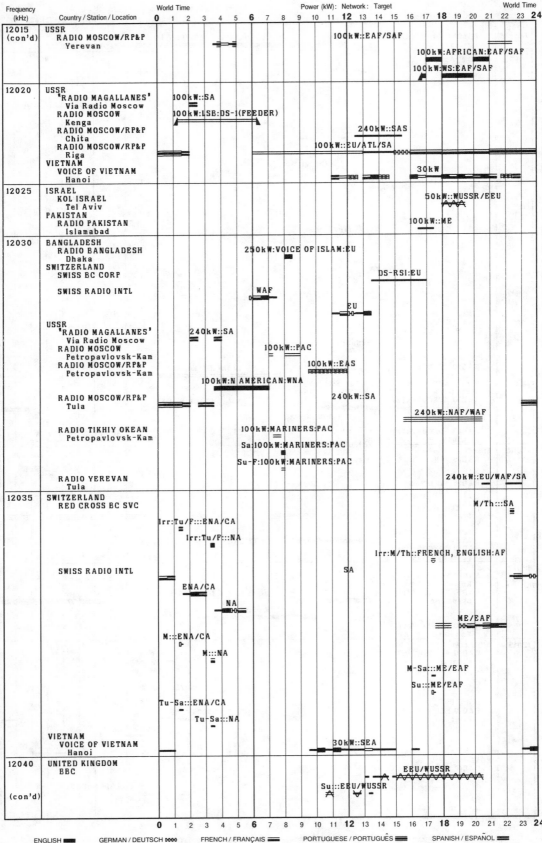

Frequency (kHz)	Country / Station / Location	World Time	Power (kW): Network: Target	World Time

12015 (con'd) — USSR — RADIO MOSCOW/RP&P — Yerevan — 100kW::EAF/SAF — 100kW:AFRICAN:EAF/SAF — 100kW:WS:EAF/SAF

12020 — USSR — 'RADIO MAGALLANES' Via Radio Moscow — 100kW::SA — RADIO MOSCOW Kenga — 100kW:LSB:DS-1(FEEDER) — RADIO MOSCOW/RP&P Chita — 240kW::SAS — RADIO MOSCOW/RP&P Riga — 100kW::EU/ATL/SA — VIETNAM — VOICE OF VIETNAM Hanoi — 30kW

12025 — ISRAEL — KOL ISRAEL Tel Aviv — 50kW::WUSSR/EEU — PAKISTAN — RADIO PAKISTAN Islamabad — 100kW::ME

12030 — BANGLADESH — RADIO BANGLADESH Dhaka — 250kW:VOICE OF ISLAM:EU — SWITZERLAND — SWISS BC CORP — DS-RSI:EU — SWISS RADIO INTL — WAF — EU — USSR — 'RADIO MAGALLANES' Via Radio Moscow — 240kW::SA — RADIO MOSCOW Petropavlovsk-Kam — 100kW::PAC — RADIO MOSCOW/RP&P Petropavlovsk-Kam — 100kW::EAS — 100kW:N AMERICAN:WNA — RADIO MOSCOW/RP&P Tula — 240kW::SA — 240kW::NAF/WAF — RADIO TIKHIY OKEAN Petropavlovsk-Kam — 100kW:MARINERS:PAC — Sa:100kW:MARINERS:PAC — Su-F:100kW:MARINERS:PAC — RADIO YEREVAN Tula — 240kW::EU/WAF/SA

12035 — SWITZERLAND — RED CROSS BC SVC — M/Th:::SA — Irr:Tu/F:::ENA/CA — Irr:Tu/F:::NA — Irr:M/Th::FRENCH, ENGLISH:AF — SWISS RADIO INTL — SA — ENA/CA — NA — ME/EAF — M:::ENA/CA — M:::NA — M-Sa:::ME/EAF — Su:::ME/EAF — Tu-Sa:::ENA/CA — Tu-Sa:::NA — VIETNAM — VOICE OF VIETNAM Hanoi — 30kW::SEA

12040 (con'd) — UNITED KINGDOM — BBC — EEU/WUSSR — Su:::EEU/WUSSR

ENGLISH ▬ GERMAN / DEUTSCH ∞∞∞ FRENCH / FRANÇAIS ▭▭▭ PORTUGUESE / PORTUGUÊS ≡≡≡ SPANISH / ESPAÑOL ▬

ARABIC / عربى ≣ RUSSIAN / РУССКИИ ═══ CHINESE / 中文 □□□□ JAPANESE / 日本語 ▬▬▬ MULTILINGUAL ∞∞∞ OTHER ▬

SUMMER ONLY (J) WINTER ONLY (D) JAMMING /\/\ or / or \ EARLIEST HEARD ◢ LATEST HEARD ◣ + TENTATIVE

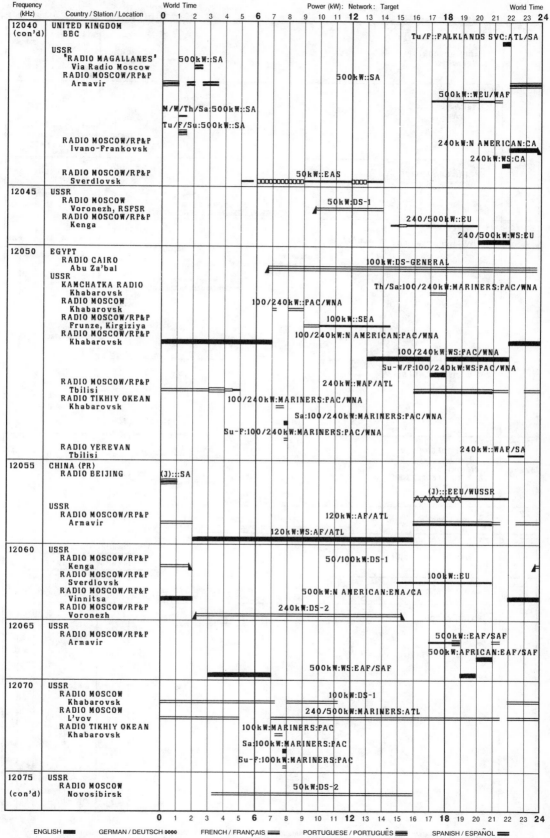

| Frequency (kHz) | Country / Station / Location | Power (kW) : Network : Target |

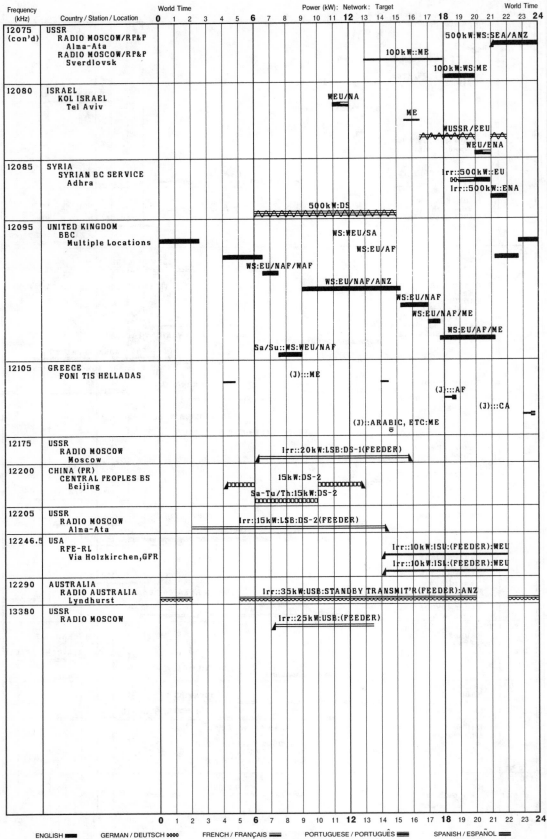

Frequency (kHz)	Country / Station / Location
12075 (con'd)	USSR — RADIO MOSCOW/RP&P Alma-Ata; 500kW:WS:SEA/ANZ. RADIO MOSCOW/RP&P Sverdlovsk; 100kW::ME; 100kW:WS:ME
12080	ISRAEL — KOL ISRAEL Tel Aviv; WEU/NA; ME; WUSSR/EEU; WEU/ENA
12085	SYRIA — SYRIAN BC SERVICE Adhra; Irr::500kW::EU; Irr::500kW::ENA; 500kW:DS
12095	UNITED KINGDOM — BBC Multiple Locations; WS:WEU/SA; WS:EU/AF; WS:EU/NAF/WAF; WS:EU/NAF/ANZ; WS:EU/NAF; WS:EU/NAF/ME; WS:EU/AF/ME; Sa/Su::WS:WEU/NAF
12105	GREECE — FONI TIS HELLADAS; (J):::ME; (J):::AF; (J)::CA; (J)::ARABIC, ETC:ME
12175	USSR — RADIO MOSCOW Moscow; Irr::20kW:LSB:DS-1(FEEDER)
12200	CHINA (PR) — CENTRAL PEOPLES BS Beijing; 15kW:DS-2; Sa-Tu/Th:15kW:DS-2
12205	USSR — RADIO MOSCOW Alma-Ata; Irr::15kW:LSB:DS-2(FEEDER)
12246.5	USA — RFE-RL Via Holzkirchen,GFR; Irr::10kW:ISU:(FEEDER):WEU; Irr::10kW:ISL:(FEEDER):WEU
12290	AUSTRALIA — RADIO AUSTRALIA Lyndhurst; Irr::35kW:USB:STANDBY TRANSMIT'R(FEEDER):ANZ
13380	USSR — RADIO MOSCOW; Irr::25kW:USB:(FEEDER)

Power (kW): Network: Target

World Time: 0 1 2 3 4 5 6 7 8 9 10 11 12 13 14 15 16 17 18 19 20 21 22 23 24

ENGLISH ▬▬   GERMAN / DEUTSCH ০০০০   FRENCH / FRANÇAIS ▬▬   PORTUGUESE / PORTUGUÊS ▬▬   SPANISH / ESPAÑOL ▬▬
ARABIC / عربي ▬▬   RUSSIAN / РУССКИЙ ▬▬   CHINESE / 中文 ০০০০   JAPANESE / 日本語 ▬▬   MULTILINGUAL ০০০০   OTHER ▬▬
SUMMER ONLY (J)   WINTER ONLY (D)   JAMMING /\/\ or / or \   EARLIEST HEARD ◢   LATEST HEARD ◣   + TENTATIVE

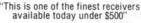

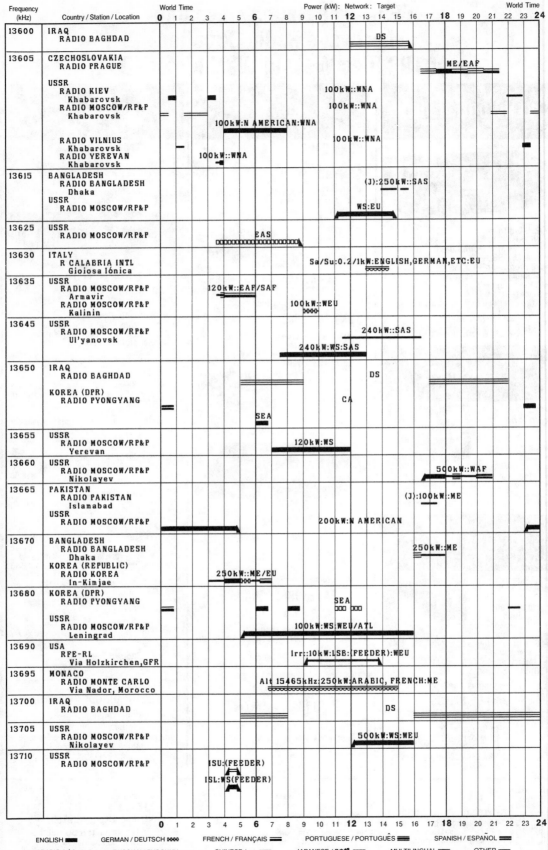

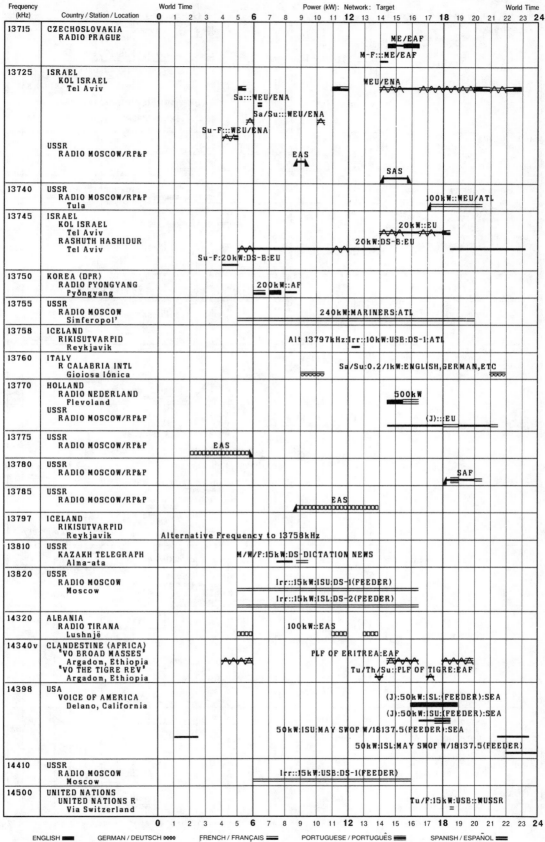

Frequency (kHz)	Country / Station / Location	0	1	2	3	4	5	6	7	8	9	10	11	12	13	14	15	16	17	18	19	20	21	22	23	24

13715 CZECHOSLOVAKIA RADIO PRAGUE — ME/EAF; M-F:::ME/EAF

13725 ISRAEL KOL ISRAEL Tel Aviv — Sa:::WEU/ENA; Sa/Su:::WEU/ENA; Su-F:::WEU/ENA; WEU/ENA
USSR RADIO MOSCOW/RP&P — EAS; SAS

13740 USSR RADIO MOSCOW/RP&P Tula — 100kW::WEU/ATL

13745 ISRAEL KOL ISRAEL Tel Aviv — 20kW::EU
RASHUTH HASHIDUR Tel Aviv — 20kW:DS-B:EU; Su-F:20kW:DS-B:EU

13750 KOREA (DPR) RADIO PYONGYANG Pyŏngyang — 200kW::AF

13755 USSR RADIO MOSCOW Simferopol' — 240kW:MARINERS:ATL

13758 ICELAND RIKISUTVARPID Reykjavik — Alt 13797kHz:Irr::10kW:USB:DS-1:ATL

13760 ITALY R CALABRIA INTL Gioiosa Iónica — Sa/Su:0.2/1kW:ENGLISH,GERMAN,ETC

13770 HOLLAND RADIO NEDERLAND Flevoland — 500kW
USSR RADIO MOSCOW/RP&P — (J):::EU

13775 USSR RADIO MOSCOW/RP&P — EAS

13780 USSR RADIO MOSCOW/RP&P — SAF

13785 USSR RADIO MOSCOW/RP&P — EAS

13797 ICELAND RIKISUTVARPID Reykjavik — Alternative Frequency to 13758kHz

13810 USSR KAZAKH TELEGRAPH Alma-ata — M/W/F:15kW:DS-DICTATION NEWS

13820 USSR RADIO MOSCOW Moscow — Irr::15kW:ISU:DS-1(FEEDER); Irr::15kW:ISL:DS-2(FEEDER)

14320 ALBANIA RADIO TIRANA Lushnjë — 100kW::EAS

14340v CLANDESTINE (AFRICA) "VO BROAD MASSES" Argadom, Ethiopia — PLF OF ERITREA:EAF
"VO THE TIGRE REV" Argadom, Ethiopia — Tu/Th/Su:PLF OF TIGRE:EAF

14398 USA VOICE OF AMERICA Delano, California — (J):50kW:ISL:(FEEDER):SEA; (J):50kW:ISU:(FEEDER):SEA; 50kW:ISU:MAY SWOP W/18137.5(FEEDER):SEA; 50kW:ISL:MAY SWOP W/18137.5(FEEDER)

14410 USSR RADIO MOSCOW Moscow — Irr::15kW:USB:DS-1(FEEDER)

14500 UNITED NATIONS UNITED NATIONS R Via Switzerland — Tu/F:15kW:USB::WUSSR

| | | 0 | 1 | 2 | 3 | 4 | 5 | 6 | 7 | 8 | 9 | 10 | 11 | 12 | 13 | 14 | 15 | 16 | 17 | 18 | 19 | 20 | 21 | 22 | 23 | 24 |

ENGLISH ▰▰▰   GERMAN / DEUTSCH ०००o   FRENCH / FRANÇAIS ▭▭▭   PORTUGUESE / PORTUGUÊS ▰▰▰   SPANISH / ESPAÑOL ▰▰▰

ARABIC /ﻉﺭﺏ ▰▰▰   RUSSIAN / РУССКИИ ▰▰▰   CHINESE / 中文 ००००   JAPANESE / 日本語 ▰▰▰   MULTILINGUAL ००००   OTHER ▬▬

SUMMER ONLY (J)   WINTER ONLY (D)   JAMMING /\/\ or / or \   EARLIEST HEARD ◢   LATEST HEARD ◣   + TENTATIVE

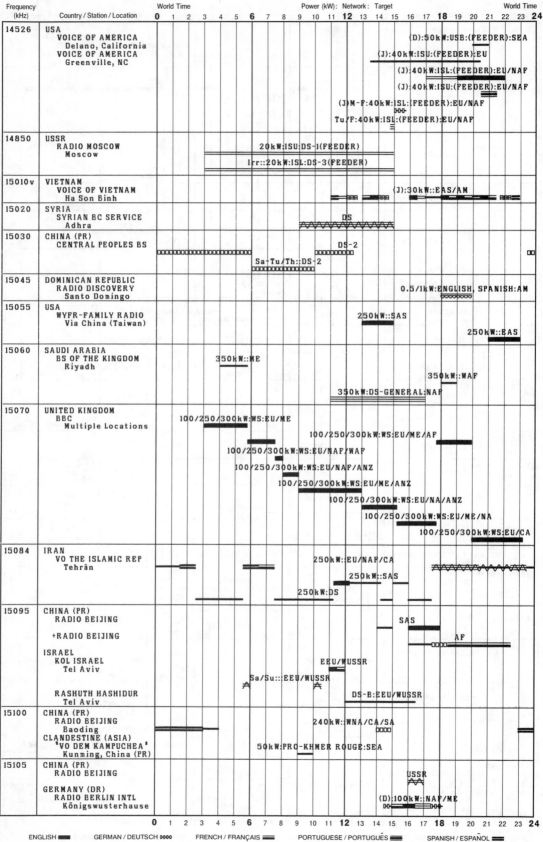

Frequency
(kHz)   Country / Station / Location

14526 USA
       VOICE OF AMERICA
         Delano, California
       VOICE OF AMERICA
         Greenville, NC
       (D):50kW:USB:(FEEDER):SEA
       (J):40kW:ISU:(FEEDER):EU
       (J):40kW:ISL:(FEEDER):EU/NAF
       (J):40kW:ISU:(FEEDER):EU/NAF
       (J)M–F:40kW:ISL:(FEEDER):EU/NAF
       Tu/F:40kW:ISL:(FEEDER):EU/NAF

14850 USSR
       RADIO MOSCOW
         Moscow
       20kW:ISU:DS–1(FEEDER)
       Irr::20kW:ISL:DS–3(FEEDER)

15010v VIETNAM
       VOICE OF VIETNAM
         Ha Son Binh
       (J):30kW::EAS/AM

15020 SYRIA
       SYRIAN BC SERVICE
         Adhra
       DS

15030 CHINA (PR)
       CENTRAL PEOPLES BS
       DS–2
       Sa–Tu/Th::DS–2

15045 DOMINICAN REPUBLIC
       RADIO DISCOVERY
         Santo Domingo
       0.5/1kW:ENGLISH, SPANISH:AM

15055 USA
       WYFR–FAMILY RADIO
         Via China (Taiwan)
       250kW::SAS
       250kW::EAS

15060 SAUDI ARABIA
       BS OF THE KINGDOM
         Riyadh
       350kW::ME
       350kW::WAF
       350kW:DS–GENERAL:NAF

15070 UNITED KINGDOM
       BBC
         Multiple Locations
       100/250/300kW:WS:EU/ME
       100/250/300kW:WS:EU/ME/AF
       100/250/300kW:WS:EU/NAF/WAF
       100/250/300kW:WS:EU/NAF/ANZ
       100/250/300kW:WS:EU/ME/ANZ
       100/250/300kW:WS:EU/NA/ANZ
       100/250/300kW:WS:EU/ME/NA
       100/250/300kW:WS:EU/CA

15084 IRAN
       VO THE ISLAMIC REP
         Tehrān
       250kW::EU/NAF/CA
       250kW::SAS
       250kW:DS

15095 CHINA (PR)
       RADIO BEIJING
       SAS
       +RADIO BEIJING
       AF
       ISRAEL
       KOL ISRAEL
         Tel Aviv
       EEU/WUSSR
       Sa/Su:::EEU/WUSSR
       RASHUTH HASHIDUR
         Tel Aviv
       DS–B:EEU/WUSSR

15100 CHINA (PR)
       RADIO BEIJING
         Baoding
       240kW::WNA/CA/SA
       CLANDESTINE (ASIA)
       'VO DEM KAMPUCHEA'
         Kunming, China (PR)
       50kW:PRO–KHMER ROUGE:SEA

15105 CHINA (PR)
       RADIO BEIJING
       USSR
       GERMANY (DR)
       RADIO BERLIN INTL
         Königswusterhause
       (D):100kW::NAF/ME

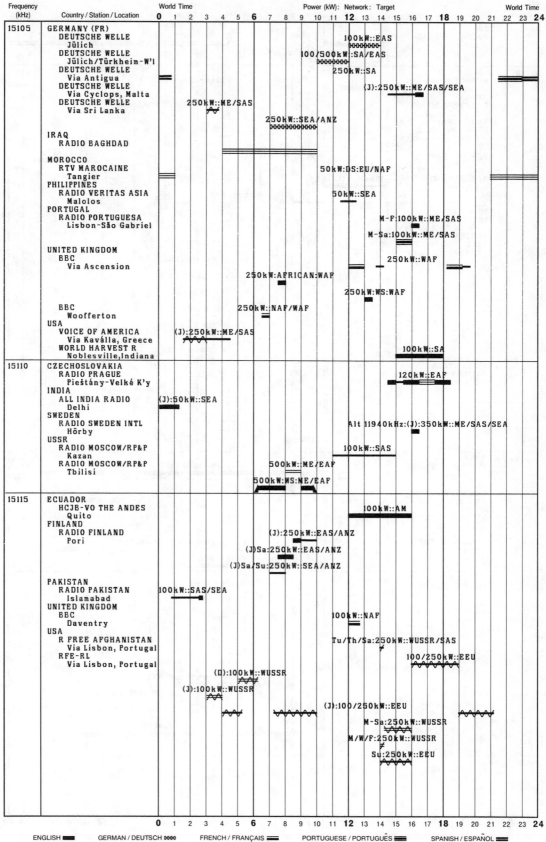

Frequency (kHz)	Country / Station / Location	Schedule

15105

GERMANY (FR)
- DEUTSCHE WELLE / Jülich — 100kW::EAS
- DEUTSCHE WELLE / Jülich/Türkheim-W'l — 100/500kW::SA/EAS
- DEUTSCHE WELLE / Via Antigua — 250kW::SA
- DEUTSCHE WELLE / Via Cyclops, Malta — (J):250kW::ME/SAS/SEA
- DEUTSCHE WELLE / Via Sri Lanka — 250kW::ME/SAS
- 250kW::SEA/ANZ

IRAQ
- RADIO BAGHDAD

MOROCCO
- RTV MAROCAINE / Tangier — 50kW:DS:EU/NAF

PHILIPPINES
- RADIO VERITAS ASIA / Malolos — 50kW::SEA

PORTUGAL
- RADIO PORTUGUESA / Lisbon-São Gabriel — M-F:100kW::ME/SAS
- M-Sa:100kW::ME/SAS

UNITED KINGDOM
- BBC / Via Ascension — 250kW::WAF
- 250kW:AFRICAN:WAF
- 250kW:WS:WAF
- BBC / Woofferton — 250kW::NAF/WAF

USA
- VOICE OF AMERICA / Via Kaválla, Greece — (J):250kW::ME/SAS
- WORLD HARVEST R / Noblesville,Indiana — 100kW::SA

15110

CZECHOSLOVAKIA
- RADIO PRAGUE / Pieštány-Velké K'y — 120kW::EAF

INDIA
- ALL INDIA RADIO / Delhi — (J):50kW::SEA

SWEDEN
- RADIO SWEDEN INTL / Hörby — Alt 11940kHz:(J):350kW::ME/SAS/SEA

USSR
- RADIO MOSCOW/RP&P / Kazan — 100kW::SAS
- RADIO MOSCOW/RP&P / Tbilisi — 500kW::ME/EAF
- 500kW:WS:NE/EAF

15115

ECUADOR
- HCJB-VO THE ANDES / Quito — 100kW::AM

FINLAND
- RADIO FINLAND / Pori — (J):250kW::EAS/ANZ
- (J)Sa:250kW::EAS/ANZ
- (J)Sa/Su:250kW::SEA/ANZ

PAKISTAN
- RADIO PAKISTAN / Islamabad — 100kW::SAS/SEA

UNITED KINGDOM
- BBC / Daventry — 100kW::NAF

USA
- R FREE AFGHANISTAN / Via Lisbon, Portugal — Tu/Th/Sa:250kW::WUSSR/SAS
- RFE-RL / Via Lisbon, Portugal — 100/250kW::EEU
- (D):100kW::WUSSR
- (J):100kW::WUSSR
- (J):100/250kW::EEU
- M-Sa:250kW::WUSSR
- M/W/F:250kW::WUSSR
- Su:250kW::EEU

ENGLISH ▬▬ GERMAN / DEUTSCH ◊◊◊◊ FRENCH / FRANÇAIS ═══ PORTUGUESE / PORTUGUÊS ▬▬ SPANISH / ESPAÑOL ▬▬

ARABIC / ﻉﻒﻉ ≡≡ RUSSIAN / РУССКИИ ═══ CHINESE / ✳✳ ▢▢▢▢ JAPANESE / 日本語 ▬▬▬ MULTILINGUAL ▭▭▭ OTHER ▬▬

SUMMER ONLY (J) WINTER ONLY (D) JAMMING ∧∧ or / or \ EARLIEST HEARD ◢ LATEST HEARD ◥ + TENTATIVE

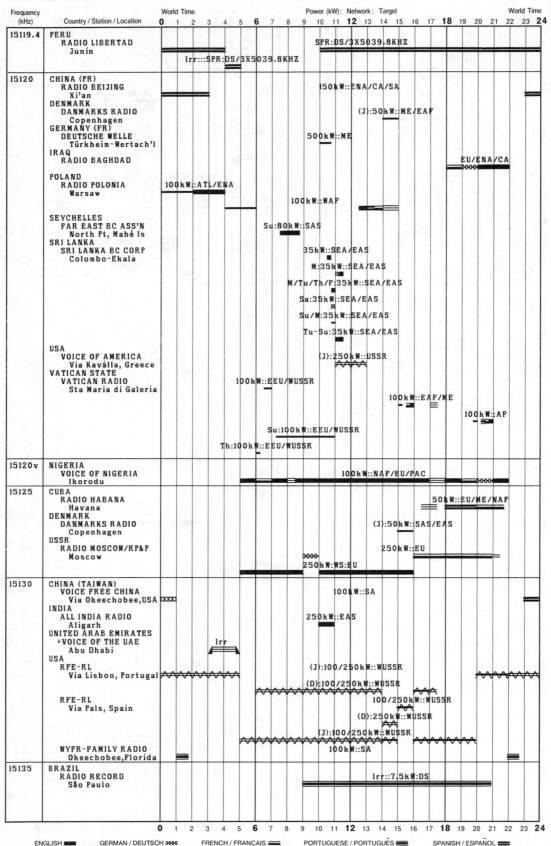

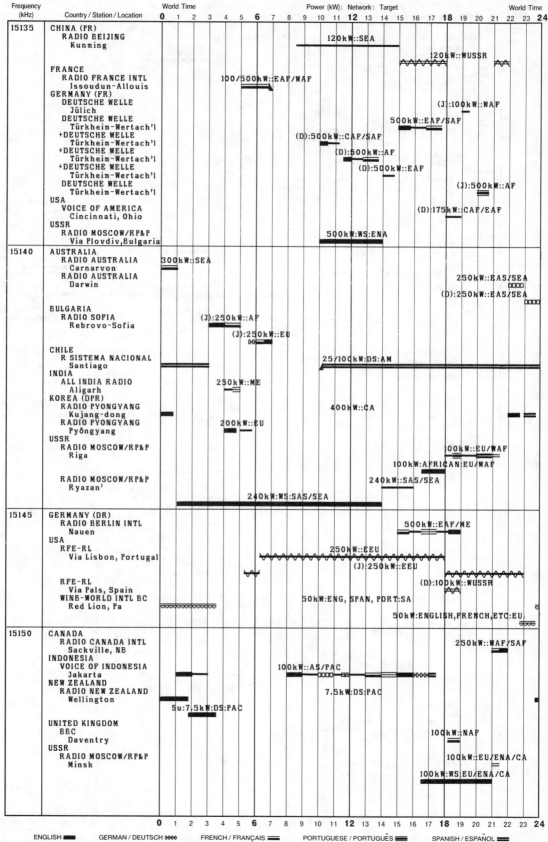

Frequency (kHz)	Country / Station / Location	Power (kW): Network: Target
15135	CHINA (PR) RADIO BEIJING Kunming	120kW::SEA / 120kW::WUSSR
	FRANCE RADIO FRANCE INTL Issoudun-Allouis	100/500kW::EAF/WAF
	GERMANY (FR) DEUTSCHE WELLE Jülich	(J):100kW::WAF
	DEUTSCHE WELLE Türkheim-Wertach'l	500kW::EAF/SAF
	+DEUTSCHE WELLE Türkheim-Wertach'l	(D):500kW::CAF/SAF
	+DEUTSCHE WELLE Türkheim-Wertach'l	(D):500kW::AF
	+DEUTSCHE WELLE Türkheim-Wertach'l	(D):500kW::EAF
	DEUTSCHE WELLE Türkheim-Wertach'l	(J):500kW::AF
	USA VOICE OF AMERICA Cincinnati, Ohio	(D):175kW::CAF/EAF
	USSR RADIO MOSCOW/RP&P Via Plovdiv, Bulgaria	500kW:WS:ENA
15140	AUSTRALIA RADIO AUSTRALIA Carnarvon	300kW::SEA
	RADIO AUSTRALIA Darwin	250kW::EAS/SEA / (D):250kW::EAS/SEA
	BULGARIA RADIO SOFIA Rebrovo-Sofia	(J):250kW::AF / (J):250kW::EU
	CHILE R SISTEMA NACIONAL Santiago	25/100kW:DS:AM
	INDIA ALL INDIA RADIO Aligarh	250kW::ME
	KOREA (DPR) RADIO PYONGYANG Kujang-dong	400kW::CA
	RADIO PYONGYANG Pyŏngyang	200kW::EU
	USSR RADIO MOSCOW/RP&P Riga	100kW::EU/WAF / 100kW:AFRICAN:EU/WAF
	RADIO MOSCOW/RP&P Ryazan'	240kW::SAS/SEA / 240kW:WS:SAS/SEA
15145	GERMANY (DR) RADIO BERLIN INTL Nauen	500kW::EAF/ME
	USA RFE-RL Via Lisbon, Portugal	250kW::EEU / (J):250kW::EEU
	RFE-RL Via Pals, Spain	(D):100kW::WUSSR
	WINB-WORLD INTL BC Red Lion, Pa	50kW:ENG, SPAN, PORT:SA / 50kW:ENGLISH,FRENCH,ETC:EU
15150	CANADA RADIO CANADA INTL Sackville, NB	250kW::WAF/SAF
	INDONESIA VOICE OF INDONESIA Jakarta	100kW::AS/PAC
	NEW ZEALAND RADIO NEW ZEALAND Wellington	7.5kW:DS:PAC / Su:7.5kW:DS:PAC
	UNITED KINGDOM BBC Daventry	100kW::NAF
	USSR RADIO MOSCOW/RP&P Minsk	100kW::EU/ENA/CA / 100kW:WS:EU/ENA/CA

ENGLISH ▪▪▪   GERMAN / DEUTSCH ◊◊◊◊   FRENCH / FRANÇAIS ══   PORTUGUESE / PORTUGUÊS ▤▤   SPANISH / ESPAÑOL ══

ARABIC / ﺏﺮﻋ ═══   RUSSIAN / РУССКИИ ═══   CHINESE / 中文 ◊◊◊◊   JAPANESE / 日本語 ▦▦   MULTILINGUAL ∞∞   OTHER ──

SUMMER ONLY (J)   WINTER ONLY (D)   JAMMING ∧∧ or / or \   EARLIEST HEARD ◢   LATEST HEARD ◣   + TENTATIVE

Frequency (kHz) / Country / Station / Location	Schedule (World Time)
15150 USSR — RADIO MOSCOW/RP&P — Multiple Locations	240/500kW::EAF/EU/ATL; 240/500kW:WS:EAF/EU/ATL
15155 BRAZIL — RADIO NACIONAL — Brasília	250kW::EU
DENMARK — DANMARKS RADIO — Copenhagen	(J)M-F:50kW:DS:EU/WAF
ECUADOR — HCJB-VO THE ANDES — Quito	100kW::NA/CA
EGYPT — RADIO CAIRO — Kafr Silim-Abis	250kW::EAF
FRANCE — RADIO FRANCE INTL — Issoudun-Allouis	100kW::EAF
USA — VOICE OF AMERICA — Via Philippines	250kW::EAS; (J):50kW::SEA
USSR — RADIO MOSCOW/RP&P — Chita	500kW::EAS; 500kW:WS:EAS/ANZ
15160 ALGERIA — RTV ALGERIENNE — Algiers	100kW:DS:ME/WUSSR
AUSTRALIA — RADIO AUSTRALIA — Shepparton	100kW::PAC/EAS; 100kW::PAC
CANADA — RADIO CANADA INTL — Via Sines, Portugal	250kW::EEU/WUSSR
ECUADOR — HCJB-VO THE ANDES — Quito	100kW::CA/WNA
GERMANY (FR) — DEUTSCHE WELLE — Jülich	100kW::SEA/ANZ
GERMANY (FR) — DEUTSCHE WELLE — Via Sines, Portugal	(J):250kW::EEU
HUNGARY — RADIO BUDAPEST — Szekésfehérvár	20kW::SEA/ANZ; 20kW::EU; M-F:20kW::EU; M-F:20kW::SEA/ANZ; M-Sa:20kW::EU; Sa:20kW::EU; Sa/Su:20kW::EU; Su:20kW::EU; Su-F:20kW::EU
INDIA — ALL INDIA RADIO — Delhi	100kW:DS:ENGLISH, ETC
KOREA (DPR) — RADIO PYONGYANG — Kujang-dong	400kW::CA; 200kW::EAS; 200kW::SEA
TURKEY — TURKISH RTV CORP — Ankara	(J)::ME
USA — VOICE OF AMERICA — Greenville, NC	M-F:250kW:FEED:CA/SA
USA — VOICE OF AMERICA — Via Kaválla, Greece	(J):250kW::SAS
USA — VOICE OF AMERICA — Via Philippines	50kW::SAS/SEA
USA — VOICE OF THE OAS — Cincinnati, Ohio	250kW::CA/SA

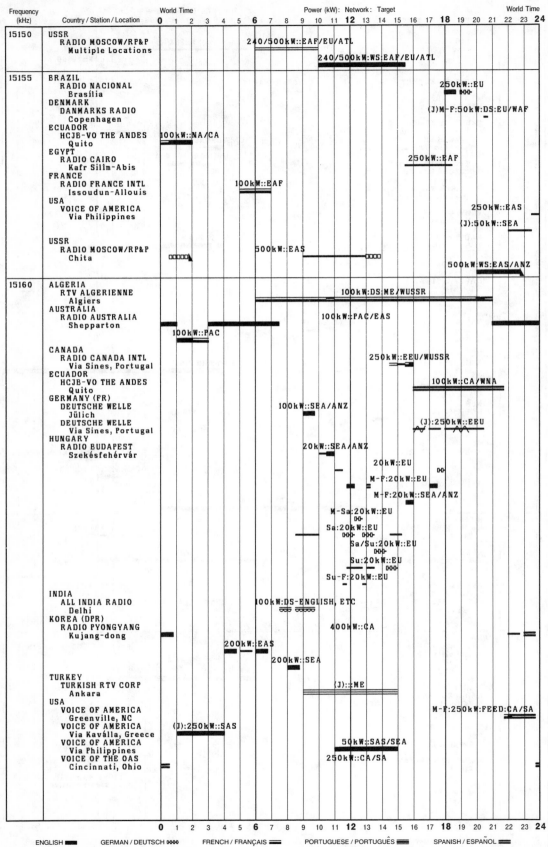

ENGLISH ▬▬   GERMAN / DEUTSCH ◊◊◊◊   FRENCH / FRANÇAIS ═══   PORTUGUESE / PORTUGUÊS ▓▓▓   SPANISH / ESPAÑOL ▬▬

ARABIC / ﺔﻴﺑﺮﻋ ▬▬   RUSSIAN / РУССКИИ ═══   CHINESE / 中文 ◊◊◊◊   JAPANESE / 日本語 ▓▓▓   MULTILINGUAL ▒▒▒   OTHER ▬

SUMMER ONLY (J)   WINTER ONLY (D)   JAMMING ∧∧ or / or \   EARLIEST HEARD ◢   LATEST HEARD ◣   + TENTATIVE

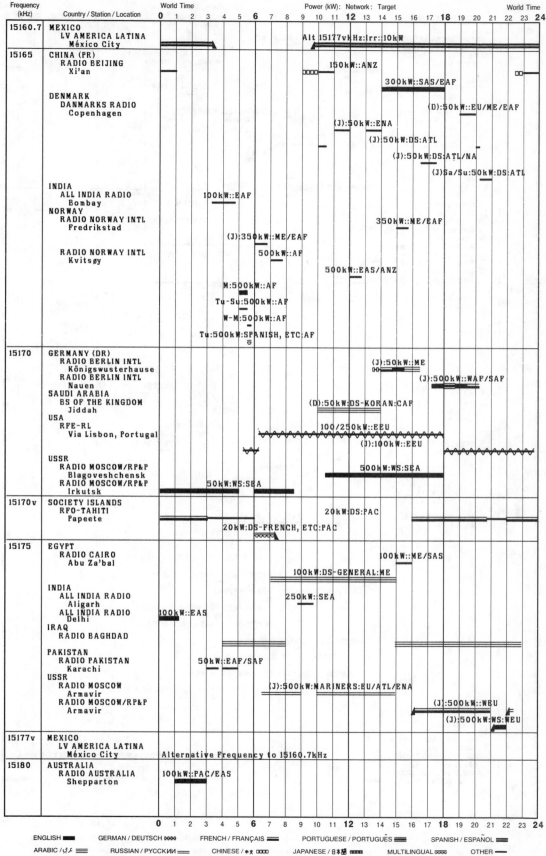

ENGLISH ▬ **GERMAN / DEUTSCH** ▭▭▭ **FRENCH / FRANÇAIS** ══ **PORTUGUESE / PORTUGUÊS** ▬ **SPANISH / ESPAÑOL** ══

ARABIC / يخ ▓ **RUSSIAN / РУССКИИ** ══ **CHINESE / 中文** ▭▭▭ **JAPANESE / 日本語** ▬▬▬ **MULTILINGUAL** ▬▬▬ **OTHER** ▬

SUMMER ONLY (J)   **WINTER ONLY (D)**   **JAMMING** ∧∧ or / or \   **EARLIEST HEARD** ◢   **LATEST HEARD** ◣   ✦ **TENTATIVE**

Frequency (kHz)	Country / Station / Location	Power (kW): Network: Target

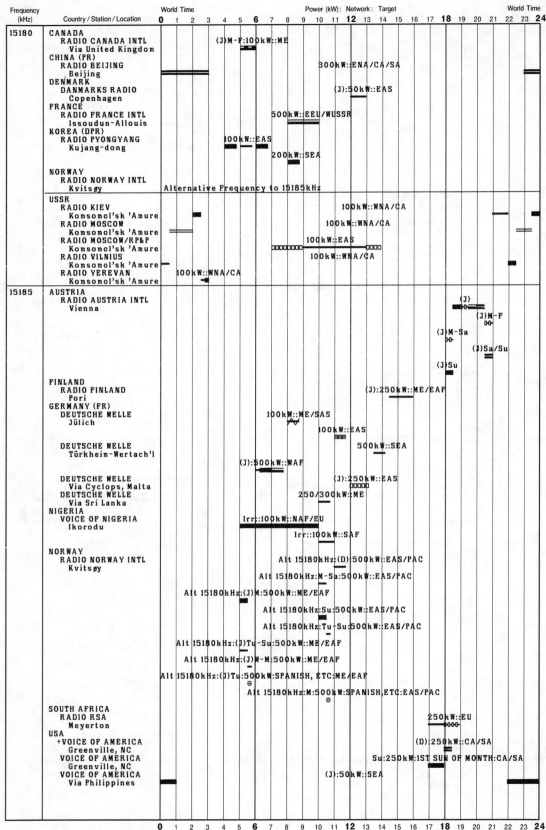

15180

CANADA
RADIO CANADA INTL
Via United Kingdom
(J)M–F:100kW::ME

CHINA (PR)
RADIO BEIJING
Beijing
300kW::ENA/CA/SA

DENMARK
DANMARKS RADIO
Copenhagen
(J):50kW::EAS

FRANCE
RADIO FRANCE INTL
Issoudun-Allouis
500kW::EEU/WUSSR

KOREA (DPR)
RADIO PYONGYANG
Kujang-dong
100kW::EAS
200kW::SEA

NORWAY
RADIO NORWAY INTL
Kvitsøy
Alternative Frequency to 15185kHz

USSR
RADIO KIEV
Komsomol'sk 'Amure
100kW::WNA/CA
RADIO MOSCOW
Komsomol'sk 'Amure
100kW::WNA/CA
RADIO MOSCOW/RP&P
Komsomol'sk 'Amure
100kW::EAS
RADIO VILNIUS
Komsomol'sk 'Amure
100kW::WNA/CA
RADIO YEREVAN
Komsomol'sk 'Amure
100kW::WNA/CA

15185

AUSTRIA
RADIO AUSTRIA INTL
Vienna
(J)
(J)M–F
(J)M–Sa
(J)Sa/Su
(J)Su

FINLAND
RADIO FINLAND
Pori
(J):250kW::ME/EAF

GERMANY (FR)
DEUTSCHE WELLE
Jülich
100kW::ME/SAS
100kW::EAS
500kW::SEA

DEUTSCHE WELLE
Türkheim-Wertach'l
(J):500kW::WAF

DEUTSCHE WELLE
Via Cyclops, Malta
(J):250kW::EAS

DEUTSCHE WELLE
Via Sri Lanka
250/300kW::ME

NIGERIA
VOICE OF NIGERIA
Ikorodu
Irr::100kW::NAF/EU
Irr::100kW::SAF

NORWAY
RADIO NORWAY INTL
Kvitsøy
Alt 15180kHz:(D)500kW::EAS/PAC
Alt 15180kHz:M–Sa:500kW::EAS/PAC
Alt 15180kHz:(J)M:500kW::ME/EAF
Alt 15180kHz:Su:500kW::EAS/PAC
Alt 15180kHz:Tu–Su:500kW::EAS/PAC
Alt 15180kHz:(J)Tu–Su:500kW::ME/EAF
Alt 15180kHz:(J)M–M:500kW::ME/EAF
Alt 15180kHz:(J)Tu:500kW:SPANISH, ETC:ME/EAF
Alt 15180kHz:M:500kW:SPANISH,ETC:EAS/PAC

SOUTH AFRICA
RADIO RSA
Meyerton
250kW::EU

USA
+VOICE OF AMERICA
Greenville, NC
(D):250kW::CA/SA
VOICE OF AMERICA
Greenville, NC
Su:250kW:1ST SUN OF MONTH:CA/SA
VOICE OF AMERICA
Via Philippines
(J):50kW::SEA

ENGLISH ▬▬ GERMAN / DEUTSCH ◊◊◊◊ FRENCH / FRANÇAIS ═══ PORTUGUESE / PORTUGUÊS ▬▬ SPANISH / ESPAÑOL ▬▬

ARABIC /ﻰﺑﺮﻋ ≡≡ RUSSIAN / РУССКИИ ▬▬ CHINESE / 中文 ◊◊◊◊ JAPANESE / 日本語 ▬▬▬ MULTILINGUAL ▬▬▬ OTHER ▬▬

SUMMER ONLY (J)   WINTER ONLY (D)   JAMMING /\/\ or / or \   EARLIEST HEARD ◢   LATEST HEARD ◣   + TENTATIVE

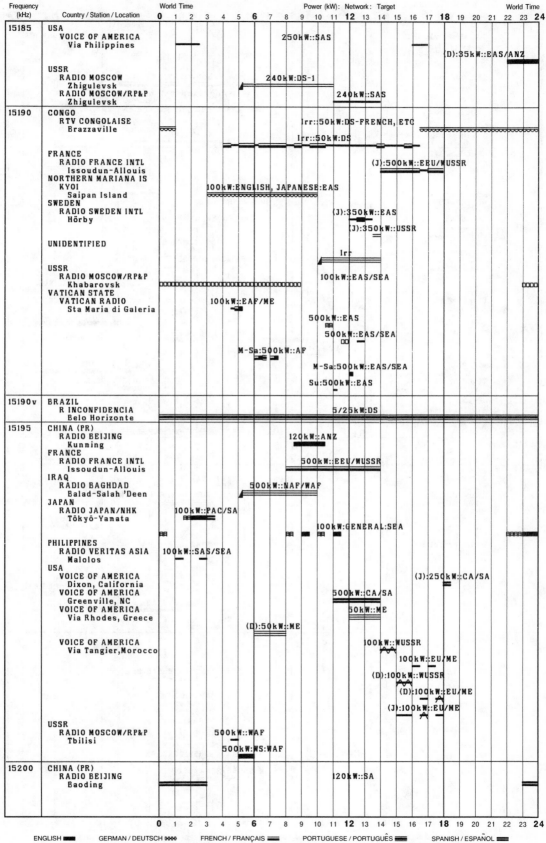

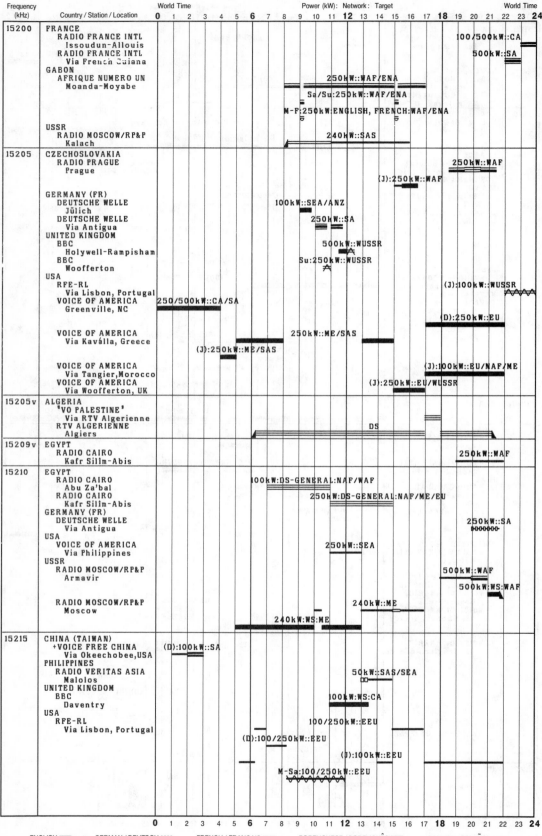

Frequency (kHz)	Country / Station / Location	Power (kW): Network: Target

15200 FRANCE
RADIO FRANCE INTL — Issoudun-Allouis — 100/500kW::CA
RADIO FRANCE INTL — Via French Guiana — 500kW::SA
GABON
AFRIQUE NUMERO UN — Moanda-Moyabe — 250kW::WAF/ENA — Sa/Su:250kW::WAF/ENA — M-F:250kW:ENGLISH, FRENCH:WAF/ENA
USSR
RADIO MOSCOW/RP&P — Kalach — 240kW::SAS

15205 CZECHOSLOVAKIA
RADIO PRAGUE — Prague — 250kW::WAF — (J):250kW::WAF
GERMANY (FR)
DEUTSCHE WELLE — Jülich — 100kW::SEA/ANZ
DEUTSCHE WELLE — Via Antigua — 250kW::SA
UNITED KINGDOM
BBC — Holywell-Rampisham — 500kW::WUSSR
BBC — Woofferton — Su:250kW::WUSSR
USA
RFE-RL — Via Lisbon, Portugal — (J):100kW::WUSSR
VOICE OF AMERICA — Greenville, NC — 250/500kW::CA/SA — (D):250kW::EU
VOICE OF AMERICA — Via Kaválla, Greece — 250kW::ME/SAS — (J):250kW::ME/SAS
VOICE OF AMERICA — Via Tangier,Morocco — (J):100kW::EU/NAF/ME
VOICE OF AMERICA — Via Woofferton, UK — (J):250kW::EU/WUSSR

15205v ALGERIA
"VO PALESTINE" — Via RTV Algerienne
RTV ALGERIENNE — Algiers — DS

15209v EGYPT
RADIO CAIRO — Kafr Silîm-Abis — 250kW::WAF

15210 EGYPT
RADIO CAIRO — Abu Za'bal — 100kW:DS-GENERAL:NAF/WAF
RADIO CAIRO — Kafr Silîm-Abis — 250kW:DS-GENERAL:NAF/ME/EU
GERMANY (FR)
DEUTSCHE WELLE — Via Antigua — 250kW::SA
USA
VOICE OF AMERICA — Via Philippines — 250kW::SEA
USSR
RADIO MOSCOW/RP&P — Armavir — 500kW::WAF — 500kW:WS:WAF
RADIO MOSCOW/RP&P — Moscow — 240kW::ME — 240kW:WS:ME

15215 CHINA (TAIWAN)
+VOICE FREE CHINA — Via Okeechobee,USA — (D):100kW::SA
PHILIPPINES
RADIO VERITAS ASIA — Malolos — 50kW::SAS/SEA
UNITED KINGDOM
BBC — Daventry — 100kW:WS:CA
USA
RFE-RL — Via Lisbon, Portugal — 100/250kW::EEU — (D):100/250kW::EEU — (J):100kW::EEU — M-Sa:100/250kW::EEU

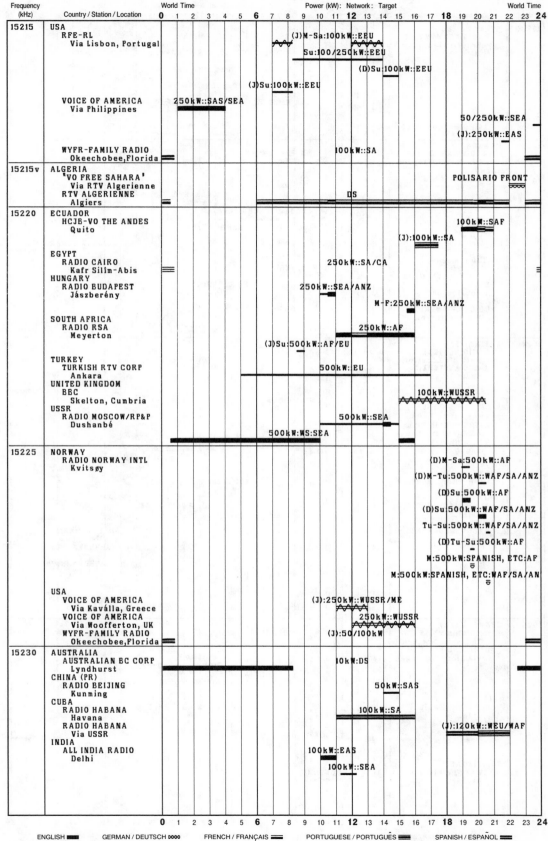

Frequency (kHz)	Country / Station / Location	World Time 0-24 / Power (kW): Network: Target
15215	USA RFE-RL Via Lisbon, Portugal	(J)M-Sa:100kW::EEU; Su:100/250kW::EEU; (D)Su:100kW::EEU; (J)Su:100kW::EEU
	VOICE OF AMERICA Via Philippines	250kW::SAS/SEA; 50/250kW::SEA; (J):250kW::EAS
	WYFR-FAMILY RADIO Okeechobee,Florida	100kW::SA
15215v	ALGERIA 'VO FREE SAHARA' Via RTV Algerienne	POLISARIO FRONT
	RTV ALGERIENNE Algiers	DS
15220	ECUADOR HCJB-VO THE ANDES Quito	100kW::SAF; (J):100kW::SA
	EGYPT RADIO CAIRO Kafr Silim-Abis	250kW::SA/CA
	HUNGARY RADIO BUDAPEST Jászberény	250kW::SEA/ANZ; M-F:250kW::SEA/ANZ
	SOUTH AFRICA RADIO RSA Meyerton	250kW::AF; (J)Su:500kW::AF/EU
	TURKEY TURKISH RTV CORP Ankara	500kW::EU
	UNITED KINGDOM BBC Skelton, Cumbria	100kW::WUSSR
	USSR RADIO MOSCOW/RP&P Dushanbé	500kW::SEA; 500kW:WS:SEA
15225	NORWAY RADIO NORWAY INTL Kvitsøy	(D)M-Sa:500kW::AF; (D)M-Tu:500kW::WAF/SA/ANZ; (D)Su:500kW::AF; (D)Su:500kW::WAF/SA/ANZ; Tu-Su:500kW::WAF/SA/ANZ; (D)Tu-Su:500kW::AF; M:500kW:SPANISH,ETC:AF; M:500kW:SPANISH,ETC:WAF/SA/AN
	USA VOICE OF AMERICA Via Kaválla, Greece	(J):250kW::WUSSR/ME
	VOICE OF AMERICA Via Woofferton, UK	250kW::WUSSR
	WYFR-FAMILY RADIO Okeechobee,Florida	(J):50/100kW
15230	AUSTRALIA AUSTRALIAN BC CORP Lyndhurst	10kW:DS
	CHINA (PR) RADIO BEIJING Kunming	50kW::SAS
	CUBA RADIO HABANA Havana	100kW::SA
	RADIO HABANA Via USSR	(J):120kW::WEU/WAF
	INDIA ALL INDIA RADIO Delhi	100kW::EAS; 100kW::SEA

ENGLISH ▬ GERMAN / DEUTSCH ꝏꝏ FRENCH / FRANÇAIS ═ PORTUGUESE / PORTUGUÊS ▬ SPANISH / ESPAÑOL ═

ARABIC /جزء ≡ RUSSIAN / РУССКИЙ ═ CHINESE / 中文 ꝏꝏ JAPANESE / 日本語 ▬ MULTILINGUAL ▭▭ OTHER —

SUMMER ONLY (J) WINTER ONLY (D) JAMMING /\/\ or / or \ EARLIEST HEARD ◢ LATEST HEARD ◣ + TENTATIVE

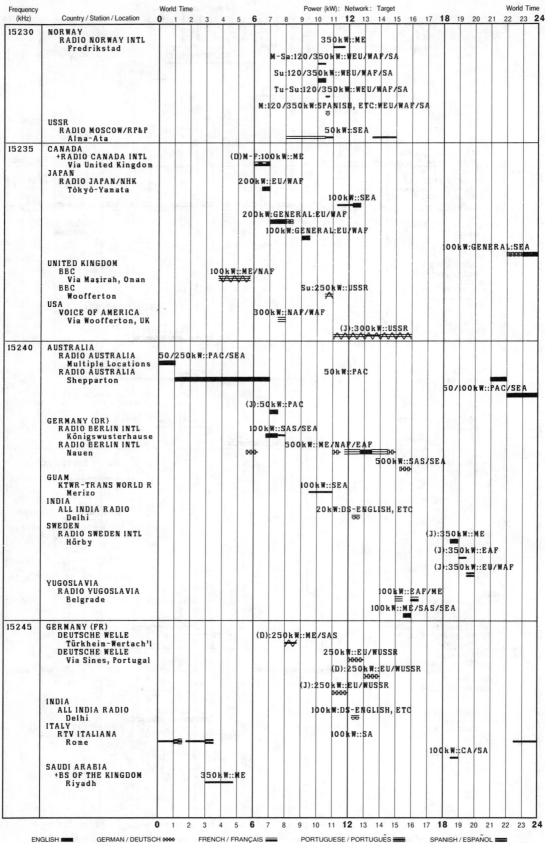

Frequency (kHz)	Country / Station / Location	Details
15230	**NORWAY** RADIO NORWAY INTL Fredrikstad	350kW::ME
		M-Sa:120/350kW::WEU/WAF/SA
		Su:120/350kW::WEU/WAF/SA
		Tu-Su:120/350kW::WEU/WAF/SA
		M:120/350kW:SPANISH, ETC:WEU/WAF/SA
	USSR RADIO MOSCOW/RP&P Alma-Ata	50kW::SEA
15235	**CANADA** +RADIO CANADA INTL Via United Kingdom	(D)M-F:100kW::ME
	JAPAN RADIO JAPAN/NHK Tōkyō-Yamata	200kW::EU/WAF
		100kW::SEA
		200kW:GENERAL:EU/WAF
		100kW:GENERAL:EU/WAF
		100kW:GENERAL:SEA
	UNITED KINGDOM BBC Via Maṣirah, Oman	100kW::ME/NAF
	BBC Woofferton	Su:250kW::USSR
	USA VOICE OF AMERICA Via Woofferton, UK	300kW::NAF/WAF
		(J):300kW::USSR
15240	**AUSTRALIA** RADIO AUSTRALIA Multiple Locations	50/250kW::PAC/SEA
	RADIO AUSTRALIA Shepparton	50kW::PAC
		50/100kW::PAC/SEA
		(J):50kW::PAC
	GERMANY (DR) RADIO BERLIN INTL Königswusterhause	100kW::SAS/SEA
	RADIO BERLIN INTL Nauen	500kW::ME/NAF/EAF
		500kW::SAS/SEA
	GUAM KTWR-TRANS WORLD R Merizo	100kW::SEA
	INDIA ALL INDIA RADIO Delhi	20kW:DS-ENGLISH, ETC
	SWEDEN RADIO SWEDEN INTL Hörby	(J):350kW::ME
		(J):350kW::EAF
		(J):350kW::EU/WAF
	YUGOSLAVIA RADIO YUGOSLAVIA Belgrade	100kW::EAF/ME
		100kW::ME/SAS/SEA
15245	**GERMANY (FR)** DEUTSCHE WELLE Türkheim-Wertach'l	(D):250kW::ME/SAS
	DEUTSCHE WELLE Via Sines, Portugal	250kW::EU/WUSSR
		(D):250kW::EU/WUSSR
		(J):250kW::EU/WUSSR
	INDIA ALL INDIA RADIO Delhi	100kW:DS-ENGLISH, ETC
	ITALY RTV ITALIANA Rome	100kW::SA
		100kW::CA/SA
	SAUDI ARABIA +BS OF THE KINGDOM Riyadh	350kW::ME

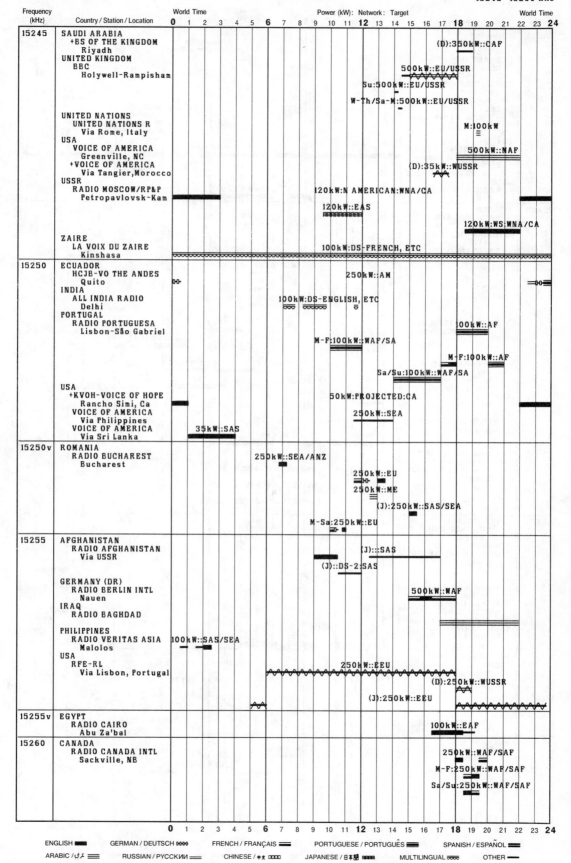

Frequency (kHz)	Country / Station / Location	Power (kW): Network: Target
15245	SAUDI ARABIA +BS OF THE KINGDOM Riyadh	(D):350kW::CAF
	UNITED KINGDOM BBC Holywell-Rampisham	500kW::EU/USSR Su:500kW::EU/USSR W-Th/Sa-M:500kW::EU/USSR
	UNITED NATIONS UNITED NATIONS R Via Rome, Italy	M:100kW
	USA VOICE OF AMERICA Greenville, NC	500kW::NAF
	+VOICE OF AMERICA Via Tangier,Morocco	(D):35kW::WUSSR
	USSR RADIO MOSCOW/RP&P Petropavlovsk-Kam	120kW:N AMERICAN:WNA/CA 120kW::EAS 120kW:WS:WNA/CA
	ZAIRE LA VOIX DU ZAIRE Kinshasa	100kW:DS-FRENCH, ETC
15250	ECUADOR HCJB-VO THE ANDES Quito	250kW::AM
	INDIA ALL INDIA RADIO Delhi	100kW:DS-ENGLISH, ETC
	PORTUGAL RADIO PORTUGUESA Lisbon-São Gabriel	100kW::AF M-F:100kW::WAF/SA M-F:100kW::AF Sa/Su:100kW::WAF/SA
	USA +KVOH-VOICE OF HOPE Rancho Simi, Ca	50kW:PROJECTED:CA
	VOICE OF AMERICA Via Philippines	250kW::SEA
	VOICE OF AMERICA Via Sri Lanka	35kW::SAS
15250v	ROMANIA RADIO BUCHAREST Bucharest	250kW::SEA/ANZ 250kW::EU 250kW::ME (J):250kW::SAS/SEA M-Sa:250kW::EU
15255	AFGHANISTAN RADIO AFGHANISTAN Via USSR	(J):::SAS (J)::DS-2:SAS
	GERMANY (DR) RADIO BERLIN INTL Nauen	500kW::WAF
	IRAQ RADIO BAGHDAD	
	PHILIPPINES RADIO VERITAS ASIA Malolos	100kW::SAS/SEA
	USA RFE-RL Via Lisbon, Portugal	250kW::EEU (D):250kW::WUSSR (J):250kW::EEU
15255v	EGYPT RADIO CAIRO Abu Za'bal	100kW::EAF
15260	CANADA RADIO CANADA INTL Sackville, NB	250kW::WAF/SAF M-F:250kW::WAF/SAF Sa/Su:250kW::WAF/SAF

World Time: 0 1 2 3 4 5 6 7 8 9 10 11 12 13 14 15 16 17 18 19 20 21 22 23 24

ENGLISH ▬▬ GERMAN / DEUTSCH ◊◊◊◊ FRENCH / FRANÇAIS ═══ PORTUGUESE / PORTUGUÊS ▬▬ SPANISH / ESPAÑOL ═══

ARABIC / ﻉﺮﺑ ≡≡≡ RUSSIAN / РУССКИИ ══ CHINESE / 中文 ◊◊◊◊ JAPANESE / 日本語 ▬▬▬ MULTILINGUAL ▭▭▭ OTHER ▬▬

SUMMER ONLY (J) WINTER ONLY (D) JAMMING /\/\ or / or \ EARLIEST HEARD ◢ LATEST HEARD ◣ + TENTATIVE

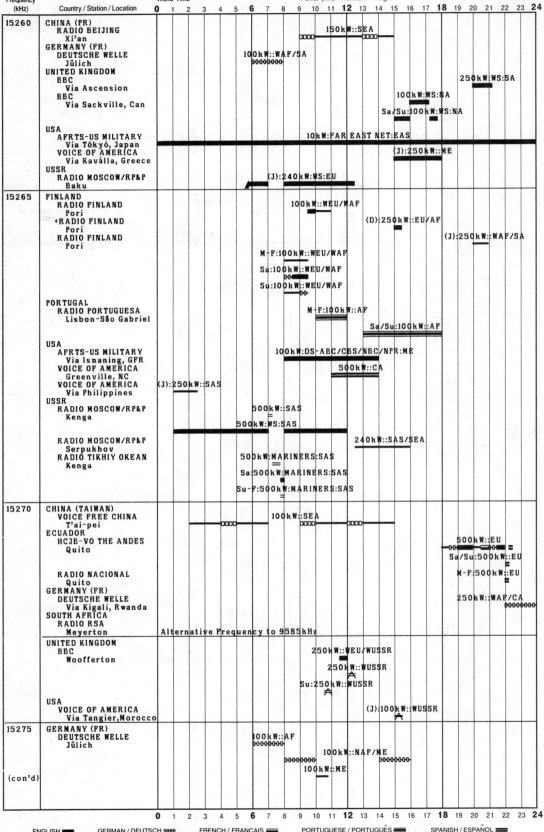

Frequency (kHz)	Country / Station / Location	World Time 0 ... 12 ... 24	Power (kW) : Network : Target
15260	CHINA (PR) RADIO BEIJING — Xi'an		150kW::SEA
	GERMANY (FR) DEUTSCHE WELLE — Jülich		100kW::WAF/SA
	UNITED KINGDOM BBC — Via Ascension		250kW:WS:SA
	BBC — Via Sackville, Can		100kW:WS:NA / Sa/Su:100kW:WS:NA
	USA AFRTS-US MILITARY — Via Tōkyō, Japan		10kW:FAR EAST NET:EAS
	VOICE OF AMERICA — Via Kaválla, Greece		(J):250kW::ME
	USSR RADIO MOSCOW/RP&P — Baku		(J):240kW:WS:EU
15265	FINLAND RADIO FINLAND — Pori		100kW::WEU/WAF
	+RADIO FINLAND — Pori		(D):250kW::EU/AF
	RADIO FINLAND — Pori		(J):250kW::WAF/SA
			M-F:100kW::WEU/WAF
			Sa:100kW::WEU/WAF
			Su:100kW::WEU/WAF
	PORTUGAL RADIO PORTUGUESA — Lisbon-São Gabriel		M-F:100kW::AF
			Sa/Su:100kW::AF
	USA AFRTS-US MILITARY — Via Ismaning, GFR		100kW:DS-ABC/CBS/NBC/NPR:ME
	VOICE OF AMERICA — Greenville, NC		500kW::CA
	VOICE OF AMERICA — Via Philippines		(J):250kW::SAS
	USSR RADIO MOSCOW/RP&P — Kenga		500kW::SAS
			500kW:WS:SAS
	RADIO MOSCOW/RP&P — Serpukhov		240kW::SAS/SEA
	RADIO TIKHIY OKEAN — Kenga		500kW:MARINERS:SAS
			Sa:500kW:MARINERS:SAS
			Su-F:500kW:MARINERS:SAS
15270	CHINA (TAIWAN) VOICE FREE CHINA — T'ai-pei		100kW::SEA
	ECUADOR HCJB-VO THE ANDES — Quito		500kW::EU
			Sa/Su:500kW::EU
	RADIO NACIONAL — Quito		M-F:500kW::EU
	GERMANY (FR) DEUTSCHE WELLE — Via Kigali, Rwanda		250kW::WAF/CA
	SOUTH AFRICA RADIO RSA — Meyerton	Alternative Frequency to 9585kHz	
	UNITED KINGDOM BBC — Woofferton		250kW::WEU/WUSSR
			250kW::WUSSR
			Su:250kW::WUSSR
	USA VOICE OF AMERICA — Via Tangier, Morocco		(J):100kW::WUSSR
15275	GERMANY (FR) DEUTSCHE WELLE — Jülich		100kW::AF
			100kW::NAF/ME
(con'd)			100kW::ME

World Time: 0 1 2 3 4 5 6 7 8 9 10 11 12 13 14 15 16 17 18 19 20 21 22 23 24

ENGLISH ▰▰▰   GERMAN / DEUTSCH ००००   FRENCH / FRANÇAIS ▭▭▭   PORTUGUESE / PORTUGUÊS ▰▰▰   SPANISH / ESPAÑOL ▰▰▰

ARABIC /ئ ٤ ≡   RUSSIAN / РУССКИИ ▭▭   CHINESE / ✦✚ ००००   JAPANESE / 日本語 ▰▰▰   MULTILINGUAL ▧▧▧   OTHER ▬

SUMMER ONLY (J)   WINTER ONLY (D)   JAMMING ∧∧∧ or / or \   EARLIEST HEARD ◢   LATEST HEARD ◣   + TENTATIVE

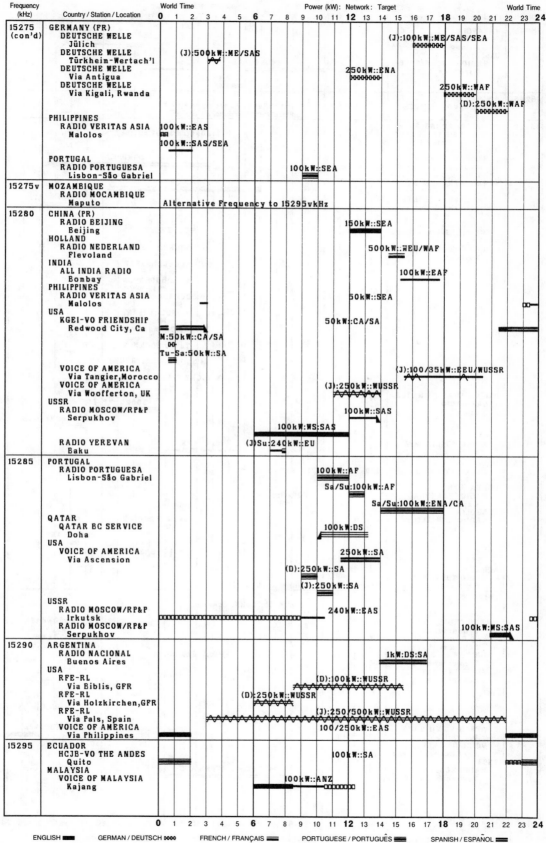

ENGLISH ▬▬ GERMAN / DEUTSCH ◊◊◊◊ FRENCH / FRANÇAIS ═══ PORTUGUESE / PORTUGUÊS ▭▭ SPANISH / ESPAÑOL ▬▬

ARABIC /ف ف ═══ RUSSIAN / РУССКИИ ═══ CHINESE / 中文 ◻◻◻◻ JAPANESE / 日本語 ▬▬▬ MULTILINGUAL ▭▭▭ OTHER ▬▬▬

SUMMER ONLY (J) WINTER ONLY (D) JAMMING ∧∧ or / or \ EARLIEST HEARD ◢ LATEST HEARD ◣ + TENTATIVE

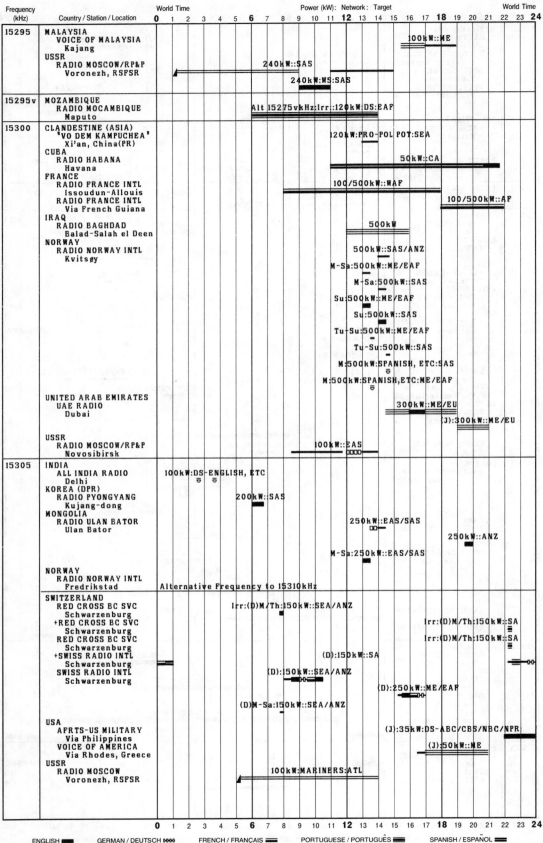

Frequency (kHz)	Country / Station / Location	World Time 0 1 2 3 4 5 6 7 8 9 10 11 **12** 13 14 15 16 17 **18** 19 20 21 22 23 **24**

15295	MALAYSIA
	    VOICE OF MALAYSIA
	      Kajang
		100kW::ME

	USSR
	    RADIO MOSCOW/RP&P
	      Voronezh, RSFSR
		240kW::SAS
		240kW:WS:SAS

15295v	MOZAMBIQUE
	    RADIO MOCAMBIQUE
	      Maputo
		Alt 15275vkHz:Irr::120kW:DS:EAF

15300	CLANDESTINE (ASIA)
	    'VO DEM KAMPUCHEA'
	      Xi'an, China(PR)
		120kW:PRO-POL POT:SEA

	CUBA
	    RADIO HABANA
	      Havana
		50kW::CA

	FRANCE
	    RADIO FRANCE INTL
	      Issoudun-Allouis
		100/500kW::WAF

	RADIO FRANCE INTL Via French Guiana	100/500kW::AF

	IRAQ
	    RADIO BAGHDAD
	      Balad-Salah el Deen
		500kW

	NORWAY
	    RADIO NORWAY INTL
	      Kvitsøy
		500kW::SAS/ANZ
		M-Sa:500kW::ME/EAF
		M-Sa:500kW::SAS
		Su:500kW::ME/EAF
		Su:500kW::SAS
		Tu-Su:500kW::ME/EAF
		Tu-Su:500kW::SAS
		M:500kW:SPANISH, ETC:SAS
		M:500kW:SPANISH,ETC:ME/EAF

	UNITED ARAB EMIRATES
	    UAE RADIO
	      Dubai
		300kW::ME/EU
		(J):300kW::ME/EU

	USSR
	    RADIO MOSCOW/RP&P
	      Novosibirsk
		100kW::EAS

15305	INDIA
	    ALL INDIA RADIO
	      Delhi
		100kW:DS-ENGLISH, ETC

	KOREA (DPR)
	    RADIO PYONGYANG
	      Kujang-dong
		200kW::SAS

	MONGOLIA
	    RADIO ULAN BATOR
	      Ulan Bator
		250kW::EAS/SAS
		250kW::ANZ
		M-Sa:250kW::EAS/SAS

	NORWAY
	    RADIO NORWAY INTL
	      Fredrikstad
		Alternative Frequency to 15310kHz

	SWITZERLAND
	    RED CROSS BC SVC
	      Schwarzenburg
		Irr:(D)M/Th:150kW::SEA/ANZ

	+RED CROSS BC SVC Schwarzenburg	Irr:(D)M/Th:150kW::SA
	RED CROSS BC SVC Schwarzenburg	Irr:(D)M/Th:150kW::SA
	+SWISS RADIO INTL Schwarzenburg	(D):150kW::SA
	SWISS RADIO INTL Schwarzenburg	(D):150kW::SEA/ANZ (D):250kW::ME/EAF (D)M-Sa:150kW::SEA/ANZ

	USA
	    AFRTS-US MILITARY
	      Via Philippines
		(J):35kW:DS-ABC/CBS/NBC/NPR

	VOICE OF AMERICA Via Rhodes, Greece	(J):50kW::ME

	USSR
	    RADIO MOSCOW
	      Voronezh, RSFSR
		100kW:MARINERS:ATL

World Time 0 1 2 3 4 5 **6** 7 8 9 10 11 **12** 13 14 15 16 17 **18** 19 20 21 22 23 **24**

ENGLISH ▄▄▄   GERMAN / DEUTSCH ⋈⋈⋈   FRENCH / FRANÇAIS ≡≡≡   PORTUGUESE / PORTUGUÊS ≡≡≡   SPANISH / ESPAÑOL ▭▭▭

ARABIC / عربى ≣≣≣   RUSSIAN / РУССКИИ ═══   CHINESE / 中文 ▭▭▭▭   JAPANESE / 日本語 ▤▤▤▤   MULTILINGUAL ▨▨▨▨   OTHER ▬▬▬

SUMMER ONLY (J)   WINTER ONLY (D)   JAMMING ∧∧∧ or / or \   EARLIEST HEARD ◢   LATEST HEARD ◣   + TENTATIVE

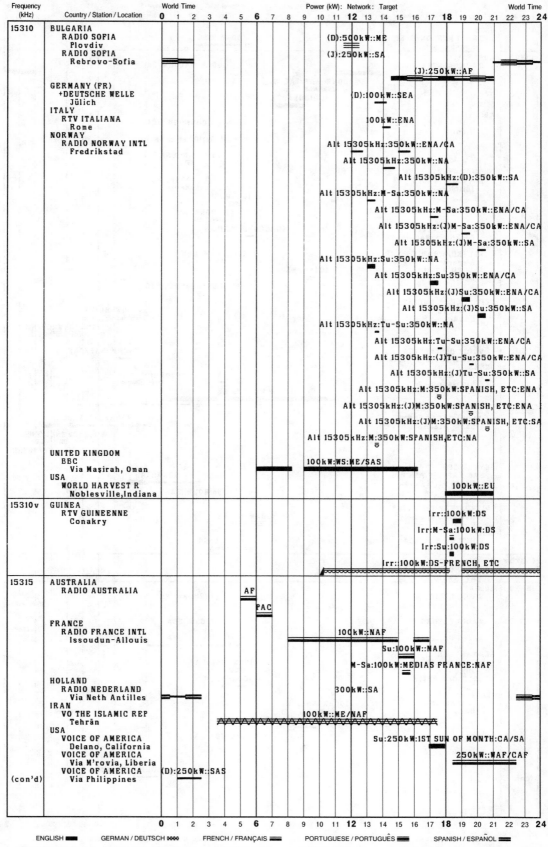

Frequency (kHz)	Country / Station / Location	World Time / Power (kW): Network: Target
15310	**BULGARIA**	
	RADIO SOFIA — Plovdiv	(D):500kW::ME
	RADIO SOFIA — Rebrovo-Sofia	(J):250kW::SA
		(J):250kW::AF
	GERMANY (FR)	
	+DEUTSCHE WELLE — Jülich	(D):100kW::SEA
	ITALY	
	RTV ITALIANA — Rome	100kW::ENA
	NORWAY	
	RADIO NORWAY INTL — Fredrikstad	Alt 15305kHz:350kW::ENA/CA
		Alt 15305kHz:350kW::NA
		Alt 15305kHz:(D)350kW::SA
		Alt 15305kHz:M-Sa:350kW::NA
		Alt 15305kHz:M-Sa:350kW::ENA/CA
		Alt 15305kHz:(J)M-Sa:350kW::ENA/CA
		Alt 15305kHz:(J)M-Sa:350kW::SA
		Alt 15305kHz:Su:350kW::NA
		Alt 15305kHz:Su:350kW::ENA/CA
		Alt 15305kHz:(J)Su:350kW::ENA/CA
		Alt 15305kHz:(J)Su:350kW::SA
		Alt 15305kHz:Tu-Su:350kW::NA
		Alt 15305kHz:Tu-Su:350kW::ENA/CA
		Alt 15305kHz:(J)Tu-Su:350kW::ENA/CA
		Alt 15305kHz:(J)Tu-Su:350kW::SA
		Alt 15305kHz:M:350kW:SPANISH, ETC:ENA
		Alt 15305kHz:(J)M:350kW:SPANISH, ETC:ENA
		Alt 15305kHz:(J)M:350kW:SPANISH, ETC:SA
		Alt 15305kHz:M:350kW:SPANISH,ETC:NA
	UNITED KINGDOM	
	BBC — Via Maṣirah, Oman	100kW:WS:ME/SAS
	USA	
	WORLD HARVEST R — Noblesville,Indiana	100kW::EU
15310v	**GUINEA**	
	RTV GUINEENNE — Conakry	Irr::100kW:DS
		Irr:M-Sa:100kW:DS
		Irr:Su:100kW:DS
		Irr::100kW:DS-FRENCH, ETC
15315	**AUSTRALIA**	
	RADIO AUSTRALIA	AF
		PAC
	FRANCE	
	RADIO FRANCE INTL — Issoudun-Allouis	100kW::NAF
		Su:100kW::NAF
		M-Sa:100kW:MEDIAS FRANCE:NAF
	HOLLAND	
	RADIO NEDERLAND — Via Neth Antilles	300kW::SA
	IRAN	
	VO THE ISLAMIC REP — Tehrän	100kW::ME/NAF
	USA	
	VOICE OF AMERICA — Delano, California	Su:250kW:1ST SUN OF MONTH:CA/SA
	VOICE OF AMERICA — Via M'rovia, Liberia	250kW::WAF/CAF
(con'd)	VOICE OF AMERICA — Via Philippines	(D):250kW::SAS

ENGLISH ▬▬ GERMAN / DEUTSCH ▭▭▭ FRENCH / FRANÇAIS ▭▭▭ PORTUGUESE / PORTUGUÊS ▬▬ SPANISH / ESPAÑOL ▬▬
ARABIC / ﻉ ﻝ ≡ RUSSIAN / РУССКИИ ═══ CHINESE / 中文 ▯▯▯ JAPANESE / 日本語 ▦▦▦ MULTILINGUAL ▭▭▭ OTHER ▬▬
SUMMER ONLY (J) WINTER ONLY (D) JAMMING /\/\ or / or \ EARLIEST HEARD ◢ LATEST HEARD ◣ + TENTATIVE

Frequency (kHz)	Country / Station / Location	World Time 0-24	Power (kW): Network: Target

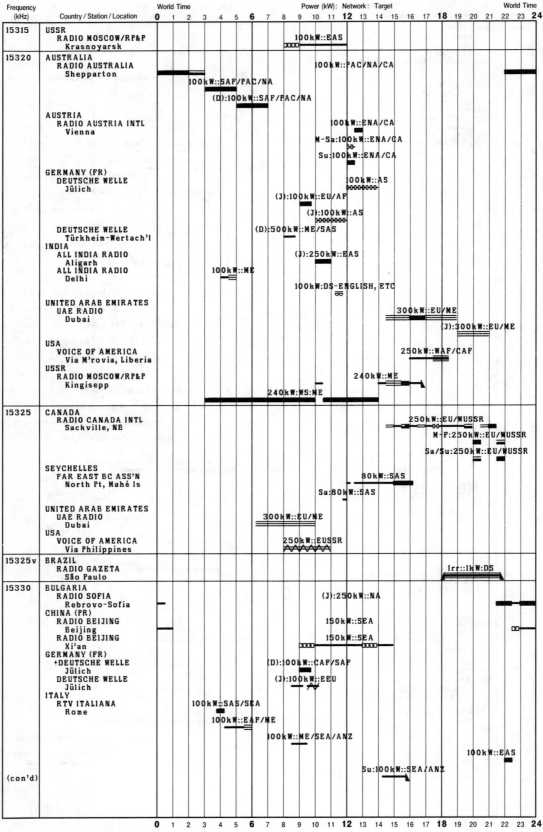

15315 — USSR — RADIO MOSCOW/RP&P — Krasnoyarsk — 100kW::EAS

15320 — AUSTRALIA — RADIO AUSTRALIA — Shepparton — 100kW::PAC/NA/CA; 100kW::SAF/PAC/NA; (D):100kW::SAF/PAC/NA

AUSTRIA — RADIO AUSTRIA INTL — Vienna — 100kW::ENA/CA; M-Sa:100kW::ENA/CA; Su:100kW::ENA/CA

GERMANY (FR) — DEUTSCHE WELLE — Jülich — 100kW::AS; (J):100kW::EU/AF; (J):100kW::AS

DEUTSCHE WELLE — Türkheim-Wertach'l — (D):500kW::ME/SAS

INDIA — ALL INDIA RADIO — Aligarh — (J):250kW::EAS

ALL INDIA RADIO — Delhi — 100kW::ME; 100kW:DS-ENGLISH, ETC

UNITED ARAB EMIRATES — UAE RADIO — Dubai — 300kW::EU/ME; (J):300kW::EU/ME

USA — VOICE OF AMERICA — Via M'rovia, Liberia — 250kW::WAF/CAF

USSR — RADIO MOSCOW/RP&P — Kingisepp — 240kW::ME; 240kW::WS:ME

15325 — CANADA — RADIO CANADA INTL — Sackville, NB — 250kW::EU/WUSSR; M-F:250kW::EU/WUSSR; Sa/Su:250kW::EU/WUSSR

SEYCHELLES — FAR EAST BC ASS'N — North Pt, Mahé Is — 80kW::SAS; Sa:80kW::SAS

UNITED ARAB EMIRATES — UAE RADIO — Dubai — 300kW::EU/ME

USA — VOICE OF AMERICA — Via Philippines — 250kW::EUSSR

15325v — BRAZIL — RADIO GAZETA — São Paulo — Irr::1kW:DS

15330 — BULGARIA — RADIO SOFIA — Rebrovo-Sofia — (J):250kW::NA

CHINA (PR) — RADIO BEIJING — Beijing — 150kW::SEA

RADIO BEIJING — Xi'an — 150kW::SEA

GERMANY (FR) — +DEUTSCHE WELLE — Jülich — (D):100kW::CAF/SAF

DEUTSCHE WELLE — Jülich — (J):100kW::EEU

ITALY — RTV ITALIANA — Rome — 100kW::SAS/SEA; 100kW::EAF/ME; 100kW::ME/SEA/ANZ; 100kW::EAS; Su:100kW::SEA/ANZ

(con'd)

ENGLISH ▬▬ GERMAN / DEUTSCH ◊◊◊◊ FRENCH / FRANÇAIS ══ PORTUGUESE / PORTUGUÊS ▬ SPANISH / ESPAÑOL ▬
ARABIC ══ RUSSIAN / РУССКИИ ══ CHINESE ◻◻◻◻ JAPANESE ▦▦ MULTILINGUAL ▤▤ OTHER —
SUMMER ONLY (J) WINTER ONLY (D) JAMMING /\/\ or / or \ EARLIEST HEARD ◢ LATEST HEARD ◣ + TENTATIVE

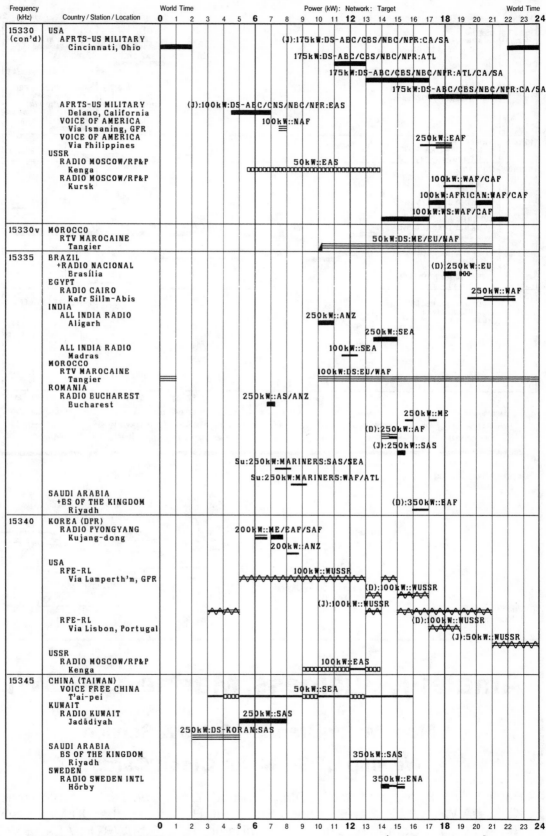

Frequency (kHz)	Country / Station / Location	Power (kW) : Network : Target

15330 (con'd)
USA
  AFRTS-US MILITARY Cincinnati, Ohio — (J):175kW:DS-ABC/CBS/NBC/NPR:CA/SA / 175kW:DS-ABC/CBS/NBC/NPR:ATL / 175kW:DS-ABC/CBS/NBC/NPR:ATL/CA/SA / 175kW:DS-ABC/CBS/NBC/NPR:CA/SA
  AFRTS-US MILITARY Delano, California — (J):100kW:DS-ABC/CNS/NBC/NPR:EAS
  VOICE OF AMERICA Via Ismaning, GFR — 100kW::NAF
  VOICE OF AMERICA Via Philippines — 250kW::EAF
USSR
  RADIO MOSCOW/RP&P Kenga — 50kW::EAS
  RADIO MOSCOW/RP&P Kursk — 100kW::WAF/CAF / 100kW:AFRICAN:WAF/CAF / 100kW:WS:WAF/CAF

15330v
MOROCCO
  RTV MAROCAINE Tangier — 50kW:DS:ME/EU/NAF

15335
BRAZIL
  +RADIO NACIONAL Brasília — (D) 250kW::EU
EGYPT
  RADIO CAIRO Kafr Silim-Abis — 250kW::WAF
INDIA
  ALL INDIA RADIO Aligarh — 250kW::ANZ
  ALL INDIA RADIO Madras — 250kW::SEA / 100kW::SEA
MOROCCO
  RTV MAROCAINE Tangier — 100kW:DS:EU/WAF
ROMANIA
  RADIO BUCHAREST Bucharest — 250kW::AS/ANZ / 250kW::ME / (D):250kW::AF / (J):250kW::SAS / Su:250kW:MARINERS:SAS/SEA / Su:250kW:MARINERS:WAF/ATL
SAUDI ARABIA
  +BS OF THE KINGDOM Riyadh — (D):350kW::EAF

15340
KOREA (DPR)
  RADIO PYONGYANG Kujang-dong — 200kW::ME/EAF/SAF / 200kW::ANZ
USA
  RFE-RL Via Lamperth'm, GFR — 100kW::WUSSR / (D):100kW::WUSSR / (J):100kW::WUSSR
  RFE-RL Via Lisbon, Portugal — (D):100kW::WUSSR / (J):50kW::WUSSR
USSR
  RADIO MOSCOW/RP&P Kenga — 100kW::EAS

15345
CHINA (TAIWAN)
  VOICE FREE CHINA T'ai-pei — 50kW::SEA
KUWAIT
  RADIO KUWAIT Jadādiyah — 250kW::SAS / 250kW:DS-KORAN:SAS
SAUDI ARABIA
  BS OF THE KINGDOM Riyadh — 350kW::SAS
SWEDEN
  RADIO SWEDEN INTL Hörby — 350kW::ENA

ENGLISH ▬▬ GERMAN / DEUTSCH ◊◊◊◊ FRENCH / FRANÇAIS ═══ PORTUGUESE / PORTUGUÊS ▬▬ SPANISH / ESPAÑOL ▬▬
ARABIC / ﻉﺏﻉ ═══ RUSSIAN / РУССКИИ ═══ CHINESE / ⋆⋆ ◻◻◻◻ JAPANESE / 日本語 ▤▤▤ MULTILINGUAL ◻◻◻◻ OTHER ▬▬
SUMMER ONLY (J) WINTER ONLY (D) JAMMING /\/\ or / or \ EARLIEST HEARD ◢ LATEST HEARD ◣ + TENTATIVE

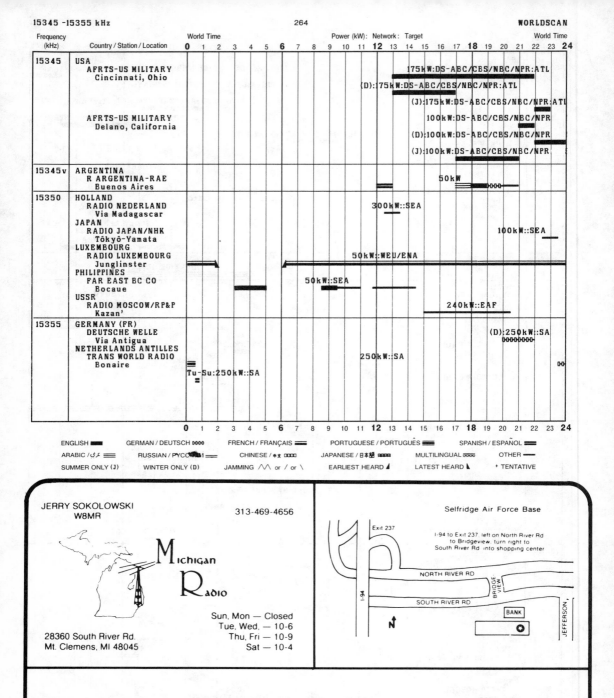

Frequency (kHz)	Country / Station / Location	Power (kW): Network: Target
15345	USA AFRTS–US MILITARY Cincinnati, Ohio	175kW:DS-ABC/CBS/NBC/NPR:ATL (D):175kW:DS-ABC/CBS/NBC/NPR:ATL (J):175kW:DS-ABC/CBS/NBC/NPR:ATL
	AFRTS–US MILITARY Delano, California	100kW:DS-ABC/CBS/NBC/NPR (D):100kW:DS-ABC/CBS/NBC/NPR (J):100kW:DS-ABC/CBS/NBC/NPR
15345v	ARGENTINA R ARGENTINA-RAE Buenos Aires	50kW
15350	HOLLAND RADIO NEDERLAND Via Madagascar	300kW::SEA
	JAPAN RADIO JAPAN/NHK Tōkyō-Yamata	100kW::SEA
	LUXEMBOURG RADIO LUXEMBOURG Junglinster	50kW::WEU/ENA
	PHILIPPINES FAR EAST BC CO Bocaue	50kW::SEA
	USSR RADIO MOSCOW/RP&P Kazan'	240kW::EAF
15355	GERMANY (FR) DEUTSCHE WELLE Via Antigua	(D):250kW::SA
	NETHERLANDS ANTILLES TRANS WORLD RADIO Bonaire	250kW::SA Tu-Su:250kW::SA

World Time: 0 1 2 3 4 5 6 7 8 9 10 11 12 13 14 15 16 17 18 19 20 21 22 23 24

Legend:

ENGLISH ▬▬   GERMAN / DEUTSCH ⋈⋈⋈⋈   FRENCH / FRANÇAIS ▬▬   PORTUGUESE / PORTUGUÊS ▤▤   SPANISH / ESPAÑOL ▬▬

ARABIC / عربية ▬▬   RUSSIAN / РУССО ▬▬   CHINESE / 中文 ▭▭▭▭   JAPANESE / 日本語 ▦▦▦▦   MULTILINGUAL ▨▨▨▨   OTHER ▬▬

SUMMER ONLY (J)   WINTER ONLY (D)   JAMMING /\/\ or / or \   EARLIEST HEARD ◢   LATEST HEARD ◣   + TENTATIVE

Frequency (kHz)	Country / Station / Location	World Time ... Power (kW) : Network : Target ... World Time

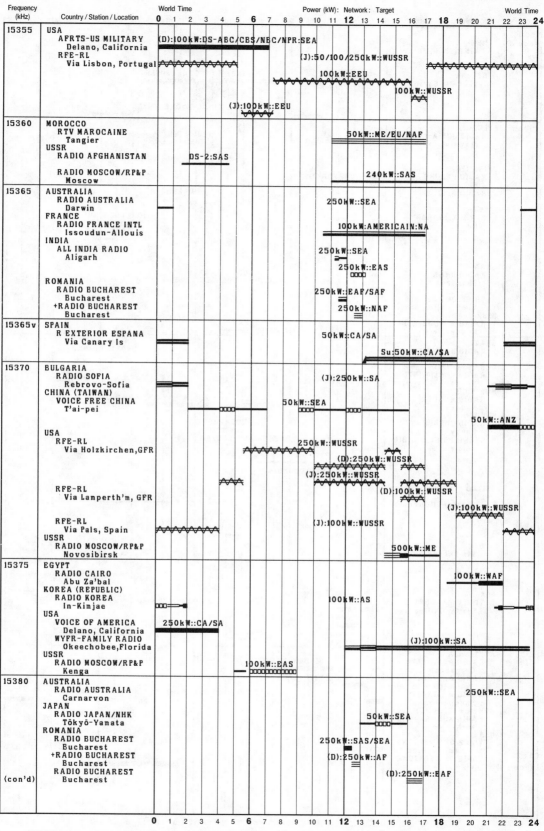

15355

USA
AFRTS-US MILITARY
Delano, California
(D):100kW:DS-ABC/CBS/NBC/NPR:SEA
RFE-RL
Via Lisbon, Portugal
(J):50/100/250kW::WUSSR
100kW::EEU
100kW::WUSSR
(J):100kW::EEU

15360

MOROCCO
RTV MAROCAINE
Tangier
50kW::ME/EU/NAF
USSR
RADIO AFGHANISTAN
DS-2:SAS
RADIO MOSCOW/RP&P
Moscow
240kW::SAS

15365

AUSTRALIA
RADIO AUSTRALIA
Darwin
250kW::SEA
FRANCE
RADIO FRANCE INTL
Issoudun-Allouis
100kW:AMERICAIN:NA
INDIA
ALL INDIA RADIO
Aligarh
250kW::SEA
250kW::EAS
ROMANIA
RADIO BUCHAREST
Bucharest
250kW::EAF/SAF
+RADIO BUCHAREST
Bucharest
250kW::NAF

15365v

SPAIN
R EXTERIOR ESPANA
Via Canary Is
50kW::CA/SA
Su:50kW::CA/SA

15370

BULGARIA
RADIO SOFIA
Rebrovo-Sofia
(J):250kW::SA
CHINA (TAIWAN)
VOICE FREE CHINA
T'ai-pei
50kW::SEA
50kW::ANZ
USA
RFE-RL
Via Holzkirchen,GFR
250kW::WUSSR
(D):250kW::WUSSR
(J):250kW::WUSSR
RFE-RL
Via Lamperth'm, GFR
(D):100kW::WUSSR
(J):100kW::WUSSR
RFE-RL
Via Pals, Spain
(J):100kW::WUSSR
USSR
RADIO MOSCOW/RP&P
Novosibirsk
500kW::ME

15375

EGYPT
RADIO CAIRO
Abu Za'bal
100kW::WAF
KOREA (REPUBLIC)
RADIO KOREA
In-Kimjae
100kW::AS
USA
VOICE OF AMERICA
Delano, California
250kW::CA/SA
WYFR-FAMILY RADIO
Okeechobee,Florida
(J):100kW::SA
USSR
RADIO MOSCOW/RP&P
Kenga
100kW::EAS

15380

AUSTRALIA
RADIO AUSTRALIA
Carnarvon
250kW::SEA
JAPAN
RADIO JAPAN/NHK
Tōkyō-Yamata
50kW::SEA
ROMANIA
RADIO BUCHAREST
Bucharest
250kW::SAS/SEA
+RADIO BUCHAREST
Bucharest
(D):250kW::AF
(con'd)
RADIO BUCHAREST
Bucharest
(D):250kW::EAF

ENGLISH ▬   GERMAN / DEUTSCH ▒▒▒   FRENCH / FRANÇAIS ═══   PORTUGUESE / PORTUGUÊS ═══   SPANISH / ESPAÑOL ═══

ARABIC /ﻉﺭﻉ ≣   RUSSIAN / РУССКИИ ═══   CHINESE / 中文 ▒▒▒   JAPANESE / 日本語 ▒▒▒   MULTILINGUAL ▒▒▒   OTHER ▬

SUMMER ONLY (J)   WINTER ONLY (D)   JAMMING ∧∧ or / or \   EARLIEST HEARD ◢   LATEST HEARD ◣   + TENTATIVE

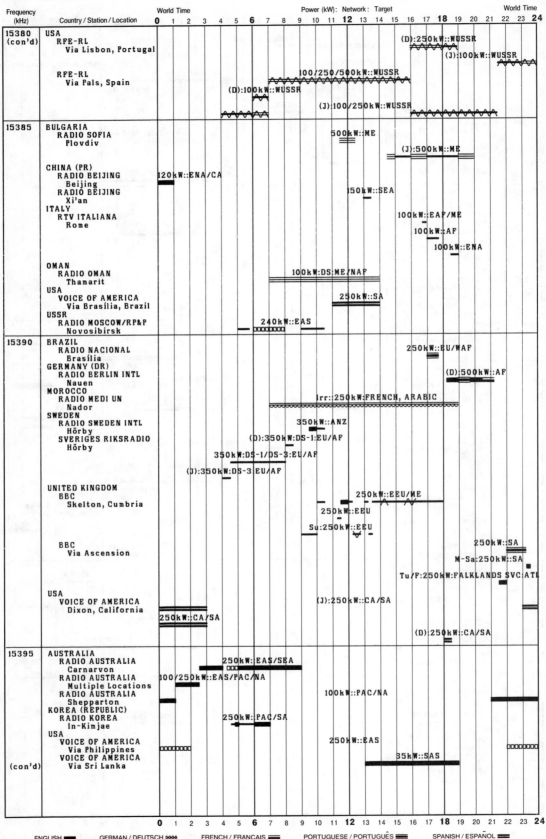

Frequency (kHz)	Country / Station / Location	Power (kW): Network: Target
15380 (con'd)	USA RFE-RL Via Lisbon, Portugal	(D):250kW::WUSSR / (J):100kW::WUSSR
	RFE-RL Via Pals, Spain	100/250/500kW::WUSSR / (D):100kW::WUSSR / (J):100/250kW::WUSSR
15385	BULGARIA RADIO SOFIA Plovdiv	500kW::ME / (J):500kW::ME
	CHINA (PR) RADIO BEIJING Beijing	120kW::ENA/CA
	RADIO BEIJING Xi'an	150kW::SEA
	ITALY RTV ITALIANA Rome	100kW::EAF/ME / 100kW::AF / 100kW::ENA
	OMAN RADIO OMAN Thamarit	100kW:DS:ME/NAF
	USA VOICE OF AMERICA Via Brasília, Brazil	250kW::SA
	USSR RADIO MOSCOW/RP&P Novosibirsk	240kW::EAS
15390	BRAZIL RADIO NACIONAL Brasília	250kW::EU/WAF
	GERMANY (DR) RADIO BERLIN INTL Nauen	(D):500kW::AF
	MOROCCO RADIO MEDI UN Nador	Irr::250kW:FRENCH, ARABIC
	SWEDEN RADIO SWEDEN INTL Hörby	350kW::ANZ
	SVERIGES RIKSRADIO Hörby	(D):350kW:DS-1:EU/AF / 350kW:DS-1/DS-3:EU/AF / (J):350kW:DS-3 EU/AF
	UNITED KINGDOM BBC Skelton, Cumbria	250kW::EEU/ME / 250kW::EEU / Su:250kW::EEU
	BBC Via Ascension	250kW::SA / M-Sa:250kW::SA / Tu/F:250kW:FALKLANDS SVC:ATL
	USA VOICE OF AMERICA Dixon, California	(J):250kW::CA/SA / 250kW::CA/SA / (D):250kW::CA/SA
15395	AUSTRALIA RADIO AUSTRALIA Carnarvon	250kW::EAS/SEA
	RADIO AUSTRALIA Multiple Locations	100/250kW::EAS/PAC/NA
	RADIO AUSTRALIA Shepparton	100kW::PAC/NA
	KOREA (REPUBLIC) RADIO KOREA In-Kimjae	250kW::PAC/SA
	USA VOICE OF AMERICA Via Philippines	250kW::EAS
(con'd)	VOICE OF AMERICA Via Sri Lanka	35kW::SAS

ENGLISH ▬   GERMAN / DEUTSCH ००००   FRENCH / FRANÇAIS ═   PORTUGUESE / PORTUGUÊS ═   SPANISH / ESPAÑOL ═

ARABIC /ﺑﺮ ═   RUSSIAN / РУССКИИ ═   CHINESE / 中文 ०००   JAPANESE / 日本語 ▬   MULTILINGUAL ᑐᑐᑐ   OTHER ▬

SUMMER ONLY (J)   WINTER ONLY (D)   JAMMING ∧∧ or / or \   EARLIEST HEARD ◢   LATEST HEARD ◣   + TENTATIVE

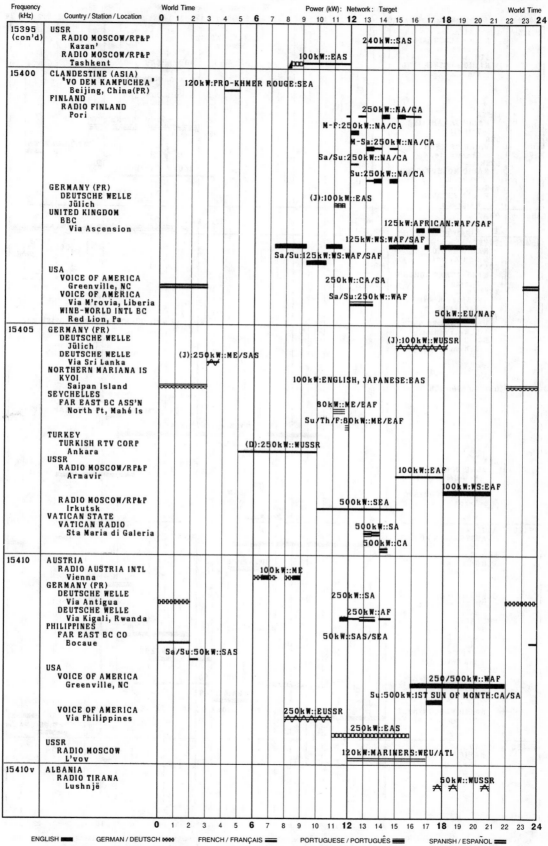

15395 (con'd) — USSR
- RADIO MOSCOW/RP&P, Kazan' — 240kW::SAS
- RADIO MOSCOW/RP&P, Tashkent — 100kW::EAS

15400
- CLANDESTINE (ASIA) — 'VO DEM KAMPUCHEA', Beijing, China(PR) — 120kW:PRO-KHMER ROUGE:SEA
- FINLAND — RADIO FINLAND, Pori — 250kW::NA/CA; M-F:250kW::NA/CA; M-Sa:250kW::NA/CA; Sa/Su:250kW::NA/CA; Su:250kW::NA/CA
- GERMANY (FR) — DEUTSCHE WELLE, Jülich — (J):100kW::EAS
- UNITED KINGDOM — BBC, Via Ascension — 125kW:AFRICAN:WAF/SAF; 125kW:WS:WAF/SAF; Sa/Su:125kW:WS:WAF/SAF
- USA — VOICE OF AMERICA, Greenville, NC — 250kW::CA/SA
- VOICE OF AMERICA, Via M'rovia, Liberia — Sa/Su:250kW::WAF
- WINB-WORLD INTL BC, Red Lion, Pa — 50kW::EU/NAF

15405
- GERMANY (FR) — DEUTSCHE WELLE, Jülich — (J):100kW::WUSSR
- DEUTSCHE WELLE, Via Sri Lanka — (J):250kW::ME/SAS
- NORTHERN MARIANA IS — KYOI, Saipan Island — 100kW:ENGLISH, JAPANESE:EAS
- SEYCHELLES — FAR EAST BC ASS'N, North Pt, Mahé Is — 80kW::ME/EAF; Su/Th/F:80kW::ME/EAF
- TURKEY — TURKISH RTV CORP, Ankara — (D):250kW::WUSSR
- USSR — RADIO MOSCOW/RP&P, Armavir — 100kW::EAF; 100kW:WS:EAF
- RADIO MOSCOW/RP&P, Irkutsk — 500kW::SEA
- VATICAN STATE — VATICAN RADIO, Sta Maria di Galeria — 500kW::SA; 500kW::CA

15410
- AUSTRIA — RADIO AUSTRIA INTL, Vienna — 100kW::ME
- GERMANY (FR) — DEUTSCHE WELLE, Via Antigua — 250kW::SA
- DEUTSCHE WELLE, Via Kigali, Rwanda — 250kW::AF
- PHILIPPINES — FAR EAST BC CO, Bocaue — 50kW::SAS/SEA; Sa/Su:50kW::SAS
- USA — VOICE OF AMERICA, Greenville, NC — 250/500kW::WAF; Su:500kW:1ST SUN OF MONTH:CA/SA
- VOICE OF AMERICA, Via Philippines — 250kW::EUSSR; 250kW::EAS
- USSR — RADIO MOSCOW, L'vov — 120kW:MARINERS:WEU/ATL

15410v
- ALBANIA — RADIO TIRANA, Lushnjë — 50kW::WUSSR

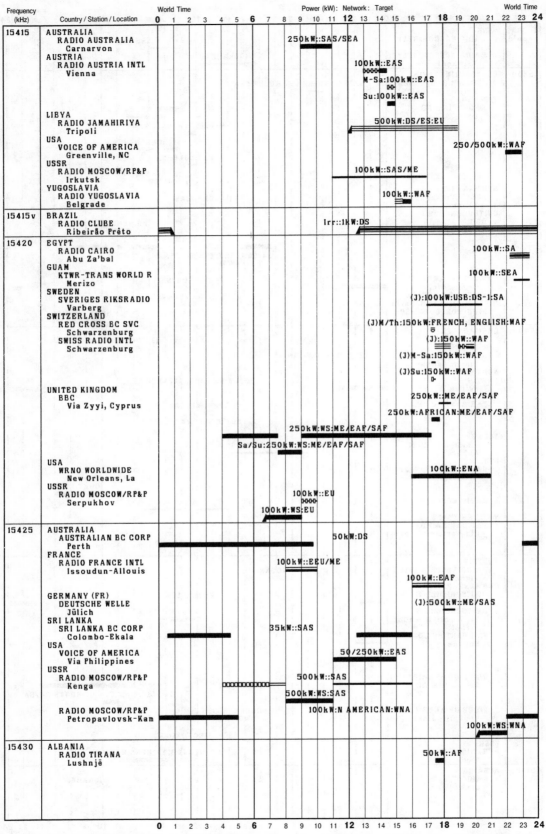

Frequency (kHz)	Country / Station / Location	Schedule (World Time / Power (kW) : Network : Target)
15415	AUSTRALIA RADIO AUSTRALIA Carnarvon	250kW::SAS/SEA
	AUSTRIA RADIO AUSTRIA INTL Vienna	100kW::EAS M-Sa:100kW::EAS Su:100kW::EAS
	LIBYA RADIO JAMAHIRIYA Tripoli	500kW:DS/ES:EU
	USA VOICE OF AMERICA Greenville, NC	250/500kW::WAF
	USSR RADIO MOSCOW/RP&P Irkutsk	100kW::SAS/ME
	YUGOSLAVIA RADIO YUGOSLAVIA Belgrade	100kW::WAF
15415v	BRAZIL RADIO CLUBE Ribeirão Prêto	Irr::1kW:DS
15420	EGYPT RADIO CAIRO Abu Za'bal	100kW::SA
	GUAM KTWR-TRANS WORLD R Merizo	100kW::SEA
	SWEDEN SVERIGES RIKSRADIO Varberg	(J):100kW:USB:DS-1:SA
	SWITZERLAND RED CROSS BC SVC Schwarzenburg	(J)M/Th:150kW:FRENCH, ENGLISH:WAF
	SWISS RADIO INTL Schwarzenburg	(J):150kW::WAF (J)M-Sa:150kW::WAF (J)Su:150kW::WAF
	UNITED KINGDOM BBC Via Zyyi, Cyprus	250kW::ME/EAF/SAF 250kW:AFRICAN:ME/EAF/SAF 250kW:WS:ME/EAF/SAF Sa/Su:250kW:WS:ME/EAF/SAF
	USA WRNO WORLDWIDE New Orleans, La	100kW::ENA
	USSR RADIO MOSCOW/RP&P Serpukhov	100kW::EU 100kW:WS:EU
15425	AUSTRALIA AUSTRALIAN BC CORP Perth	50kW:DS
	FRANCE RADIO FRANCE INTL Issoudun-Allouis	100kW::EEU/ME 100kW::EAF
	GERMANY (FR) DEUTSCHE WELLE Jülich	(J):500kW::ME/SAS
	SRI LANKA SRI LANKA BC CORP Colombo-Ekala	35kW::SAS
	USA VOICE OF AMERICA Via Philippines	50/250kW::EAS
	USSR RADIO MOSCOW/RP&P Kenga	500kW::SAS 500kW:WS:SAS
	RADIO MOSCOW/RP&P Petropavlovsk-Kam	100kW:N AMERICAN:WNA 100kW:WS:WNA
15430	ALBANIA RADIO TIRANA Lushnjë	50kW::AF

World Time: 0 1 2 3 4 5 6 7 8 9 10 11 12 13 14 15 16 17 18 19 20 21 22 23 24

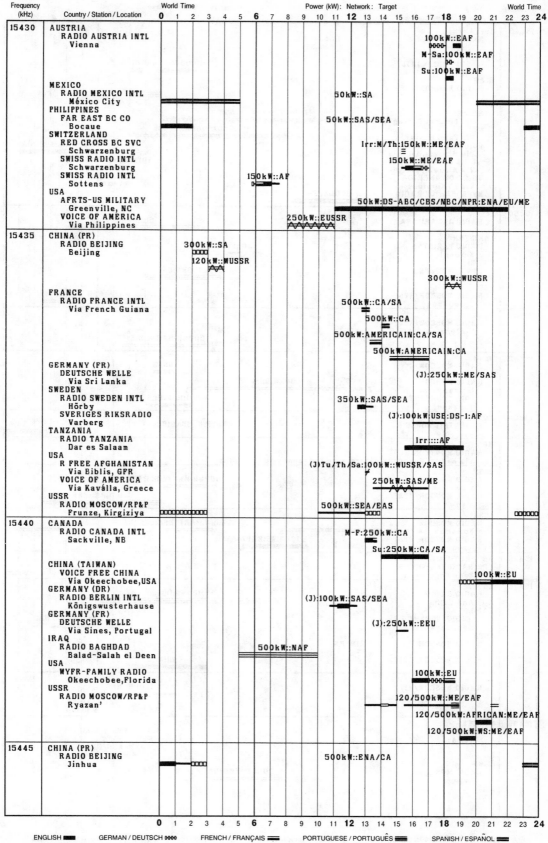

Frequency (kHz)	Country / Station / Location	Power (kW): Network : Target
15430	AUSTRIA	
	RADIO AUSTRIA INTL / Vienna	100kW::EAF; M-Sa:100kW::EAF; Su:100kW::EAF
	MEXICO	
	RADIO MEXICO INTL / México City	50kW::SA
	PHILIPPINES	
	FAR EAST BC CO / Bocaue	50kW::SAS/SEA
	SWITZERLAND	
	RED CROSS BC SVC / Schwarzenburg	Irr:M/Th:150kW::ME/EAF
	SWISS RADIO INTL / Schwarzenburg	150kW::ME/EAF
	SWISS RADIO INTL / Sottens	150kW::AF
	USA	
	AFRTS-US MILITARY / Greenville, NC	50kW::DS-ABC/CBS/NBC/NPR:ENA/EU/ME
	VOICE OF AMERICA / Via Philippines	250kW::EUSSR
15435	CHINA (PR)	
	RADIO BEIJING / Beijing	300kW::SA; 120kW::WUSSR; 300kW::WUSSR
	FRANCE	
	RADIO FRANCE INTL / Via French Guiana	500kW::CA/SA; 500kW::CA; 500kW:AMERICAIN:CA/SA; 500kW:AMERICAIN:CA
	GERMANY (FR)	
	DEUTSCHE WELLE / Via Sri Lanka	(J):250kW::ME/SAS
	SWEDEN	
	RADIO SWEDEN INTL / Hörby	350kW::SAS/SEA
	SVERIGES RIKSRADIO / Varberg	(J):100kW:USE:DS-1:AF
	TANZANIA	
	RADIO TANZANIA / Dar es Salaam	Irr:::AF
	USA	
	R FREE AFGHANISTAN / Via Biblis, GFR	(J)Tu/Th/Sa:100kW::WUSSR/SAS
	VOICE OF AMERICA / Via Kaválla, Greece	250kW::SAS/ME
	USSR	
	RADIO MOSCOW/RP&P / Frunze, Kirgiziya	500kW::SEA/EAS
15440	CANADA	
	RADIO CANADA INTL / Sackville, NB	M-F:250kW::CA; Su:250kW::CA/SA
	CHINA (TAIWAN)	
	VOICE FREE CHINA / Via Okeechobee, USA	100kW::EU
	GERMANY (DR)	
	RADIO BERLIN INTL / Königswusterhause	(J):100kW::SAS/SEA
	GERMANY (FR)	
	DEUTSCHE WELLE / Via Sines, Portugal	(J):250kW::EEU
	IRAQ	
	RADIO BAGHDAD / Balad-Salah el Deen	500kW::NAF
	USA	
	WYFR-FAMILY RADIO / Okeechobee, Florida	100kW::EU
	USSR	
	RADIO MOSCOW/RP&P / Ryazan'	120/500kW::ME/EAF; 120/500kW:AFRICAN:ME/EAF; 120/500kW:WS:ME/EAF
15445	CHINA (PR)	
	RADIO BEIJING / Jinhua	500kW::ENA/CA

ENGLISH ■■■	GERMAN / DEUTSCH ◊◊◊◊	FRENCH / FRANÇAIS ══	PORTUGUESE / PORTUGUÊS ▤	SPANISH / ESPAÑOL ▥
ARABIC / علم ≡	RUSSIAN / РУССКИИ ══	CHINESE / 中文 ◊◊◊◊	JAPANESE / 日本語 ▦▦▦	MULTILINGUAL ▨▨	OTHER ──
SUMMER ONLY (J)	WINTER ONLY (D)	JAMMING /\/\ or / or \	EARLIEST HEARD ◢	LATEST HEARD ◣	⁺ TENTATIVE

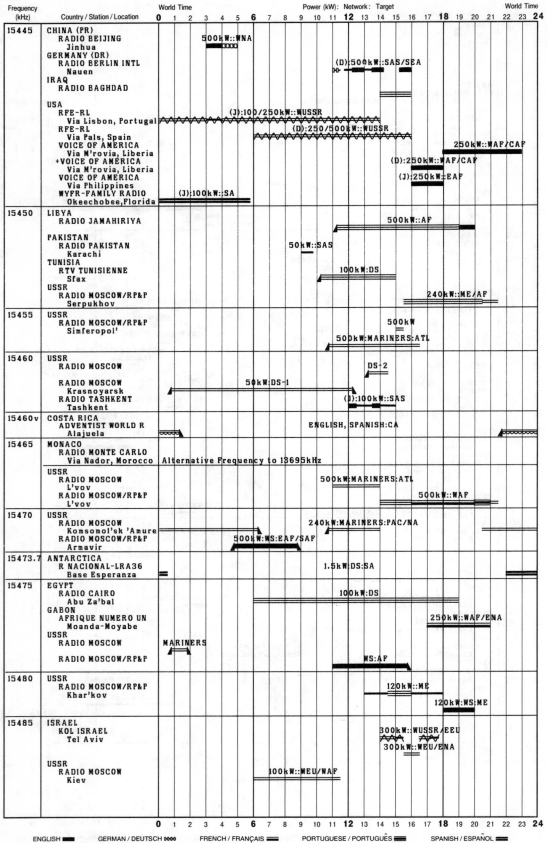

Frequency (kHz)	Country / Station / Location	Power (kW): Network: Target	World Time
15445	CHINA (PR) RADIO BEIJING Jinhua	500kW::WNA	
	GERMANY (DR) RADIO BERLIN INTL Nauen	(D):500kW::SAS/SEA	
	IRAQ RADIO BAGHDAD		
	USA RFE-RL Via Lisbon, Portugal	(J):100/250kW::WUSSR	
	RFE-RL Via Pals, Spain	(D):250/500kW::WUSSR	
	VOICE OF AMERICA Via M'rovia, Liberia	250kW::WAF/CAF	
	+VOICE OF AMERICA Via M'rovia, Liberia	(D):250kW::WAF/CAF	
	VOICE OF AMERICA Via Philippines	(J):250kW::EAF	
	WYFR-FAMILY RADIO Okeechobee,Florida	(J):100kW::SA	
15450	LIBYA RADIO JAMAHIRIYA	500kW::AF	
	PAKISTAN RADIO PAKISTAN Karachi	50kW::SAS	
	TUNISIA RTV TUNISIENNE Sfax	100kW:DS	
	USSR RADIO MOSCOW/RP&P Serpukhov	240kW::ME/AF	
15455	USSR RADIO MOSCOW/RP&P Simferopol'	500kW / 500kW:MARINERS:ATL	
15460	USSR RADIO MOSCOW	DS-2	
	RADIO MOSCOW Krasnoyarsk	50kW:DS-1	
	RADIO TASHKENT Tashkent	(D):100kW::SAS	
15460v	COSTA RICA ADVENTIST WORLD R Alajuela	ENGLISH, SPANISH:CA	
15465	MONACO RADIO MONTE CARLO Via Nador, Morocco	Alternative Frequency to 13695kHz	
	USSR RADIO MOSCOW L'vov	500kW:MARINERS:ATL	
	RADIO MOSCOW/RP&P L'vov	500kW::WAF	
15470	USSR RADIO MOSCOW Komsomol'sk 'Amure	240kW:MARINERS:PAC/NA	
	RADIO MOSCOW/RP&P Armavir	500kW:WS:EAF/SAF	
15473.7	ANTARCTICA R NACIONAL-LRA36 Base Esperanza	1.5kW:DS:SA	
15475	EGYPT RADIO CAIRO Abu Za'bal	100kW:DS	
	GABON AFRIQUE NUMERO UN Moanda-Moyabe	250kW::WAF/ENA	
	USSR RADIO MOSCOW	MARINERS	
	RADIO MOSCOW/RP&P	WS:AF	
15480	USSR RADIO MOSCOW/RP&P Khar'kov	120kW::ME	
		120kW:WS:ME	
15485	ISRAEL KOL ISRAEL Tel Aviv	300kW::WUSSR/EEU / 300kW::WEU/ENA	
	USSR RADIO MOSCOW Kiev	100kW::WEU/WAF	

ENGLISH ▬▬▬   GERMAN / DEUTSCH ◊◊◊◊   FRENCH / FRANÇAIS ═══   PORTUGUESE / PORTUGUÊS ▤▤▤   SPANISH / ESPAÑOL ▬▬▬

ARABIC /ϳ∫ ═══   RUSSIAN / РУССКИИ ═══   CHINESE / 中文 ◊◊◊◊   JAPANESE / 日本語 ▦▦▦   MULTILINGUAL ▨▨▨   OTHER ▬▬

SUMMER ONLY (J)   WINTER ONLY (D)   JAMMING ∧∧ or / or \   EARLIEST HEARD ◢   LATEST HEARD ◣   + TENTATIVE

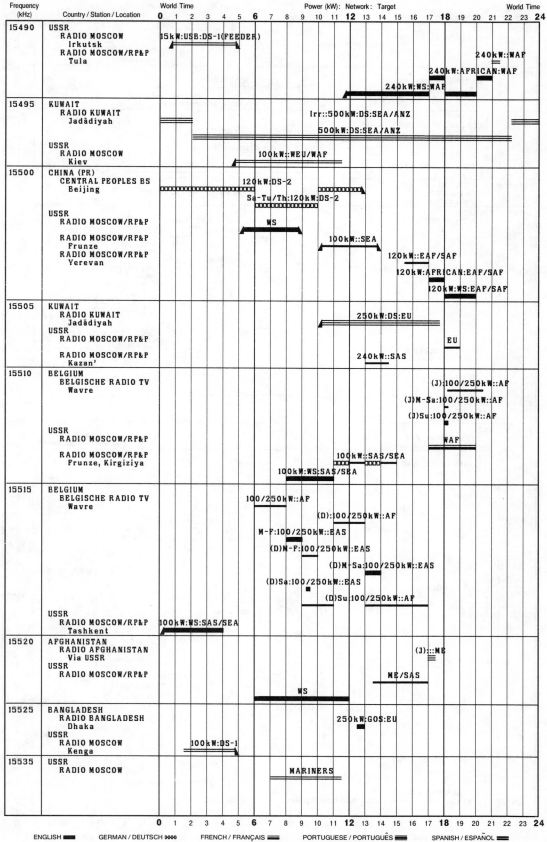

Frequency (kHz)	Country / Station / Location				Power (kW): Network: Target				

(chart rows, World Time 0–24)

15490 — USSR
- RADIO MOSCOW, Irkutsk — 15kW:USB:DS-1(FEEDER)
- RADIO MOSCOW/RP&P, Tula — 240kW::WAF / 240kW:AFRICAN:WAF / 240kW:WS:WAF

15495 — KUWAIT
- RADIO KUWAIT, Jadādiyah — Irr::500kW:DS:SEA/ANZ / 500kW:DS:SEA/ANZ
- USSR RADIO MOSCOW, Kiev — 100kW::WEU/WAF

15500 — CHINA (PR)
- CENTRAL PEOPLES BS, Beijing — 120kW:DS-2 / Sa-Tu/Th:120kW:DS-2
- USSR RADIO MOSCOW/RP&P — WS
- RADIO MOSCOW/RP&P, Frunze — 100kW::SEA
- RADIO MOSCOW/RP&P, Yerevan — 120kW::EAF/SAF / 120kW:AFRICAN:EAF/SAF / 120kW:WS:EAF/SAF

15505 — KUWAIT
- RADIO KUWAIT, Jadādiyah — 250kW:DS:EU
- USSR RADIO MOSCOW/RP&P — EU
- RADIO MOSCOW/RP&P, Kazan' — 240kW::SAS

15510 — BELGIUM
- BELGISCHE RADIO TV, Wavre — (J):100/250kW::AF / (J)M-Sa:100/250kW::AF / (J)Su:100/250kW::AF
- USSR RADIO MOSCOW/RP&P — WAF
- RADIO MOSCOW/RP&P, Frunze, Kirgiziya — 100kW::SAS/SEA / 100kW:WS:SAS/SEA

15515 — BELGIUM
- BELGISCHE RADIO TV, Wavre — 100/250kW::AF / (D):100/250kW::AF / M-F:100/250kW::EAS / (D)M-F:100/250kW::EAS / (D)M-Sa:100/250kW::EAS / (D)Sa:100/250kW::EAS / (D)Su:100/250kW::AF
- USSR RADIO MOSCOW/RP&P, Tashkent — 100kW:WS:SAS/SEA

15520 — AFGHANISTAN
- RADIO AFGHANISTAN, Via USSR — (J):::ME
- USSR RADIO MOSCOW/RP&P — ME/SAS / WS

15525 — BANGLADESH
- RADIO BANGLADESH, Dhaka — 250kW:GOS:EU
- USSR RADIO MOSCOW, Kenga — 100kW:DS-1

15535 — USSR
- RADIO MOSCOW — MARINERS

ENGLISH ▬▬▬   GERMAN / DEUTSCH ◊◊◊◊   FRENCH / FRANÇAIS ═══   PORTUGUESE / PORTUGUÊS ▬▬▬   SPANISH / ESPAÑOL ═══
ARABIC / عربى ═══   RUSSIAN / РУССКИИ ═══   CHINESE / 中文 ◻◻◻◻   JAPANESE / 日本語 ▬▬▬   MULTILINGUAL ◦◦◦◦   OTHER ▬▬
SUMMER ONLY (J)   WINTER ONLY (D)   JAMMING ⋀⋀ or / or \   EARLIEST HEARD ◢   LATEST HEARD ◣   + TENTATIVE

Frequency (kHz)	Country / Station / Location	Power (kW): Network: Target

World Time (0 1 2 3 4 5 6 7 8 9 10 11 12 13 14 15 16 17 18 19 20 21 22 23 24)

15535 — USSR, RADIO MOSCOW/RP&P
- WS

15540 — USSR, RADIO MOSCOW/RP&P, Minsk
- 100kW::ME
- 100kW:WS:ME

15550 — CHINA (PR), CENTRAL PEOPLES BS, Beijing
- 15kW:DS-1
- W-M:15kW:DS-1

15550 — USSR, RADIO MOSCOW/RP&P, L'vov
- 500kW::ME/SAS

15555 — CLANDESTINE (M EAST), 'VO LIB OF IRAN', Abu Za'bal, Egypt
- 100kW:ANTI-KHOMEYNI:ME

15560 — HOLLAND, RADIO NEDERLAND, Flevoland
- 500kW::EAS
- 500kW::CAF
- 500kW::SEA
- 500kW::SAS/SEA
- 500kW::ME
- 500kW::ME/EAF
- 500kW::WAF
- (J):500kW::EU/ME

15560 — RADIO NEDERLAND, Via Neth Antilles
- 300kW::WAF
- 300kW::SA
- Su:300kW::WNA

15565 — PAKISTAN, RADIO PAKISTAN, Islamabad
- 100kW::ME/NAF

15566 — USA, WYFR-FAMILY RADIO, Okeechobee, Florida
- 100kW::EU

15570 — HOLLAND, RADIO NEDERLAND, Via Madagascar
- 300kW::SAS
- (D):300kW::EAF

15570 — SWITZERLAND, RED CROSS BC SVC
- Irr:M/Th:::ANZ/SEA
- Irr:M/Th:::AS
- Irr:M/Th:::SAS/SEA
- Irr:M/Th:::ME/EAF
- Irr:M/Th:::SA/CA

SWISS RADIO INTL
- SA/CA
- ANZ
- AS
- SAS/SEA
- (J):::ME/EAF
- M-Sa:::ANZ
- M-Sa:::SAS/SEA
- M-Sa:::SA/CA
- Su:::SAS/SEA
- Su:::SA/CA

15570 — USSR, RADIO MOSCOW/RP&P
- WAF
- WS:WAF

(con'd) — RADIO MOSCOW/RP&P, Khabarovsk
- 100kW::EAS

World Time (0 1 2 3 4 5 6 7 8 9 10 11 12 13 14 15 16 17 18 19 20 21 22 23 24)

ENGLISH ▰▰▰ GERMAN / DEUTSCH ००० FRENCH / FRANÇAIS ≡≡≡ PORTUGUESE / PORTUGUÊS ≡≡≡ SPANISH / ESPAÑOL ≡≡≡

ARABIC / ٱلع ≡≡≡ RUSSIAN / РУССКИИ ═══ CHINESE / 中文 ०००० JAPANESE / 日本語 ▰▰▰ MULTILINGUAL ०००० OTHER ▬▬

SUMMER ONLY (J) WINTER ONLY (D) JAMMING ∧∧∧ or / or \ EARLIEST HEARD ◢ LATEST HEARD ◣ + TENTATIVE

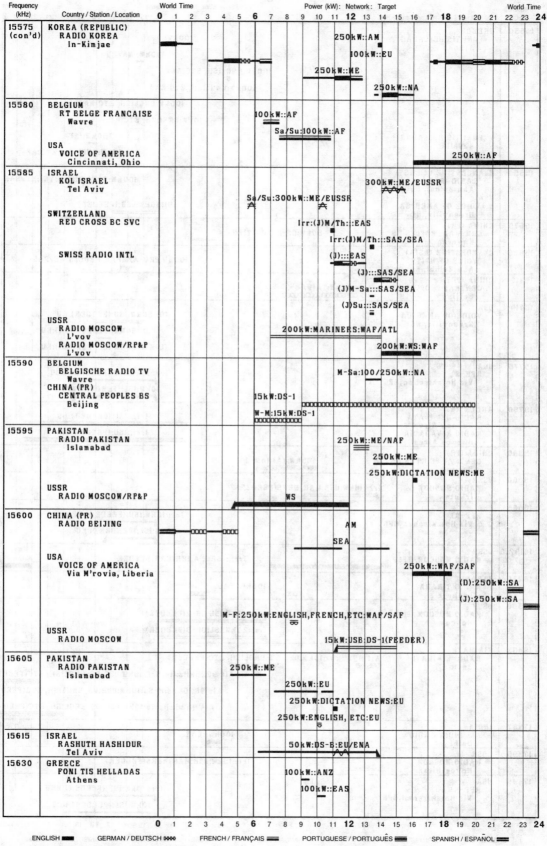

Frequency (kHz)	Country / Station / Location	World Time / Power (kW): Network: Target

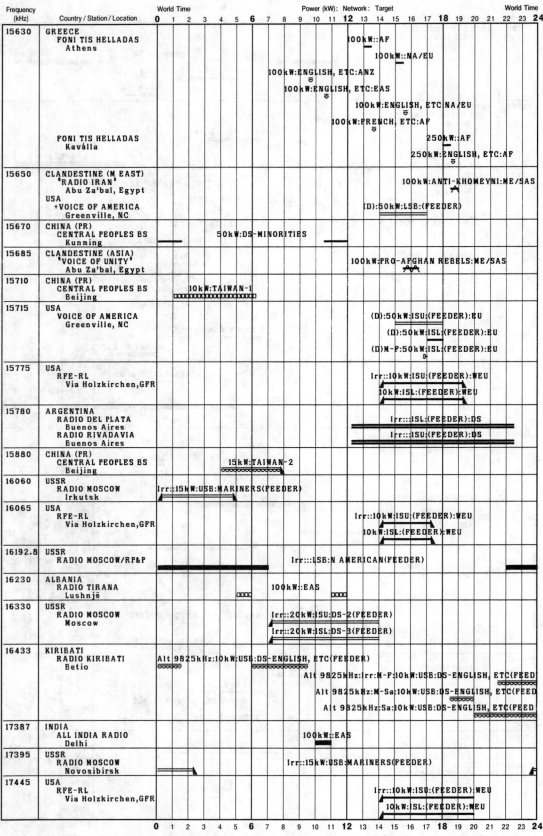

15630 GREECE — FONI TIS HELLADAS, Athens
- 100kW::AF
- 100kW::NA/EU
- 100kW:ENGLISH, ETC:ANZ
- 100kW:ENGLISH, ETC:EAS
- 100kW:ENGLISH, ETC NA/EU
- 100kW:FRENCH, ETC:AF

FONI TIS HELLADAS, Kaválla
- 250kW::AF
- 250kW:ENGLISH, ETC:AF

15650 CLANDESTINE (M EAST) 'RADIO IRAN', Abu Za'bal, Egypt
- 100kW:ANTI-KHOMEYNI:ME/SAS

USA +VOICE OF AMERICA, Greenville, NC
- (D):50kW:LSB:(FEEDER)

15670 CHINA (PR) CENTRAL PEOPLES BS, Kunming
- 50kW:DS-MINORITIES

15685 CLANDESTINE (ASIA) 'VOICE OF UNITY', Abu Za'bal, Egypt
- 100kW:PRO-AFGHAN REBELS:ME/SAS

15710 CHINA (PR) CENTRAL PEOPLES BS, Beijing
- 10kW:TAIWAN-1

15715 USA VOICE OF AMERICA, Greenville, NC
- (D):50kW:ISU:(FEEDER):EU
- (D):50kW:ISL:(FEEDER):EU
- (D)M-F:50kW:ISL:(FEEDER):EU

15775 USA RFE-RL, Via Holzkirchen, GFR
- Irr::10kW:ISU:(FEEDER):WEU
- 10kW:ISL:(FEEDER):WEU

15780 ARGENTINA RADIO DEL PLATA, Buenos Aires
- Irr:::ISL:(FEEDER):DS

RADIO RIVADAVIA, Buenos Aires
- Irr:::ISU:(FEEDER):DS

15880 CHINA (PR) CENTRAL PEOPLES BS, Beijing
- 15kW:TAIWAN-2

16060 USSR RADIO MOSCOW, Irkutsk
- Irr::15kW:USB:MARINERS(FEEDER)

16065 USA RFE-RL, Via Holzkirchen, GFR
- Irr::10kW:ISU:(FEEDER):WEU
- 10kW:ISL:(FEEDER):WEU

16192.8 USSR RADIO MOSCOW/RP&P
- Irr:::LSB:N AMERICAN(FEEDER)

16230 ALBANIA RADIO TIRANA, Lushnjë
- 100kW::EAS

16330 USSR RADIO MOSCOW, Moscow
- Irr::20kW:ISU:DS-2(FEEDER)
- Irr::20kW:ISL:DS-3(FEEDER)

16433 KIRIBATI RADIO KIRIBATI, Betio
- Alt 9825kHz:10kW:USB:DS-ENGLISH, ETC(FEEDER)
- Alt 9825kHz:Irr:M-F:10kW:USB:DS-ENGLISH, ETC(FEED
- Alt 9825kHz:M-Sa:10kW:USB:DS-ENGLISH, ETC(FEED
- Alt 9825kHz:Sa:10kW:USB:DS-ENGLISH, ETC(FEED

17387 INDIA ALL INDIA RADIO, Delhi
- 100kW::EAS

17395 USSR RADIO MOSCOW, Novosibirsk
- Irr::15kW:USB:MARINERS(FEEDER)

17445 USA RFE-RL, Via Holzkirchen, GFR
- Irr::10kW:ISU:(FEEDER):WEU
- 10kW:ISL:(FEEDER):WEU

ENGLISH ▬▬ GERMAN / DEUTSCH ◊◊◊◊ FRENCH / FRANÇAIS ▭▭▭ PORTUGUESE / PORTUGUÊS ▰▰▰ SPANISH / ESPAÑOL ▰▰▰
ARABIC /ﻉﺏﻉ ▤▤▤ RUSSIAN / РУССКИИ ▬▬ CHINESE / 中文 ◻◻◻◻ JAPANESE / 日本語 ▦▦▦ MULTILINGUAL ◻◻◻◻ OTHER ▬
SUMMER ONLY (J) WINTER ONLY (D) JAMMING ∧∧ or / or \ EARLIEST HEARD ◢ LATEST HEARD ◥ + TENTATIVE

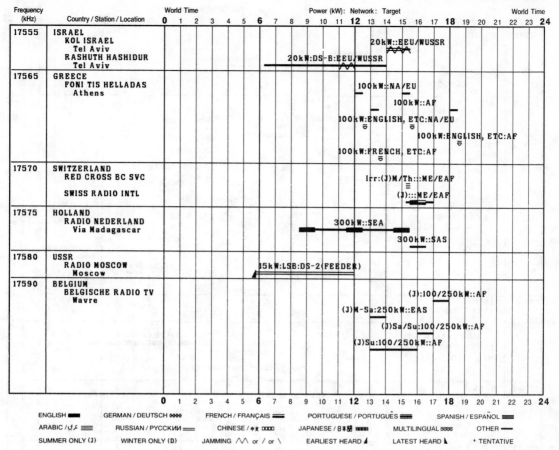

Frequency (kHz)	Country / Station / Location	World Time — Power (kW): Network: Target
17555	ISRAEL — KOL ISRAEL, Tel Aviv	20kW::EEU/WUSSR (13–14)
	RASHUTH HASHIDUR, Tel Aviv	20kW:DS-B:EEU/WUSSR (6–13)
17565	GREECE — FONI TIS HELLADAS, Athens	100kW::NA/EU (14–15)
		100kW::AF (15–17)
		100kW:ENGLISH, ETC:NA/EU (13–15)
		100kW:ENGLISH, ETC:AF (16–18)
		100kW:FRENCH, ETC:AF (13–14)
17570	SWITZERLAND — RED CROSS BC SVC	Irr:(J)M/Th:::ME/EAF (14)
	SWISS RADIO INTL	(J):::ME/EAF (15)
17575	HOLLAND — RADIO NEDERLAND, Via Madagascar	300kW::SEA (9–13)
		300kW::SAS (14–16)
17580	USSR — RADIO MOSCOW, Moscow	15kW:LSB:DS-2(FEEDER) (6–12)
17590	BELGIUM — BELGISCHE RADIO TV, Wavre	(J):100/250kW::AF (16–18)
		(J)M-Sa:250kW::EAS (13–17)
		(J)Sa/Su:100/250kW::AF (15–17)
		(J)Su:100/250kW::AF (14–17)

ENGLISH ▬▬   GERMAN / DEUTSCH ᗯᗯᗯᗯ   FRENCH / FRANÇAIS ▬▬   PORTUGUESE / PORTUGUÊS ▬▬   SPANISH / ESPAÑOL ▬▬

ARABIC / ﺓﻑ ≡   RUSSIAN / РУССКИИ ═   CHINESE / 中文 ᗐᗐᗐᗐ   JAPANESE / 日本語 ▩▩▩   MULTILINGUAL ᗧᗧᗧᗧ   OTHER ▬

SUMMER ONLY (J)   WINTER ONLY (D)   JAMMING ∧∧ or / or \   EARLIEST HEARD ◢   LATEST HEARD ◣   + TENTATIVE

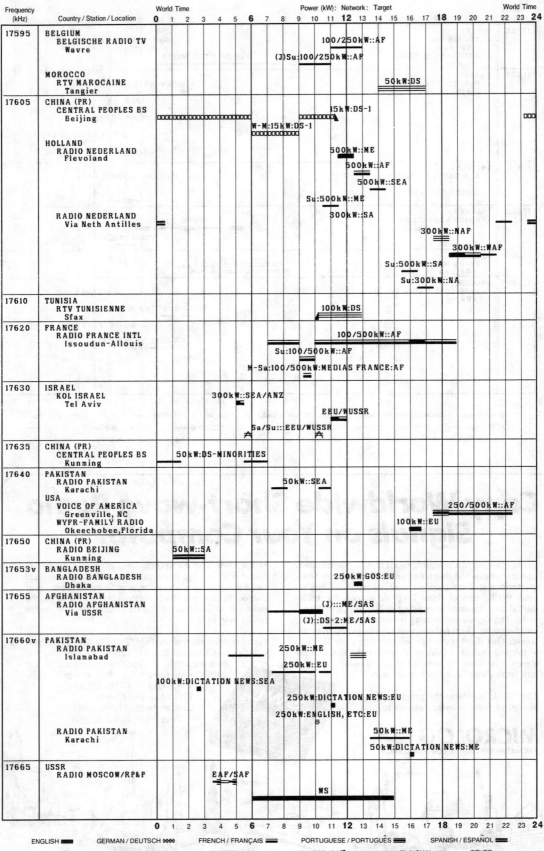

Frequency (kHz)	Country / Station / Location	Schedule (World Time)
17595	BELGIUM BELGISCHE RADIO TV Wavre	100/250kW::AF; (J)Su:100/250kW::AF
	MOROCCO RTV MAROCAINE Tangier	50kW:DS
17605	CHINA (PR) CENTRAL PEOPLES BS Beijing	15kW:DS-1; W-M:15kW:DS-1
	HOLLAND RADIO NEDERLAND Flevoland	500kW::ME; 500kW::AF; 500kW::SEA; Su:500kW::ME; 300kW::SA
	RADIO NEDERLAND Via Neth Antilles	300kW::NAF; 300kW::WAF; Su:500kW::SA; Su:300kW::NA
17610	TUNISIA RTV TUNISIENNE Sfax	100kW:DS
17620	FRANCE RADIO FRANCE INTL Issoudun-Allouis	100/500kW::AF; Su:100/500kW::AF; M-Sa:100/500kW:MEDIAS FRANCE:AF
17630	ISRAEL KOL ISRAEL Tel Aviv	300kW::SEA/ANZ; EEU/WUSSR; Sa/Su:::EEU/WUSSR
17635	CHINA (PR) CENTRAL PEOPLES BS Kunming	50kW:DS-MINORITIES
17640	PAKISTAN RADIO PAKISTAN Karachi	50kW::SEA
	USA VOICE OF AMERICA Greenville, NC	250/500kW::AF
	WYFR-FAMILY RADIO Okeechobee,Florida	100kW::EU
17650	CHINA (PR) RADIO BEIJING Kunming	50kW::SA
17653v	BANGLADESH RADIO BANGLADESH Dhaka	250kW:GOS:EU
17655	AFGHANISTAN RADIO AFGHANISTAN Via USSR	(J):::ME/SAS; (J)::DS-2:ME/SAS
17660v	PAKISTAN RADIO PAKISTAN Islamabad	250kW::ME; 250kW::EU; 100kW:DICTATION NEWS:SEA; 250kW:DICTATION NEWS:EU; 250kW:ENGLISH, ETC:EU
	RADIO PAKISTAN Karachi	50kW::ME; 50kW:DICTATION NEWS:ME
17665	USSR RADIO MOSCOW/RP&P	EAF/SAF; WS

ENGLISH ▬▬   GERMAN / DEUTSCH ००००   FRENCH / FRANÇAIS ═══   PORTUGUESE / PORTUGUÊS ▬▬   SPANISH / ESPAÑOL ▬▬

ARABIC / ٷﺀ ≡≡≡   RUSSIAN / РУССКИИ ═══   CHINESE / ◆✗ ००००   JAPANESE / 日本語 ▬▬▬   MULTILINGUAL ౷౷౷౷   OTHER ▬▬

SUMMER ONLY (J)   WINTER ONLY (D)   JAMMING /\/\ or / or \   EARLIEST HEARD ◢   LATEST HEARD ◣   ⁺ TENTATIVE

Frequency (kHz)	Country / Station / Location	World Time 0–24 / Power (kW): Network: Target
17669	EGYPT RADIO CAIRO Abu Za'bal	100kW:DS-GENERAL
17675	BELGIUM RT BELGE FRANCAISE Wavre	250kW:DS/ES:AF Su:250kW:DS/ES:AF
	EGYPT RADIO CAIRO Kafr Silîm-Abis	250kW::SAS/SEA
	USSR RADIO MOSCOW/RP&P	SAS WS:SAS
17680	CHINA (PR) RADIO BEIJING Beijing RADIO BEIJING Kunming	500kW::ENA/CA/SA 120kW::SEA
	USSR RADIO MOSCOW/RP&P Dushanbé	500kW::ME/NAF/WAF 500kW:WS:ME/NAF/WAF
17685	BELGIUM RT BELGE FRANCAISE Wavre	250kW:DS/ES:AF Sa/Su:250kW:DS/ES:AF
	ISRAEL KOL ISRAEL Tel Aviv	20kW::EU Sa/Su:20kW::EU
17690	EGYPT RADIO CAIRO Kafr Silîm-Abis	250kW::SAS
	USSR RADIO MOSCOW/RP&P	SAS
17695	UNITED KINGDOM BBC	EU/ME/USSR WUSSR EEU Su:::EU/ME Su:::WUSSR Su:::EEU
17700	USSR RADIO MOSCOW/RP&P	EAF WS
17705	CZECHOSLOVAKIA RADIO PRAGUE Pieštány-Velké K'y	250kW::AF M-F:250kW::AF
	GERMANY (DR) RADIO BERLIN INTL Nauen	(J):500kW::SAS/SEA (J):100kW::SAS/SEA
	INDIA ALL INDIA RADIO Delhi	50kW::ANZ 50kW:DS-ENGLISH, ETC
	IRAQ RADIO BAGHDAD Balad-Salah el Deen	500kW
	NEW ZEALAND +RADIO NEW ZEALAND Wellington	(D):7.5kW::PAC
	UNITED KINGDOM BBC Daventry	250kW:WS:WAF
(con'd)	USA VOICE OF AMERICA Dixon, California	(J):250kW::CA/SA

ENGLISH ▬▬   GERMAN / DEUTSCH ००००   FRENCH / FRANÇAIS ═══   PORTUGUESE / PORTUGUÊS ▬▬   SPANISH / ESPAÑOL ═══

ARABIC / ﻋﺮﺑﻲ ═══   RUSSIAN / РУССКИИ ═══   CHINESE / 中文 ००००   JAPANESE / 日本語 ▬▬   MULTILINGUAL ▭▭   OTHER ▬

SUMMER ONLY (J)   WINTER ONLY (D)   JAMMING /\/\ or / or \   EARLIEST HEARD ◢   LATEST HEARD ◣   + TENTATIVE

Frequency (kHz)	Country / Station / Location	World Time 0–24 / Power (kW): Network: Target

17705 (con'd)

USA
VOICE OF AMERICA
Via M'rovia, Liberia
250kW::AF
(D):250kW::AF

17710

CHINA (PR)
CENTRAL PEOPLES BS
Beijing
50kW:DS-2
Sa-Tu/Th:50kW:DS-2

HUNGARY
RADIO BUDAPEST
EU
M-F:::EU
M-Sa:::EU
Sa::EU
Sa/Su:::EU
Su:::EU
Su-F:::EU

RADIO BUDAPEST
Jászberény
250kW::SEA/ANZ
M-F:250kW::SEA/ANZ

ISRAEL
KOL ISRAEL
Tel Aviv
300kW::WUSSR/EEU
Sa/Su:300kW::WUSSR/EEU

UNITED KINGDOM
BBC
Via Singapore
250kW::EAS
250kW:WS:EAS

USA
VOICE OF AMERICA
Via Brasília, Brazil
250kW::SA

USSR
RADIO HABANA
L'vov
200kW::AF
RADIO MOSCOW
Moscow
240kW::EU/ATL
240kW:MARINERS:SAS

RADIO MOSCOW/RP&P
Novosibirsk
100kW::EAS

17714v

COLOMBIA
RADIO NACIONAL
Bogotá
Alt 17869vkHz::Irr::25kW:DS

17715

AUSTRALIA
RADIO AUSTRALIA
Carnarvon
300kW::SAS/SEA
GERMANY (FR)
DEUTSCHE WELLE
Jülich
100kW::ME
DEUTSCHE WELLE
Via Antigua
250kW::SA
ITALY
RTV ITALIANA
Rome
100kW::ENA
Su:100kW::ENA

UNITED KINGDOM
BBC
Multiple Locations
100kW::EU/ME/NAF
BBC
Skelton, Cumbria
100kW::EU/ME
Su:100kW::EEU

USA
VOICE OF AMERICA
Greenville, NC
(J):250kW::CA/SA

17720

CHINA (TAIWAN)
VOICE FREE CHINA
T'ai-pei
50/100kW::SEA
EGYPT
RADIO CAIRO
Kafr Sillm-Abis
250kW::SA
FRANCE
RADIO FRANCE INTL
Issoudun-Allouis
500kW:AMERICAIN:CA
SAUDI ARABIA
BS OF THE KINGDOM
Riyadh
350kW::SEA
USSR
RADIO MOSCOW/RP&P
Khabarovsk
100kW:WS:PAC

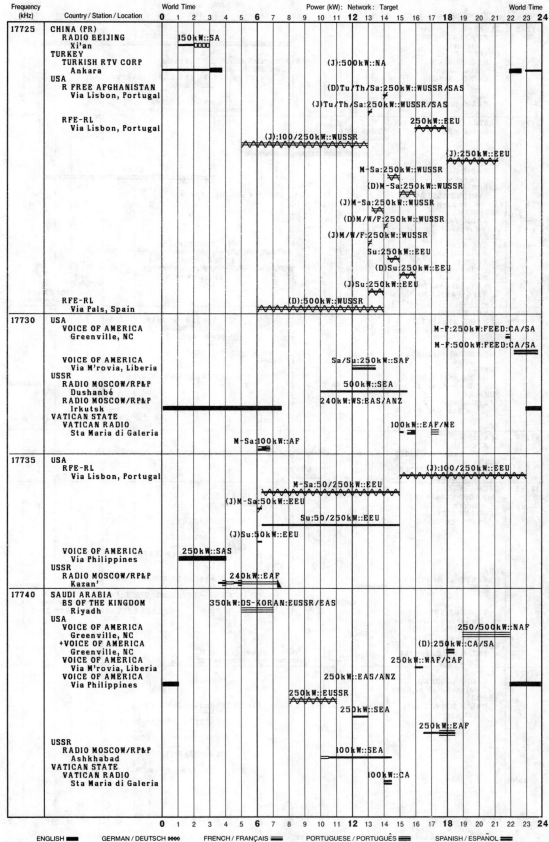

Frequency (kHz)	Country / Station / Location	
17725	CHINA (PR)	
	RADIO BEIJING	150kW::SA
	Xi'an	
	TURKEY	
	TURKISH RTV CORP	(J):500kW::NA
	Ankara	
	USA	
	R FREE AFGHANISTAN	(D)Tu/Th/Sa:250kW::WUSSR/SAS
	Via Lisbon, Portugal	(J)Tu/Th/Sa:250kW::WUSSR/SAS
		250kW::EEU
	RFE-RL	
	Via Lisbon, Portugal	(J):100/250kW::WUSSR
		(J):250kW::EEU
		M-Sa:250kW::WUSSR
		(D)M-Sa:250kW::WUSSR
		(J)M-Sa:250kW::WUSSR
		(D)M/W/F:250kW::WUSSR
		(J)M/W/F:250kW::WUSSR
		Su:250kW::EEU
		(D)Su:250kW::EEU
		(J)Su:250kW::EEU
	RFE-RL	
	Via Pals, Spain	(D):500kW::WUSSR
17730	USA	
	VOICE OF AMERICA	M-F:250kW:FEED:CA/SA
	Greenville, NC	M-F:500kW:FEED:CA/SA
	VOICE OF AMERICA	Sa/Su:250kW::SAF
	Via M'rovia, Liberia	
	USSR	
	RADIO MOSCOW/RP&P	500kW::SEA
	Dushanbé	
	RADIO MOSCOW/RP&P	240kW:WS:EAS/ANZ
	Irkutsk	
	VATICAN STATE	
	VATICAN RADIO	100kW::EAF/ME
	Sta Maria di Galeria	
		M-Sa:100kW::AF
17735	USA	
	RFE-RL	(J):100/250kW::EEU
	Via Lisbon, Portugal	
		M-Sa:50/250kW::EEU
		(J)M-Sa:50kW::EEU
		Su:50/250kW::EEU
		(J)Su:50kW::EEU
	VOICE OF AMERICA	250kW::SAS
	Via Philippines	
	USSR	
	RADIO MOSCOW/RP&P	240kW::EAF
	Kazan'	
17740	SAUDI ARABIA	
	BS OF THE KINGDOM	350kW:DS-KORAN:EUSSR/EAS
	Riyadh	
	USA	
	VOICE OF AMERICA	250/500kW::NAF
	Greenville, NC	
	+VOICE OF AMERICA	(D):250kW::CA/SA
	Greenville, NC	
	VOICE OF AMERICA	250kW::WAF/CAF
	Via M'rovia, Liberia	
	VOICE OF AMERICA	250kW::EAS/ANZ
	Via Philippines	
		250kW::EUSSR
		250kW::SEA
		250kW::EAF
	USSR	
	RADIO MOSCOW/RP&P	100kW::SEA
	Ashkhabad	
	VATICAN STATE	
	VATICAN RADIO	100kW::CA
	Sta Maria di Galeria	

World Time: 0 1 2 3 4 5 6 7 8 9 10 11 **12** 13 14 15 16 17 **18** 19 20 21 22 23 **24**

Power (kW): Network: Target

ENGLISH ▬▬ GERMAN / DEUTSCH ◊◊◊◊ FRENCH / FRANÇAIS ═══ PORTUGUESE / PORTUGUÊS ▤▤▤ SPANISH / ESPAÑOL ═══

ARABIC /ﻉﺭﻉ ≣≣ RUSSIAN / РУССКИИ ═══ CHINESE / ★★ ◊◊◊◊ JAPANESE / 日本語 ▦▦▦ MULTILINGUAL ∽∽∽∽ OTHER ▬▬

SUMMER ONLY (J)   WINTER ONLY (D)   JAMMING ∧∧ or / or \   EARLIEST HEARD ◢   LATEST HEARD ◣   + TENTATIVE

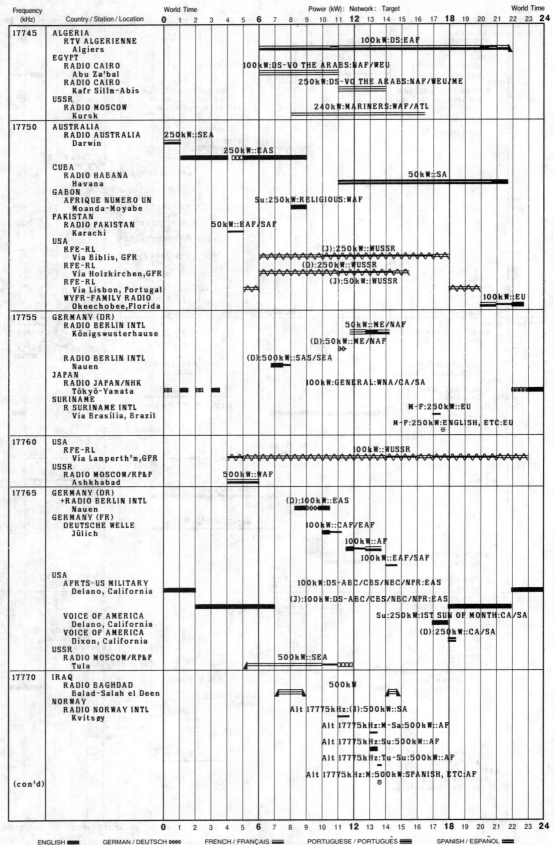

Frequency (kHz)	Country / Station / Location	World Time 0–24
17745	**ALGERIA**	
	RTV ALGERIENNE	100kW:DS:EAF
	Algiers	
	EGYPT	
	RADIO CAIRO	100kW:DS-VO THE ARABS:NAF/WEU
	Abu Za'bal	
	RADIO CAIRO	250kW:DS-VO THE ARABS:NAF/WEU/ME
	Kafr Silim-Abis	
	USSR	
	RADIO MOSCOW	240kW:MARINERS:WAF/ATL
	Kursk	
17750	**AUSTRALIA**	
	RADIO AUSTRALIA	250kW::SEA
	Darwin	250kW::EAS
	CUBA	
	RADIO HABANA	50kW::SA
	Havana	
	GABON	
	AFRIQUE NUMERO UN	Su:250kW:RELIGIOUS:WAF
	Moanda-Moyabe	
	PAKISTAN	
	RADIO PAKISTAN	50kW::EAF/SAF
	Karachi	
	USA	
	RFE-RL	(J):250kW::WUSSR
	Via Biblis, GFR	
	RFE-RL	(D):250kW::WUSSR
	Via Holzkirchen,GFR	
	RFE-RL	(J):50kW::WUSSR
	Via Lisbon, Portugal	
	WYFR-FAMILY RADIO	100kW::EU
	Okeechobee,Florida	
17755	**GERMANY (DR)**	
	RADIO BERLIN INTL	50kW::ME/NAF
	Königswusterhause	(D):50kW::ME/NAF
	RADIO BERLIN INTL	(D):500kW::SAS/SEA
	Nauen	
	JAPAN	
	RADIO JAPAN/NHK	100kW:GENERAL:WNA/CA/SA
	Tōkyō-Yamata	
	SURINAME	
	R SURINAME INTL	M-F:250kW::EU
	Via Brasília, Brazil	M-F:250kW:ENGLISH, ETC:EU
17760	**USA**	
	RFE-RL	100kW::WUSSR
	Via Lamperth'm,GFR	
	USSR	
	RADIO MOSCOW/RP&P	500kW::WAF
	Ashkhabad	
17765	**GERMANY (DR)**	
	+RADIO BERLIN INTL	(D):100kW::EAS
	Nauen	
	GERMANY (FR)	
	DEUTSCHE WELLE	100kW::CAF/EAF
	Jülich	100kW::AF
		100kW::EAF/SAF
	USA	
	AFRTS-US MILITARY	100kW:DS-ABC/CBS/NBC/NPR:EAS
	Delano, California	(J):100kW:DS-ABC/CBS/NBC/NPR:EAS
	VOICE OF AMERICA	Su:250kW:1ST SUN OF MONTH:CA/SA
	Delano, California	
	VOICE OF AMERICA	(D):250kW::CA/SA
	Dixon, California	
	USSR	
	RADIO MOSCOW/RP&P	500kW::SEA
	Tula	
17770	**IRAQ**	
	RADIO BAGHDAD	500kW
	Balad-Salah el Deen	
	NORWAY	
	RADIO NORWAY INTL	Alt 17775kHz:(J):500kW::SA
	Kvitsøy	Alt 17775kHz:M-Sa:500kW::AF
		Alt 17775kHz:Su:500kW::AF
		Alt 17775kHz:Tu-Su:500kW::AF
	(con'd)	Alt 17775kHz:M:500kW:SPANISH, ETC:AF

ENGLISH ▬▬   GERMAN / DEUTSCH ◊◊◊◊   FRENCH / FRANÇAIS ═══   PORTUGUESE / PORTUGUÊS ▬▬   SPANISH / ESPAÑOL ═══

ARABIC /ﻉﺭﺏ ═══   RUSSIAN / РУССКИИ ═══   CHINESE / 中文 ◊◊◊◊   JAPANESE / 日本語 ▬▬▬   MULTILINGUAL ▭▭▭   OTHER ▬

SUMMER ONLY (J)   WINTER ONLY (D)   JAMMING ∧∧ or / or \   EARLIEST HEARD ◢   LATEST HEARD ◣   + TENTATIVE

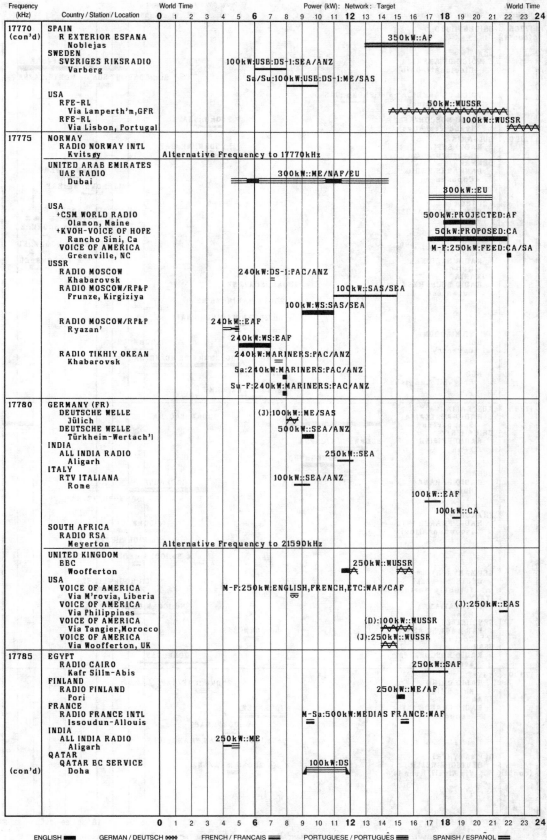

Frequency (kHz)	Country / Station / Location	Power (kW) : Network : Target (World Time 0–24)
17770 (con'd)	**SPAIN** R EXTERIOR ESPANA Noblejas	350kW::AF (13–18)
	SWEDEN SVERIGES RIKSRADIO Varberg	100kW:USB:DS-1:SEA/ANZ (4–8) Sa/Su:100kW:USB:DS-1:ME/SAS (6–9)
	USA RFE-RL Via Lamperth'm,GFR	50kW::WUSSR (13–18)
	RFE-RL Via Lisbon, Portugal	100kW::WUSSR (21–24)
17775	**NORWAY** RADIO NORWAY INTL Kvitsøy	Alternative Frequency to 17770kHz
	UNITED ARAB EMIRATES UAE RADIO Dubai	300kW::ME/NAF/EU (6–11)
		300kW::EU (18–21)
	USA +CSM WORLD RADIO Olamon, Maine	500kW:PROJECTED:AF (13–17)
	+KVOH-VOICE OF HOPE Rancho Simi, Ca	50kW:PROPOSED:CA (13–16)
	VOICE OF AMERICA Greenville, NC	M-F:250kW:FEED:CA/SA (13–17)
	USSR RADIO MOSCOW Khabarovsk	240kW:DS-1:PAC/ANZ (6–10)
	RADIO MOSCOW/RP&P Frunze, Kirgiziya	100kW::SAS/SEA (11–14) 100kW:WS:SAS/SEA (8–11)
	RADIO MOSCOW/RP&P Ryazan'	240kW::EAF (4–7) 240kW:WS:EAF (4–8)
	RADIO TIKHIY OKEAN Khabarovsk	240kW:MARINERS:PAC/ANZ (5–9) Sa:240kW:MARINERS:PAC/ANZ (6–9) Su-F:240kW:MARINERS:PAC/ANZ (6–9)
17780	**GERMANY (FR)** DEUTSCHE WELLE Jülich	(J)100kW::ME/SAS (6–8)
	DEUTSCHE WELLE Türkheim-Wertach'l	500kW::SEA/ANZ (6–9)
	INDIA ALL INDIA RADIO Aligarh	250kW::SEA (9–12)
	ITALY RTV ITALIANA Rome	100kW::SEA/ANZ (6–9) 100kW::EAF (16–18) 100kW::CA (17–19)
	SOUTH AFRICA RADIO RSA Meyerton	Alternative Frequency to 21590kHz
	UNITED KINGDOM BBC Woofferton	250kW::WUSSR (13–15)
	USA VOICE OF AMERICA Via M'rovia, Liberia	M-F:250kW:ENGLISH,FRENCH,ETC:WAF/CAF (4–10)
	VOICE OF AMERICA Via Philippines	(J):250kW::EAS (21–22)
	VOICE OF AMERICA Via Tangier,Morocco	(D):100kW::WUSSR (13–15)
	VOICE OF AMERICA Via Woofferton, UK	(J):250kW::WUSSR (13–15)
17785	**EGYPT** RADIO CAIRO Kafr Silim-Abis	250kW::SAF (13–17)
	FINLAND RADIO FINLAND Pori	250kW::ME/AF (14–16)
	FRANCE RADIO FRANCE INTL Issoudun-Allouis	M-Sa:500kW:MEDIAS FRANCE:WAF (9–11)
	INDIA ALL INDIA RADIO Aligarh	250kW::ME (4–6)
(con'd)	**QATAR** QATAR BC SERVICE Doha	100kW:DS (9–12)

ENGLISH ■■■   GERMAN / DEUTSCH ০০০০   FRENCH / FRANÇAIS ═══   PORTUGUESE / PORTUGUÊS ≡≡≡   SPANISH / ESPAÑOL ▬▬▬

ARABIC / العربية ≡≡≡   RUSSIAN / РУССКИИ ═══   CHINESE / 中文 ০০০০   JAPANESE / 日本語 ▬▬▬   MULTILINGUAL ০০০০   OTHER ───

SUMMER ONLY (J)   WINTER ONLY (D)   JAMMING ∧∧∧ or / or \   EARLIEST HEARD ◢   LATEST HEARD ◣   + TENTATIVE

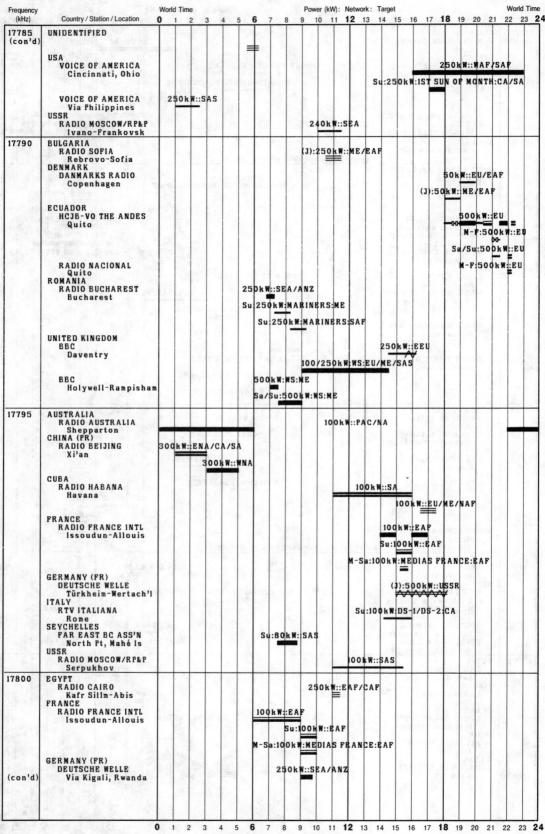

Frequency (kHz)	Country / Station / Location	Schedule notes
17785 (con'd)	UNIDENTIFIED	
	USA	
	VOICE OF AMERICA — Cincinnati, Ohio	250kW::WAF/SAF; Su:250kW:IST SUN OF MONTH:CA/SA
	VOICE OF AMERICA — Via Philippines	250kW::SAS
	USSR	
	RADIO MOSCOW/RP&P — Ivano-Frankovsk	240kW::SEA
17790	BULGARIA	
	RADIO SOFIA — Rebrovo-Sofia	(J):250kW::ME/EAF
	DENMARK	
	DANMARKS RADIO — Copenhagen	50kW::EU/EAF; (J):50kW::ME/EAF
	ECUADOR	
	HCJB-VO THE ANDES — Quito	500kW::EU; M-F:500kW::EU; Sa/Su:500kW::EU; M-F:500kW::EU
	RADIO NACIONAL — Quito	
	ROMANIA	
	RADIO BUCHAREST — Bucharest	250kW::SEA/ANZ; Su:250kW:MARINERS:ME; Su:250kW:MARINERS:SAF
	UNITED KINGDOM	
	BBC — Daventry	250kW::EEU; 100/250kW:WS:EU/ME/SAS
	BBC — Holywell-Rampisham	500kW:WS:ME; Sa/Su:500kW:WS:ME
17795	AUSTRALIA	
	RADIO AUSTRALIA — Shepparton	100kW::PAC/NA
	CHINA (PR)	
	RADIO BEIJING — Xi'an	300kW::ENA/CA/SA; 300kW::WNA
	CUBA	
	RADIO HABANA — Havana	100kW::SA; 100kW::EU/ME/NAF
	FRANCE	
	RADIO FRANCE INTL — Issoudun-Allouis	100kW::EAF; Su:100kW::EAF; M-Sa:100kW:MEDIAS FRANCE:EAF
	GERMANY (FR)	
	DEUTSCHE WELLE — Türkheim-Wertach'l	(J):500kW::USSR
	ITALY	
	RTV ITALIANA — Rome	Su:100kW:DS-1/DS-2:CA
	SEYCHELLES	
	FAR EAST BC ASS'N — North Pt, Mahé Is	Su:80kW:SAS
	USSR	
	RADIO MOSCOW/RP&P — Serpukhov	100kW::SAS
17800	EGYPT	
	RADIO CAIRO — Kafr Sillm-Abis	250kW::EAF/CAF
	FRANCE	
	RADIO FRANCE INTL — Issoudun-Allouis	100kW::EAF; Su:100kW::EAF; M-Sa:100kW:MEDIAS FRANCE:EAF
	GERMANY (FR)	
(con'd)	DEUTSCHE WELLE — Via Kigali, Rwanda	250kW::SEA/ANZ

World Time: 0 1 2 3 4 5 6 7 8 9 10 11 12 13 14 15 16 17 18 19 20 21 22 23 24

Power (kW): Network: Target

ENGLISH ▬▬ GERMAN / DEUTSCH ◊◊◊◊ FRENCH / FRANÇAIS ═══ PORTUGUESE / PORTUGUÊS ▤▤ SPANISH / ESPAÑOL ▬▬

ARABIC / عربى ≡≡ RUSSIAN / РУССКИИ ══ CHINESE / 中文 ◊◊◊◊ JAPANESE / 日本語 ▦▦ MULTILINGUAL ▒▒▒ OTHER ▬▬

SUMMER ONLY (J) WINTER ONLY (D) JAMMING ∧∧ or / or \ EARLIEST HEARD ◢ LATEST HEARD ◣ + TENTATIVE

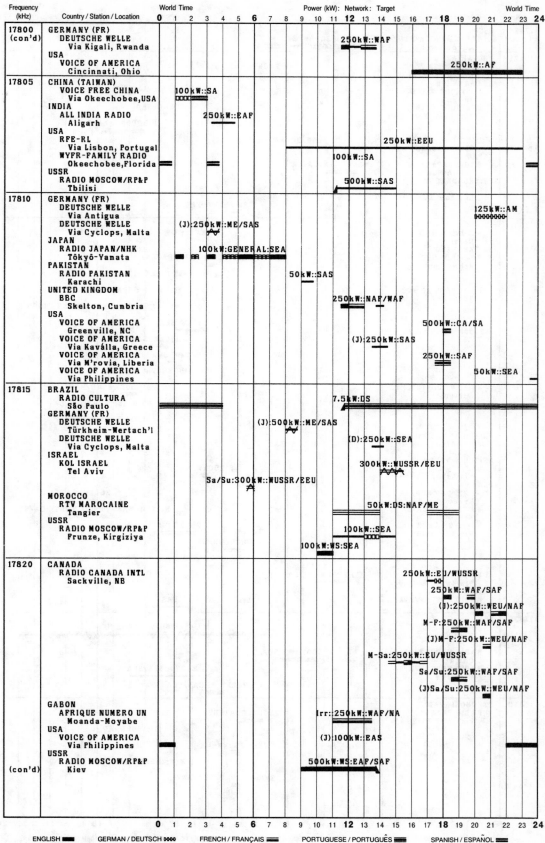

Frequency (kHz)	Country / Station / Location	Power (kW) : Network : Target

17800 (con'd)
GERMANY (FR)
DEUTSCHE WELLE
Via Kigali, Rwanda — 250kW::WAF (12–14)
USA
VOICE OF AMERICA
Cincinnati, Ohio — 250kW::AF (16–22)

17805
CHINA (TAIWAN)
VOICE FREE CHINA
Via Okeechobee, USA — 100kW::SA (0–1)
INDIA
ALL INDIA RADIO
Aligarh — 250kW::EAF (3–4)
USA
RFE-RL
Via Lisbon, Portugal — 250kW::EEU (8–22)
WYFR-FAMILY RADIO
Okeechobee, Florida — 100kW::SA (11–12)
USSR
RADIO MOSCOW/RP&P
Tbilisi — 500kW::SAS (11–14)

17810
GERMANY (FR)
DEUTSCHE WELLE
Via Antigua — 125kW::AM (22–23)
DEUTSCHE WELLE
Via Cyclops, Malta — (J):250kW::ME/SAS (3–6)
JAPAN
RADIO JAPAN/NHK
Tōkyō-Yamata — 100kW:GENERAL:SEA (1–7)
PAKISTAN
RADIO PAKISTAN
Karachi — 50kW::SAS (8–9)
UNITED KINGDOM
BBC
Skelton, Cumbria — 250kW::NAF/WAF (11–13)
USA
VOICE OF AMERICA
Greenville, NC — 500kW::CA/SA (16–17)
VOICE OF AMERICA
Via Kaválla, Greece — (J):250kW::SAS (12–14)
VOICE OF AMERICA
Via M'rovia, Liberia — 250kW::SAF (16–17)
VOICE OF AMERICA
Via Philippines — 50kW::SEA (22–24)

17815
BRAZIL
RADIO CULTURA
São Paulo — 7.5kW:DS (0–24)
GERMANY (FR)
DEUTSCHE WELLE
Türkheim-Wertach'l — (J):500kW::ME/SAS (5–6)
DEUTSCHE WELLE
Via Cyclops, Malta — (D):250kW::SEA (12–14)
ISRAEL
KOL ISRAEL
Tel Aviv — 300kW::WUSSR/EEU (12–14)
Sa/Su:300kW::WUSSR/EEU (5–6)
MOROCCO
RTV MAROCAINE
Tangier — 50kW:DS:NAF/ME (12–14)
USSR
RADIO MOSCOW/RP&P
Frunze, Kirgiziya — 100kW::SEA (11–13)
100kW:WS:SEA (9–11)

17820
CANADA
RADIO CANADA INTL
Sackville, NB — 250kW::EU/WUSSR (16–17)
250kW::WAF/SAF (18–19)
(J):250kW::WEU/NAF (19–21)
M-F:250kW::WAF/SAF (18–19)
(J)M-F:250kW::WEU/NAF (19–21)
M-Sa:250kW::EU/WUSSR (16–18)
Sa/Su:250kW::WAF/SAF (19–20)
(J)Sa/Su:250kW::WEU/NAF (20–21)
GABON
AFRIQUE NUMERO UN
Moanda-Moyabe — Irr:250kW::WAF/NA (11–14)
USA
VOICE OF AMERICA
Via Philippines — (J):100kW::EAS (0–1)
USSR
RADIO MOSCOW/RP&P
(con'd) Kiev — 500kW:WS:EAF/SAF (9–14)

ENGLISH ▬▬   GERMAN / DEUTSCH ✕✕✕✕   FRENCH / FRANÇAIS ══   PORTUGUESE / PORTUGUÊS ▬   SPANISH / ESPAÑOL ▭

ARABIC /ﻉﺭﻉ ═   RUSSIAN / РУССКИИ ══   CHINESE / ✕★ ✕✕✕✕   JAPANESE / 日本語 ▬▬   MULTILINGUAL ▭▭▭▭   OTHER ▬

SUMMER ONLY (J)   WINTER ONLY (D)   JAMMING ∧∧ or / or \   EARLIEST HEARD ◢   LATEST HEARD ◣   + TENTATIVE

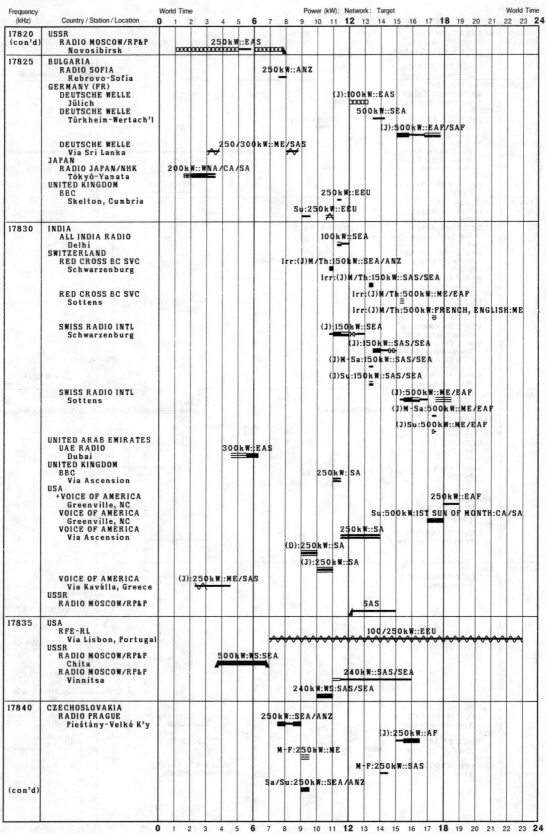

Frequency
(kHz)

Country / Station / Location

World Time
0 1 2 3 4 5 6 7 8 9 10 11 12 13 14 15 16 17 18 19 20 21 22 23 24

Power (kW): Network: Target

World Time

Frequency (kHz)	Country / Station / Location	Schedule
17820 (con'd)	USSR RADIO MOSCOW/RP&P Novosibirsk	250kW::EAS
17825	BULGARIA RADIO SOFIA Rebrovo-Sofia	250kW::ANZ
	GERMANY (FR) DEUTSCHE WELLE Jülich	(J):100kW::EAS
	DEUTSCHE WELLE Türkheim-Wertach'l	500kW::SEA / (J):500kW::EAF/SAF
	DEUTSCHE WELLE Via Sri Lanka	250/300kW::ME/SAS
	JAPAN RADIO JAPAN/NHK Tōkyō-Yamata	200kW::WNA/CA/SA
	UNITED KINGDOM BBC Skelton, Cumbria	250kW::EEU / Su:250kW::EEU
17830	INDIA ALL INDIA RADIO Delhi	100kW::SEA
	SWITZERLAND RED CROSS BC SVC Schwarzenburg	Irr:(J)M/Th:150kW::SEA/ANZ / Irr:(J)M/Th:150kW::SAS/SEA
	RED CROSS BC SVC Sottens	Irr:(J)M/Th:500kW::ME/EAF / Irr:(J)M/Th:500kW:FRENCH, ENGLISH:ME
	SWISS RADIO INTL Schwarzenburg	(J):150kW::SEA / (J):150kW::SAS/SEA / (J)M-Sa:150kW::SAS/SEA / (J)Su:150kW::SAS/SEA
	SWISS RADIO INTL Sottens	(J):500kW::ME/EAF / (J)M-Sa:500kW::ME/EAF / (J)Su:500kW::ME/EAF
	UNITED ARAB EMIRATES UAE RADIO Dubai	300kW::EAS
	UNITED KINGDOM BBC Via Ascension	250kW::SA
	USA +VOICE OF AMERICA Greenville, NC	250kW::EAF
	VOICE OF AMERICA Greenville, NC	Su:500kW:1ST SUN OF MONTH:CA/SA
	VOICE OF AMERICA Via Ascension	250kW::SA / (D):250kW::SA / (J):250kW::SA
	VOICE OF AMERICA Via Kaválla, Greece	(J):250kW::ME/SAS
	USSR RADIO MOSCOW/RP&P	SAS
17835	USA RFE-RL Via Lisbon, Portugal	100/250kW::EEU
	USSR RADIO MOSCOW/RP&P Chita	500kW:WS:SEA
	RADIO MOSCOW/RP&P Vinnitsa	240kW::SAS/SEA / 240kW:WS:SAS/SEA
17840	CZECHOSLOVAKIA RADIO PRAGUE Piešťany-Velké K'y	250kW::SEA/ANZ / (J):250kW::AF / M-F:250kW::ME / M-F:250kW::SAS / Sa/Su:250kW::SEA/ANZ
(con'd)		

ENGLISH ▄▄▄   GERMAN / DEUTSCH ◊◊◊◊   FRENCH / FRANÇAIS ═══   PORTUGUESE / PORTUGUÊS ▤▤   SPANISH / ESPAÑOL ▬▬

ARABIC /ﻉﺭ ≣≣   RUSSIAN / РУССКИЙ ═══   CHINESE /✦✗ ◊◊◊◊   JAPANESE / 日本語 ▬▬▬   MULTILINGUAL ▤▤▤   OTHER ▬▬

SUMMER ONLY (J)   WINTER ONLY (D)   JAMMING ∧∧ or / or \   EARLIEST HEARD ◢   LATEST HEARD ◣   + TENTATIVE

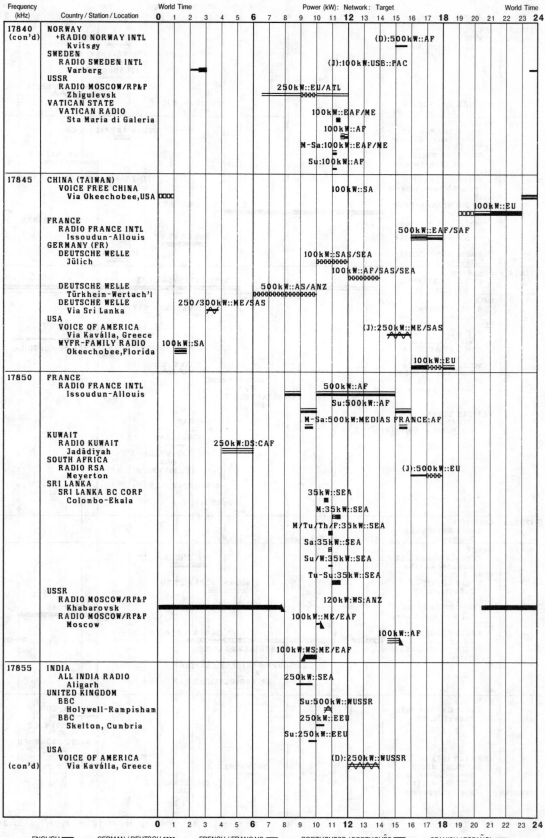

Frequency (kHz)	Country / Station / Location	World Time 0 1 2 3 4 5 6 7 8 9 10 11 12 13 14 15 16 17 18 19 20 21 22 23 24 Power (kW): Network: Target
17840 (con'd)	NORWAY +RADIO NORWAY INTL Kvitsøy	(D):500kW::AF
	SWEDEN RADIO SWEDEN INTL Varberg	(J):100kW:USB::PAC
	USSR RADIO MOSCOW/RP&P Zhigulevsk	250kW::EU/ATL
	VATICAN STATE VATICAN RADIO Sta Maria di Galeria	100kW::EAF/ME
		100kW::AF
		M-Sa:100kW::EAF/ME
		Su:100kW::AF
17845	CHINA (TAIWAN) VOICE FREE CHINA Via Okeechobee,USA	100kW::SA
		100kW::EU
	FRANCE RADIO FRANCE INTL Issoudun-Allouis	500kW::EAF/SAF
	GERMANY (FR) DEUTSCHE WELLE Jülich	100kW::SAS/SEA
		100kW::AF/SAS/SEA
	DEUTSCHE WELLE Türkheim-Wertach'l	500kW::AS/ANZ
	DEUTSCHE WELLE Via Sri Lanka	250/300kW::ME/SAS
	USA VOICE OF AMERICA Via Kaválla, Greece	(J):250kW::ME/SAS
	WYFR-FAMILY RADIO Okeechobee,Florida	100kW::SA
		100kW::EU
17850	FRANCE RADIO FRANCE INTL Issoudun-Allouis	500kW::AF
		Su:500kW::AF
		M-Sa:500kW:MEDIAS FRANCE:AF
	KUWAIT RADIO KUWAIT Jadādiyah	250kW:DS:CAF
	SOUTH AFRICA RADIO RSA Meyerton	(J):500kW::EU
	SRI LANKA SRI LANKA BC CORP Colombo-Ekala	35kW::SEA
		M:35kW::SEA
		M/Tu/Th/F:35kW::SEA
		Sa:35kW::SEA
		Su/W:35kW::SEA
		Tu-Su:35kW::SEA
	USSR RADIO MOSCOW/RP&P Khabarovsk	120kW:WS:ANZ
	RADIO MOSCOW/RP&P Moscow	100kW::ME/EAF
		100kW::AF
		100kW:WS:ME/EAF
17855	INDIA ALL INDIA RADIO Aligarh	250kW::SEA
	UNITED KINGDOM BBC Holywell-Rampisham	Su:500kW::WUSSR
	BBC Skelton, Cumbria	250kW::EEU
		Su:250kW::EEU
(con'd)	USA VOICE OF AMERICA Via Kaválla, Greece	(D):250kW::WUSSR

ENGLISH ▄▄▄	GERMAN / DEUTSCH ◊◊◊◊	FRENCH / FRANÇAIS ▰▰▰	PORTUGUESE / PORTUGUÊS ▰▰▰	SPANISH / ESPAÑOL ▰▰▰
ARABIC /ﻉﻉ ▰▰▰	RUSSIAN / РУССКИИ ▰▰▰	CHINESE / ▰▰ ◊◊◊◊	JAPANESE / 日本語 ▰▰▰	MULTILINGUAL ▤▤▤	OTHER ▬
SUMMER ONLY (J)	WINTER ONLY (D)	JAMMING /\/\ or / or \	EARLIEST HEARD ◢	LATEST HEARD ◣	+ TENTATIVE

Frequency (kHz) / Country / Station / Location	World Time 0–24 / Power (kW): Network: Target
17855 (con'd) USA	
VOICE OF AMERICA Via Tangier, Morocco	100/35kW::WUSSR (at ~16–18)
	(D):100/35kW::WUSSR (at ~17–18)
	(J):35kW::EEU (at ~16–17)
	(J):35kW::EEU/WUSSR (at ~18–21)
VOICE OF AMERICA Via Woofferton, UK	(J):300kW::WUSSR (at ~11–13)
17860 FRANCE	
RADIO FRANCE INTL Via French Guiana	500kW:AMERICAIN:CA (at ~15–17)
GERMANY (FR) DEUTSCHE WELLE Via Kigali, Rwanda	250kW::WAF/CA (at ~18–20)
USA VOICE OF AMERICA Via M'rovia, Liberia	(J):250kW::CAF/EAF (at ~15–17)
USSR RADIO MOSCOW/RP&P Chita	500kW:WS:SEA (at ~0–11)
	500kW::SEA (at ~22–23)
RADIO MOSCOW/RP&P L'vov	500kW:WS:ME (at ~11–13)
RADIO MOSCOW/RP&P Leningrad	100kW::WAF (at ~15–17)
17864.4 COLOMBIA	
LA VOZ CENTAUROS Villavicencio	SPR:DS/3X5954.8KHZ (at ~0–15)
17865 POLAND	
RADIO POLONIA Warsaw	100kW::NAF/WAF (at ~13–15)
USA RFE-RL Via Pals, Spain	50kW::EEU (at ~18–23)
VOICE OF AMERICA Greenville, NC	Su:250/500kW:1ST SUN OF MONTH:LA (at ~16–18)
VOICE OF AMERICA Via Kaválla, Greece	250kW::WUSSR/ME (at ~13–15)
VOICE OF AMERICA Via Philippines	100kW::EUSSR (at ~9–11)
	(J):100kW::EUSSR (at ~8–10)
VATICAN STATE VATICAN RADIO Sta Maria di Galeria	100kW::EAS (at ~11)
	100kW::SEA (at ~12)
	100kW::SA (at ~13)
	100kW::CA (at ~13–14)
	M-Sa:100kW::EAS (at ~11)
	Su:100kW::EAS (at ~11)
17869v COLOMBIA	
RADIO NACIONAL Bogotá	Alternative Frequency to 17714vkHz
17870 GABON	
AFRIQUE NUMERO UN Moanda-Moyabe	Irr::250kW (at ~11–13)
KUWAIT RADIO KUWAIT Jadãdiyah	Alt 17885kHz:250kW:DS:EU (at ~9–11)
USA VOICE OF AMERICA Via M'rovia, Liberia	250kW::AF (at ~16–23)
USSR RADIO MOSCOW/RP&P Chita	500kW::EAS/SEA (at ~0–13, 22–23)
RADIO TIKHIY OKEAN Chita	500kW:MARINERS:EAS/SEA (at ~6–8)
	Sa:500kW:MARINERS:EAS/SEA (at ~8)
	Su-F:500kW:MARINERS:EAS/SEA (at ~8)
17875 CANADA	
RADIO CANADA INTL Sackville, NB	250kW::EU (at ~18–20)
	M-F:250kW::EU (at ~19–20)
	Sa/Su:250kW::EU (at ~20–21)
GERMANY (FR) DEUTSCHE WELLE Türkheim-Wertach'l	500kW::ME (at ~7–8)
DEUTSCHE WELLE (con'd) Via Cyclops, Malta	(J):250kW::EAS (at ~12)

ENGLISH ▬▬ GERMAN / DEUTSCH ◊◊◊◊ FRENCH / FRANÇAIS ═══ PORTUGUESE / PORTUGUÊS ▬▬ SPANISH / ESPAÑOL ▬▬

ARABIC / عربى ═══ RUSSIAN / РУССКИИ ═══ CHINESE / 中文 ◊◊◊◊ JAPANESE / 日本語 ▬▬ MULTILINGUAL ▦▦▦ OTHER ▬▬

SUMMER ONLY (J) WINTER ONLY (D) JAMMING /\/\ or / or \ EARLIEST HEARD ◢ LATEST HEARD ◣ + TENTATIVE

Frequency (kHz)	Country / Station / Location	World Time / Power (kW): Network: Target

World Time scale: 0 1 2 3 4 5 6 7 8 9 10 11 12 13 14 15 16 17 18 19 20 21 22 23 24

17875 (con'd)
GERMANY (FR)
  DEUTSCHE WELLE
    Via Sines, Portugal — (D):250kW::USSR
      (J):250kW::EEU
  DEUTSCHE WELLE
    Via Sri Lanka — (D):250kW::ME
INDIA
  ALL INDIA RADIO
    Aligarh — 250kW::ANZ
SEYCHELLES
  FAR EAST BC ASS'N
    North Pt, Mahé Is — 80kW::ME/EAF
    Su/Th/F:80kW::ME/EAF
USSR
  RADIO MOSCOW/RP&P
    Vinnitsa — 100kW:WS:EU

17875v
BRAZIL
  RADIO MEC
    Rio de Janeiro — 7.5kW:DS

17880
GERMANY (DR)
  +RADIO BERLIN INTL
    Königswusterhause — (D):500kW::SAS/SEA
  +RADIO BERLIN INTL
    Nauen — (D):500kW::SAS/SEA
NORTHERN MARIANA IS
  KFBS-FAR EAST BC
    Saipan Island — (J):100kW::SAS
PORTUGAL
  RADIO PORTUGUESA
    Lisbon-São Gabriel — M-F:100kW::AF
TURKEY
  TURKISH RTV CORP
    Ankara — Alternative Frequency to 17885kHz
UNITED KINGDOM
  BBC
    Via Ascension — 250kW:AFRICAN:SAF
    250kW:WS:SAF
  BBC
    Via Singapore — 250kW:WS:EAS
USSR
  RADIO MOSCOW/RP&P
    Tula — 100kW::ME/SAS
    100kW:WS:ME/SAS

17885
KUWAIT
  RADIO KUWAIT
    Jadādiyah — Alternative Frequency to 17870kHz
TURKEY
  TURKISH RTV CORP
    Ankara — Alt 17880kHz:250kW::ME/SAS
UNITED KINGDOM
  BBC
    Via Ascension — 250kW:WS:SAF
USA
  RFE-RL
    Via Pals, Spain — 250kW::WUSSR
  VOICE OF AMERICA
    Via Brasília, Brazil — 250kW::SA
USSR
  RADIO MOSCOW/RP&P
    Irkutsk — 240kW::EAS
  RADIO MOSCOW/RP&P
    Tbilisi — 240kW:WS:AF

17890
ECUADOR
  HCJB-VO THE ANDES
    Quito — 100kW::NA/CA
    100kW::SA
SPAIN
  R EXTERIOR ESPANA
    Noblejas — 350kW::EAF/ME
USSR
  RADIO MOSCOW/RP&P
    Armavir — 100kW::ME/SAS

17895
KUWAIT
  RADIO KUWAIT
    Jadādiyah — 250kW::SAS
LIBYA
  RADIO JAMAHIRIYA
    Tripoli — 500kW:DS:ES:NAF/ME/SAS
USA
  RFE-RL
    Via Lisbon, Portugal — 50kW::WUSSR
  RFE-RL
    Via Pals, Spain — 250/500kW::WUSSR
    100/250kW::WUSSR

World Time scale: 0 1 2 3 4 5 6 7 8 9 10 11 12 13 14 15 16 17 18 19 20 21 22 23 24

ENGLISH ▬▬   GERMAN / DEUTSCH ००००   FRENCH / FRANÇAIS ══   PORTUGUESE / PORTUGUÊS ▤   SPANISH / ESPAÑOL ══

ARABIC /العربية ☰   RUSSIAN / РУССКИИ ══   CHINESE / 中文 ០០០០   JAPANESE / 日本語 ▦▦   MULTILINGUAL ০০০০   OTHER ▬

SUMMER ONLY (J)   WINTER ONLY (D)   JAMMING /\/\ or / or \   EARLIEST HEARD ◢   LATEST HEARD ◣   + TENTATIVE

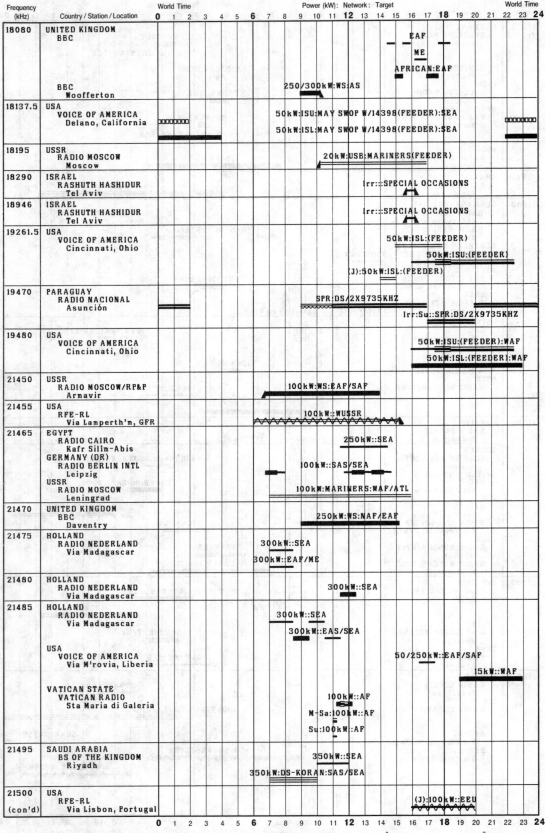

Frequency (kHz)	Country / Station / Location	Schedule (World Time)
18080	UNITED KINGDOM BBC	EAF / ME / AFRICAN:EAF
	BBC Woofferton	250/300kW:WS:AS
18137.5	USA VOICE OF AMERICA Delano, California	50kW:ISU:MAY SWOP W/14398(FEEDER):SEA / 50kW:ISL:MAY SWOP W/14398(FEEDER):SEA
18195	USSR RADIO MOSCOW Moscow	20kW:USB:MARINERS(FEEDER)
18290	ISRAEL RASHUTH HASHIDUR Tel Aviv	Irr:::SPECIAL OCCASIONS
18946	ISRAEL RASHUTH HASHIDUR Tel Aviv	Irr:::SPECIAL OCCASIONS
19261.5	USA VOICE OF AMERICA Cincinnati, Ohio	50kW:ISL:(FEEDER) / 50kW:ISU:(FEEDER) / (J):50kW:ISL:(FEEDER)
19470	PARAGUAY RADIO NACIONAL Asunción	SPR:DS/2X9735KHZ / Irr:Su:SPR:DS/2X9735KHZ
19480	USA VOICE OF AMERICA Cincinnati, Ohio	50kW:ISU:(FEEDER):WAF / 50kW:ISL:(FEEDER):WAF
21450	USSR RADIO MOSCOW/RP&P Armavir	100kW:WS:EAF/SAF
21455	USA RFE-RL Via Lamperth'm, GFR	100kW::WUSSR
21465	EGYPT RADIO CAIRO Kafr Silim-Abis	250kW::SEA
	GERMANY (DR) RADIO BERLIN INTL Leipzig	100kW::SAS/SEA
	USSR RADIO MOSCOW Leningrad	100kW:MARINERS:WAF/ATL
21470	UNITED KINGDOM BBC Daventry	250kW:WS:NAF/EAF
21475	HOLLAND RADIO NEDERLAND Via Madagascar	300kW::SEA / 300kW::EAF/ME
21480	HOLLAND RADIO NEDERLAND Via Madagascar	300kW::SEA
21485	HOLLAND RADIO NEDERLAND Via Madagascar	300kW::SEA / 300kW::EAS/SEA
	USA VOICE OF AMERICA Via M'rovia, Liberia	50/250kW::EAF/SAF / 15kW::WAF
	VATICAN STATE VATICAN RADIO Sta Maria di Galeria	100kW::AF / M-Sa:100kW::AF / Su:100kW::AF
21495	SAUDI ARABIA BS OF THE KINGDOM Riyadh	350kW::SEA / 350kW:DS-KORAN:SAS/SEA
21500 (con'd)	USA RFE-RL Via Lisbon, Portugal	(J):100kW::EEU

Power (kW): Network: Target

ENGLISH ▬▬▬   GERMAN / DEUTSCH ០០០០   FRENCH / FRANÇAIS ═══   PORTUGUESE / PORTUGUÊS ▬▬▬   SPANISH / ESPAÑOL ▬▬▬

ARABIC / بربي ≡≡≡   RUSSIAN / РУССКИИ ═══   CHINESE / ✷✵ ០០០   JAPANESE / 日本語 ▬▬▬   MULTILINGUAL ០០០០   OTHER ▬▬▬

SUMMER ONLY (J)   WINTER ONLY (D)   JAMMING ΛΛ or / or \   EARLIEST HEARD ◢   LATEST HEARD ◥   + TENTATIVE

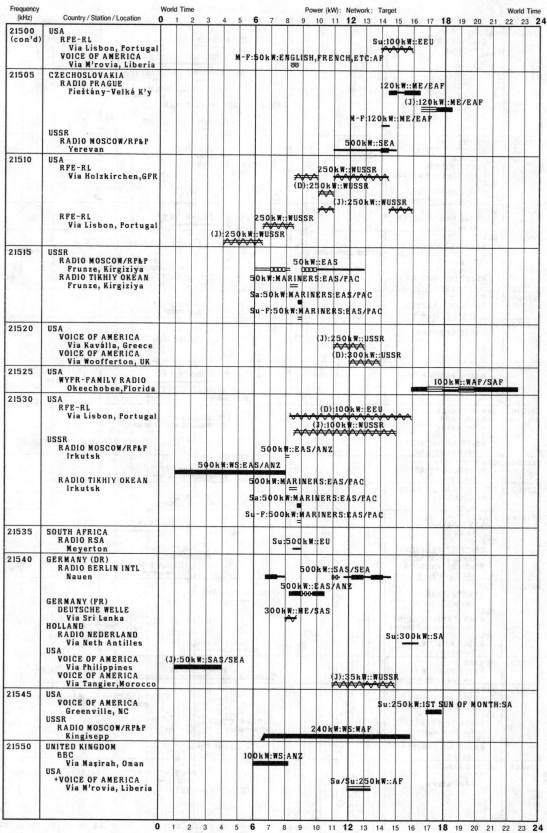

Frequency (kHz)	Country / Station / Location	World Time 0–24 — Power (kW): Network: Target
21500 (con'd)	USA	
	RFE-RL Via Lisbon, Portugal	Su:100kW::EEU
	VOICE OF AMERICA Via M'rovia, Liberia	M-F:50kW:ENGLISH,FRENCH,ETC:AF
21505	CZECHOSLOVAKIA	
	RADIO PRAGUE Pieštány-Velké K'y	120kW::ME/EAF
		(J):120kW::ME/EAF
		M-F:120kW::ME/EAF
	USSR	
	RADIO MOSCOW/RP&P Yerevan	500kW::SEA
21510	USA	
	RFE-RL Via Holzkirchen,GFR	250kW::WUSSR
		(D):250kW::WUSSR
		(J):250kW::WUSSR
	RFE-RL Via Lisbon, Portugal	250kW::WUSSR
		(J):250kW::WUSSR
21515	USSR	
	RADIO MOSCOW/RP&P Frunze, Kirgiziya	50kW::EAS
	RADIO TIKHIY OKEAN Frunze, Kirgiziya	50kW:MARINERS:EAS/PAC
		Sa:50kW:MARINERS:EAS/PAC
		Su-F:50kW:MARINERS:EAS/PAC
21520	USA	
	VOICE OF AMERICA Via Kaválla, Greece	(J):250kW::USSR
	VOICE OF AMERICA Via Woofferton, UK	(D):300kW::USSR
21525	USA	
	WYFR-FAMILY RADIO Okeechobee,Florida	100kW::WAF/SAF
21530	USA	
	RFE-RL Via Lisbon, Portugal	(D):100kW::EEU
		(J):100kW::WUSSR
	USSR	
	RADIO MOSCOW/RP&P Irkutsk	500kW::EAS/ANZ
		500kW:WS:EAS/ANZ
	RADIO TIKHIY OKEAN Irkutsk	500kW:MARINERS:EAS/PAC
		Sa:500kW:MARINERS:EAS/PAC
		Su-F:500kW:MARINERS:EAS/PAC
21535	SOUTH AFRICA	
	RADIO RSA Meyerton	Su:500kW::EU
21540	GERMANY (DR)	
	RADIO BERLIN INTL Nauen	500kW::SAS/SEA
		500kW::EAS/ANZ
	GERMANY (FR)	
	DEUTSCHE WELLE Via Sri Lanka	300kW::ME/SAS
	HOLLAND	
	RADIO NEDERLAND Via Neth Antilles	Su:300kW::SA
	USA	
	VOICE OF AMERICA Via Philippines	(J):50kW::SAS/SEA
	VOICE OF AMERICA Via Tangier,Morocco	(J):35kW::WUSSR
21545	USA	
	VOICE OF AMERICA Greenville, NC	Su:250kW:1ST SUN OF MONTH:SA
	USSR	
	RADIO MOSCOW/RP&P Kingisepp	240kW:WS:WAF
21550	UNITED KINGDOM	
	BBC Via Maşirah, Oman	100kW:WS:ANZ
	USA	
	+VOICE OF AMERICA Via M'rovia, Liberia	Sa/Su:250kW::AF

ENGLISH — GERMAN / DEUTSCH — FRENCH / FRANÇAIS — PORTUGUESE / PORTUGUÊS — SPANISH / ESPAÑOL
ARABIC / عربي — RUSSIAN / РУССКИИ — CHINESE / 中文 — JAPANESE / 日本語 — MULTILINGUAL — OTHER
SUMMER ONLY (J) — WINTER ONLY (D) — JAMMING /\/\ or / or \ — EARLIEST HEARD — LATEST HEARD — + TENTATIVE

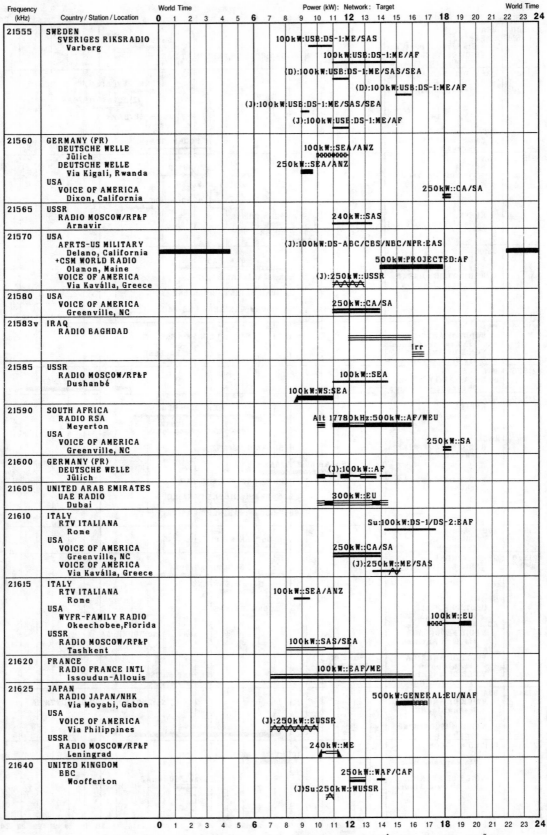

Frequency (kHz)	Country / Station / Location		World Time / Power (kW): Network: Target
21555	SWEDEN	SVERIGES RIKSRADIO Varberg	100kW:USB:DS-1:ME/SAS 100kW:USB:DS-1:ME/AF (D):100kW:USB:DS-1:ME/SAS/SEA (D):100kW:USB:DS-1:ME/AF (J):100kW:USB:DS-1:ME/SAS/SEA (J):100kW:USB:DS-1:ME/AF
21560	GERMANY (FR)	DEUTSCHE WELLE Jülich	100kW::SEA/ANZ
	DEUTSCHE WELLE	Via Kigali, Rwanda	250kW::SEA/ANZ
	USA	VOICE OF AMERICA Dixon, California	250kW::CA/SA
21565	USSR	RADIO MOSCOW/RP&P Armavir	240kW::SAS
21570	USA	AFRTS-US MILITARY Delano, California	(J):100kW:DS-ABC/CBS/NBC/NPR:EAS
	+CSM WORLD RADIO	Olamon, Maine	500kW:PROJECTED:AF
	VOICE OF AMERICA	Via Kaválla, Greece	(J):250kW::USSR
21580	USA	VOICE OF AMERICA Greenville, NC	250kW::CA/SA
21583v	IRAQ	RADIO BAGHDAD	Irr
21585	USSR	RADIO MOSCOW/RP&P Dushanbé	100kW::SEA
			100kW:WS:SEA
21590	SOUTH AFRICA	RADIO RSA Meyerton	Alt 17780kHz:500kW::AF/WEU
	USA	VOICE OF AMERICA Greenville, NC	250kW::SA
21600	GERMANY (FR)	DEUTSCHE WELLE Jülich	(J):100kW::AF
21605	UNITED ARAB EMIRATES	UAE RADIO Dubai	300kW::EU
21610	ITALY	RTV ITALIANA Rome	Su:100kW:DS-1/DS-2:EAF
	USA	VOICE OF AMERICA Greenville, NC	250kW::CA/SA
	VOICE OF AMERICA	Via Kaválla, Greece	(J):250kW::ME/SAS
21615	ITALY	RTV ITALIANA Rome	100kW::SEA/ANZ
	USA	WYFR-FAMILY RADIO Okeechobee, Florida	100kW::EU
	USSR	RADIO MOSCOW/RP&P Tashkent	100kW::SAS/SEA
21620	FRANCE	RADIO FRANCE INTL Issoudun-Allouis	100kW::EAF/ME
21625	JAPAN	RADIO JAPAN/NHK Via Moyabi, Gabon	500kW:GENERAL:EU/NAF
	USA	VOICE OF AMERICA Via Philippines	(J):250kW::EUSSR
	USSR	RADIO MOSCOW/RP&P Leningrad	240kW::ME
21640	UNITED KINGDOM	BBC Woofferton	250kW::WAF/CAF
			(J)Su:250kW::WUSSR

ENGLISH ▬▬ GERMAN / DEUTSCH ◇◇◇◇ FRENCH / FRANÇAIS ▬▬ PORTUGUESE / PORTUGUÉS ▬▬ SPANISH / ESPAÑOL ▬▬

ARABIC / العربية ▬▬ RUSSIAN / РУССКИИ ▬▬ CHINESE / 中文 ◻◻◻◻ JAPANESE / 日本語 ▬▬ MULTILINGUAL ◻◻◻◻ OTHER ▬

SUMMER ONLY (J) WINTER ONLY (D) JAMMING ∧∧ or / or \ EARLIEST HEARD ◢ LATEST HEARD ◣ + TENTATIVE

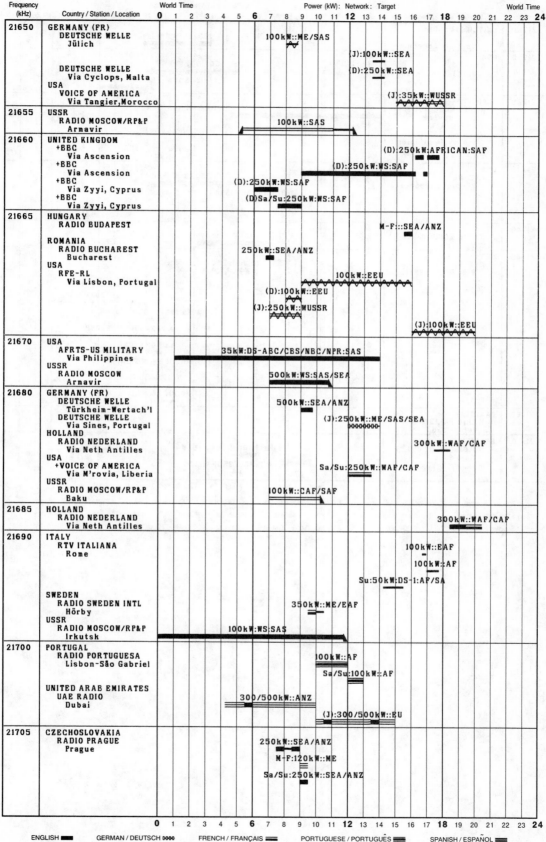

Frequency (kHz)	Country / Station / Location	Power (kW): Network: Target
21650	GERMANY (FR) DEUTSCHE WELLE Jülich	100kW::ME/SAS
		(J):100kW::SEA
	DEUTSCHE WELLE Via Cyclops, Malta	(D):250kW::SEA
	USA VOICE OF AMERICA Via Tangier,Morocco	(J):35kW::WUSSR
21655	USSR RADIO MOSCOW/RP&P Armavir	100kW::SAS
21660	UNITED KINGDOM +BBC Via Ascension	(D):250kW:AFRICAN:SAF
	+BBC Via Ascension	(D):250kW:WS:SAF
	+BBC Via Zyyi, Cyprus	(D):250kW:WS:SAF
	+BBC Via Zyyi, Cyprus	(D)Sa/Su:250kW:WS:SAF
21665	HUNGARY RADIO BUDAPEST	M-F:::SEA/ANZ
	ROMANIA RADIO BUCHAREST Bucharest	250kW::SEA/ANZ
	USA RFE-RL Via Lisbon, Portugal	100kW::EEU
		(D):100kW::EEU
		(J):250kW::WUSSR
		(J):100kW::EEU
21670	USA AFRTS-US MILITARY Via Philippines	35kW:DS-ABC/CBS/NBC/NPR:SAS
	USSR RADIO MOSCOW Armavir	500kW:WS:SAS/SEA
21680	GERMANY (FR) DEUTSCHE WELLE Türkheim-Wertach'l	500kW::SEA/ANZ
	DEUTSCHE WELLE Via Sines, Portugal	(J):250kW::ME/SAS/SEA
	HOLLAND RADIO NEDERLAND Via Neth Antilles	300kW::WAF/CAF
	USA +VOICE OF AMERICA Via M'rovia, Liberia	Sa/Su:250kW::WAF/CAF
	USSR RADIO MOSCOW/RP&P Baku	100kW::CAF/SAF
21685	HOLLAND RADIO NEDERLAND Via Neth Antilles	300kW::WAF/CAF
21690	ITALY RTV ITALIANA Rome	100kW::EAF
		100kW::AF
		Su:50kW:DS-1:AF/SA
	SWEDEN RADIO SWEDEN INTL Hörby	350kW::ME/EAF
	USSR RADIO MOSCOW/RP&P Irkutsk	100kW:WS:SAS
21700	PORTUGAL RADIO PORTUGUESA Lisbon-São Gabriel	100kW::AF
		Sa/Su:100kW::AF
	UNITED ARAB EMIRATES UAE RADIO Dubai	300/500kW::ANZ
		(J):300/500kW::EU
21705	CZECHOSLOVAKIA RADIO PRAGUE Prague	250kW::SEA/ANZ
		M-F:120kW::ME
		Sa/Su:250kW::SEA/ANZ

World Time 0 1 2 3 4 5 6 7 8 9 10 11 12 13 14 15 16 17 18 19 20 21 22 23 24

ENGLISH — GERMAN / DEUTSCH — FRENCH / FRANÇAIS — PORTUGUESE / PORTUGUÊS — SPANISH / ESPAÑOL — ARABIC / عربي — RUSSIAN / РУССКИЙ — CHINESE / 中文 — JAPANESE / 日本語 — MULTILINGUAL — OTHER — SUMMER ONLY (J) — WINTER ONLY (D) — JAMMING /\/\ or / or \ — EARLIEST HEARD — LATEST HEARD — + TENTATIVE

Frequency (kHz)	Country / Station / Location	World Time 0 1 2 3 4 5 6 7 8 9 10 11 12 13 14 15 16 17 18 19 20 21 22 23 24
21710	UNITED KINGDOM BBC Multiple Locations	100/250kW:WS:ME/AF
21720	USA RFE-RL Via Lisbon, Portugal	50/100kW::EEU (J):50kW::EEU
21725	USSR RADIO MOSCOW/RP&P Vladivostok VATICAN STATE VATICAN RADIO Sta Maria di Galeria	500kW:WS:SAS/SEA 500kW::SA 500kW::CA/SA
21735	USA RFE-RL Via Lisbon, Portugal	250kW::WUSSR (D):250kW::WUSSR (J):250kW::WUSSR
21740	USSR RADIO MOSCOW/RP&P Yerevan	100kW:WS:EAF
21745	USA RFE-RL Via Lisbon, Portugal	100/250kW::WUSSR 100kW::EEU (J):100kW::EEU M-Sa:100/250kW::WUSSR (D)M-Sa:100kW::WUSSR Su:100kW::EEU (D)Su:250kW::WUSSR (D)Su:100kW::EEU (J)Su:100kW::EEU
21765	PAKISTAN RADIO PAKISTAN Islamabad	100kW::SEA
21810	BELGIUM BELGISCHE RADIO TV Wavre	(J)M-F:100/250kW::EAS (J)Sa:100/250kW::EAS

World Time 0 1 2 3 4 5 6 7 8 9 10 11 12 13 14 15 16 17 18 19 20 21 22 23 24

ENGLISH ▬ GERMAN / DEUTSCH ◊◊◊◊ FRENCH / FRANÇAIS ▬ PORTUGUESE / PORTUGUÊS ▬ SPANISH / ESPAÑOL ▬
ARABIC / عربى ▬ RUSSIAN / РУССКИИ ▬ CHINESE / 中文 □□□□ JAPANESE / 日本語 ▬ MULTILINGUAL ▬ OTHER ▬
SUMMER ONLY (J) WINTER ONLY (D) JAMMING /\/\ or / or \ EARLIEST HEARD ◢ LATEST HEARD ◣ + TENTATIVE

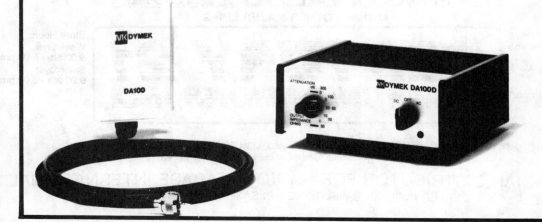

TALK IS CHEAP!
We put our promises in writing for you...

Lowest Price Guaranteed!

It is our policy to provide the very best value for your purchase dollar. You will **never** pay more at Century 21 Communications! If within 30 days of your purchase anyone else in Canada advertises for sale the same equipment under similar conditions of sale at a lower price, we will cheerfully refund the difference in full, with proof of lower price. Guaranteed **lowest** price at Century 21 Communications!

Customer Satisfaction Guaranteed!

Century 21 Communications intends to be Canada's largest independent supplier of amateur and commercial communications equipment. It is the aim of every employee to ensure that you are completely satisfied with your purchase. If you have any problems or questions please inform us and we will be glad to assist you in any way possible.

Service You Can Count On!

Century 21 Communications has an on-premises service facility for service of amateur, commercial, cellular and marine communications equipment. We are an authorized dealer and service centre for most major lines. We also have drive-in installation bays for in-vehicle installations. We service what we sell! And we do it well!

"No-Hassle" Extended Warranty!

We believe in the quality and reliability of the equipment we sell. We provide a no-cost extended warranty on all amateur equipment which covers needed repairs long after the manufacturer's warranty expires. And if your equipment legitimately needs service more than three times under warranty we will gladly replace it with a new piece of equipment, free of charge! You can buy with confidence at Century 21 Communications!

Before You Pick Your Rig— Pick Our Brains!

We are all radio amateurs — some with 20 years of experience. All of us keep up with the latest technology and we enjoy talking about it! So, whether you are an experienced amateur, or just a beginner, you'll find that we will be happy to take the time to explain anything you want to know. **AND**, since we carry **ALL** major lines of amateur radio equipment you will get an unbiased opinion! Pick our brains before you pick your rig!

Free Delivery!

In keeping with our policy of offering the very best values to hams across Canada we will deliver your purchase of any transceiver, anywhere in Canada, free of charge! (Some remote destinations excepted).

Why Settle For Less?

Authorized Dealers For
KENWOOD YAESU ICOM
AND ALL OTHER MAJOR LINES

Please send two 34¢ stamps for free catalogue.

Murray Lampert
VE3HI
Owner

Store Hours:
Weekdays:
9:00 am - 5:00 pm
Saturdays:
9:00 am - 3:00 pm

4610 Dufferin Street, Unit 20-B, Downsview, Ontario, M3H 5S4 • Telephone: (416) 736-0717
(Just north of Finch Avenue. Take the Allen Expressway from Hwy. 401)

CANADIAN DISTRIBUTOR FOR RADIO DATABASE INTERNATIONAL
DEALER INQUIRIES WELCOME—PLEASE WRITE OR CALL!

RADIO
DATABASE
INTERNATIONAL

1987 BUYER'S GUIDE
TO
WORLD-BAND RADIOS

RDI RATINGS OF OVERALL PERFORMANCE

***** Superb
**** Excellent
*** Very Good
** Good
* Fairly Good

No stars = Fair (F), Poor (P) or Unacceptable (U)

CLASSEMENT GENERAL RDI

***** Superbe
**** Excellent
*** **Très Bon**
** Bon
* Assez Bon

Non Etoilé = Moyen (F), Médiocre (P) ou Inacceptable (U)

CLASIFICACION GENERAL RDI

***** **Magnífico**
**** Sobresaliente
*** Muy Bueno
** Bueno
* Bastante Bueno

Sin estrellas = Regular (F), Mediocre (P) o Inaceptable (U)

EINTEILUNG IN KLASSEN RDI

***** Ausgezeichnet
**** Vorzüglich
*** Sehr Gut
** Gut
* Ziemlich Gut

Ohne Sternen = Nicht Sehr Gut (F), Schlecht (P) oder Unannehmbar (U)

RDI SWL/DX 用総合評価

***** 超優秀
**** 優秀
*** 秀
** 優
* 良

星なし： （Ｆ）可， （Ｐ）不良， （Ｕ）不可

RDI BUYER'S GUIDE TO PORTABLE WORLD RECEIVERS

Ever since Sony introduced its pioneering ICF-2001 portable shortwave radio back in 1980, world radio listening hasn't been the same. Gone forever are the days of large, clunky receivers, their dozens of tubes smoking and glowing angrily in the dark. Gone, too, are the days of having to guess at what frequency you're tuned in to. Today, high-tech computer-type circuitry makes it a real joy to look up a frequency in your RADIO DATABASE INTERNATIONAL, punch it in, then sit back and enjoy.

Now, seven years after the unveiling of the ICF-2001, a wide range of advanced-technology portable receivers is available worldwide to suit every need.

We have carefully tested, firsthand, each model listed in the **RDI Buyer's Guide**, adhering to the no-nonsense standard of integrity and accuracy that have been our hallmark since 1977.

To facilitate comparing prices among competing models, US "list" price is usually given, as that country has one of the world's broadest selections of world receivers. These prices thus serve as an effective worldwide index to relative price differences once adjustments are made for local commercial and tariff considerations.

RDI scours the earth for interesting new models of world receivers. For models we have tested that are not found in North America, the price given is that in the country where the receiver was obtained.

The following self-contained portables are listed in descending order of suitability as devices for listening to worldwide shortwave radio broadcasts. Test results are based on self-contained operation using batteries and built-in antennas.

*** Sony ICF-2010/ICF-2001D $389.95

Top-rated Sony ICF-2010/ICF-2001D

The best portable on the market today, this innovative and advanced Sony world-band receiver — called the ICF-2010 within North America, the ICF-2001D elsewhere — provides very good shortwave, as well as mediumwave AM, perfor-

mance. FM performance, as is often the case with Sony world receivers, is less exemplary.

Much of this superior performance results from an enhanced-fidelity concept with the cumbersome title of "synchronous exalted-carrier selectable side-band" (ECSS-s). This advanced technique reduces distortion and interference, making listening more pleasurable than is possible on most conventional world receivers, even though Sony has not provided an audio stage or speaker equal to the aural potential of ECSS-s.

The '2010/'2001D is compact enough to be suitable for almost any kind of traveling. Yet, it incorporates nearly every feature imaginable to gladden the hearts of world radio aficionados, as well as travelers. For example, there are elaborate clock/alarm/sleep facilities and a dial light to aid the traveling world radio listener, along with a multitude of computer "memories" in which you can store your favorite channels, then bring them back later at the push of a button.

Early production samples suffered from excessive "hiss" when the ECSS-s circuitry was switched in. It appears as if this has been reduced, albeit at the expense of high-frequency audio response. A more consistent drawback has been in the casual alignment of ECSS-s circuitry at the factory (see box). Another has been in the overly-wide "wide" bandwidth that lets in too much interference from stations on adjacent channels.

Sony tells us they are aware of these difficulties and should have them remedied in due course. But, even without these minor mid-course corrections, the Sony ICF-2010/ICF-2001D is the pick of the lot in a portable.

Oddly, despite healthy demand for the radio in the United States, Sony appears to be having significant distribution problems with the ICF-2010. One Sony sales representative informed RDI that the company is importing only a modest quantity of '2010's — well below observed demand — into the country each month.

As a result, at the time of this writing, this excellent portable is often unavailable in the US. Fortunately, in other countries distribution appears to be keeping pace with consumer demand.

A complete test report on the Sony ICF-2010/ICF-2001D is available via *RDI White Paper*.

*** Panasonic RF-9000/National DR-90
$3,800.00

Ridiculously overpriced and grossly overweight, this gilt-edged entry from Panasonic nevertheless performs quite well, overall. Its audio quality, in particular, helps make shortwave listening pleasurable. Some design oversights notwithstanding, the RF-9000/DR-90 comes equipped with nearly every feature imaginable, making the set some-

Panasonic's hefty RF-9000 "Portable"

thing of a gadgeteer's delight — or shortwave circus freak show.

The behemoth RF-9000/DR-90 — a portable in name only — should sell well at such outlets as Neiman-Marcus, nestled alongside platinum bidets and wolf's nose fur coats. For those seeking a more satisfactory marriage of treasure and result, better overall performance — audio quality excepted — can be found at a fraction of the cost in Japan Radio's superb new NRD-525 tabletop receiver, which is actually considerably lighter than Panasonic's entry into the portable refrigerator look-alike market.

*** Grundig Satellit 600 $650.00

The Grundig Satellit 600 is a nominally portable model in need of Weight Watchers that nonetheless provides above-average overall performance, plus unusually pleasant audio quality and a wide array of useful features. These range from a 24-hour clock-/alarm to keypad tuning to programmable channel memories. FM performance similarly is superior.

As is the case with nearly every portable tested, the '600 — which lacks the relatively tight "skirt" selectivity of the top-rated Sony ICF-2010/ICF-

Grundig's pleasant-sounding Satellit 600

2001D, above — is not really up to the rigors of fishing for faint "DX" catches from within congested bands. However, for general shortwave listening, the results are pleasing. Lifelong broadcaster Arnold Hartley, an IBS panelist with some fifty-odd years of shortwave listening experience, considers the '600 among the most pleasant sets he has ever used for listening to world radio programs.

Although — perhaps surprisingly — the European-made '600 costs far less than does the Japanese-made Panasonic RF-9000/DR-90, its audio quality is fully comparable, making it a relatively affordable alternative for armchair world radio listening.

A complete test report is available via *RDI White Paper.*

*** Grundig Satellit 650 About $675

Not tested, but appears to be functionally similar to the Satellit 600, preceding, save that it tunes to 30, rather than 26.1, MHz, and has color-coded controls — a small, but desirable, touch to make operation less confusing.

** Philips/Magnavox D2999 $399.00

The current version of this recent large-sized entry from Philips of Holland performs very nicely not only on shortwave, but also on FM and other local bands. Its audio quality is well above average, as well, making it in many ways comparable to the Grundig Satellit 600/650.

A complete test report appears elsewhere in this edition of RADIO DATABASE INTERNATIONAL.

** Philips D2935 About $169.00
(outside North America only)

A simplified and more compact version of the Philips/Magnavox D2999, preceding, the D2935 — currently not available in North America — is unquestionably the best value today in Europe for a high-performance shortwave portable.

A complete test report may be found in "Affordable Portable I" elsewhere in this RADIO DATABASE INTERNATIONAL.

** Sony ICF-2002/ICF-7600D $269.95

A traveler's delight, the paperback-sized Sony ICF-2002 — called the ICF-7600D outside North America — delivers more performance than does any other portable in its size class. Its only significant drawback is its modest sensitivity, which limits its use in receiving faint shortwave stations.

For the traveler, there are 24-hour clock/alarm/sleep facilities. Favorite stations can also be stored for later immediate recall by pushing a button, as on a car radio.

On the other hand, no dial light is included. Also not included is a tuning knob. Instead, elevator-type up-down "slewing" buttons tune in single-channel (5 kHz) increments...not the best arrangement, but more than adequate.

Sony's ICF-2002/ICF-7600D judged best for air travel.

For the regular air traveler, the ICF-2002/ICF-7600D's combination of performance, features and size make it an obvious choice.

** General Electric World Monitor $235.00
(US only)

An upgraded version of Panasonic's discontinued model RF-2600, the GE World Monitor II — available, often discounted, only in the US and on American military bases worldwide — is second only to Philips' D2935, above, as the preferred choice for the newcomer to world radio listening.

As to whether the World Monitor will continue in the General Electric line throughout 1987, we have had three answers from GE: yes, no and maybe. However, there are indications that the supply of radios on hand is sufficient to last some time.

The World Monitor's only significant drawbacks are modest frequency stability — although rarely such that it needs retuning — and a tendency to produce repeat signals ("images") 6 MHz down. For example, a station on 17605 kHz will tend to pop up again — albeit much more weakly — as a false signal on 11605 kHz. But in most other respects — notably audio quality — it produces results on a par with more costly world receivers.

For air travel, the World Monitor is larger and heavier than many other portables, such as those produced by Sony. It lacks some of the snazzier "bells and whistles", such as programmable channel memories, found on a number of newer models such as the Philips D2935. However, this relative simplicity makes for fewer things to go wrong, which in part accounts for the World Monitor's above-average record of reliability.

Unlike most small portables, the World Monitor comes equipped with an inboard dual-voltage ac power supply, an analog signal-strength meter, plus a light to illuminate both that meter and the digital frequency readout. The World Monitor also provides unusually strong, clear audio, making it pleasant for listening to local and world stations, alike.

Incidentally, although this GE receiver is officially termed the World Monitor II, the packing cartons and other printed matter simply refer to it as the World Monitor.

For a more complete report on the GE World Monitor, see "Affordable Portable III", found elsewhere in this RADIO DATABASE INTERNATIONAL.

** Panasonic RF-3100/National DR-31 $399.95

Panasonic RF-3100

According to a former consultant to Panasonic in Japan, the engineering crew that designed the classic RF-2800/RF-2900 and RF-2200 world receivers in the late 1970's was reassigned in the early 1980's to design Panasonic computer hardware.

The RF-3100/DR-31 was among Panasonic's first efforts emanating from the replacement radio engineering team. The results signaled a perceptible slip in the performance of Panasonic's radios.

Although the '3100/'31 possesses superior audio quality and worthy FM performance, in other respects its performance is less substantial. Unfortunately, it's too large for traveling and eats batteries like candy.

The Panasonic RF-3100 is a perfectly acceptable world receiver, but not equal to alternative models available at the same or lower prices.

* Embassy Ambassador 2020 $279.95

Produced for the US firm of Electronic Equipment Bank by the Taiwanese manufacturer, Sangean Electronics, Inc., the Ambassador 2020 is essentially identical to the Sangean ATS-803, save that the Ambassador utilitzes two switchable bandwidths instead of the one found on the '803. List price notwithstanding, the actual selling price is expected to be under $200.

A complete test report may be found in "Affordable Portable II" in this RADIO DATABASE INTERNATIONAL.

* Eska RX33   DM598 (roughly $290)
in West Germany

The Eska RX33 is scheduled to be produced for the Swedish firm of EDVIS by the Taiwanese firm of Sangean Electronics, Inc. Not tested or seen by us as yet, the '33 appears to be essentially identical to the Embassy Ambassador 2020, preceding.

Radio West informs us that they are to be the US distributor; that an upgraded RX33II is also planned; and that the actual selling price in the US will be comparable to that of the Ambassador 2020, reviewed in "Affordable Portable II" in this RADIO DATABASE INTERNATIONAL.

* Sangean ATS-803 $299.95

The feature-laden Sangean ATS-803 provides fairly good performance at a reasonably affordable price. The reason is that the actual selling price in the US thus far has been around $180, making it comparable in price to the General Electric World Monitor.

A complete test report may be found in "Affordable Portable II" in this RADIO DATABASE INTERNATIONAL.

* Supertech SR-16H   Around $125.00
(Europe only)

Essentially identical to the Sangean ATS-803, preceding, the Supertech SR-16H sells in Western Europe for approximately the equivalent of $100-125.

At the current selling price, the Supertech SR-16 is a genuine bargain for thrifty shortwave listening in Europe.

A complete test report may be found in "Affordable Portable II" in this RADIO DATABASE INTERNATIONAL.

* Sony ICF-4910/ICF-4900 $99.95

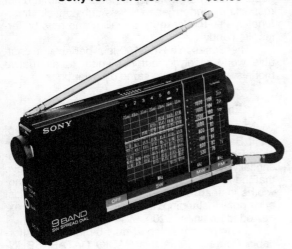

Sony's ICF-4910/ICF-4900 pocket portable

Another of Sony's little innovations, the ICF-4910, known outside North America as the ICF-4900, provides quite decent world radio performance in a box not much larger than a pack of cigarettes. As a result, it is a favorite among globe-

trotters who travel with an absolute minimum of baggage.

The '4910/'4900 covers most, but not all, of the shortwave spectrum, and it does so without benefit of a digital frequency readout.

The '4910/'4900 is the only miniature world portable that is selective and effective in reducing repeat ("image") signals. What this means is that the station you're trying to hear is almost certainly going to sound better on the '4910/'4900 than on, say, the Silver XF1900, below.

Additionally, the '4910/'4900 is reasonably sensitive, allowing it to bring in some of the juicy weaker signals that elude a number of other models of world-band portables. Although the speaker is flea-sized, the overall audio quality is not too unpleasant when taken in small doses.

The truth is, however, that listening to the Sony ICF-4910/ICF-4900 day-in-and day-out can wear your aural patience thin. But for the weight-conscious traveler, it provides an acceptable alternative to larger and more costly portables.

(F) Toshiba RP-F11   About $125
(outside US only)

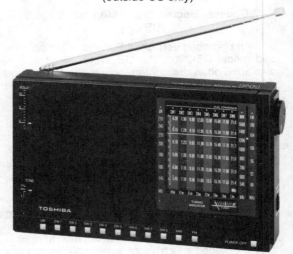

Toshiba RP-F11 compact. Available in Europe, but hard to find in US.

Similar in many respects to Panasonic's discontinued RF-B50, Toshiba's variation covers more of the shortwave spectrum, is more apt to be able to receive weak stations and comes with a genuine signal strength meter...a rarity in compact travel portables.

Unfortunately, the RP-F11 suffers from inadequate IF rejection, with the result that false signals sometimes pop up into what would otherwise be pleasant reception. Also unfortunately — at least for Americans — the RP-F11 is no longer available in the US.

Additionally, the RP-F11 lacks the degree of selectivity found on virtually all of Sony's small portables. Nevertheless, the Toshiba RP-F11 provides reasonably good all-around performance at a fair price, especially for listeners who concentrate on tuning clear-channel stations that are relatively free from interference from nearby stations — a rarity in today's world of international radio.

(F) Sony ICF-7600A/ICF-7600AW $179.95

Sony ICF-7600A/ICF-7600AW compact

Very similar to the Toshiba RP-F11 in size, shape and performance...save that the Toshiba covers more of the shortwave spectrum, and thus is able to pick up more world radio stations. Too, the Sony lacks a genuine signal-strength meter.

Because Sony products are widely distributed in certain countries, and the '7600 is more sensitive to weak signals than is Sony's more sophisticated ICF-2002/ICF-7600D, the '7600A has become a favorite of foreign journalists in parts of Africa and Asia. Perhaps more to the point, members of the fourth estate are not traditionally enamored of high technology and thus welcome the '7600A's lack of digital readout, programmable channel memories and the like.

(F) Silver XF1900 About $125.00 (Europe only)

Silver XF1900

A few years ago, the then-new Silver XF1900 offered good value in a simple world radio portable with digital frequency readout. Nowadays, there are simply too many better choices available for the XF1900 to continue to be attractive.

Although the XF1900 provides fairly good audio, a 24-hour clock/alarm and a dial light, it performs suboptimally in terms of rejecting interference from nearby sources, as well as suppression of repeat ("image") signals. All this means that the same broadcast that comes in clearly on a better model may be disturbed by a cacophony of noise on the XF1900.

In all, the XF1900 continues to be a decent buy. But it's not equal to the comparably priced Super-tech SR-16, much less the worthy Philips D2935, both of which are also available in Europe.

(F) Grundig Yacht Boy 700 $249.00

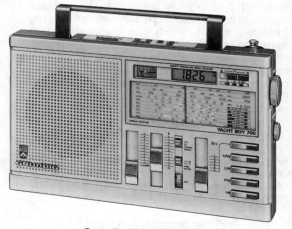

Grundig Yacht Boy 700

Hardly Grundig's pride of the fleet, the Yacht Boy 700 is insensitive to weak signals, uninspiring in its ability to reject interference from adjacent stations, and possesses inadequate rejection of repeat ("image") signals. In short, it picks up fewer stations than it should, and those stations that it receives tend to be disrupted with unnecessary interference.

All this notwithstanding, the '700 has a number of commendable features: digital frequency readout, a 24-hour clock/timer, analog signal-strength meter, built-in dual-voltage ac power supply, a dial light, and above-average audio power.

In recent years, Grundig gradually has been upgrading the technological caliber of its world receivers. Hopefully, in due course the Yacht Boy series, which is by now seriously out-of-date, will be the beneficiary of this effort.

(FP) Philips D1835 About $55.00
(outside North America only)

Similar in appearance to the Sony ICF-7600A, the Philips D1835 is the lowest-priced entry in that company's recent attempt to reenter the shortwave listening market with vigor.

Low-cost Philips D1835

Lowest-rated Realistic DX-360

Unfortunately, it lacks sensitivity to weak signals; is prone to allow interference from adjacent signals to bother reception; and suffers from repeat ("image") signals, which also cause unnecessary disruption to otherwise-clear signals.

Its coverage of the international shortwave bands is fairly complete, although it skips the tropical bands and 75 meter international band altogether. Its frequency readout, although not digital, is reasonably accurate for a set in its class.

In Europe, which is where the lion's share of D1835's are likely to be sold, the proliferation of strong world radio signals tends to make high sensitivity unnecessary. This, combined with the set's very low price, allows it to fill a niche in the low end of the European world receiver market...its mediocre performance notwithstanding.

(FP) Sangean SG-789 $99.95

A very small travel portable with analog, rather than digital, frequency readout, the Sangean SG-789 covers most of the international and tropical world radio bands. Given the availability of the smaller and far better Sony ICF-4910/ICF-4900, above, the '789 has little to commend it.

(FP) Embassy Diplomat 4950 $99.95

Virtually identical to the Sangean SG-789, preceding, but distributed by the US firm of Electronic Equipment Bank.

(P) Sangean ATS-801 $179.95

Lacking coverage of the upper portion of the shortwave spectrum, the Sangean ATS-801 is so unselective as to be nearly useless for reception of world radio signals. Its tuning system is dreadfully slow, and as if this weren't enough repeat ("image") signals proliferate and battery consumption is disconcertingly high.

(P) Tandy/Radio Shack Realistic DX-360
$99.95

Bringing up the rear, alas, is the one radio that is the most widely distributed in the world, Radio

Shack's Realistic DX-360. A greatly stripped-down version of an already bad radio, the Silver XF1900, above, the DX-360 has neither digital nor reasonable analog frequency readout. As a result, when you turn on the DX-360, you have no idea where you are on the band. In an effort to make the radio truly a dog, Radio Shack also stripped off the XF1900's clock/timer, sleep control and longwave band.

Radio Shack knows wheat from chaff. Its former model DX-400 world receiver was a very fine world-band portable, indeed. Yet, it was dropped in 1985, while the DX-360 was retained. Hopefully, we will see a revival of more interesting world receivers in the future from this omnipresent organization. In the meantime, the DX-360 should be avoided.

The following models have reportedly been discontinued, but may still be available new in some retail outlets. Prices are in the range of actual or estimated sale prices as of the time RADIO DATABASE INTERNATIONAL went to press. Because these are discontinued models, prices vary widely and interesting bargains can sometimes be struck with retailers seeking to unload outdated inventory.

**** Sony CRF-1 About $1,000.00

The best-performing portable ever made, the CRF-1 never has been a volume seller, first, because of its staggering list price of $1,795; and, second, because its operating controls are archaic and cumbersome to operate.

The CRF-1 is no travel portable. Instead, it's a pretty large semi-professional communications receiver suited to field portable applications. Nearly every aspect of performance is top-drawer — dynamic range, selectivity, sensitivity, image rejection...the works. Only the "wide" bandwidth — which is too wide to be of any use for receiving world radio signals — disappoints, although audio quality is only about average for a high-end portable.

The DXer who can strike a handsome bargain on a new CRF-1 is a lucky person, indeed.

** Panasonic RF-2900/National DR-29
About $175.00

Very similar to the General Electric World Monitor II, in its day the RF-2900/DR-29 was *the* affordable portable to own. Especially interesting a the high-performance version sold in the United Kingdom a few years back.

At the right price, the RF-2900/DR-29 is still a good choice for a newcomer's first world receiver. For more details, see the description of the GE World Monitor II.

** Sony ICF-2001 $169.95 in New York, more in Europe

Shortly after Panasonic introduced its RF-2800/RF-2900 portables, Sony in 1980 came out with its long-awaited response, the ICF-2001. Although, overall, the '2001 did not really outperform the Panasonic entries, it was much more compact, and thus suitable for air travel. More importantly, it dispensed with traditional analog tuning circuits, replacing them with synthesized tuning derived from computer technology. In so doing, Sony opened the door to a new era in international radio listening.

In many ways, the '2001 is still a desirable receiver. Yet, such has been the rush to progress that its shortcomings now make it a relatively poor buy in the bustling marketplace of the late 1980's. It's unselective, letting in interference from adjacent signals, and the keypad used for accessing stations directly is prone to failure. Its battery consumption is so great that it is sometimes referred to as the "battery monster".

Otherwise, in most respects it's like its shrunken successor, the ICF-2002/ICF-7600D, above, except that the '2002/'7600D is a bit less sensitive and much more selective.

Still, at the right price the Sony ICF-2001 continues to be a reasonably attractive choice.

** Panasonic RF-2200/National DR-22 $179.95

Today, digital frequency displays are as *de rigeur* to world-band radio as color is to television. But Panasonic's RF-2200/DR-22 is one of a shrinking number full-sized world portables that does not come equipped with this "must have" feature. Note, however, that the radio is a a veteran model that goes back some ten years before its discontinuance in late 1985. Its performance and audio quality is similar to that of the General Electric World Monitor, above, to which the '2200/'22 adds something unique: a fully rotatable mediumwave AM antenna. As a result, it's a favorite among mediumwave AM enthusiasts who still savor the romance of listening to faraway domestic stations.

It's also used as a direction finder by electric utilities trying to locate sources of electrical interference, as well as by boaters navigating coarsely by mediumwave AM radio signals.

The rub is that in lieu of a straightforward digital frequency readout, for shortwave the '2200/'22 utilizes an unbelievable Rube Goldberg array of spinning metal discs, compensation controls and a "whistle" circuit that changes pitch to allow the listener to ascertain what channel is being heard. Some fun, eh?

For direction-finders or devotees of radio with ample patience and a peculiar mechanical bent, this is adequate. But for nearly everybody else, the complexity of trying to tune in a shortwave signal on the RF-2200/DR-22 is just too much to handle.

* Panasonic RF-B50 $149.95.

Pricey for what it is, the Panasonic RF-B50 is unusual for a compact portable in that it provides two switchable bandwidth choices: wide for listening to local stations, narrow for tuning about the worldwide shortwave bands. Audio quality, as well as overall FM and mediumwave AM performance, are above average for a compact.

The RF-B50 covers most, but not all, of the shortwave broadcasting spectrum. It utilizes an analog, rather than digital, frequency readout that can be off by as much as 15 kHz, or three shortwave broadcast channels. However, for most casual applications this degree of resolution is adequate.

Unfortunately, on shortwave the 'B50 suffers from a lack of sensitivity with its built-in antenna. As a result, weak stations are difficult to bring in. Although the 'B50 is effective in reducing common types of repeat signals ("images"), the lack of adequate rejection of which results in the intrusion of various undesired signals, including those from passing aircraft, which makes the 'B50 inappropriate for use on or near flight paths.

According to Panasonic, the RF-B50 has now been replaced by the model RF-B20 ($99.95), not tested.

* Sharp FV-610GB   Under $170

Somewhat tardily, in 1983, Sharp decided to plunge into the portable world receiver market. Their entries were poorly promoted, hard to find, and did not stand apart from the pack sufficiently for sales to take off. As a result, except for the bargain bin, Sharp world receivers are a thing of the past.

Their top-end model, the FV-610GB (sold in various parts of the world with different suffix letters), is notable mainly for its relatively high sensitivity and propensity to "overload". Thus, the '610 has found favor in parts of the world, such as the Americas and the Pacific, where signal strengths tend to be relatively low.

Coverage of the shortwave spectrum is incomplete, but adequate for most applications. Selectivity is only fair, allowing some interference from adjacent signals to disturb listening to favorite programs. And the tuning knob is vague and unresponsive.

Aside from the various Sangean models, the Sharp FV-610GB is the only world receiver tested that comes equipped with stereo FM, albeit that stereo listening is via earphones only. Also to its credit, the '610 incorporates digital frequency readout, a 24-hour clock/timer with sleep control, plus a dial light for nighttime listening.

For someone outside Europe seeking a portable world receiver with the ability to pull out relatively weak stations, the FV-610GB may still be a good choice...provided the price is right.

* Panasonic RF-6300/National DR-63
Around $350.00

Originally introduced at the then-hefty price of $700, the RF-6300/DR-63 — along with the RF-799, below — were two of Panasonic's great engineering flops.

Viewed positively, the '6300/'63 has pleasant audio for listening to world and local broadcasts alike. It also includes twelve programmable channel memories to allow favorite stations to be brought up at the push of a button. In principle, at any rate.

Unfortunately, in practice the '6300/'63 includes something rarely encountered this side of a radio museum: a manual front-end selectivity range switch. So when you push the button for your favorite station, it will appear only if that switch is cranked to the correct range position. Too, every time you alter the range-switch setting, the set jumps to a predetermined frequency, such as 5500 or 16000 kHz, from which the frustrated listener must tune laboriously to where he wishes to be.

Selectivity, despite two switchable settings, is mediocre. Neither sensitivity nor dynamic range are appropriate to a set anywhere in this price class.

It makes little economic sense to pay the current going price for the '6300/'63 when comparable sums can buy any of a number of truly delightful world receivers.

(F) Kenwood R-11/Trio R-11   Under $125

Virtually identical to the Toshiba RP-F11, above...if you can find one.

(F) Grundig Satellit 300   Under $250

Another flawed design that failed to catch on in the marketplace, the Grundig Satellit 300 is longer on features than it is on performance.

The '300's fundamental shortcoming is that it is insensitive to weak signals. But beyond that lies shortwave performance that is uninspiring in nearly every respect.

What is worthy on the '300 is its audio quality, ergonomics and FM performance. Tuning is very flexible, being via a variable-rate incremental-tuning knob, keypad, band slewing and programmable channel memories. A 24-hour clock-timer is also included, along with a dial light for nighttime listening. An inboard dual-voltage power supply allows the set to be used on ac power nearly anywhere in the world, and a genuine analog signal-strength meter is included.

The Satellit 300 is scheduled to be replaced by the Satellit 400 International in the near future.

(F) Sharp FV-310GB   Under $140

Identical to the Sharp FV-610GB, above, except that it lacks digital frequency readout, clock/timer and stereo FM. What a deal.

(F) Grundig Yacht Boy 650   Under $200

The Grundig Yacht Boy 650 covers most, but not all, of the shortwave spectrum in use by world broadcasters. Frequency readout is both analog and digital, with the latter sharing a 24-hour clock/timer. Unusual for such a compact set is the presence of a dual-voltage inboard ac power supply — a real convenience for the world traveler.

As is the custom with Grundig receivers, audio quality is above average in quality and strength. FM performance is similarly commendable. As for shortwave broadcasts, performance is only so-so, overall.

The Yacht Boy '650 will probably be of interest mainly to air travelers interested in its many features, rather than optimum shortwave performance.

(F) Panasonic RF-799   Under $300

Panasonic's attempt to compete with Sony's ICF-2001 was a real flop. Whoever designed the RF-799 apparently had little knowledge or appreciation of what shortwave listening is all about.

The truth is that this set could have been a real winner. Panasonic has a reputation for producing reliable products and, at the time of the '799's unveiling, the Sony '2001 was suffering from problems with keypad failure and high battery consumption.

Features are in profusion: digital readout, keypad tuning, programmable-channel memories, inboard dual-voltage ac power supply, clock/alarm, sleep timer and dial light.

Closer inspection reveals design shortcomings. Low-cost circuitry — inappropriate in a $300 receiver — allows repeat ("image") signals to appear to disturb reception of desired stations. Tuning is in single-channel (5 kHz) increments, as with the Sony ICF-2002/ICF-7600D. However, unlike the Sony, the '799 has no fine-tuning provision to interpolate between 5 kHz points. This makes it impossible to detune slightly to reduce interference, plus makes it difficult to receive properly "split-channel" broadcasters, such as All India Radio on 9912 kHz.

The '799 covers only portions of the shortwave spectrum, and those portions that were skipped include some of the choicest segments — notably 9.0-9.5 MHz — used by such major world broadcasters as the BBC.

It's hard to justify purchasing such a flawed piece of equipment when so many more desirable models are freely available today at the same or lower cost.

(P) Panasonic RF-9/Panasonic RF-9L/National Micro 00 $99.95

This miniature radio, similar in appearance to Sony's respectable ICF-4910/ICF-4900, has only size working in its favor. Unselective with repeat ("image") signals aplenty; lacking complete coverage of the shortwave spectrum; and crowned by really bad audio; the RF-9/RF-9L/Micro 00 brings back the nightmare of what shortwave used to sound like before Sony, Panasonic and others revolutionized shortwave listening with advanced-technology portables less than a decade ago.

RDI BUYER'S GUIDE TO TABLETOP WORLD RECEIVERS

Most of us become acquainted with world radio by purchasing a low-cost portable world radio. This is a common-sense way to test the waters, even if most inexpensive portables tend to provide a somewhat disappointing introduction to international broadcasting.

Once the wonders of world radio have been explored, the audible squeals and other drawbacks of low-cost, low-technology portables take their toll on most listeners' patience. They either throw in the towel or move up to one of the more advanced portables, such as the well-rated models reviewed elsewhere in this RADIO DATABASE INTERNATIONAL.

Tabletop Radios Sought for High Performance

Results with state-of-the-art portables can be satisfying, indeed. But, for some, satisfying isn't good enough. They seek the best the marketplace has to offer, so turn to tabletop world radios...receivers, if you prefer.

Is this the way to go? Do tabletop models really outperform high-technology portables?

Drawbacks Amidst The Virtues

Yes, the best tabletop models do tend to outperform the best portables...at least for those trying to hear certain types of difficult signals. But these high performers also exact a stiff financial tribute. Additionally, they're usually not self-contained, forcing you to go through the rignamarole of affixing an external antenna.

The drawbacks of tabletop models are not inadvertent. Steep prices result from the production of a more intricate piece of equipment, as well as the relative lack of economies of scale resulting from specialized, low-volume production. As to most tabletop radios' lack of a built-in antenna, this is because the best results for perfectionistic world listening are brought about by an external antenna — preferably outdoors — just as with a television set (for more on this topic, see articles elsewhere in thie RADIO DATABASE INTERNATIONAL).

Still, costly tabletop radios tend to reflect their origin as designs based on nonpublic applications — listening to ships at sea and the like — in which audio quality is not of primary importance. These voice-oriented radios are known as "communications receivers", although hyperbole-prone advertisers often use this same term to describe pedestrian models that are anything but suited to such tasks.

So, for the individual fond of listening to music over powerful world radio stations, certain sophisticated tabletop models can be a poorer choice than one of the better portables designed to reproduce faithfully voice and music programs alike.

Variations in Price and Performance

Tabletop models, like portables, come with a wide variation in price and performance. One — the Sony ICF-6800W — provides high-quality overall performance with audio quality that is especially pleasant. Provided you don't feel the need for jet-cockpit-type controls, it's an excellent choice for listening to music and voice programs day-in-and-day-out...even though in some respects it is not so well suited as other models for snaring really tough, faint signals.

For those more interested in "DXing" — the art of tuning flyspeck signals — audio quality is of less compelling importance. The range of choices for DXing is considerable, ranging from the top-rated Japan Radio NRD-525 — reviewed in detail elsewhere in this edition of RADIO DATABASE INTERNATIONAL — to the popular ICOM IC-R71 to less-costly models from Yaesu and Trio-Kenwood.

Because they are targeted to an elite of world radio listeners, tabletop models tend to be harder to find than are most portables. For example, in the US Sony all but hides its ICF-6800W — and, alas, many other models, as well — from consumers. But the good news is that many of the electronics specialty firms that do carry these tabletop world receivers also provide useful consumer advice and service after the sale.

How They Perform

The following tabletop radios, all of which are priced in the US at under $1,000, are listed in descending order of suitability as devices for listening to world shortwave broadcasts. Keep in mind that if you listen mainly to weaker stations — or speech, such as newscasts — audio quality will be of less importance than if you listen to musical programs over strong, clear stations.

**** ICOM IC-R71 $949.00

ICOM's IC-R71A, popular for "DXing"

Because of its high level of communications-receiver performance, the IC-R71 series (IC-R71A, etc.) has become popular among radio enthusiasts chasing after the really weak, tough catches to be found among the over-1,000 channels of world radio broadcasting. The 'R71 performs very well and incorporates a host of advanced electronic features.

What the 'R71 does not provide is audio quality. Distortion at some audio frequencies approaches 30%, making long-term listening unnecessarily tiring. Numerous tiny, cramped controls also diminish user pleasure.

Judging from letters received at RADIO DATABASE INTERNATIONAL, the quqlity-control problems that characterized the predecessor model, the 'R70, have been overcome. Accordingly, for reception of tough signals the 'R71 provides an alternative to the Japan Radio NRD-525, NRD-515 and NRD-93 models reviewed elsewhere in this RADIO DATABASE INTERNATIONAL ("When Money Is No Object").

The 'R71 is also a favorite among electronics experimenters who relish modifying its electronics circuitry to obtain enhanced performance. Sometimes this produces results that are more "sizzle than steak", but in other instances the improvements are audible and worthwhile. Certain of these alterations, which tend to be frowned upon by the factory, are obtainable through world radio specialty firms in North America and Europe.

The now-pricey 'R71 is a radio enthusiast's set, and to that extent makes an excellent choice for snaring tough "catches". Those more concerned with pleasant reproduction of music and other programs from major broadcasters may wish to consider, instead, the Sony ICF-6800W, aas well as the two models from Yaesu and Kenwood.

A complete test report on the ICOM IC-R71A is available via *RDI White Paper*.

*** Sony ICF-6800W $719.95

Sony's ICF-6800W provides exceptionally pleasant results

Arguably the most agreeable radio extant for everyday listening to shortwave broadcasts, the Sony ICF-6800W manages to make do nicely without most of the "bells and whistles" found on other models of high-performance world radios. Rather, the '6800 stands out by providing unusually well-rounded and pleasant results, along with uncomplicated, straightforward operation. In particular, its audio quality is well above average, and circuit noise — "hiss" — is essentially nonexistent. Both bass and treble tone controls are included, as well.

Another unusual plus with the '6800 is that it operates off either ac power or batteries. It's also fully self-contained, with features from antennas to a reading light being built in. This allows the quasi-portable '6800 to be moved easily from room-to-room, as well as outdoors — or even tossed into the car on trips.

The '6800's chief shortcoming lies in its dynamic range, which is the most limited of any currently available tabletop model tested. This can result in "overloading", with stations sounding as though they're piled on top of each other when they really aren't. So in strong-signal areas, such as Europe, high-gain external antennas should be avoided. On the other hand, with the built-in antenna the '6800 works fine in nearly any part of the world.

An additional drawback — common among mid-priced world radio models — is that the '6800's wider bandwidth is far too wide for useful reception of all but a distinct minority of stations operating well away from adjacent sources of interference. Its narrow filter, on the other hand, works very well. Added to this is the '6800's ability to be detuned slightly without causing high distortion, thus allowing the narrow filter to be unusually flexible in reducing interference while broadening reception of high audio frequencies.

The '6800 has all the sex appeal of a shoebox. As a result, some dealers and consumers — accustomed as they are to high-tech world radios garlanded with blinking lights and banks of controls — tend to give the '6800 short shrift.

In the US an additional problem is that, in the **past couple of years, Sony has all but rationed its** meager imports of world radios available to dealers. As a result, dealers are often out of stock of various Sony models and — understandably — tend to steer buyers to competing models. Still, in time the patient and persistent consumer can obtain a '6800.

Those in the US having difficulties locating a '6800 can call Sony's Consumer Information number: 800-222-7669. If this fails, you can write Product Planning, Sony General Consumer Audio, Park Ridge NJ 07656. Fortunately, outside the US Sony world-band radios appear to be available more or less in concert with consumer demand.

For traditionalists who treasure high-quality audio quality in a high-performance tabletop receiver, the '6800 is an obvious choice. The Sony ICF-6800W tends to be discounted more heavily than are most other tabletop models. As a result, in many countries the '6800 is one of the more affordable tabletop world radios available to careful shoppers.

*** Yaesu FRG-8800 $599.95

All electronics design is based on compromise relating to what the consumer is willing to pay. A properly balanced design allows the various functions to operate at a similar level so there are no great weaknesses in given aspects of performance or the range of features offered.

Balance is the chief characteristic of the Yaesu FRG-8800's design. A good compromise model when you want above-average audio quality, but

Yaesu FRG-8800 provides good performance for the money

don't wish to forego such advanced operating features as keypad frequency entry and pushbutton channel memories, the attractively priced Yaesu FRG-8800 provides worthy all-around performance with audio that is not tiring. The sensible layout of the front panel and operating controls make the set enjoyable to operate, as well.

The '8800 is more than adequate for most world radio listeners' needs. Still, in some respects it is not what it could be. Of its two bandwidths, the narrower is sufficient for most shortwave listening applications, but the wider is too broad to be of use except for listening to the minority of world radio stations operating "in the clear".

As of presstime, the '8800 has not seen a price rise since its inception in late 1984, notwithstanding that the yen has risen dramatically during that time. So long as this situation remains in effect, the '8800 should be considered a better-than-average value.

A complete test report on the Yaesu FRG-8800 is available via *RDI White Paper*.

** Kenwood R-2000/Trio R-2000 $649.95

Trio-Kenwood R-2000

The R-2000 — sold variously under the brand names "Kenwood" and "Trio" — is another good compromise model for those seeking advanced operating features, above-average audio quality and generally good performance. The R-2000's front panel is sensibly laid out for user-friendly operation of the wide variety of controls. Operating this set is a pleasure.

The R-2000 provides pleasant results, but suffers from mediocre dynamic range and front-end selectivity that can result, among other things, in "overloading" under some circumstances — particularly when a substantial external antenna is used in those parts of the world, such as Europe, where received signal strengths tend to be high. Another drawback is that the '2000's tuning is in 50 Hz increments only — more than adequate for typi-

cal world radio listening uses, but rather coarse for certain communications types of reception.

As with most tabletop models tested, the "wide" bandwidth position is too wide to be of real use in tuning world radio stations. But to compound the problem, the narrow filter is rather tight for day-to-day listening.

Withal, the R-2000 is a pleasure to operate and provides generally good performance in receiving world radio programs, although it is not the optimum choice for "DXing" or receiving communications-type signals.

(F) Heathkit/Zenith SW-7800 (Revised) $349.95

Heathkit/Zenith's disappointing SW-7800

Poor in its original incarnation circa 1984, but upgraded after a period of modest re-engineering, the Heathkit SW-7800 is unique in that it comes available only as a kit which the buyer must assemble from instructions that are all but foolproof.

Alas, the end result of dozens of hours of soldering and snipping is a world radio that is far below the level of performance of any other model tested. Nevertheless, its relatively affordable price — the lowest of any tabletop tested — plus its role as a widely-distributed kit, allow it to fill niches that would otherwise be vacant.

If kits aren't your special passion, you should consider, instead, for one of the better-rated portables or tabletop models.

A complete test report on the Heathkit/Zenith SW-7800 (Revised) is available via *RDI White Paper*.

Discontinued Models

A number of discontinued models still are available new on dealer shelves. However, unlike discontinued portables, discontinued tabletop models are rarely heavily discounted beyond pre-discontinuation levels. Indeed, in the case of some prized models, prices may be higher than they were when the sets were still in the manufacturer's catalog.

Here's a glance at some of the more recently discontinued models you might come across in your wanderings through electronics stores...

** Kenwood R-1000/Trio R-1000   About $500

The first of Kenwood's modern world radios to come on the market, the R-1000 — also sold under the brand name "Trio" — was an early favorite among DX aficionados and electronics experimenters. Indeed, Radio West in the US acquired its reputation in equipment modification mainly because of its alterations to the R-1000's circuitry.

Although the current Kenwood R-2000 is in many ways a more modern receiver than the older R-1000, the '1000 is less prone to overloading, and thus continues to be preferred when long antennas are used, for example.

*** McKay Dymek DR 101-6   Under $1,000

The best of the receivers produced by the firm of McKay Dymek before it was taken over by Stoner Communications, the DR 101-6 manages to incorporate McKay's innovative ideas, such as a variable-rate slewing knob, without certain of the drawbacks evidenced on the earlier versions of the DR 22 and DR 33 series (see below).

As with other models in the McKay line, the DR 101-6 comes equipped with a substandard speaker and mediocre front-end selectivity. But with a worthy external speaker the end result can be quite pleasant.

*** Yaesu FRG-7700   About $550

Similar in performance to the newer FRG-8800 (see above), but lacking many of the '8800's "bells and whistles", the '7700 — which has three bandwidths — can be an attractive alternative when it is priced to move.

** McKay Dymek DR 33-C $995.00

Some years ago, McKay Dymek, an innovative California firm, decided to produce world radio receivers/tuners that would look like and interface with conventional stereo hi-fi components. Thus, the reasoning went, world radio tuners would take their places alongside their popular FM brethren.

The earliest models, the DR 22 and DR 33 series, were not entirely successful, even though they did have the appearance of hi-fi components. The problem — obvious in retrospect — lay in trying to market an exotic, but low-fidelity, medium to consumers specifically seeking equipment producing the *ne plus ultra* in aural fidelity.

Various novel approaches were tried in order to make world radio more palatable to the uninitiated, but the end result was akin to putting sugar on vegetables to make them palatable to hamburger-loving kids.

The whole concept was rooted in erroneous assumptions, so the '22 and '33 never really took off. However, before selling out to Stoner Communications, McKay did come up with an improved model, the DR 101-C (see above).

A small quantity of the final version of the DR 33-C — the DR 33-C/6 — is still on hand at Stoner Communications' warehouse. Presumably it incorporates improvements over the earlier version of the DR 33-C we tested some years back.

* Bearcat/Uniden DX1000 $649.00

When Bearcat, long known as a pioneer in the manufacture of scanning devices, announced its first world receiver, it was expected that something advanced and quite special would emerge. Instead, what appeared was a thoroughly serviceable, but uninspiring, radio seemingly designed to be produced at minimal cost.

Given the alternatives, there is really no reason to select this overpriced model unless extenuating circumstances, such as the availability of parts and service in your country, make it appropriate. As of presstime, the DX1000, discontinued in 1986, continues to be available at some dealers in North America and Europe. According to Uniden, there are no plans for that firm to re-enter the world radio market.

* Kenwood R-600/Trio R-600   About $400

Kenwood's bargain receiver, the R-600 — also sold under the "Trio" name — provides decent, uncomplicated world radio reception with a minimum of operating controls and features.

Introduced on the market long after the appearance of the R-1000, and as high-technology portables were present as competition, the R-600 was too little, too late. At present, there is no satisfactory tabletop set in the '600's price range, but Lowe's planned HF-125 (see "Coming Up!" elsewhere in this RDI) at least has the potential of being an effective replacement.

* Panasonic RF-4900/National DR-49 About $500

An otherwise-modest performer with surprisingly pleasant audio quality, the Panasonic RF-4900 — also sold as the National DR-49 — operates off both ac power and batteries.

Because the '4900 was so widely distributed, it still turns up new every now and then in various parts of the world, such as Asia and Latin America.

THE PHILIPS/MAGNAVOX D2999: TURNING A PUMPKIN INTO CINDERELLA

Consumers who were unfortunate enough to have, in the fall of 1985, spent $400 on the Philips/Magnavox D2999 found themselves with a world-band radio that was all but useless. False signals, generated by poor circuitry within the receiver, showed up everywhere on the dial. To say that the D2999 made world radio listening confusing, frustrating and downright unpleasant would be an understatement. It was one of the worst sets we had ever tested.

Philips management, to its credit, reacted to this state of affairs by recalling the entire lot of receivers. Anyone who had purchased a D2999 was given the option of having his set upgraded, at no cost, for improved performance. Today, the D2999 is once again on the market, but in revised form.

Multiband Field Portable

The Philips/Magnavox D2999 — which covers longwave and mediumwave AM, as well as the complete world radio spectrum — is a *field portable*...that is, fully self-contained, yet too large and heavy for convenient travel. As befits a device intended for use worldwide, it operates not only from batteries, but also on 120/240V ac power. The potential for power line hum has been minimized by placing the entire ac/dc power supply inboard.

Front-End Selectivity Improved

Front-end selectivity — the curse of the original D2999 — is improved in the cleaned-up version, even though it remains substandard for a model in its price class. A good external antenna still allows vestigial false shortwave signals to be generated in the higher reaches of the shortwave spectrum, such as the 13, 16 and 19 meter bands. Within the 11 meter band, even mediumwave AM signals appear. Withal, front-end selectivity is now acceptable.

Excellent Sensitivity

On the other hand, sensitivity — even with only the built-in telescopic antenna — is nothing short of excellent. Dynamic range is at least average for a set in this class, allowing outdoor antennas to be used in many parts of the world. However, in Europe overloading may occur with an outdoor antenna under certain conditions, such as when you're tuning the 49 meter band at night.

Reasonable Selectivity

There are two bandwidths. The wider is excessively wide for most world radio listening situations, but allows for pleasant listening to local stations and to the occasional shortwave broadcast out in the clear. The narrower width works well under more typical conditions.

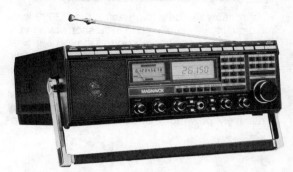

Philips/Magnavox D2999 Portable

Controls Well Thought Out

Some painstaking and creative thought went into the design of the cabinet and controls of the D2999. With a few exceptions, even the smallest detail has been attended to carefully.

Its synthesized tuning arrangement — which tunes and reads out to the nearest kHz — is very complete. There's a foolproof keypad to select any desired frequency with a minimum of button-pushing. Added to this are a scanner of sorts and sixteen memories in which to store your favorite stations.

There's a real variable rate tuning knob. When you give it a good flick, it shifts into overdrive and takes off. The knob assembly also has detents that produce one "click" per kHz (10 kHz on FM) tuned at normal speed. This provides a tuning aid to the visually impaired as well as enhanced "feel" for bandscanning.

The top of the set has a handy row of buttons to allow you to get right to whichever meter band you'd like to scan. Next to each button is a red light-emitting diode (LED) which glows if you're tuned to that band. If you're between bands, two LED's light up — one for each of the bands astraddle where you're tuned.

The D2999 incorporates an analog meter for battery and signal strength, along with a clock/timer that operates in either 24 or 12 hour format but, alas, does not display seconds. For $400, though, you shouldn't find, as you do with the D2999 and a distressingly large number of other models, including the Sangean ATS-803, that the clock shares the front-panel display with the frequency readout. This means you can see the time or frequency — but not both — at the same time.

The D2999's liquid-crystal display and signal/battery strength meter are illuminated — a plus for nocturnal listening — and the long, beefy carrying handle also works as an effective "tilt leg" to prop the '2999 to a pleasant angle once the set is laid down for listening. The rugged, lengthy (160 cm/63") telescopic antenna swivels in discrete increments a full 360 degrees — a nice touch, especially for optimum FM reception. Indeed, this is as worthy a built-in antenna as we've come across in some time.

Commendable Audio Quality

Arguably the best thing about the D2999 is its audio quality — usually good for a shortwave radio. The separate bass/treble controls have been well engineered to allow the listener to shape the audio frequency response to suit the varied demands of high-fidelity FM, on one hand, and the reduced-bandwidth response of longwave, mediumwave AM and shortwave, on the other. Two speakers, fed by a relatively powerful monaural amplifier, are pro-

vided — one atop the cabinet, the other (switchable) in front — to disperse the sound as appropriate throughout the listening area. Although there is a trace of hiss, it's not objectionable.

Revised D2999 Provides Enjoyable Listening

Overall, the cleaned-up version of the D2999 is not only an improvement over the original attempt, but is actually a worthy world-band radio in its own right. For those who listen mainly to the major shortwave broadcasters, the Philips/Magnavox D2999 is straightforward to operate and provides aurally pleasant results.

AFFORDABLE PORTABLE I: PHILIPS D2935

Now that advanced technology has brought world radio more into the mainstream of consumer electronics, what consumers find missing is real value. Noisy, inexpensive low-tech portables perform dreadfully — not surprising, after all, as something more sophisticated than a souped-up AM radio is needed to receive signals properly from thousands of kilometers away. The newer high-tech models, on the other hand, often perform splendidly, but usually hit the pocketbook with a wallop.

Good Values Appearing

Does a good world radio *have* to cost as much as a VCR?

Not any more. While a number of firms, such as Sony, are forging ahead into the frontiers of technology, other companies are making their mark by taking existing advanced technology and producing quite good radios at surprisingly affordable prices.

Probably the best example of this emanates from the large Dutch conglomerate of Philips. To almost everyone's surprise, it came up with a fairly good low-cost travel portable in 1986. That radio, the D2935, provides worthy performance except for selectivity...a shortcoming that — at a price Philips quotes as equivalent to only $160 — many consumers have been willing to overlook.

1987 Model Features Major Improvement

Now, as we go to press, Philips informs us that the D2935 is being produced for 1987 with improved selectivity. We haven't been able to test the revised model — it doesn't exist yet — but Philips engineers inform us that the D2935's new bandwidth filter is the same as that already used in the larger D2999 portable's "narrow" bandwidth position. As we analyzed this filter in our tests of the D2999 (see findings elsewhere in this RDI), we have been able to form a tentative judgement as to how the 1987 D2935 should perform.

The Philips D2935 is about midway in size between the General Electric World Monitor II (reviewed elsewhere in this RDI) and Sony's new ICF-2010 and 2001D portables. And, like the World Monitor, the D2935 operates not only off batteries, but also from 120 and 240 volt ac current. This allows it to be used in nearly any part of the world — a plus for those who spend long period of time in different countries.

Flexible Tuning Configuration

As the descendant of the '2999, the '2935 is a decent piece of equipment. It has keypad direct frequency entry and programmable channel memories, along with the customary tuning knob. Actually, the keypad and other pushbutton controls aren't "buttons" at all. Instead, they're only markings printed on a sheet of Mylar. You "dent" the markings with your finger, just as you do on some microwave ovens, to make your choices.

Affordable Portable I: Philips D2935

This has plusses and minuses. The major minus is that the Mylar sheet is less comfortable and precise to operate than are regular buttons. The plus is that dirt, water and sand can't get inside the radio as easily. This makes the '2935 unusually well-suited to use around water and on beaches.

The tuning knob is unusual for a portable in that it's variable-rate: the faster you tune, the faster the rate of tuning. If you tune carefully, this can be a plus. But if you tune too fast, the radio jumps frequency by no less than 100 kHz, forcing you to back up and retune. The tuning knob also has detents that produce one click per kHz. This is helpful for anyone, but especially those with visual impairment.

Performance Above Average

The '2935 includes a midpower audio stage with a single tone control and a fairly good speaker. The end result is above-average audio quality, although not fully equal to the exceptional standards of the larger Philips/Magnavox D2999, Grundig S-600/S650 or Sony's very fine ICF-6800W. The only quirk is that every now and then the audio output on both our test units became unusually low, but revived unaccountably to normal level once we twiddled the tuning knob.

Shortwave frequency readout — to the nearest kHz — is via a liquid-crystal display, which can be lit at the touch of a button. Signal strength is indicated by five light-emitting diodes (LED's).

Overall, shortwave performance is quite good for a portable. Useable sensitivity with the built-in antenna is fairly good, although there is less sensitivity and more "hiss" than there is with the '2999. That's because the '2999 has an unusually long built-in telescopic antenna as compared to that of the '2935.

The set is quite stable, too. Once a station is tuned in, it doesn't need to be retuned. For a portable, dynamic range is fairly good, even though front-end selectivity is mediocre. So as long as the built-in antenna is used, most listeners won't hear "funnies" mixing in with the station they're trying to hear.

Selectivity on existing samples of the '2935 has been quite poor except for the minority of world radio stations that operate in the clear. Selectivity with the forthcoming 1987 version, using the D2999's "narrow" filter, should be more than adequate, based on our tests with the existing D2999. Still, we miss the switchable dual-bandwidth feature found on many other models of world radios. With two choices, you can have you cake and eat it too: "wide" for maximum fidelity when there is little or no interference; "narrow" to reduce or eliminate interference when you're tuning crowded bands. But, at $160, compromises are inevitable.

FM performance is very good, overall. Mediumwave AM performance with the new version should be less exciting because only one bandwidth is used, and it's geared to reception of world radio stations. In some locations the D2935 produces a 3 kHz howl on 560 kHz. This was found on both our test units in Philadelphia, but not elsewhere, suggesting that the problem results from a peculiar combination of local mediumwave AM signals mixing to cause a spurious signal on 563 kHz.

Distribution not Worldwide

Within Europe, the D2935 appears to be widely available through Philips well-honed system of distribution. However, in the US neither Philips nor its American subsidiary, Magnavox, appears to be experienced in the marketing and distribution of high-technology world radios. With Magnavox, the situation is particularly confusing. One dealer reports that he was told by his Magnavox distributor that the D2935 was available for immediate shipment to dealers. The dealer prepaid for a quantity of radios, supposedly to be received in a few days, only to be told some weeks later that the set didn't exist in the US, after all. Another dealer reports that he was told by Magnavox that the minimum dealer order quantity for the D2935 would be several *hundred radios*.

The reason for Magnavox's apparent lack of enthusiasm for the D2935 appears to relate to the way the company is set up. Even though world portable radios such as this are known to sell twenty-to-sixty thousand units per year in the US, a Magnavox spokesman has indicated to RDI that the market for world radio in the US simply is not there in sufficient quantity to be of interest to a firm the size of Magnavox. Additionally, Magnavox's distribution channels are not geared to world radio sales, which largely take place in specialty stores and electronics/camera outlets, and changing them is more bother than it's worth.

So, for now, the Philips D2935 is available only in Europe and selected other world markets. However, in due course the Philips D2935 could appear on the US "grey market" or Magnavox could alter its stance.

Distinguishing the Two Versions

How can you distinguish the earlier D2935 from the improved version? According to Philips, the 1987 version is to have a recessed on-off power switch, whereas the original version's equivalent switch protrudes from the radio's cabinet by about 3 mm. (1/8").

A final bonus is that the D2935 is manufactured by Philips at its Hong Kong facility. This bargain-priced set thus is not tied to the Land of the Rising Yen, so its price is likely to remain relatively stable throughout 1987.

AFFORDABLE PORTABLE II: TAIWAN'S NEWEST AMBASSADOR

With the Japanese yen — and thus Japanese world radios — rising in price, budget-conscious world radio listeners have begun taking a closer look at offerings from countries whose exports are unaffected by the upward spiral of the yen. The chief beneficiary of this consumer shift has been Taiwan, although nearby Hong Kong has also appeared under the "Philips" and "Magnavox" brand labels (see reports elsewhere in this RDI).

The hub of this new activity is Sangean Electronics Inc. in Taipei. For the past couple of years, now, a variety of world radios has been turned out by this firm under a variety of brand names as well as "Sangean."

Sangean Model Appears in Many Guises

The pride of the Sangean fleet — and the only of their products worthy of serious consideration by the world radio listener — is the Sangean ATS-803. This midsized travel portable contains many state-of-the-art features, along with reasonably good performance and pleasant audio quality. At least as important is its affordable selling price: between $150-290 in Europe and North America.

The standard Sangean ATS-803, which is also sold in Europe as the Supertech SR-16H (about $125) and in North America by Sears under its own brand name (about $210), covers European longwave, worldwide mediumwave AM, FM stereo 87.5-108 MHz, plus the entire shortwave world radio spectrum. Tuning is via conventional knob, direct-entry keypad, programmable channel memories and scanner. The '803 is fully portable and self-contained, being well-suited to use during travels, as well as in the home. It's powered not only by batteries, but also by an outboard worldwide dual-voltage ac converter. It comes equipped with a liquid-crystal display for precise frequency readout so you can tell immediately what channel you're tuned to, plus a five-LED signal-strength indicator. A dial light, bass and treble tone controls, sleep-delay timer, clock-alarm/timer, and power lock (to keep the set from accidentally turning on during travels) round out the '803's list of features.

The '803's performance has many plusses. For one thing, it's very stable — essentially drift-free. Pick a frequency, punch it in and it stays there. Sensitivity with the built-in antenna is quite good, too. So the set can bring in, without problem, a variety of weak and strong stations. Because its dynamic range is fairly good, it works well in just about any part of the world.

Single Bandwidth Major Drawback

There is only one major drawback: its bandwidth filter is unselective. This means that when you're trying to pluck one signal from a band full of competing stations, you'll probably hear more interference than you should. Lesser drawbacks include a "thumping" sound when tuning up and down the bands, distorted "breakthrough" of local FM stations into the world radio spectrum, plus some hum

Affordable Portable II: Sangean ATS-803

when the outboard ac converter is used in lieu of batteries.

So there the story ends: the Taiwanese manufacture a decent radio that, because of this oversight with the bandwidth filter, is, in the end, only passable. Wrong! And the rest of the story reads like a detective novel.

Given the fact that the '803's only really big problem is this overly wide filter, it came as a bit of a shock when an experimenter opened one of the radios and found — a second filter, this one much better than the first. But it only worked when the radio's scanner was turned on. And the scanner in the '803 is virtually useless. So what to do? End of story?

Dual-Bandwidth Versions Created

In the US, Electronic Equipment Bank decided this was just so much foolishness. So it contracted with Sangean to manufacture for EEB a custom-made version of the '803 with a switch to allow the user to select *either* of the two bandwidth filters: "wide" for full fidelity with stations in the clear; "narrow" for stations hemmed in by interference.

The name for this new radio: Ambassador 2020. It "lists" for $279.95, but actually sells for under $200. EEB indicates the '2020 will be sold not only by their firm, but also by a worldwide network of retail dealers.

We tested a pre-production sample of the '2020, and the difference between it and the standard '803 is considerable. With dual selectivity, the '2020 is a much more versatile device...and far kinder to the ears.

EDVIS, a Swedish firm that formerly operated under the name ESKAB, is also having something similar, the ESKA model RX-33 (DM598 — about $290 — in Germany), performed by Sangean, and surely other firms will follow in due course. EDVIS also plans to modify further the RX-33 in Sweden in the near future.

If history is any guide, Taiwanese world radio manufacturing will follow a progressive learning curve. In the meantime, the Embassay Ambassador 2020 now provides worthwhile results at a reasonable price *vis-a-vis* the Japanese competition.

AFFORDABLE PORTABLE III: GENERAL ELECTRIC WORLD MONITOR

Even in the fast lane of high technology, the newest isn't always the best for your needs. Take, for example, the General Electric World Monitor radio, the original design for which dates back a good decade.

Original Design from Panasonic

The original version of the World Monitor was found not under the GE label, but rather under those of Panasonic and National. Introduced variously as the Panasonic RF-2600 and National Panasonic DR-26, it fared poorly in the marketplace, having failed to distinguish itself adequately from its established sibling, the successful RF-2900/DR-29, from which its design was adapted. The '2900/'29, in turn, was derived from the Panasonic RF-2800/National Panasonic DR-28, which appeared on the market around 1977.

Matsushita — the parent company of Panasonic and National — yanked the slow-selling '2600/'26 from its lines and began producing it in improved guise for General Electric starting in 1982.

Unsurprisingly, the World Monitor lacks nearly all the "bells and whistles" found in state-of-the-art world radios. Here are not to be found programmable channel memories, keypad tuning, scanning circuitry, "slewing" controls, timer...or even a lowly digital clock. Instead, the World Monitor represents a successful twilight entry into the then-emerging generation of high-tech radios.

Good All-Around Performance

So, while its tuning is not synthesized, it does have a digital frequency readout to tell you what channel you're hearing, as well as a genuine analog signal/battery-strength meter. It also incorporates circuitry to reduce certain types of interference and "false" signals. It is reasonably selective, as well, using two bandwidths to allow the listener to choose the more suitable setting depending on what's being received. It's sturdy and portable, with dual-voltage ac power built in. Perhaps best of all, its audio quality is well above average, even by today's standards. As an added bonus, it receives FM and mediumwave AM signals unusually well.

Affordable Portable III: GE's World Monitor

Amidst all these cheers, there are drawbacks. Its elder technology of unsynthesized gear-and-pulley tuning results in drift, so sometimes the tuning knob needs re-tweaking even after a station has been properly tuned in. And "repeat" signals tend to appear 6 MHz below where they should. For example, the BBC on 9410 kHz may sometimes be disturbed by a false "repeat" signal from 15410 kHz. And although the World Monitor is portable, by today's standards it is considered bulky for air travel.

Affordable Price, but Not Found Worldwide

Arguably the best news is its selling price, which usually is under $200. This makes it an obvious choice for thrifty listeners seeking worthy performance without the complexities of computer-derived operating controls.

A catch? Of course. In mirror-image of the Philips D2935 (see report elsewhere in this RDI), the **General Electric World Monitor is distributed** *only* in the US and its possessions, along with official US "PX" stores worldwide. And GE has no intention of changing this pattern any time in the forseeable future. Turnabout, after all, is fair play.

ONWARD BACKWARD!

Say that you've decided to buy a car. You go to the car dealer, make a selection, sign the contract, then trot out to the lot to pick up your pride and joy. When you see it, you gasp. "Wait a minute", you say, "There's no steering wheel!" "Oh," says the salesman, "I *am* sorry. But the Mooseracer 9000-HP doesn't come with a steering wheel. It's for people who only drive in a straight line."

So it is with a couple of slightly eccentric world-band radios. You take it for granted that any radio can be tuned — steered — to the appropriate frequency. Not necessarily so. Some tiny firms can't afford the stiff research and development costs associated with designing a first-rate frequency synthesizer suitable for tuning up and down the shortwave bands. So they take a hoary, but affordable, route: fixed crystal-controlled channels.

What this means is that you have to limit your listening to a tiny number of favorite channels. The other 98% of what the world has to say simply won't be heard unless you purchase new crystals, then disembowel the receiver to install them. And what better way to enjoy a few hours with your shortwave radio than cursing the BBC for changing frequency to 9515 kHz — a crystal you don't have installed — right in the middle of a three-hour reading of Dante's *Inferno*. There you are, screwdriver clenched in hand, sweat rolling down your brow as you fumble to find that one crystal from among the dozens you keep in a cavernous drawer by the radio.

What this means is that these sets — for all but a limited number of applications — are as useful as belly-button lint.

Liniplex F1

If there were a world radio "Apertyx Award" — named after the hairy, wingless and utterly useless bird of "B.C." comic strip fame — it would have to go to the very British and pleasantly eccentric Liniplex F1, reviewed in depth in last year's RADIO DATABASE INTERNATIONAL. On one hand, the F1 incorporates innovative ECSS-s circuitry with far greater enhanced-fidelity potential than is possessed by any other receiver on the market today. Yet, this superb circuitry is followed by one of the most pedestrian audio stages and ear-bending tinny

Liniplex F1 Non-Tunable World Radio

speakers to be found anywhere, which chokes off all the benfit of ECSS-s reception.

The radio performs, overall, quite well in receiving shortwave stations. Yet, this ability is next to pointless, as the F1 receives only up to nine fixed channels. Notwithstanding that it carries a budget-busting price tag roughly equivalent to $800.

The Liniplex is an excellent performer when its audio is fed to an outboard preamp/amp/speaker system. If enhanced-fidelity world listening is what you're looking for, the F1 merits consideration — providing, of course, that you're willing to make do with hearing the same nine channels day, after day, after day.

A more successful application for the Liniplex F1 has been with radio stations' receiving a limited number of world radio channels for local rebroadcast.

ESKA RX12PL

Possibly — but doubtfully — still available from either the Swedish (EDVIS) or Danish (ESKA Communications Systems A/S) offshoot of the now-defunct Danish firm of ESKA Elektronik A/S, the hand-held model RX12PL provides fairly good overall performance and tunes up to twelve (gasp!) fixed channels. If it is still available, the RX12PL should be priced new in the vicinity of the equivalent of $200-300, including crystals and associated hardware. Not a bad choice if you don't mind listening to the same twelve channels day-in and day-out.

According to ESKA Communications Systems, the tunable semi-professional model RX99PL portable tested by RDI last year has been discontinued.

WHEN MONEY IS NO OBJECT: FOUR CHOICE PLUMS

With world radio, money literally talks...with more voices, more clarity, more reliability.

Following are four choice plums — all currently available tabletop models — from the world of world radio. Probably our most encouraging finding is that Japan Radio's superb NRD-525 is the least costly of the lot. It also comes equipped with nearly every feature imaginable as standard equipment, rather than as extra-cost options.

Few dealers carry these de luxe models, but those that do almost invariably provide exceptional customer support and service arrangements.

***** Japan Radio NRD-93 $7,995.00

The Ne Plus Ultra, Japan Radio's NRD-93

A sterling professional device in terms of both price and quality, the Japan Radio NRD-93 — conceived primarily for maritime use — is notable more for its hardiness and superb quality of construction than for its performance, which is not markedly different from that of its far less costly sibling models, the Japan Radio NRD-525 and NRD-515. With scanner and other options, the price of the '93 can easily top the heady figure of $9,000! Obviously, this is not the Volkswagen of radios.

Its highly advanced scanner, by the way, is a robust version of that found in the new Japan Radio NRD-525 (see "Hot Knobs: Japan Radio's NRD-525" in this RADIO DATABASE INTERNATIONAL). This excellent accessory allows the '93 to be all but fully automated.

Where money is no object — but reliability and ease of repair are *musts* — this "yachtsman's friend" is one of the world's finest choices, just as it is for use on shore, and provides superior audio quality to boot. Parts and service are available at leading ports, as well as radio specialty firms, worldwide.

A complete test report on the Japan Radio NRD-93 is available via *RDI White Paper*.

***** Japan Radio NRD-525 $1,285.00

An excellent blend of near-professional design, features and performance oriented to the dedicated shortwave listener, Japan Radio's NRD-525 is a superb and relatively affordable choice for those listening to and "DXing" tough catches from afar. Audio quality is reasonable, but assuredly not in the same class as that of Sony's ICF-6800W (see "Buyer's Guide to Tabletop World Receivers" elsewhere in this RDI).

A complete test report appears elsewhere in this edition of RADIO DATABASE INTERNATIONAL.

***** Japan Radio NRD-515   About $1,500

Japan Radio's Rugged NRD-515

Very nearly a professional-caliber communications receiver, the Japan Radio NRD-515 is built like a fortress and provides intelligible signal reception under all but the most excruciating situations. With options, the price can exceed $2,000.

Operation is straightforward and pleasant, making the '515 well-suited to day-in-and-day-out manual surveillance and scanning of the bands. Nevertheless, the '515's sibling, the NRD-525, is more appropriate to the needs of most world radio aficionados, as the '515's woolly audio is not well-suited to the reproduction of music.

A complete test report on the Japan Radio NRD-515 is available via *RDI White Paper*.

***** Racal RA6790/GM   Over $5,000

A thoroughly professional receiver widely used for military and surveillance operations, this pricey US-made version of a British receiver performs superbly, especially in strong-signal environments, but lacks many of the operating features found on most other modern world receivers. Too, its keypad tuning arrangement is suboptimal.

One unusual feature it does have is BITE (built-in test equipment). However, in our tests BITE served no useful purpose when service difficulties arose.

The '6790 and a variety of related British- and US-made models — some of which are priced in the five figures and include advanced operating controls and scanner circuits — occasionally appear, new and used, at greatly reduced prices in such places as Canada, where they are quickly snapped up by zealous radio enthusiasts.

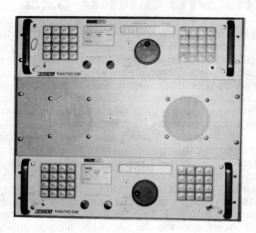

*A Pair of RACAL RA6790/GM Receivers
Used by Radio Canada International
Courtesy RCI*

Discontinued Models

When gilt-edged sets are withdrawn from a manufacturer's catalogue, the market price is liable to do anything from stay constant to drop dramatically. Here and there, some gems are still available in the nooks and crannies of radioland. Among them...

***** Drake R4245 $1,000-3,000

Arguably the finest set ever produced for "serious" DXing, the US-made Drake R4245 is characterized by unusual operating flexibility, clumsiness of operation and the ability to flush out nearly any signal that makes it to your antenna.

The reaction of most users to the R4245 is the same as that of most people to Margaret Thatcher's Administration: you either love it or you hate it. If you relish tweaking a variety of controls to obtain subtle enhancement of signal quality, you will embrace the R4245. If you prefer to have the radio do these chores for you, forget it.

In 1985, Jordanian King Hussein's army bought out the last of Drake's R4245 factory inventory, presumably not to "DX" Brazilian tropical band stations. Jordanian conscripts take note!

***** Drake R-7/Drake R-7A $600-1,600

*Drake R-7/R-7A
Drake's Vernerable R-7/R-7A*

Very similar to the Drake R4245, but no less quirky, the R-7/R-7A is inferior only in frequency stability.

On very, very rare occasion, samples of the R-7 and R-7A are still found new. For a brief golden period, they were also being offered on the used market at bargain prices when if-it's-newer-it's-better types dumped their Drakes in favor of the then-latest-kid-on-the-block, the ICOM R-70.

Even today, used R-7's in excellent condition can be found for well under $1,000, an important price consideration being whether a variety of voice bandwidth filters (e.g., 6, 4, 3 kHz) have been installed to complement the 2.3 kHz filter that came standard with the set when it was new. Otherwise, new filters may be obtained from the Drake factory or Sherwood Engineering.

HOT KNOBS: JAPAN RADIO'S NRD-525

To the professional, $1,300 for a receiver is absurdly cheap. To the world radio listener, it's a fortune. But for those who can afford it, there is an unusual world-band radio that's worth a close look: the $1,285 Japan Radio NRD-525.

To give you an idea of just how much the engineers at Japan Radio have stuffed into this box, consider merely one of its standard-equipment features, the scanner. The '525's scanning function performs comparably to that of the NDH-93, an accessory for the $8,000 Japan Radio NRD-93 professional receiver and an exquisite piece of equipment in its own right (see "When Price Is No Object"). The price of the NDH-93 scanner alone? Nearly $1,000. The entire NRD-525 — scanner and all — cost $1,200. It's almost like buying the scanner and getting the radio for free!

Whether any radio is worth over $1,000 is another matter. It's a judgment call — your call — to which we can only add that the '525 is so well built that it'll probably still be working many years from now. If you keep your '525 for only fifteen years, the annual cost comes to only about $80.

Computer-Type Modular Design Facilitates Repair

In comparison with its older cousin, the quasi-professional NRD-515, the '525 is something quite different. For one thing, its plastic front panel and controls give it an uncanny resemblance to the $600 Yaesu FRG-8800. On the other hand, the '525 — unlike the '515 — does incorporate professional-type plug-in circuit boards, even if the shielding panels between those boards are pretty flimsy.

These computer-type boards definitely facilitate repair...even if the '525 is unlikely to need much in the way of service. Although the '525 has no BITE (built-in test equipment), many malfunctions can be traced to a given board by the nature of the symptoms. This allows you to send a single board, rather than the complete receiver, to a repair facility. Another service plus is that the front panel snaps loose for immediate access. It, too, can be forwarded for repair. In fact, the entire radio can be disassembled down to the last board in a matter of minutes.

Parts Quality Generally Excellent

Parts quality of the '525 is generally excellent, but compromises have been made in trying to keep costs down. For example, shielding is generally insufficient to provide a signal completely free from unwanted interaction among circuits within the radio. And, as with the '515, ceramic and consumer-grade mechanical voice bandwidth filters are used.

The use of tiny surface-mounted devices (SMD's, or "chip" parts) — such as resistors, capacitors, diodes and transistors — is another of the secrets of how Japan Radio has managed to create a receiver of this caliber for just over $1,000. SMD's, which lack the customary wire leads or tabs, are

less costly for manufacturers to install. While they are more reliable than conventional parts, they are also more difficult to replace, as each is glued to the circuit board. Obtaining these unusual parts may also be a problem. Again, though, plug-in boards overcome both these drawbacks by allowing you to simply pull out the offending board and mail it in to an authorized Japan Radio repair facility.

In the end, however, parts really shouldn't be a problem, as their quality — and the quality of parts assembly — of the '525 is such that it simply stands apart from other receivers produced for the consumer market. Universal Radio in the US informs us that, in 1986, 5% of early-production samples came from the factory with a shielding "can" not properly grounded, and one unit came with a board improperly seated. Aside from these factory defects — now routinely looked for as part of Universal's pre-sale checks — no other problems have arisen to date. This tends to confirm our engineering analysis that the '525 will be more reliable than average.

Factory Alignment Initially Suboptimal

On the other hand, our tests of two '525's — both from the initial production run of some fifty units — indicate that factory alignment during early production was less precise that it should have been. As a result, there has been a higher-than-desirable variation in performance from sample-to-sample. Presumably this problem — disappointing but, alas, not unusual in early production runs of complex equipment — will diminish as production "settles in", like shoes, over time.

Excellent Ergonomics

A good receiver, like a good motor car, should have its operating controls laid out so they are logically located and easy to use. The '525 has countless "bells and whistles", which is one of the set's chief attractions. With so much operating power placed in the hands of the user, the '525 challenges the operator to tweak the last erg of performance out of the receiver.

In order to provide the user with such a high degree of operating flexibility, Japan Radio did not take the usual expedient route and clutter up the '525's front panel with minuscule controls. Instead, its designers freed up valuable front panel space for many of the '525's new functions. Creative engineering and design have also allowed the '525's roster of controls to perform comfortably and logically. Too, most of the '525's controls — the keypad buttons excepted — have above-average "feel".

As the '525 comes from the factory, it is programmed such that the user has to offset manually, with the main tuning or RIT controls, for reception of lower sideband (LSB) and upper sideband (USB). In the original version of the owner's manual, nothing was mentioned about this odd procedure. Fortunately, the newly-printed owner's manual explains,

Japan Radio's Hot New HRD-525

on page 19, how this can be avoided by a simple keyboard command. We tested this on our second test receiver, and it works as it should.

A visual annoyance is that the front panel's digital signal-strength meter, only marginally accurate to begin with, is as jumpy as a grasshopper in a parched wheat field. More positively apropros the front panel, the '525 tunes and displays frequencies to the nearest 10 Hz — a degree of precision found in few other world radios.

Exceptionally Flexible Tuning

The '525 gives the user every means imaginable to tune in a signal, short of shipping out each radio with a trained monkey. Not only is there the traditional tuning knob — the mainstay of any operator-controlled receiver — there are also up-down slewing buttons to aid in rapid bandscanning, a keypad for direct frequency selection, a professional-caliber scanner and no less than 200 programmable channel memories.

Much of the reason for the '525's superb fine tuning is that the set's knob tunes very slowly. At the other extreme, for zipping up and down the bands quickly, the up-down slewing buttons work well. However, some operators have expressed disappointment that an intermediate tuning or slewing rate had not been provided.

Homebrew Spooks, Anyone?

Although we did not attempt to create software to test the '525, the receiver is potentially well suited to light-duty surveillance use, not to mention whatever computer-controlled mischief shortwave-listening hackers may devise. Indeed, the '525 opens up the possibility of eavesdropping computer freaks' becoming miniature "National Security Agencies", using homebrew artificial intelligence software, personal computers and the '525 to poke about the radio spectrum for all manner of juicy information, such as eavesdropping on Air Force One to hear Ronald Reagan cancelling his son's American Express card.

Exceptional Stability Improves
Reception Quality

The Japan Radio NRD-525 is an exceptionally stable receiver by any measure. As such, it is unusually well suited to reception of certain types of

communications-type signals: Ships at sea, that sort of thing.

More to the point of what most of us are interested in, the '525's high stability also makes it well-suited to unattended reception of world radio signals through — hang on! — "manual exalted-carrier selectable-sideband (ECSS)". What this mouthful means is that you can listen to one side — rather than both, as is the usual case — of a signal, thus avoiding interference from a station alongside the one you're trying to hear.

The reason for this is simple: world radio signals consist of two identical Siamese-twin-like parts. With certain radios, you can listen to just one of those two parts — the quieter one.

Why Siamese-twin transmissions? Isn't that silly, not to mention wasteful?

Wasteful, yes. Silly, no. This twofer approach allows world radio signals to be received without heavy distortion on inexpensive radios. But for over a thousand bucks things can be done differently.

Alas, there is no synchronous (automatic) ECSS — a disappointment in a newly designed receiver of this caliber, especially inasmuch as Sony's midpriced ICF-2010/ICF-2001D includes it.

High-Tech Automated Operation

The '525's relatively sophisticated scanner, plus a timer and related controls, allow for dedicated listening to a favorite station. For regular listeners to the BBC World Service or other multi-frequencied giants, this can mean all but "hands off" listening nearly around the clock. Similarly, listeners can leave the '525 on, even with spouses and youngsters around, knowing their beloved station will either come in automatically or the set will become silent.

Here's how that scanner works. You pick a group of adjacent programmable memory channels (there are a total of 200 such channels, so it's easy to find vacant groups), then store a different frequency for your favorite station in each channel. For example, with the BBC World Service, if you're in Europe you might store 5975 kHz in channel 110, 9410 kHz in channel 111, 12095 kHz in channel 112, 15070 kHz in channel 113, and so on.

You decide what you wish as a minimum acceptable level of signal strength, then set a special control to that level. You further decide how long during scanning you want the scanner to "sample" each channel (with world radio broadcasts, a fairly long sample time is needed to avoid having the scanner "tricked" by fade troughs). As backup, you can also set the squelch at a level just above that of the radio background noise on a vacant channel.

You then instruct the scanner so that it scans only those four channels (110-113, inclusive) then relax. From now on, you will hear the BBC World Service or your other favorite station without having to get up and keep fiddling with the radio every time a channel peters out or goes off the air.

It sounds like a load of fuss and bother, but it's not — the whole exercise takes less than a minute, and once it's set, it's set for good unless you choose to change it.

Actually, the '525 can provide robotic ECSS reception, too. This is because the '525 also allows you to program the mode into each memory channel.

Say, you want to use the scanner to listen regularly to the BBC on 12095 kHz, but there's a howl coming from a signal on 12098 kHz. ECSS can reject this. Simply (using the preceding example again) store in channel 112: "12095.00 kHz LSB" ("L" in "LSB" stands for the lower half of the signal).

That's all. Fron now on, only the lower half of the BBC's signal will be received by the scanner, and the howl on the "high" side will have vanished.

The '525's built-in timer can be used to turn the set on and off each day, adding further to the set's robotic capabilities. Too, the timer is designed to control your tape recorder at the same time.

So, this state-of-the-art radio will select your channels, tune and retune them for high-quality reception, turn itself on and off, and even record your favorite programs for you when you're not home-...just like a good VCR.

Passband Tuning Helps Improve Reception Quality

The '525 contains a passband tuning control to help reduce interference and improve audio fidelity. For example, if a signal is "boomy", the passband tuning control can be adjusted to an outer edge of the signal to incorporate more high ("treble") audio frequencies and fewer low ("bass") audio frequencies.

This sort of flexibility is a real aid not only in hearing difficult stations, but also in listening to music and voice programs from major world broadcasters.

Good Selectivity Adds to Listening Pleasure

Every receiver needs at least one bandwidth filter, preferably more, to select the desired station out of the morass of competing stations on the air. A bandwidth filter acts as does a cattle chute, the objective being to let through only one bull — or station — at a time.

The dilemma in the overcrowded shortwave bands is that with a wide filter you may get good audio quality, but too much interference from adjacent stations. With a narrow filter, you might eliminate that adjacent interference, but then you degrade audio quality. As the amount of interference varies considerably from station-to-station and even hour-to-hour, a worthy receiver for serious world radio listening should include as many voice bandwidth choices as is economically feasible to provide the optimum tradeoff between audio quality and interference. This point is not academic, inasmuch as high-quality bandwidth filters are currently among the most expensive parts of a receiver.

For voice and music, the '525 comes with filters that provide two bandwidths: 5.7 and 2.2 kHz. Both bandwidth filters have very fine performance char-

acteristics, but in a radio of this caliber a bandwidth roughly midpoint between these two is called for.

There are circuit provisions for just such a third filter. Although no suitable filter is presently available from Japan Radio, various dealers will install, at extra cost, a high-quality Collins 3.8 kHz filter for this purpose.

Excellent Noise Blanker

The '525 includes a noise blanker that, in the "wide" position, is unusually effective in alleviating disruption of reception by the *rat-a-tat-tat* of Soviet "Woodpecker" over-the-horizon radar transmissions.

Audio Quality About Average

One of the unwelcome surprises with "supersets" is that they tend to have mediocre audio reproduction. This is not so illogical as it might seem at first blush, as sets costing thousands of dollars are not typically purchased by world radio aficionados but, instead, by military and similar organizations. These outfits could care less about hearing Stravinsky. What they want is audio shaped to reproduce speech intelligibly. Like a telephone.

The '525, in this context, stands out positively, although there is a slight persistent "hiss" audible in the background. Additionally, if an unshielded antenna lead-in is used, digital-circuit whine can be heard, like the "hiss", at low level.

This assessement of how the '525 "sounds" may seem like damnation with faint praise, and to some extent it is. But when compared, say, to Japan Radio's own NRD-515, the '525 is almost an aural treat.

The bottom line is that for listening to both voice and music programs, the '525's audio quality is more than adequate. But it is not in the same league as that of such consumer-oriented models as the Sony ICF-6800W, Philips/Magnavox D2999 or Grundig Satellit 600.

Variable Notch Filter Kills Unwanted "Whistles"

World radio has never been a high-fidelity medium, and still isn't. But, step by step, advanced technology and improved broadcasting techniques have been raising the quality of reception to the point where it is now, at times and with the right radio, comparable to that of local mediumwave AM stations.

One such aural aid is the notch filter. Unlike most improvements in world radio, this is nothing fresh from the likes of Bell Labs. Rather, notch filters have been around for decades, but faded from use in the last twenty years or so except on models produced by the R.L. Drake Company and, more recently, ICOM. Thankfully, Japan Radio has picked up on the concept and included it to good effect in the '525.

In the tropical bands (2-5.7 MHz), which are shared by a potpourri of broadcast and non-broadcast signals alike, this filter is effective in reducing heterodyne — "whistle" — interference up to 3 kHz away on either side and in any mode. And reduce interference it does, by -40 dB on the first of our two test units (although by only -30 dB on the second).

Points for Unusual Applications

As is the custom with Japan Radio receivers, the '525 utilizes diodes designed to protect the radio's innards against static damage. As a result, cross-modulation — characterized by signals appearing where they shouldn't be — tends to arise when the receiver is operated very near to powerful radio transmitters. In these unusual instances, this may be cleared up by having a service technician disable the diodes, then install in their place an effective replacement static-protection device, such as the Alpha-Delta "Transi-Trap".

For those living in very high signal areas, such as parts of Europe, it is worth noting that the '525's dynamic range, while very good, is such that under extreme conditions — e.g., the 49 meter band at night with a high-gain antenna — the '525 will be very slightly less resistant to overloading than are some other highly rated world radios. Otherwise, the '525's dynamic range is comfortably more than adequate for use on shortwave. Similarly, certain laboratory measurements — of ultimate rejection and blocking — suggest that the '525, while well-suited to listening to world radio broadcasts, is not fully tailored either to professional applications or to the "DXing" of certain types of tough, distant mediumwave AM stations.

The Bottom Line

Do you need to spend over a thousand dollars to have a first-rate receiver for listening to shortwave broadcasts?

Of course not. You can make do very nicely with a Sony ICF-6800W, for example, which costs half as much. But there is no receiver other than the '525 we have tested that quite equals its combination of excellence of performance, reasonably good audio, "intelligent" hands-off operation, high-quality parts and assembly, flexibility, ease of operation-...and just plain fun.

An unabridged, 20-page *RDI White Paper,* containing full laboratory measurements and other findings of interest to the current or prospective owner of the Japan Radio NRD 525, is available from Radio Database International.

COMING UP!

A vigorous rub of our crystal ball shows a number of juicy offerings expected to appear on the world radio market during 1987. Among these are...

KENWOOD R-5000/TRIO R-5000
$800–1,000 range

For some time, listeners have squawked because Trio-Kenwood has not been turning out world band radios that provide the same high level of performance as that found in the receiver sections of the Trio-Kenwood transceiver line sold to "hams".

The squeaky wheel gets the oil, so Kenwood will be responding by introducing the new R-5000 world-band radio sometime in early 1987. Among other things, it is to feature 100 memories programmable both by frequency and mode, keypad tuning, and a scanner. A variety of standard and optional bandwidths will be offered, as well.

The Kenwood R-5000 should perform similarly to the receiver section of the Kenwood TS-440S. If so, it will be of no small interest to serious world radio listeners.

TEN-TEC RX235 $549.00

In mid-1986, we tested an early prototype of this frill-free US-made model, originally scheduled

Ten-Tac's New RX325, a US-Made Model

to be introduced shortly after our tests. We have not published our findings, however, as following the results of the RDI laboratory tests the manufacturer decided to redesign and upgrade various circuits and operating controls to improve performance and ease of operation.

As of presstime, the new date for introduction of the RX235 had not been specified. However, production is expected to commence sometime in the very near future.

LOWE HF-125   About £350 (equivalent to roughly $450)

Untested by us as of presstime, the British-made HF-125 appears, "on paper", to be designed to provide above-average, but no-nonsense, performance with few frills at a price somewhere on the sunny side of most people's pocketbooks.

Introduction is expected to take place sometime during the first half of 1987.

SONY "X"...SONY "Y"...SONY "Z"

Tantalizing rumors from Japan suggest that Sony has at least one — perhaps as many as three — new models scheduled to be added to its world radio stable for 1987. High technology and advanced features are expected to be hallmarks of these models, one of which is likely to replace the discontinued CRF-1 portable (see "Guide to Portable World Receivers").

Introduction is expected to take place no later than early 1987.

Shortly after these models appear on the market, RADIO DATABASE INTERNATIONAL will conduct in-depth laboratory and "hands-on" tests to ascertain their worth. The full breadth of our findings and measurements will appear in separate *RDI White Papers*, which may be obtained from RDI dealers worldwide.

EXTERNAL ANTENNAS: DO THEY HELP?

There is a WW II movie, *Voice of Terror*, in which British sleuths struggle to overcome the effects of a German clandestine radio station. A hero of the film is none other than...a shortwave set. Not what we think of today as a world-band set. No, this was big — kind of a truck with dials.

That's what "real" shortwave receivers used to be like. They were fed by lengthy outdoor antennas resembling props from another movie — *The Web of the Giant Spider*. One of this genre was the "Zepp" — so-called because Zeppelin dirigibles trailed them a good 25 meters or yards across the sky. In fact, smile-a-mile antennas were once so commonplace that, even today, they're what spring to mind when oldtimers think of shortwave.

Unfortunately, the same people who today become curious about shortwave when they see today's handy, compact world-radio sets are still put off by the mistaken idea that they need to fill their back yard with enormous lengths of antenna wire.

Outdoor Antennas Usually Unnecessary

The truth is that the majority of world radio listeners need no antenna at all other than their radio's own built-in telescopic "whip". This sort of antenna works fine, so long as your set is reasonably sensitive and you are not into listening to flea-powered stations.

But if you are trying to snare faint stations — or if you live in a concrete/steel building — you should consider something fancier. Too, if you're using a first-rate communications receiver, you'll want an equally first-rate antenna so your receiver can reach its full potential.

Antennas for Simple Portables

What's your radio like? If you have one of those $29.95 combination all-band/clock-radio/stir-the-soup models that can't even handle the signals coming in through its built-in antenna, all a fancy separate antenna is going to do is provide you with a gruesome result called "overloading"...a mish-mash of stations all heard at once because of your radio's dimestore innards. Either buy a better set or take up another pastime, such as collecting belly button lint.

But even costlier portables (some field portables excepted) often don't take kindly to high-gain external antennas. These radios were designed to work at their peak with built-in antennas, so a minimalist approach usually works best.

If you live in a house and have a portable that you'd like to coax a bit more out of, there's an easy solution. Run several meters or yards of just about any kind of insulated wire — doorbell wire is fine — through your listening room's window. Connect one end high up on a nearby structure or tree, the other end either to the set's external antenna input (if it has one) or directly to the built-in antenna, using a

garden-variety "alligator" clip such as is found at electronics parts stores.

Assuming the wire is plastic-coated, you can get away with tying it around a tree limb or whatever. But a much better solution is to isolate your antenna fully from the signal-absorbing tree or structure by using an insulator. Inexpensive ceramic or plastic insulators for this purpose can also be found at electronics parts stores. If your antenna is short and lightweight, an ordinary plastic hair curler will do.

Wrap the far end of your antenna wire through one of the holes in an insulator. Tie a piece of cord through the insulator's other hole, then wrap that cord around a high tree or structure.

Do the same thing at the antenna's near end, then run the antenna's lead-in wire to your set (or — better — its gas-type lightning arrestor), and you're ready to unearth the hard-to-hear secrets of world radio.

In any event, use common sense. Don't drape the thing under or over a 36,000-volt power line unless you're planning to do a circus audition for the role of Crispy the Cadaver. And forget trying to be a modern-day Ben Franklin. When there's lightning nearby, disconnect your antenna. And, if you have overhead power lines, unplug your radio, TV, computer and anything else you value.

If you're using a simple portable in a high-rise apartment, the best accessory antenna is an ordinary inexpensive automobile "whip" (there's no need to get anything fancier) available at auto supply stores.

But why buy an antenna that's just like the one already built into your radio?

The reason is simple. The concrete-and-steel walls of a high-rise building act as a "shield", keeping out radio signals. An outdoor accessory antenna is needed to catch signals *before* they are made faint by trying to pass through the building's outer walls.

Secure an automobile "whip" antenna firmly to your window frame or balcony railing so that it points away from the signal-absorbing building, like a flagpole, then run a wire from the antenna to your radio. This allows your set to be fed healthy outdoor signals unhampered by your building's metal-and-concrete shielding. If neighbors cast suspicious glances, hang a small flag from the antenna.

Worthy Receivers Need Worthy Antennas

Many high-quality receivers don't even come with built-in antennas, as radio engineers know that such elementary devices are inadequate for sophisticated receivers. So, even if your superset has its own antenna, you should contemplate something better

Why? While simple portables can do only so much because of the cost of the components crammed inside their tiny cases, costly receivers are often capable of superb performance. They can handle strong signals from high-gain antennas without "overloading", and in so doing improve the signal-to-noise ratios of the signals you hear.

Signal-to-noise ratios are important because increasing signal strength means little if you also increase background noise by a like amount. These noises can include the local variety — appliances, fluorescent lights, computers, dimmers, and the like — as well as "hiss" and other circuit noises within your receiver. The winning formula, then, is not just more signal strength, but less noise with respect to that signal strength. A well-located high-quality antenna improves signal-to-noise by capturing radio signals out in the fresh air, away from the home's environment of potentially noisy electrical wiring and appliances. And the stronger signals coming coming from a high-gain antenna into your set reduce the audibility of your set's own circuit noise.

Passive vs. Active Antennas

There are two basic types of antennas: "passive" and "active". A passive antenna consists of a healthy stretch of wire or other metal to provide a healthy signal directly to the receiver without the need for electrical amplification. An active antenna, on the other hand, typically uses a much shorter rod or wire, plus one or more stages of electrical amplification to make up for the relatively low signal gain of the stubby rod or wire.

Active antennas are convenient because they are compact. In apartments, this is ideal. Even some landed homeowners like them because they're easier to erect than are lengthy wire antennas.

But active antennas have three performance drawbacks. First, their short antenna elements fail to provide the signal-to-noise enhancement that comes when longer elements are used. Second, the antenna's amplifier can generate noise of its own. So, while there are some first-rate active antennas on the market today, these are not the antennas of choice except when installation of a first-rate passive antenna is not feasible. Third, many active antennas have mediocre front-end selectivity, and thus are prone to comingling signals from local AM or FM stations with those of world radio stations. This makes them inappropriate for use in the very urban areas in which apartment dwellers tend to be concentrated.

For the wise owner of high-quality receiving gear, there is really no choice — it's dictated by where he lives. An apartment dweller will go with an active antenna simply because there's no room outdoors to erect a long outdoor antenna.

As to the house dweller who can string up 10-20 meters or yards of outdoor wire antenna, he will find that a passive antenna provides results superior to those obtained by even the most elegant of active antennas. Quite simply, passive antennas have more exposed surface area and thus don't

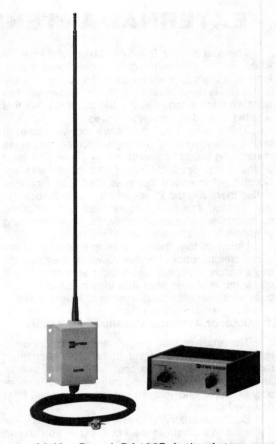

McKay Dymek DA100D Active Antenna

need potentially problemsome electronic amplification in order to do their job.

The Best Shortwave Antennas

Best of the *active* antennas is the excellent, but relatively costly, McKay Dymek DA100D (Stoner

Top-Rated "Eavesdropper" Passive Antenna

Communications). Because of its superior front-end selectivity, it's particularly well-suited for use in tough urban or other areas where there are strong local AM or FM stations.

Also of interest are the KRS AA-1 (Radio West), the MFJ-1024 (MFJ Enterprises) and the line of active antennas from Datong (Datong Electronics Limited). Additionally, a number of new active antennas have appeared recently. Among these are the Palomar PA-351 (Palomar Engineers) and the Grove PRE3 (Grove Enterprises). Most sell for between $100-160 in the US, usually more elsewhere.

Two of the best passive antenna types are the trap-dipole, such as the "Eavesdropper", and the inverted-L. See the accompanying antenna article for details.

Receive the world's short wave bands with only one antenna and one feed line!

11 Meters (25.6 to 26.1 MHz)
13 Meters (21.45 to 21.75 MHz)
16 Meters (17.7 to 17.9 MHz)
19 Meters (15.1 to 15.45 MHz)
25 Meters (11.7 to 11.975 MHz)
31 Meters (9.5 to 9.775 MHz)
41 Meters (7.1 to 7.3 MHz)
49 Meters (5.95 to 6.2 MHz)
60 Meters (4.75 to 5.06 MHz)

Only

$64.50

plus shipping

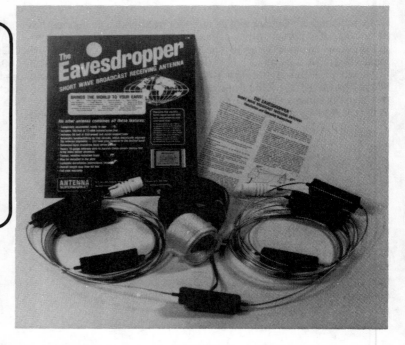

No other antenna combines all these features:

- **Completely assembled, ready to use**
- **Includes 100 feet of 72-ohm transmission line**
- **Includes 50 feet of 450-pound test nylon support rope**
- **Automatic bandswitching by trap circuits, which electrically separate the antenna segments — just tune your receiver to the desired band!**
- **Balanced input minimizes local noise pickup**
- **Heavy 14-gauge antenna wire to survive those severe storms that bring down lesser antennas**
- **Sealed, weather-resistant traps**
- **May be installed in the attic**
- **Complete installation instructions included**
- **Overall length less than 43 feet**
- **Full year warranty**

TO ORDER:
Please patronize your stocking dealer. We both need him to survive. If no luck there, you may order direct, certified funds or C.O.D. Add $3.50 for UPS Cont. U.S. C.O.D.'s cash only. Dealer inquiries invited.

Carried in stock by many progressive dealers
Used in 45 countries we know of as of 1983
Large SASE or 3 IRC's (foreign) for brochure

ANTENNA
SUPERMARKET

P. O. Box 563, Palatine, Illinois 60067 U.S.A.   MADE IN U.S.A.

Manufacturers of Quality Short Wave Listening Antenna Systems

HOW TO CHOOSE AND INSTALL A FIRST-RATE OUTDOOR ANTENNA

It used to be that owning a shortwave radio also meant having to deal with an outside antenna. For decades, listeners were forced to risk their lives climbing tall ladders, braving the elements and risking getting tangled in hundreds of feet of unruly wire. Today, shortwave radios are so advanced that most not only don't need outside antennas — their performance can be reduced by them.

Buy or Build?

Once you've decided that you really want or need an outside antenna for your radio, you've got to decide whether you want to buy one or build it yourself. There are plenty of articles and books available on the subject, but the antennas recommended are almost always far more complicated than necessary and often based on designs originally intended for other applications (e.g., amateur radio or military transmissions). As a result, these books and articles are widely read, but rarely acted upon.

The vast majority of those who choose to erect an outdoor antenna opt for the classic "inverted-L" design. In the inverted-L, the antenna forms one leg and the cable connecting it to your receiver the other. It's inexpensive, covers the entire shortwave spectrum, and — if constructed and installed properly — can last for decades. Its measurements are noncritical, too, so if you want to build one you don't need a degree in electronics and a houseful of computers to do the job.

What the Pros Use

If you have ever have the pleasure of visiting an official shortwave monitoring site, you'll undoubtedly notice a wide variety of antenna types in use. For example, the Canadian government's monitoring site at Stittsville, Ontario makes use of three types: lengthy inverted-L antennas, a rotatable log-periodic antenna, and an innovative (and costly) Hermes Canadian-made configuration of hoop-shaped loop antennas. For best reception results, the no-nonsense veteran monitors at Stittsville prefer the exotic Hermes loop system, followed by the inverted-L's, and only lastly the one that, "on paper", should be best: the expensive and complex log periodic.

If You Buy...

For the listener who doesn't have $25,000 to spend on his own Hermes loop system, or the land to construct it on, a properly designed trap dipole is the best choice. Unfortunately, it's just not practical to build such an antenna from scratch — it's too complicated. So if you want it, buy it.

The best of the lot is the "Eavesdropper". One of its plusses is that it resists rust, leakage and corrosion, and so keeps performing well as time goes by.

Hermes Professional Loop Antennas (Courtesy RCI)

As for constructing your own antenna, there are two potential advantages.

First, you can choose the quality of materials. This allows you to save money or optimize quality — but not both — as compared with what's available commercially.

Second, if you have a large spread of free land, you can erect some absolutely awesome antennas — up to 60 meters or yards long. These are much longer than those commercially available. If you use Copperweld wire, you can go for an even *longer* antenna. Tests at the RADIO DATABASE INTERNATIONAL monitoring facility in Pennsylvania show that such "longwire" inverted-L antennas provide a superior signal-to-noise ratio.

For example, one RDI inverted-L is 67 meters in length. This provides one wavelength for the 60, 49 and 41 meter bands; two wavelengths for the 31 and 25 meter bands; three wavelengths for the 19 and 21 meter bands; four wavelengths for the 16 meter band, and five wavelengths for the 13 meter band.

The inverted-L is such a simple antenna that many people construct their own from scrap parts and material available locally. However, inverted-L kits are commercially available for the equivalent of $10-20. These are handy, inasmuch as all the parts are together in one package, ready to assemble.

In any case, the principles, hazards and donkey work of erecting an outdoor antenna are pretty

Andy's Having A Ball . . .

and you can too!

Andy is a Ham Radio operator and he's having the time of his life talking to new and old friends in this country and around the world.

You can do it too! Join Andy as he communicates with the world. Enjoy the many unique and exclusive amateur bands . . . the millions of frequencies that Hams are allowed to use. Choose the frequency and time of day that are just right to talk to anywhere you wish. Only Amateur Radio operators get this kind of freedom of choice. And if it's friends you're looking to meet and talk

with, Amateur radio is the hobby for you. The world is waiting for you.

If you'd like to be part of the fun . . . if you'd like to feel the excitement . . . we can help you. We've got all the information you'll need to get your Ham license. Let us help you join more than a million other Hams around the world and here at home. Who are we? We're the American Radio Relay League, a non-profit representative organization of Amateur Radio operators.

For information on becoming a Ham operator write to:

AMERICAN RADIO RELAY LEAGUE

Dept. RI, 225 Main Street
Newington, Conn. 06111.

much the same, regardless of whether the antenna is long or short, store-bought or home constructed. So read on, even if you are getting a ready-made antenna...

If You Build...

What Materials You'll Need

If you're purchasing a commercial antenna, it will have nearly everything you'll need to proceed with erection except a lightning protector and associated hardware. Still, if your antenna is even reasonably long, you may wish to consider the counterweight approach detailed below. This protects your antenna from excess stretching or breakage in bad weather — especially icestorms, which can make short work of an inflexible antenna.

Constructing an Inverted-L Antenna

If you're constructing an inverted-L antenna from scratch, you'll need the following:

—Copper antenna wire, unspliced, preferably 14 or 12 gauge. In principle, stranded is superior to solid; in practice, for receiving, any difference in results appear to be indiscernable. Insulated wire is superior for short antennas, but for most applications the lighter weight of uninsulated — or, better, "enameled" — wire makes it preferable.

Copperweld is a copper-clad steel wire. It has great tensile strength for long antennas (40+ meters or yards). However, it's springy stuff that's hard to work with, not unlike handling an unruly boa constrictor. Even worse, Copperweld can be rendered less effective by sharp kinks anywhere along the length of its copper-clad exterior, so treat this "snake" gently.

—Lead-in wire (or coaxial cable), unspliced. Simple weather-resistant insulated copper wire of about the same thickness as the antenna wire provides the greatest efficiency and makes a logical connection to your receiver's high-impedance input (if it has one).

There are pros and cons in making the decision whether to use insulated wire or coax. You'll loose more of the incoming signal using coaxial cable, but it can reduce noise if that noise emanates from near or within the room your radio is in — for example, from your radio's digital circuitry.

An inverted-L tends to have high impedance, whereas coaxial cable typically has low impedance (coaxial cable and modern receivers both typically have impedances of 50-75 ohms). The added mismatch of impedence brought about by coaxial cable can further exacerbate lead-in loss of signal. So unless you have a noise problem, ordinary single wire should work best.

—Coax-Seal (or silicon caulking) to protect outdoor connections from corrosion.

—Two sausage-shaped insulators, preferably ceramic, with one hole at each end. These should

Advanced Lightning Protectors
Protect Listeners and Equipment Alike

be strong enough to handle any anticipated strain, but remember that even small ceramic insulators have remarkable strength. Insulators the size of a link of breakfast sausage thus are usually more than sufficient for antennas of up to 35 meters or yards in length.

—An effective lightning and static protector. This is essential unless you live where there is no nearby lightning, no snow storms, and no sand storms...all of which generate static charges strong enough to send your radio — or you — to the clinic. These are manufactured by Alpha-Delta Communications, Inc., as well as the R.L. Drake Company. Beware the cheaper "spark-gap" lightning arrestors, such as the "Blitz Bug." These are fine for protecting tube-type equipment, electrical motors, and the like, but they let through too much static current to be used safely with most solid-state equipment.

—A copper-clad ground rod, at least 1.5 meters or 5 feet in length. A dedicated ground is needed both to reduce the chances of lightning damage and to minimize hum and noise in your radio.

—A length of ground wire, preferably copper, to run from your lightning protector to a ground rod.

—A cast (not strap) copper-clad or copper-alloy ground clamp suitable to be affixed to the ground rod. This and the preceding two items are available from any electrical supply house.

—Three connectors: two to go in and out of your lightning protector, a third to go into your radio's antenna input (that last connector usually comes with your radio as standard equipment).

—A suitable length of strong weather-resistant rope for "guying"; that is, connecting the antenna to trees or structures.

—A strong marine or other weatherproof pulley capable of turning freely after years of being exposed to the elements. It should be capable of handling the thickness of the aforementioned rope.

—Three strong, weather-resistant eyelets. These come either threaded for wood, threaded for nuts, or bracketed for flush mounting.

—Hefty brass — or at least plated — screws for any eyelets that may be flush-mounted.

—A sturdy, weatherproof ballast container with a single side-to-side metal handle on to. The container, which is to be used as a counterweight, needs to be suitable for holding stones, bricks, scrap metal or other ballast. In a pinch, a bucket will do. For long, heavy antennas a second container or bucket may be needed. If a bucket is used, heavy-gauge aluminum foil will also be needed in colder climates to act as a cover against weighty snow and ice accumulating inside.

Where to Obtain Antenna Materials

If you are fortunate enough to live near a ham radio store or electronics outlet carrying a wide variety of wiring, insulators and the like, you know where to head. Fortunately, in the US, there is a mail-order firm — Universal Radio — that carries just about everything imaginable for the wire antenna constructionist. They offer 14-gauge stranded copper wire, 12 gauge enameled solid copper wire, 14/12-gauge Copperweld, coaxial cable, coaxial-cable seal, insulators, connectors, ground wire, ground rods, ground clamps and Transi-Trap lightning protectors. About the only antenna parts they don't offer are weatherproof cable/rope, pulleys, eyelets and counterweights — all of which you should be able to obtain locally.

Tools You'll Need

—A sturdy ladder of suitable length.
—A long, flat screwdriver.
—Wire cutters or wire-cutting pliers.
—A soldering iron or gun of reasonable wattage.
—A hank of rosin-flux solder.
—A pocket knife to strip and clean wire for soldering.
—A sledge hammer to drive in the ground rod.
—Optional: A wood-screw starter or hand drill to make easier the insertion of wood eyelets or screws.

Precautionary Note

There are a number of potential pitfalls that go along with erecting antennas. It can be a risky business. Respect heights. Be careful of electrical wires. Use crepe or other rubber-sole/rubber-heel shoes, and don't work or walk on wet or other slick surfaces. If you are holding the ladder, don't stand directly underneath your partner, lest you be beaned by falling tools or parts...or even your falling partner. And above all, avoid setting up your antenna near power lines!

If you think this sounds Mickey Mouse, check with ham or CB groups to see how many of their members have spent time in the hospital — or worse — because of accidents while erecting antennas. If you have any doubt whatsoever about your ability to erect an antenna safely, either hire a tree man or other bonded professional to do the job, or make do with a simpler antenna.

Step-by-Step: How to Install Your Outdoor Antenna

1. Pick two distant points — one near your listening room — at which the ends of your new antenna are to be affixed. These and the line-of-sight between should be as far as possible from electrical power lines and other sources of noise. The antenna cannot be allowed to run under, over or near an electrical power line.
2. Thoroughly wash your hands with oil-free soap. Grungy hands degrade solder bonds.
3. Scrape clean 2 cm/1" of one end of the antenna wire and 2 cm/1" from one end of the lead-in wire.
4. Line up the cleaned ends in parallel with the wire tips facing in the same direction.
5. Using your hands and pliers, tightly twist together the two cleaned ends to form a "pigtail".
6. Solder the "pigtail". To solder properly, do not melt the solder by placing it against the iron or gun tip. Instead, place the hot iron or gun at one end of the cleaned "pigtail", then hold the solder against the other end of the "pigtail" about 2 cm/1" away. Thus, when the solder finally melts, it will flow smoothly throughout the entire preheated "pigtail". Remove the solder, then the iron or gun, and let nature cool off the joint for thirty seconds or so. Be patient — don't blow.
7. Stick this "pigtail", plus another several centimeters or few inches more of the wires, through a hole in an insulator. Depending on the insulator design (some have recesses for wrapping wires, some don't), either wrap and twist securely this wiring to the insulator or back over to the antenna wire itself. When you are through, there whould be no tugging that can take place on the soldered "pigtail". Solder is to provide a secure electrical, not physical, connection.
8. Using Coax-Seal (or silicon caulking), cover the "pigtail" to protect the joint from moisture and air.
9. Cut a piece of weather-resistant rope to a length equal to the sum of the distance from the hook to the outer edge of the tree's branches, plus an amount equal to the anticipated outward growth of those branches over the years, plus another 30 cm/1 foot or so.
10. Pass one end of that piece of rope through the remaining hole in the insulator that is already connected to one end of the antenna. Secure the rope to the insulator, using a hangman's or other robust knot that tightens as the rope becomes taut.
11. At the mounting point nearer your listening room, affix an eyelet as high as possible. Keep in mind that if an inverted-L antenna slopes, the lower end will point to the direction favoring signals, adding to directivity.
12. Using the other end of the rope already affixed to the antenna, secure the rope to the mounted eyelet as in step 10.

13. Repeat step 11 for the remaining mounting point.

14. Cut a piece of weather-resistant rope just long enough to go through that eyelet and the eyehole of the pulley, leaving only a small gap between the eyelet and pulley.

15. Tie together the eyelet and pulley, leaving a small gap and using a robust knot that tightens as the rope becomes taut.

16. Pass the other end of the antenna wire through one end of the remaining insulator. Determine where you want the antenna to end, ensuring it will be well away from tree-branch tips even in the years of tree growth to come. Tighten the wire securely around the insulator and/or twist it over the antenna wire coming into the insulator.

17. Securely tie a substantial length of weatherproof rope to the remaining hole in the insulator.

18. Pass that rope through the pulley, then down to the ground.

19. Affix the remaining eyelet to a point about one meter or yard above the ground and directly below the eyelet connected to the pulley.

20. Pull the rope until the antenna is reasonably taut — not violin-string tight, yet not sagging unduly in the middle.

21. If your ballast container is a bucket, drill or puncture the bottom generously to create an exit for rainfall.

22. Tie your ballast container to the rope about 1 meter or yard from the ground. Fill the container with ballast until the antenna is just held taut by ballast alone. If the container is a bucket, cover it with heavy-gauge aluminum foil to keep out solid precipitation.

23. From the tie-point in the preceding step, leave a length of rope roughly equal to the height of the antenna. Cut the rope at this point, then secure the end to the eyelet one meter or yard above the ground. This will allow you to lower and raise the antenna in the future; e.g., to make repairs or dispatch obtrusive new tree growth.

24. Following the instructions that come with your radio and lightning protector, affix the necessary three connectors.

You are now ready to enjoy years of improved shortwave listening using your ballast-protected external antenna!

SUMMARY OF WORLD BROADCASTING ACTIVITY
(Total Spectrum Occupancy in Hours per Week)

Fully 161 of the world's countries, from the giant Soviet Union to tiny Bhutan — plus various extralegal stations — broadcast within the world radio shortwave spectrum. This spectrum is divided into two parts: the Tropical bands from 2.2-3.9 and 4.0-5.73 MHz; and the International bands from 3.9-4.0 and 5.73-26.1 MHz.

Although the Tropical bands consist largely of broadcasts intended for domestic consumption, the nature of shortwave is such that they are often heard thousands of kilometers away.

The International bands consist mainly of powerful broadcasts intended for audiences abroad.

Nevertheless, many domestic stations operate here, as well, and also can be heard for great distances.

Jamming consists of deliberate interference directed against a broadcaster by those who do not wish the programs to be heard. The jammed hours given here are listed alongside the "victim" country, not the country actually doing the jamming.

Countries listed are those responsible for the broadcast material. Thus, Radio Moscow, for example, is listed under "USSR" whether it is aired from transmitters in the Soviet Union, Bulgaria, Cuba or whathaveyou.

	Country	Tropical Hours	International Hours	Total Hours	Total Jammed
1	USSR	5342	34277	39619	None
2	USA	None	18544	18544	8613
3	CHINA (PR)	5236	12294	17530	957
4	BRAZIL	9805	5493	15298	None
5	PERU	4396	2990	7386	None
6	INDONESIA	4952	1736	6688	None
7	GERMANY (FR)	None	4732	4732	437
8	UNITED KINGDOM	None	4165	4165	688
9	ECUADOR	2353	1394	3747	None
10	KOREA (DPR)	1618	1907	3525	None
11	BOLIVIA	2165	936	3101	None
12	AUSTRALIA	645	2383	3028	None
13	INDIA	971	1972	2943	None
14	CHINA (TAIWAN)	258	2512	2770	1251
15	FRANCE	None	2511	2511	None
16	CANADA	None	2123	2123	None
17	MALAYSIA	539	1523	2062	None
18	VENEZUELA	1759	259	2018	None
19	GERMANY (DR)	None	1994	1994	None
20	COLOMBIA	1181	769	1950	None
21	PAPUA NEW GUINEA	1383	556	1939	None
22	ALBANIA	216	1661	1877	273
23	ISRAEL	None	1830	1830	832
24	JAPAN	None	1751	1751	None
25	EGYPT	None	1691	1691	None
26	SWITZERLAND	None	1660	1660	None
27	KOREA (REPUBLIC)	None	1554	1554	9
28	NIGERIA	355	1127	1482	None
29	SOUTH AFRICA	331	1109	1440	None
30	ITALY	None	1400	1400	None
31	HOLLAND	None	1342	1342	20
32	VIETNAM	212	1120	1332	None
33	PAKISTAN	231	995	1226	28
34	CUBA	168	1047	1215	None
35	POLAND	None	1200	1200	None
36	SPAIN	None	1137	1137	None
37	ALGERIA	None	1123	1123	None
38	CZECHOSLOVAKIA	None	1112	1112	None
39	BULGARIA	None	1111	1111	None
40	MONGOLIA	667	436	1103	None
41	HUNGARY	None	1088	1088	None
42	IRAN	52	1006	1058	668
43	SINGAPORE	252	783	1035	None
44	VATICAN STATE	None	1018	1018	None
45	AUSTRIA	60	945	1005	None
46	PHILIPPINES	None	997	997	None
47	ROMANIA	None	986	986	None
48	SAUDI ARABIA	None	970	970	None
49	ANGOLA	447	502	949	None
50	AFGHANISTAN	251	687	938	15
51	IRAQ	None	938	938	66
52	ARGENTINA	30	855	885	None
53	KUWAIT	None	833	833	None
54	SRI LANKA	298	512	810	None
55	COSTA RICA	292	464	756	None
56	TURKEY	None	756	756	1
57	MOZAMBIQUE	152	557	709	None
58	LIBYA	None	658	658	115
59	SWEDEN	None	635	635	None
60	ZAMBIA	112	518	630	None
61	CHILE	None	619	619	None
62	GUATEMALA	493	110	603	None
63	THAILAND	106	472	578	None
64	COLOMBIA	266	309	575	None
65	UNITED ARAB EMIRATES	None	564	564	None
66	GREECE	None	557	557	3
67	YEMEN (PDR)	113	413	526	None
68	TANZANIA	185	340	525	None
69	CAMEROON	231	294	525	None
70	MOROCCO	None	525	525	None
71	PORTUGAL	None	524	524	None
72	BELGIUM	None	498	498	None
73	CLANDESTINE (ASIA)	166	325	491	80
74	YUGOSLAVIA	None	483	483	None
75	FINLAND	None	474	474	None
76	GABON	139	309	448	None
77	SOCIETY ISLANDS	None	448	448	None
78	NICARAGUA	None	385	385	None
79	CLANDESTINE (AFRICA)	97	286	383	199
80	TUNISIA	None	373	373	None
81	CLANDESTINE (C AMER)	50	322	372	96
82	URUGUAY	None	366	366	None
83	CLANDESTINE (M EAST)	181	184	365	262
84	NORTHERN MARIANA IS	None	362	362	None
85	HONDURAS	236	119	355	None
86	GUINEA	101	254	355	None
87	SYRIA	None	353	353	232
88	BOTSWANA	164	184	348	None
89	LIBERIA	156	189	345	None
90	SWAZILAND	115	228	343	None
91	NAMIBIA	337	None	337	None
92	BANGLADESH	63	267	330	None
93	NORWAY	None	316	316	None
94	OMAN	None	314	314	None
95	LAOS	61	248	309	None
96	ZAIRE	115	193	308	None
97	MALAWI	90	212	302	None
98	LUXEMBOURG	None	297	297	None
99	SENEGAL	55	238	293	None
100	NIGER	115	173	288	None
101	GHANA	232	40	272	None
102	MADAGASCAR	164	105	269	None
103	GUAM	None	268	268	None
104	UNIDENTIFIED	None	267	267	156
105	JORDAN	None	256	256	None
106	TOGO	155	100	255	None
107	MALI	47	207	254	None
108	ETHIOPIA	None	234	234	3
109	MONACO	None	229	229	27
110	YEMEN (REPUBLIC)	None	226	226	None
111	VANUATU	None	224	224	None
112	KENYA	115	101	216	None
113	SEYCHELLES	None	206	206	None
114	MEXICO	49	154	203	None

	Country	Tropical Hours	International Hours	Total Hours	Total Jammed		Country	Tropical Hours	International Hours	Total Hours	Total Jammed
115	SOLOMON IS	126	77	203	None	144	LEBANON	None	122	122	None
116	QATAR	None	192	192	None	145	GREENLAND	None	120	120	None
117	SUDAN	126	64	190	None	146	NETHERLANDS ANTILLES	None	113	113	None
118	IVORY COAST	None	189	189	None	147	RWANDA	109	None	109	None
119	FRENCH GUIANA	107	77	184	None	148	CYPRUS	None	108	108	None
120	LESOTHO	133	46	179	None	149	KAMPUCHEA (CAMBODIA)	None	108	108	None
121	EQUATORIAL GUINEA	55	119	174	None	150	CLANDESTINE (EUROPE)	None	107	107	None
122	PARAGUAY	None	172	172	None	151	RWANDA	None	105	105	None
123	COOK ISLANDS	None	168	168	None	152	BENIN	104	None	104	None
124	CLANDESTINE (N AMER)	None	168	168	None	153	MAURITANIA	63	39	102	None
125	UGANDA	85	81	166	None	154	DENMARK	None	92	92	None
126	ZIMBABWE	22	143	165	None	155	LESOTHO	None	87	87	None
127	CHAD	127	32	159	None	156	DJIBOUTI (JIBUTI)	83	None	83	None
128	NEW ZEALAND	None	156	156	None	157	COMOROS	35	46	81	None
129	NEW CALEDONIA	36	119	155	None	158	CENTRAL AFRICAN REP	72	None	72	None
130	BURMA	51	101	152	None	159	CAPE VERDE	None	71	71	None
131	SOMALIA	None	151	151	None	160	IRELAND	None	70	70	None
132	SURINAME	147	3	150	None	161	KIRIBATI	None	51	51	None
133	DOMINICAN REPUBLIC	None	150	150	None	162	PIRATE (S AMERICA)	15	33	48	None
134	FALKLAND ISLANDS	74	74	148	None	163	MALTA	None	34	34	None
135	NEPAL	147	None	147	None	164	ICELAND	None	24	24	None
136	ANTARCTICA	None	146	146	None	165	BHUTAN	18	3	21	None
137	GUYANA	None	134	134	None	166	TRISTAN DA CUNHA	15	None	15	None
138	BELIZE	133	None	133	None	167	TANZANIA	None	14	14	None
139	BURKINA FASO	78	52	130	None	168	PIRATE (PACIFIC)	None	3	3	None
140	SIERRA LEONE	None	130	130	None	169	CLANDESTINE (S AMER)	None	2	2	None
141	MAURITIUS	42	84	126	None	170	SAO TOME E PRINCIPE	1	None	1	None
142	HAITI	125	None	125	None	171	UNITED NATIONS	None	1	1	None
143	BURUNDI	73	51	124	None						

THE RDI PHOTOFILE

World radio: the battleground of ideas. France's former minister of agriculture, Michael Rocard (left) is interviewed by Victor Andriananjason for broadcast over the United Nations' network of stations.

WRNO Worldwide brought listeners live coverage of the entertainment events at the World's Fair in New Orleans.

Dave Rosenthal hosts the astronomy program Skyline, *part of the daily Radio Earth broadcast on WHRI.*

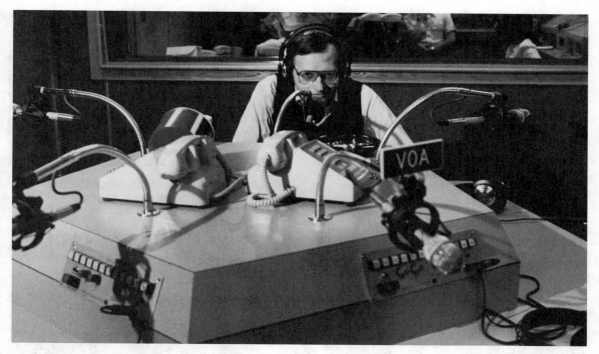

U.S. talk show host Larry King also conducts an international telephone call-in show on the Voice of America.

Radio Canada International's Ian Mc Farland at the site of Radio Milano International in Italy.

Every year, several stations leave and return to the shortwave bands, adding to the panorama of news, views and entertainment. The voice of the Maldives, above, is currently off the air.

The radio and television building, located on the Nile River in Cairo, is the home of Radio Cairo, Egypt's international radio station.

Jeff White, formerly of Radio Earth International and now vice president of World Radio Network, S.A. (Radio Clarin, Radio Discovery) toasts his listeners.

Willis Conover, host of the VOA's long-running jazz show, is virtually unknown in his home town of Washington, D.C. When visiting Eastern Europe, however, his plane is often met by mobs of listeners.

Tom Meyer is host of Radio Netherland's popular weekly musical variety show, Happy Station. The show first came on the air in the 1920's.

LEXICON OF TERMS

Alt—Alternative Frequency: Frequency that may be irregularly or unexpectedly brought into use in lieu of the regularly scheduled frequency.

AV—A Voz.

BC—Broadcasting, Broadcasting Company, Broadcasting Corporation.

BS—Broadcasting Service, Broadcasting Station.

Cd—Ciudad.

Channel—The norm for channel spacing within the shortwave broadcasting spectrum is 5.0 kHz. A small proportion of stations does not operate within this norm, so RDI provides frequency resolution to better than one kHz to aid in station location and identification.

Cl—Club, Clube.

Country—Country designations of officially recognized nations are those of the International Telecommunication Union. Unofficial broadcasters and geographical entities are included for reference purposes only and do not imply endorsement or recognition by IBS or the ITU.

Cu, Cult—Cultura, Cultural, Culture.

(D)—Winter schedule only.

DS—Domestic Service.

Ed, Educ—Educational, Educação, Educadora.

Em—Emissora, Emisora, Emissor, Emetteur.

EP—Emissor Provincial.

ER—Emissor Regional.

ES—External Service.

F—Friday.

Fade-in, Fade-out—If the RDI monitoring team cannot establish the definite sign-on (or sign-off) of a station, the earliest (or latest) time the station could be traced is entered, instead, as the fade-in (or fade-out) time.

Feeder, shortwave—A Fixed service (point-to-point) transmission, usually in single or independent sideband mode, beamed to a relay site. Although not intended for reception by the public, shortwave feeder transmissions, which can be received on better communications receivers, sometimes provide the best or only means for reception of a particular broadcaster at a given time. For this reason, selected shortwave feeder data is included in RDI, even though any given actual useage may be irregular. Transmission modes for shortwave feeders are:

    LSB—Lower Sideband (single-sideband signal)

    ISL—Lower Sideband (of independent-sideband signal)

    USB—Upper Sideband (single-sideband signal)

    ISU—Upper Sideband (of independent-sideband signal)

    RAM—Double Sideband, Reduced Carrier signal

FR—Federal Republic.

Frequency—The measurement most widely accepted to indicate the location of a station within the radio spectrum. Frequency is most often expressed in kilohertz (kHz) or Megahertz (MHz), although wavelength is still used in Eastern Europe and certain other parts of the world. The frequency of a station may be determined from the wavelength via the following formula: Frequency (kHz) = 299,792/Wavelength (Meters). Also, cf. "Wavelength" and "Channel".

Irr—Irregular operation or hours of operation; i.e., schedule tends to be unpredictable.

Is—Island(s).

(J)—Summer schedule only.

Jamming—Deliberate interference to a transmission with the intent of making reception impossible. The vast majority of jamming currently emanates from the Soviet Union and its Eastern European allies and is directed against broadcasts in Armenian, Azerbaijani, Belorussian, Bulgarian, Czech, Estonian, Georgian, Hebrew, Latvian, Lithuanian, Polish, Russian, Slovak, Tatar-Bashkir, Turkestani, Ukrainian, and Yiddish. Soviet/Eastern European jamming consists largely of a sound not unlike that of a roomful of truck or lorry engines roaring away. Coded messages appear now and then amidst the roaring, and in some instances distorted programming from the Soviet "Mayak" (DS-2) home service is mixed in, as well. One means to cope with jamming interference is to determine which bands are most likely to provide good reception from the part of the world you wish to hear, while at the same time are not likely to provide good reception from the Soviet Union and Eastern Europe. Directional antennas also can improve the signal-to-jamming ratio under certain circumstances.

kHz—Kilohertz (cf. Frequency).

kW—Kilowatt(s) (cf. Power).

Loc—Local.

Location—The physical location of the transmitter/antenna complex. This location may not correspond to the location of the studios in which the broadcasts are prepared. Data on location names are derived, in most instances, from the Map Section of the 1983 Comprehensive Edition of *The Times Atlas of the World*. As transmitter complexes of major international broadcasters are sometimes located in sparsely populated areas, the exact transmitter site may be up to several kilometers from the location indicated. Those in need of precise transmitter geographical coordinates should contact the Publications Department of the ITU.

LV—La Voix, La Voz.

M—Monday.

MHz—Megahertz (cf. Frequency).

Multilingual—A combination of any "graphics language" (Arabic, Chinese, English, French, German, Japanese, Portuguese, Russian, Spanish) with another language. Thus, a transmission in English and Urdu would be designated as Multilingual, rather than English, whereas a transmission in Tamil and Urdu would be designated as Other.

N—New, Nueva, Nuevo, Nouvelle, Nacional, National.

Nac—Nacional.

Nat, Natl—National, Nationale.

Network—The network or service of a broadcast. Domestic Service transmissions are always so indicated by "DS".

Non-AM Mode—Transmission in other than the conventional double-sideband-with-carrier ("AM") mode (see "Feeder, shortwave" for list of non-AM modes).

PBS—People's Broadcasting Station.

Power—RF output power, i.e. before amplification by the antenna, in kilowatts (kW). The present range of powers in use for shortwave broadcasting is 0.04-600 kW.

PR—People's Republic.

PS—Provincial Station, Pangsong.

Pto—Puerto, Pôrto.

R—Radio, Radiodiffusion, Radiodifusora, Radiodifusão, Radiofonikos, Radiostansiya, Radyo, Radyosu, etc.

Reg—Regional.

Relay—Extraterritorial transmission facility, usually fed by recording, satellite, or shortwave feeder (cf.).

Rep—Republic, République, Republica.

RT, RTV—Radiodiffusion Télévision, Radio Télévision, etc.

RN—Cf. R and N.

RS—Radio Station, Radiostantsiya, Radiofonikos Stathmos.

S—San, Santa, Santo, São, Saint.

Sa—Saturday.

Shortwave Spectrum—The shortwave, or High-Frequency, spectrum is that portion of the radio spectrum that lies between 3-30 MHz (3,000-30,000 kHz); however, common useage places the shortwave spectrum between roughly 2-30 MHz. Although broadcasting takes place throughout the shortwave spectrum (between-band broadcasting is known as "out-of-band" broadcasting, which is sometimes permitted under the Rules and Regulations of the ITU), the recently-adopted—but not yet fully implemented—nominal ITU shortwave broadcasting band parameters are (worldwide unless otherwise indicated):

120 Meter Band:
2300-2498 kHz (Tropical Domestic Broadcasting only)

90 Meter Band:
3200-3400 kHz (Tropical Domestic Broadcasting only)

75 Meter Band:
3900-3950 kHz (Asia & Pacific only)
3950-4000 kHz (except Americas)

60 Meter Band:
4750-4995 kHz (Tropical Domestic Broadcasting only)
5005-5060 kHz (Tropical Domestic Broadcasting only)

49 Meter Band:
5950-6200 kHz

41 Meter Band:
7100-7300 kHz (except Americas)

31 Meter Band:
9500-9900 kHz

25 Meter Band:
11650-12050 kHz

21 Meter Band:
13600-13800 kHz

19 Meter Band:
15100-15600 kHz

16 Meter Band:
17550-17900 kHz

13 Meter Band:
21450-21850 kHz

11 Meter Band:
25670-26100 kHz (25600-26100 kHz until 7/89)

St—Saint.

Sta—Santa.

Sto—Santo.

Su—Sunday.

Target—The international geographical entities to which a transmission is beamed, provided it is intended to be heard outside the country. Targets are as follows:

AF—Africa
AM—Americas
ANZ—Australia & New Zealand
AS—Asia
ATL—Atlantic
CA—Central America, Carribean & Mexico
CAF—Central Africa
EAF—Eastern Africa
EAS—Eastern Asia
EEU—Eastern Europe
ENA—Eastern North America
EU—Europe
EUSSR—Eastern USSR
ME—Middle East
NA—North America
NAF—Northern Africa
PAC—Pacific
SA—South America
SAF—Southern Africa
SAS—Southern Asia
SEA—South-East Asia
USSR—USSR
WAF—Western Africa
WEU—Western Europe
WNA—Western North America
WUSSR—Western USSR

(+) Tent—Tentative, i.e. uncertain of accuracy of certain listed details, e.g. exact station name.

Th—Thursday.

Tu—Tuesday.

UTC—Coordinated Universal Time, a/k/a Greenwich Mean Time (GMT) or Zulu (Z): the 24-hour international broadcasting reference, based on the time standard of the Greenwich Observatory in the U.K. The difference between UTC and local time may be determined by listening for routine UTC announcements aired by international broadcasters. Some shortwave radios and digital watches come equipped with a 24-hour time standard to eliminate the necessity to convert local time to UTC.

v—Variable frequency, i.e. one that is unstable or drifting.

Vo—Voice of.

W—Wednesday.

Wavelength—A vintage alternative to Frequency (cf.) to express the location of a station within the radio spectrum. The wavelength of a station may be determined via the following formula: Wavelength (Meters) = 299,792/Frequency (kHz). This formula may also be used to ascertain the metre band of a particular station (cf. Shortwave Spectrum).

WS—World Service.

For countries where savings time is used, schedules may vary by an hour during winter.

GUIDE TO GRAPHICS FORMAT

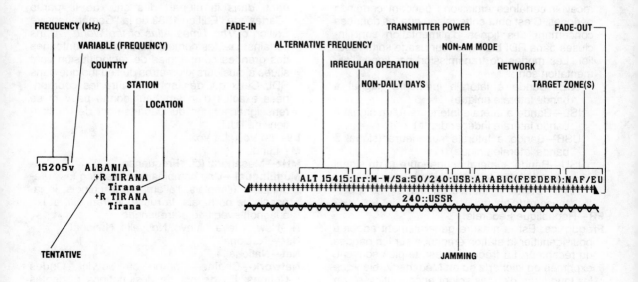

LEXIQUE

Alt—Alternative.

AV—A Voz.

BC—Broadcasting, Broadcasting Company, Broadcasting Corporation.

BS—Broadcasting Service, Broadcasting Station.

Cd—Ciudad.

Canal—La norme pour l'espace réservé à un canal est de 5 kHz. Un petit nombre de stations ne suivent pas cette norme. Pour celà, RDI publie une résolution de fréquence supérieure à un kilohertz afin de faciliter l'identification de la station émettrice.

Cl—Club, Clube.

Cu, Cult—Cultura, Culture.

(D)—Horaire uniquement pour l'hiver.

DS—Service Local.

Em—Emissora, Emisora, Emissor, Emetteur.

EP—Emetteur Provincial.

ER—Emetteur Régional.

Fade-in, Fade-out—Debut et fin d' Ecoute—Si les moniteurs qui suivent les stations de radiodiffusion ne peuvent pas établir, d'une manière certaine, les débuts ou les fins d'émission, ils fournissent à **Database** les horaires les plus tôt (pour le début) et les plus tard (pour la fin) des emissions qu'ils ont pu entendre sur la station en question.

F—Vendredi.

Feeder, Shortwave—Ligne d'alimentation, ondes courtes. Consiste en une émission d'un point fixe à un autre, généralement en bandes latérales indépendantes ou bandes latérales uniques, dirigée vers un relais à partir d'un pays ou se situe la station de radiodiffusion. Bien que cette méthode de transmission ne soit pas destinée à être captée par le public, les transmissions d'ondes courtes par ligne d'alimentation peuvent être captées par certains récepteurs qui permettent parfois un meilleur, ou même le seul, moyen de recevoir certaines émissions pendant certaines périodes. C'est pour cette raison que les données concernant des lignes d'alimentation sont incluses dans RDI bien que leur usage soit irrégulier. Les modes de transmission par ligne d'alimentation sont:

    LSB—Bande à latérale inferieure (signal à bande latérale unique)

    ISL—Bande à latérale inferieure (d'un signal à bande latérale indépendante)

    USB—Bande à latérale superieure (signal à bande latérale unique)

    ISU—Bande à latérale superieure (d'un signal à bande latérale indépendante)

    RAM—Bande à latérale double, signal à porteuse reduite.

FR—République Fédérale.

Fréquence: Est la mesure généralement adoptée pour identifier la station émettrice sur les bandes du récepteur. La fréquence est, le plus souvent, exprimée en kilohertz ou en Mégahertz, bien que les longueurs d'ondes soient encore utilisées en Europe et dans certains autres pays. Les longueurs d'ondes sont exprimées en mètres. Les formules suivantes permettent de passer d'une mesure à l'autre:

    Fréquence en kilohertz = 299,792/Longueur d'onde en métres.

Irr—Opération ou heures d'opération irrégulières.

Is—Iles.

(J)—Horaire uniquement pour l'été.

Jamming—Brouillage—Interférence provoquée délibérément pour rendre la réception soit impossible, soit très difficile. La grande majorité des brouillages provient de l'Union Soviétique ou des pays de l'Europe de l'Est et est dirigée contre des émissions en arménien, azerbaijani, biellorusse, bulgare, estonien, georgien, hébreu, latvien, lituanien, polonais, russe, slovaque, tartar-bashkir, tchèque, turkestan, ukrainien et yiddish. Les brouillages en provenance de l'URSS et de l'Europe de l'Est produisent un bruit similaire à des ronflements de moteurs. De temps à autre, des messages codés ou même des programmes altérés provenant du service "Mayak" (DS-2) de l'URSS apparaissent parmi ces brouillages. L'un des moyens de surmonter ces difficultés de réception est d'utiliser les bandes les plus susceptibles de donner une bonne réception du pays que vous désirez écouter et qui, aux mêmes heures, ont le moins de possibilité de donner une bonne réception de l'Union Soviétique ou des pays de l'Europe de l'Est. Une antenne directionelle peut, dans certaines conditions, améliorer le rapport signal/brouillage.

kHz—kilohertz (cf. "Frequence").

kW—kilowatt (s), (cf. "Puissance").

Location—Le lieu ou est situé le complexe emetteur/antenne. Ce "site" ne correspond pas nécessairement à celui des studios qui préparent les programmes. Les sites publiés par RDI proviennent, dans la plupart des cas, de la partie "Cartes" de l'Edition 1983 de la "Comprehensive Edition of *The Times Atlas of the World*". Dans certains cas, les complexes émetteurs/antennes des grandes compagnies de radiodiffusion sont situés à plusieurs kilométres du lieu indiqué dans RDI. Ceux qui désirent connaître les coordonnées exactes d'un émetteur donné peuvent se renseigner auprès du Département de Publications de l'UIT.

LV—La Voix, La Voz.

M—Lundi.

MHz—Mégahertz (cf. "Frequence").

Multilingual—Une combinaison des langues "graphiques" (l'anglais, l'allemand, le chinois, le japonais, le portugais, la russe, le français, et l'espagnol) avec une autre langue.

N—New, Nueva, Nuevo, Nouvelle, National.

Nac—Nacional.

Nat—National.

Network—Chaîne—Chaîne ou Service Ondes Courtes. En dehors de désignations évidentes telles que "Service Mondial". Les services locaux d'ondes courtes sont indiqués par "DS."

Pays—Les noms de pays publiés dans RDI sont ceux spécifiés par l'UIT. Certaines stations non-officielles et autres entités géographiques sont incluses pour référence mais n'indiquent d'aucune manière l'endossement ou la reconnaissance de ces stations de la part, soit de IBS, soit de UIT.

PBS—Station national ou local de Radiodiffision de la République populaire de Chine.

Power—Puissance—La puissance RF d'émission en kilowatts avant l'amplification par l'antenne. Actuellement, les puissances utilisées en émission se situent entre 0,04 et 600 kW.

PR—République Populaire.

Pto—Puerto.

R—Radio, Radiodiffusion, Radiodiffusora, Radiodifusão, Radiostantsiya, Radyo, Radyosu, etc.

Relais—Est une installation extraterritoriale généralement alimentée par des enregistrements, par satellite ou par ligne d'alimentation, ondes courtes.

Rep—République.

RTV—Radiodiffussion Télévision.

RN—Cf. R and N.

S—Sa, Santa, Santo, São, Saint.

Spectre Ondes Courtes—Le spectre ondes courtes ou haute fréquence est la partie du spectre radiodiffusé entre 3 et 30 Mhz (3.000-30.000 kHz); cependant, l'usage le plus fréquent est approximativement entre 2 et 30 MHz. Bien que les radiodiffusions aient lieu sur toutes les bandes ondes courtes, les bandes désignées par UIT pour la radiodiffusion ondes courtes sont: (Mondialement à moins qu'il e soit indiqué autrement):

Bande 120 Mètres:
2300-2498 kHz (Zones tropicales exclusivement).

Bande 90 Mètres:
3200-3400 kHz (Zones tropicales exclusivement).

Bande 75 Mètres:
3900-3950 kHz (Asie et Pacifique seulement).
3850-4000 kHz (a l'exception des Amériques).

Bande 60 Mètres:
4750-4995 kHz (Zones tropicales exclusivement).
5005-5060 kHz (Zones tropicales exclusivement).

Bande 49 Mètres:
5950-6200 kHz

Bande 41 Mètres:
7100-7300 kHz (sauf les Amériques)

Bande 31 Mètres:
9500-9900 kHz

Bande 25 Mètres:
11650-12050 kHz

Bande 21 Mètres:
13600-13800 kHz

Bande 19 Mètres:
15100-15600 kHz

Bande 16 Mètres:
17550-17900 kHz

Bande 13 Mètres:
21450-21850 kHz

Bande 11 Mètres:
25670-26100 kHz (25600-26100 kHz jusqu'à 7/89)

Sta—Santa.

Sto—Santo.

Su—Dimanche.

Objectif—L'entité internationale vers laquelle l'émission est dirigée, avec l'intention que l'émission soit entendue à l'etranger. Les objectifs sont les suivants:

> AF—Afrique.
> AM—Amériques.
> ANZ—Australie et Nouvelle-Zélande.
> AS—Asie.
> ATL—Atlantique.
> CA—Amérique Centrale, les Caraïbes et le Mexique.
> CAF—Afrique Centrale.
> EAF—Afrique de l'Est.
> EAS—Asie de l'Est.
> EEU—Europe de l'Est.
> ENA—L'Est de l'Amérique du Nord.
> EU—Europe.
> EUSSR—Partie Est de l'URSS.
> ME—Moyen Orient.
> NA—Amérique du Nord.
> NAF—Afrique du Nord.
> PAC—Pacifique.
> SA—Amérique du Sud.
> SAF—Region sud Africaine
> SAS—Sud de l'Asie.
> SEA—Sud-Est de l'Asie.
> USSR—URSS.
> WAF—Afrique de l'Ouest
> WEU—Europe de l'Ouest.
> WNA—Ouest de l'Amérique du Nord.
> WUSSR—Ouest de l'URSS.

Th—Jeudi.

Tu—Mardi.

UTC—Heure Universelle Coordonnée: Heure Internationale de reférence pour les radiodiffusions, basée sur l'heure standard du méridien de l'Observatoire de Greenwich (GMT) en Angleterre. Les Chaînes Internationales de Radiodiffusion annoncent regulièrement la différence entre l'heure locale et l'Heure Universelle Coordonnée. Certains récepteurs ou montres digitales sont munis d'un cadran 24-heures qui permet de connaître la relation entre l'heure locale et celle de UTC.

V—Fréquence variable.

Vo—Voix de.

W—Mercredi.

Wavelength—Longueur d'Onde. Exprime la place qu'occupe une station sur le spectre radiodiffusé. Un terme maintenant moins souvent utilisé que le terme fréquence. Longueur d'onde et fréquence sont liés par la formule:

> Longueur d'onde en Mètres = 299,792 divisé par la fréquence en kHz.

Cette formule peut, naturellement, être utilisée pour déterminer la Bande en Mètres d'une station.

WS—Service Mondial.

LÉXICO DE TÉRMINOS

Alt—Frecuencia alternativa: una frecuencia cuyo uso sea imprevisto o irregular y en lugar de la frecuencia asignada.

AV—A Voz.

BC—Broadcasting, Broadcasting Company, Broadcasting Corporation.

BCS, BS—Broadcasting Service, Broadcasting Station.

Cd—Ciudad.

Channel—Canal. La norma para la separación de canales dentro de la gama de radiodifusión de onda corta es de 5.0 kHz. Un pequeño porcentaje de estaciones no opera dentro de esta norma, así que el RDI proporciona resolución de frecuencia de menos de un kilohertz, para facilitar la ubicación e identificación de las estaciones.

Cl—Club, Clube.

Country—País. Las designaciones, en el caso de las naciones oficialmente reconocidas, son las de la Unión Internacional de Telecomunicaciones. Emisoras y entidades geográficas no oficiales se incluyen para los fines de referencia y no presupone ningún apoyo o reconocimiento por parte de la IBS o UIT.

Cu, Cult—Cultura, Cultural, Culture.

(D)—Indica que los detalles refieren solamente al período "D" que corresponde al invierno en el hemisferio del norte y al verano en los paises del sur.

DS—Domestic Service (Servicio Doméstico).

Ed, Educ—Educação, Educadora.

Em—Emissora, Emisora, Emissor, Emetteur.

EP—Emissor Provincial.

ER—Emissor Regional.

ES—External Service (Servicio al Exterior).

F—Friday (Viernes)

Fade-in, Fade-out—Si el equipo de monitores del RDI no puede establecer definitivamente el comienzo (o fin) de una transmisión, se entra en cambio la hora más temprana (o tarde) en que pudo rastrearse la estación, eso es, la hora del 'fade-in' (o 'fade-out').

Feeder, shortwave—Una transmision de servicio fijo (punto a punto) usualmente en modo de banda lateral única o independiente, dirigida a la estación de redifusión desde el país de origen de la transmisión. Aunque no destinadas para la recepcion general, las transmisiones de eslabón de onda corta, que pueden ser recibidas por los mejores receptores de comunicaciones, a veces proporcionan la mejor o única oportunidad para la recepción de una emisora determinada a una hora dada. Por esta razón se incluyen en el RDI datos sobre esta tipo de transmisión, aunque el uso actual no sea regular. Los modos de transmisión para los eslabones de onda corta son:

> LSB—Banda lateral inferior (señal banda lateral única)
>
> ISL—Banda lateral inferior (de una señal banda lateral independiente)

> USB—Banda lateral superior (señal banda lateral única)
>
> ISU—Banda lateral superior (de una señal banda lateral independiente)
>
> RAM—Banda lateral doble, con la portadora reducida.

FR—Federal Republic (República Federal)

Frequency—Frecuencia. La medida más ampliamente aceptada para indicar la ubicación de una estación dentro de la gama radial. La frecuencia se expresa más a menudo en kilohertz (kHz) o Megahertz (MHz), aunque la longitud de onda se utiliza todavía en Europa oriental y algunas otras partes del mundo. La frecuencia de una estación puede determinarse de la siguiente fórmula:

> Frecuencia (kHz) = 299,792 ÷ Longitud de onda (metros).

Vease también 'Wavelength' y 'Channel'.

Irr—Operación irregular; horas de operación irregulares.

Is—Isla(s).

(J)—Indica que los detalles refieren solamente al período "J" que corresponde al verano en el hemisferio del norte y al invierno en los pais del sur.

Jamming—Interferencia intencional a una transmisión con el propósito de hacer imposible la recepción de la misma. La gran mayoría del jamming proviene de la Unión Soviética y sus aliados de Europa oriental, y es dirigida contra emisiones en armenio, azerbaijano, beloruso, búlgaro, checo, estonio, georgiano, hebreo, letón, lituano, polaco, ruso, slovaco, tatar-bashkir, turquestano, ucraniano e yiddish. El jamming proveniente de la URSS y Europa oriental consiste mayormente de un ruido no muy diferente de lo de un depósito lleno de camiones los cuales tienen sus motores en plena marcha. De vez en cuando se agrega a este ruido algunos mensajes en clave o programación distorsionada del servicio doméstico soviético, Mayak (DS-2). Una forma de contender con la interferencia jamming es determinar cuales de las bandas podrían ser las más apropiadas para proporcionar buena recepción de la parte del mundo que se quiere escuchar, mientras que al mismo tiempo no darían buena recepción de la Unión Soviética y Europa oriental. Antenas direccionales también pueden mejorar la razón de señal a jamming, bajo ciertas circunstancias.

kHz—Kilohertz (vease 'Frequency').

kW—Kilovatio(s) (vease 'Power').

Loc—Local.

Location—La ubicación física del complejo transmisor/antena. Esta ubicación pudiera no corresponder a la de los estudios donde se preparan los programas. Los datos sobre los nombres geográficos se completan en su mayoría de la Edición Comprensiva (1983) del *Times Atlas of the World*. Como sucede a veces que los complejos de transmisores de las emisoras internacionales más grandes se encuentran en áreas de escasa población, el sitio exacto del transmisor podría estar a varios kilometros de la localidad indicada. Esas personas que necesitan coordinados geográficos precisos deben ponerse en contacto con el Departamento de Publicaciones de la UIT.

LV—La Voix, La Voz.

M—Monday (Lunes)

MHz—Megahertz (vease 'Frequency').

Multilingual—Una combinación de cualquier idioma representado por símbolo gráfico (alemán, árabe, chino, español, francés, inglés, japonés, portugués, o ruso) con otro idioma. Asi una transmisión en español y quechua sería designada como 'Multilingual', mientras que una emisión en quechua y aymara sería designada como 'Other' (= Otro).

N—New, Nueva, Nuevo, Nouvelle, Novo, Nova, Nacional, National, Nationale.

Nac—Nacional.

Nat—National, Nationale.

Network—La red o el servicio de una emisión. Transmisiones de servicios domésticos son indicadas por "DS".

Non-AM Mode—Transmisión en otro modo que el convencional 'AM' (banda lateral doble con portadora). (Vease 'Feeder, shortwave' para una lista de modos no AM.)

PBS—People's Broadcasting Station (Estación de Radiodifusión del Pueblo)

Power—La potencia de salida de RF (radio-frecuencia), eso es, antes de la amplificación por la antena, en kilovatios (kW). La gama actual de potencias en uso para la radiodifusión de onda corta es 0.04-600 kW.

PR—People's Republic (República Popular)

PS—Provincial Station (Estación Provincial), Pangsong.

Pto—Puerto, Pôrto.

R—Radio, Radiodiffusion, Radiodifusora, Radiodifusión, Radiodifusão, Radioemisora, Radiofonikos, Radiostantsiya, Radyo, Radyosu, etc.

Reg—Regional.

Relay—Instalaciones transmisoras extraterritoriales que retransmiten programas recibidos por satélite, eslabón de onda corta, o en forma de grabación.

Rep—Republic, República, République.

RT, RTV—Radiodiffusion Télévision, Radio Television, etc.

RN—Vease R y N.

S—San, Santa, Santo, São, Saint.

Sa—Saturday (Sábado).

Shortwave Spectrum—La gama de onda corta, o alta frecuencia, es esa porción de la gama radial que se encuentra entre 3 y 30 MHz (3,000-30,000 kHz); sin embargo, de ordinario se ubica la gama de onda corta entre 2 y 30 MHz aproximadamente. Aunque la radiodifusión tiene lugar en toda la gama de onda corta, los recién adoptados—pero no aun plenamente implementados—parametros nominales de la UIT para la radiodifusión de onda corta son (mundialmente, salvo ser indicado de otra manera):

Banda de 120 metros:
2300-2498 kHz (Zonas tropicales solamente)
Banda de 90 metros:
3200-3400 kHz (Zonas tropicales solamente)
Banda de 75 metros:
3900-3950 kHz (Asia & Pacífico solamente)
3950-4000 kHz (excepto las Américas)
Banda de 60 metros:
4750-4995 kHz (Zonas tropicales solamente)
5005-5060 kHz (Zonas tropicales solamente)
Banda de 49 metros:
5950-6200 kHz
Banda de 41 metros:
7100-7300 kHz (excepto las Américas)
Banda de 31 metros:
9500-9900 kHz
Banda de 25 metros:
11650-12050 kHz
Banda de 21 metros:
13600-13800 kHz
Banda de 19 metros:
15100-15600 kHz
Banda de 16 metros:
17550-17900 kHz
Banda de 13 metros:
21450-21850 kHz
Banda de 11 metros:
25600-26100 kHz (25670-26100 kHz desde Julio de 1989)

St—Saint.

Sta—Santa.

Sto—Santo.

Su—Sunday (Domingo)

Target—Las entidades geográficas internacionales a las cuales se dirige una transmisión, con tal que está destinada fuera del país de origen. Las zonas de recepcion son las siguientes:

AF—África
AM—Américas
ANZ—Australia & Nueva Zelandia
AS—Asia
ATL—Atlántico
CA—América Central, Caribe & México
CAF—África Central
EAF—África Oriental
EAS—Asia Oriental
EEU—Europa Oriental
ENA—América del Norte (Este)
EU—Europa
EUSSR—URSS Oriental
ME—Oriente Medio
NA—América del Norte
NAF—África del Norte
PAC—Pacífico
SA—América del Sur
SAF—África Meridional
SAS—Sud Asia
SEA—Asia (Sudeste)
USSR—URSS
WAF—África Occidental
WEU—Europa Occidental
WNA—America del Norte (Oeste)
WUSSR—URSS Occidental

Th—Thursday (Jueves).

Tu—Tuesday (Martes).

UTC—Hora Universal Coordinada, también conocida como Hora Meridiano de Greenwich (GMT) o Zulu (Z): la referencia internacional de 24 horas para la radiodifusión, basada en el marco de tiempo del Observatorio de Greenwich en el Reino Unido. La diferencia entre UTC y la horo local puede determinarse escuchando los avisos rutinarios de la hora UTC transmitidos por emisoras internacionales.

v—Frecuencia variable, eso es, una que es inestable.

Vo—Voice of (Voz de).

W—Wednesday (Miércoles).

Wavelength—Longitud de onda. Una alternativa antigua a 'Frecuencia' (vease) para precisar la ubicación de la estación dentro de la gama radial. La longitud de onda de una estación puede determinarse atravéz de la siguiente fórmula: Longitud de onda (metros) = 299,792 ÷ Frecuencia (kHz). Esta fórmula puede utilizarse también para precisar la banda (en metros) de una estación determinada (vease 'Shortwave Spectrum').

WS—World Service (Servicio Mundial).

(+) Tent—Tentativo (-a); eso es, la exactitud de algunos detalles (p.ej. el nombre exacto de la estación) está incierta.

GLOSSAR

Channel; Kanal—Die Norm für den Abstand verschiedener Sendungen im Kurzwellenspektrum ist 5.0 kHz. Da aber ein kleiner Teil der Stationen nicht gemäss dieser Norm funktioniert, bietet **Database** Frequenzgenauigkeit von besser als einem kHz für die Lage und Identifizierung von Stationen.

Country; Land—Die Namen für die verschiedenen Länder sind diejenigen der ITU. Inoffizielle Sender und geographische Einheiten werden nur zur Bequemlichkeit erwähnt und bedeuten nicht formale Anerkennung oder Endorsement von IBS oder ITU.

Fade-in, Fade-out; Hineinschwinden, Herausschwinden—Falls die Moniteure der Databasis nicht den Anfang oder das Ende einer Sendung genau bestimmen können, dann wird die früheste oder späteste Zeit angegeben, wann die Station gehört werden kann. Dies wird als "fade-in" oder "fade-out" Zeit charakterisiert.

Feeder, shortwave; Kurzwellenspeisesender oder Versorger—Eine Punkt-zu-Punkt bestimmte Sendung zu einer Relaisstation, gewöhnlich durch einzelnes oder unabhängiges Seitenband. Manchmal kommt es vor, dass gewisse Rundfunkprogramme am besten oder nur durch "feeder" gehört werden können, obgleich sie eigentlich nicht für die Oeffentlichkeit beabsichtsind und auch bessere Empfänger benötigen. Aus diesem Grunde enthält RDI Information über Kurzwellen "feeder", obwohl es möglich ist, dass tatsächlicher Gebrauch nicht immer regelmässig ist.

Sendearten für Kurzwellen "feeder" sind wie folgt:

LSB—Lower Sideband (single-sideband signal); Unteres Seitenband

USB—Upper Sideband (single-sideband signal); Oberes Seitenband

ISL—Lower Sideband (of independent-sideband signal); Unteres Seitenband (von einem unabhängigen Seitenband Signal)

ISU—Upper Sideband (of independent sideband signal); Oberes Seitenband (von einem unabhängigen Seitenband Signal)

RAM—Double Sideband, reduced carrier signal; Doppeltes Seitenband, reduziertes Träger Signal

Anmerkung: Mittelwellen Sendungen, die hauptsächlich dem Inlandsdienst dienen, bestehen aus einem Träger (carrier) und zwei Seitenbändern, die beide dieselbe Information als Spiegelbilder enthalten. Diese Sendeart wird AM genannt und wird auch auf Kurzwelle gebraucht. Indem ein Rundfunksender nur ein Seitenband oder sogar auch keinen Träger gebraucht, spart er Energie, oder falls er doch noch mehr kW gebraucht, dann reicht die Sendung weiter stärker und klarer.

Frequency; Frequenz—Das weitverbreitetste Mass, um die Lage einer Sendung innerhalb des Radiospektrums anzugeben. In Osteuropa und einigen anderen Teilen der Welt wird jedoch noch Wellenlänge gebraucht. Frequenz wird hauptsächlich in Kilohertz (kHz) oder Megahertz (MHz) ausgedrückt. Die Frequenz einer Sendung kann durch die folgende Formel von der Wellenlänge errechnet werden: Frequenz (kHz) = 299,792/Wellenlänge (Meter). Vgl. "Wavelength" (Wellenlänge) und "Channel" (Kanal).

Jamming; Mischmaschen—Die Störung einer Sendung mit der Absicht ihren Empfang unmöglich zu machen. In der Hauptsache kommt "Jamming" heutzutage von der Sowjetunion und ihren osteuropäischen Verbündeten. Es ist gegen Sendungen in den folgenden Sprachen dirigiert: Armenisch, Aserbeidschanisch, Belorussisch, Bulgarisch, Tschechisch, Estonisch, Georgisch, Hebräisch, Lettisch, Litauisch, Polnisch, Russisch, Slowakisch, Tatarisch-Baschkirisch, Turkestanisch, Ukrainisch und Jiddisch. Sowjetisch-osteuropäisches Mischmaschen bestetht hauptsächlich aus einem Geräusch wie von vielen, lauten Maschinen. Manchmal kann man Identifikationen in dem Morsealphabet hören oder seltener auch verzerrte Programme des Sowjetischen "Mayak" (DS-2) Inlandsdienstes. Ein Mittel zur Minimierung oder zum Abschwächen des Mischmaschens besteht in der Benutzung des Kurtzwelleverbreitung. Man tut dies, indem man herausfindet, welche Bände wahrscheinlich guten Empfang für den Teil der Welt geben, den man hören will; aber zur selben Zeit wahrscheinlich nicht guten Empfang von der Sowjetunion oder Osteuropa. Durch Antennen, die auf verschiedene Richtungen eingestellt werden können, kann man zuweilen auch die Beziehung zwischen Signal und "Jamming" unter gewissen Umständen verbessern.

Location; Standort—Der Platz, wo sich die Sendeanlagen, einschliesslich des Senders und der Antennen, befinden. Dieser mag nicht derselbe sein wie derjenige der Studios, wo die Rundfunkprogramme hergestellt werden. Data für die Namen von Standorten wurden in der Hauptsache mit Hilfe der Karten in *The Times Atlas of the World,* 1983 Comprehensive Edition, vorbereitet.

Network; Rundfunknetz—Der Dienst oder Service einer Rundfunkorganisation. Ausser solchen offensichtlichen Anwendungen wie 'Weltdienst' kann dieser Ausdruck sich auf Sprachen beziehen, wenn dies nicht durch die graphischen Symbole für Arabisch, Chinesisch, Englisch, Französisch, Deutsch, Japanisch, Portugiesisch, Russisch, und Spanisch angegeben ist. Inlandsdienste sind durch 'DS' (Domestic Service) bezeichnet.

Non-AM Mode—Siehe Feeder.

Power; Kraft—Senderleistung in Kilowatt (kW) vor der Amplifikation durch die Antenne. Zur Zeit gebrauchen Kurzwellensender von 0,04 bis 600 kW, aber manchmal werden zwei Sender mit nur kleinen Unterschieden in der Richtung gebraucht.

Relay; Relais—Ausserterritoriale Sendestation, gewöhnlich durch Tonbänder, Satelliten oder Kurzwellendienst versorgt (vgl. 'Feeder').

Shortwave Spectrum; Kurzwellenspektrum— Gemäss der wissenschaftlichen Definition liegt das Kurzwellen—oder Hochfrequenzspektrum zwischen 3 und 30 MHz oder 3,000 und 30,000 kHz. Gewöhnlicher Gebrauch diktiert jedoch, dass es ungefähr zwischen 2 und 30 MHz liegt. In der Praxis kann man Rundfunksendungen fast überall im Kurzwellenspektrum finden. Aber gemäss vor kurzem angenommenen Prinzipien der ITU sind, mit gewissen Begrenzungen, die in den Klammern angegeben sind, die folgenden die nominalen Parameter für Kurzwellen Rundfunkbände. Es ist jedoch auch in Betracht zu ziehen, dass diese noch nicht ganz offiziell genehmigt sind, wenngleich *de facto* verschiedene Rundfunksender sie schon z.Z. gebrauchen.

120 Meterband:
2300-2498 kHz (nur tropische Zone)
90 Meterband:
3200-3400 kHz (nur tropische Zone)
75 Meterband:
3900-3950 kHz (nur Asien und Pazifik)
3950-4000 kHz (mit Ausnahme Amerikas)
60 Meterband:
4750-4995 kHz (nur tropische Zone)
5000-5060 kHz (nur tropische Zone)
49 Meterband:
5950-6200 kHz
41 Meterband:
7100-7300 kHz (mit Ausnahme Amerikas)

31 Meterband:
9500-9900 kHz
25 Meterband:
11650-12050 kHz
21 Meterband:
13600-13800 kHz
19 Meterband:
15100-15600 kHz
16 Meterband:
17550-17900 kHz
13 Meterband:
21450-21850 kHz
11 Meterband:
25600-26100 kHz
25670-26100 kHz (Anfangend Juli, 1989)

UTC—Coordinated Universal Time; Koordinierte Universalzeit; auch Greenwich Mean Time (GMT) oder Zulu (Z) genannt; die 24-stündige internationale Rundfunkreferenz, die sich auf das Observatorium von Greenwich in Grossbritannien basiert. Man kann den Unterschied zw. UTC und örtlicher Zeit bestimmen, indem man internationalen Rundfunksendungen zuhört. Einige Kurzwellenempfänger und Digitaluhren können auf das vierundzwanzigstündige Format gesetzt werden, sodass man nicht umrechnen braucht.

Wavelength; Wellenlänge—Ein veraltender Ausdruck anstatt Frequenz (vgl. 'Frequency'), um die Lage einer Sendung im Radiospektrum anzugeben. Die Wellenlänge einer Sendung kann durch die folgende Formel errechnet werden: Wellenlänge (Meter) = 299,792/Frequenz (kHz). Diese Formel kann auch gebraucht werden, um das Meterband einer Sendung zu bestimmen (vgl. 'Shortwave Spectrum').

ABKUERZUNGEN

Alt—Alternate; abwechselnd, alternativ

AV—A Voz

BC—Broadcasting; Rundfunksendung-sender, oder gesellschaft

BCS, BS—Broadcasting Service; Rundfunkdienst

Cd—Ciudad; City; Stadt

CI—Club; Clube; Klub

Cu—Cult-Culture; Cultura; Kultur

(D)—Winter

DS—Domestic Service; Inlandsdienst

Ed—Educacão, Educadora.

Em—Emissora, Emisora; Emetteur Strahlung

ES—External Service, Auslandsdienst

FR—Federal Republic; Bundesrepublik

F—Friday; Freitag

Hz—hertz—A unit of frequency equal to one cycle per second; Eine Frequenzeinheit, die eine Schwingung pro Sekunde bezeichnet

Irr—Irregular operation or hours of operation; unregelmässige Sendung

Is—Island(s); Insel(n)

(J)—Sommer

kHz—Kilohertz 1,000 Hertz (cf. Frequency); vgl. Frequenz

kW—Kilowatt(s) (cf. Power); Stärke, Senderleistung (vgl. "Power")

LV—La Voix, La Voz; die Stimme

M—Monday; Montag

MHz—Megahertz 1,000 kHz (cf. Frequency); vgl. Frequenz

N—New; Nueva; Nuevo; Nouvelle; Novo, Nova, Nacional, Nationale; Neu

Nac—Nacional; National

Nat—National, Nationale

PBS—People's Broadcasting Station Volksrundfunkstation

PR—People's Republic; Volksrepublik

Pto—Puerto Pôrto; Hafen

R—Radio, Radiodiffusion, Radiodifusora, Radiodifusíon, Radiodifusão, Radioemisora, Radiofonikos, Radiostantsiya, Radyo, Radyosu, etc.

Rep—Republic; República; République; Republik

RT, RTV—Radiodiffusion Télévision, Radio Television, etc.

S—San, Santa, Santo, São, Saint; in Heiligennamen verschiedener Sprachen und auf solche zurückgehenden Ortsnamen

Sa—Saturday; Sonnabend, Samstag

St—Saint; vgl. S

Sta—Santa, vgl. S

Sto—Santo, vgl. S

Su—Sunday; Sonntag

Target—Zielgebiet, spez. die internationalen geographischen Gebiete für die eine Sendung beabsichtigt ist, falls sie ausserhalb des Landes gehört werden soll:

    AF—Africa; Afrika

    AM—Americas; die amerikanischen Kontinente

    ANZ—Australia & New Zealand; Australien u. Neuseeland

    AS—Asia; Asien

    ATL—Atlantic; Atlantik

    CA—Central America, Carribean & Mexico; Mittelamerika, Karibik u. Mexiko

    CAF—Central Africa; Zentralafrika

    EAF—Eastern Africa; Ostafrika

    EAS—Eastern Asia; Ostasien

    EEU—Eastern Europe; Osteuropa

    ENA—Eastern North America; Ostnordamerika

    EU—Europe; Europa

    EUSSR—Eastern USSR; UdSSR (Ost)

    ME—Middle East; Nahost

    NA—North America; Nordamerika

    NAF—Northern Africa; Nordafrika

    PAC—Pacific; Pazifik

    SA—South America; Südamerika

    SAF—Southern Africa; Südliches Afrika

    SAS—Southern Asia; Sadasien

    SEA—South East Asia; Sudostasien

    USSR—USSR; UdSSR

    WAF—Western Africa; Westafrika

    WEU—Western Europe; Westeuropa

    WNA—Western North America; Westnordamerika

    WUSSR—Western USSR; UdSSR (West)

Th—Thursday; Donnerstag.

Tu—Tuesday; Dienstag.

v—Variable frequency; variierende Frequenz, d.h. eine, die nicht stabil ist oder sich verändert.

Vo—Voice of . . . Die Stimme von . . .

WS—World Service; Weltdienst

用　語・略　語　表

Alt −Alternate.代替の（周波数など）。
定期放送の周波数の代りに突然，又は不定期に使われる周波数。

AV −A Voz.………の 。（ブラジルあるいはポルトガル語系の放送局名に使われる）

BC −Broadcasting, Broadcasting Company, Broadcasting Corporation 放送又は放送会社。

BS −Broadcasting Service.放送サービス。

Cd −Ciudad.市，あるいは町。

Channel −短波放送バンド内のチャンネル間隔の標準は5kHzです。幾つかの局がこの標準によらずに運用しているので，本データベースでは，1kHzかそれ以上良好な読み取り精度で周波数を確認し，放送局名あるいは局所在地の確認を容易にしています。

Cl −Club, Clube. クラブ。（放送局名にも使われている）

Country −国名の呼び方はITU方式に従っています。非公式な放送局（地下局など）や地名も参考情報として含めてありますが，これはIBSやITUがこれらの局や地名を認知したことを意味するものではありません。

Cu,Cult −Cultura, Culture.文化。（教育局などの放送局名に使われる）

（D）冬スケジュールのみ

DS −Domestic Service.国内サービス，国内向け放送。

Ed,Educ −Educational, Educa çao, Educadora.教育（局）

Em −Emissora, Emisora, Emissor.放送(局)

EP −Emissor Provincial 州向け放送。

ER −Emissor Regional.地域放送。

ES −External Service.外国向け放送。

F −Friday.金曜日。

Fade−in,Fade−ont −データベース・モニタ・チームが，局の開始（又は終了）時間を確認できない場合，確認できる最も早い（又は遅い）時間を「フェード・イン」（又は「フェード・アウト」）時間として用いています。

Feeder,shortwave −番組作成国から中継局向けに通常は単一側波帯又は独立側波帯で，固定局送信による番組中継が行われており，これをフィーダと呼んでいます。これは一般聴取者向けではありませんが，通信形受信機を用いて良好に受信できることが多く，ある局を受信しようとした場合，時間によってはフィーダの方が良く聞こえたり，フィーダのみしか聞こえないということさえあります。このため，本データベースでは，定期放送より送信時間は少ないにしても，その有効性を考慮してフィーダの情報も含めてあります。
短波フィーダの送信モードは次の5つに分かれています。

    LSB−下側単一側波帯信号
    ISL−下側独立側波帯信号
    UBS−上側単一側波帯信号
    ISU−上側独立側波帯信号
    RAM−両側独立搬送波信号

FR −Federal Republic.連邦共和国。

Frequency −無線スペクトラムの中の局の位置を測定するため最も広く使われている単位です。日本語では「周波数」。周波数は一般にはキロヘルツ（kHz），又はメガヘルツ（MHz）で表わされます。東欧諸国等では未だ「波長」で局の存在を示すところがあります。周波数と波長の換算は，

    周波数（kHz）＝299,792／波長（メータ）で計算できます。
Wave LengthとChannelの項も参照。

Irr −Irregular operation or hours of operation.不定期放送。

Is −Island(s).島。

（J）夏スケジュールのみ

Jamming −ジャミングとは，放送を受信できないように送信される妨害信号のことです。現在行なわれているジャミングの大多数は，ソ連および東欧諸国から発せられており，妨害されている言語は，アルメニア語，アゼルバイジャン語，バイエルロシア語，ブルガリア語，チェコ語，エストニア語，ギオルジニア語，ヘブライ語，ラトビア語，リトアニア語，ポーランド語，ロシア語，スロバク語，タタール・バシキール語，トルキスタン語，ウクライナ語，そしてイディッシュ語です。ソ連／東欧諸国のジャミングは，大形トラックがエンジンをウーウー言わせて走り去っていくような音を発しており，唸り音の中にコード符号が時々入ることがあり，又，ソ連の国内向け放送「MAYAK」のプログラムが極端に歪んだ音で混入される場合もあります。
ジャミングの影響を最も少く受信するためには，電波伝ぱ予報などのデータを用い，聞こうとしている局に最適の周波数でかつソ連／東欧方向から伝ぱんしにくい周波数を選ぶことです。場合によっては，指向性アンテナで信号・ジャミング比を向上することが出来ます。

KHz −Kilohertz.キロヘルツ

KW −Kilowatt.キロワット

Loc −Local.地方向け。

Location −送信所の地図上の場所を指しています。この場所は，番組の制作されるスタジオとは必ずしも一致していません。地名については，The Time Atlas of the World の1983年Comprehensive Edition 地図編からとっています。主要国際放送局の送信所は，特に人家の無いような場所に設置されていますので，実際の送信施設の場所は，地名で表示された所から場所により数kmも離れているかも知れません。送信所の正確な座標位置（緯度，経度）をお知りになりたい方はITUの出版部（Publication/Department）にお問い合せて下さい。

LV −La Voix, La Voz.……の声。（中南米の放送局名に使われる。）

M −Monday.月曜日。

MHz −Megahertz.メガヘルツ。

Multilingual −グラフィック表示の言語（アラビア語，英，仏，独，日，露，ポルトガル，スペインの各言語）と他の言語の組み合せ。例えば英語とウルド語の送信では英語でなく「Multilingual」と表示しています。尚

グラフィック表示でないタミル語とウルド語の送信では，「Other」で表示しています。

N－New, Nueva, Nuevo, Nouvelle,（新）。Nacional, National（国有，国立）

Nac－Nacional. 国有，国立。

Nat , Natl－National. 国有，国立。

Network－ネットワークは放送網，或いは放送サービスを意味しています。尚，国内向け放送は「DS」で表示されています。

Non-AM Mode－従来の両側波帯方式（AM）以外の送信を指しています。（Feeder, shortwave の項参照）

PBS－People's Broadcasting Service. 人民放送サービス。

Power－高周波出力，即ちアンテナ入力部の電力のことでキロワット（kW）で表示されます。現在，短波放送で使われている電力は，0.04－500kWの範囲です。

PR－People's Republic. 人民共和国。

PS－Provincial Station, Pangsong. 地方局。

Pto－Puerto.（ポート）港の意。地名に多い。例 Puerto Rico.

R－Radio, Radiodiffusion, Radiodiffusora, Radiodiffusao, Radiodifusao, Radiostantsiya, Radyo, Radyosu, etc. ラジオ，放送（局）。

Reg.－Regional. 地域向け。

Relay－中継所。自国外の送信設備を指すことが多く，録音番組，衛星中継又は短波フィーダによる番組を送出しています。

Rep－Republic, Republique, Republica. 共和国。

RT , RTV－Radiodiffusion Television, Radio Television, etc. ラジオ，テレビ放送局。

RN－Cf. R and N. RとNの項参照。Radio Nacional（国営放送局）などと使います。

RS－Radio Station, Radiostantsiya, Radiofonikos Stathmos, ラジオ放送局。

S－San, Santa, Santo, Sao, Saint, 聖……と使う。地名ではそのまま

Sa－Saturday. 土曜日。

Shortwave Spectrum－日本語でいう短波は，英語でShortwaveあるいはHigh-Frequencyと表現され，その無線スペクトルは，3－30MHz（3,000－30,000kHz）と規定されています。しかし一般には2－30MHzの波を短波と通称することが多いようです。短波スペクトラムのいろいろな部分で短波放送は行われていますが，最近採用された（未だ完全実施には至っていないが）ITU短波放送帯の標準は，次の通りです。

120Mバンド2300－2498kHz
　　　　　　　（トロピカル・ゾーンのみ）
90Mバンド3200－3400kHz
　　　　　　　（トロピカル・ゾーンのみ）
75Mバンド3900－3950kHz
　　　　　　　（アジア太平洋地域のみ）
　　　　　　　3950－4000kHz（大陸を除く）
60Mバンド4750－4995kHz
　　　　　　　（トロピカル・ゾーンのみ）
　　　　　　　5005－5060kHz
　　　　　　　（トロピカル・ゾーンのみ）
49Mバンド5950－6200kHz
41Mバンド7100－7300kHz（米大陸を除く）
31Mバンド9500－9900kHz
25Mバンド11650－12050kHz
21Mバンド13600－13800kHz
19Mバンド15100－15600kHz
16Mバンド17550－17900kHz
13Mバンド21450－21850kHz
11Mバンド25600－26100kHz
　　　　　　　25670－26100kHz（86年7月から）

St－Saint. セイント。聖……の意。Sの項参照。

Sta－Santa. サンタ。聖……の意。Sの項参照。

Sto－Santo. サント。聖……の意。Sの項参照。

Su－Sunday 日曜日。

Target－放送が外国で聞かれることを意図している場合の放送対象地域／対象国のことをターゲットと言います。ターゲットは下記の略称で表わされています。

AF　－Africaアフリカ向け。

AM　－Americasアメリカ大陸向け。

ANZ－Australia & New Zealand オーストラリア向け。

AS　－Asiaアジア向け。

ATL－Atlantic 大西洋地域向け。

CA　－Central America, Carribean & Mexico 中央アメリカ，カリブ，メキシコ向け。

CAF－Central Africa中央アフリカ向け。

EAF－Eastern Africa東アフリカ向け。

EAS－Eastern Asia東アジア向け。

EEU－Eastern Europe東ヨーロッパ向け。

ENA－Eastern North America北米東部向け。

EU　－Europeヨーロッパ向け。

EUSSR－Eastern USSR ソ連東部向け。

ME　－Middle East中東向け。

NA　－North America北米向け。

NAF－Northern Africa北アフリカ向け。

PAC－Pacific太平洋地域向け。

SA　－South America南米向け。

SAF－Southern Africa南アフリカ向け。

SAS－Southern Asia南アジア。

SEA－South-East Asia東南アジア向け。

USSR－USSR ソ連向け。

WAF－Western Africa西アフリカ向け。

WEU－Western Europe西ヨーロッパ向け。

WNA－Western North America北米西部向け。

WUSSR－Western USSR ソ連西部向け。

(+)**Tent**－Tentative. 暫定。記載されている内容の

一部，例えば正式局名などが不確かなもの。

Th — Thursday. 木曜日。

Tu — Tuesday. 火曜日。

UTC — 協定世界時と訳されており，グリニッジ標準時（GMT）やズル時（Z）と同意語です。英国のグリニッジ天文台の時間標準をもとにした２４時間方式の時間表示です。ＵＴＣと自分の地方標準時の差は，国際放送局が定期的にアナウンスするＵＴＣ時間を聞くことにより計算できます。最近の短波受信機の中には，２４時間のＵＴＣを表示するものも出て来ています。

V — Variable frequency. 即ち不安定な漂同する周波数です。

Vo — Voice of. ……の声。（放送局名に使われる。）

W — Wednesday. 水曜日。

Wavelength — 波長。無線スペクトラムの中の局の位置を測定するための，旧式な単位，表現方法です。放送局の波長は

波長（M）＝299,792／周波数（kHz）で計算できます。この式は，或る局が何メータ・バンドに出ているかを確めるときにも使えます。（Short Wave Spectrum の項参照）

WS — World Service. ワールド・サービス。（全世界カバーの放送）

World Time — UTCの項参照

夏時間を使用している国では，スケジュール上夏と冬で１時間の差のある場合があります。

グラフ表示へのガイド

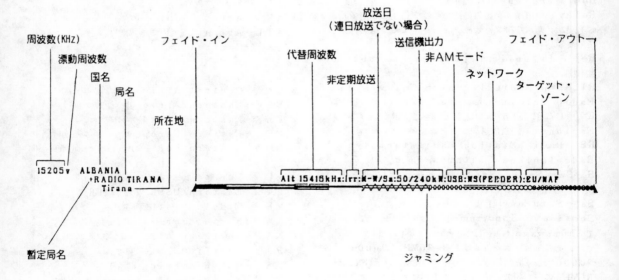

DIRECTORY OF ADVERTISERS

Advertising Representative

Mary Kroszner
IBS, Ltd.
Box 300
Penn's Park, PA 18943 USA
Tel. (215) 794-8252

Typesetting & Makeup: Graphic Arts Composition
Printing & Binding: Science Press